Boris Pasternak

VOLUME 2

This concluding volume of Christopher Barnes's acclaimed biography of the Russian poet and prose-writer Boris Pasternak covers the period from 1928 to his death, during which he wrote the famous *Doctor Zhivago* and was awarded the Nobel Prize for Literature. Drawing on archive material, eyewitness accounts and an unprecedented range of biographical and background information, Barnes brings to light many aspects of Pasternak's personality and private life, while illuminating his relations with Stalin, the Communist régime and the literary establishment. There is a detailed discussion of Pasternak's original writing (with ample quotation in English translation), and his translations of Goethe, Shakespeare and others. The growth story of *Doctor Zhivago* is traced, and the personal and political implications of the novel's controversial publication explored. The biography concludes with discussion of Pasternak's Nobel Prize award, final years and death, and a brief account of his artistic legacy.

From reviews of Volume 1 of *Boris Pasternak: A Literary Biography*

'Painstakingly researched, elegantly produced and illustrated and gracefully written . . . This first volume, which covers the years 1890 to 1928, runs to more than 500 pages, and when the second volume appears we will have the most complete biography of the poet in any language. One is tempted to use the word definitive – at least for the present generation – in the case of this book.'
David Bethea, *The New York Times Book Review*

'Christopher Barnes's "Literary Biography", of which this solid work is the first of two volumes, will certainly become the standard and indispensable guide for students not only of the poet but of his age and literary milieu.'
John Bayley, *London Review of Books*

'Christopher Barnes's biography, first volume in a projected two-volume study, is very nearly everything that a literary biography should be, scholarly, judicious, thought-provoking, and in command of its many sources.'
Poetry Review

'In this extraordinary book, Barnes does for Boris Pasternak what Joseph Frank, in his brilliant multivolume study, did for Fyodor Dostoevsky – i.e., combine meticulous scholarship with a broad understanding of the times and weave both into an enthralling account of the writer's life and works.'
Choice

'Barnes's book is admirably full and scholarly; it is also self-effacing; he does not offer judgments, but seeks to understand and situate the young Pasternak in his time, against a background of European symbolism, futurism and revolution.'
The Scotsman

'. . . an impressively thorough and sensitive account of Pasternak's life in the period up to 1928, with a well judged balance between the private and the public . . . In all, this volume conveys a sharp and consistent intuition of a complex poetic personality.'
The Slavonic and East European Review

'Christopher Barnes's book . . . rests on a mountain of scholarly research: when completed, it is likely to become the definitive reference work to Pasternak's life.'
The Sunday Times

S. Oganesyan, 'Boris Pasternak', portrait on wood

Boris Pasternak
A Literary Biography

VOLUME 2
1928–1960

CHRISTOPHER BARNES

PUBLISHED BY THE PRESS SYNDICATE OF THE UNIVERSITY OF CAMBRIDGE
The Pitt Building, Trumpington Street, Cambridge CB2 1RP, United Kingdom

CAMBRIDGE UNIVERSITY PRESS
The Edinburgh Building, Cambridge CB2 2RU, United Kingdom
40 West 20th Street, New York, NY 10011–4211, USA
10 Stamford Road, Oakleigh, Melbourne 3166, Australia

First published 1998

Printed in the United Kingdom at the University Press, Cambridge

Typeset in 10/12.5pt Galliard   [CE]

A catalogue record for this book is available from the British Library.

ISBN 0 521 25958 4 hardback

In memory of my beloved father
William Barnes
(1906–96)

Contents

Contents

Illustrations

Preface

The loose threads left hanging in 1928, at the end of volume I of this biography, were symptomatic of a somewhat arbitrary break in the story of Pasternak's life and creativity. With advancing years the author became increasingly dismissive about his earlier literary achievement, yet in both of his autobiographies Pasternak dwelt at length on his childhood, youth and early professional career and drew regular sustenance from the legacy he had inherited as well as from his own past. In this sense, despite its crises and reversals, his life possessed an organic wholeness.

Nevertheless, in the later 1920s Pasternak was pursued by a vaguely perceived but unambiguous sense of impending finality. Personal and family circumstances, the natural force of artistic evolution, as well as events in Russian political, social and cultural life, coincided to make the turn of the decade into a general biographical watershed for Pasternak. Some of these changes are recounted in the first few chapters below. Moreover, the sum total of these transformations affected not just the substance of Pasternak's life but also the manner in which its story can be told. Apart from a selective reticence about some personal matters, his sense of inadequacy to compose – let alone force through the censorship – any coherent account of the Stalinist period explained the abrupt curtailment of his *Autobiographical Essay* written in the 1950s (see volume I, x–xi). Pasternak's own inability to articulate, and his evident malaise and faltering creative output during this carnivorous period of Russian history were signs of a problem that has not been fully overcome in the present narrative. By contrast with volume I, we thus have no continuous autobiographical accounts to flesh out and illustrate our story. Largely thanks to Lazar Fleishman and Evgenii Borisovich Pasternak, this biographical segment is no longer perceived as a mere series of melodramatic prominences, or in the terms of memoirists with a penchant for confabulation (Vilyam-Vilmont), with a personal agenda (such as Ivinskaya), or who (like Gladkov, Maslenikova and others) were largely reliant on what Pasternak himself told them and saw their own role in the retailing of this. However, one still regrets that Pasternak never had his Boswell, or a constant companion with the intellect and accurate recall of a Nadezhda Mandelstam.

Despite the availability of private family correspondence or recollections by intimate eyewitnesses, some still alive, the fabric of this account of the 1930s and later years is qualitatively different from what was achieved with Pasternak's earlier life. One reason lies in the major conundrums that remain unsolved: the actions and opinions of many official personages now deceased were wrapped in secrecy, destroyed, or never committed to paper, and even in the present age of open archives they are beyond our reach. Furthermore, some of Pasternak's more intriguing contacts – with Bukharin, Pilnyak or Fadeyev – were largely in the form of *viva voce* exchanges whose details were never recorded.

Pasternak's personality also, inevitably, tantalises his biographers. If in younger years he showed a waywardness and obscurity that emerged mainly in his poetic personality, this in the thirties and afterwards was extended to real-life situations, major issues and public attitudes, resulting in a baffling (and perhaps partly protective) choreography of naïveté and mystification. Frequently, too, as Hingley and other biographers have noted, Pasternak showed a propensity for being mortified by personal and historical circumstance, only to be 'reborn', or to survive and seemingly accept the intolerable. The present account of his life makes no claim to explain or 'iron out' every such paradox. Generally, though, and despite everything, Pasternak was not one to turn his back on experiences, personalities, and on his own past; this ability to assimilate explains many factors in his life – his view of the political regime, of artistic creativity, his dealings with women and with often perfidious friends such as Aseyev, Fadeyev, Fedin and Feltrinelli. Ultimately his life story was one of organic growth.

As in his youthful piano-playing, Pasternak in many of his life's activities remained an inspired and sometimes naive improviser. Cunning intelligence, foresight and causation are not always in evidence in his artistic or everyday behaviour; I have often therefore been content to 'tell the story' rather than force a conceptualised view of his behaviour. Thus, there seemed no masterful intelligence behind his handling of the *Zhivago* and Nobel Prize affairs. Nor does there seem to be a final answer to the question of his survival during the Stalinist regime when so many more conformist contemporaries perished. While some persuasive factors are considered, there was an element of sheer good fortune in play; Pasternak had no complete answer, and in 1956 needed urgent reassurance from Isaiah Berlin that no one believed he could ever have 'done something for *them*'.

Pasternak's resort to translation work during the mid 1930s, war period and later 1940s, adds a further layer of enigma to his literary personality. Although his best translations of Shakespeare and Goethe were genuinely inspired, his selection and interpretation of other men's writings was, at best, an indirect key to his own life and thought. At worst, translation work was, as he later told Zoya Maslenikova, a form of existence at the expense of other people's thought. In any event, for lengthy periods during the years covered by this book, there is neither the volume nor continuity of autobiographically based writing that assisted my efforts in volume I.

As in the discussion of Pasternak's earlier works, the approach here is descriptive rather than critical, although evaluative remarks are not excluded. There is no separate lengthy discussion of Pasternak's novel (I have tried to avoid what Gerald S. Smith calls a 'Zhivago-telic' view of his career), and an account of its gradual composition is included, with discussion of only a handful of critical assessments with which Pasternak was personally familiar.

Work on the present volume has been greatly facilitated by earlier mono-graphers and memoirists. In particular, I have profited from Lazar Fleishman's biographical studies centred on the writer's professional activities and their political implications, and from Evgenii Pasternak and his wife's many publica-tions, in addition to his own invaluable *Materials for a Biography* (*Materialy dlya biografii*). Of the biographies that appeared before the release of new information in the latter days of the Soviet period, Ronald Hingley's life of Pasternak remains especially admirable. Thanks to recent liberated publishing conditions in Russia, and to the 1990 centenary of Pasternak's birth, there has been a spate of archival, memoir, interpretative and bibliographic publications on which I have been able to draw. In fact, in view of the abundance of material now available, both the narrative and the notes and bibliography in this second volume are very selective. More than in volume I, the apparatus serves as only a partial guide to further reading. Partly for this reason, it would be wrong to claim infallibility or final authority for this account of Pasternak's life; we are now at a stage where only triple- and multi-volume treatment could do justice to the wealth of accumulated detail and understanding. While working on these two volumes, I have not wanted for good advice and for a rich supply of first-hand information – particularly from Elena and Evgenii Pasternak, and various of Pasternak's other relatives, friends and correspondents. For errors of fact or judgement that have slipped through the net I take sole responsibility.

The transliteration and typographical procedures established in volume I are adhered to in this second volume. A brief reminder: versions of Russian names in the text represent a compromise between accepted renderings (if they exist) and the dictates of elegance and consistency. Quotation of Russian in the narrative text and the notes and bibliography, however, use the transliteration system employed in the journal *Oxford Slavonic Papers*.

Affectionate diminutive versions of Russian forenames are by and large avoided with one or two exceptions, e.g. Aunt 'Asya' Freidenberg. The form 'Zhenya' was in currency among family and friends to refer both to Pasternak's first wife Evgeniya Vladimirovna and to their son Evgenii. To avoid confusion in this account, Evgeniya is always referred to by her full name; 'Zhenya'is applied only to her son during his childhood and youth. Pasternak's two sisters were long resident in England, and are referred to by the English forms Josephine and Lydia, instead of the Russian Zhozefina and Lidiya. Fyodor Karlovich Pasternak ('Fedya') also had Austrian and English hypostases, as Friedrich and Frederick, and he is variously referred to depending on context.

Titles of plays, books and other publications are italicised and in English, with the Russian original in brackets on their first occurrence. Foreign-language newspapers and journals retain their original Russian (or other) titles. Even though not always issued as separate books, the major works of Pasternak, including stories, poetic cycles, longer narrative *poemy*, articles and essays, are usually italicised. Translations are in every case my own, except where stated otherwise. The omission of text from quotations is indicated by [. . .].

Since publication of volume I of this Biography, a five-volume edition of Pasternak's works – *Sobranie sochinenii v pyati tomakh* – has appeared in Moscow, and this will clearly for many years to come be the authoritative textual source. Its appearance supersedes the earlier Michigan University Press *Sochineniya* (1961), the 'Biblioteka poeta' *Stikhotvoreniya i poemy* (1965), *Vozdushnye puti* (1982), and *Izbrannoe* which were main sources of reference in volume I. For consistency's sake we have adhered to our established page-reference practice, but have in each case appended page references to the five-volume edition. Thus, bracketed page references within the text will usually consist of three elements: a volume number in Roman numerals followed by a page number, referring to *Sochineniya* (1961); a reference consisting of *SP* or *VP* followed by a number, referring to *Stikhotvoreniya i poemy* (1965) or *Vozdushnye puti* (1982); and the letters *SS* followed by a Roman numeral, which locate the reference in the five-volume *Sobranie sochinenii*. Although the Feltrinelli text of Pasternak's novel is faulted in some textual details, reference is made to it where relevant, for consistency's sake with volume I. Citations from *Doctor Zhivago* are thus usually indicated by *DZh* plus page number, denoting the 1957 Feltrinelli edition, followed by a page reference to the fully authenticated text in volume III of *Sobranie sochinenii*.

The bibliography of belletristic writings by Pasternak at the end of this book does not attempt to catalogue all his lifetime publications, but simply lists the main posthumous collected editions giving access to texts and their variants. A detailed account of archival versions, successive editions, and the publication story of individual works can be reconstructed from the bibliographies and the apparatus in these various collected works.

Similarly, no attempt is made to list all the lifetime and posthumous editions of Pasternak's translations. Information on these can be gleaned from other separate major bibliographical sources listed on p. 440, and from monographs and other sources given in the end notes.

Although containing 345 letters, volume V of *Sobranie sochinenii v pyati tomakh* presents only part of Pasternak's enormous correspondence. The bibliographic section at the end of the present book forms a supplement to that fifth volume and includes most of the important additional published correspondence relating to the second half of Pasternak's life.

I would like here to reiterate my gratitude to all the many individuals who assisted me with the first volume of this work. Many of these have continued to provide me with help in completing the present volume. Among them, some notable mentions must be made.

In Moscow, Elena and Evgenii Pasternak have now helped me for close on thirty-five years with various endeavours bound up with their father/father-in-law, and they more than anyone else have made this work possible by their friendship, encouragement, countless hours of consultations, and hospitality during the writing of this book. To the 'Oxford Pasternaks' and members of the Pasternak Trust, and notably to Ann Pasternak Slater, I also wish to express my warm thanks – for their help with illustrations and many factual queries. Vyacheslav Ivanov kindly agreed to be interrogated for many hours during his guest professorship in Toronto in 1991. To Rimma Salys I am immensely grateful for her help in unravelling texts and queries concerned with the Pasternak family correspondence. I thank Jacqueline de Proyart for her generous time and trouble in discussing with me various aspects of Pasternak's latter years and for checking large sections of my manuscript.

In ways too numerous and varied to recount, the following persons have also provided me with assistance, and I hereby wish to thank: Nicholas Anning, Sergei Averintsev, Olga Bakich, the late Sir Isaiah Berlin, Miriam Berlin, Amiya Chakravarty, Marietta Chudakova, Helen Coates (assistant to Leonard Berstein), Mikhail Gasparov, Rostislav Gergel, Yurii Glazov, Henry Hardy, Peter Haworth, Solomon Ioffe, Boris Katz, Charles Lock, Lev Loseff, Michael Makin, Leonid Maximenkov, the late Igor Monin, Aleksandr Parnis, Sergei Pavlov, Konstantin Polivanov, Ella Pereslegina, Irina Podgaetskaya,

Maria Rashkovskaya, Evgenii Rashkovsky, Galina Rylkova, Norman Shneidman, Aleksandra Sviridova, Roman Timenchik, the late Alan Moray Williams, and Irma Yudina.

Among those who were thanked in volume I, I would also like to state my particular appreciation again to Boyara Aroutunova, Neil Cornwell, Richard Davies, Martin Dewhirst, Lazar Fleishman, Henry Gifford, Jane Grayson, Bengt Jangfeldt, Angela Livingstone, Roger Keys, Anna Ljunggren, John Malmstad, Gordon McVay, Aleksandr Parnis, Donald Rayfield, Aleksandr Zholkovsky.

While at work on this volume, I was fortunate to receive various material and financial support from the Center for Russian Studies at Harvard University, the Canadian Social Sciences and Humanities Research Committee, the University of Toronto Centre for Russian and East European Studies, the Faculty of Arts and Science and the Department of Slavic Languages and Literatures in the University of Toronto.

I have been strongly dependent on, and am grateful to, the staff of various libraries, in particular: the Russian (former Lenin) State Library and Gorky Institute of World Literature in Moscow, the University Library of St Andrews, Scotland, the Leeds Russian Archive, the Robarts Library in the University of Toronto, the Widener Library of Harvard University, the University Libraries of Colorado at Boulder, the Nobel Library of the Swedish Academy, and the University of Michigan Press archives.

At Cambridge University Press I enjoyed the support and sympathetic interest of Katharina Brett and latterly of Linda Bree and Con Coroneos, who together invested much patience and good counsel in preparing this Biography for publication.

Finally, closer to home, my predicament in relation to near and dear ones has often seemed well reflected in the horseback ponderings of the hero of Pasternak's *District Behind the Lines*, which could be paraphrased as follows:

I rode at walking pace, and thought of my family and of the wife to whom I was returning. And as I thought of them, I found myself reflecting that they would never know I had been thinking of them on the way. They would believe that I did not love them sufficiently, and that the love they desired of me was something I felt only for other things – things remote, like solitude, my book, or the pacing of the horse. Yet I would be powerless to explain to them that all this *was them* . . .

I hope that all those who have supported me in this endeavour will find themselves at least partly rewarded in the pages that follow.

Acknowledgements

The dust-jacket portrait is from a woodcut by S. Oganesyan. The photograph of Pasternak in his study is reproduced with grateful thanks to David Floyd. Gordon McVay kindly provided the pictures of Zinaida and Boris Pasternak with Leonid Pasternak and Kruchenykh, and of Pasternak with Bannikov, Ivinskaya and her daughter. The remaining pictures appear by kind courtesy of the Pasternak Trust.

1

The crisis of the lyric

'To a Friend'

Was it not clear? After prodding the darkness,
Daylight would always have scattered the gloom.
Am I such a monster? Is not the gladness
Of thousands more vital than joys of the few?

And is it not true that my personal measure
Is the Five-Year Plan, its rise and its fall?
Yet what can I do with my rib-cage's pressure
And with my inertia, most sluggish of all?

In vain in our day, when the Soviet's at work
By high passion all seats on the stage have been taken.
But the poet has forsaken the place they reserved.
When that place is not vacant, the poet is in danger.

(1931)

On 11 October 1976, Boris Pasternak's younger son Leonid died at the wheel of his car while it was standing at the junction of Manège Square and Moscow's Nikitskaya Bolshaya (formerly Herzen) Street. The cause of death was a sudden heart attack; Leonid was aged thirty-eight. Grieved at his death in the prime of life, his family and friends were also struck by the tragic near-coincidence of life and literature. At almost the same age, in August 1929, and only a few hundred yards away, on the corner of Nikitskaya and Gazetny Lane, Pasternak's fictional hero Yurii Zhivago boarded the streetcar in which he suffered his own fatal heart attack. Minutes later, as he rushed for the open air and collapsed lifeless on the pavement, Zhivago was briefly observed by an elderly passer-by. He had last met Mademoiselle Fleury, a one-time retainer at Melyuzeyev, during the First World War. As a Swiss national, she was now heading for her embassy to collect the visa that would allow her to leave Bolshevik Russia and return to her homeland.[1]

If blind coincidence linked the location of Leonid Pasternak's death with his father's novel, the episode described in *Doctor Zhivago* was bound up with the author's own life by a multitude of strands, both factual and emblematic. Mademoiselle Fleury was based on the Vysotsky family governess he had known in his youth. In 1929, one of his family's own former servants, Olga Schweingruber, had approached him for help in contacting her daughter who had emigrated to Switzerland, and the request was passed on via his parents in Berlin.[2] Meanwhile the departure of Mesdames Fleury and Schweingruber was in a more general way symbolic of the bifurcating destinies of Russian and western European culture in the later 1920s.

The death of Yurii Zhivago in 1929 was also a retrospective figurative statement on the predicament of Pasternak himself – that of an essentially non-Soviet sensibility doomed to labour in an increasingly antagonistic milieu. As the end of the decade approached, Pasternak was haunted by a sense of the imminent destruction of his own moral and material world. The earlier chapters of his autobiography *Safe Conduct* had shown a proclivity for viewing his whole life as a pattern of crises, epiphanies, and deaths followed by renewal and rebirth. From now on, however, this ceased to be a mere poetic metaphor and acquired an increasingly dense factual underlay, lending a unifying fatal quality to the remainder of his life. The fact that Pasternak artistically survived the ensuing cataclysms, as well as outliving his fictional alter ego by over thirty years, was a tribute to his vitality, but also in some measure to sheer good fortune.

In the late 1920s motifs of death and destruction were many, not just in Pasternak's literary work but in his own life and the lives of those around him. As his later autobiographical essay of the 1950s explained, after the poetical earlier work of Babel, Fedin, Pilnyak, Vsevolod Ivanov, and even Sholokhov, this period coincided with 'the last years of Mayakovsky's life, when nobody's poetry was left, neither his own, nor anyone else's, when Esenin hanged himself, and when, put more simply, literature ceased to be' (II, 43–4; *VP*, 457; *SS*, IV, 337).

Pasternak talked here of literature in general, but the genre that suffered first and most grievously was his native medium of lyric verse. From the mid 1920s, official promotion of the epic, public, and monumental, and the strident advocacy of a 'proletarian' culture created an environment uncongenial to the 'private' lyric. Pasternak had in 1923 diagnosed its affliction by a 'Malady Sublime'; Mandelstam's verses proclaimed their creator as a 'sick son of the age'; by the mid 1920s there was an acute shortage of publishing outlets for lyric verse; and many poets (including even the émigrée Tsvetaeva) registered a general trend towards the narrative *poema*.

By 1928, the journal *Molodaya gvardiya* (The Young Guard) signalled a general alarm in its printed discussion of the question: 'Is there a crisis in contemporary poetry?' The 'Lefist' Aseyev and 'proletarian' poets Bezymensky and Rodov concurred that there was. Ilya Selvinsky also observed that while the epic and verse drama were in buoyant state, the lyric muse was languishing: Pasternak had abandoned his earlier manner in favour of 'artistically dubious exercises on the theme of the year 1905'; Tikhonov was offering a perplexed mélange of constructivist and Pasternakian lyric device; and Aseyev had unaccountably reverted to the quite alien 'newspaper genre'. As Selvinsky concluded, the lyric was in crisis because it craved for the return of its own germane 'themes of love, death and landscape'. A few months later, the journal *Na literaturnom postu* (On Literary Guard) offered a 'proletarian' wrap-up of the discussion by stating that it was hard to talk of a 'crisis' in poetry when it had never flourished anyway: 'the interest in verses in the first few years after October [1917] was an indicator not of their strength but of our literary impotence'![3]

In the time ahead it was one of Pasternak's main concerns to preserve the thematic elements that Selvinsky claimed were vital to the lyric genre. It was true, he had made concessions to the spirit of the age. The mid 1920s showed his increasing reversion to poetic translation as a livelihood (volume 1, 368), and his embrace of 'public' narrative and historical subject matter demonstrated a half-reluctant determination to be an integral part of his age. Yet *Malady Sublime* (1923) offered an essentially lyric treatment of epic motifs, and even the narrative span of *Lieutenant Shmidt* and *Spektorsky* preserved subjective, autobiographical elements as well as Pasternak's recognisably lyric metaphor.[4] Now, in the later 1920s, deprived of sympathetic external stimulus, and concerned as he was for his very survival as a creative personality, it was perhaps natural that Pasternak turned to the autobiographic retrospectives of *Safe Conduct* and *Spektorsky*, and also re-examined the fountainhead of earlier lyric inspiration by reworking the poems of *Over the Barriers*, first published in 1917 (volume 1, 406 ff).

As Pasternak later commented, in this refashioned version the title of *Over the Barriers* became the name of a period or manner that brought together poems of various years containing 'a predominance of objective thematism and a momentary picturesque quality depicting movement'.[5] Another factor in the revision process was the elimination or rewriting of any poems marked by excessive lugubriety. The new book indeed had some of the exultant mood of *My Sister Life*. Some basic principles animating Pasternak's verse in 1917–18 thus still held good in the late 1920s. *Safe Conduct* provided evidence of this, and the lasting validity of his 'Propositions' on art penned in 1918 was confirmed in 1929 when he offered them to Vityazev for reprinting in a projected Leningrad miscellany.[6]

In 1928–9, reviews of Pasternak's narrative poems *The Year 1905* and *Lieutenant Shmidt* were still appearing,[7] and critical appreciation of *Over the Barriers* (1929) was coloured by awareness of these works and involved discussion of the new book's contrasting lyrical and epic qualities. V. Aleksandrov in the 'proletarian' journal *Na literaturnom postu* mentioned the poet's mastery in relating elements of a distant past to the modern day, while A. Manfred, writing in *Kniga i revolyutsiya* (Books and Revolution) observed a new expressive clarity, a token of future prospects and of Pasternak's 'growing into the revolution'.[8] Reviewing the revised book in *Literaturnaya gazeta*, Pasternak's friend Konstantin Loks observed his new ability to name objects and phenomena by 'their proper names'; also, while questioning the justification for some revisions, he noted a greater thematic precision and epic structure of images as evidence of Pasternak's 'unified and logical development'. However, by observing Pasternak's persistent subjective imagery with a consequent occasional incomprehensibility, Loks unfortunately highlighted a feature which loomed large in orthodox Party critiques of Pasternak over the next few years. A foretaste of this was apparent also in another review which cited the new conclusion of *Malady Sublime* and pronounced that Pasternak was still no poet for the masses, and that he remained a fascinating 'verbal lab assistant' (*laborantom slova*) and 'armchair thinker' of an intelligentsia which had adopted a doomed view of the revolution.[9]

Despite various attempts to see Pasternak's overall growth from lyric to epic poet, *Over the Barriers* was thus recognisable as an essentially *lyrical* statement – not so much a retreat as the revisitation of a lyrical past in the light of a hard-won maturity. Within two years Pasternak would discover new sources of the love, death and landscape which Selvinsky maintained were vital for the lyric to survive. Meanwhile, the crisis of the lyric in the late 1920s was due largely to causes lying beyond literature. As Lazar Fleishman observes, Pasternak's revision of his older book was a personal way of escaping the dictates of inimical social and cultural surroundings.[10] Yet parts of the rewritten book were actually confrontational – notably the revised ending of *Malady Sublime*; and the tone and subject matter of several other poems implicitly commented on current social and cultural issues. (volume I, 403, 411–12)

Along with a few other books such as Mandelstam's *Verses (Stikhi)* and Spassky's *Special Features (Osobye primety)*, *Over the Barriers* constituted a form of moral statement by its very appearance. In congratulating Spassky on his book in September 1930, Pasternak observed that even to be read as a lyricist was now a rare achievement, since 'contemporary life suggests to the lyricist neither a common language nor anything else. It does no more than tolerate him. He is a sort of extra-territorial entity within it.' To engage in lyric verse was thus to recognise a moral imperative that was stronger than the individual and his efforts.[11] The stance of *Dichter in dürftiger Zeit*, however, inevitably affected even Pasternak's overall view of the validity of lyric verse. His feelings were reflected in a rueful letter of May 1929 to Nikolai Tikhonov in Leningrad:

Right now poetic language, which in various proportions consists of Khlebnikov, you and myself, is becoming and now strikes me as neutral, unadopted and routine. I have ceased to hear it; it leaves me neither hot nor cold; and if I ceased working I would be distressed and scared.

Meanwhile Pasternak disparaged the many literary time-servers:

As regards people who at an advanced age are stuck fast in forms and means, one can state quite simply: they have contented themselves with the mere threshold of art, its initial and superficial part. I find it awful to watch when women turn up at the dairy with petrol cans: why, one wonders, did they choose to come here of all places?[12]

Despite the comical image to convey the incongruous demands now made on poets and poetry, there was little in Pasternak's predicament or in the social atmosphere that smacked of humour.

The Shakhty trial in spring of 1928 initiated a new round of political terror, ending the relative liberalism of the mid 1920s and signalling a major shift in socio-political climate. After destruction of the Trotskyite left, the Bukharinite right remained. All of this had cultural consequences. RAPP (the Russian Association of Proletarian Writers) quickly interpreted Stalin's warning of a 'rightist' threat as applying also to the literary field, and a new literary campaign opened up in December following Friche's report on 'Bourgeois tendencies in modern literature and the tasks of criticism'. The literary rightists were identified as the so-called 'fellow travellers' (*poputchiki*). Along with many such independent writers, Pasternak was made 'nervous and depressed almost to the point of physical sickness' by the new campaign.[13]

Ever since the Central Committee resolution 'On Party Policy in the Field of Literature' in 1925, the existence of non-aligned litterateurs had been defended by the Communist Party, and this protection had assisted the continuing vitality and variety of Russian literature. However, the Federation of Soviet Writers' Organisations (FOSP) and its publishing house 'Federatsiya', initially created to support the resolution, had emerged as upholders of the aggressive mediocrity so feared by Pasternak in his first response to the

1925 resolution (volume I, 344–5). By the late 1920s the fruits of this were apparent. Symptomatic was editor Boris Guber's remark to Pasternak explaining that one of Spassky's books had been rejected for publication because it was 'too good for "Federatsiya"'. This was said without any irony, and Pasternak was amazed only at the open cynicism of Guber's self-fulfilling prophecy.[14]

Although nominally independent, in its role as ideological vigilante, RAPP took its cue from the Party Central Committee for each new policy, effectively reinforcing the official censorship and assisting a centrally mounted campaign of suppression and enforced orthodoxy that embraced virtually all of public life.

In April 1929 the collectivisation of agriculture was proclaimed, and over the next few years its violent enactment ruined the rural economy and destroyed the lives of millions. The same month the first industrial Five-Year Plan was approved. After discovery of the alleged rightist menace, a new purge of the Party was begun, and in order to destroy opposition, real or imaginary, the punitive organs were expanded and the GULag (General Directorate of Camps) was set up, controlled by OGPU (United State Political Directorate) or secret police. Campaigns of public persecution, show trials and the execution of supposed saboteurs and counter-revolutionaries became regular features of public life, and the vastly expanded security organs were charged with new duties involving penetration of every public institution, including all cultural organisations. Over the next few years, the resulting mechanism of information and denunciation decimated almost every trace of independent cultural activity. In spring of 1929 a press campaign against the Academy of Sciences because of its alleged apolitical stance resulted in dismissals and arrests; the directorate of several theatres including the Moscow Arts Theatre was replaced; and in music and the fine arts a crudely aggressive 'proletarian' policy was imposed.

The literary witch-hunts and other upheavals of 1929 closely affected several colleagues and friends of Pasternak, although he himself was not targeted. These events included the press vilification of Ivan Kataev and Andrei Platonov. Both writers were personally known to Pasternak via the literary circle grouped around Pilnyak. Platonov's alleged offence lay in preaching anarchism, nihilism and petty-bourgeois ideology, and in allowing a generalised 'humanism' in his works to dominate over healthy – and more truly 'humane' – proletarian class hatred.[15] In May of 1929, the Central Committee itself intervened to censure the journal *Molodaya gvardiya* for printing 'The Barefooted Truth' ('Bosaya pravda') by Artem Vesyoly, which was identified as a tendentious lampoon of Soviet reality. In July, following a secret police search of his apartment, confiscation of manuscripts, hounding in the press and the banning of all his plays, Bulgakov wrote the first of three protest letters to the leadership; it was only after a letter to Stalin in March 1930 that he was allowed to resume his professional activities.[16]

It was in this setting that Pasternak in May of 1929 became involved again in the problematic life of Mandelstam. In 1928 Mandelstam had been exculpated after a publisher's error credited him as translator rather than mere editor of an edition of *Till Eulenspiegel*. But after publishing an article in which he condemned the entire working conditions of translators and editors, Mandelstam was savaged and the old affair raked up in a malicious *Literaturnaya gazeta* feuilleton by David Zaslavsky. In the ensuing row, Pasternak signed a letter defending Mandelstam, and also addressed the executive bureau of FOSP in conciliatory vein. Yet, as Pasternak confided to Tikhonov, despite its supposed independence an official organ such as *Literaturnaya gazeta* would never issue an apology or retraction, and he regretted Mandelstam's tenacity in refusing to 'purify the air' and end the matter.[17] At this point Pasternak's part in the affair ceased. Matters simmered on until December, however, when FOSP finally adopted his very proposal: that Mandelstam should accept some responsibility for the initial confusion, and Zaslavsky's vindictive article should be regarded as a mistake. After threatening to resign from FOSP, Mandelstam left for Armenia, where, away from the poisoned literary milieu of Moscow, he recovered his composure and eventually started writing poetry again.[18]

Despite the background of alarming events in 1928–9, Pasternak's frequent doomsday statements to family and friends did not always square with the levity with which he reported them. In regard to his artistic predicament, he seemed to be facing an impasse. For all his earlier desire to participate in his age, the revelation of some new events and circumstances was not only forbidden, but even defied description. Provisionally, Pasternak's resort was to revise and complete earlier unfinished projects in anticipation of the end of his creative life. As he told his mother in spring of 1928, 'I only need to write myself out before the age of forty or forty-one, and then it is all too apparent that somewhere around that time I shall snuff it [*okachuryus*]'.[19]

In January 1929, with the revision of *Over the Barriers* almost complete, Pasternak dismissed his recent attainments and bemoaned that for over a month he had been living on publishers' advances. As he now set to work on a prose extension of *Spektorsky*, he was aware of the grim onus of being at a focal point where individual creativity intersected with history and with a simple need to earn a living and feed a family. As he observed to his parents in January 1929,

Sometimes one is forced to digress into works and reflections that are unproductive and not directly needed, under the influence of rumours and conversations. You listen to them and obey, because this is [. . .] the State talking, and I cannot fail to obey it, because I believe in its future sooner than in my own. In a few days' time, though, I shall set to work, because I cannot go on like this with one debt after another.[20]

Shortly afterwards, having gained some forward inertia with a prose story, Pasternak envisaged completing current projects within eighteen months, 'so that by the age of forty, this cycle will be complete and I can then either die peacefully or else carry on living and then, as it were, start again on a new cycle'.[21]

Pasternak completed his prose *Story* and *Spektorsky* in 1929, and the following year continued successfully with *Safe Conduct*. By now nothing survived of the exultant mood in which *My Sister Life* and other early works were produced. Pasternak's photographer friend Lev Gornung heard him comment: 'There are people who write joyfully. But not everyone. For Gogol all writing was a tragedy. And I write only from unhappiness, and it has always been like that. [. . .] Viewed absolutely soberly and rationally from the viewpoint of modern requirements, all my writings are madness.'[22]

Pasternak's opaque forebodings continued into 1930. In the darkest of moods on realising that even foreign travel would offer no relief, he told his cousin Olga Freidenberg:

I am not seriously ill with anything. Nothing directly threatens me. But I am haunted more and more often by a sense of the end, and it emanates from the most decisive thing in my case – from observation of my own work. It has run up against the past and I am powerless to shift it from the spot: I had no part in creating the present and I feel no lively affection for it.

It is by no means a new discovery that every man has his limits and everything comes to an end. But it is painful to convince oneself of this in one's own case. I have no prospects, I have no idea what will become of me.[23]

In 1926 Pasternak had told Tsvetaeva of plans to round off and complete three chapters of a story that had appeared in 1922. The following year, Gorky reminded him of the high expectations of him as a prose writer and enquired about his progress. But it was late January of 1929 before he set *Spektorsky* aside again in order to fulfil his long-postponed plan.[24]

'In draft it has the title "Revolution",' he told the scholar and editor Pavel Medvedev. 'It will run to three or four printer's signatures, but maybe more, and it will form one link of *Spektorsky*, i.e. in it I propose dealing narratively with the entire martial and civilian-cum-military episode that would be difficult to unravel in verse.' A note detailing this plan in similar terms appeared that spring in *Na literaturnom postu*.[25]

Progress with the story was not halted by occasional compulsions to write poetry. As explained in a letter to Akhmatova in April, this included some special poetic addresses to individuals – Akhmatova herself, Tsvetaeva, the Meyerholds and others – which were to appear in the May issue of *Krasnaya nov'* and figured in the new version of *Over the Barriers*.[26] Pasternak's creative routine was also simplified by his wife's departure in late April for a month's holiday in Gaspra in the Crimea. After which, the only distractions were young Zhenya's bout of mumps and a flying visit by Olya Freidenberg who came to give a lecture at the Communist Academy and stayed over at the Pasternaks' apartment.[27]

In the second half of May, the prose story was complete and Pasternak read it to an enthusiastic gathering at Pilnyak's home at the end of the month. As he told his cousin, this was actually just 'the first part (one quarter of the planned whole)' which back in January he envisaged as a large-scale novel.[28] The completed 'quarter' thus had the proportions of a novella. It was extracted in the journal *Krasnaya niva* (The Red Cornfield), no. 30, and in *Literaturnaya gazeta* on 15 July. The complete work was then printed in the July issue of *Novy mir*; later, in 1934, a separate book edition illustrated by Konashevich was issued in Leningrad.

The Russian title '*Povest*'' – meaning a tale, story or narrative – both described the genre of the work and at the same time referred to the 'story within a story', composed and described by the central hero as the plot unfolded.

The *Story* had a hero, Sergei (Seryozha) Spektorsky, and a number of other characters who were featured also in the verse narrative *Spektorsky*. In the opening lines Pasternak actually recalled this and pointed out that *Spektorsky* and the present offering in prose breathed 'one and the same life' (II, 151; *VP*, 136; *SS*, IV, 99).

The intended 'martial theme' was not realised, and the *Story* in fact emerged as less 'revolutionary' in theme than *Spektorsky*. Shortly after arriving in Usolye to stay at his sister Natasha's in early 1916, Sergei Spektorsky falls asleep. Most of the story is then taken up with his dream recollections of earlier and prewar events, and only in the final pages does he reawake to the realities of 1916. The setting of the story was familiar to Pasternak from his own visit to that area on the Kama in 1915. The central dreamed episode also derived closely from authorial experience. The hero, a recent graduate and aspiring young Moscow writer, is appointed as resident tutor to the son of the wealthy Fresteln family. Similarities between the characters and their real-life prototypes in the Philipp household on Prechistenka where Pasternak worked as tutor in 1915 were so striking that, as he told his father in a letter, 'it will be impossible to show [the story] either to Walter [i.e. Walter Philipp, who like the Pasternak parents had emigrated to Berlin] or to Pepa [Boris Zbarsky] or the Sinyakovs because although I have said nothing bad, it will be clear to them where all this derived from'.[29]

While living at the Frestelns, Spektorsky becomes involved emotionally with Anna Arild, Madame Fresteln's Danish lady companion, and spiritually – with Sashka, a whore with a heart of gold from the Tverskaya-Yamskaya red-light district. Compassion for these women rouses his ambition to use the wealth he hopes to acquire from authorship in order to redeem all of Moscow's suffering and exploited women. This he projects into a fictional tale whose inspired drafting is described, and which partially reflects the character and concerns of Pasternak as a young man. The story within the *Story* tells of Y-3, the cypher and pseudonym of a gifted poet-musician who auctions himself off to the highest bidding patron as a way of financially realising his talents and thus fulfilling his charitable ambitions.

The various episodes of the story represent a bundle of narrative wisps rather than a coherent plot. A sense of overall structure is provided by the setting and temporal frame. Spektorsky's lyrical dream of 1914 – that 'last summer when life still appeared to heed individuals, and when to love anything in the world was easier and more natural than to hate' – is mounted in the descriptive frame of a ruder, military and mechanised reality, all of which might have figured more prominently had Pasternak realised his initial conception. Spektorsky arrives at Usolye by the same train as Fardybasov, a sailor on furlough. The latter appears only briefly, but his coarse energy, broad stride, and love of the hunt evoke memories of the Bolshevik Polivanov in the story *Aerial Ways* (1924), and of the ominous hunting motifs in Pasternak's verse of the late 1920s.[30] At the end of the *Story*, Spektorsky awakes in time for supper at his sister's, when he is introduced to their friend Lemokh. An embodiment of the new martial age and mentality, Lemokh confronts the hero as 'something lofty and alien that stripped Sergei of all value from top to toe. Here was a personification of the masculine spirit of fact, the most modest yet most dread of all spirits' (II, 201; *VP*, 189; *SS*, IV, 147). Lemokh too was autobiographically based – on Pasternak's impressions of Socialist Revolutionary member Boris Zbarsky with whom he had close dealings during World War 1.[31]

Of the larger unrealised conception of the *Story* we know something from what Pasternak told Nikolai Vilyam shortly after the work appeared in *Novy mir*. Pasternak intended following up Spektorsky's relations with Anna Arild, which would end only with her departure in 1918 to her native Denmark. Several pages were to be devoted to the younger Lemokh brother who appeared only fleetingly in the *Story*. Wounded in the war, he was to return to the front and perish in the Russian advance initiated by Kerensky in 1917. The sailor Fardybasov was also planned to reappear and 'plunge into the revolution hook, line and sinker'.[32]

The hero's reluctance to confront mentally the age of war and revolution was symptomatic of the author's own seeming incapacity to deal narratively with the revolutionary aftermath of the First World War, and it was later evidenced also in Pasternak's attempts at a novel in the 1930s. The *Story*'s incomplete state probably explained why it was barely noticed by contemporary Soviet and émigré critics. When it appeared in summer of 1929, Pasternak himself was dismissive. 'In a literary sense it's not much of a work,' he told Raisa Lomonosova, and contrasted it with other splendid items in the same issue of *Novy mir*, such as an instalment of Aleksei Tolstoy's *Peter the First (Petr pervyi)*.[33] Only one contemporary Soviet review note described the work as 'original and brilliant in its artistry', while in Paris Adamovich dismissed the *Story* as 'a certain Hamlet-like young man's memories of his life in Moscow as tutor in a rich merchant's house, and of his love for the lady of the house's companion'.[34] In its extant form the *Story* shared the fragmentary and episodic quality of *Spektorsky*. There were echoes too of earlier literary models. Natasha and Lemokh had a tantalisingly half-concealed prehistory of revolutionary activity, and together with Spektorsky seemed poised at the end for some deeper embroilment in history – all this seemed redolent of Pushkin's revolutionary plans for *Evgenii Onegin* beyond the confines of the novel, or Pierre Bezukhov's adumbrated Decembrist future. Lemokh too was an evident avatar of Rakhmetov in Chernyshevsky's *What is to Be Done? (Chto delat'?)*, and of various Bolshevik literary 'iron men', as well as prefiguring Antipov in Pasternak's own *Doctor Zhivago*. But the plot of the *Story* as printed ran up against an opaque and imponderable future. As such it reflected the impasse that haunted Pasternak when writing it and became further reinforced in light of public events in 1929.

Aside from the slow strangulation of art by political overseers, several of Pasternak's literary projects in the late 1920s carried their own intimations of mortality. The impact of Rilke's death was still not written out of his system. The first part of *Safe Conduct*, stemming from a projected memorial note on Rilke, appeared in issue no. 8 for 1929 of *Zvezda* magazine together with a translation of Rilke's Requiem 'Für Wolf Graf von Kalckreuth' (volume 1, 397–8). Pasternak announced this translation plan in a letter to his parents on 3 April 1929 and also detailed his father to discover more information on the poet Kalckreuth's suicide from Rilke's widow, Clara Westhoff.[35] At her request, relayed back by his father, Boris made copies of Rilke's letters to him and sent them to Berlin with writer Ovadii Savich as courier so as to permit their inclusion in the forthcoming Insel Verlag edition of Rilke. The translation of the Kalckreuth Requiem was finished in June 1929 and another translation in the same genre, 'Für eine Freundin' (to the memory of artist Paula Modersohn-Becker) occupied Pasternak during July. In these requiems, both dedicated to two talented artists who failed to realise their promise, Pasternak found a further reflection of his own experience of the inordinate problems of being a writer; implicit in this was a realisation that in Soviet Russia the price of creativity, or of failure, might indeed be an early death.[36]

Pasternak's attachment to Rilke's memory as the model for a fulfilled creative life was also reflected in a general nostalgia for European culture, contacts with which were increasingly attenuated. Rilke was of course irreplaceable, yet several bonds with other foreign writers helped sustain morale during trials at home and perennial postponements of foreign travel. Pasternak's main cultural interests had a Germanic slant, but at the turn of the decade new links emerged with French writers. One Sunday in early November of 1928 Pilnyak brought the French poet Charles Vildrac to see him. Pasternak took an immediate liking to him and wrote enthusiastic letters of introduction for him to Bely and Tikhonov in Leningrad. On 15 November, Pasternak also attended a Vildrac evening at the Moscow Union of Writers and described him to Olya Freidenberg as 'a splendid poet of the Romain Rolland "humane" type'.[37]

Shortly afterwards, Pasternak received touching signs of Rolland's own attention. Both of them shared a common love of music and reverence for Tolstoy. Rolland's links with the Russian literary community blossomed in the later twenties after getting to know Maria Kudasheva, whom he was to marry in 1934. His twenty-volume collected works in Russian translation began appearing in 1930. Kudasheva had known Pasternak since the mid 1910s when some of her verse appeared in the *Second Tsentrifuga Miscellany*. It was at her prompting that Rolland in late 1929 sent Pasternak the third volume of *L'Âme enchantée* (1927) with an inscription which, as Pasternak reported to his parents, brought tears to his eyes:

À Boris Pasternak. Au jeune frère de la rive du ciel où le soleil se lève. Le vieux frère de la rive où se couche le soleil. Bon jour. Bon an, bonne traversée de l'un à l'autre bord! Villeneuve, l'an qui s'en va.   Romain Rolland.[38]

Shortly afterwards, Pasternak wrote Rolland a letter full of gratitude and veneration; later, in summer of 1930 after completing reading *L'Âme enchantée*, he wrote him again and received a reply in August. As Pasternak told Lomonosova, 'it was amazing. His letter was just as if from you, or M[arina]

I[vanovna Tsvetaeva], or Sv[yatopolk] M[irsky]. Quite independently of us, how much integrality there is in that which surrounds our life and makes contact with it!' In what Rolland called 'the age of Icarus' (l'âge d'Icare), his interest and support meant much to Pasternak and were shortly followed by another signal favour.[39]

Pasternak in 1928 still rated Tsvetaeva as his favourite and closest contemporary poet.[40] But after the climax of 1926, his epistolary romance with her had waned, and her own increasingly rare letters to him bore the mark of fatigue. On 31 December 1929, she wrote:

Boris, with you I fear all words, that is my reason for not writing. Because apart from words we have nothing, we are doomed to use them. Because everything with everyone else goes on without words, through the air [. . .] With us our every letter is a last letter. One letter is the last before we meet, another – the last one altogether. Perhaps everything starts anew each time because we write rarely. The soul feeds on life, – but here the soul feeds on the soul, self-gluttony, inescapability [. . .] Only now – when it is still on the point of hurting! – do I realise how much I have forgotten you (myself). You are buried within me – like the Rheingold – until the time comes . . .[41]

Although their correspondence had flagged, Tsvetaeva was similarly interred in Pasternak's mind. He continued to show concern for her fate, and in 1929 and 1930, without his wife Evgeniya's knowledge, arranged to have money sent to her via Lomonosova.[42] Tsvetaeva also figured twice, alongside Akhmatova and the Meyerholds, in a bouquet of dedicated verse printed in no. 5 of *Krasnaya nov'* for 1929. The first poem was untitled, but was headed by her initials in a 1931 re-edition of *Over the Barriers*. The poem reinforced Pasternak's sense of the poet's organic oneness with time. Anonymously, the poet is ever-present like a smouldering layer of underground peat. And when this spontaneously ignites beneath the earth, then '. . . as of peat, our grandchildren will say: / There burns the epoch of such and such . . .' (I, 225; *SP*, 201; *SS*, I, 229). Another untitled poem was an acrostych on Tsvetaeva's name and drew a parallel between the sudden elemental incongruity of snow in April and 'the poet's perplexity and person'. Like an earlier acrostych dedicated to Tsvetaeva, the poem also hinted at the poet's risk of violent death.[43]

Pasternak's poetic messages eventually elicited a response in Tsvetaeva's poem 'Homesickness' ('Toska po rodine') in 1934. Meanwhile her sister Anastasia became dedicatee of the 'Malady Sublime' section of *Over the Barriers*. As Pasternak told his wife, this was to recompense her difficult life and give her 'something like a revolutionary commendation'.[44]

Foreign visitors and correspondence did not fully assuage Pasternak's tantalising desire to travel however. A period in Western Europe would benefit his wife's shaky health, a family reunion was long overdue, and he himself longed to escape the hardships of Moscow daily life and regenerate his creative energies. All this was a perennial leitmotif in correspondence with family and friends. Yet all Pasternak's foreign correspondence was sewn through with strands of phraseology on the theme 'not just yet'. The urge to press on with current literary projects, reinforced by financial need, always took precedence. As he told his parents in May 1929, he felt powerless to resist a creative impetus that seemed set to turn the prose *Story* into a full-length novel:

My success, i.e. the seriousness of what I have done, frightens me like some historical side-effect. I understand all this well and can change nothing [. . .] I myself have to stay here all this year. I cannot manage the work I have started on in less than a year. One might recall that any great creativity bears tragedy within it. So here is mine [. . .] Love and disaster – these are the only two forces that remain on a scene that has been cleared of trifles.[45]

For the same reasons Pasternak turned down an invitation from VOKS (the All-Union Society for Cultural Links) to visit Warsaw, all expenses paid, in December of 1929.[46] Meanwhile, as time and advancing age took their toll, the Berlin Pasternaks awaited a family reunion with increasing urgency. No letters or visits from regular travellers such as Zbarsky or Dr.Lev Levin compensated for this, and invitations and hopes were often uttered. 'I feel like a heart to heart talk with you,' Leonid wrote. 'But the everyday thread of all sorts of "business" gets pulled so taut that there's no room for anything else.' In the wake of the American 'crash', the German economic situation also gave cause for alarm. Leonid still hoped for improvements however, and as he put it, 'still remain[ed] on the captain's bridge'.[47]

Meanwhile family correspondence in 1929 centred on: Aleksandr's architectural award; a daughter Elena (Helen) born to Josephine in Munich, the Pasternak parents' fortieth wedding anniversary in February; transfer of the Rilke letters and forwarding to Berlin of books and other property; supplies of clothing, tea and cocoa needed in Moscow; inclusion of Boris' *Aerial Ways* in a German edition of *Dreißig neue Erzähler*, and the transfer of gifts from Leonid and Rozalia to relatives in Russia. The system evolved for this involved Boris' forwarding items or money in roubles to Aunt Klara, Uncle Osip and others, while his parents deposited an equivalent amount in a German bank account. By May 1929 Pasternak had accumulated 1,600 Deutsche Mark, which were retained in a Munich bank in reserve for the moment when he and his family came to visit. These funds were eventually used by Evgeniya in 1931.

Traumatic public events and material hardships formed a detectable undercurrent in family correspondence. Problems were aggravated by their total insolubility and by 'the inconceivability of our general Russian daily life in recent years'. On the other hand, as Pasternak admitted to Lomonosova, 'I submit in almost feminine fashion to things that are elusive but dispersed in the air, basic, and affect everyone [. . .] It is hardest of all to imagine my own life and that of people of my ilk and in my position.'[48]

All this, as he appreciated, had to be seen in context and proportion. His letter of 2 January 1930 to Lydia, for instance detailed physical trials at home and family illnesses, but went on to allude to much graver matters. 'Everyone now is living under great pressure,' he assured his sister.

But the press under which townsfolk live is simply a *privilege* compared with what is going on in the countryside. Measures of broad-ranging, epochal significance are in progress there, and only someone who is blind could not to see what unprecedented prospects this is leading to nationwide. But probably one would need to be a muzhik in order to *dare* think about this, i.e. one would have to experience these surgical transformations on oneself. Sounding off on this theme from the sideline is even more immoral than writing about war from the rear. And this is what the air here is full of . . .

By comparison with this, Pasternak maintained, there was 'absolutely nothing to write about in this uninterrupted, smooth and industrious life of ours'.

Seen in clearer focus, the Pasternaks' daily life was arduous indeed. While staying at her cousin's in late April 1929, Olga Freidenberg witnessed the intolerable life of the communal apartment, where 'tenants treated Borya in an offhand manner, with their fifteen primus stoves, with the toilet permanently under siege', and with life going on in the bathroom, hallway and corridor.[49] Details of this misery were spelled out by Pasternak in a questionnaire sent in December 1928 to the Board of the All-Russian Union of Writers in the hope of being rehoused in a newly built writers' block in Nashchokinsky Lane. It described a total of twenty residents (six families) lodged in one apartment, an unheated corridor, an enforced existence in two corridor-like rooms made by partitioning Leonid's former studio, his artist wife's need of studio facilities, and his own work and fearful discomfort in the family dining room and his ability to concentrate only out of 'extreme sublimated despair'. Pasternak's request for better accommodation was received by the Union on 4 January and forthwith turned down.[50]

Another factor in the Pasternaks' cramped existence was their growing son. At four he was already learning to read, and was 'a trickster and an oaf rolled into one', but very dear and spoilt only by his freckles, his mother reported in 1928.[51] Boris' observations on Zhenya to his cousin Olga were also marked by their difficult living conditions:

He is both mischievous and at the same time an arrant melancholic. Egoistic to the point of heartlessness, yet also with a feminine affection. Probably he has been spoiled, but I don't follow who can have spoilt him and with what. He has a by no means sweet existence in the present arrangement of Moscow apartments, and the same setup prevents my understanding what is wrong with him or what it is that he lacks.[52]

According to his sister Lydia, Boris too was obsessed by Zhenya's freckles, and although his parents later remonstrated with him, the subject became a lifelong *idée fixe*.[53] He was also upset when Zhenya acquired signs of a Jewish accent and intonation through chattering with their neighbours the Frishmans. There was much relief therefore when an educated Russian lady took charge of the boy's education.

In addition to lessons in 'rhythmics' with Aleksandra Andreyevna Egiz (a friend of the Pasternak parents), in his sixth year Zhenya was put in the hands of a governess-cum-tutor whose personality imprinted itself to some extent on the life of the whole family. In Pasternak's description, Elizaveta Mikhailovna Stetsenko was 'an intelligent, ironic, sixty-year old lady of lofty origins and from a family connected with Lermontov'.[54] She was of noble birth and retained a stately bearing, trim appearance and commanding presence. In her youth she had seen life at the imperial court. (Some of her impressions about the doomed Romanov regime were recounted to Pasternak and found their way into part III of *Safe Conduct*.[55]) Her first husband Dmitrii Lopukhin and their son Georgii had both perished in the First World War, and she had later married a family friend and cavalry officer, Ippolit Stetsenko, who with Kirov's approval had been transferred to Moscow. There, in an apartment at 10 Mertvy (now Ostrovsky) Lane, she taught Zhenya Pasternak the rudiments of French and was eventually entrusted with the whole of his early education. She accompanied the family on vacation in 1929 and her genial formative influence has remained a vivid lifelong memory for Pasternak's son. Later, in the mid 1930s, Stetsenko went to the Shervinsky household, to help supervise the poet's granddaughter Anyuta, who later married the violist Druzhinin.[56]

Throughout the late 1920s Evgeniya Pasternak had been in poor health. Her nervous and physical exhaustion were the result of a demanding life-style – the strain of caring for a family while pursuing her artistic activities. (At Vkhutemas she studied along with a constellation of young artists such as Chuikov, Nissky and Romadin who were all to make names for themselves.) All this was aggravated by inadequate medical treatment and there were fears lest she succumb to tuberculosis, like many at that time. After the blow of her mother's illness and death in late 1928, Evgeniya interrupted her studies.[57] A month's recuperation on her own in the Crimea in spring of 1929 greatly improved her condition, and she was able to resume studying in the autumn and hastened to complete her graduation diploma work by the end of the year. Pasternak described to his father the canvas she produced on an industrial subject, and also commented on the appalling domestic work conditions with no space even to set up her easel.[58]

Evgeniya Pasternak's professional ambition and her need to work, *faute de mieux*, in the awful confines of the Volkhonka apartment did not favour family cohesion. Her own aspirations ran up against Boris' even stronger artistic ego. Observing both his father and Evgeniya convinced him that certain traits of the hermit were an integral part of the painter's mentality; Evgeniya too discerned her own similarity of temper to her father-in-law.[59] Boris' growing sense of incompatibility with another powerful artistic nature increased his own guilt feelings at his behaviour towards Evgeniya. Doubtless, his work on the Requiem 'Für eine Freundin' and his awareness of Paula Modersohn-Becker's sacrifice and of parallels with Rilke's own earlier estrangement from an artist wife also made an impact on him. All this conspired to undermine relations between Boris and Evgeniya. For a short while yet their marriage remained intact however.[60]

On the 30 May, two days before Evgeniya's return from Gaspra, Pasternak handed his manuscript of the completed prose *Story* to the typist. His satisfaction was tempered by awareness that the whole project for a novel could take another year to complete.[61] Despite a generous gift of 650 Deutsche Mark from Leonid, hopes of foreign travel were shelved again. Apart from artistic commitments, Boris had suffered most of the spring from what at first resembled pyrrheia, but which X-rays later revealed to be a cyst of the lower jaw. A ninety-minute operation involving removal of several teeth was carried out in the third week of June. In the jargon of the time, Pasternak described this to Tikhonov as the 'industrialisation' of his jaw.[62] The aftermath, involving stitches and wadding, made speech almost impossible for two weeks. When his twenty-two-year-old cousin Osip came to visit from Orekhovo-Zuevo, Pasternak had to communicate mainly by notes written in an exercise book. It was his first meeting with Osip, and he liked his quiet, independent manner and noted an identifiable Pasternakian 'abstractness and absent-mindedness'.[63]

Throughout June Evgeniya nursed Boris devotedly. Meanwhile she was assisted in the kitchen by Yulia Frishman, the aunt of their neighbour Stella Adelson, who stepped in after the Pasternaks' housekeeper left. After his recovery, Evgeniya and son were dispatched, on 8 July, to Mozhaisk for the family holiday. Boris himself remained a few days to attend a post-operational check-up and to finish his translation of the second Rilke Requiem. Then, on 17 June he left to join his family.[64]

The Pasternaks spent their holiday in the Ognevsky Ravine, six kilometers from Mozhaisk. Their accommodation was in a large wooden house owned by the ancient historian Professor Dmitrii Konchalovsky. There, during the summer months, with one dishwasher as assistant, Konchalovsky's wife ran an informal guesthouse for some twenty visitors. Konchalovsky's father, the well-known publisher, had collaborated with Leonid Pasternak on the Lermontov jubilee edition back in 1891, and thanks to this old family connection the Pasternaks received special attention. Among the other boarders they met there were the Berg family, last encountered on holiday at Mereküla in 1910.[65]

Despite an initial mild indisposition that went around the family, they enjoyed their two-month holiday. Boris continued working in relaxed surroundings and read various items such as Medvedev's recent work on Formalist critical method and Tynyanov's book *The Death of Vazir-Mukhtar (Smert' Vazir-Mukhtara)* sent by the author as a gift back in February.[66] He also paid one or two visits back into town, to arrange details for publication of part one of *Safe Conduct* in the journal *Zvezda*.[67]

The Pasternaks returned to Moscow in September, and Boris now worked to complete his verse narrative *Spektorsky* and other projects. He spent an unsociable autumn and saw few literary friends, although on one rare outing, to the Meyerholds', he made the acquaintance of the composer Prokofiev who was visiting his home country.[68] Family correspondence also languished during the autumn, and on 7 December Leonid Pasternak sent an anxious and reproachful postcard: 'Even you, Borya, have stopped writing . . . Are you well? What has happened? Are you really so busy? We too are busy and things are not always cheery, on top of which there is our age. Yet still we manage . . .'

There were good reasons for Pasternak's dejected silence. Apart from general pressures against 'fellow-travelling' artists, the whole literary community had been affected by an issue that broke in the press in August 1929, while the Pasternaks were on holiday. During the 1920s it had been Soviet authors' frequent practice to publish works abroad so as to secure international copyright (the USSR not being signatory to any International Copyright Convention), as well as in order to circumvent official censorship. In this way Zamyatin's anti-utopian novel *We (My)* came out in English translation in America in 1924, and was then excerpted by the Prague émigré journal *Volya Rossii* (Liberty of Russia) in 1927; Pilnyak's novella *Mahogany (Krasnoe derevo)* appeared with Petropolis publishers in Berlin in spring of 1929. Now, on 26 August, the Soviet press, including *Literaturnaya gazeta*, accused the two authors of major acts of treachery, involving anti-Soviet slander and collaboration with White-Guardist elements.

The campaign of vilification lasted several weeks, gathering momentum as new voices joined the abusive chorus, including Mayakovsky speaking on behalf of Ref (Revolutionary Front of Art). In fact, although an example was made of just two writers, there were dozens of nominal offenders, including Pasternak himself: part of *Lieutenant Shmidt* was printed in the same issue of *Volya Rossii* where extracts of Zamyatin's novel had appeared.[69] The reason for choosing Pilnyak and Zamyatin was their prominence (they were respectively chairman and former chairman of the Moscow and Leningrad Writers' Unions), and their names were bywords for all that was best in the free, innovatory literature of the 1920s. As the campaign unfurled, however, new offenders were named and further reputations tainted, including those of Bulgakov, Ehrenburg, Vsevolod Ivanov, Kaverin, Klychkov, Leonov, Nikitin, Platonov and Tynyanov. Despite his own technical offence, however, Pasternak was not publicly indicted.

Apart from the violence and duration of the verbal onslaught, the campaign displayed some sinister new features. First, the writers' organisations not only failed to defend but joined in the attack on their members. Secondly, the whole affair had the character of a Party- and state-organised campaign and it left the entire 'fellow-traveller' writing community in a state of fear and insecurity. The campaign finally sputtered to a conclusion only in the winter of 1929–30. This was partly thanks to Gorky, who spent the period 12 September to 23 October in Russia and, though no admirer of Pilnyak, called a halt to the vicious campaign which was all too redolent of earlier Bolshevik terror tactics.[70]

Zamyatin throughout the affair remained proudly unrepentant. His letter to *Literaturnaya gazeta* demonstrated the farcical, 'rigged' nature of the campaign; although in late September he was vindicated by a meeting of the local branch, he resigned from the Leningrad Writers' Union in protest. Gorky spoke on his behalf with both Stalin and Yagoda, head of OGPU, and following a letter of June 1931 to Stalin requesting permission to emigrate, Zamyatin left Russia and settled in France.[71]

Pilnyak too was forced to resign from the Moscow Writers' Union on 7 September. Pasternak took his case closely to heart. Not only did he regard Pilnyak and Fedin as the most congenial of modern authors (while acknowledging Babel and Vsevolod Ivanov as more brilliant),[72] but they shared stylistic features in common and a substantial warmth of personal relations. First acquainted in 1921, they had pursued slightly divergent paths in mid-decade, when Pilnyak travelled extensively, visiting Egypt, Japan, and various European countries, including Germany where he met up with Pasternak's parents. From 1928 onward, however, Pilnyak figured regularly in Pasternak's circle of friends. He was the dedicatee of chapters 6 and 7 of *Spektorsky*, published in 1928 in *Krasnaya nov'*, and his story 'City of the Winds' ('Gorod vetrov') completed that summer was inscribed to Pasternak. As Pasternak told Tikhonov in June of 1929, apart from himself Pilnyak was the only one 'with whom I find things simply enjoyable [. . .] He is probably the only person I constantly met up with throughout the winter'.[73]

As one of Russia's acknowledged leading writers, Pilnyak lived in some luxury. At his house on Moscow's 2nd Yamskoye Polye Street, he offered frequent and lavish entertainment to guests from Russia and abroad, and also ran a regular cénacle for young authors. On his many visits there, both alone and with his family, Pasternak admired the lifestyle and also some of the realia from the controversial novella *Mahogany*. As he gushingly told his sister Josephine in spring of 1929, Pilnyak had 'a gorgeous little cottage, a magnificent Great Dane brought from Egypt, a fine collection of old books, and mahogany furniture bought for a song at various times and in various obscure spots like Uglich or Putivl'.[74]

Pasternak's sense of divorcement from official literature probably explained why not a single figure from the Moscow literary scene of the 1920s appeared in *Doctor Zhivago*. Nor was it an accident that the hero's fictional expiry in August of 1929 coincided exactly with the start of the Pilnyak–Zamyatin scandal. Like many liberal colleagues, Pasternak was deeply affected by the whole affair. At an extraordinary meeting of the Moscow branch of the Union in September, he had vainly spoken in a spirit of compromise, urging that the public significance of Pilnyak's action be dissociated from any assessment of him as a person, and on 21 September he joined Pilnyak in declaring his resignation from the Union.[75]

Later on, Pasternak also put pen to paper in Pilnyak's defence. The manuscript of the poem 'To a Friend' (above p.1) was probably composed in summer 1930 and actually addressed 'To Boris Pilnyak'. The poem was published in the fourth issue of *Novy mir* for 1931 and in a reprint that year of *Over the Barriers*. Though written as a statement of solidarity with Pilnyak, its *published* title (altered by the official censor) actually enhanced its relevance to any writers under assault.[76] For several years afterwards the poem drew hostile comment from Pasternak's orthodox colleagues and critics and paradoxically appeared more provocative than the stance of Pilnyak himself. The latter's resignation of the Moscow branch chairmanship, public recantation, and

20

penitential letter to Stalin secured for him a remission and continued span as a privileged publishing author until his eventual arrest in 1937.[77]

Even as the campaign against Pilnyak, Zamyatin and other 'fellow travellers' lost impetus, a new rigidity became apparent. On 1 September, Lunacharsky was removed as a Commissar of Enlightenment patently too liberal for the new iron age. Pressure by RAPP, Ref, and other proletarians continued against non-aligned writers, and *Pravda* on 4 December published a first official announcement that RAPP was indeed the sole spokesman for Party policy on literary matters. The same month *Na literaturnom postu* printed a grandly sycophantic message signed by twenty-one leading 'proletarians', thanking Stalin for his advice and instruction on literary matters.[78]

The day after the *Pravda* announcement, Pasternak wrote to air his views on the new situation to Tikhonov and expressed evident agreement with some of the latter's apprehensions (Tikhonov's own letter has been lost):

I am sure that literature is not required by anyone, and only in this do I see a virtue of the epoch. I would rejoice at this if they would only state this openly, wind up the publishing houses and close down *Lit[eraturnaya]gazeta* and the lit[erary] sections of others. I merely reserve the right to he irritated that they don't do that, and that in order to distract the public gaze we are placed in the position of children and even treated indulgently.[79]

Recent events and changing times inevitably left their trace on the final pages of *Spektorsky*, which was completed in autumn of 1929. A draft sketch from the work, originally titled 'Farewell to Romanticism' ('Proshchanie s romantikoi') and later altered to 'Twenty Verses with a Preface' ('Dvatsat' strof s predisloviem'), had appeared in *Over the Barriers* in October and contained a nostalgic echo of the prose *Story*, recollecting how

> I lived in those days when on flat earth
> Old men were pardoned and forgiven,
> Dawnlight indulged all youths,
> And evening urged them on to glory.

But that more genial age had ended with the outbreak of World War –

> When, aiming at adults,
> Through a smoking gruel like a veil
> Rifles rippled, ready stacked,
> And Krupp steel swelled . . .   (I, 244; *SP*, 218; *SS*, II, 252–3)

Work on the final pages of *Spektorsky* moved on apace in the late summer and autumn. But recent changes – external and within the poet – now created problems. As Lev Gornung recorded, Pasternak had at one time 'believed that

21

he would be able to link up the end of "Spektorsky" with his projected plan –
by sending the hero off to work, for example'. Now, however, such a
conclusion would 'contradict everything'.[80]

Chapter 7 of *Spektorsky*, which appeared in 1928, was marked only as the
'end of part one'. But the final two chapters added in autumn of 1929 brought
the narrative to an obviously foreshortened conclusion and some material had
meanwhile strayed into the prose *Story*, although without justifying its projected revolutionary theme. In fact, *Spektorsky*'s final two chapters came closer
to that subject and Pasternak himself believed the most successful part of the
work was chapter 9 with its evocation of revolution as a revolt of the spirit of
outraged womanhood.[81]

Chapter 8 opens by alluding to the passage of six years, to 'showers of events
that darkened Jupiter's brow', and to the Civil War and 'age of cavemen'. The
action plays in Moscow, but personalities and plot are lost amid an impressionistic frieze of historical event and urban snowscape. The 'end of literature',
imminent in 1929, is projected back into revolution-torn Moscow. There, in
chapter 9, 'from early morn there roams a group of cranks', one of whom is
Sergei Spektorsky:

> These were men of literature. Their Union
> Of Writers had been detailed to sort through
> A load of state-seized freight and furniture
> Stored in the sheds of former transport bureaux.
>
> (I, 310; *SP*, 337; *SS*, I, 368)

As these men go about their task, their faces 'dead as clichés', amid the lumber
one of them uncovers some former property of Sergei's one-time inamorata
Maria Ilyina. Sergei listens as a colleague reels off the inventory, which includes
photos and notebooks recognisable as his own. The figure of Maria in earlier
chapters was based partly on Tsvetaeva, and in this passage Pasternak now
evidently played out the motif of his exhausted romance with her.[82]

Eventually the narrator himself runs across Spektorsky who lures him back
to his communal apartment near Kursky Station, which is inhabited by a social
assortment typical of the era – a student, a seamstress, a singer, a 'man in office'
and a former Socialist Revolutionary. Olga Bukhteyeva then suddenly appears
in order to visit the Party man. Awaiting his return, she sees and recognises her
former lover Spektorsky, and the narrator overhears their exchanges. Bukhteyeva is now transformed as a tough woman of the revolution (a female
equivalent of Lemokh senior in the *Story*) and wears the leather jacket of a
Cheka or Party agent. Frivolously brandishing her revolver, she morally
annihilates the unprepossessing Spektorsky, after which the narrator drifts off

22

to sleep and awakes to find that both she and his hero have disappeared without trace. So ends the narrative, clearly establishing its wayward hero as a cathartic self-image of the traumatised author. Spektorsky vanishes from the revolutionary narrative just as Pasternak seemed poised to opt out of revolutionary literature.[83]

The two final chapters of the work were printed in the twelfth issue of *Krasnaya nov'* for 1929. But there were problems in securing a complete book edition. In sending the manuscript to Medvedev at Lengiz publishers, Pasternak's covering letter of 6 November anticipated the difficulties that would arise from the 'ineffectual' character of Sergei Spektorsky.

Despite his own satisfaction with the sections on revolution,[84] of the whole work Pasternak admitted to Medvedev: 'I know it is not a success, but I don't know whether its publication is conceivable.' *Spektorsky* was indeed an innocently 'fellow-travelling' work, i.e. neither 'proletarian' nor obviously counter-revolutionary. But Pasternak's hope of a continued liberal cultural milieu favouring such writing was disappointed. As he explained to Medvedev,

I was expecting some ordinary social transformations as a result of which the possibility of an individual story might be restored, that is, a story of individual characters [. . .] I began with some hope that life's shattered homogeneity and its tangible evidential nature would be restored in the course of years, not decades [. . .] And whatever my own insignificance, such a move would have given me strength – and its growth, accompanied by the vital growth of general moral forces, is the sole story of the lyric poet.[85]

Since 1925, however, when the previous ordinance concerning non-Party literature was issued, much had changed. Apoliticism was now a sin of commission. And while the *Story*, set before the year 1917, had found page space in the non-aligned journal *Krasnaya nov'*, the tale of an ideological drifter such as Spektorsky was unwelcome at any of the increasingly politicised Soviet publishing houses. In a letter to the author Lengiz expressed its misgivings over *Spektorsky* due to the 'inclarity of its social tendencies'.[86] Suggestions were made for overcoming this, but Pasternak rejected them in various messages to Medvedev in November and early December 1929.[87] Finally, on the 19 December he informed Lengiz that he was annulling their contract. To Medvedev he expressed indignation that the publishers had insisted on the 'letter of ideology' as if this were the letter of the contract – 'as though the contract itself stated that [. . .] the terror would not be terrible. As though in the contract I said I was ready to depict the revolution as an event culturally matured [*vynoshennoe*] at Com[munist] Academy meetings.' A postscript in Pasternak's letter sounded further notes of dejected finality: 'How many false careers there are all around, how many false reputations and false pretensions. And am I really the most outrageous example in *this* series of phenomena?' Regarding the heightened autobiographic nature of his recent work, Pasternak claimed to be

'accounting for myself as if in answer to an accusation, because I have long had an awkward and ambivalent feeling. I must round off this whole series of explanatory writings, and then I shall be free for a good long time and will give up writing. Indeed, I would have done so by now already without finishing anything, had it not been for my family . . .[88]

The cancellation of his contract with Lengiz caused Pasternak acute financial problems: he had only just paid back another 500 rouble advance from Gosizdat in anticipation of revenues from *Spektorsky*. A joyless year thus went out amid professional setbacks, financial straits, and cold weather. Pasternak wrote laconically to his elder sister's family: 'A happy new year to you all and to our parents in Berlin! As is our custom, we are late with our greetings, but this time it is pardonable, since this year we are neither celebrating nor recognising any New Year.'[89] As part of a crackdown on relics of bourgeois culture, there was a new state ban on any traditional celebrations. All festive phenomena, from Christmas trees to campanology, were prohibited; bells were removed from belfries, and more churches were closed in an intensified atheist campaign. All this was accompanied by threats of new famine as the first results of collectivisation became apparent.

2

Time of Plague

'Ballade'

The depot garages all shudder.
Then – distant as a dice – a church's glimmer.
Over the parkland – showers of topaz.
The summer lightning cauldron simmers.
Tobacco scents the park, the pathways
And crowds. Bees drone among the throng.
Stormcloud tatters and an aria fragment.
Still the Dnieper, nightbound Podol.

'He's here!' the message flies among the elms.
Unsleeping fragrances of matthiolas
Suddenly grow heavy in the air
As if some climax is approaching.
'He's here!' – from pair to pair it passes.
'He's here!' – it lisps from bole to bole.
Lightning inundation! Rainstorm rage!
Yet still the Dnieper, nightbound Podol.

Peal after peal and passagework.
Then, sudden, Chopin's funebral phrase
Like a sickened eagle strains
Up to the milky nimbus of the spheres.
Beneath – the reek of monkey-puzzle trees.
But, dulled on achievement of their goal,
And fingering the hillside from below
Are Dnieper, stillness, nightbound Podol.

The eagle's flight – like a progressing tale.
Allurements of southern resins linger,
And all the ecstasies and prayers
For both the fair sex and the stronger.
A song of Icarus' flight and fall.
But gently ash flakes from the hills,
And deaf as a convict on the Kara is
The unmoving Dnieper, nightbound Podol.

Harri, this ballade I present to you.
And fancy's flights, arbitrary and skittish
Ne'er touched these lines devoted to your gifts.
What is lodged there is an act of witness.
I shall record and never squander:
The blizzard of midnight matthiolas,
The park, the riverside, the concert,
The Dnieper, calm, nightbound Podol.

(1930)

Genrikh Neigauz, the well-known concert pianist and teacher, was born in 1888 in Elizavetgrad (later renamed Kirovograd) in the southern Ukraine, where his parents ran a music school. His mother was of Polish extraction, related to the composer Szymanowski, and his father was German; Neigauz himself (known also by the German version of his name: Heinrich Neuhaus) was trained partly in Germany and had studied under Heinrich Barth in Berlin before the First World War. His imaginative flair combined with a 'Teutonic' intellectual grasp quickly established him as one of the finest musicians of his age. After teaching successively at the conservatoires of Tiflis and Kiev (where his junior friend and occasional duet partner was Vladimir Horowitz) he was in 1922 appointed to a professorship at the Moscow Conservatoire.[1]

Neigauz brought with him to Moscow his young wife Zinaida, who had studied the piano in Elizavetgrad with his elder sister Natalya and later with Genrikh himself. Although never active professionally, Zinaida was an accomplished pianist and a regular duet partner with her husband, who respected her musical judgement. In Moscow in the mid 1920s the Neigauzes had two sons, Adrian and Stanislav; the latter was to become a celebrated pianist in his own right.[2]

In Kiev, the Neigauzes had been friends of the philosophical historian Valentin Asmus. Like Neigauz, he was of partly German origin. After graduating at Kiev University in 1919, he established an early reputation as an academic philosopher, logician and aesthetician, as well as working in the field of literature. In 1927 he and his family also moved to Moscow. There, at various times he worked at the Red Professorial Institute, the Moscow Institute of Philosophy, Literature and History, Moscow State University (from 1939 onwards), and the USSR Academy of Sciences' Institute of Philosophy.[3]

It was Asmus' wife Irina who introduced the Neigauzes and her own family to Boris Pasternak. She herself became a Pasternak devotee in 1928 after discovering a copy of the 1917 edition of *Over the Barriers*, and she passed on her enthusiasm to her husband and Genrikh Neigauz. Some time in the winter of 1928–29 Irina Asmus saw and recognised Pasternak at a tramway stop, and after introducing herself invited him to their apartment home on Zubovsky Boulevard. Pasternak duly came and sat through the night in animated conversation with his hosts and Genrikh Neigauz, in the course of which he inspired the whole company with the fire of his personality, intellect and eloquence.[4]

A week later Pasternak invited the Asmuses and Neigauzes to his Volkhonka home. During the evening there was animated discussion, piano-playing by Neigauz and Pasternak's recitation of recent verse. Apart from cultural interests in common there was a rapport among their company which Pasternak later described as the families' 'six-hearted union'.[5]

Pasternak had already heard Neigauz play in the concert hall and he was thrilled again that evening by his new friend's private performance. The pleasure was to be repeated often during the next several years, as also was that of post-concert gatherings with Neigauz and friends, when the company repaired either to the Volkhonka or to the Neigauzes' home on Trubnikovsky Lane for food and drink. One such occasion following a duet recital with Keneman lasted all night, and its refreshments, ample libations, recitations, music and foxtrot dancing were colourfully described in a letter to Pasternak's parents. On another occasion cheese and wurst brought from a concert tour in Germany were provided by Leningrad pianist Maria Yudina. On Neigauz's urging Pasternak first heard her play on 5 January 1929; afterwards they met and maintained a lifelong friendship especially after her removal to Moscow in the mid 1930s. At their first encounter Pasternak was astonished by Yudina's playing and also by her 'eccentricities'. As he told his sister Josephine, she was 'mystically inclined, wears penitential bonds under her dress and plays like that'.[6]

Early in their friendship, Pasternak gave Neigauz a manuscript copy of his own youthful piano sonata of 1909, and there was talk of a public performance. However Pasternak was opposed to the performing of a 'composer who never was'; regrettably, one result of regular communion with professional musicians during the 1930s was that he himself almost gave up playing the piano.

Unlike her husband, Zinaida Neigauz had relatively unsophisticated literary tastes extending no further than the verse of Blok. She recalled being conquered by Pasternak's personality, but as a poet his complexity was beyond her. She told him so and he laughingly (and as it emerged, prophetically) agreed to write more simply. According to Zinaida, only Evgeniya Pasternak failed to enjoy their communal gatherings and quite evidently the two of them took against one another from the outset. Initially this clouded Zinaida's attitude towards Boris himself, and for the meanwhile she paid no further visits to the Volkhonka, although Genrikh, Pasternak and the Asmuses continued meeting frequently. Very soon, unilaterally, Irina Asmus became infatuated with Pasternak. Her husband was aware of the situation but remained well disposed to Boris, who was innocent of any provocation. Nevertheless, his capacity for rapt attentiveness reinforced the impact of his personality, and as he later admitted to Raisa Lomonosova, 'Quite apart from friendship, I have never experienced even *attention* without some admixture of love.'[7]

The year 1930 in Russian literary history has been termed the 'Year of Acquiescence', that is, literature's final submission to control by political authority. That year Stalin for the first time personally intervened in literary discussions and called for nothing to be printed that diverged from the viewpoint of the state. As the accredited Party representative in literary matters, RAPP connived at the disbandment not just of 'fellow-travelling' literary groups – the Constructivists, Pereval, and critical followers of Pereverzev – but also of 'proletarian' groups such as Kuznitsa (The Smithy) and Mayakovsky's Ref.[8] Russian literature was now required to assist actively in reinforcing Party policy. In the first instance, in mid 1930, this involved approving a new orgy of terror against those accused of counter-revolutionary subversion and 'wrecking'. Those charged included groups of engineers, academics, clergymen, former Mensheviks, members of an 'Industrial Party' (Prompartiya), and others alleged to be plotting an anti-Stalin coup. Writers were expected to join in the chorus of condemnation that greeted the November trials; Gorky was commissioned to write a play on the 'wrecker' theme; and *Literaturnaya gazeta* on 4 December printed several writers' letters demanding death sentences for the accused engineers.

Now, in addition to a total ban on oppositional publications, 'positive coercion' was brought to bear on the writing community. Silence in itself became suspect, and a readiness to join in vilifying trial defendants became a test of political reliability, especially for literary 'fellow travellers'. To encourage doubters, literary misdemeanours such as those of Pilnyak and Zamyatin, or of alleged 'kulak' sympathisers like Klychkov and Klyuev, were now likened to the crimes of class enemies in other walks of life. While many colleagues competed in the accusatory chorus, Pasternak took the risk of staying silent and limited himself to signing a fairly innocuous collective letter that defended Gorky against West European press attacks on his attitude to the Industrial Party trials.[9] In fact Pasternak was deeply troubled by literary and political events, and he only hinted at his true feelings in a letter to Andrei Bely in November of 1930. Discussing the plight of the exiled and destitute former Symbolist editor and translator Sergei Polyakov, he told Bely:

The entire last few days I have kept reading your *Petersburg* and the various ministers from *Notes of an Eccentric*. What an awful Nemesis, which was already captured by Dostoevsky. Yet your own and his (Dostoevsky's) phantasmagorias have been surpassed by reality [. . .] Swift screwed up, didn't he? He didn't know the right time and place to be born.[10]

Paradoxically, while frenzied publicity was demanded for the Moscow show trials, a wall of secrecy surrounded a host of other 'unofficial' arrests, internments and executions that accompanied the reign of terror. To break that silence put those who uttered and received such messages at risk, and foreign correspondence required special caution because of postal censorship. A letter to Pasternak's father in late March of 1930 used Aesopic language to describe the recent execution of a young friend 'who perished from the same illness as the first husband of Liza [i.e. Louis, husband of Pasternak's cousin Liza Hosiasson]. From all that I have said you will realise how terrible this incident is. He was just 28 years old. They say [. . .] he thought too much, which sometimes leads to this form of meningitis.'[11]

Vladimir Sillov was a literary scholar, poet, teacher and one-time member of Mayakovsky's Lef. Pasternak had been on good terms with him and his wife since 1922, although he had seen little of them after leaving Lef. It was in mid March, at the première of Mayakovsky's *The Bathhouse*, that he heard from Semyon Kirsanov of Sillov's arrest in early January and execution on 16 February.[12] In a letter to Nikolai Chukovsky in Leningrad Pasternak characterised Sillov and the need to conceal his fate with almost alarming frankness. Among the Lef fraternity, Sillov struck him as 'a singularly honest, vital, reproachfully noble example of a moral novelty which I never pursued since it was totally unfathomable and alien to my turn of mind [. . .] There was only one man who for a moment gave probability to that impossible and enforced myth, and that was V. A. Sillov.' Pasternak's letter also reflected on the recent requirement that

when we lose people close to us we are obliged to pretend they are alive, and we are unable to remember them and say that they are not there. If my letter could cause you any unpleasantness, please do not spare me. Return it to me as the guilty party. I will then provide my full signature. (Normally I sign illegibly or with initials only.)[13]

After resigning from Lef in 1927, Pasternak made vain attempts to seek Mayakovsky's understanding for his own need to preserve integrity and sense of involvement in an organic culture untainted by politics. In the late 1920s their meetings were very infrequent, and it was after a gap of nearly two years that Pasternak and his wife attended Mayakovsky's party to let in the New Year of 1929.[14] None of this had affected his personal affection and admiration for Mayakovsky. A revised version of 'Windmills' ('Mel′nitsy') submitted in August 1928 to *Novy mir* was inscribed to Mayakovsky as a tribute to the gargantuan aspect of his genius. A whole section of the revised *Over the Barriers* was dedicated to him, and another poem full of admiration, regrets and hopes, was originally planned for inclusion.[15]

Pasternak also preserved a personal sympathy for Nikolai Aseyev, who emerged as Mayakovsky's most loyal disciple. He deplored Aseyev's omission from Vladimir Pozner's survey of modern Russian literature, although realising that like Mayakovsky he had compromised his talent and failed to solve the dilemma of 'whether to suffer without illusions or to prosper while deceiving oneself and others'.[16] Ideology aside, however, Pasternak also showed genuine concern when Aseyev developed acute tuberculosis in 1929 and began spitting blood; fortunately he was treated in time and cured, and lived into the early 1960s.[17]

During 1929–30 Mayakovsky showed increasing signs of a mental and artistic crisis. While Pasternak resigned from Lef in order to preserve his freedom, in September 1928 Mayakovsky abandoned it in submission to even more rigorous political control, forswearing his modernist habits and announcing a new programme 'to rehabilitate the novel and Rembrandt'. After mid 1928 the efforts of RAPP and the censor were supplemented by secret police penetration of all literary groups and organisations. The Brik family apartment then effectively became, in Pasternak's expression, 'a department of the OGPU', patronised personally by Yakov Agranov, who was assistant head of the Special Section concerned with infiltration of the literary intelligentsia.[18]

Mayakovsky's new 'Revolutionary Front of Art' (Ref) created in May 1929 pursued only journalistic goals: Mayakovsky himself contributed nothing except propaganda doggerel for the press, and Ref went out of existence before ever conducting any meaningful activity. In summer and autumn of 1929 he lent his voice to various official schemes, vehemently condemning 'fellow traveller' apoliticism in literature and publishing a personal denunciation of Pilnyak.[19] This vociferous conformism disguised a new crisis in Mayakovsky's personal life, and officialdom were now uncertain of his reliability and orthodoxy. In the autumn of 1929 he was refused an exit visa to visit his lady friend Tatyana Yakovleva in Paris. Quite apart from frustrating his romantic ambitions, this prohibition demonstrated he was no longer one of the privileged elite, and for the next few months he made frantic attempts to

30

reestablish his political credibility. In September, at a plenary session of the RAPP directorate he proclaimed his and Ref's unanimous support of RAPP, and at final rehearsals for *The Bathhouse* he offered otiose assurances that he regarded himself first and foremost as a 'Party worker'.[20] Finally, after the dissolution of Ref, on 6 February he announced his intention to join RAPP and thus bade farewell to all his longstanding literary companions; none of the new company in which he found himself was a kindred spirit.[21]

Whilst Mayakovsky's literary isolation aggravated his psychological crisis, Pasternak had a resigned and half-humorous attitude towards what he described as his own 'constant attraction towards an elegant solitude'.[22] This 'isolationism' provoked ambivalent reactions in several colleagues, and even Pilnyak, who appreciated it as the only honourable position for a contemporary writer, publicly criticised Pasternak for it.[23]

Pasternak and Mayakovsky evidently met for the last time in early 1930 at the home of Meyerhold. The poet Evgenii Dolmatovsky recalled Mayakovsky's attacking him for his semi-infantile 'Akhmatova-like' poetic style, at which Pasternak sprang to his defence.[24] Beyond that, nothing is known of that last encounter. However, several witnesses recorded their penultimate meeting at a social gathering in late 1929 which had a more final quality. The Pasternaks saw in the New Year of 1930 at the Asmuses' home, when Neigauz played to the guests and Pasternak recited the 'New Year' episode from *Spektorsky*.[25] But in deference to the ban on bourgeois festivities, Mayakovsky held his 'New Year' party at the Briks' on 30 December, when he also celebrated the twentieth anniversary of his literary début. Towards morning, when most guests had already left, Pasternak turned up with Viktor Shklovsky to pay his respects and stayed only briefly. Lev Kassil's slightly belletrised and disputed version reported Pasternak in a friendly and conciliatory mood and Mayakovsky rebuffing him in the third person: 'He'd better go. He's still understood nothing. He thinks it [i.e. friendship] is like a button: today you pull it off and tomorrow sew it on again [. . .] People are being torn out of my flesh . . .' Other slightly differing accounts recall Pasternak leaving the dining room in perplexity and despair and gazing blankly ahead while Mayakovsky stood in lowering martial pose, hands in pockets and chewing a cigarette butt. To Galina Katanyan it appeared that a quarrel had taken place.[26]

Pasternak may have seen Mayakovsky one final time on March 16 at the Moscow première of *The Bathhouse* at Meyerhold's theatre, but there was no recorded contact between them. The play was panned as a slander of Soviet society and taken off after only a few performances. This defeat at the hands of the literary theatrical press was the final blow to Mayakovsky. At 10.15 am on

14 April, he committed suicide with a gunshot to the head at his studio in Lubyansky Passage.

According to *Safe Conduct*, Pasternak's first reaction on hearing the news by phone later that morning was to call up Sillov's widow who had apparently attempted suicide herself after her husband's execution: 'Something prompted me that this shock would provide an outlet for her own grief.' He met Olga Sillova at the entrance to Lubyansky Passage around midday. As they arrived at Mayakovsky's apartment the body was borne out under wraps to a waiting ambulance and taken to the Briks' apartment in Gendrikov Lane. Pasternak went there by cab with Olga Sillova, and he was later observed wandering blindly about the room and collapsing in sobs against each person he encountered. His later memoir recorded snapshots of Aseyev weeping, Kirsanov sobbing uncontrollably, Mayakovsky's mother, and his sister Olga hysterically attempting to talk with her brother. Mayakovsky lay on his side with his face to the wall, covered by a sheet up to his chin. 'Proudly turned away from everyone, even as he lay there, even in his sleep, he stubbornly strained to get away and escape.'[27]

The dynamism imprinted on the dead man's countenance found explosive expression again in the poem 'The Poet's Death' ('Smert' poeta') which Pasternak later wrote in his memory. Beyond this, the event had a stunning and immediate impact on Pasternak's other literary undertakings, as well as a longer-term shaping influence on his career in the 1930s.

Pasternak's major project during the first months of 1930 was the completion of *Safe Conduct*, part one of which was written two years earlier and published in 1929 (volume I, 396–8). Though normally rendered as 'Safe Conduct', the Russian title more accurately signified a 'preservation order' – a document issued in the early Soviet period to confirm ownership, or protect certain objects from nationalisation or revolutionary vandalism. Yet the contents 'preserved' here were not those of conventional memoirs or autobiography. Pasternak said little about his parentage and family; and only sparse information was offered on his personal life, professional career, social milieu and historical background. Instead, the book was structured around a series of autobiographic episodes recording Pasternak's passions, romantic and cultural, and their successive sifting, ending in an abnegation of the revolutionary Mayakovsky, and in the latter's own suicidal self-rejection.

Over time, the nature of the material scheduled for inclusion in Pasternak's book had changed. Unlike part I, which crystallised earlier,[28] the second and third parts, devoted mainly to his sojourns in Marburg and Venice in 1912 and his dealings with Mayakovsky, were heavily coloured by the events and specific moods of 1929–30. In part I the Rilkean essence of Pasternak's philosophy was set in relief by the destructive theories of Lef (volume I, 315–17); in parts II and especially III the practical realisation of Lef's extremist theories was shown as part of an aggressive state policy inimical to art in general. Similarly, although nominally concerned with Mayakovsky, 'the last year of the poet' discussed in part III was understood to be archetypal and to reflect a sense of finality which darkened every aspect of life at the end of the decade.[29] *Safe Conduct* was thus in some sense a farewell statement. As Pasternak reminded his sister Lydia in February 1930, part I was written in 1927:

Times then were quite different. But it already contains something that is increasing year by year and is killing me. I have started weighing down my writing with valedictory theoretical insertions, like testamentary truths, in a constantly haunting anticipation of my coming demise – whether complete, physical, or partial and natural, or finally unwilled and arbitrary.[30]

The revised version of one of Pasternak's earliest poems ended in a programmatic statement that 'the more randomly, the surer / Poems are forming out of sobs.'[31] Similarly in part II of *Safe Conduct*, several discourses on artistic philosophy reinforced the randomness of Pasternak's whole autobiographic approach:

Art [. . .] cannot be arbitrarily directed where one wishes like a telescope. Focussed on reality dislocated by feeling, art is the record of this dislocation and it copies it from nature [. . .] Details gain in brilliance, losing their independence of meaning. Any one can be replaced by another, and any one is precious. (II, 243; *VP*, 231; *SS*, IV, 187–8)

Earlier in the work Pasternak stated that even an honest man's attempt to speak the truth lagged behind and distorted reality, whereas 'in art man falls silent and the image speaks out. And it emerges that only the image keeps pace with the progress of nature' (II, 235; *VP*, 223; *SS*, IV, 179). All this described how Pasternak's earlier lyric verse had come into being, and while he worked on *Safe Conduct*, in early 1930, a second edition of *Two Books* appeared as a living reminder of this. This poetics was juxtaposed and contrasted with the causal mind-set of the Marburg Neo-Kantian philosophical school. Implicitly, though, Pasternak's philosophy of art contradicted not just the 'literature of fact' conceived by Chuzhak and other Lef extremists, but the whole notion of an art created in 'causal' response to 'proletarian' state directive.

Written during a renewed official atheist campaign in the USSR, part II of Pasternak's book encoded several heretical innuendi against the literal-mindedness that fired this aggressive atheism. Recalling Saint Elizabeth of Hungary's life in Marburg, he described her spiritual ward as 'a tyrant, that is a man without imagination'. Later, to illustrate the continuity of world culture,

Pasternak chose an example that was provocatively anachronistic: surveying the religious art of Venice, he observed that 'the Bible is not so much a book with a hard and fast text as a notebook of humanity [. . .] The history of culture is a chain of equations in images connecting and pairing up the known with the next unknown' (II, 263; *VP*, 252; *SS*, IV, 208). The religious image had an implicit primacy that eluded even honest attempts to speak a Marxist truth.

The pungent relevance of *Safe Conduct* to the Soviet here-and-now also distinguished it from conventional reminiscences, and it explained a compelling drive to complete and publish the book. This took precedence over any thoughts of foreign travel or family visits to Berlin, and in this respect at least the book had a precision of purpose quite different from the 'arbitrariness' of lyric verse.[32] In later sections of *Safe Conduct* an obliquity of statement barely disguised the unmentionable truth.

The most controversial section of part II of *Safe Conduct* was an Aesopic parallel between the Venice of the Doges and the Soviet state with its secret police activities. In Venice the postbox for depositing secret denunciations on the censor's stairway was shaped like a lion's maw. As Pasternak recorded, this 'bocca di leone' inspired terror in people's hearts, while at the same time 'it became a mark of ill-breeding to mention persons who had disappeared into that exquisitely sculpted aperture except when the authorities themselves had expressed regret in this regard'.[33] In part I of his book Pasternak had breached etiquette by mentioning his exiled friend Durylin.[34] A worse offence in part III was the allusion by initials to the regime's innocent victim Vladimir Sillov. *Safe Conduct* also cocked an Aesopic snook at the whole modern Soviet state and its notion of 'social command' as a prime motive force of artistry: Venetian art was described as having eluded and deceived the tyrannical palace-dwellers who commissioned it, for 'the language of the palaces emerged as the language of oblivion [. . .] the palaces remained' (II, 261; *VP*, 250; *SS*, IV, 206).

The suicide of Mayakovsky had itself been a flagrant act of deception and defiance of the Soviet state. Official commentators pronounced his death as due to incidental factors and out of keeping with his revolutionary heroic poetic stance. But Pasternak described even his facial expression in death as one of truculent disdain, and his suicide as a final act of romantic self-dramatisation. While Pasternak allegedly abandoned the 'romantic manner' – a notion of the poet's life conceived as 'spectacle' – Esenin and Mayakovsky, he claimed, had intensified it, their suicides forming a consummation of their poetics.

In the third section of *Safe Conduct*, several other phenomena described as belonging to the pre-revolutionary or early Soviet era were in fact referable to the very recent past. Thus, the apoliticism of modern 'fellow travellers' who were currently being lashed was described as characteristic of Pasternak's generation in the 1910s. Also, at a time when Gorky and Mayakovsky's mutual animosity was well known, Pasternak wickedly yoked them together, recalling Mayakovsky's claim that Gorky had led him to discover the 'social theme' and the art of working 'in measured portions' – i.e. in a manner consistent with 'social command', but barely compatible with wayward inspiration.[35]

Safe Conduct dismissed Mayakovsky's pre-war entourage as a 'random, hastily assembled and always indecently mediocre clique', and implicitly this applied also to his adherents in the 1920s. This was driven home in Pasternak's poem on 'The Poet's Death' which consciously echoed Lermontov's invective against an order that had assassinated Pushkin. Pasternak's first version of the poem concluded by describing Mayakovsky as having 'erased from the earth' the friends and 'scum' (*mraz'*) who held him dear. For *Novy mir*'s editor Polonsky, who was by now politically vulnerable, this was too outspoken. He had required a change of title for Pasternak's poem to Pilnyak, and now commissioned a milder conclusion to 'The Poet's Death', although even the version printed in the first issue for 1931 was not inoffensive:

> Your gunshot was akin to Etna
> Among the foothills' set of cowards.[36]

Aseyev correctly identified himself in these lines and was deeply offended.[37] In *Safe Conduct* Pasternak paid tribute to Aseyev's pre-revolutionary virtues of imagination, sensitivity and musicality, but commented laconically that 'in art, as also in life, we pursued different things'.[38] Over the next several years, Aseyev was to reward Pasternak by playing Salieri to his Mozart. Pasternak, however, refused to fall out with him and preferred expressions of exaggerated admiration to animosities.

In spring of 1930 Pasternak repeated to his parents his promise to Evgeniya that once the next chapter of *Safe Conduct* was written, he would set about organising a visit to Germany. By now his wife was ailing again. Her chest condition had worsened over the winter and doctors urged a rest cure in Western Europe. One passing thought was to take up Raisa Lomonosova's offer and send Evgeniya to visit her in Pasadena, California; alternatively – to his parents in Berlin, where he would join them in a few months' time, once *Safe Conduct* was complete.[39]

These plans were upstaged by Mayakovsky's suicide on 14 April, and it took Pasternak another year to complete his book. Verbal enquiries about an exit permit for the whole family to leave Russia had meanwhile drawn a negative response. The fact that more and more travellers stayed in the West because of Soviet conditions was viewed with disfavour. An influential sponsor was needed, and Pasternak turned to Karl Radek, an acquaintance from Berlin days in 1922–3. Radek's approaches also produced a refusal however, and in alarm Pasternak now appealed to Gorky. His letter of 31 May explained his request in almost overtly political terms:

It has been hard for me to work recently, especially this winter when the city has lapsed into a situation of such crazy and totally unjustified privilege compared with what has been happening in the countryside, and city-dwellers have been invited to go visit the victims and congratulate them on their shocks and disasters. Until this last winter I was so minded that, whatever the urge to travel to the West, I would not leave until I completed what I had started. I enticed myself with this as a promised reward and it was this that kept me going.

Now, though, I sense that there is no point in deluding myself. Nothing will come of all this, I overestimated my resistance and maybe my strength. I cannot achieve anything worthwhile and no delays are going to help. Something has broken inside me. I do not know when this was, but I have recently been aware of it. I have decided not to delay matters. Perhaps a trip will set me right if I have not yet mentally come to a final full-stop.

I have made some efforts and in the very initial steps I took I became convinced that without your support I shall not be granted permission to leave. So this is my request: please help me.[40]

In his reply received on 19 June, the elder writer minced no words and turned Pasternak down in a display of high-handed feebleness. Reluctant to back a lost cause, he seized on the lame but barely relevant political excuse that too many recent travellers had been making anti-Soviet statements, and regretted that this would make the release of other writers abroad more difficult. 'It has always been the case that decent folk have had to pay for the deeds of scoundrels,' he told Pasternak, 'and now your turn has come.'[41]

Gorky's answer was a self-fulfilling prophecy, at least so far as his help could be counted on. Pasternak made no attempt to press his case and instead intended to try again in the autumn – at least for his wife and son since (as he told Lydia) 'the main obstacle evidently lies in me'.[42] Meanwhile Gorky's betrayal was a blow to his pride. Under its fresh impact he reported his misfortune to Tsvetaeva. 'Not to let *Pasternak* out is a piece of idiocy and ingratitude,' Tsvetaeva commented to Raisa Lomonosova.[43]

Further insult was added to Pasternak's injury when attempts to secure visas only for his wife and son met with bureaucratic stonewalling. Pasternak felt humiliated and exasperated, partly because 'they don't turn you down directly. Instead they are emphatically friendly and show respect as they let things trail on [. . .] for years until I myself ask for the matter to be buried so as to put an end to the uncertainty.'[44] In answer to his complaint Lomonosova offered to approach her one-time 'great friend' Aleksandra Kollontai.[45] Meanwhile, Pasternak had expressed his frustration and disappointment to Romain Rolland in July. 'Cher ami, ' Rolland wrote back, 'Je sens la douleur de votre lettre, et j'en suis pénétré. Ce que je pourrai faire pour l'atténuer, je le ferai. Mais dominez vos sentiments! Même votre art y gagnera . . .'[46] Rolland was as good as his word. An idea that Rabindranath Tagore might act as advocate while visiting Moscow fell through. But shortly after that Rolland talked to Lunacharsky in Geneva in January 1931, and despite the latter's waning influence, he was eventually able to secure exit visas for Evgeniya Pasternak and Zhenya.[47]

In summer of 1930, the Pasternaks had considered various holiday plans. Artist and musician Anna Troyanovskaya invited them to her dacha near Maloyaroslavets where earlier in the decade the composer Medtner and artist Robert Falk had sojourned, but the offer was not taken up.[48] However, for the last few years the Asmuses and Neigauzes had spent summer together in the Kiev region, and Irina Asmus urged that the Pasternaks join them. One attraction was the likelihood of better supplies than were available in Russia following the collectivisation. In early May, Zinaida Neigauz, who had a head for practical matters, went to reconnoitre, make bookings and report back. Four villas were thus reserved for the Asmus, Neigauz and Pasternak families and for Aleksandr Pasternak and his wife, at the dacha settlement of Irpen, twenty-three kilometres from Kiev.[49]

At the end of May the Neigauzes and Asmuses travelled to Irpen. With them went Pasternak's wife and son, together with Elizaveta Stetsenko, and a multitude of pots, pans, bedding and other household effects done up in bundles. Boris stayed on in Moscow to put various matters in order and collect some money. After Gorky's letter arrived on the 19th, however, there was nothing more to detain him; he arrived in Irpen on 22 June.[50]

As at Gelendzhik, Evgeniya was initially unimpressed with Irpen, although Nikolai Vilyam who came to visit in August recalled it as a great beauty spot.[51] The villas stood in their own grounds amid mixed woodland; the Pasternaks' plot of land boasted a gigantic spreading oaktree of which Evgeniya made an oilpainting. On the outskirts of the wood, oxen grazed in the languid heat, and in the distance were the shaded banks of the River Irpen, reached by crossing a field overgrown with wormwood and savory. Hoopoes trundled along the woodland paths; other birdlife included storks, herons and oreoles; and there was an abundance of snakes and squirrels.[52]

The all-season villas were solidly built and spacious. Pasternak was reminded of the family dacha at Raiki in 1907–9. Their house stood near to that of the Asmuses, and was deliberately selected by Zinaida, as she recalled, on some inner prompting to avoid too close proximity to the Pasternaks.[53]

The Neigauzes had taken a house next door to that of Aleksandr and Irina Pasternak. A grand piano was specially ordered from Kiev, and like the rest of their luggage, it arrived by horse and cart. This enabled Neigauz to work on new repertoire and prepare for his summer concerts in Kiev.[54]

Evgeniya Pasternak had recently graduated from Vkhutein (Higher Art and Technical Institute) and continued her painting activities at Irpen. In one of Pasternak's poems she was the artist whose 'countenance, forehead and smile' were recorded as she painted in her smock, spattering the grass with oil-colour and smoking those 'packets of poison / Which bear the name "Basma" and bring threats of asthma'.[55] Apart from the oak tree, while in Irpen she produced several sketches and portraits, including one of Zinaida Neigauz.[56]

Neigauz's main concert of the summer was on the open-air stage of Kiev's Kupechesky Garden on 15 August, and was attended by the entire party from Irpen and friends from in town. Impressions of the occasion figured in Pasternak's poetic 'Ballade' dedicated to Neigauz (above, pp. 25–6). As the August night drew on, thunderclouds gathered. Neigauz played the Chopin E minor concerto to great acclaim. But at the end of the performance came a blinding flash of lightning, peals of thunder, and the heavens opened. Soloist and orchestra remained sheltered under the platform canopy; an intent audience, however, consented to get saturated and hear the music out, taking flight only at the end, during Borodin's Polovtsian Dances.[57]

Apart from that gala occasion, the whole summer's ravishing impressions were coloured by Neigauz's piano playing – especially his interpretations of Brahms and Chopin – and several of Pasternak's poems contained echoes of this. There was also much talk of matters musical, in addition to discussions on philosophy, literature, recitation of poetry, and open-air living in good company.

While at Irpen the four families enjoyed visits from friends in Kiev, such as Leonid Vysheslavsky, poet Nikolai Ushakov and the family of the scholar Evgenii Perlin. The sisters of Aleksandr Pasternak's wife also came to visit, and later on, in early August came her recently widowed brother Nikolai.[58] There had also been discussion in letters of a visit by Olga Freidenberg and her mother, but nothing came of this. Nevertheless, as Boris later told his cousin, 'It was an entrancing summer with splendid friends in a splendid setting. And [. . .] my work suddenly somehow revived in the sunshine, and I had not worked so well for a long, long time as I did in Irpen.'[59]

Pasternak sketched or completed several lyric poems marked by the realia and emotions of that summer. He also successfully revisited the manuscript of *Spektorsky*, some chapters were refashioned, and a new introduction was written, linking the hero with the circumstances of Pasternak's own life in 1924 when the work was begun (volume I, 336). The complete revised manuscript was submitted in September and was used for the eventual book edition in 1931.[60]

While in Irpen Pasternak also finished reading Rolland's *L'Âme enchantée* and became interested in Proust again. In July he wrote asking Josephine to send him *Du côté de chez Swann* and *Le corde de Guermantes*. As he told her, 'Until now I was *afraid* to read Proust, it was all so close to me. Now that I have nothing to lose [. . .] there is nothing left in me for Proust to influence.'[61] Perhaps, indeed, the influence was faint, but there remained some powerful affinities between Pasternak and Proust which some later scholars have explored.[62]

In one respect, there was an unreality about that Irpen summer. As Olga Freidenberg later heard, it was 'a world of complete detachment and isolation, like the solitude in Hamsun's *Hunger*'.[63] Reminders of a cruel outside world reached the dacha community only seldom – as, for instance, when a commission visited every villa in the settlement to 'remove valuables' as part of the rural collectivisation process, which included taxing and dispossessing all members of the well-to-do 'kulak' peasant population.[64] In fact, as the poem 'Summer' ('Leto') later recalled, the Irpen visitors realised that in effect they were attending 'an age-old prototype banquet – / A feast, as in Plato, in time of plague'. The subject of Plato's 'Symposium' or 'Banquet' evidently figured in conversations there, and this image was elaborated in greater detail in Pasternak's poem and later discussed in Nikolai Vilyam's memoirs: Plato's Diotima was Irina Asmus, to whom the poem was originally dedicated and who evidently mistook it as a form of amorous declaration by Pasternak. In fact, as the poem stated, he sought refuge in a toast 'to friendship, my salvation!' The poem 'Summer' also introduced a character from Pushkin's *Feast in a Time of Plague*:

> And is it Mary the harp-player's scheming
> Caused Arabian hurricanes at fortune's behest
> To yield to her hand and set the harp ringing
> In a pledge that is final: there is no death?
>
> (I, 333; SP, 356; SS, I, 389)

Mary the harpist here, as Vilyam showed, was Zinaida Neigauz, and the poem 'Summer' thus alluded not just to the continued Platonic Dialogue on beauty and immortality, but hinted too at the unspoken amorous underlay that enhanced the atmosphere of Irpen and relit a spark of poetic creativity.[65]

Zinaida Neigauz's memoirs later related more of what transpired on the emotional front in Irpen. Irina Asmus' infatuation with Pasternak became increasingly obvious, although he himself was drawn more towards the Neigauzes, and 'accidentally on purpose' staged several meetings with Zinaida *à deux*. Though a pianist by training she was an essentially prosaic and practical person, and Pasternak was first of all enthralled not only by her musicality or Italianate attractiveness but by her adroitness with saucepan, iron and scrubbing brush. While Genrikh remained in the artistic clouds and was challenged by tasks as simple as making tea, Zinaida was exercised on the domestic front by two young sons aged three and four. Pasternak, for his part, enjoyed and appreciated the minutiae of her domestic activity. He maintained that 'a poetic nature should love the round of daily life and that some poetic splendour could always be found in this', and he perceived in Zinaida a kindred spirit in her ability to move with ease from the keyboard to her saucepans, which, he claimed, 'breathed true poetry'.[66]

Zinaida suspected something unnatural in this eloquently expressed 'kinship' and avoided the Pasternaks – partly because she disliked Evgeniya, whom she regarded as spoilt, lethargic and indulgent. The contrast between the two women in this respect doubtless increased Zinaida's seeming attractiveness to Boris. He continued hovering around the Neigauz dacha, eager to hear Genrikh practising and alert to any chance of assisting her with gathering firewood, retrieving a bucket from the wellshaft, or sniffing her fresh ironing.[67] Irina Asmus became aware of Boris's crush on Zinaida and suffered in consequence. If aware of these emotional undercurrents, Evgeniya registered no response – it was not the first time Boris had aroused her jealousy.

In September the holidays came to an end. The Asmuses left first, and the Neigauzes departed last of all together with the Pasternaks. The joint packing operation was assisted by Zinaida's practical bent, later celebrated in a little poem, 'Could I have wished for a life that's sweeter . . .' ('Zhizni l' mne khotelos' slashche . . .') Its manuscript, which she preserved, also contained a musical quote from Brahms's C sharp minor intermezzo, opus 117, part of Genrikh's summer repertoire.[68]

The Moscow-bound train left Kiev at 9 pm on 21 September. Zinaida's sons and husband were asleep already when she stepped out to smoke in the corridor. There she was joined by Boris and the two of them talked for almost three hours. Now for the first time she detected a note of urgency and seriousness in the compliments he paid to both her looks and moral qualities. Fending off the tributes, she attempted to dampen his ardour by recounting an episode from her earlier life. From the age of fifteen she had been the mistress of her own cousin, who was then aged forty-five. At the time it struck her as 'the ultimate great passion', but she was left with guilt feelings that later tormented her. However, she little realised that in Pasternak she was dealing with one who thrived on a sense of pity for outraged womanhood. Shortly afterwards he described her as 'a beauty of the Mary Queen of Scots type, judging by [. . .] her fate'.[69] Her story thus had the opposite effect to the one she expected. 'I knew as much all the time!' Pasternak replied. 'Of course, you'll find it hard to believe, but when I first heard all this, I'd already guessed what you went through.' She thereupon bade him goodnight and retired.[70]

More details of Zinaida's early life emerged later, and they were retailed in family correspondence. Her father had been a military engineer and had turned fifty when he married her eighteen-year-old mother, who was of partly Italian descent. Zinaida, the third daughter of the marriage, was born in Petersburg in 1897. She grew up in a noisy household at Sablino, near the capital. Her father died when she was ten and his pension would not stretch to finance two families. Her mother moved into town and scraped to send her daughter to the Smolny Institute for girls. At fifteen Zinaida fell for her much older cousin, Nikolai Melitinsky, who rented a flat for their trysts – an arrangement that continued for three years. During this period she began intensive music studies, and later, after the Revolution, she went on to study the piano with the Neigauzes in Elizavetgrad.[71] The story of Zinaida's youth, however, made a deep impression on Pasternak. In 1931 he wrote to his sister Josephine about her 'person, character, fate and destiny which combine everything that is feminine with such force, as in the Magdalene'.[72] Much later, elements of Zinaida's biography figured in the novel *Doctor Zhivago*, in the story of Lara and Komarovsky.

3

New Love and Second Birth

All loving is a cross to bear, yet
Your beauty has no convolution,
And the secret of your splendour
Is like our puzzled life's solution.

In spring we hear the stir of dreams,
Of rustling truths and news awaking.
And from such origins you come,
Selfless as the air – your meaning.

It's easy to wake up and see,
And rid one's heart of verbal litter;
To live henceforth a life that's free
Of trash is quite a simple matter.

(1931)

After the previous winter's setback with *Spektorsky* it was with some diffidence that Pasternak on 28 September submitted his revised version to GIKhL (State Publishers of Artistic Literature). 'Probably it won't see the light of day', he told Olga Freidenberg. 'The censors have started shredding me in repeated editions, and to make up for their previous lack of attention, they now show it to excess and even start digging their teeth into manuscripts that have not yet been published.'[1] Not all was despair and gloom however. A public reading in autumn 1930 in the House of Scholars on Kropotkinskaya Street was a huge success.[2] Despite apprehensions, the revised book version of *Spektorsky* was accepted and appeared in the ideologically more relaxed year of 1931, although it was never separately reprinted during Pasternak's lifetime. The work's new introduction was taken by *Novy mir*, where it appeared in the last issue for 1930. Meanwhile the final issue of *Krasnaya nov'* for 1930 included the two new poetic 'Ballades', and Pasternak pressed on with the third and final part of *Safe Conduct*.

In family correspondence with Berlin, apart from Pasternak's dejection and general complaints of life's difficulties, there was barely a hint of the disturbing issues dominating Russian public life. Family news from Germany centred on items such as the birth of a son Karl (Charles) to Josephine and her husband, Leonid's sojourn with Gerhart Hauptmann at Agnetendorf and sketches for a portrait of the German author,[3] and Lydia's own poems in German and Russian which were sent to Boris and pleased him. Also forwarded to Moscow by Josephine, and received on 26 December, was a recent issue of the Cambridge magazine *Experiment*, which included some verse translations and an essay on Pasternak by George Reavey. This was Pasternak's effective début in English letters; Reavey, whose mother was Russian and who had lived in Russia as a child, also corresponded with Pasternak in 1930–33 and later translated more of his work.[4]

German visas for Evgeniya and Zhenya were announced as ready for collection in late November. By this time, however, dramatic undercurrents in Pasternak's private life began to surface in correspondence. There was alarm in Berlin at his seeming impatience for Evgeniya's departure. Nothing was spelt out to his parents at this stage, [5] but the Neigauz and Pasternak family drama meanwhile moved on apace.

Soon after returning from Irpen, Pasternak caused mayhem in both families. Without even establishing a consensus of mutual feeling with Zinaida, he confessed his love for her to his wife. Evgeniya was agonised and incensed, concluding immediately that their marriage was ruined; she told Boris he must leave, and was further offended by his seeming acquiescence.[6] Pasternak also paid the Neigauzes a visit, bringing the text of the two 'Ballades' as a gift, and made a similar declaratory announcement to Genrikh. In their ensuing discussion both men evidently shed tears. Pasternak declared his devotion to Genrikh and his love for Zinaida. He said he was incapable of contemplating life without her, and at the same time he had no idea of a solution to their problems in real life . . . Zinaida laughed the whole issue aside and suggested they should meet with Boris less often. Their encounters that autumn were indeed rarer and occurred mainly at the Asmuses. Irina Asmus inevitably learned of the situation and her friendship towards Zinaida cooled in consequence. Zinaida meanwhile sensed 'a grandiose feeling' for Boris rising within her, although aware that all this was cruel to both their families and to the Asmuses.[7]

On 1 January 1931 Genrikh Neigauz was scheduled to leave on an extended concert tour of Siberia. After his departure Boris began calling on Zinaida as often as three times per day. He averred that he intended leaving Evgeniya and he was not put out by Zinaida's stated resolve to stay with her own family.

Pasternak kept his word and in mid January moved out of the Volkhonka apartment. For about three weeks he lodged with the Asmuses on Zubovsky Boulevard, where he managed to complete the writing of *Safe Conduct*.[8] Until late December he and Zinaida had still been on formal '*vy*' terms; in January, though, Pasternak pressed his suit and relations with Zinaida ripened to the point where they decided on engagement. This was recorded in a circumstantial poem addressed to her à propos of the funeral and memorial concert they attended on 21 January for Feliks Blumenfeld, the uncle and one-time teacher of Genrikh Neigauz.[9]

In early February, Pasternak moved and lodged for three months with the Pilnyaks. The politically and professionally rehabilitated master of the house was away in the USA until April, but Pasternak was allowed to sleep in his study. Well looked after by Pilnyak's actress wife and mother-in-law, he enjoyed the comfortable surroundings, good fare, and the company of Aida the Great Dane, and eventually of Pilnyak himself.[10]

During March Pasternak also for the first time stayed overnight with Zinaida at the Trubnikovsky Lane apartment. Following this, overwhelmed by her guilty passion, Zinaida wrote to her husband and confessed all. The news shattered Neigauz, so much so that he stopped playing in the middle of one recital and left the platform in tears. The remainder of his Siberian tour was cancelled and he returned to Moscow on 22 March.[11]

Shaken though Neigauz was, he was a by no means innocent party. Zinaida's eventual break with him was eased by his own infidelities. In 1929, in fact, he had sired a daughter by his former fiancée Militsa Borodkina. In the mid 1930s he married her and later jokingly referred to his amorous affairs as being conducted 'in rondo form'.[12]

For many months Zinaida was torn by a sense of family duty and guilt at breaking up her own and the Pasternaks' marriage on the one hand, and by her overwhelming infatuation with Boris on the other. Pasternak's own talent for paradox and original thought patterns meanwhile enhanced everyone's confusion. In a state of 'guilty innocence' and naive exaltation, apparent from his letters to Zinaida, he believed it possible to preserve good relations with both her and Evgeniya, as well as with Genrikh Neigauz. The complexion of his feelings was described in a letter to his parents in March 1931, which broke a long silence and briefly outlined the situation. Schematically its theses were: I am unworthy of Zinaida whom I love eternally; I have caused Evgeniya unspeakable suffering and I am innocent; though in love with Zinaida, I am not leaving Evgeniya; Evgeniya loves me so much because she does not understand me. Pasternak concluded that Evgeniya needed rest and freedom – freedom to realise herself professionally in a way hitherto impossible; he did not exclude the resumption of a full conjugal life some time in the future, and meanwhile undertook to provide full support for her and their son.[13]

After moving out, Pasternak continued visiting his wife and son every few days and to all appearances maintained a strong affection for Evgeniya. They were seen together at Sofronitsky's piano recital in the Large Hall of the Conservatoire in mid January, and in the spring Sergei Bobrov still thought it possible to reconcile them.[14]

None of this was concealed from Zinaida who still struggled between family commitment and powerful feeling for Boris. When she quizzed Nikolai Vilyam he told her Boris 'never loved anyone so strongly as he loves you'. Pasternak was however still capable of waxing ecstatic to her about Evgeniya's virtues. A letter of May told Zinaida how he was filled with pain . . . 'pain at her [Evgeniya's] plight, not the pain of longing [. . .] I have known few people whom it was so worth loving and so necessary to love as her – and not just for her moral qualities, but also for her looks: for the story of her looks, the fate of those looks and their metamorphosis.'[15] To Pasternak both Evgeniya and Zinaida were women of arresting, but quite contrasting beauty. An unfinished afterword to *Safe Conduct* described Evgeniya's smile as flooding her face with light . . . 'and then one felt like bathing in her face. And since she always needed this illumination in order to be beautiful, so she needed happiness in order to please'. Zinaida's face by contrast seemed more lovely when caught in situations where other beauty would fade . . . 'this is femininity itself, a coarse lump of unbreakable pride, extracted from the quarries of creation . . .' (II, 343–4; *VP*, 480; *SS*, IV, 787).

Despite Pasternak's nomadic life in early 1931, the working conditions at his friends' were very conducive to creativity. By late February the completed manuscript of *Safe Conduct* was with the typist, and Pasternak planned to send one copy to Leningrad with Zamyatin who was paying a final visit to Moscow before leaving the country.[16] Poetic inspiration flowed again, fired partly by his new love. A bouquet of nine lyrics written in March and April appeared in the eighth issue of *Novy mir*, together they later formed section 3 of *Second Birth*. Three of them were on the spring thaw theme; others celebrated moments in the romantic calendar of the last year with memories of Irpen, impressions of Neigauz's playing and departure for Siberia, etc. Another poem was probably written in early summer to wish 'bon voyage' to Evgeniya, and there were three ardent love poems to Zinaida. The juxtaposition of these verses aroused the puzzled distaste of Akhmatova when she read them. The poems to Zinaida she described as the work of a 'distraught suitor' . . . 'And what nasty verses to his former wife! "It's not our life, not a heartfelt union /

We're breaking, but a mutual deceit." He apologises to one woman and runs to the other with a posy . . .'[17]

Evident particularly in the love lyrics was a new simplicity and clarity, which became an actual theme of the poems themselves (above, p. 42). A selection of these verses was recited by Pasternak at the *Novy mir* editorial offices in a programme of readings featuring Antokolsky, Aseyev, Kirsanov and others. His other engagements that spring included presentation and discussion of *Spektorsky* at the offices of GIKhL on 14 March. The discussion on that occasion largely decided the published fate of the work. Shklovsky alone spoke in its wholehearted defence. Several speakers criticised the loose-woven story-line and the central hero's lack of revolutionary consciousness. A report on the debate in *Literaturnaya gazeta* typified the general official attitude to Pasternak in the early 1930s. While noting *Spektorsky*'s poetic value, the reporter observed a draught of 'decadence, decline and autumnal feelings' emanating from its intricate texture and stated that the poem inadequately reflected the spirit of the modern age.[18]

A fortnight later, on March 28, at the FOSP clubroom on Vorovsky Street Pasternak again read from *Spektorsky*. This time public applause was dampened from the platform. Pasternak's performance was later described by various witnesses, among whom the theatre scholar Vitalii Vilenkin recalled that chairman Vsevolod Vishnevsky did not disguise his displeasure at the massive ovation Pasternak harvested, and he shouted at the audience: 'Such hysterics! Control yourselves! Exactly what is it that you're applauding?!'[19]

Publication of *Spektorsky* went ahead in early July, but negative verdicts were reiterated during 1931–2 by establishment RAPP-ists such as Prozorov and Selivanovsky.[20] Symptomatic of a general inability to 'read the text' in the case of a sophisticated poet such as Pasternak was Tarasenkov's conflation of the characters of Maria Ilyina and Olga Bukhteyeva in his discussion of *Spektorsky* in the journal *Zvezda*.[21]

The upcoming anniversary of Mayakovsky's death and Pasternak's recent completion of *Safe Conduct* occasioned various other public appearances, including one at the FOSP club on 6 April. At another discussion at the All-Russian Union of Poets, Pasternak reiterated some of his published remarks on Mayakovsky, notably his idea that the lyric poet operates against, and even needs the resistance of, the state.[22] To mark the anniversary *Literaturnaya gazeta* also carried the Mayakovsky chapters from *Safe Conduct*.[23]

At a Mayakovsky memorial meeting in Moscow University Pasternak added some further remarks on the status of poetry and its creators which were relevant to his own stance in the years ahead:

If one takes everything written by a poet, however much a genius he be, it could never be of equal force to the role played by him. This role will always be greater, because of all the arts the phenomenon of poetry is the most formalised [. . .] It communicates to you certain values, and in them we see a response to what [. . .] we term immortality. This essentially is the most precious mark of our species [. . .] The most thoroughbred expression of these formal qualities is the poet [who] dedicates his life to recalling these qualities and gives his own self up to the grinding of this theme.[24]

Thus Pasternak suggested that Mayakovsky's innate revolutionary quality sounded a note of integrity which the Russian revolution as officially recognised should try to preserve and imitate – 'a tone to which we ourselves have not yet risen'. All this pointed controversially to the idea of the poet and the spirit of revolution as oppositional forces ranged against the state. It also inevitably contrasted with any view of literature as a 'carbon copy' of reality, or as a record of facts and philosophies generated by the socialist state.

The final chapters of *Safe Conduct* plus some recent verse were read to a small company while Pasternak was staying at Pilnyak's home in April. That month *Novy mir* also finally printed the poem to Pilnyak arising from the 1929 campaign against him. It remained acutely relevant to Pilnyak's status: since the scandal subsided, he had contrived to reoccupy his earlier place of favour; his journey to America with Stalin's assent was a sign of that precarious rehabilitation.[25]

On the morning of 29 April while still at the Pilnyaks, Pasternak wrote another controversial poem which he described to Zinaida as 'unpoetic [. . .] but very much against the grain'.[26] On the evening of 29 April he read the poem in question to a well-lubricated company at Pilnyak's, whereupon Aleksandr Voronsky embraced him and said he would soon become the 'Black Saviour [*Chernyi Spas*] of the age – a sectarian, forbidden image'.[27]

It is not certain exactly which 'unpoetic' *vers de circonstances* were involved here.[28] It seems possible, though, that it was the poem beginning and ending as follows:

> Not one day's passed – a century or more,
> Yet strong is temptation, as of old,
> To gaze unflinching, without fear,
> With hope of glorious things and good.
> [. . .]
> Yet only now has come the time to say,
> While mindful of our different generation:
> The dawn of Great Peter's glorious days
> Was dark with mutiny and executions.

So never falter, forward march,
By this bold parallel consoled,
While you're alive, no bygone relic,
Before posterity condoles.　　　　(I, 360; *SP*, 377; *SS*, I, 421)

The implied addressee of the final stanza here was Stalin himself, and the poem
was the start of a sporadic dialogue that Pasternak maintained – or imagined
himself to be conducting – with Stalin during the 1930s. The poem was also a
sign of a newly regained artistic equilibrium and continuing belief in breathing
the 'air of history' – a history now embodied and personified by the figure of
Stalin himself. The poem was one of a group designated in manuscript as a
'Civic Triad' ('Grazhdanskaya triada') and published in *Novy mir*, no. 5 for
1932. A new buoyancy of spirit emerged in another of the poems, which
announced that:

. . . like cabbage-rose' wet scent,
The ripened years' fermented spirit
Will burst forth, loud itself express,
Declare its presence willy-nilly.　　(I, 358; *SP*, 377; *SS*, I, 420)

The controversial aspect of 'Not one day's passed . . .' was concealed in a
hallowed precedent. The poem evoked and partly paraphrased Pushkin's
'Stanzas' ('Stansy') of 1826 addressed to Nicholas I whose accession was
greeted by the Decembrist revolt, followed by reprisals against its ringleaders
and by a regime of rigid oppression. Addressing Nicholas, Pushkin referred to
the even earlier revolt of Kremlin guards (the Streltsy) which had not inhibited
the spirit of generosity which allegedly obtained under Peter the Great. Stalin's
personal reaction to the verse went unrecorded, but Pasternak's donning the
mantle of Pushkin hinted at an attempt to establish a protective aura. The
provocative equation of Nicholas and Stalin's oppressive regimes doubtless
explained why after the poem's appearance in *Second Birth* (1932) Pasternak
withdrew it from subsequent reprints. As he told Kruchenykh, he himself and
not the censor had suppressed it. First of all, it was 'unpoetic' and, paradoxically, the very fact of a dialogue with Stalin created the illusion of his closeness
to the regime.[29] Also excluded from the 1934 *Second Birth* were two other
poems of this period, probably because they expressed a by then disappointed
optimism that the 'strong ones' of this earth would destroy 'the final ulcers
that afflict us'.[30]

After securing all permits and tickets for Evgeniya and their son, Pasternak
moved back to the Volkhonka for twenty-four hours and on 5 May saw them
off on the train bound for Berlin. His 'bon voyage' poem promised that

Evgeniya would 'straighten like a bud in sunlight' – a hope which she maybe also shared.[31] For many months however she remained emotionally distraught at the rupture of their marriage. She had plans for a prolonged absence and, after staying with Pasternak's parents in Berlin, expected to go to Paris where her former teacher Robert Falk was now based. Eventually, with her father-in-law's help, she hoped to establish herself as an independent artist. Unfortunately, this was not to be. Beyond a few portrait commissions, she had no source of earnings in Berlin, and the uncertain economic climate in Germany prevented Leonid from helping or employing her to assist him.[32]

A letter in the same spirit as Pasternak's farewell poem was sent to Evgeniya the day after her departure,[33] and further similar messages to Berlin followed. To his sister Josephine Pasternak maintained his lasting affection for Evgeniya and his love for Zinaida, regretting that other people perceived such feelings as mutually exclusive simply because 'the majority of human heads are not constructed like textbooks of formal logic'.[34] In this respect his parents' and Evgeniya's minds were no different from the majority. After a spate of confusing and upsetting messages from Boris to Evgeniya, Leonid in December sent him a reproachful letter, noting his talent for tormenting equivocation:

Your letters have the character of someone genuinely in love whereas reality and the facts speak the very opposite [. . .] Have the courage not to be duplicitous towards her. This is killing her [. . .] It's clear after all that you are offering her friendship – in which case speak and act more precisely . . .[35]

In the summer of 1931, after a short sojourn in Berlin, Evgeniya went off alone to stay at a tubercular clinic in Schömberg in the Black Forest. Her son was meanwhile taken by his grandparents to Josephine's in Munich, and all of them including her family then went to stay in a boarding house on the Schliersee.[36]

The week after Evgeniya's departure, there was a three-sided discussion between Pasternak and the Neigauzes at which Zinaida declared that she needed time and space in order to 'sort herself out'. The younger son Stanislav (Stasik, or 'Lyalya' as he was fondly known) was left in the care of Genrikh with assistance from a nanny, and she meanwhile took the elder boy Adrian ('Adik') with her by train to Kiev, where she stayed with the daughter-in-law of her friends the Perlins. While there she made music with a young violinist and aspiring poet, Lev Ozerov, who later became a colleague of Pasternak's.[37] In her wake Pasternak sent a series of long letters in which, she recalled, he 'increasingly conquered me by the power of his love and profundity of his intellect'.[38] As in Pasternak's earlier love letters, the whole of surrounding reality was depicted as a function of his feeling. With his regained confidence in modern history, this produced some quaint touches of incongruity. Of their love amidst obstacles and adversity he declared:

I believe in you and I always know: you are the close partner of a great Russian creativity, lyrical in these years of socialist construction, inwardly terribly similar to it, its very sister.[39]

In the same thoughtlessly expansive spirit, proclaiming a new full life of unshackled feeling, Pasternak even allowed that Zinaida might eventually be led back to Genrikh. The latter indeed visited her during a concert trip to Kiev.[40] In his wake, however, came Boris himself on a flying visit in late May, to reassert the claims of passion.[41]

On 27 May Pasternak had to be back in Moscow, and on the next day he left by train on a visit to the Urals, his first trip there since the First World War. With some reluctance he allowed Polonsky, the *Novy mir* editor, to co-opt him to a small 'brigade' of writers, including Gladkov, Malyshkin and the graphic artist Vasilii Svarog, who were to visit new industrial sites at Chelyabinsk, Kuznetsk and Magnitogorsk. Under the Five-Year Plan many artists were sent on missions to gather material and inspiration for socialist creativity. The inclusion of Pasternak and other prominent names in this particular party was an urgent matter of prestige for Polonsky. The aim was to parry attacks on his journal and improve its image by a show of support for socialist construction enterprises. (Unfortunately, this initiative did not prevent his removal from the chief editor's post later in 1931.)[42]

Pasternak forewarned Polonsky that he was not available for the full three-week programme, and he limited his visit to Chelyabinsk. There he was duly impressed by the scale of the new tractor factory and the 'Cyclopian plans and production that will start when once the factories are built'.[43] What failed to come alive for him was any correlation between reality and the stilted hyperbolic rhetoric used to describe such projects in official statements back in Moscow. For writers fired with propagandistic zeal the journey might have served some purpose; for Pasternak it was impossible:

Ordinary human stupidity nowhere emerges in such herd-like standardisation as in the setting of this trip. It was worth coming even for this. I always thought the sterility of urban campaigning language was a distorted echo of some other language in which truth maybe expressed itself locally. But I have been convinced otherwise [. . .] Behind everything that repelled me with its vacuity and vulgarity there was nothing ennobling or illuminating other than organised mediocrity . . .[44]

As Evgenii Pasternak suggests, probably the only material his father derived from the visit was a ganglion of impressions later used to characterise Terentyev, a Party activist depicted in some prose sketches of the later 1930s and who seemed unable to communicate other than by clichés. Apart from official sightseeing and travel, Pasternak gave poetry readings in the regional public library, to a youth group, and in the offices of the Chelyabinsk Tractor Plant newspaper.[45] On 7 June he was back again in Moscow.

While Pasternak was repulsed by the evidence of universal conformism, other free-thinking writers too were far from quiescent. On returning to Moscow he heard of a meeting organised by Gorky at his home on 30 May at which his own name had figured. The aim of the gathering – to reconcile 'fellow travellers' and the members of RAPP – had not been achieved.

In a fit of passion and as a challenge to officialdom, Aleksei Tolstoy and Vs[evolod] Ivanov proposed a toast to 'our premier poet'. Everyone looked at Bubnov, the People's Commissar for Enlightenment, who said that I 'am not one of them', i.e. not a revolutionary. Tolstoy then shouted that they would very soon drive even him to become a monarchist – which in the presence of government members was a rather daring statement.[46]

Bubnov's allegation emerged as a promise of the treatment Pasternak would receive at the hands of literary officials later in the year. Meanwhile, other events proved emotionally more engrossing.

Pasternak returned from Chelyabinsk in time for Genrikh Neigauz's recital on 8 June. Afterwards the two of them met up at the Asmuses. There the company sat and talked, Pasternak read from Tsvetaeva's narrative poem *The Ratcatcher (Krysolov)*, after which he and Genrikh went for a walk through Moscow in the early hours. In the next few days Pasternak reported that 'Garrik and I are again like brothers.'[47] Neigauz was meanwhile mending his relations with Militsa Borodkina.

Various plans were entertained for spending the summer with Zinaida in the Kiev or Moscow region. However, a better alternative emerged from contacts with the Georgian poet Paolo Yashvili. Pasternak had met him and his wife in Moscow in late 1930 thanks to an introduction by Andrei Bely, and they had had further dealings and correspondence during the winter and spring.[48] Now, on ·12 June, a letter from Yashvili confirmed an earlier invitation to Pasternak and Zinaida to come to Georgia for a few months to live and work. As Pasternak commented, the one drawback of Yashvili's suggestion was that it all sounded too good to be true.[49]

Prior to departure in mid July, Pasternak busied himself gathering funds and sorting out his chaotic and neglected financial affairs. Also, since Aleksandr Pasternak and family were shortly moving to an apartment in a new block that

he himself had helped design on Gogolevsky Boulevard, Pasternak hoped –
with support from Kalinin, the Russian President – to acquire the extra living
space to accommodate Zinaida and her two sons upon their return. These
various activities combined with urban seasonal impressions in the draft of a
poem that Pasternak sent to Zinaida at the end of the month.[50] As he reported,
'I have become so impregnated with your presence that the April wave of
inspiration came alive again and I have drafted an item or two . . .'[51]

The poem included with Pasternak's letter was also a repost to Irina Asmus.
She had reacted scornfully to news of Zinaida's affair, and on a visit to Kiev had
maintained that her union with Pasternak blighted a great poet's creativity.
The truth was quite different, at least in the short term. 'Poetry had returned
as though pardoned', a whole new collection was burgeoning, and Pasternak
told Zinaida he expected to see 'her' book completed by the autumn.[52]

After a few days together in Kiev, Pasternak took Zinaida and her son Adrian
by train to Georgia, arriving in Tiflis at daybreak on 14 July. The three months
spent in Georgia were an enthralling and unforgettable experience of what
became Pasternak's confessed 'second homeland'. Recalling his sojourn a year
later, he told Yashvili that Tiflis 'together with everyone I saw there and with
everything that I brought there and took away will for ever be for me what
Chopin, Scriabin, Marburg, Venice and Rilke were – one of the chapters of
Safe Conduct that will last me the whole of life'.[53] This appendix to *Safe
Conduct* was later condensed in the final episode of an autobiographical essay
written in the mid 1950s. In this Georgian revelation,

Everything was new, and everything was astounding. The dark overhanging masses of
stone mountain at the end of every street vista in Tiflis. The life of the poorer
population that spilled out from the yards onto the street – gaudy and frank, bolder and
less concealed than in the north. The symbolism of folk legends, full of mysticism and
messianism, encouraging a life of fantasy and [. . .] making every man a poet. The lofty
culture of progressive society and an intellectual life which in those years was already
rare in its intensity. The elegant corners of Tiflis, reminiscent of Petersburg, the first-
floor window grills, twisted in the shape of lyres and baskets, the picturesque back-
streets. And following on one's heels and everywhere striking the ear came the rattle of
tambourines, beating out lezghinka rhythms. The goat-like bleat of bagpipes and some
other instruments, the onset of evening in a southern town, full of stars and aromas
coming from gardens, confectioners and coffee-houses.

(II, 49; *VP*, 463–4; *SS*, IV, 342–3)

For almost every Russian poet impressions of Georgia have fallen on fertile
ground. Like Italy for the Germans, the Caucasus in the nineteenth century
captivated the Russian Romantic imagination; Pushkin and Lermontov re-

sponded to its scenery and colourful vitality, and Belinsky commented that 'the Caucasus seems to have been fated to become the cradle of poetic talents, the inspiration and mentor of their muses, their poetic homeland.'[54] To the 'Caucasian' Lermontov Pasternak was introduced by his own father's illustrations to *Mtsyri* and other poems. The opening dedication of *My Sister Life* had been 'To the Demon's Memory' ('Pamyati Demona'), and now one of Pasternak's new Georgian poems almost suggested the primacy of Lermontov's text over the real scene in which

> The rivers' confluence
> Might not have taken place.
> But for the text's sake it occurred
> In one of the Junker's notebooks
> At the instant when *en route*
> We fly into the embrace of Lermontov's lines.[55]

Pasternak's Caucasian journey also brought an encounter with living modern literature. As their base in Tiflis, he, Zinaida and Adrian had use of the poet Grigol Robikadze's apartment (Robikadze and his wife were in Berlin, where they eventually defected and made common cause with the Nazis).[56] Initially however they stayed with Yashvili and his wife Tamara. To greet the visitors on their first evening Yashvili summoned a company of fellow poets including Gaprindashvili, Nadiradze and Tabidze, all founder-members of the former Blue Horns post-symbolist group. During the 1920s these Georgian poets had made their mark in Moscow, and had already played host to personalities such as Bely, Esenin and Mayakovsky. Yashvili had brought from Moscow enraptured accounts of Pasternak which were now amply justified. Tabidze's wife Nina recalled his charm and inspired recitation at their first meeting. Zinaida she found attractive, lively and good company, although 'in her whole manner one sensed a concealed suffering and sorrow'.[57]

Among the company on that first evening, Pasternak was most struck by the contrasting pair of Tabidze and Yashvili. The latter had a Mayakovskian flamboyance. As raconteur and master of dazzling rhetoric, he was most readily associated with 'urban situations, rooms, discussions, public speeches'. Tabidze's element was nature, 'rural scenes, the openness of flowering plains, waves of the sea'. Similarly their verse, once Pasternak got to know it. Yashvili's poetry displayed an extravagant passion. Based on unexpected and keen observation, for Pasternak it had some features of the prose of Bely, Hamsun and Proust. Also, matching the simplicity of his own new verse, it seemed filled with air, space and movement. Tabidze, by contrast, seemed inward-looking and 'summoned you into the depths of his rich soul, full of intuitions and premonitions'. In Tabidze's 'sense of inexhaustible lyrical potential underlying every poem, a preponderance of things unsaid [. . .] over those expressed', lay a strong kinship with Pasternak, who was later to translate him with special empathy and understanding.[58] At their first meeting, Georgian poets recited from their own verse, and as Pasternak later wrote in his 'Travel Notes' ('Putevye zapiski'):

> Without knowing your stanzas,
> Yet enamoured of their source,
> Your translation yet to be
> I fathomed without words.   (*SP*, 390; *SS*, II, 17)

On leaving for Moscow in the autumn, Pasternak took with him several interlinear glosses of Yashvili and Tabidze and began work on the task of producing Russian versions.[59]

With their new friends, Pasternak and Zinaida visited places close to the capital such as Dzhavari and Mtskheta. There were also outings to Kakhetia, Tsinandali and the former estate of the poet Chavchavadze. After returning from Kakhetia, the heat in Tiflis became so unbearable that the entire company left the capital for Kodzhory (forty minutes by car) whose scenic splendour Bely had described to Pasternak in 1928.[60] There they spent most of August staying in the Kurort Hotel, where Bely had stayed. From Kodzhory they were taken by their Georgian friends on visits to Abastumani, the Udzo monastery with its nightingales and the soaring Ker-Ogla fortress. There was also a visit to the poet Leonidze at Bakuryani, and their torchlight supper in the woods and Tabidze's after-dinner speech later figured in Pasternak's poetic 'Travel Notes' and later autobiographical essay, as well as in Nina Tabidze's memoirs.[61]

In September Yashvili took his guests to the seaside villa resort of Kobulety for a further month. There they stayed in the same hotel as poets Bessarion ('Beso') Zhgenti and Simon Chikovani – the latter a 'future master of the brilliant picturesque image' and lifelong friend of Pasternak.[62] At Kobulety Pasternak's party fed in the government dining room, from where they regularly salvaged bread and other morsels for Chikovani and Zhgenti, who were forced to dine in the more plebeian Kursaal. In the mornings Pasternak worked on the poetic cycle 'Waves' ('Volny') with which his new collection was to open. These and various other new lyrics quickly became familiar to all their Georgian poet friends who, as Zinaida recalled, knew them by heart within two or three days after Pasternak first recited them. At the end of their seaside stay, Pasternak and family returned to Tiflis by train together with Chikovani.[63]

For a long time while in Georgia, Pasternak and Zinaida heard very little from their respective families. There were only two or three letters from Genrikh Neigauz, who was staying with his parents in Elizavetgrad and wrote full of apprehension lest some accident should leave them lying dead at the foot of a Caucasian gorge.[64] Boris also had a letter from Josephine in late July and replied with nostalgic thoughts of his son, thanks for Josephine's concern for his family, and a renewed exposition of his feelings for Evgeniya.[65] The latter also figured in some revised poetic thoughts 'while climbing in the Caucasus':

> When summits cause the heart to falter
> And mountains' censers swing,
> Do you think, my distant one,
> You failed to please me?
> And in the Alps of Germany
> Where crags clink glasses just as here,
> Although the echoes there are fainter,
> Do you think you've somehow failed?

All of which led to a perturbed rumination on the hardness of life and a realisation that 'To fashion one's own fate is harder / Than cutting water with a pair of scissors.'[66]

Despite Pasternak's new buoyancy of mood, material conditions in Georgia were far from luxurious. Food and clothing were scarce and expensive, and the visitors' survival was due entirely to 'miracle-working friends' who provided hospitality, fixed advances from publishers and offered loans – it took Pasternak two years to pay off an advance of 1,000 roubles from Tabidze and an even larger one from Yashvili.[67] Meanwhile a new prospect of earnings had appeared: a contract from 'Zakkniga' (Transcaucasian Books) was signed up with editor Garegin Bebutov literally on the Tiflis station platform as Pasternak headed back for Moscow on 16 October; three new poems headed 'Tiflis' were printed in the Georgian bi-weekly *Tempy* (Tempi) and in modified form they later appeared in *Second Birth*.[68] In August a contract was also drawn up with the Leningrad Writers' publishing house for an edition of collected works which, though later cancelled, for the time being provided payments in regular monthly instalments;[69] the hope of foreign translations of *Safe Conduct* was a further encouraging prospect.

The discovery of Georgia completed Pasternak's brief poetic renaissance in the early 1930s. He found there much that had disappeared from the cultural, social and political scene in Moscow. Here was a still vital, independent national culture which had not been utterly tainted or stultified. Georgian literary life was still steered and dominated by powerful artistic personalities rather than by a blinkered bureaucracy and clamorous time-servers. Here, too, Pasternak was surrounded by smiling and appreciative colleagues in a lush and spectacular setting, where the rigours of a collectivised economy were mollified by a genial climate and hospitable people.

Although, as his biographer Ronald Hingley comments, Pasternak showed a continuous lifelong tendency to proclaim himself born anew,[70] it is true to say that in Georgia he was genuinely reborn as a poet. 'The Poet's Death', a new love, and the Georgian landscape completed the array of ingredients which, according to Selvinsky, were vital for the lyric to flourish once again.

In Kobulety Pasternak had begun assembling the poetic collection *Second Birth*. The prefatory cycle 'Waves' was essentially a programmatic statement:

> Here will be everything: the lived-through
> And that whereby I'm still alive,
> My aspirations and foundations
> And real-life scenes that crossed my sight.
>
> (I, 319; *SP*, 343; *SS*, II, 374

The ranging vision of the poet takes in all of Kobulety's 'gigantic eight-verst spread of beach', 'nocturnal Poti', 'glinting Batum'. Yet unlike earlier lyrics, these ravishing depictions are now identified explicitly as projections of the poet's inner life and outward deeds. His own 'wave crests of experience' run towards him along with the Black Sea surf. The central sections of 'Waves' chart the poet's journey from Vladikavkaz along the Georgian Military Highway, with lyrical scenes interlaced and mingling with philosophical reflection. From the lugubrious expanse of his home apartment, to which in section 2 he looks forward to returning, there is also a vision of Moscow which the poet promises to (and thereby does) 'set into words' as it 'creeps and smokes, is elevated and constructed':

> And I'll accept you as my harness
> For the sake of madness yet to be,
> That you'll record me as though conning verses,
> Committing me as fact to memory.   (I, 321; *SP*, 345; *SS*, I, 376)

Thus the poet enters the life and awareness of his city – another new and larger form of the immortality achieved in earlier love poetry and proclaimed still in 'My beauty, your whole form . . .' ('Krasavitsa moya, vsya stat′ . . .')

But in *Second Birth* something has changed in the underlying poetic system or creative process, which is no longer founded on metaphor, dislocation of landscape by feeling, or randomness of imagery. As one of the love poems announces, now 'Not as a vagrant, / As kinsman I'll enter my native tongue'.[71]

After the opening poem of travel and philosophy, the following sections contain poems of the Irpen summer, amorous outpourings from Moscow and Kiev, and the new Georgian verses. If not exultant in its observations, almost all this poetry demonstrates a confident confrontation of new challenges including – by implication – Russia's drastic new historical transformations. Sections 6 and 7, however, carried post-Georgian verses of a quite different sort, reflecting the poet's tragic view of a carnivorous age, and his despair and suffering in a complex marital situation.

The opening poem of section 6 reinvoked two of Pasternak's familiar images: the barbarity of ancient Rome as a metaphor for the socialist state, and the image of the actor as an emblem for the poet.[72] The poem carried Mayakovskian associations, and it now proclaimed Pasternak's destiny to play out a dramatic role whose performance could lead to death, although in a different cause from Mayakovsky's. The newly written poem (which partly prefigured the *Zhivago* poem 'Hamlet') was glossed in a letter to Josephine of February 1932, in which Pasternak explained how

one is born again and what a prisoner of time this fate makes one, this discovery of oneself among communal property, this non-freedom nurtured by warmth on every side. Because herein lies the age-old cruelty of an unhappy Russia: when she bestows her love on anyone, the chosen one can never escape her gaze. As she watches, he, as it were, ends up before her in a Roman arena, and in return for her love is obliged to provide some spectacle. And if no one has managed to escape this, what can I say when Russia finds that loving me is made so extremely difficult, like Germany's love for Heine [. . .] I have described for you not my *motives*, but my reality, my existence that moves along with motive. I have identified my duty towards destiny.[73]

Next in the sequence was a poem that talked of a promise by powerful men to eliminate our last ulcers. Hardly an optimistic poem, it contained the image of two female faces shining lantern-like amid the hardships of the construction plan, and of attempts to live for the future when the 'new man' has run us over with the cartwheel of his 'project'.[74] The final, seventh section of *Second Birth* contained the other two poems of the 'Civic Triad'. A concluding item reprinted from the Tiflis journal *Tempy* linked Pasternak's 'wounding by the female lot' with his current joy at being 'reduced to nought / In revolutionary liberty'.[75]

Of all Pasternak's books, *Second Birth* was the one that least delighted not only the author but even kindly disposed and compatible colleagues such as Akhmatova and Mandelstam. Pasternak's own dissatisfaction was registered on a copy of the second edition inscribed to Elizaveta Stetsenko and recording that 'it contains too many traces of how one *should not* act, either in life, or in the less responsible field of art'.[76] The book contained lines that were variously inspired, lovely, and compellingly doom-laden, although as a whole it lacked a central conceptual or structural frame. The discoursiveness of 'Waves' and desire to embrace 'everything' were both expressive and symptomatic of this. The sections, too, were not links in a progressive sequence, nor were they always coherent as episodes; often they merely reflected the grouping of poems in their initial journal publication.

Most striking in the expression of *Second Birth* was its 'unheard-of simplicity'. This pursuit – like some 'heresy' and one step away from total muteness – is described as a feature of naturalness experienced by all great poets.[77] But if one recalls the final valedictory nature of *Safe Conduct* with its poetics based on 'dislocation' and metaphoric refraction, the change of style in *Second Birth* seems surprising. In Pasternak's new verse there is seeming evidence of a desire to reach a wider audience on issues of general moment, and a hint at an earlier half-humorous undertaking to write in a way that Zinaida might appreciate! However, probably of more significance is a mature poet's natural gravitation towards a hard-won serene clarity. At approximately the same time, the theme of a 'most arduous simplicity' was picked up by Sergei Spassky in *Yes* (*Da*), his next poetry book published in Leningrad in 1934. Several other near-contemporary authors sought a new simplicity in the 1930s, including such names as Babel, Olesha, Zabolotsky and Zoshchenko. Moreover, there would soon be strong external pressures to encourage both this pursuit as well as the 'total muteness' that lay beyond it.[78]

4

A Prisoner of Time

Oh, had I known the way of things
When I embarked on my début,
That blood-spurting lines of verse can kill,
Choke to death and flood the throat.

All jokes with such an undertone
Would have been renounced outright.
My beginnings were so long ago,
My first commitment was so slight.

Yet growing age, like ancient Rome,
In place of childish tricks and jests
Requires no read-through of the role
But wants the player done to death.

When passion high dictates the lines,
It sends a slave out on the stage.
And then, as art comes to an end,
We feel the breath of soil and fate.

(1931)

After the warmth of Georgia, Moscow in October was bitterly cold. The travellers were met at the station by Stanislav's nanny who brought winter coats for Zinaida and Adrian. Zinaida felt uncomfortable about moving into the Volkhonka apartment, which was still the official home of Evgeniya. But there was no alternative: at that time free accommodation was not to be found in Moscow. Shortly after they settled in, Genrikh Neigauz paid a visit and later, in conversation with Boris, agreed that Stanislav should come to join his mother.[1]

In Moscow Pasternak continued and completed the poems of *Second Birth*. In November he and Zinaida also spent a few days in Leningrad searching for a possible home and visiting relatives and friends. It was the Freidenbergs' first

59

contact with Zinaida, and they had difficulty in accepting her. Pasternak himself was unsure of the impact she had made. As he reported to Josephine, 'she always returns from the hairdresser disfigured like a freshly polished boot, and before any formal events (including a visit to my aunt's) she goes and has her hair permed'.[2] While in Leningrad Pasternak also met up with Tabidze and Yashvili and introduced them to Akhmatova. With them he also travelled out to Tsarskoye Tselo to see Andrei Bely; that summer Bely had followed other examples and had written to Stalin protesting his exclusion from published literature.[3]   •

In early December 1931, the Cathedral of Christ Saviour, just opposite Pasternak's Volkhonka apartment, was detonated by the Soviet authorities to clear a site for a projected Palace of Soviets. The explosion shook the whole house, raising dust and smashing windows. The same month a bomb blast of another sort hit the literary scene. Early in December, Polonsky was dismissed as editor of *Novy mir* for alleged 'right-wing opportunism' and pandering to 'fellow travellers'. He was replaced by Ivan Gronsky, who although not a totally oppressive personality (*viz.* his support for Pilnyak's rehabilitation), was a grey and orthodox figure compared with his predecessor. Pasternak continued publishing with *Novy mir* and remained on good terms with Gronsky, but he was offended on Polonsky's behalf and regarded his period in office as a high point in the journal's history.[4]

In mid December the All-Russian Writers' Union held a major public meeting to discuss the so-called 'political lyric'. The programme began with Aseyev's keynote speech 'On Poetry', which displeased both liberals and left-wingers with its formalistic classification of modern poets as: innovators, eclectics and archivists. Several figures (Pasternak among them) fitted none of these categories. Pasternak himself came late, missed Aseyev's speech, and made what he himself confessed was one of his more confused utterances.[5] Later, after reading a report on the start of the conference in *Vechernyaya Moskva*, he requested the floor again to clarify his position. His two speeches were not published, but their general tenor as reported by *Literaturnaya gazeta* made clear that his views struck a discordant note:

Pasternak's speech [. . .] dismissed the fact that 'not everything has been destroyed by the revolution'. Art has been left alive as a supremely mysterious and eternal entity. But here 'there is such confusion because people keep shouting at our poets: "You must do this", "You must do that"! But the first thing to discuss should be what the poet himself requires: the age exists for man, and not man for the age.

According to the reporter, anyone else who said such things would have been hissed, but instead Pasternak was applauded, a fact that was leading him astray.

'Pasternak would do well to reflect on who it is that applauds him, and why', the report concluded.[6] In his final speech Aseyev defended himself and also offered a repost to Pasternak, mentioning his dangerous 'philosophical condition of inertia' recently demonstrated in *Spektorsky* and marking a retrograde step from his valuable Lef-inspired poem *The Year 1905*.[7]

A heavier broadside attack on Pasternak was launched on 16 December, the final day of the meeting, by Aleksei Selivanovsky, the emergent RAPP specialist on poetry. He inveighed against former Lef 'liquidators of art' and the new 'bourgeois revivalists', whose 'most blatant representative' was Pasternak. The latter's alleged proposition of 'an art that sets its own goals' was identified as a '*protest against the period of socialism*', and the action of his supporters was branded as 'objectively a *provocation* that prevents Pasternak from joining the ranks of modern revolutionary poetry'.[8]

Selivanovsky's remarks further linked Pasternak's December conference statement with the previous month's publication of *Safe Conduct* and the poem 'To a Friend'. The autobiographical essay was described as an 'open platform of idealistic bourgeois art', and Selivanovsky's verdict heralded several RAPP-inspired attacks in the same vein during the winter and spring 1931–2. The first of these was printed in the same issue of *Literaturnaya gazeta* that carried Kalm's negative report on the conference.[9]

Apart from its disappointingly small print run (only 6,200 copies), the critical panning of *Safe Conduct* was a blow to Pasternak. He regarded the work as a major profession de foi, and as he told George Reavey, 'I wrote this book not as one among many, but as an only book'.[10] It was moreover a work that he was keen to see translated and published abroad. Gorky himself had spoken encouragingly the previous summer, describing the manuscript as 'dense, furious – remarkable!' and suggesting that his wife Maria Budberg should translate it. Unfortunately, however, nothing came of this proposal.[11]

Thanks to the Mayakovsky anniversary in 1931, *Safe Conduct* received preview publicity at various public readings, including one at FOSP on 9 May when sections of part three were presented together with some recent verse.[12] However, before going to press, the book was editorially pruned 'in house' and various passages were removed concerning Venice under the Doges and the collapse of the tsarist regime (which implicitly minimised the achievement of the Bolshevik revolt).[13] However, as events of the later 1930s showed, clearance by the censor and appearance in print were no guarantee against subsequent indictment for ideological offences. Pasternak was spared this, but the threat and possibility of reprisals increased during the winter of 1931–2.

On the strength of its mere journal serialisation, at a September plenary meeting of RAPP *Safe Conduct* was listed by Selivanovsky along with other recent pernicious publications.[14] After the book appeared in November, *Literaturnaya gazeta* lumped it together with Olga Forsh's *The Crazy Vessel (Sumasshedshii korabl')* and Kaverin's *Artist Unknown (Khudozhnik neizvesten)* as examples of a bourgeois 'restoration' in literature. The same issue carried Tarasenkov's review, which found the work symptomatic of Pasternak's slothful bourgeois apoliticism. The author's origins and sympathies lay, allegedly, with the Symbolist poets, Plato, and the Neo-Kantian Hermann Cohen, and his depiction of reality reflected a mental detachment from the objective world.[15] The same negative conclusions emerged the following year when the journal *Zvezda* took Pasternak to task for his subjective idealism.[16] Similar verdicts and allusions to *Safe Conduct* together with repeated quotation from the poem 'To a Friend' made Pasternak one of the chief targets for orthodox attack during winter of 1931–32 and put paid to hopes of any reprint of his autobiography.[17]

Evgeniya Pasternak's plans for a prolonged stay in Western Europe foundered because of financial problems. In addition to the funds awaiting her in a Munich bank, she later received money from Raisa Lomonosova (against an equivalent rouble sum transferred by Boris to her husband's former wife in Russia).[18] But the 3,000 Marks promised by Gorky as the advance on a translated edition of *Safe Conduct* never materialised.[19] Pasternak was naturally concerned lest Evgeniya be stranded in Germany without funds but felt he could not write, and she too was diffident about approaching him with her problems.[20]

After recuperating in the Black Forest, Evgeniya moved to Berlin in the autumn. There she lived in the Pension Kuhr on Victoria-Luisenplatz, for which, of course, rental had to be paid. A further problem was young Evgenii's schooling: was this to be in Germany or Russia? Meanwhile there was a dearth of commissions which might have provided a livelihood, and Evgeniya felt unequipped to cope with living abroad on her own and without financial security. With funds running low, she abandoned plans to visit Paris, and ruled at even a short stay in Cambridge with the Lomonosovs. Finally, although her home had been taken over by Boris with Zinaida's family, she 'decided on the worst variant – Moscow. There at least there will be an end to all this.' On the 22 December, along with Dr Levin and family, Evgeniya and her son boarded the train for Moscow.[21]

Returning to Moscow replaced one set of problems by another. Boris ingenuously believed Evgeniya's return was 'a fatal mistake for which [his] relatives were partly to blame'.[22] Her impending arrival spelt the end of his tenure of their apartment. For the first few weeks, she and her son stayed in a cramped room in a working-class part of the Zamoskvorechye, but then moved back to the Volkhonka. Boris and Zinaida meanwhile went to stay at his brother Aleksandr's new three-room apartment on Gogolevsky Boulevard. Decorating was still going on there and conditions were cramped; the two of them slept on the floor but also occasionally stopped over at friends, and Pasternak even wrote his Leningrad poet friend Sergei Spassky asking about possible accommodation in that city.[23] Genrikh Neigauz meanwhile agreed to take the two boys to live with him at Trubnikovsky Lane, and for a while Zinaida shuttled between Gogolevsky Boulevard and her estranged husband's apartment in order to feed and care for her sons.[24]

Physical and emotional exhaustion soon took their toll however. Finally, Zinaida loaded her belongings in a sleigh-mounted cab and went back to Trubnikovsky Lane. Before leaving she asked Aleksandr to tell Boris that she still loved him dearly, but proposed ending the suffering of so many people and begged him to go back to Evgeniya and not attempt to contact her again. Genrikh agreed to Zinaida's return, if not as his wife, then as housekeeper and mother of their sons, and a moratorium was declared on all that had happened.[25]

At the end of January Pasternak did return to Evgeniya but stayed only three days. He then left again and sent his brother to implore Zinaida to return to him. Zinaida refused. Two days later Nikolai Vilyam visited the Neigauzes and told them Pasternak was beside himself with suffering, and that some form of mutual co-existence had to be found. Zinaida thereupon announced that she would take the children and live separately, since she regarded her maternal calling as stronger than all else.[26]

A mere few hours later Nina Tabidze, who was visiting Moscow, appeared at the Neigauzes evidently aghast at Zinaida's 'monstrous' abandonment of Boris. *In medias res*, after midnight, Boris himself then arrived. 'Der spät kommende Gast' was welcomed by Genrikh. Boris seemed in utter despair, having heard that the Union of Writers could provide no alternative accommodation.[27] Looking distraught, he walked straight through into the nursery and closed the door, whereupon a gulping sound was heard. By the time Zinaida dashed in, he had swallowed a whole bottle of iodine from the medicine shelf. On the advice of a doctor living on the same staircase, two litres of cold milk were poured into him, which induced repeated vomiting and thus probably saved his life. He later recalled being laid out on the settee in a disembodied state of helpless bliss. 'Actively, yet without any tension, I felt like dying, just as one feels like eating a piece of gateau', he later told Josephine.[28] For all that, Pasternak's choice of location for his action suggested it was not so much a resolute attempt to do away with himself, as a desperate semiotic gesture aimed at solving their romantic imbroglio.

Pasternak's action had dramatic effect. Genrikh Neigauz was astounded at his deed, and then catechised Zinaida: 'Well, are you satisfied? Has he now *proved* his love for you?' Genrikh at least was convinced and agreed to hand her over to Pasternak for good. Pasternak for his part insisted that she bring both children to live with them, and he promised to continue the search for housing. The following morning the four of them moved back temporarily to stay with his brother on Gogolevsky Boulevard.[29] Meanwhile the Volkhonka apartment remained at Evgeniya's disposal and she was permitted to use the personal food and goods allowance to which Pasternak was entitled as a writer.[30] Although a formal divorce was mentioned, for the time being no action was taken.

Pasternak kept his suicide attempt a fairly close secret. It was mentioned *en passant* and without details to Olga Freidenberg, Lomonosova, and a few intimate friends; only later did rumour of it spread.[31]

With time, Evgeniya Pasternak was able to put together a new life for herself, and the ensuing years were ones of successful artistic activity. Her work was regularly exhibited and purchased, and included several portraits of prominent personalities. After World War II, when commissions and exhibitions were hard to secure, she shared studio facilities with her former mentor and friend Robert Falk. Other friends who gave moral and professional support included the artist Sarra Lebedeva and the Chernyaks.[32]

Evgeniya Pasternak devoted herself mainly to her son. Although she later had one brief and unsuccessful liaison, she never fully recovered from Pasternak's desertion. To their credit, she and Boris contrived to remain on friendly terms and he assuaged some of his guilt by concern and material support for her and their son, probably paying more than Zinaida ever suspected.[33] No love was lost between Zinaida and Evgeniya, and it was evident to Chukovsky and others that for them the battle was not yet over. Several of Pasternak's friends were unhappy at his realignment. Pilnyak in particular was appalled at Zinaida's appearance, which dashed his plan to take Pasternak with him to Japan that year as a travelling companion.[34] Ironically, Pasternak's life may have been saved by missing out on that bachelors' jaunt.

Pasternak and Zinaida remained at his brother's for another three months, and the accommodation problem continued to depress him.[35] Relief was at hand however. With the help of Gorky, and of Vladimir Slyotov and Ivan Evdokimov (the latter two each surrendering some living space) he managed to secure from the Union a small unfurnished two-room flat on the ground floor of a wing of the so-called 'Herzen House' at 25 Tverskoi Boulevard.[36] Some basic furniture was supplied from Zinaida's former apartment, and she and the boys moved in mid May 1932. Boris' removal was delayed till the 22nd: Evgenii his son had a serious bout of scarlet fever, and Pasternak spent nearly a month at the Volkhonka apartment helping to care for him.[37]

Strangely, the relocation to Tverskoi Boulevard was foretold in literature. As Pasternak told his sister Josephine, when planning *Spektorsky* in 1925 he had conceived the second part in the form of notes written by the hero while living on the ground floor of a two-storey house on Tverskoi Boulevard, where the Danish Embassy was once situated. Now, as he reported, 'It is summer. Outside the window is Tverskoi Boulevard [and] I myself have landed in the half-imaginary place of a half-imaginary action.' As his immediate neighbours, Pasternak now had writers such as Afinogenov, Bolshakov, Fadeyev, Antal Hidas, Lugovskoi, Mandelstam, Platonov and Pavlenko.[38]

Despite the final blissful union with Zinaida and the convenience of the Litfond dining-room across the yard, Pasternak's problems were far from solved. He was pursued by financial difficulties and found it hard to concentrate on work. However, as he told Josephine, 'we wrap up this prose in a fog of happiness, like the smoke in a chimneyless peasant hut, so that nothing can be made out and probably we shall perish.'[39]

Another relocation soon followed. The Volkhonka apartment, enlarged by acquisition of Aleksandr Pasternak's former quarters, was too large for Evgeniya and her son, while Boris' new quarters were hopelessly cramped. It was Evgeniya's suggestion that the families exchange apartments, and Boris readily agreed. The exchange occurred in September. Evgeniya was happy to be quartered and fed on the Writers' Union premises, although she gave up her access to the privileged shopping facilities on Myasnitskaya Street.[40]

According to family correspondence in 1932, Evgenii long failed to accept that his father would not be returning to live with them. Pasternak in turn felt pangs of guilt and nostalgia for his son. At various points it was thought that the boy might go and live with his father, but his enthusiasm for this evaporated after one visit, and thereafter he saw his father only at the Volkhonka or on joint outings.[41] Zinaida understood Boris' paternal feelings and later recalled how some of this was reflected in Yurii Zhivago's moral discomfort when Lara's daughter lay in the bed his son had slept in.[42]

As the abuse directed at *Safe Conduct* continued, Pasternak reported the implications of all this in a letter to his elder sister in mid February:

At a time when my activities have been announced as an unconscious sally by the class enemy, my understanding of art is seen as a statement that it is inconceivable under socialism [. . .] all of which in our conditions is an evaluation that promises little good, when my books are prohibited in libraries . . .[43]

Shortly after writing this, Pasternak endured a savage public castigation amounting almost to a tribunal. On 6 April, FOSP held its thirteenth fortnightly literary meeting, or *dekadnik*, at which he recited 'Waves' to a large audience. The poem was familiar to many already from its January publication in *Krasnaya nov'*, but after his recitation the avalanche of hostile comment was such that the debate had to be adjourned and was wound up only on the 11th.[44] Only a partial account of it was reported in *Literaturnaya gazeta*, although a fragmentary verbatim record was retained in the archive of Moscow's Institute of World Literature (IMLI).[45]

A naively panegyric statement reversing his earlier view of Pasternak came from the young dramatist and *Znamya* editor Vishnevsky. Peretz Markish hailed Pasternak but begged him to come down from his mountain-top, and another journeyman poet Osip Kolychev praised him as a rightly influential master of form, but rejected his 'content', and he ended by wishing Pasternak would write 'a novel of our epoch' and integrate with 'our great, real world'. The heaviest attacks came from the 'soldier-poet' Máté Zalka and Aleksei Surkov however. The former identified Pasternak as a flagrant ideological enemy and attacked not only the verses he had just heard but *Safe Conduct* as well, while Surkov branded him as a 'subjective idealist' (a now established cliché of abuse). A staunch defence of Pasternak came, however, from Paolo Yashvili, still relatively little known in Moscow. He objected to Zalka's 'uncomradely approach' and intimidation tactics, and praised the truth and genuineness of 'Waves' which, he pointed out, had been largely written in his own presence. Even if expressions such as 'socialism' and 'Five-Year Plan' (*pyatiletka*) had arrived late in Pasternak's poetic vocabulary, Yashvili maintained, the honesty of such poetry was impressive.[46]

Pasternak was visibly nonplussed and depressed by the discussion. Bobrov, who normally relished the cut and thrust of a debate, recalled him as grey in the face and lost for words in his own defence. Pasternak's final statement had an explicit Tolstoyan note and at a time of executions and class warfare hinted at an awful truth:

A lot of people here used metaphoric similes – of shooting and barricades. For me this is not a metaphor. I dislike it – in a Tolstoyan way. If you feel that this is nonsense, that these are the fruits of enlightenment, then you should give everything up, and [. . .] people should give up art . . .

Pasternak cited the example of Vladimir Narbut who had seemingly abandoned poetry, and he himself had embarked on a period of silence. His speech continued: 'I don't understand the treatment of art as though it were some everyday routine: here you have this and that, and your life would be better if you did this or that. [In fact] Art [. . .] is suffering.'[47]

On 16–18 April Pasternak underwent a further personality assassination at the 'Second Working Conference' of RAPP. Here even Selivanovsky's earlier recognition of his technical mastery was slammed by Averbakh, and critic Ekaterina Troshchenko denounced him as no longer even a 'fellow traveller', but as well on the way to being a 'purveyor of the bourgeois menace'.[48]

After this treatment, it became obvious that the next consequences for Pasternak could involve more than mere verbal abuse. He was saved, though, by the announcement in *Pravda* on 24 April of a Resolution by the Party Central Committee 'On the Restructuring of Literary Organisations'. Along with other bodies RAPP was declared as disbanded in order to prepare for creation of one central organisation, the USSR Union of Writers. Pasternak made no public reaction to the news, and no private thoughts or words went on record. But his relief must have been considerable.

As soon as the *perestroika* of belles lettres was proclaimed, a complete change of atmosphere and a spirit of reconciliation were evident. It was maybe no coincidence that 24 April was the date of Gorky's return to Russia, and he now became a figurehead for the changes, if not a managerial force. At his Moscow home a large gathering of writers met to propose candidates for the Organising Committee (Orgkomitet) of a new USSR Writers' Union.[49] The major functionaries who emerged to head the new literary administration were Gronsky and the critic Valerii Kirpotin.

Not only were the witch-hunts against Pasternak and others suddenly ended, but many of RAPP's recent excesses were actually condemned, including its alleged part in the hounding of Mayakovsky. The fortunes of some prominent RAPP spokesmen such as Averbakh also began to turn. With the creation of an all-embracing Union, the discrimination between trusted communists and 'bourgeois' fellow travellers was dropped. Towards the latter a new conciliatory policy was adopted, and comradely persuasion and 'assistance with problems' were used to coax them towards the socialist citadel.

Pasternak's voice was absent from the chorus of welcome for the new policy change. As he later told Kirpotin, he felt shaken and annihilated by recent criticism of him.[50] He was not present, either, at a tea party at Gorky's house on Malaya Nikitskaya on 26 October, when new directions for Russian literature were discussed by writers, critics and editors together with a handful of Party leaders and Stalin himself. Nor did he attend the first plenary meeting of the Orgkomitet in late October. It was here that the notion of 'socialist realism' was first mooted as a general method of procedure for Soviet literature; this doctrine was nebulously equated with 'truth' and was developed – symptomatically – by a special commission on which only Gronsky represented the artistic community.[51]

Although Pasternak was an obvious beneficiary of the new situation, it was not long before he privately dismissed it as 'a stupid phantom of relative freedom, false, superficial, and perhaps incongruous in our situation'.[52] It was clear in fact that the changes, however welcome, resulted from an arbitrary bureaucratic dictat from above rather than a sensitive response to artistic needs.

The improvement in Pasternak's position was nevertheless quite tangible. In May the apartment space on Tverskoi Boulevard was made available, and in summer he was offered a visit to the Urals for himself and his family – not as a press-ganged delegation member, but now as a Party guest. On the literary front, a selection of lyrics in *Novy mir* no. 5 included the contraversial 'Not one day's passed – a century or more . . .' although without the stanza referring to uprisings and executions. In May 1932 *Literaturnaya gazeta* carried a re-evaluation of Pasternak's achievement. Although still couched in political cliché, its tone was appreciative with none of Selivanovsky's crass phraseology. Identified only as 'K.', the author was probably Kirpotin. The article described Pasternak as a sincere supporter of the revolution, although he remained a scion of the pre-revolutionary bourgeois intelligentsia characterised by individualism and a contemplative fatalism. Despite a lack of firm ideological foundations, Pasternak's revolutionary sympathy was recognised as genuine, and his transformation could be achieved once he made common cause with the society of 'builders of socialism'. In this he would find help readily at hand, for 'the working class takes splendid account of the fact that the "place of the poet" is an important and responsible post on the construction site'.[53] In November, in an article more moderately toned than earlier, Selivanovsky mentioned Pasternak as a poet still shackled to the past, beset by 'great changes' and in need of help, like others such as Antokolsky, Bely and Mandelstam.[54]

It also now proved possible for Pasternak to influence slightly the printed and public settings in which he appeared. In deference to his wish, Selivanovsky was removed as the prefator to his projected collected works, and later in the year at Pasternak's behest Tarasenkov was replaced by his friend Kornelii Zelinsky to chair his recital evening in the Polytechnic Museum.[55]

'The Urals Oblast Party Committee has invited me to the Urals for the summer on very good conditions', Pasternak told his sister Lydia on 1 June. The invitation was one of several soliciting artistic support for economic initiatives in readiness for the upcoming fifteenth anniversary of the revolution.[56] A few days later Pasternak and his new family embarked on the four-day train journey to Sverdlovsk (Ekaterinburg); with them, as children's helper, went 'Tusya' (Natalya) Blumenfeld, a cousin of Genrikh Neigauz. Evgeniya Pasternak and her son together with Elizaveta Stetsenko meanwhile went on holiday to Kislovodsk in the Caucasus.

The promised good conditions were not apparent. Initially the guests, who included composers and the second troupe of the Moscow Arts Theatre, were put up at the Ural Hotel in Sverdlovsk. Pasternak described it as 'the last word in American technology erected amid semi-Asiatic wilderness'. Sanitary conditions, though, were barrack-like, warm water was brought in buckets, and Lydia Pasternak received a graphic account of unpartitioned communal toilets where patrons were exposed to public view each time the door was opened. A compensating luxury, though, was free access to the local Party Committee dining room.

After three weeks in Sverdlovsk, the tour organiser moved the Pasternaks to a three-room villa in the grounds of a children's sanatorium by Lake Shartash. The villa turned out to be infested with bedbugs, and Pasternak alluded in a letter to various 'non-egoistic, un-dacha-like reasons' for wanting to return home. However, they stayed on and another letter to Paolo Yashvili mentioned a plan to sit down shortly and write some 'prose about all sorts of things, northern and connected with the Civil War'.[57] Some current impressions figured later in the Civil War sequence in *Doctor Zhivago*, for these were the 'un-dacha-like' observations that dominated all others, and no boat trips on the lake and other amusements could divert the visitors' attention.

At Lake Shartash Pasternak saw for himself what he earlier agonised about in letters to Lydia and to Gorky. Summer of 1932 saw the start of massive famine in rural Russia, the result of forcibly collectivising the rural economy and confiscating animals and goods from the peasantry. As Pasternak recalled, 'Russia was dying of hunger [. . .] Some people were bursting with opulence, and others like wound-up watches, seemed to live on nothing'.[58] The contrast between the luxurious cuisine of the official dining room with its caviar and cakes and the scene outside was especially sickening. Local peasants came to their window begging for alms, and Pasternak took to bringing morsels from the dining room and distributing them. Finally he gave up eating the luxurious fare altogether. He began suffering sleepless nights and was revolted at being called to witness such misery in order to write untruths about it, since the real truth could never be published.[59]

Finally, on feigned grounds of illness, Pasternak took his family back to Moscow. As they left, despite his protests, a food hamper was forced on them; he himself bought savoury pasties at the rail stations for the adults, while Zinaida surreptitiously fed the boys from the Oblast Committee hamper which later kept the entire family supplied for a month.

Pasternak announced at the Writers' Union that he was unable to write anything on what he had seen in the Urals and demanded to be sent on no more 'artistic assignments'.[60] But the writers' visit to the Urals was a publicised event and *Pravda* rebuked him for refusing to write a report: 'How is it that you, who are an intelligent man, don't realise that one must see not the facts but the tendencies?'[61]

Pasternak alluded to his summer impressions in a short 150–word 'Autobiography' written on 21 September for some now forgotten publishing purpose. In it he claimed to value most of all the Revolution's moral aspect, in a Tolstoyan sense:

Morally annihilated at first by its denunciatory excesses, I have subsequently felt annihilated by them again and again [. . .] So unspeakably severe is [life] to hundreds of thousands and millions, and so relatively gentle towards specialists and people with names. No reform can correct this dissatisfaction; for that one would have to be born different.

(*SS*, IV, 630)

In 1932 Leonid Pasternak celebrated his seventieth birthday. An exhibition marked the occasion at Berlin's Hartberg Gallery and an expanded jubilee monograph was published by Stybel with text by Max Osborn and Leonid's own autobiographical notes. In Moscow Boris was filled with 'animated, free and simple delight' at his father's jubilee and wrote him several pages of appreciative comment on the monograph.[62]

In order to avoid alarming his parents, Pasternak refrained from spelling out many unpleasant aspects of his private, professional and public life. For instance, they heard nothing about the miseries he witnessed on Lake Shartash. This factor, plus the postal censorship and sheer enormity of recent Soviet events led to increasing misprision by Pasternak's parents. In April of 1932 Boris told them that 'Now everything in the USSR is assessed from the political angle. In particular, Anatolii Vasilyevich [Lunacharsky] now has very little weight here.'[63] But the elder Pasternaks' ability to read and understand was overtaxed. After Pilnyak called to visit them while in Germany, they urged Boris to try and secure a Berlin visa, little realising the price Pilnyak had paid and would have yet to pay:

After all, your friend the prose writer, Boris (I forget his patronymic), found the right way. So follow his example and they won't refuse you – that's my firm conviction. You only need to want to [. . .] So come on, Borya, shake off this Chekhovianism [*chekhovshchina*] . . .[64]

In October 1932 a new round of mass arrests began, and the alleged 'Ryutin platform' conspiracy within the Party was exposed. Relying largely on descriptions by friends who were allowed abroad, and who paid for this partly by silence or reticence, Leonid Pasternak laboured under the impression that the Russian situation was still within the bounds of normality. 'Inspired and unbribable newspaper correspondents and such brilliant, responsible, immortal and free witnesses as B. I. [Zbarsky] and L. G. [Levin] probably support you in this opinion', Boris ironised. Yet

meanwhile the Apocalypse which you once left behind has only become more complex in its inescapability [. . .] Maybe such naive Soviet philistines as B. I. and L. G. can and do live like that – believing their faith in reason insures them against any posthumous responsibilitiy and foreboding of great catastrophes [i.e. against the idea that they could perish – CJB].[65]

Since the Tverskoi Boulevard flat had only minimal furnishings, Evgeniya took some furniture with her from the Volkhonka including Rozaliya Pasternak's grand piano. Thanks to her tolerance of semi-bohemian conditions, and through lack of funds and the need to keep working, she had survived well enough on the Volkhonka. But when Boris and family moved back in September, they found the house in an appalling state. The roof leaked, rats had gnawed and ripped away skirting boards, and many window panes were cracked or missing following the shockwave when the Cathedral of Christ Saviour was demolished. It was in this dilapidated accommodation that Pasternak received a brief visit from Svyatopolk-Mirsky who had recently returned to Moscow from exile in London.[66]

In early October, however, Zinaida wrought a transformation that amazed Boris on returning from a three-day trip to Leningrad. The windows were repaired; she had hung curtains, repaired collapsing and herniated mattresses and made a settee from one of them, and she had also polished the floors and washed and sealed the windows for the winter. Various rugs, two cupboards, and an upright piano were acquired from the household of Neigauz's parents who had recently moved from Elizavetgrad to Moscow and were living with their son in Trubnikovsky Lane.[67]

Despite initial misgivings over his scandalous elopement with Zinaida, Gustav Neigauz took a great liking to Pasternak on his first visit to his grandsons. Thereafter, despite distance and great age, he became an almost daily visitor. With him Boris was able to revive his German. Gustav himself had never learned decent Russian and spoke French with Olga his wife; she herself was able to enjoy talking in her native Polish to Leonid Pasternak's friend the elderly art critic Pavel Ettinger.[68]

After returning to the Volkhonka, Pasternak enjoyed a period of settled existence and contentment. 'I have never been so calm and happy as most recently,' he wrote his parents. And

with Zina things are so well, easy and natural, as though I had lived with her since childhood, been born and grew up with her [. . .] Many things that we considered specifically Pasternakian [. . .] I have encountered in her too, with the sole difference that in her make-up and fate words and moods play virtually no part and are replaced by actions and real-life situations.

Zinaida's earthbound practicality was well appreciated; she knew how to run domestic operations so as to leave both her successive distinguished husbands free to pursue their art. If aware that she had feet of clay, Pasternak was not yet upset by this. But there were many witnesses to Zinaida's embodiment of anti-art, including Irina Asmus and Akhmatova. If Zinaida did not actually disapprove of poetry, there were, as Hingley comments, 'abundant indications that she feared its power to upset the equilibrium of her well-managed household by provoking official disfavour'.[69]

During 11–14 October Pasternak travelled alone to Leningrad to give three solo poetry readings on successive evenings. He stayed with Sergei Spassky and his wife, and while there he discussed with editor Grigorii Sorokin the possibility of sending him some new work in prose – evidently the writing mentioned in summer correspondence with Yashvili.[70] The Freidenberg and Margulius families were found to be 'living worse and with more difficulty than last year, but with rare exceptions that is the normal situation', Pasternak reported to his father.[71]

Although himself financially pressed, from his honorarium for the readings Pasternak passed on 500 roubles to Nikolai Punin for relaying to Akhmatova, who was seriously ill and living in awful poverty. Back in Moscow he also contacted Chulkov and others with a view to helping organise medical treatment for her via the Writers' Union Orgkomitet and Narkompros.[72]

Another Petersburg poet who reappeared on Pasternak's horizon at about this time was Mandelstam. Since summer of 1931 he and his wife had been living at 25 Tverskoi Boulevard, and thus for a short period they were Pasternak's neighbours. Renewed contacts only served to highlight their incompatibility however. In particular, Mandelstam resented Pasternak's desire, evident in *Second Birth*, to maintain a dialogue with his age. His own 'Night in the courtyard . . .' ('Noch' na dvore . . .') was reputedly meant as a scathing response to Pasternak's 'My beauty, your whole form. . .' ('Krasavitsa moya, vsya stat'. . .') with its promise of eternity through love and art.[73] After a five-year silence Mandelstam had experienced a new bout of poetic inspiration and, deprived of any printed forum, he took every chance to recite his work. One such occasion, part of the new post-RAPP liberalism, was a reading organised for him at the offices of *Literaturnaya gazeta* on the 10 November. As Mandelstam's friend Khardzhiev reported, the poems recited 'were such terrifying exorcisms that many people took fright'. Pasternak evidently commented: 'I envy you your freedom. For me you are a Khlebnikov, and just as alien to me as he is. I need non-freedom.'[74] Pasternak was referring here not to political freedom,[75] but to Mandelstam's liberation arising from his exclusion from literature as a profession. Pasternak merely envied the status of the unprinted 'amateur', freed from social command and censorship, such as Khlebnikov had been, Mandelstam was, and his future hero Yurii Zhivago would be.

At around the same time Mandelstam turned up one evening at Pasternak's Volkhonka apartment. Various other guests, including Tikhonov and some Georgians, asked the host to recite. But when Pasternak briefly paused, Mandelstam himself began declaiming and took up the rest of the evening with his recital. The captive audience was perplexed, and Zinaida was shocked at his disrespect for her husband. Pasternak, however, was more struck by the morbid extremity of his behaviour. There were soon to be further evidence of this.[76]

Second Birth appeared with Federatsiya in August of 1932 in an edition of 5,200 copies. Three major reviews were by specialists writing from post-RAPP socialist positions. Prozorov gave an optimistic prognosis of Pasternak's development but noted a continuing subjectivity and irrational imagery at variance with 'real life'. Only in the book's final section was there a semblance of movement in step with the times, though evidently as an act of self-abnegation, and visions of the future were drawn hesitantly and hazily.[77]

After slating the subjective idealism of *Safe Conduct* Tarasenkov greeted *Second Birth* as a milestone in Pasternak's liberation from this disorder. 'Contradictions' were observed, and if 'the distance of socialism' was near at hand it was barely tangible. Yet even the poem 'Oh, had I known the way of things . . .' was positively construed, and Tarasenkov predicted Pasternak's art would lose its tragic quality once he learned to understand socialist human relations.[78]

A further article, commissioned by *Literaturnaya gazeta* from the scholars Khardzhiev and Trenin surveyed Pasternak's development in the context of poetic modernism. The paper's editors were perplexed at this neo-Lefist eructation and replaced it with an essay by Selivanovsky, claiming this reflected Pasternak's own wish. With gleeful cynicism Pasternak confirmed to the authors that 'what is needed at present is the most primitive panegyric'.[79] However reluctant to see his aberrant Futurist work rehearsed, Pasternak must have found Selivanovsky's essay far more offensive, and his letter to Khardzhiev and Trenin merely reflected the state of *Literaturnaya gazeta*.[80]

Selivanovsky's article was a demonstration of 'RAPP with its teeth pulled'. It noted the still unrealistic, intimate nature of Pasternak's dialogue with socialism, hopes were held out for a genuine 'second birth' if only the poet could escape his 'bourgeois individualism', which was doomed in an age of socialist revolution.[81] Variations on these ideas kept appearing during the mid 1930s and formed the basis for Selivanovsky's entry on Pasternak in the *Literaturnaya Entsiklopediya* in 1934.[82] Selivanovsky effectively articulated the official line on Pasternak's work for several years to come, basing it on a series of supposedly typical quotations from poems such as 'About these Verses' ('Pro eti stikhi'), 'To a Friend', etc. Characteristic was Miller-Budnitskaya's review of Pasternak's *Poems in One Volume (Stikhotvoreniya v odnom tome)* and the prose selection *Aerial Ways (Vozdushnye puti)* published in 1933, in which the critic noted Pasternak's doom-laden bourgeois view of revolution as a destructive force, and his fetishisation of an art that conflicted with its epoch.[83] The fossilisation of such views was of course encouraged by continual reprints of Pasternak and a virtual absence of new verse following *Second Birth*. Similarly with his prose. Reviewing the *Aerial Ways* anthology, the critic Nusinov noted the stories' divorcement from Soviet reality and regrettable indulgence in 'literary reminiscences'.[84]

Apart from a handful of émigré assessments,[85] the only relatively jargon-free critique of *Second Birth* appeared in a survey article by Pasternak's friend, the constructivist theoretician Kornelii Zelinsky. His 'Lyric Notebook' in the almanac *The Sixteenth Year (God shestnadtsaty)* discussed the book alongside verse by Bagritsky and Smelyakov. Unlike other reviewers, Zelinsky identified *Second Birth*, despite its title, as the end of a natural line of development. However, he discerned evident signs of an artistic crisis or impasse, and *Second Birth* evidenced an extension of thematic range but no real 'growth towards socialism'. Pasternak's virtual poetic silence for the next three years confirmed this and contradicted any view of a seeming embracement of socialism.[86]

After Pasternak's initial poetic addresses to Stalin, another event later in 1932

helped enhance the myth of some mystical communion between poet and
ruler. In the night of 8–9 November, following a celebration of the fifteenth
October revolution anniversary, Stalin's wife, Nadezhda Alliluyeva, died. The
brief *Pravda* announcement on the 10th and absence of further report
suggested there was something to hide. Available evidence and most conjectures point to suicide. In despair at her non-functional marriage to a
preoccupied, coarse and despotic husband, and at the Kremlin clique's cynical
indifference to the misery inflicted by their policies, Alliluyeva had a semi-
public contretemps with Stalin at Voroshilov's home on the evening of the 8th
and refused to join in a toast. She retired for the night and domestic staff found
her next morning with a fatal shot-wound. A suicide note to Stalin allegedly
reviewed the personal and political grounds for her desperate act. These details
and reconstruction of event and motive emerged later over several decades.[87]
At the time there was only whispered conjecture that Alliluyeva's death was
not from natural causes, and Pasternak himself added a baffling convolution to
the mystery. Among the flurry of tributes, *Literaturnaya gazeta* published a
collective letter from a group of writers on the 17 November, expressing bland
condolences to Stalin 'on the death of Nadezhda Alliluyeva, who gave all her
strength to the cause of liberating millions of oppressed humanity, the cause
that you yourself lead and for which we are ready to surrender our own lives as
confirmation of the uncrushable vitality of this cause'. There followed thirty-
three signatures by various men and women of letters in seeming random
order. Immediately below them was one individual response:

I share in the feelings of my comrades. On the evening before I had for the first time
thought about Stalin deeply and intently as an artist. In the morning I read the news. I
am shaken as if I had actually been there, lived through and seen everything.

Boris Pasternak.

This postscript was a strange disruption of the collective condolatory genre
and it seems surprising that it was printed in this form. Much later Pasternak
reported that he refused to sign the collective message and 'wrote Stalin a long
letter on the occasion of Alliluyeva's death'.[88] There is no evidence of such a
letter having been sent or received however.

Pasternak's postscript contained no echo of official phraseology, and was also
mystifying in its content, lacking any statement of sharing in the premier's loss. As
Pasternak later told Isaiah Berlin, during the hours when Alliluyeva died, he had
'had a creative night', although he left no clue about the fruits of this creativity.[89]
Alliluyeva was unknown to Pasternak personally, but in life and literature he had
already shown a fascination with certain real and fictional 'women of the
revolution', and he was also adept at typecasting women in a role of suffering.[90]

His own recent brush with suicide had sharpened his awareness of the despair that drives people to such action. Most significantly, Pasternak's message seemed calculated to hint mysteriously at some special insight that made him a vicarious party to Stalin's motives, emotions and presumed sense of guilt. It thus hinted at Pasternak's search for a *yurodivy*-like role with licence to allude to awful truths – like the 'holy fool' in *Boris Godunov* – while enjoying protection from reprisal.[91]

If Pasternak's message to Stalin evoked no direct response, his other dealings with sinister forces behind the regime suggest that his word was listened to.

At a literary gathering held, presumably, at about this time and in honour of the OGPU, Aleksei Tolstoy recalled some dozen poets' reciting dithyrambs to this institution, followed by Pasternak's reading of some of his recent verse, which brought the ceremony to a discordant and premature close. Despite a private accolade afterwards from Ordzhonikidze, the government representative, Pasternak and others believed that he risked arrest.[92] Pasternak evidently said as much to Aleksei Tolstoy, and wrote openly to Lomonosova about his perceived dissidence:

Here they do not like eulogising anything apart from revolutionary politics, and anything introverted, anarcho-individualistic and independent is treated with all the more hostility, the greater its strength in each individual case.[93]

Awareness of his situation failed to intimidate Pasternak however. When mass arrests of 'opponents' began again following defeat of the alleged Ryutin conspiracy, in late 1932 the OGPU expanded its activity. In December, Pasternak renewed his earlier tenuous contacts with Agranov, the OGPU agent who in the 1920s had frequented the Brik-Mayakovsky circle and at that time expressed interest in getting to know him too. A pretext arose following the arrest and sentence on conspiracy charges of Viktor Anastasyev, son of the late Feliks Blumenfeld. When his pianist wife and young daughter were suddenly given ten days' notice to leave Moscow as relatives of an 'enemy of the people', Pasternak sent them five hundred roubles via Tusya Blumenfeld. Later, when they called to thank him, he agreed to approach Agranov, on whom rescindment of the eviction order depended. Without disputing the charges against her husband, Pasternak was able to obtain two three-month extensions of their Moscow residence permit, followed by issue of a permanent passport when all residents were eventually reregistered. Despite changing times, he thus continued his intercessions for victims of the system, as in the early 1920s. Later, in 1934, following his appeal to President Kalinin, Anastasyev's hard labour sentence was commuted from ten to five years, but before release he was resentenced and executed in 1939.[94]

The Nazi assumption of power in Germany in early 1933 further jeopardised communication among the separated Pasternak family. As Boris told his parents on 5 March that year:

Now it will surely be impossible to correspond: suspicion is bound to increase on both sides. That is why I am writing more openly than at any time, and directly on the subject, so that in future, if this letter reaches you and nothing happens to me, we can limit ourselves to mutual information about our health [. . .] Let me know whether I should continue writing you in Russian, or better in German. Should it be inconvenient to correspond as before, for practice I could write you in my foul broken French.

Until May of 1933, when he lapsed back into Russian, Boris did write several letters in French, so as not to draw attention to his parents as citizens of a hostile communist state. How much mail was perlustrated on either side is uncertain; by no means all Pasternak's messages reached Berlin. As he told his father in April, 'le nombre des malheurs n'amoindrit'. There were in fact several cases like that of Anastasyev where Pasternak found himself spending considerable time and effort on various solicitations, and he hardly worked as a result.[95]

In light of German events, and quite independently of one another, Boris in Moscow and the Freidenbergs in Leningrad invited Leonid and Rozaliya Pasternak back to Russia in spring of 1933. Boris' telegram was sent as soon as news broke of Nazi measures against Jews and socialists. A following letter cautioned, however, 'Dans tous les cas avant d'adopter une décision quelconque considérez bien les difficultés accrues de la vie d'ici, dont l'habitude vous aurait fait ressentir leur étrangeté au double.'[96] Discussion of plans for a return to Russia continued into the autumn, including mention of an official invitation, transport arrangements for Leonid's pictures, the possibility of the Soviet Embassy in Berlin storing or dispatching belongings, etc. In May a visitor to Moscow from Germany 'of totally Arian provenance' reported his country had become a madhouse. On the other hand, Lydia, as a Jewish foreigner, was still employed as a psychologist in Munich, and holiday photos on the beach later in the summer showed no evidence of any tragedy.[97] It also became clear that after cautioning messages from Boris and Olga Freidenberg the Pasternak parents were in no hurry to return to Russia.[98]

As it emerged, being foreign subjects the Pasternaks were unlikely to be disadvantaged by residing in Germany. Meanwhile, in 1934 Lydia became engaged to Eliot Slater, an English psychologist working in the same Munich institute as herself, and she eventually left with him for England. Josephine's husband, an Austrian citizen, remained in his post with the Deutsche Vereins-

bank in Munich and he and his family were untouched until the Anschluß of
Austria in 1938. Boris remained alert to the potential menace of Nazism,
however, and as he told cousin Olga, he remained hopeful that he could
'surreptitiously coax our people in the indicated direction', i.e. back to
Russia.[99]

Revival of the internal passport system in winter of 1932–33 coincided closely
with revision of the ration system and of legislation covering family depen-
dants, all of which affected the Moscow Pasternaks. It precipitated an official
divorce between Boris and Evgeniya, thus enabling her to secure an independent claim to the Tverskoi Boulevard apartment; this in turn allowed Boris and
Zinaida to register their relationship officially. However, the new rulings
caused problems for Neigauz's relatives and for the Frishmans and others, and
for Zinaida's aunt, who spent several weeks with her and Boris in early 1933
and was now forced to return to her home in Tula.[100]

In autumn of 1933 Evgenii Pasternak began attending school in the
Patriarch Pools area of Moscow and made good progress. The school's
vermin- and vice-ridden location and the risk of encounters with teenage
hoodlums caused concern, but no untoward incidents occurred. In October
Zhenya also joined the Young Pioneer movement and evidently approached
this with conscientious gravity. As Boris told his sister Lydia in October, 'It's a
strange thing and it would take long to explain, but even this fills me with a
certain positive excitement'.[101]

Following the summer trip to the Urals, Pasternak only resumed writing in the
winter of 1932–33. Correspondence with friends at home and abroad was also
semi-dormant, and Pasternak figured rarely on the professional or literary
social scene. Despite this, reprints or compilations from earlier books continued appearing in the post-RAPP 'thaw'. *The Year 1905* was republished by
the Leningrad Writers' Publishing House in 1932. The next year saw the
Moscow publication of *Selected Verse (Izbrannye stikhi)* and *Longer Poems
(Poemy)* with Sovetskaya literatura, and the prose anthology *Aerial Ways* with
GIKhL. Meanwhile *Poems in One Volume* appeared in Leningrad, although
this was the mere salvaged remnant of a more ambitious project.

In January 1933 Pasternak was told by the Leningrad Writers' Publishing
House that his five-volume collected works had been cancelled; the *Poems in
One Volume* appeared simply in order not to waste what had already been
typeset. Then, in early March 1933, he was told that *Safe Conduct* was to be
excluded from the *Aerial Ways* collection.[102] 'Comradely' treatment of non-
Party writers now involved Pasternak's own self-censorship and -suppression.

As he told Gorky in a last-ditch attempt to rescue *Safe Conduct*, the Party Central Committee's Kultprop section had cancelled his collected works as a general policy decision; now it was proposed that Pasternak himself withdraw *Safe Conduct* 'on the pretext that it was received with disapproval by the writing community, and that it would be uncomradely of me to disdain their disapproval.'[103] Pasternak pointed out that poets such as Aseyev and Zharov had had collected editions published, and he thus hoped for a similar favour in his own instance. Gorky blustered to his secretary Kryuchkov but was evidently powerless to reverse an official decision.[104] *Safe Conduct* was banned and was not reprinted in Russia till the early 1980s.

In February 1933 the Orgkomitet of the Writers' Union held its second plenary session in preparation for a general First Congress. During the proceedings Stalin was proclaimed by Gronsky as progenitor of the new 'socialist realism'.[105] The agenda also included discussion of the theatre, with Lunacharsky among the keynote speakers; consideration of the status of the Writers' Union; and reports by committees on the three Caucasian republics.[106] There is no record of Pasternak's active participation, but he certainly attended the session on drama and was disturbed by Lunacharsky's speech. As he reported to his father, 'After his stroke and half under death sentence, aged and changed, [Lunacharsky] made a public speech to the writers on drama, a bloody and revolutionary speech full of hatred and threats – and this almost on the edge of the grave. I listened in horror and with inexpressible pity for him.'[107]

Leonid Pasternak had hoped Lunacharsky would assist with distributing his jubilee commemorative volume in Russia and asked his son to approach him. But Lunacharsky's speech and observable condition made it clear that he was not to be taxed with such requests. Apart from a few gift copies, Leonid's anniversary album failed to reach Russian readers for a quite different reason: the unsold editions were destroyed at one of the ritual Nazi burnings of Jewish and other 'decadent' literature on 10 May 1933, and the few surviving copies were lost when the family left Germany later in the decade.

On 4 April 1933 Pasternak attended an evening given by the young peasant poet Pavel Vasilyev in the *Novy mir* editorial offices. Vasilyev's arrival in town in 1932 and his progress through the capital had a *succès de scandale* similar to that of Esenin. Despite his temporary detention for disorderly conduct and a censorship ban, Gronsky and others attempted to rescue this 'kulak' literary phenomenon for Soviet literature. Pasternak never showed any partiality for the rural lyric but his impression of Vasilyev was of 'a great gift with an undoubtedly great future'.[108] His statement after the recital went unrecorded, but its tenor, afterwards summarised by Nusinov, was: 'if it is necessary for a writer to reshape himself organically, then woe betide our literature'. Received opinion by now, however, was that natural talent required ideological supervision.[109]

On 12 April Pasternak made a more telling public statement at a memorial evening on the second anniversary of Mayakovsky's suicide held in Moscow University. His impromptu speech again echoed ideas expressed in the last section of *Safe Conduct*, which quite contradicted the orthodox 'life-asserting' official view of Mayakovsky. According to Pasternak the theme of suicide was there in all his texts, and his death was a gigantomaniac enactment of this. Even more controversial was Pasternak's claim that Mayakovsky's 'spontaneous revolutionary quality' had a vitality that rivalled the 'officially recognised tone of our revolution' which Pasternak had long regarded as a suffocating piece of dogma. (volume I, 348–9) At the memorial gathering Pasternak's views were vehemently countered by subsequent speakers including Aseyev, Bezymensky, Osip Brik and Kirsanov, and he then returned to apologise for his 'inclarity' that led his 'former friends' (!) to attribute such primitive ideas to him.[110]

The First Congress of the Writers' Union was originally scheduled for June 1933, but that date was put back as plans developed. Factors causing the delay were: political events in Germany and an increasing collaboration with French intellectuals that raised the likely international profile of the Congress; increasingly complex elaborations of the theory and practice of 'socialist realism'; and a growing sense of the role of Soviet national minority literatures. The Congress was thus postponed till summer of 1934.

During 1933 there were various changes in the Orgkomitet, and finally Gorky who had returned to Russia in mid May was created chairman to breathe life into the flagging committee stage of the preparations. His relations with Stalin had reached their cordial apogee, and this was conjecturally a reason for the new and relatively liberal atmosphere in the country at large.[111]

As part of the preparations, Pasternak was at first drafted to a large group headed by Panfyorov to examine the literature of the RSFSR. Pilnyak then suggested the tantalising prospect of an expedition party to visit Azerbaidzhan and Pasternak suddenly became interested. However, Pilnyak had remained on good terms with Evgeniya Pasternak, and Boris bowed out after her secondment to the group as official illustrator. (Her reputation was by now rising, and in the early summer she had made portraits of most of the Red Army command.)[112]

Pasternak then tried hard in September to secure inclusion in a Georgian expeditionary group to be led by Pavlenko and planned to include Kirpotin, Kolosov, and friends such as Tynyanov, Tikhonov and the scholar and translator Viktor Goltsev. Like Pasternak, both Tynyanov and Tikhonov had been in Georgia before. Pasternak's eagerness stemmed less from his bureaucratic ambitions than from a desire to produce some new Georgian poetic translations;[113] for this he required further interlinear translations since his rudimentary Georgian left him unable to fathom a complex poetic text. On 6 October he sent Zhgenti a handful of translations from Tabidze and Yashvili based on glosses he collected two years before, and he requested further such material from Tabidze, Chikovani or any others recommended. The plan was to produce a complete translated anthology of Georgian verse and a contract was signed providing for delivery of a manuscript by January 1934.[114]

The interlinear cribs were not quick to appear however, and Pasternak realised he was dealing with southern indolence. 'They are terrible idlers,' he told his sister Lydia, 'which lets me down with the publishers and reduces my earnings, since I am forced to sit twiddling my thumbs while those folk in the Caucasus get moving.'[115] Using Yashvili as courier, Pasternak wrote again to Tabidze, requesting materials from himself and a list of other prominent names to which Yashvili made a few of his own additions.[116]

The Georgian visitation travelled by train via Kharkov and Rostov, arriving in Tiflis on 17 November. To the originally scheduled members Kaverin and Olga Forsh had been added. In Tiflis the party stayed at the Orianta Hotel where Pasternak had Goltsev and Tikhonov as congenial room-mates.[117] On the programme were visits to Kutaisi and Imeretia, and in Tiflis there were reunions with Tabidze, Yashvili, Leonidze and other friends, including artist Lado Gudiashvili. Other events recalled by Nina Tabidze included a meeting over supper with actors from the Rustaveli Theatre.[118] A rapid visit was also paid to Gadzha where it was possible to buy grapes, dates, apples and pears, only rarely available in Moscow from the writers' special distribution centre. Otherwise the same shortages and high prices were in evidence as in 1931. But Pasternak was again struck by the contrast between life in Tiflis and Moscow: 'As before the town has a European patina, and everyone can see that houses and streets are for living people and not for phantoms and formulas.'[119] The official programme of meetings with the Caucasian Culture and Propaganda Department was irksome of course, but Pasternak pleaded in vain with Pavlenko to be released early and left with the rest of the group on 29 November.

In Tiflis Pasternak and Tikhonov negotiated a joint contract with Zakgiz publishers for a volume of translated *Poets of Georgia (Poety Gruzii)* that appeared there the following year. It was a significant event: apart from occasional examples by Balmont, Gorodetsky and Mandelstam, Pasternak and Tikhonov became the first systematic translators of Georgian into Russian. During his stay, however, Pasternak realised that his own choice of verse for translation was not at all to the taste of local officials, who preferred civic verse to lyrics and distrusted the old masters of the Blue Horns group. Although convinced of the superiority of Tabidze and Yashvili, he found them excluded from the list of authors officially sponsored. As he commented in a letter, 'I would have great success here if I rejected them. But my loyalty to them will be all the livelier for that.'[120]

Pasternak's support of his talented and original friends was not in vain, and some of the finest Georgian lyrics survived in his translated editions. The Tabidze renderings particularly showed a re-creative inspiration and virtual symbiosis of two kindred poetic natures. Other items drew more on sheer professionalism. They included Yashvili's and Mitsishvili's floridly oriental odic addresses to Stalin. These works had been created as part of the nascent Stalin 'personality cult' that began in the winter of 1933–34 partly in preparation for the 17th Party Congress.[121] However, there was an element of compromise in Pasternak's agreement to translate such work, as also in his assurance to Zhgenti that Yashvili's 1924 poem 'On the Death of Lenin' was 'astounding'.[122]

Despite the rewards of translating some remarkable poets, Pasternak was aware that 'for a litterateur the switch from original work is a step downhill and a retreat'.[123] A similar view of translation was shared by Mandelstam. In Akhmatova's presence he told Pasternak in autumn of 1933 that 'Your complete collected works will consist of twelve volumes of verse translation and one volume of your own poems.'[124] This of course rubbed in the recent cancellation of Pasternak's collected works and reflected the two men's capacity for offending one another. That autumn Mandelstam was livid at Pasternak's intended encouraging remark when he acquired new quarters in Nashchokinsky Lane. To the assurance that 'Now you've got an apartment – you can write poetry', Mandelstam responded with a poem of barely disguised fury: 'The apartment is quiet as paper. . .'[125]

As a known implacable enemy of the system, Mandelstam had by now made his last lifetime appearance in print. Pasternak however was an optimist and his translation project seemed a justifiable if secondary professional activity involving a positive 'engagement' with contemporary reality.[126] Indeed, for the time being he was ready to comply in the hope that something good would emerge over and above the interference with liberty and dead conformism. In October 1934 he wrote the following to his father's sister in Leningrad:

I am fearfully glad of our consensus which has formed in our different towns without persuasion, and for mutually unknown reasons and in different situations. It is, after all, this which characterises our times. Whether in Party purges, or as a measure of artistic or real-life assessments, or in the awareness and language of children, already a certain as yet unnamed truth is forming, which constitutes the rightness of the system and also the temporary excessiveness of its elusive novelty.

Some nocturnal conversation of the nineties has dragged on and become real life. Though charming in its original half-madness amid clouds of tobacco smoke, how can this raving of the Russian revolutionary nobility not seem like madness? And the conversation has become a part of the geographical map and is so tangible! But the world has seen nothing more aristocratic and liberated than this naked boorish reality of ours which is still being cursed and evokes groans – you are right, aunty.[127]

Such a belief in 'consensus' was for Mandelstam an abnormality that visited him only in moments of mental sickness. Nadezhda Mandelstam described this as a 'desire to be reconciled with reality and seek justification for it [. . .] as though at such moments he was under hypnosis. He would then say that he wanted to be with everyone and feared to be left out of the revolution and to miss through shortsightedness the noble thing that was being carried out before our eyes [. . .] This feeling was experienced by many of our contemporaries, among them some very worthy people like Pasternak.[128]

Mandelstam's intolerance meanwhile placed him beyond the pale of Soviet literature and now jeopardised his very survival. In *Safe Conduct*, Pasternak talked of an art that could survive by 'deceiving' the regime that commissioned it. Mandelstam's poetry encroached on a perilous area, whoever, where there was no saving aesthetic ambiguity. His exercises in the genre of political satire dated from the dawn of the Bolshevik era, and he recited an outrageous new example to Pasternak on a walk through the Tverskaya-Yamskaya region in early 1934. The poem was a verse portrait of Stalin, the 'Kremlin's man of the mountains', whose 'thick fingers are fatty as maggots / And words, heavy as lead weights, are right and true. / His cockroach whiskers leer / And his boottops gleam. / And around him a rabble of thin-necked leaders [. . .] half-men. . .'[129]

In safer times, both earlier and later on, Pasternak occasionally composed such verse. Artistically his efforts were weaker than Mandelstam's best, and he had a low regard for the genre. On this occasion, however, he was terrified and angry at having been made an unwitting audience to such treasonable verse. 'What you have just recited to me bears no relation to literature or poetry', he told Mandelstam. 'It isn't a literary fact, but an act of suicide which I disapprove of and I want no part in it. You didn't recite anything to me. I didn't hear anything. I beg you not to recite it to anyone else.'[130] This was an aspect of Mandelstam's non-professional freedom that Pasternak did not envy. He also took exception to a racial aspersion in the poem's reference to the 'broad chest of the Ossetian': 'How could he write verses like that – he's a Jew after all!' was his later comment to Nadezhda Mandelstam – a remark understandable in terms of Pasternak's own complex-ridden Jewishness, his current warmth towards Caucasian friends and – for the time being – respectful consensus with the Stalinist regime.[131]

5

Congress, Consensus and Confrontation

'A Word about Poetry'

Poetry will forever remain a pinnacle more illustrious than the highest Alps, yet one which lies in the grass beneath our feet, so that we need only bend in order to see it and pluck it from the ground. It will forever be too simple to be discussed at meetings. It will forever be an organic function of the happiness of men filled with the blessed gift of rational speech, so that the more happiness there is on earth, the easier it will be to be an artist.

(1935)

Tired after Georgian junketing and committee work, Pasternak returned from Tiflis to a winter of family illnesses and inconvenience. Both his stepsons fell sick with a succession of children's ailments; no firewood was available over the New Year period, and for a week the house had no water supply.[1]

In early January Viktor Goltsev turned up with some newly received Georgian cribs for Pasternak to work on. On 8 January, however, came a further interruption following news of Andrei Bely's death from arterio-sclerosis at the age of fifty-three. That day, together with other adherents of the former Free Philosophical Association (Vol'fila), Pasternak sat several hours with Bely's widow. As a long-standing friend and admirer, he was placed on a six-man commission entrusted with the funeral arrangements. He signed the death announcement in *Literaturnaya gazeta*; he was in the guard of honour and spoke at the civil memorial ceremony at the Writers' Union on the evening of the 9th; and he was a coffin-bearer at the funeral and cremation next day. Later in the month, he sat on a committee that met in Kamenev's office at Academia Publishers to discuss a possible complete edition of Bely's verse.[2]

Together with Pilnyak and Sannikov, Pasternak also signed an obituary in *Izvestiya*. It described Bely's work as 'a brilliant contribution to both Russian and world literature' and as having created an entire literary school and left its mark on all subsequent literature. Acknowledging themselves as Bely's pupils,

the three signatories recognised his place among 'revolutionary phenomena' –
a judgement strongly at variance with Marxist opinion, but quite in keeping
with the revolutionary spirit Pasternak admired and recently reaffirmed with
reference to Mayakovsky.[3]

The Bely obituary was so unorthodox that *Izvestiya* next day published a
major article by Kamenev correcting its errors and relegating the deceased to
his proper obscure place in the past. A week later *Literaturnaya gazeta* also
noted the reactionary nature of the obituary notice. Significantly, Pasternak's
name was never cited as a party to the offence – which in negative terms was a
sign of favour.[4] The obituary was for him a purely formal if slightly polemical
statement, and it exaggerated his own sense of debt to Bely. Very shortly
afterwards he told Akhmatova that 'He [Bely] is alien to me, but I will not
yield him up to *them*.'[5] By 'them' Pasternak meant the orthodox literary
bureaucracy. However, there was no sense at this stage that the new Writers'
Union was part of 'their' apparatus. Indeed Pasternak's next remark to
Akhmatova was to urge her to apply for membership. Her response was a
puzzling silence and eloquent drumming of the fingers.[6]

Meanwhile the spate of new editions of Pasternak continued with a new
Selected Poems (Izbrannye stikhotvoreniya), and further efforts were made to
groom him as an establishment personality despite the recent ban on his
collected works. He continued on the editorial committee of the 'Poet's
Library' editions, chaired by Gorky, and in January he was coopted to a
committee preparing Russian editions of Georgian verse. He accepted these
duties reluctantly. As he told his parents, 'they fuss over me quite undeservedly', despite the fact that 'I have not a single revolutionary virtue, and not one
public one. I'd just like to sit quiet and unnoticed and write some good
works.' Requests and commissions continued however, including various
ceremonial and ideologically marked activity such as signing an article in
support of the recent Austrian workers' uprising, or co-signing a message to
welcome Bulgarian communists Dmitrov, Popov and Tanev who arrived after
their acquittal of causing the Berlin Reichstag fire.[7] Aware of what might
happen if his and his parents' situations were reversed, Pasternak was concerned about repercussions for them in Germany. No adverse consequences
were noted though, and Leonid Pasternak wrote confirming that 'auntie'
('*tyotya*') had raised no complaint.[8]

A sense of his parents' vulnerability aroused Pasternak's fear of their visit to
Russia, and he further postponed his own travel plans. As he told Josephine:

If I belonged wholly to myself, i.e. if I was just a private individual, I might even now go
off to Switzerland to see Rolland and try to invite them there. Or else I might call on
them en route for France. But in my situation, to go anywhere means having something

to say, or undertaking to say something immediately on returning. That is why I cannot come to see you [. . .] Indirectly you would make it necessary for me to keep quiet about my trip – a problem which is quite beyond me and unnatural, my fate being what it is.[9]

The potential rewards for Pasternak's agreement to have his life manipu-lated and to become an official functionary were considerable. For the previous tax year his declared earnings had topped 29,000 roubles, and as he realised, there were further chances to reconstruct his life, purchase property, and double or even triple his earnings, and free himself from dependence on contracts by repeatedly reprinting one and the same thing. But, as he told his parents, he resisted such blandishments as immoral. Apart from which: 'I love life and art too much in all their authentic prosaic quality, and I would find it boring and vacuous [. . .] beyond that golden frontier where the chance opens up to acquire gramophones, American closets, rare libraries, etc., and I refuse.'[10]

During the winter, however, Pasternak virtually abandoned original writing. He told Grigorii Sorokin, 'I am up to my ears in translating from Georgian, which is often even enjoyable and absorbing'.[11] The immediate aim was to complete Vazha Pshavela's epic *The Snake-Eater (Zmeeed)* and the Georgian lyric collection in time for the summer Writers' Congress. Under such pressure, as he told his Tiflis editor, 'I am working on everything at once, I am not going for walks, I don't read any books. For two months I haven't even seen my son who lives only twenty minutes' ride from here.'[12]

Under such pressure an intriguing project of the previous winter finally collapsed. The Leningrad State Opera and Ballet Theatre had invited Pasternak to produce a Russian libretto of Wagner's *Der Ring des Nibelungen*, and in January 1933 he had borrowed the score from his pianist friend Samuil Feinberg. Now the plan was aborted and a thousand roubles had to be returned to the theatre.[13]

However, when excavations began for the new Moscow metro in the courtyard and nearby street, something akin to a set for *Götterdämmerung* was created on Pasternak's doorstep – or, as he told Folyan, 'something halfway between the German town of Essen and a Grecian Tartarus'.[14] The metro construction in fact continued beyond the year end, and by autumn of 1934 some of its domestic consequences included prolific filth, cracked walls, collapsing floors, and infestation by rats.[15]

In the first months of 1934 Pasternak's Georgian verse translations appeared in almanacs and journals such as *Krasnaya nov'*, *Molodaya gvardiya*, *Novy mir*, *Tridtsat' dnei* (Thirty Days), as well as *Izvestiya* and *Literaturnaya gazeta*.

Later, in October *The Snake Eater* appeared with Sovetsky pisatel (Soviet Author) publishers, and the following year the same publisher produced his *Georgian Lyricists (Gruzinskie liriki)*; at the same time *Poets of Georgia* translated jointly by Pasternak and Tikhonov appeared with Zakgiz in Tiflis.

Pasternak's mood and attitude towards this work varied considerably from day to day. He was irked that 'his' Georgian miscellany contained two mandatory odes to Stalin by Yashvili and Mitsishvili and other items reflecting official taste. 'Most upsetting is that I cannot work at all seriously,' he complained to his parents. 'I have been translating Georgian poets, but this is not work, although these items (nothing but sh..!)[*odno d{er'mo}!*] have been feeding me.'[16] On the other hand, to Spassky who was also busy translating, he enthused over their shared pleasure: 'How much blazing, dramatic, mutually shared truth there is in the fact that without prior agreement four poets, under the effect of *one and the same law* which moulded their lives these past years, have *so eagerly* seized on this opportunity and write *such* Russian verse, deriving stimulus and justification from Georgia!'[17] Pasternak also later wrote in similar terms to Tabidze, grateful for this '*admission* to a close participation in the affairs of history, and an involvement in its future [. . .] the broad and boundless love affair of a few specially fortunate people beneath a sky that decks them with the significance of one common date.'[18]

The warmth of the official embrace and attempts to 'adopt' Pasternak[19] were accompanied in spring of 1934 by reminders of his still ambivalent position however. On 13 May the new Writers' Union began enrolling members and Pasternak was among the first batch of names processed by the commission.[20] On the same day, Aseyev also made one of his routine attempts to undermine his colleague's reputation while maintaining an elaborate cordiality which Pasternak went along with sooner than precipitate a quarrel.[21] Aseyev who had recently been appointed as Orgkomitet spokesman on poetry and at a preliminary meeting for an All-Union Conference of Poets, reported on the state of the art as he perceived it, awarding marks to Russian poets on the degree of their commitment to the 'thematics of Soviet reality'. In this scheme Pasternak fell in the worst, 'minus three', category recognised by its 'motivated rejection' of this theme.[22] The report raised such controversy that Pasternak found himself in strange alliance with other speakers such as Osip Brik, Kirsanov and Surkov, and he himself offered a deft rebuttal. The awarding of good marks, he maintained, smacked of the infant school; he disliked Aseyev's uncomradely attitude and his formalistic categorisations reminiscent of Lef. Moreover, 'in art, as distinct from history, our time has not yet been identified by name'.[23] A few days later the critic Tarasenkov supported Pasternak by citing *Second Birth* as an example of an indeed successful lyrical engagement with socialism.[24]

In the early hours of 14 May, secret police agents appeared at Mandelstam's apartment in Nashchokinsky Lane with an arrest warrant signed by Yagoda. In the presence of his wife and of Akhmatova, who had arrived on a visit from Leningrad the previous day, the apartment was searched, after which Mandelstam was taken to the Lubyanka. Pasternak heard news of this from Akhmatova later that day.[25]

Akhmatova went on Mandelstam's behalf to see Pilnyak, and via the actor Ruslanov who knew Enukidze's secretary, she obtained an audience with the Chairman of the All-Union Central Executive Committee.[26] Nadezhda Mandelstam on the same day contacted Bukharin, who was well disposed to her husband and had helped them obtain their apartment in 1933.

At Nadezhda's request, Pasternak also tried to contact Bukharin. Not finding him at the *Izvestiya* editor's office, he left a note recording his deep concern and requesting Bukharin's urgent intervention. On Nadezhda's initiative he also spoke with the poet Demyan Bedny, who probably heard no details but surmised the nature of Mandelstam's offence and advised against getting involved.[27] At this stage there was no information about any indictment: Mandelstam could have been detained for his verses and views quite apart from the Stalin lampoon, particularly after recently slapping the establishment author Aleksei Tolstoy across the face in public over an old grievance involving his wife.[28] Significantly Pasternak made no attempt to intercede via Agranov: if indeed the case involved Mandelstam's poetic calumny of Stalin, only highest-level intervention could be effective. Moreover, Agranov probably had evidence on everyone who had heard Mandelstam's poem – an attempt to intercede via OGPU could backfire on the petitioner.

For all Mandelstam's recent inhinged and exasperating behaviour, Pasternak retained a compassionate admiration for him and had continued making friendly calls long after Mandelstam struck the Volkhonka off his visiting list following his encounter with Zinaida. Despite Akhmatova's approaches, her name by now belonged to bourgeois literary history and carried little clout. Pasternak's word was still listened to, and his approach to Bukharin proved crucial in helping Mandelstam.

Equally vital was Bukharin's own status and personality. Having lived down his reputation as a right-wing oppositionist, he was appointed editor of *Izvestiya* in February 1934 in succession to Gronsky. Unlike most of the leadership, Bukharin combined an angularity of intellect with artistic sensitivity and a sense of humour. Ever since 1925 when he helped draft the Party resolution legitimising 'fellow traveller' literature, he had advocated non-interference in culture by the Party, and his general stance was close to that of Gorky. When he took over *Izvestiya*, the paper acquired a refreshing new scientific, educational, and cultural dimension. New contributors included a constellation of poets among whom Pasternak was the brightest star. Although no connoisseur of literary modernism, Bukharin responded to Pasternak's own integrity, independence and seeming willingness to collaborate with the new order. Within a fortnight of his appointment Pasternak made his début in *Izvestiya* with some Georgian translations – not 'approved' civic verses, but favourite lyrics by Yashvili and Tabidze.[29]

The impact of Pasternak's and Bukharin's action was felt within two weeks of Mandelstam's arrest. The offending verses never circulated in writing, but they were pieced together during OGPU investigations and were presented to Bukharin when he spoke with Yagoda about the case. After Bukharin's intercession, however, the official view of the poem as equivalent to a terrorist act was revised. Nadezhda Mandelstam was summoned and told of her husband's sentence with the instruction to 'isolate but preserve'. He was condemned to three years' exile in the outback town of Cherdyn in Perm Oblast, a few hundred miles north east of Moscow, where his wife was permitted to join him.[30]

Mandelstam's case might have rested there. His detention and transport under guard to Cherdyn aggravated an incipient psychosis however. He had tried slitting his veins while in prison and in Cherdyn he was admitted to hospital, where he evaded attempts to restrain him and jumped from a window in another vain suicide attempt. Thereupon Nadezhda cabled the Party Central Committee, requesting commutement of his sentence and permission for psychiatric treatment. At this point Stalin intervened personally and in the 'liberal' role he had already played in the cases of Pilnyak, Zamyatin, and Bulgakov. The number of cities banned to Mandelstam was reduced to twelve, and shortly afterwards he elected to reside in Voronezh to the south of Moscow. Immediately prior to this alleviation of his sentence, however, Stalin made a personal telephone call to Pasternak which was probably occasioned by Bukharin's note mentioning that 'Pasternak too is worried'.[31]

Stalin's phone call to Pasternak occurred in the second week of June 1934. His direct telephone calls to writers were rare events and invariably had a signal impact on the fate of that individual. Just as when Bulgakov received a call in April 1930, Stalin's phone call left Pasternak acutely dissatisfied with his own answers and with a lingering anxiety to continue the conversation and clarify his position.[32] However, in the short term, as with Bulgakov, the phone call enhanced his public standing.

An entire folklore sprang up around Stalin's call to Pasternak. Versions and interpretations have proliferated and they unnecessarily complicate the story so far as we can know it. Pasternak himself was the sole informed source concerning the phone conversation, and third- or fourth-hand interpretations stemming from his account are unreliable. Those who heard the story direct from him at the time were few: Nadezhda Mandelstam, her brother, and the poet and translator Georgii Shengeli.[33] Later, in 1945 and the 1950s, so as to correct distortions and clarify the historical record, Pasternak recounted the episode to various individuals, but with commentary that was eventually conflated with the original words spoken.[34]

Pasternak's telephone was in the corridor of the communal apartment and conversations could thus be overheard. Zinaida was at the time prostrate with pneumonia and unreliable as a witness; a neighbour, Stella Adelson, overheard Pasternak's side of the conversation but by the time she talked about it in the 1960s her recall was very incomplete; Nikolai Vilyam's subsequent claim to have been present that day as a dinner guest of the Pasternaks is unbelievable if only because of Zinaida's condition, and his account is more fragmentary than the fuller and closely congruent records kept by Akhmatova and Nadezhda Mandelstam.[35] It is their versions and the reconstruction by Evgenii and Elena Pasternak that offer the least contaminated account.

In the second half of 11 June, Pasternak was called to the phone and a male voice announced that Stalin wished to speak with him. In the early 1930s there was a brand of popular black humour based on telephone take-offs, and Pasternak at first thought some trickster was on the line. However, the voice (Stalin's secretary Poskryobyshev) gave a number for Pasternak to dial, which he did.

According to Zinaida, Pasternak behaved with his normal composure and began with his ritual complaint about distractions and extraneous noise in the communal corridor. Stalin immediately turned the conversation to Mandelstam and gave a reassurance that his case was being reviewed and that a favourable decision could be expected. He then asked why Pasternak had not petitioned on Mandelstam's behalf, or approached writers' organisations or himself. 'If I was a poet and my friend was in trouble, I would move heaven and earth in order to help him . . .'

Pasternak ignored the last remark. (But for his appeal to Bukharin, Stalin would not have known to telephone him at all.) He replied that since 1927 – i.e. since the creation of FOSP – these organisations had not concerned themselves with such matters.

91

'But after all he is your friend?' Stalin persisted. To clarify their relations and with a half-jesting hint at the distance between himself and Mandelstam, Pasternak responded that poets are like women and therefore always jealous of one another.

'But he is a master of his art, a master?' Stalin continued, to which Pasternak replied, 'But that isn't the point.' By this time he felt increasingly uncomfortable. After all, Stalin did not require him as intermediary to inform Mandelstam that his sentence would be lightened; furthermore, that information was conveyed at the very start of the conversation. The exchanges thus had some other aim. In the leader's queries about their friendship and Mandelstam's poetic mastery Pasternak sensed a menacing attempt to probe him as a potential accomplice, and to establish whether he knew of the offensive verses. To pursue that topic could have disastrous consequences. Pasternak realised he was in effect talking to his own interrogator, and he had the fortunate presence of mind to divert the conversation: 'But that isn't the point . . . Why do we keep on about Mandelstam? I have long wanted to meet with you for a serious discussion.'

'What about?' Stalin asked.

'About life and death.'

Thereupon Stalin hung up, bored, nonplussed or irritated at the prospect of a mind-bending verbal tangle with the poet-*yurodivy*. Pasternak too was taken aback by the abrupt end to their exchange. Had it continued, he might have attempted some representation to Stalin about recent infamies committed without his knowledge. He was denied the chance however. He attempted to redial the Kremlin number but reached only Poskryobyshev who said that Stalin was busy. Since the conversation had been overheard by neighbours, Pasternak asked whether he was allowed to speak about it with others, and was told that was his own affair.[36]

At the time of the phone call, the Mandelstams were still in Cherdyn. Pasternak was not asked to pass on any message and he made no attempt to contact them. He did however call Nadezhda Mandelstam's brother Evgenii Khazin, and without mentioning the phone call assured him of his sense that Osip's case would be favourably reviewed. The revised sentence was meanwhile communicated directly to Cherdyn, and the Mandelstams relocated to Voronezh. On a visit to Moscow later in the summer, Nadezhda was sick with typhoid and dysentery, and only heard of Pasternak's talk with Stalin on a later visit, quite by chance, from Shengeli. At this point Pasternak gave her a verbatim account of the Kremlin phone call. In the Mandelstams' and Akhmatova's view he had acquitted himself with credit.[37]

Pasternak's conversation with Stalin acquired powerful resonance in the literary community. He evidently recounted the incident to Ilya Ehrenburg who had just arrived from Paris with Malraux in tow, ready for the Writers' Congress. A few others were also told and the news spread like wildfire among Moscow's literati. Stalin's use of the word 'master' was later conjectured to have supplied the title of Bulgakov's novel *The Master and Margarita*.[38] Certainly the fact of the phone call was seen as a mark of favour. Zinaida recalled how they were suddenly treated with a new deference by staff and employees at the Writers' Union restaurant and elsewhere.[39] That same month Pasternak's stock also rose by association – as translator of Yashvili's ode to Stalin printed in the current issue of *Krasnaya nov'*.[40]

A few days after the phone call, a glowing picture of Pasternak's new official status was painted in a family letter:

. . . The attitude to me (in the most varied and directly *opposing* sections of society) is very favourable. Last week I was even (for the first time in life) called up on the phone by St.[alin] himself, and you can imagine what that means. I haven't even told young Zhenya about it, so easily does this fact lend itself to exploitation, even independently of the will of the person concerned. I. e. if one does *not* conceal it, one could fall into such a way of artificial ease.[41]

As Pasternak realised, it was really Bukharin's intervention that secured commutement of Mandelstam's sentence. Gratitude for this as well as for their more overt collaboration in *Izvestiya* prompted him to dedicate the 'Waves' cycle to Bukharin in the 1934 re-edition of *Second Birth*. At Bukharin's express request, some further lines on the imperialist character of the Caucasian campaign were also added.[42] As he told Lomonosova, 'At the time I was signing up *Sec[ond] B[irth]* for publication and hastily inscribed to him a piece that bore no relation to him and was terribly personal!! Then I forgot about it!!! See what stupid things one sometimes does. What can I do about it now?'[43] Meanwhile, Bukharin's position was strong, and there were no dark clouds on Pasternak's horizon. In terms of professional success *he* was the acknowledged 'master'.

For the summer of 1934 Pasternak took his wife, stepsons and Tusya Blumenfeld to a holiday centre at Odoev, south of Moscow. Several other writers and their families were also staying there in the mansion house which stood on a former landed estate on the river Upa, not far from the samovar town of Tula.

On 14 August Pasternak returned to Moscow by train with author Nikolai Shestakov for the start of the Writers' Congress. To avoid the filth and

93

inconvenience of the Volkhonka metro construction, he stayed round the corner at his brother Aleksandr's. The brothers saw little of one another however. As a member of the Presidium platform party, Boris left each morning and returned at night in the early hours; lunch was provided for delegates on a costfree token system at the former Filippov Café; between various sessions there was much socialising, and Pasternak spent his time mainly with Babel, Tynyanov, Tabidze and his wife Nina. The evening sessions were followed by 'nocturnal fêtings' in various restaurants, and Pasternak usually returned to Gogolevsky Boulevard between four and six in the morning.[44]

The First Congress of the Soviet Writers' Union opened on 17 August in the Moscow Hall of Columns and ran through to the end of the month. From the Party managerial viewpoint a chief aim of the Congress was to proclaim, impose, and secure acceptance of, the doctrine of 'socialist realism' as an aesthetic norm for all Soviet writers. Insofar as that was achieved, no further gathering was needed, and indeed none was held until after Stalin's death. Among the delegates themselves the issue of Party control underlay the whole proceedings, and there were two opposing camps of opinion: those in favour of Party dictatorship in literary matters, and the 'liberal' camp which aligned Gorky, Bukharin and most of the former 'fellow-travellers' including Pasternak.[45]

The Congress was attended by some two score foreign guests, including celebrities such as Louis Aragon, Jean-Richard Bloch, Oskar Maria Graf, André Malraux, Klaus Mann and Ernst Toller; several other international figures sent greetings to the Congress. From within the USSR, apart from republican literary delegates, there was substantial Communist Party representation, including Central Committee secretary Zhdanov who gave an important keynote speech; Radek discussed world literature and the mission of proletarian art; and Bukharin spoke 'On Poetry, Poetics and the Tasks of Poetic Creativity in the USSR'.

The Congress programme included thematic sessions to discuss prose, poetic and theatrical genres, children's literature, literatures of the Soviet republics, and the national and international functions of Soviet literature especially in light of the new fascist threat. The whole event passed off with much fanfare and interludes to hear greetings from parading delegations of students, workers, military, and collective farmers. During one such pageant Pasternak had one of his *yurodivy* turns and sprang from his seat to assist a female metro construction worker as she paraded past with some heavy cutting tool; for several seconds, to the amusement of onlookers, the two of them wrestled for possession of the instrument. Later, in his speech, Pasternak described this display of 'intellectual sentimentality' as caused by a sudden alleged sense of kinship with her as 'an old and close friend' – partly no doubt in view of the excavation's proximity to his own doorstep.[46]

'The opening of the Congress [. . .] scared us all off with its tedium – it was too solemn and official. But now each day is more interesting than the last, now the discussions have begun, ' Pasternak reported on 22 August.[47] The most engaging events for him began the previous day, when after a restaurant lunch with Neigauz and Yashvili, he presided at a session with Bloch, Chukovsky, Ehrenburg, Kassil and Isai Lezhnev as principal speakers. Immediately afterwards there was a special meeting with Georgian delegates at the Writers' House, where Pasternak and Tikhonov joined Tabidze and Yashvili and read some of their recent translations.[48] A further opportunity to read from his recent work came on 26 August at a 'Soviet Literature Festival' in Gorky Park; on that occasion he met and talked with the German delegate Oskar Maria Graf.[49]

The Georgian delegation caused a sensation at the Congress and established their major place in Soviet literary culture; this was partly due to speakers such as Toroshelidze and Sandro Euli, who affirmed their entire group's sympathy with Bukharin's keynote speech, and thereby aligned them with the whole Gorky–Bukharin faction. Pasternak's association with the Georgians was just one aspect of his personal triumph at the Congress.[50] André Malraux was only one of several speakers who proclaimed him as the rightful successor to Mayakovsky as Russia's premier poet. Ehrenburg cited the two poets as examples of the sophistication of Soviet socialist literature, which he contrasted with the simplistic directives emanating from the new literary establishment, and he criticised the primitive, imitative 'bourgeois' qualities that were concomitants of the Marxist-inspired drive against 'formalism'.[51]

Ehrenburg's point was taken up with even greater vehemence by Bukharin in his three-hour speech on 28 August. In a review of Russian verse since the Revolution he dismissed the outmoded primitive tendentiousness of the proletarian poets; he also expressed restrained criticism of Mayakovsky and played down the 'agitational' aspect of his work, thus offending the epigones led by Aseyev. For Bukharin the best of modern poetry was personified by Pasternak, Selvinsky and Tikhonov. While praising Pasternak's 'revolutionary works of profound sincerity',[52] he avoided mindless eulogising. Thus, Pasternak's 'retreat into the pearly shell of individual experience' was a protest against the old order, yet while accepting the revolution, he was seen as remote from the 'peculiar technicism of the age, the noise of battle and the passion of campaigning'. There was little appreciation here of Pasternak's recent work, but even a qualified accolade for him was incidental to Bukharin's main aim.

Genuine poetry, he opined, could be apprehended only via imagery and feelings rooted deep within the textual fabric – an argument directed against the placard and agitational genre perpetuated by the Mayakovskians. Aseyev struck Bukharin as not untalented, but he embodied an aspect of Mayakovsky that was rudimentary and no longer 'relevant'.[53] A supporting speech in much the same key as Bukharin's was given by Tikhonov.

Bukharin's speech was received by many as a hopeful sign of reconciliation between the regime and the intelligentsia, and many of the audience were excited at the seeming prospect of an artistic liberation.[54] However, there was a powerful backlash from the orthodox camp, led by the communist poet Surkov, a vociferous parvenu opposed to any suggestion that agitational verse was *passé*. After a tribute to his poetic mastery, Surkov felt 'compelled to say that for a large group of our poets [. . .] the work of Pasternak is an unsuitable point of orientation in their growth'.[55] Later several other poets – Aseyev, Bedny, Bezymensky, Kirsanov and Zharov – spoke up supporting Surkov against Bukharin's 'rearguard apoliticism' and divorcement of literature from the 'basic needs of the day', although only Bezymensky took specific issue with Pasternak.

Two days later, Bukharin returned to the podium and responded, but with such vitriolic and demagogic vehemence that Stetsky, head of the Central Committee Cultural Section, who had spoken in conciliatory vein, filed a complaint with the Politburo. Details of this were not publicised, but in the wake of the conference it became clear that Bukharin had overstepped the mark and been reproved. Shortly afterwards he was withdrawn altogether from literary affairs and transferred in February 1935 to head a commission charged with drafting a new national Constitution.[56]

Meanwhile, Pasternak and his most earnest concerns stood outside the framework of Congress discussions. This was clear from his speech on the evening of 29 August, which never directly addressed the issues raised by other speakers and offered a typical Pasternakian *mélange* of rhapsody and obliquity. Without discussing its technique or 'tasks', he presented a new definition of poetry which could be discovered in any genuine artistic engagement with the living people and issues of the day. His opening sentences expressed 'joy at the fact that this noble poetic language is born spontaneously in our dialogue with the modern age'. In this sense he likened poetry to prose –

prose, not in the sense of someone's complete prose works, but prose itself, the voice of prose, prose in action not belletristic narrative [. . .] the language of organic fact [. . .] And of course, like everything else in this world, it can be good or bad depending on whether we preserve it undistorted or contrive somehow to spoil it.

(III, 631–2; *SS*, IV, 217)

None of this directly challenged orthodox theory or opinion. At the end of his speech, though, Pasternak discussed his own position and the threat to artistic freedom posed by accepting Party patronage and its material blandishments. In effect he rehearsed again the right established by Venetian art to stand apart from those who commissioned it:

If fortune smiles on any of us, we may become prosperous (though may we be spared the riches that corrupt). 'Do not lose touch with the masses', are the Party's words on such occasions. But [. . .] my meaning is exactly the same when I say: 'Do not sacrifice personality for position.' In the great warmth that the people and the state surround us with there is too great a danger of becoming a socialist overlord. So let us withdraw a little from this affection for the sake of the source that directly bestows it, for the sake of our great, real and fruitful love for our country and the great men of our age.[57]

Pasternak's message was not lost on his audience, and although opinions of it varied,[58] he was accorded an ovation reflecting the warmth of all the tributes he received from other speakers. Yet despite the accolade, his enthusiastic response to some speakers, and a delighted smile that constantly played on his face as he sat on the platform,[59] Pasternak found much of the Congress disturbing, especially the duel between freedom and aggressive servility, personified by Bukharin and Surkov. Nor was this limited to the realm of poetry. The voices of several perplexed prose writers also sounded from the podium: Olesha was confused by the problems of focusing on a new socialist reality, and Babel had defined a style for the Bolshevik epoch as 'full of fire, passion, strength and jollity', evidently far removed from socialist realist stereotypes.[60]

Pasternak's private verdict on the Congress was unambiguously negative. Returning from one of the later sessions together with Budantsev and Emilii Mindlin, he admitted his high hopes had been dashed. Evidently he 'expected speeches with a generous philosophical content and believed the Congress would turn into a meeting of Russian thinkers'. But Gorky's speech had sounded like a lone voice, the most important issues affecting Russian literature had simply not been addressed, and Pasternak claimed to be 'mortally depressed'. To which Platonov commented that he 'would have been in that state regardless of what was said at the Congress. It's entirely a matter of Pasternak's own character [. . .] Of course it's hard for Boris Leonidovich . . . but it's hard for everyone . . .'[61]

Pasternak did not stay to the very end of the Congress. On 31 August, he left after Stetsky's speech and took the train back to Odoev to resume his holiday. He was absent for the final session and for Gorky's concluding address. He missed the elections to the Board of the new Union, but his name was proposed in absentia by Fadeyev and unanimously accepted. He also missed out on the first plenary meeting of the new Board. At it the Party official Aleksandr Shcherbakov was appointed as First Secretary and later in the triumphant wake of the Congress Pasternak cultivated cordial relations with him and other Board members such as Fadeyev, Fedin, Stavsky, and Surkov. Nevertheless, in such company, he was doomed to spiritual isolation.[62]

Owing to the disruptive metro excavations and house repairs, the family came back from Odoev only in early October. Even before returning, though, Pasternak suspected the implications of his recent elevation to office and the clash of interests at the Congress. In a worried letter to Spassky he confessed that 'the attitude towards me at the Congress was an utter surprise. All this is far more complex than you can imagine. And most of all, in the *indirectness* of the motives linking these things with me, it is much greyer and less festive.'[63] His apprehensions were realised that autumn when he was hurled into the maelstrom of literary bureaucratic life. Public speaking engagements were few, but included a Lermontov evening at Writers' House on 26 October, when he observed apologetically that he was aware of having written nothing serious to date about 'this remarkable age of ours'. Later, on 22 November, at the same venue he read from his recent translation of Vazha Pshavela.[64] But the official distractions and calls on his attention raised a howl of complaint in a letter to the Freidenbergs:

This is a crazy life, not a single free moment [. . .] I'd love to forget about everything and escape somewhere for a year or two. I desperately want to work. I'd like to write, at least and for the first time, something worthwhile, in prose, something human, grey, boring and modest, something large and nourishing. But it's impossible. There is an orgy of phone calls demanding me everywhere, as though I were society's kept woman. I battle against it and turn everything down. Yet time and energy go on these refusals. How sad and shameful . . .[65]

Amidst the abuse of his status as an officially accredited litterateur, the very notion of being a 'professional' poet became distasteful to Pasternak. In autumn of 1934 he treated Lomonosova to an account of his thoughts and feelings:

[. . .] I cannot stand even the word 'poet', let alone the tang of perfumery, confectionery and barber's shop which common understanding introduces into this grey, severe and crazily prosaic domain, even in a revolutionary state. One could pay no attention to it, except that people who seek solitude are looked on as criminals. In addition to which, there was a congress of writers here at which they were so nice to me that this faithfulness to myself [. . .] appears like ingratitude on my part.[66]

In fact, Pasternak yearned simply to engage in the creativity that alone justified his poetic profession. In this respect he envied his sister Josephine who in autumn of 1934 began sending to him and Stella Adelson examples of her original poetry. Between spring and the end of 1934 she had written over eighty poems.[67] Although he cautioned her against publishing under the name Pasternak,[68] on reading his sister's poems, Boris was astounded by the maturity and power achieved by a non-professional litterateur. Her main strength he perceived in her firm grasp on everyday life; in this lay the nobility and assurance of her style even if it lacked originality. 'And that, ' he told her, 'is why you are a real poet and person, and why I call your literary illusions *unnecessary*.'[69]

The freedom and sincerity available to Josephine as an amateur, contrasted with the non-freedom of the professional, increasingly preoccupied Pasternak. It explained, inter alia, his envy of Mandelstam, and his later novel as the story of a poet virtually unknown and unpublished in his lifetime. Josephine Pasternak's life as a wife and mother, and later as an exiled refugee, helped her to heed her brother's advice. Just before leaving Germany in 1938, she published a collection of her verse in Berlin under the title *Coordinates (Koordinaty)*. Her *nom de plume*, Anna Nei, coincided closely (although, she claimed, accidentally) with the heroine of Ehrenburg's novel *The Love of Jeanne Nei*. Later a facsimile reprint under her own name appeared in Munich in the 1970s.[70]

First signs of Pasternak's energetic, if sporadic, work on a new novel project are datable to late November of 1932. Pasternak had no clear timescale for its completion. Nor, as he told Lomonosova, had he any special public expecta-tions of the work and intended writing it just for his personal satisfaction.[71] The idea of a setting in the Urals was prompted by his recent visits there in 1931–32. Shortly after the 1934 Congress, Pasternak also called on Boris Zbarsky to check some facts and recollections from the time they spent there together during the War.[72] Some thematic strands evidently survived from the prose *Story*[73] and from the novel of which *Zhenya Luvers' Childhood* had formed part. That novel had been finally abandoned in spring of 1932, when Pasternak left the Volkhonka and burned the manuscript. Nikolai Vilyam recalled being shown a pile of papers forming 'my ill-fated novel' and Pasternak's explanation: 'The only pieces with life in them were the two opening chapters where Zhenya Luvers is still just a girl [. . .] How did the novel end? It ended with the years during which I actually wrote it – at the end of 1918, but basically in 1919.'[74]

The new novel which Pasternak now embarked upon was to contain impressions of his Moscow childhood and motifs from the early emotional biography of Zinaida his wife. (The extent to which this story affected him emerged in a letter of 1932 in which he compared her fate with that of his sister Josephine who at thirteen fell in love with Nikolai, the twenty-seven-year old nephew of the composer Scriabin; the story never followed the sordid pattern of Zinaida's affair, but there were some parallels, and it apparently left Josephine incapable of any wholehearted love thereafter.)[75]

On 4 March 1933 Pasternak wrote to Gorky telling him that for the last several years he had dreamed of a prose work which would fit 'like the lid of a box' on all his unfinished strands of plot and human fates of the last few years. The work was evidently highly diffuse and developing spontaneously, but no part could be published until the whole was complete, which would take at least a year.[76] In late 1934 there was still no end in sight. 'It is extending in breadth and in depth and getting more dense, and I cannot lay it down for a single day,' Pasternak told his parents, and continued:

I am now hastily turning myself into a prose writer of the Dickensian type, and later if I have the strength into a poet of a Pushkinian sort. Do not imagine that I think of comparing myself with them. I refer to them to give you an idea of the internal transformation.

I could put the same thing in a different way. I have become a particle of my time and state, and its interests have become my own.[77]

The Dickensian ideal was evidently explained at that time in conversation with Nikolai Vilyam. Pasternak had been rereading *A Tale of Two Cities*, and over supper talked at length on the subject of its plot set between cities in peace and revolution. 'If only one could write a novel like that, but set in our time! It's a splendid subject!' (Dickens' novel remained a seminal work for Pasternak's novelistic endeavours, and it later left a tangible trace on the plot and imagery of *Doctor Zhivago*.[78])

In January 1935, confidence in the novel project prompted Pasternak to take out a 1,000-rouble advance, and he stopped writing in order to read up on the history of the Civil War that formed the background to his narrative. The expanding plot began to have consequences for his poetry too. As he told Zinaida, 'the more it expands, the more it materialises in what has been written [. . .] this work brings me to the possibility of somehow in the future writing verse in a new way – not in the sense of an absolute *novelty* in this projected poetry, but of a future simplicity that would be unthinkable without disturbing the sequence of acquired habit.'[79] Meanwhile, however, the problems of writing prose in a new simple idiom led to much frustration. Indeed, compared with writing poetry, Pasternak found it 'such tough going that my attraction towards it is probably a pernicious delusion, and it produces nothing but stagnation, marching on the spot, and copying out one and the same thing fifty times over, and every time it reduces me to despair. Probably I am expecting something unreasonable from it and from myself, or maybe I don't really know what I want . . .'[80]

As a 'particle' of his time and state, Pasternak was drawn increasingly into public activities. In 1934 there was a new edition of *Second Birth*, a volume of *Selected Verse*, and a book edition of the prose *Story*, as well as numerous translations. In mid December 1934 and February 1935 there were also Writers' Union Board meetings. At the second of these, where problems of literary criticism were discussed, his (unrecorded) remarks on the subject of critical honesty were deemed too 'abstract' and Shcherbakov promptly pointed this out.[81] For the anniversary of Bely's death, Pasternak was detailed to arrange a memorial evening at the Writers' Union, which involved a round of phone calls to the Meyerholds, Vishnevsky, pianist Maria Yudina and others, in addition to making his own speech.[82] Shortly afterwards he was also persuaded by Shcherbakov to appear at the out-of-town settlement of Maleyevka where a two-month school for young writers was in progress. Here he talked again about poetry and Mayakovsky in terms recognisable from *Safe Conduct*; 'correct' official comment was provided by Surkov and other trusted Union figures.[83] At the end of January, Pasternak spoke at a poetry evening given by Dmitrii Petrovsky, to which Aseyev, Lugovskoi and Svyatopolk-Mirsky also contributed.[84]

In February 1935 there was a new Georgian visitation, including Euli, Grishashvili, Kaladze, Tabidze and Yashvili. Pasternak was involved in poetry evenings with them at the Mayakovsky Club on 9 February, and later in the Writers' Union. The Georgian visitors then moved on to Leningrad accompanied by various Moscow writers including Pasternak who took Zinaida with him. At the Leningrad Mayakovsky Club on the 12th, Chukovsky enthused over the Georgians' 'oriental' declamations, by contrast with which Pasternak seemed to recite in a 'throw-away' manner, as if to say 'I realise this is garbage and that my work is no good, but if you are such idiots, what can one do?'[85]

In Leningrad the company stayed in the Severnaya Hotel, which had been one of Zinaida's teenage trysting places with her cousin. She mentioned this to Nina Tabidze who later innocently alluded to it and touched off a bout of enraged jealousy on Pasternak's part. Zinaida was by now increasingly aware of his sensitivity in regard to her past. At about this time he destroyed Melitinsky's photograph which his daughter brought to her as a gift following his death,[86] and the story of Zinaida's youthful liaison became an obsession which, while providing literary material, began robbing Pasternak of sleep and eventually triggered a mental depression.

After returning from Leningrad, Pasternak attended morning and evening sessions at a Union plenary meeting, which involved further banquets and 'nocturnal libations'.[87] Tabidze and Yashvili stayed on in town at the Metropol Hotel. While there, Yashvili attended an international chess tournament with Lasker, Capablanca and other celebrities and took Evgenii Pasternak to some of the sessions where they collected autographs.[88]

Family correspondence of mid April reported meeting Gordon Craig at a matinée première in Meyerhold's theatre. Along with him the Pasternaks were afterwards invited to Meyerhold's together with composer Sergei Prokofiev and Dmitrii Svyatopolk-Mirsky. The latter struck Pasternak as 'the perfect figure of Nekhlyudov who has sprung out of Tolstoy's works with all the complexity and moral tension of his biography'.[89]

On 8 April, at a birthday party for Larisa Trenyova, Pasternak brushed aside her suggestion of a toast to Veresaev, and obstinately insisted on drinking the health of Bulgakov. Whatever his merits, Veresaev was a natural, legitimate phenomenon: 'There are laws to explain his existence,' Pasternak said, 'whereas Bulgakov has no laws adequate to explain him.'[90] The social and cultural incongruity of Mirsky and Bulgakov was symptomatic of the times.

The year end of 1934 had been marked by ominous events in public life. In the realm of literature two enlightened figures were eclipsed when Radek and Bukharin failed to be proposed for membership of the Writers' Union Board.[91] More sinister, however, was the assassination of Kirov in Leningrad on 1 December, which unleashed a new period of terror. A message of 'Grief and Anger' appeared the next day in *Izvestiya*, signed by Pasternak together with Ehrenburg, Leonov, Lidin and Novikov-Priboi. His signature also appeared under a collective letter in *Novy mir* proclaiming 'We shall carry his banner forward!'[92] Immediately following Kirov's murder, which had been secretly orchestrated from the Kremlin, mass arrests and executions of alleged terrorists were announced. On 16 December Kamenev and Zinovyev were indicted and arrested, and capital sentence of their entire supposed conspiratorial group was announced in mid January. Kamenev had been a Presidium member of the Writers' Union, and his closeness to Gorky impaired the latter's relations with Stalin, which took an irreversible downturn.[93] During a new orgy of arrests in December and January various 'proletarian' litterateurs were also interned, and a wave of apprehension and fear of denunciation gripped almost every public institution.

The terror naturally gagged all public, and most private, expression of the horror it aroused. Pasternak's mid-April letter to Spassky alluded vaguely to the fact that 'Leningrad circumstances, and recently Moscow ones also', had considerably affected him.[94] Some of his buoyancy of the previous year persisted however. In April he told Olga Freidenberg that despite everything he was still 'filled with faith in everything that is happening here. Many things strike one by their craziness and every now and then one gets a surprise. All the same, with our Russian resources still basically unchanged, people never took such a distant and worthy view of things and from such vital and live foundations.'[95]

In the spring of 1935 Pasternak began suffering from nervous exhaustion, sleeplessness and severe depression. His condition seemed unrelated to public events however, and resulted from a marital crisis due to his jealous fixation about Zinaida's teenage affair with Melitinsky. (This story had also blighted her first months of marriage to Neigauz during World War I and led to a showdown after Melitinsky arrived back from the Front.[96]) Zinaida was powerless to allay Boris' irrational anxieties. When he met Josephine in June, he expatiated frenziedly about his wife's biography,[97] and a semi-hysterical letter to Zinaida in July stated without evident pretext: 'My heart is filled with anguish and I weep at night in my dreams because some magic force is taking you away from me [. . .] I don't know why this has happened and I am prepared for something utterly dreadful. When you betray me I shall die . . .' In conversation later on he also paranoically recalled the 'semi-debauched set-up in hotels' which always reminded him of the cause of his misery.[98]

Pasternak's depression was aggravated by professional problems: the evolutionary dilemmas of a poet attempting to become a prose-writer; the irritating distraction of official duties; and the false impression of productivity caused by mere reprints of old work (*Poems in One Volume* were reissued by GIKhL in 1935 and 1936) and by a flow of translated contributions to volumes such as *Verse and Songs of Oriental Peoples about Stalin, Young Georgia,* a *Collection of Young Writers' Works from Soviet Socialist Georgia,* and so forth.[99]

Finally, in late April, in an attempt to compose himself and recover, Pasternak went with Zinaida to the Writers' country sanatorium at Uzkoye to the south-east of Moscow. Doctors there identified an 'acute and neglected neurasthenia' and talked of hospitalising him.[100] From Uzkoye, he still carried out a few professional engagements: reciting at the Writers' Union on 10 May together with Antokolsky, Gorodetsky, Shervinsky and others, when he read translations from the Armenian poet Akopyan (produced, like his Georgian versions, from glosses), and speaking on 15 May at a Presidium meeting where he expressed surprise that he was at all in vogue at a time when he was utterly unproductive and felt more like 'a corpse that had been well and truly buried'.[101]

It soon became clear that Zinaida's company was not assisting Pasternak's recovery. After a short stay in town he therefore went alone to the sanatorium at Bolshevo, north-east of Moscow, while Zinaida took the boys and Tusya Blumenfeld and her niece to a dacha in Zagoryanka, 3–4 kilometers away.[102] In June came a letter from Tabidze inviting Pasternak to come alone to Tbilisi and recuperate, but he was in no condition for such a journey. Further medical examination showed an enlargening of the heart, and Pasternak was advised to alter his life style. 'They've told me to stop smoking', he told Raisa Lomonosova, 'to develop a slow (senatorial) gait and not lift any weights.'[103] None of this came easily; but for several months Pasternak did limit himself to no more than six *papirosy* a day.

Despite his obsession with Zinaida's prehistory, it was the artistic frustration that increasingly preyed on his mind. He later told Valentin Asmus that

I wanted to do something for the glory of the entourage that so indulged me, something that was realisable [. . .] The problem was insoluble. It was like squaring the circle, I struck up against the insolubility of an intention that cloaked all horizons and barred all avenues. I was going mad and perishing. It is surprising I recovered . . .[104]

In late June Pasternak's convalescence at Bolshevo was interrupted. The Paris Congress of Writers in Defence of Culture was convoked on the initiative of several liberal and left-wing European authors to express concern at the threat posed by Nazi Germany. Leading initiators were the French writers Barbusse, Gide and Malraux, with organisational back-up from Jean-Richard Bloch, Guilloux, René Blech and Moussinac, and others including the *Izvestiya* correspondent in Paris, Ilya Ehrenburg.[105]

The 230 delegates from thirty-five different countries who gathered from 21 to 25 June in the Palais de la Mutualité included many international celebrities. The main figures from France were Aragon, Barbusse, Bloch, Cocteau, Malraux; German émigrés included Brecht, Leon Feuchtwanger, Heinrich Mann, Anna Seghers, Ernst Toller; from England came W. H. Auden, E. M. Forster, Aldous Huxley; from the USA, Sherwood Anderson, Waldo Frank, Sinclair Lewis. Gorky was nominated to lead the Soviet delegation but backed down on health grounds, although possibly the authorities forbade his visit, fearing a revival of his platform at the 1934 Congress.[106] The Kremlin viewed the Paris event as a Soviet propaganda exercise and sent Shcherbakov to supervise the delegation. As nominal leader replacing Gorky, Mikhail Koltsov was appointed, and the twenty-strong Soviet party included Vsevolod Ivanov, Karavaeva, Kirshon, Yakub Kolas, Mikitenko, Panfyorov, Tikhonov and Aleksei Tolstoy.

The Soviet delegation's arrival in Paris without both Gorky and Pasternak caused dismay. Malraux immediately suggested inviting Pasternak and was supported in this by Ehrenburg; Gustav Regler proposed adding Babel's name. Koltsov took up the matter with the Soviet Embassy in the hope of securing the two writers' arrival before the end of the conference.[107]

Once approved, Malraux's polite request became a peremptory order. Pasternak was visited at Bolshevo by Union representatives who refused to accept ill-health as grounds for refusal. He was forced to travel into Moscow, and in Zinaida's presence called up Stalin's secretary protesting his illness. Poskryobyshev's reply was 'If there was a war and you were called to serve, would you go?' Pasternak said yes, and was told: 'Regard yourself as having been called to serve.' Zinaida too encouraged her husband, believing the change of scene and his inevitable personal success would assist recovery. Next day another official arrived by car to take Pasternak into town and fit him out, and a hat, two shirts and an ill-fitting off-the-peg suit were acquired.[108]

As a concession to Pasternak's condition he was allowed to travel by train rather than fly. Together with Babel he set off on 21 June. Babel later reported that during the journey he was driven almost crazy by Pasternak's complaints about his sickness, and the futility of peace congresses as a means of saving culture.[109] There was a respite however. A few hours' stopover in Berlin was scheduled, and a telegram had been sent to Munich where Pasternak's parents were staying with Josephine's family. Age and ill-health prevented Leonid and his wife from travelling at short notice, but Josephine and her husband took the overnight train to Berlin and opened up her parents' apartment in Motzstraße. There Pasternak and Babel arrived by taxi around midday on 23 June. Babel stayed only briefly then went off leaving Boris with his relatives.[110]

For Josephine and Frederick their reunion was overclouded by Boris' obvious state of depression: he frequently burst into tears and wanted only to sleep. Two or three hours on the couch with curtains drawn brought some relief, although the Soviet Embassy confirmed there was no question of an overnight stay. There was just time for a restaurant meal and a few hours' conversation. Family news was exchanged, and Boris talked in bursts about his illness and plans for a new novel based on the teenage humiliations of Zinaida – a 'veiled beauty in the private rooms of night restaurants [. . .] so young, so unspeakably attractive'. Josephine was surprised at Boris' interest in such mawkish subject matter, and as they talked in a hotel lounge, she had a sense of some profound artistic and psychological transformation taking place in her brother. During their conversation Frederick passed on to him an earnest request from his parents that he should do and say nothing in Paris that might jeopardise their security in the Third Reich. Before leaving, Boris also talked on the phone with his parents in Munich and promised to stop off and see

105

them on the return journey. In the early evening Josephine and her husband waved Pasternak and Babel off on the train from Friedrichstraße.[111]

Pasternak appeared at the Congress in the evening of Monday, 24 June, entering the hall during Tikhonov's address. According to Ehrenburg, the Leningrad poet talked of 'the loftiness of Soviet poetry', and as he went on to speak of Pasternak's poetry, the hall gave a standing ovation to 'a poet who by his whole life had proved that supreme artistry and elevated conscience are not in conflict'.[112] In his dispatches from the Congress, there was evidence that Ehrenburg endeavoured to stress the impact of Babel and Pasternak on this sophisticated literary audience. Pasternak was honourably mentioned in speeches by both Ehrenburg and Panfyorov, and when his turn came to speak he was introduced by Malraux as 'one of the greatest poets of our time'.[113]

Whatever the Soviet delegation's contribution to the success of the conference, their orations on 'Socialist Realism' or 'The Poetry of Struggle and Victory' suggest a tonality in which both Babel and Pasternak's speeches were quite out of key. Babel gave a brilliant impromptu address in flawless French which was either unrecorded or deemed unsuitable for the Soviet edition of the Congress proceedings published in 1936. Pasternak's speech was memorable in a different way. His whole demeanour was in keeping with his parents' request and Gustav Regler recalled his 'strange, far-away look' and said that he talked with 'the shyness of a released prisoner'.[114] In the train Pasternak had drafted a speech in French which like his travel conversation dwelt on the subject of his illness and the futility of conferences and organisations. After reading it, Ehrenburg found both its content and antiquated idiom unsuitable. He and Babel thereupon sat down with Pasternak in a café and helped him draft a few words about the stuff and essence of poetry which coincided with his own genuine private agenda, and they also quickly translated one of his poems.[115]

Pasternak's short speech in French emerged as marginal to the theme of the Congress, and illustrated the nature of a free culture rather than campaigning for it. He later claimed to have enunciated ideas based on the original draft of his speech: 'Don't organise yourselves! Organisation is the death of art. Only personal independence is important. In 1789, 1848 and 1917 writers were not organised in defence of anything, nor against anything. I beg you: Don't organise yourselves!' The published text (above p. 85) was a reconstruction from memory by Tikhonov and Tsvetaeva of only part of this speech. Pasternak was irritated when he saw the printed version, which he claimed was pruned of all serious thoughts and made him look infantile.[116] His speech from the podium was followed by a recitation and by Malraux's reading of a translation of 'Thus they begin. . .' The audience responded with a long and rapturous ovation.[117]

One result of the Congress was the creation of a 112-strong Bureau to further and reinforce the achievements of the Paris meeting. Pasternak was one of the twelve Soviet authors elected, although he never functioned in this capacity, and the only Soviet activists were the two members of the Secretariat, Koltsov and Ehrenburg, who later attended a meeting in London in July of 1936. (The Second Congress was held in July 1937, with Ehrenburg, Koltsov, Mikitenko, Aleksei Tolstoy and others attending from the USSR; Pasternak was not delegated or re-elected to the Bureau; by that time he had ceased all part in literary administration.)

During his ten days in Paris Pasternak spent little time with other members of the Soviet delegation. He was not at the ceremonial opening of Boulevard Maxime Gorki in the suburb of Villejuif on 30 June; he was absent from a Soviet literary evening held shortly after the Congress closed; and on a trip to Versailles he saw two or three rooms of the Palais then opted out, feeling unwell. His unsociability was evidently noted. He ascribed it to his mental condition and later regretted having turned down an invitation from Klaus Mann, Regler and Weinert to dine with Heinrich Mann, and Malraux's offer to introduce him to Paul Valéry.[118]

While avoiding formal events, Pasternak ventured out from the Madison Hotel on the Boulevard St Germain for meetings with émigré friends. Artist Yurii Annenkov drove him and Zamyatin around Paris in his car and at Pasternak's request took him to the Faubourg St Denis to see the tombs of the French kings, and the house on rue Campagne Première where Rilke had lived. Annenkov also pointed out the Hotel Istria where Mayakovsky always stayed. At the Café Rotonde they discovered Ilya Ehrenburg, a regular denizen, and the three of them spent most of the evening discussing art and artists.[119] Letters to Zinaida also detailed Pasternak's meetings with artists Mikhail Larionov and Natalya Goncharova with whom he and Bobrov had been friends in the 1910s, with Ida Vysotskaya, the author Ovadii Savich and his wife, and his father's diplomat friend Vladimir Potyomkin. With the latter he evidently discussed the possibility of a further few weeks' recuperative stay in Paris, but the idea was not pursued.[120]

Especially crucial was Pasternak's renewed encounter in Paris with Tsvetaeva after three years of non-communication. She attended the Congress, and Pasternak presented her to members of the Soviet delegation among whom Tikhonov in particular charmed her.[121] The reunion with Pasternak was another of her lifelong series of 'non-meetings'.[122] Although the emotional tension of their earlier involvement had evaporated, she had written on him in the early 1930s and retained a moral claim on his attention, if only as an artist; and she was disappointed. His dithyrambs about Zinaida and preoccupation with restocking her wardrobe at Paris clothing stores irritated her, and before he and his companions left, she herself departed on 28 June for La Favière in the southern département of Var. Amid her exasperation she sensed his own tormented state but failed to comprehend. As she told Tikhonov: 'I wept because as I watched, Boris, the best lyric poet of our time, betrayed Lyricism by referring to his whole self and everything in him as a malady. Maybe a "sublime" one, but he didn't even say that . . .'[123] Later in the summer Tsvetaeva also wrote Pasternak; his reply in October was in a low key and conveyed that their intense association was now part of history. As Ariadna Efron commented, her mother 'recognised only *expression*, and did not understand *depressions*', regarding them as a piece of self-indulgence. Her romantic image of the male required heroism, with no place for fear or suffering.[124]

Tsvetaeva was probably also vexed by Pasternak's failure (unlike Tikhonov) to encourage her thoughts of returning to Russia. When asked his view, he 'had no definite opinion on this account, and didn't know what to advise her'. Whatever hints he made were not picked up. She quite missed the irony of his assurance that she would 'get to love the collective farms'. But she was isolated and unappreciated on the émigré literary scene, and was being pressured to return by her husband who asked Pasternak not to discourage this idea. (Strangely, Pasternak was thus ideologically gagged on both sides – by his family's request and by Sergei Efron.) In 1932 Efron had joined the Union of Friends of the Soviet Motherland, an NKVD front organisation to facilitate repatriation of émigrés, and he was shortly to become involved in further clandestine activities.[125] Tsvetaeva probably suspected little of this, and Pasternak knew nothing. After she left, her daughter Ariadna and husband called on him at his hotel and he had further chance to get to know them. For Sergei Efron – a 'charming, sensitive and steadfast man' – he acquired a considerable affection. Ariadna later recalled only the Parisian heat, the writer Lakhuti roaming hotel corridors semi-clothed, and Pasternak amid a setting of stores, bookshops and oranges.[126]

Pasternak did not see his parents on the return journey. After the Congress, the Soviet delegation returned by sea via London and Leningrad rather than cross Germany and risk some Nazi provocation. In subsequent rueful family correspondence, he claimed that he was mentally unfit to return to Moscow independently and that a foolish pride prevented his appearing before them in such a dejected state.[127] In October, Tsvetaeva chided him for his thoughtlessness, but as he assured her daughter Ariadna, 'I firmly believed there would be another chance in more suitable conditions [. . .] There has been a lot of this kind of thing in my life, but I swear it is not from lack of concern or love!'[128]

Although some Soviet delegates stayed on in Paris, Pasternak joined the group that left for England in the early morning of 4 July. The previous day he sent a telegram to the Lomonosovs, who were able to trace him in London via the Soviet Embassy on the 5th. Over the next couple of days they showed him the sights of London and also had a psychologist friend Dr Rickman examine him. Rickman's verdict, conveyed in Lomonosova's next letter, was that Pasternak would definitely recover: 'You are a strong-willed person, but you should try and become just a little thicker-skinned. Doctors and medicine can help very little in this.'[129] Pasternak in turn vowed to assert himself more strongly 'in a new apartment that I shall obtain no matter how', in work 'more independent than the efforts in which the whole of last winter was spent', and 'with a form of social behaviour that diverges more sharply from my recent compromises with our present-day uniformity'.[130]

While at sea between Tilbury and Leningrad, on board the *Jan Rudzutak*, Pasternak's cabin partner was their Party supervisor. Shcherbakov was a rotund bureaucrat with glasses and swept-back hair, who cultivated an image of grave authority. His position as Union Secretary was reinforced in May of 1935 when he took charge of the entire Central Commitee Cultural Section; prior to that he was propaganda chief in the Gorky Region; after further transfer in 1936 he subsequently became Central Committee Secretary and political manager of the Red Army and Sovinformburo.[131] Affected by the rough crossing and his disturbed psyche, Pasternak apparently talked at Shcherbakov relentlessly until the latter pleaded with him to allow them both to sleep. In the morning Pasternak panicked and tried to recall whether his nocturnal rantings had compromised him or others. But at breakfast Shcherbakov's vacant gaze was reassuring: 'No, he had understood nothing at all! Simply nothing! What good fortune!'[132]

In Leningrad Pasternak was met off the ship by his friend Chernyak, who was working in the local archives that summer. Chernyak was alarmed at his condition and spoke with Shcherbakov who was sympathetic and promised to help.[133] Probably Shcherbakov indeed assisted Pasternak beyond the bounds of duty, which required him to provide a detailed report on each delegation member's behaviour. Shcherbakov doubtless thought him genuinely unhinged, and Pasternak subsequently owed a lot to this diagnosis which reinforced his credentials as a *yurodivy* and enhanced his protective aura.[134]

After disembarking the delegation returned directly to Moscow by train.

Still in disarray, Pasternak called up the Freidenbergs, and his aunt and cousin ushered him back to their apartment where he planned to rest for a week or so before returning home. Meanwhile, Zinaida met the returning party in Moscow, heard of Boris' condition and on Shcherbakov's advice set off immediately for Leningrad. She also secured a letter from Shcherbakov to the Leningrad Customs requesting release of Pasternak's impounded luggage: apart from children's toys, his sole purchases abroad were gifts for Zinaida – a manicure set, shoes and knitted dresses – and the Customs had been suspicious of all this female tackle![135]

Zinaida's appearance sabotaged the Freidenbergs' plans for Boris' recuperation, and they were miffed when he departed with her. Although Zinaida claimed he immediately began sleeping well once she appeared, his behaviour seems to have continued erratic – Akhmatova later claimed that he three times proposed to her while in Leningrad, having just arrived fresh from an 'affair' with Tsvetaeva in Paris![136]

Pasternak and his wife stayed a week in the Evropeiskaya Hotel before going back to Moscow. On 16 July with the help of Shcherbakov's letter, all his impounded luggage and gifts were released without duty. That same night they took the train and arrived in Moscow next morning. Zinaida took her husband directly out to Bolshevo where he remained and rested till the end of August.[137]

While staying in Leningrad Pasternak missed an invitation to meet Romain Rolland at Gorky's dacha, and on 29 July he failed to attend another meeting with members of the newly founded Poets' Section of the Writers' Union. When the section was set up in spring, he had argued with Gorky against the sense of 'organising' creativity, he had no contribution to make, and his statement at the Congress had reinforced that position.[138] Meanwhile, nothing disturbed the peace of Bolshevo. Zinaida returned to town and Pasternak's letter to her gave account of various meetings and conversations, including with Surkov and the English physicist Paul Dirac, a friend of Pyotr Kapitsa who in 1934 had returned from his exile in Cambridge.[139]

In late summer of 1935 Pasternak showed signs of recovery. Although sleeping fitfully, he had started work again, and 'the internal hell that I inhabited for four months has ended', he reported to Zinaida. 'I don't know how firm and final this is, but if all goes well, I shall be the same regular happy man I have always been'.[140] By late October his parents heard that he was 'better in every way' and would be 'really fine if only the process of writing were not so closely bound up with smoking'. Nevertheless his daily ration of half a dozen cigarettes did not impair productivity.[141]

Apart from work on his novel, Pasternak also produced verse translations for inclusion in Babel's edition of André Gide's 'Fresh Nourishment' ('La Nourriture Nouvelle'), and some original verse also began·to flow in response to heartening news and circumstances.[142] In October he heard of the appearance in Prague of a volume of his verse in Czech translation by the poet Josef Hora.[143] Offprints of the edition delighted him, and he sent an exultant letter to Hora in mid November. 'After many many years you have caused me, as I did twenty years ago, to experience for the first time the exciting marvel of poetic incarnation, and however you achieved this (even by sorcery) the scale of my astonished gratitude must be apparent to you.'[144]

December of 1935 also saw publication of a Czech translation of *Safe Conduct* by Svatava Pírková-Jakobson together with an afterword by her husband Roman Jakobson.[145] In 1935 Jakobson's 'Marginal Notes on the Prose of the Poet Pasternak' drew some of their ideas (without acknowledgement) from Pasternak's own early article 'The Wasserman Test' (1914); this was later recognised as a seminal work in Pasternak studies and central to Jakobson's own literary-critical opus.[146] The poem of autumn 1935 in which Pasternak celebrated his Czech début had overtones that were amplified by the context and moment of its publication in 1936 (below, p. 125).

Pasternak's encomium at the Soviet Writers' Congress was echoed throughout 1935 in the domestic literary press. In April Oblomievsky's article gave an intelligent evaluation of his whole oeuvre.[147] In August the young critic Yaropolk Semyonov printed an appreciative article in *Literaturnaya gazeta*,[148] and in the October issue of *Zvezda* Tarasenkov changed his earlier tone, pointing out that 'subjectivity' was not to be confused with 'idealism' (in the negative Marxist-philosophical sense), nor did intimate sensitivity exclude the objective world: 'Why so crudely and so vulgarly identify philosophy with the artist's creative devices?'[149] In the twelfth issue of *Znamya*, Svyatopolk-Mirsky maintained that Pasternak's recent endorsement by the Writers' Congress was not a vindication of 'pure' lyricism without social content, but of the poet's 'faith in his own talent' and existence as a 'law unto himself'.[150] At an evening in his own honour in November at the *Znamya* editorial offices, Ehrenburg reminded his audience that Pasternak was recipient of one of only three standing ovations at the recent conclave in Paris.[151]

Pasternak's translated revelation of Georgian verse was also widely discussed and approved in the literary press of 1935–36. Tabidze wrote an ecstatic review which Goltsev for some reason failed to publish. Tarasenkov linked the translations with recent developments in Pasternak's original verse, while Mirsky remarked on the particular splendour of his Leonidze and Tabidze renderings, his lesser sympathy with the bold noise level of Yashvili, and minimum compatibility with Vazha Pshavela.[152]

Mirsky's view was closely echoed by one of Pasternak's translatees, Valerian Gaprindashvili, who at the First All-Union Conference of Translators in January 1936 explained:

Pasternak does not paint a copy but a portrait of the original. You look at your portrait twin and are surprised at your own features. Of course, the clothing of a foreign tongue and the music of another man's verse have transformed you, but you are grateful to the magician who has introduced you in different guise into the populous and triumphant world of Russian poetry.[153]

A slightly different tack was pursued by Kornelii Zelinsky, editor of the volume of *Georgian Lyricists*. He viewed the splendour of the Georgian versions as a function of the translator's own poetic artistry, thus, as it were, fending off any objections on grounds of fidelity to the originals.[154]

On 25 December 1935 Pasternak read his translations at a Chikovani evening at Writers' House. Shortly afterwards, on 3–7 January, Pasternak attended the All-Union Conference of Translators at the Writers' Union together with other leading authors and translators such as Antokolsky, Lozinsky, and Zenkevich. His address to the conference described the blossoming of literary translation as a major cultural phenomenon – 'an exchange of experience [. . .] the living breath of our republics'. He discussed metrical aspects of Georgian, the general principle of working from interlinear glosses, and the Georgian translations done by himself and Tikhonov. However, he left a clear impression that he considered his main task in this area as complete, and it was for others to continue. Successors had indeed already appeared in the persons of Antokolsky, Livshitz, Spassky, Zabolotsky and others. Anticipating the bold approach of his later translations from English and German, he told the conference that

when poetry is [. . .] an artistic form rooted in the form of existence, in cases where it is impossible to render into your own native language that other language, reality and way of life, then I believe that a metronomic rendering, observing all the steps and falterings of the original is quite absurd [. . .] I believe it is sufficient to seize the spirit of this free form and convey it, observing the law of one's own language.[155]

While Pasternak castigated himself in letters to his parents for their failure to meet in summer of 1935, they also discussed the possibility of Leonid's 'exploratory' visit to Moscow, provided there was a guarantee regarding the return journey.[156] Zbarsky and the prominent art expert Abram Efros had sent Leonid an invitation to visit Moscow. The gesture was well meant but, as Boris realised, Zbarsky was by now very 'Sovietised': since 1924 he was an official representative to the League of Nations, regularly shuttling between Moscow and Western Europe, and his son born in 1930 was named Feliks in honour of Dzerzhinsky![157] Zbarsky evidently encouraged Leonid Pasternak to see a mirage of glowing professional prospects should he resettle in Moscow, although the plight of some returnee artists about whom Leonid inquired in a letter of 6 December 1935 was hardly encouraging. Although Bilibin was accepted and employed, Natan Altman lived in dire poverty and Shukhaev was later arrested and liberated only in the 1950s.

There was nevertheless a mounting urgency for the Pasternak parents to leave Germany before Soviet subjects were deported forcibly or interned. Josephine was safe while married to an Austrian citizen, and Lydia's fate became secure in 1935 when she married the English psychologist Eliot Slater who worked at the same laboratory in Munich; on 22 November the couple left for London, where they settled in Kensington. 'What a miracle sent down to us from heaven, by fate, from the Lord God – and just when everything looked so hopeless', Leonid rejoiced.[158]

Leonid and Rozaliya contemplated a family visit to England, and even Boris considered attempting to visit France or England and see his parents.[159] For reasons quite different from Zbarsky's, though, he was convinced that his parents should eventually return and live with him in Moscow.[160] Leonid Pasternak made enquiries about shipping his belongings and pictures back to Russia, and he found a sympathetic helper in the Soviet ambassador, Yakov Suritz. There was also talk of a 75th birthday exhibition in Moscow, publication of a monograph, and provision of accommodation in Moscow through the offices of Leonid's former pupil Yuvenal Slavinsky who was head of the 'Vsekhudozhnik'(All-Artists) organisation before his arrest and execution in the later 1930s.[161]

In autumn of 1935 Pasternak was aware of continuing attempts to manipulate him through 'imposed privilege' – 'as though they were deliberately inflating me [. . .] for some unknown purpose, and all this is done by alien hands without my agreement'.[162] Relief was at hand, however. Pasternak's autobiographical essay of the mid 1950s recalled two catchphrases of the time originating from Stalin. Firstly, that 'Life is now better, Life is more merry' (an utterance printed on 22 November, 1935). Secondly, that 'Mayakovsky was and remains the best and most talented poet of our epoch'. This *ex cathedra* pronouncement published in *Pravda* on 5 December ended the dispute that started at the 1934 Congress regarding Mayakovsky's posthumous status. As Pasternak realised, Stalin's definition implicitly halted the inflation of his own importance and the attempts to manipulate him. He was sufficiently relieved to write Stalin a personal letter of thanks for the fact that he could now 'live and work as before, in modest silence with its surprises and mysteries, without which I could not love life'.[163]

No reply came to that letter, but events of the time confirmed the impression of a continuing dialogue with Stalin.

On 24 October Akhmatova's husband Nikolai Punin had been arrested, and she hurried to Moscow to solicit help for him and also for her son who was interned earlier. In Moscow she stayed with the Pasternaks.[164] There are various not altogether congruent accounts of what ensued. A visit to Seifullina and her husband, the literary critic Pravdukhin, established via the latter's Central Committee contacts that a personal petition to Stalin was needed. Pilnyak evidently took Akhmatova by car to deliver this and joined her and the Pasternaks for dinner at their Volkhonka apartment. Lengthy discussions concluded that Pasternak's further supportive letter would have greater effect than Pilnyak's, and the next day at about 4 pm Pasternak deposited his letter in the Kremlin postbox. The following morning on 3 November, a phone call from Leningrad announced that Punin and Lev Gumilyov had been released and were home already; this was followed by a confirmatory call to the Pasternaks from Poskryobyshev. There was general rejoicing. Akhmatova, who was prostrate with exhaustion, was roused; on hearing the news, she uttered the one word 'Good!' then fell fast asleep again.[165]

The release of Akhmatova's family occurred in conjunction with tangible auguries of a better life in the course of 1935: food rationing in force since the late 1920s ended; restrictions on non-proletarian members of the population were lifted; traditional army ranks were restored; New Year celebrations, once banned as a bourgeois throwback, were reinstituted; moreover, there was eager anticipation of a new Constitution whose drafting committee was led by Bukharin.[166]

In a spirit of confidence and uplift, and on commission from Bukharin, Pasternak at the year end wrote two new poems marking the return of a lyricism which, in the words of one critic, had shed the intimacy and 'earthbound quality' of *Second Birth*.[167] For all his liberalism Bukharin was not averse to token displays of incense-burning before Stalin.[168] He also welcomed Pasternak's help in shoring up his own crumbling authority; Pasternak was well aware of this and happy to oblige. Bukharin's commission was for an artefact that maybe only Pasternak could supply – a humanised lyrical portrayal of Stalin that avoided the false bombast of earlier verse dedicated to the leader. Reviewing some of these verses later on, Pasternak recalled Bukharin's delight and described them as 'a sincere attempt, one of the strongest (and the last of that period), to live by the thoughts of the time and in tune with it'.[169]

The NKVD (National Commissariat of Internal Affairs, the post-1934 title of OGPU) began gathering evidence against Bukharin in 1935. In late February of 1936 he went on a foreign tour and spent two months in France, Berlin, Prague and Copenhagen helping gather up the decimated German Social Democrat archives. His conversations in Paris with such as Malraux revealed an awareness that his days of freedom were numbered.[170] *En route* through Berlin he dined with Suritz the ambassador and met Pasternak's parents. Hearing of this, Pasternak wrote to them that Bukharin, 'if he wanted and was able, should have explained to you many things that are beyond description because of their immensity. He is a remarkable, historically extra-ordinary man with . . . a fate that has turned out unjustly. I am very fond of him. Recently he has been attacked by people who cannot hold a candle to him . . . But all this cannot be explained.'[171]

Pasternak's two new poems were published in the New Year edition of *Izvestiya* and reopened his dialogue with Stalin. Possibly, as Bukharin's wife suggested, they also helped offset Stalin's jealousy after the dedication of 'Waves' to Bukharin. Together with verse by Tabidze the verses formed the poetic ingredient of a festive issue with statements by various prominent citizens reflecting on bright prospects and hopes for the year 1936.[172]

The opening lines of the first poem showered thank-yous on three millenia of history, prophets and leaders, and on endless New Year rejoicings. But there was self-irony in a recollection that during days of slaughter and cannibalism 'our double' (the poet) perpetually emitted his 'nightingale throb'; in the future too he senses that things 'great within small' will forever echo inside him

> With laughs from the banking,
> And thoughts at the plough,
> And Lenin and Stalin,
> And these verses now.[173]

The poem was reprinted once only in the April issue of *Znamya*, a journal whose literary company Pasternak found congenial.[174] More complex, con-troversial and artistically interesting was the second poem, 'The temper obstinate appeals . . .' ('Mne po dushe stroptivyi norov . . .') Its first six quatrains contained a self-portrait that reinforced the message of Pasternak's December letter to Stalin. Pasternak approves the 'temper obstinate' of the artist at the height of his powers who renounces phraseology, is shy of his own books, eschews the public gaze, yet is unable to escape a fate that exposes him to history and life in all their fullness:

Like a Gulf Stream settlement,
He's made up all of earthly warmth.
All that past the tidebreak flows
Is swilled by time into his gulf.   (III, 3; *SP*, 381; *SS*, II, 7)

The next stanzas include a portrait of Stalin identified as the 'Kremlin recluse' – 'not a man but deed incarnate' – 'Action on a global scale'. Yet despite his superhuman stature, the leader 'has remained a human'. Contrasted with this figure is the poet, utterly 'consumed by this genius of action', existing merely as a pale echo in the 'two-voiced fugue', although still believing in his own and Stalin's knowledge of one another.[175] Events of the last two years seemed to confirm this mutual awareness. However, the 'humanity' of the leader was established only at the poet's reassuring insistance and probably at Bukharin's behest; in reality the life of the Kremlin elite had long been hidden from public gaze. The portrait was in keeping, though, with the new 'human face' of socialism and nascent iconography reinforcing the cult of Stalin. Both poems were also models of a serious if wayward engagement with the theme of Stalin which avoided the clichéd panegyrics by Aleksandr Prokofiev and Zharov, as well as recent Central Asian and Caucasian bardic hymnology.[176]

Despite his personal setbacks and the obviously vicious nature of the order, Pasternak like many others continued to dissociate these from Stalin himself. To more sceptical readers the *Izvestiya* verses doubtless seemed a sign of political naïveté. Less than three weeks after they appeared, Akhmatova addressed a poem to Pasternak that talked of his endowment with 'eternal childhood' – a concealed polemical hint that escaped most subsequent readers and may even have been lost on Pasternak himself.[177]

After the second poem's reprint in the April issue of *Znamya*, its first six stanzas were salvaged and republished by Pasternak in his wartime collection *On Early Trains (Na rannikh poezdakh)*. The Stalin section was omitted however. As Evgenii Pasternak has commented, 'Bukharin made Pasternak believe in Stalin, for a time'. These verses were a tribute to a mood of consensus which was soon to pass.

Despite Stalin's penchant for literary interference, there is no evidence that Pasternak's verse ever gave him any pleasure. While observing the political mien of leading writers, scholars and cultural figures, Stalin had no use for poetry beyond its political application. Intellectual floundering in the arts he regarded as a counter-revolutionary heresy only marginally less dangerous than Trotskyism.[178] Pasternak's verses acquired some resonance in the literary community however. The very possibility of addressing the theme of Stalin in non-hagiographic mode possibly impressed Bulgakov sufficiently for him to project a play on that theme.[179]

The brighter prospects glimpsed at the New Year of 1936 were soon obscured by a new cultural oppression. With an editorial article 'Muddle instead of Music. On the Opera "Lady Macbeth of Mtsensk"' *Pravda* in late January fired the first salvo in a vicious new campaign against alleged 'formalism' in the arts. The first victim was composer Shostakovich, and the half-baked opinions in the article suggest Stalin himself had a hand in its composition following a night at the opera with other political leaders.[180] Shortly afterwards, another article attacked Shostakovich's ballet music for *The Limpid Stream (Svetlyi ruchei)*. The composer was only a convenient initial target however. The first *Pravda* article cast aspersions in various directions – theatrical 'Meyerhol-dianism' and 'trans-sense' (*zaum'*) modernist literary experimentation, with citation of offenders such as Bulgakov, Marietta Shaginyan, and artist Vladimir Lebedev. The campaign began in official papers such as *Pravda*, *Komsomol's-kaya pravda*, and *Literaturnaya gazeta*, although other publications also rallied to the call after a *Pravda* lashing on 13 February. The witch-hunt then moved under its own momentum.[181]

Borrowed initially from the critical school of the 1910–20s, the term 'formalist' had been used for abusive purpose by RAPP, and became an universal term denoting an alleged preoccupation with formal externals at the expense of 'realist' social 'content'. The appellation acquired a new lease of life after official endorsement of socialist realism and was applied to any works that were not 'simple', 'natural', and 'human', i.e. which failed to cater for the lowest common denominator of popular taste. Intellectual sophistication or originality of expression were now viewed as an artistic, ideological, and thus *political* heresy. In this way the blunt instruments of political debate were adopted to anathematise everything that was not 'popular' in every sense of the word.

Still riding the wave of official favour, Pasternak was not indicted. He was a potential offender, however, especially in view of his link with Bukharin and the terms in which Bukharin had promoted him at the 1934 Congress, preferring his complex introvert early lyrics to the 'openness' of *Second Birth*. In the opening phase of the campaign, *Pravda* on 10 February carried an editorial 'Concerning a Certain Rotten Concept' directed against Bukharin's alleged condescending and offensive notion of the term *narod* (the people), and his inability to say things nice and simply. Symptomatically, compared with the virulence of *Pravda* and *Komsomol'skaya pravda* articles, Bukharin's *Izvestiya* was cautious in tone, refraining from personal indictments, and all articles carried attributions unlike the anonymous vituperation in *Pravda*.[182]

As Pasternak commented in spring of 1936, although he was not personally abused, 'it was sufficient that friends of mine were (and still are) treated like

117

this for me to be disturbed and [. . .] angered. Everyone is confused, nobody understands anything, and everyone is afraid of something [. . .] For the last five years we – all the Bulgakovs and Fedins and Shostakoviches – have been mindlessly naive. No one will give us back these years, and there is not a lot of time left. But what can one do?'[183]

While the anti-formalist campaign was in spate, during the week beginning 10 February, the Board of the Writers' Union held a plenary session in Minsk. Pasternak took Zinaida with him, and the wives of Selvinsky and Tabidze also attended. In Minsk they enjoyed a reunion with the Georgian contingent, which included Chikovani, Leonidze, Tabidze and Yashvili, spending all their time together, looking at the town, reciting poetry and staying up late. Pasternak was also delighted at a seeming restoration of goodwill with Aseyev. The official programme was accompanied by banquetting and ceremonial pomp, none of which was to his taste, and he said so in his speech and also at a later meeting in Moscow in March.[184]

In a letter to Gorky, Surkov stated his intention to use the Minsk conference to inveigh in general against the Bukharin literary platform, exemplified by Pasternak. While pursuing that aim however, he was partly upstaged by more recent issues. The main themes of the meeting were discussion of the state of Byelorussian and Bashkirian literature, and problems of poetry. But the ideological ground-swell was provided by the ongoing anti-formalist campaign, and by the recent canonisation of Mayakovsky. Surkov's keynote speech on 13 February centred around these issues, which had all been discussed in committee with the Poets' Section, the Union Presidium, and with Gorky.[185]

À propos of Pasternak, Surkov noted his still timid attempts to engage with revolutionary reality. He claimed his popularity was based on false premises and abetted by Mirsky in particular, but refrained from making any broadside attack.[186] Other criticism Pasternak encountered included Altauzen's attack on his 'little idealistic world' defended with courage worthy of a better cause, and on the 'literary gourmets' who savoured this; Bezymensky condescendingly reproached Pasternak for his inadequate response to the age, inability to become a modern classic, and failure to travel around giving recitals; the Latvian poet, journalist and military commander Eideman regretted that Pasternak's remarkable poetic 'locomotive' hauled only one truckload instead of a whole train of useful cargo; and Vera Inber disparaged Pasternak's international standing endorsed by the recent Paris Congress and now by Ehrenburg in his speech.[187]

Several allies sprang to Pasternak's defence however. While talking about his translations Mirsky rebutted all Bezymensky's charges,[188] and the former RAPP critic Mustangova emerged as an eloquent supporter, noting how many former admirers now maintained a conspiracy of silence against Pasternak. The 'Waves' cycle and recent *Izvestiya* verses, she claimed, were 'an urgent and open poetical interpretation of the modern age, a poet's converse with his time and with himself on subjects by no means narrowly personal but bound up with major problems of our life'. This, she avered, contrasted with the lifeless compositions of more ideologically correct writers.[189]

Despite various critical jibes, Pasternak was in fact greeted with general acclamation at the conference, especially when he gave a trenchant address on 16 February. Its printed version was considerably toned down. As he told his parents,

My speech which was made colloquially, simply and impromptu (whatever came into my head), was far more daring and broadranging than what the editorial censors and I myself later made of it. When I crossed out the opening, I couldn't *with my own hand leave in* the stenographer's note of the prolonged ovation [. . .] Conversely, other people *inserted* applause for themselves when they corrected the record of their speeches.[190]

Pasternak's speech dismissed Bezymensky's demagogic arguments and recalled Pushkin and Tyutchev, who successfully travelled via the printed page without the need for recitals. Following his earlier *Propositions*, he saw his own role in reviving 'the poetry book with pages that speak by virtue of their deafening silence'. Present poetic practice, he maintained, offended a Tolstoyan notion whereby 'anything bombastically elevated and rhetorical appears superficial, useless, and sometimes even morally suspect'.[191] In this sense, he found even Surkov's measured and sober speech commendable. Pasternak also showed unrhetorical modesty in referring to his own recent work. The *Izvestiya* poems in particular he described as 'poor verses [. . .] written hastily, the devil knows how, with an ease allowable only in the pure lyric, but impermissible with themes that need to be thought out artistically' (III, 219–22; *SS*, IV, 634–7).

Pasternak's chief 'boldness' lay in the polemical substance of his recommendations. Writers were themselves largely to blame, he claimed, for clapping additional fetters on themselves: 'Deeds are required of us, yet all we do is swear our loyalty'. Pasternak disliked some other speakers' mechanistic approach to creativity: 'they spoke about verse-writing as though it were the work of some constantly functioning piece of apparatus with output proportional to the work put into it', yet genuine creative daring, essential to art, was an element that defied legislation:

119

Art without risk and spiritual sacrifice is unthinkable. Freedom and boldness of imagination must be acquired in practice [. . .] In this connection do not wait for any directives [. . .] Is it the task of the Union to say to you: be bolder? It is the task of each of us, our personal task. That is why each one is given a mind and a heart. I do not recall in our legislation any decree forbidding genius.[192]

There was a deliberate *double entendre* here: genius was a quality publicly attributed to Stalin, but one to which Pasternak probably had greater claim. This idea was elaborated with an echo of the New Year *Izvestiya* poems and leaving listeners to apply it to whomever they saw fit in typical paradoxical form: 'A genius is related to an ordinary human being [. . .] the greatest and rarest representative of that breed, its immortal expression. These are quantitative polarities of a qualitatively homogeneous, model humanity.' In between lay the mass of merely 'interesting people' striving to be extraordinary (III, 223; SS, IV, 638). Similar thoughts on typicality, mediocrity and the paradoxical 'ordinariness' of genius had been enunciated in Pasternak's note on Lili Khorazova in 1928 (volume I, 347), and they were spelled out again in one of his prose drafts of the later 1930s. Several propositions in his Minsk speech were also rehearsed in private conversations in late February of 1936.[193]

Without mentioning the anti-formalist campaign, Pasternak's speech was implicitly opposed to the 'command culture' which the campaign exemplified and which the Minsk conference sought to impose. Indeed, the regimentation of literature in Minsk was personified by the military presence of Robert Eideman and by one comrade Bichevsky who delivered a 'militant Chekist greeting' to the conference from the Soviet Union's border guards.[194]

6

Peredelkino and the Purges

Happy the man who wholly
Without a trace of otherness
Spent childhood with the lowly,
Of one blood with the commoners.

I was not of their ranks.
Yet – more than idle whimsy –
I supped from the same platter,
Became their kith and kinsman.

Since infancy, our country
Attracted such an anthem
That, if our love's requited,
We have no need of heaven.

The people are a dwelling
Such that we don't notice it.
And like the air's expanse,
Their arching vault is infinite.

They are the densest thicket
Wherein, when we were children,
The words and names were found for
Events and for inventions.

Without them you are nothing.
And like their own possession
They place beneath the chisel
Your dreams and your intentions.

(1936)

On 25 February 1936 Pasternak sent a cable to Georgian colleagues with
greetings on the fifteenth anniversary of Soviet Georgia and regretting his

121

inability to celebrate 'among people whom I love as brothers in a country that has become my second homeland'.[1]

Georgian memories contrasted starkly with present events in Moscow however. The anti-formalist campaign rolled onward, and on 23 February *Komsomol'skaya pravda* had printed 'A Frank Discussion. On the Work of Boris Pasternak'. Though avoiding outright pogrom idiom, the article identified him as a potential target for attack. Despite his Minsk announcement of an intention to reform his ways, all his familiar vices were rehearsed, including an 'escapist alienation from life's stormy floodtide'.[2] Nevertheless, Pasternak's official standing was still not seriously jeopardised. As an article in the January issue of *Zvezda* observed, his stock with fellow poets was high, despite critiques suggesting he was a subjective idealist and Neo-Kantian, and that it was 'time to liberate Pasternak from the "embellishments" applied by over-zealous scholars'.[3]

Although no formalist charges were leveled at him in the on-going campaign, Pasternak was not sanguine about surviving unbruised,[4] especially after attacks on several close friends and colleagues. An early victim, Marietta Shaginyan, protested by demonstratively handing in her Union membership card, only to find herself publicly lambasted for an overt political misdemeanour. The notorious feuilletonist David Zaslavsky went to work on her in *Pravda* on 28 February,[5] and under brutal psychological pressure, she publicly recanted. On the 9 March *Pravda* identified Bulgakov as another formalist offender, and an annihilating critique of his *Molière* at the Moscow Arts Theatre led eventually to cancellation of all productions of his plays and ended the immunity he had enjoyed since the early 1930s.[6]

Pasternak was upset and incensed at the attack on Shaginyan,[7] and did not attend the start of three weeks of debates on the anti-formalist campaign that opened at Writers' House on 10 March. Advertised as discussions, the meetings had more the character of a tribunal, with command and reprimand issued by establishment speakers and expressions of loyalty and recantation by hapless writers. Vladimir Stavsky, who was soon to take over from Shcherbakov as Union Secretary, gave the opening address 'On Formalism and Naturalism in Literature'.[8] ('Naturalism' here meant failure to conceptualise and motivate raw and often unprepossessing factual observation, and it simply made it easier to ensnare writers who could not be caught in the formalist trap. One alleged offender was Pilnyak in his new novel *Ripening of the Fruits [Sozrevanie plodov]*.) But the mechanism of accusation and confession was slow in getting under way. While Shklovsky openly admitted his formalist sins of the past, Dmitrii Petrovsky was vigorously defended by Mirsky.

Deeply offended at what he heard and read of the first session, on 12 March

Pasternak visited Tarasenkov to seek advice whether to risk his reputation by speaking up in protest. Tarasenkov was in favour, and as Pasternak later told Olga Freidenberg, he was so infuriated at the humilition of Fedin, Leonov and Pilnyak by 'utter nonentities' that the next day he stood up and 'called everything by its proper name'.[9]

Pasternak's statement on 13 March ran strongly against the intended grain of the discussions and was never printed in the literary press. Only one or two phrases became known from the vituperative rebuttals published over the next couple of days. In fact, according to a stenographer's record retained in the Institute of World Literature archive, he attacked the futile pretense of discussing what had already been decided; critics were ferreting for evidence of what any artist worthy of the name had long ago overcome – a preoccupation with form and structure; and if bald simplicity was mandatory, then the common people with their colourful phraseology and folk sayings should also be accused of formalism! Furthermore, if there were objections to ornate rhetoric, then how could one accommodate an author such as Gogol?! Pasternak went on to attack the newly promoted antagonism between creator and critic: 'Can one say to a distressed and tormented woman how dare she give birth to a girl when she was supposed to have a boy?' Pasternak also took offence at the unison haranguing of the literary community. As for the phraseology of recent articles in the press, he refused to regard them as products of reason, and found it deeply disturbing when serious grown-ups rebuked writers as though they were miscreant little boys.[10]

Pasternak's speech of 13 March was sharply rebuffed by several speakers including critics Eidelman, Kirpotin, and the Hungarian Antal Hidas, as well as by Aseyev, Dolmatovsky and Surkov.[11] Both *Komsomol'skaya pravda* and *Pravda* (which had hitherto barely mentioned Pasternak's name) also printed tendentious summaries and dismissals of his speech.[12]

Distressed, if not surprised, at the vehement response, Pasternak requested the floor again on 16 March and reduced some of the tension with a show of humour. But while regretting the awkward expression of his first speech, he in effect merely restated his views without any retraction. He also complained afterwards that while speaking, he was put off by Antal Hidas who sat in the front row shaking his head disapprovingly.[13]

Various speakers again rehearsed Pasternak's failings – his isolation from reality, modern literary progress and popular opinion and taste, his failure to appreciate the Party's and his colleagues' concern for literature, and the fact that 'the people' would find others to write for them if Pasternak was incapable.[14] Eventually, though, the discussion moved on and *Literaturnaya gazeta* later put a conciliatory construction on his statements, noting his regret

123

at his first speech and suggesting that he could be helped to 'unravel the knot of contradictions that worry him'. Indeed, 'comrade Pasternak will manage to derive from this discussion much that is of benefit to him.'[15]

Pasternak thus escaped damnation as an ideological offender. Some protective force was in play, and he told his cousin:

I encountered the genuine surprise of responsible, even official people as to why I stuck my neck out for my colleagues, when not only had nobody touched me, but no one even intended so doing. I received such a rebuttal that later – again on official prompting – some colleagues from the Union were detailed to visit me [. . .] to inquire about my health. Nobody would believe that I felt fine, and was sleeping and working well.[16]

It seems likely that some indulgence continued in force, and it is tempting to see Shcherbakov behind this.

On 5 March, prior to the discussions, Pasternak attended a dinner at Meyerhold's to welcome Malraux, who had arrived on business arising from the 1935 Paris Congress. No doubt conversation touched on the anti-formalist campaign and discussion sessions.[17] On 13 March, Malraux visited the Writers' Union. Although unable to follow the proceedings in Russian, he doubtless saw and heard stormy reaction to Pasternak's speech, and he possibly registered some concern at high level.[18] A more important role in halting the vicious campaign, however, was played by Gorky with his article 'On Formalism' published in the central press on 9 April. Although absent in the Crimea during the discussions, he was evidently moved to anger and despair at the reports. This, his last major publicist article, hinted at an analogy between the campaign and the crimes perpetrated by fascist states, which abandoned even 'bourgeois humanism' in executing protesters who dared to think honestly and independently. Gorky had envisaged the Writers' Union as a forum of independent intelligentsia opinion, but its recent lack of resistance and supine submission to dictation were, he believed, signs of a grave moral ailment.[19]

Within two months of his article's appearance, Gorky was dead. Bukharin was absent in Western Europe and his own days too were numbered. His final press article in early July also inveighed against the methods and morality of fascism in all its forms, not confined to Nazi Germany.[20] At that time Pasternak still had nearly a quarter of a century to live. But apart from a brief and untranscribed speech at the 'Pushkin' Plenum of February 1937, his statements at the anti-formalist discussions were his last recorded public verbal pronouncement (as distinct from mere readings) for many years to come.

Pasternak's idealised view of Stalin himself remained relatively unimpaired, however. His and several colleagues' radiant enthusiasm was recorded when they saw the Leader at the Komsomol Congress in the third week of April.[21] That same month the two poems on Stalin were reprinted in *Znamya*. Along with them appeared four other items, described in a letter to Tabidze as 'rubbishy little verses'.[22] One included a half-nostalgic reminiscence of a simpler age when the 'alpha and omega seemed that life and I were cut to the same pattern' (III, 139; *SP*, 555; *SS*, II, 144). The same poem celebrated the Prague edition of Pasternak's translated poems in 1935, linking this to an earlier epoch, since which 'everything has changed at root'. The examples of Dante, Tasso and other poets are no longer applicable; art now demands the 'boldness of an estimate by eye, / Attraction, strength and seizure'. The poet has been 'sawn into billets', and instead of nature and flowers of the field, it is the people who now form the 'water and the air' he breathes. Yet there is no virtue in awarding marks to the people, or in being moved by emotion. The poet's strength lies in the vehemence of his imagery:

> Crash like thunder into twigs' embrace,
> Drown folk to their depths in rain.

And his function is summarised in the final stanza:

> Your works are not distinction's proof –
> Authority will grant rewards.
> You're hempen anguish's mere bunt-line,
> You're simply rigging for the sails that soar.[23]

Another poem in the April issue of *Znamya*, which dwelt on death and immortality and on repute based not on dictat, was a rumination on the funeral of poet Nikolai Dementyev, Pasternak's one-time imitator who had committed suicide on 28 October 1935. It was first recited by Pasternak at a poetic 'Olympiad' in Moscow's Hall of Columns on 28 February 1936 as a follow-up to the Minsk conclave. Bidding farewell to Dementyev, Pasternak offered consolation to all poets still alive in history:

> Louder than odd truths and falsehoods,
> The pages of the epoch chime.
> And in the ancient book of statutes
> We are established script and sign.[24]

As in some earlier poems, life and history are evoked in arboreal images: we will not be left to lie but will reemerge and sprout, just as new branches grow. Hence the question: 'Is suicide an escape or way of salvation?'

Another poem of the *Znamya* group rehearsed the thrust of Pasternak's December letter to Stalin on the poet's right to obscurity. Like two other items, it contained Georgian reminiscenes and was inscribed to Leonidze. For its first publication, though, Pasternak removed the dedication 'lest [Leonidze] have trouble in view of the somewhat independent nature of the contents'.[25] One of the poems includes the lines:

> With you life's not a simple essay.
> There's quite enough to choke on.
> Time will preserve my calligraphy
> From the critics' curry-comb
> [. . .]
> O revolution, you're a marvel.
> At last we're both together.
> Freed from the yokes of artistry,
> From here I see you better.[26]

While relieving Leonidze of responsibility for the revolution's greater visibility from Georgia than from Moscow, Pasternak expressed similar ideas in an April letter to the Tabidzes. That spring in Tiflis, Titsian had endured an anti-formalist pummeling similar to the one meted out to Moscow writers, and felt deeply bruised and depressed. Pasternak offered him comfort, urging him to believe first and foremost in himself, as an act of 'revolutionary patriotism' because

the chemistry of your makeup dissolves everything in the world, whatever its name, at a higher degree than is accepted in the 'Literaries' [*Literaturnaya gazeta*, etc.] and 'Evenings' [*Vechernyaya Moskva*] [. . .] Believe in the revolution as a whole, in fate, in the new inclinations of your heart, the spectacle of life, and not the constructions of the Union of Writers.[27]

The Writers' Union, as Pasternak later told Olga Freidenberg, was composed largely of 'utter and complete nonentities' who are compelled to 'consider as the style and spirit of the age that inarticulate and tremulous servility to which they are condemned by [. . .] the poverty of their own mental resources'. And conversely, 'when they hear a person who regards the revolution's greatness as lying in the possibility of speaking boldly and thinking openly in its presence, and because of it, they are ready to pronounce such a view as almost counter-revolutionary.'[28]

Meanwhile, whereas Bukharin and other liberals were privately expressing their gloom while keeping face publicly, Pasternak did almost the reverse. His 'revolutionary patriotism' in letters to family and friends suggested a belief in the spirit of revolution not as a past event but as a continuing 'state of mind', which he himself had shared in the 1920s with Zamyatin, and expressed to Rilke in 1926.[29] This in itself was a source of energy and optimism. As he wrote to Lydia in April of 1936:

Oh, this impossible life! Its local absurdities, which become an obstacle for an artist, are fantastic. But the revolution must be such, as it becomes more and more the event of the age, more and more obviously emerging at the centre and heart of peoples. What price here the fates and lives that have not justified themselves? But history has unfurled here as something obstinately immense, and this is elevating. And it is sufficient to keep remembering this in order to cease looking backward and drawing up accounts.[30]

Lydia Pasternak was now established in England, but the insecurity of other family members in Germany was more and more apparent. Although an Austrian citizen and protected by a certain prominence in international banking circles, Frederick Pasternak on 5 April took Josephine and their two children for a prolonged stay in Florence, Italy, the only country to which residents of Germany were permitted to take sufficient funds for a lengthy sojourn abroad. This seemed a relatively safe, if temporary, haven as anti-Jewish measures took hold in Germany. Meanwhile Frederick continued to work in Munich and paid weekend visits by train to his family who stayed in Tuscany till the late summer.[31]

The problem of a permanent home for 74-year-old Leonid and his wife was still unsolved. Despite promises of official assistance if they returned to Moscow, Boris shared none of the optimism of Zbarsky and Ambassador Suritz.[32] However, the accommodation problem seemed resolved in spring 1936 when Pasternak was reliably promised an out-of-town dacha residence which would be ready by the summer. Additionally, there was prospect of a new apartment in a house specially commissioned for the writing community and due to be erected in Lavrushinsky Lane, just opposite the Tretyakov Gallery.[33] In the early summer Zinaida and the boys were thus able to move into an amply proportioned villa recently constructed by the Literary Fund (Litfond) at Peredelkino and made available for a very nominal rent.

Peredelkino was the site of a whole new literary villa settlement. It stood on the former estate of the Samarin family, a few stations further down the Kiev railway line from Ochakovo railhalt and Karzinkino where the Pasternaks had spent the summer of 1918.[34] The new, all-season 'winter dacha' had two storeys and six rooms, with a balcony and two terraces. Commanding a woodland view, it stood on what was eventually named Pogodin Street, and was flanked by Pilnyak's villa on the right and by the house of critic and scholar Ivan Bespalov on the left; almost directly opposite lived the Selvinskys. Among the other early settlers and neighbours there were Babel, Chukovsky, Leonov, Lidin, Seifullina, Trenyov, and the Polish exile Bruno Jasieński. From now on to the end of his life, Peredelkino remained Pasternak's main place of residence. The house had no telephone and Pasternak never sought to acquire one; he generally paid visits into town only two or three times a week to attend to business, meet friends, collect mail and send messages.

Unlike the Peredelkino villas, the town apartments in Lavrushinsky Lane were built on a cooperative basis. Despite promises, they were ready only after a year's delay, in the autumn of 1937. A five-room apartment costing 15,000–20,000 roubles was quite beyond the Pasternaks' means. However, partly with the help of an editor friend Aleksandra Ryabinina, who arranged for an extra impression of the 1935 *Poems in One Volume*,[35] 8,000 roubles were produced as deposit. Zinaida busied herself with negotiation and barter, first with the Fedins then with the stage compère Garkavi. The latter's intended two-storey penthouse pad was acquired, and it was Pasternak's idea that if his parents returned to Moscow, they could live in the Lavrushinsky apartment in which two extra rooms were created by giving up a projected internal staircase. The upper rooms with their own exit door were set aside for the boys, including a piano practice room for Stanislav; the rooms downstairs were for the adults' use, and verbal communication was possible between floors via part of the stairwell left open. (Later, during the terror of 1937–38 some neighbours speculated that Pasternak purposely created this set-up with a double escape route for 'conspiratorial purposes'!) Subsequently the cooperative purchase scheme was abandoned; the house was run by a residence committee; all deposits were returned, and as it emerged, the Pasternaks could in fact have claimed a larger five-room dwelling.[36]

The Pasternak parents were more or less resigned to returning to Moscow despite the lack of professional guarantees for Leonid. Anticipating this, the two of them undertook one last trip through Europe, including a final sortie to Paris, and to London to see Lydia's family which now included a son, Michael, born in the autumn of 1936. They spent most of November and December in England, living at the Oxford home of her parents-in-law. They were delighted by the place and the people. *En route* back to Berlin they stayed briefly in Paris where Josephine joined them for three days and where their diplomat friend Potemkin introduced them to Boris' French admirer, the author Jean-Richard Bloch.[37]

On 12 June 1936, to much fanfare, the draft of the new 'Stalin' Constitution was printed in the central press. Liberal hopes for open elections and freedom to form even a 'loyal opposition' were not upheld, and the draft seemed to offer the forms of democracy with no substance. However, the press hailed the promise of new benefits, and scores of personalities and public organisations were invited to comment and evaluate. Bukharin reinforced his alignment with

Pasternak by printing his reponse first among a series of writers' contributions in *Izvestiya* for 15 June.

Pasternak's article, 'A New Coming of Age' ('Novoe sovershennoletie') further enhanced his reputation for paradox and ambiguity – since this was only a draft constitution, he was after all dealing with merely virtual reality. The title of his response referred to the maturity supposedly achieved after two decades of Soviet rule. If the earlier constitution offered the framework of a new society, so the new one supposedly marked an 'entry into full historical life', with 'the chance to develop a soul of its own appropriate to the maturity of its structure'. The new Constitution 'transfers the task of self-awareness from the hands of the future into our own. And the name for this is freedom.'

Never – and here is the root of that blind accusation of apoliticism directed against me and a whole series of artists – never did I understand freedom as a liberation from duty, as a dispensation, as an indulgence. Never did I imagine freedom as a thing one could obtain or extract from someone else by insisting or whining. There is no force on earth that could give me freedom if I did not already possess it in embryo and if I do not myself seize it, not from God or from some manager, but from the air and from the future, from the earth and from myself, in the form of kindness and courage and full-fledged productivity, in the form of independence of weakness and of other people's calculations. And this is how I imagine socialist freedom.[38]

The personally conceived freedom of which Pasternak spoke and which he had always lived by, patently had little to do with the factual non-freedom of Soviet public life. It was a function of that euphoric revolutionary liberation which he and a few like-minded contemporaries had privately perpetuated. Tabidze clearly apprehended this: his comment on the Constitution draft was printed in *Izvestiya* on 23 June. It had an oriental exaltation absent from Pasternak's projection, but employed a similar ambiguity in condemning recent fascist excesses and destruction of free expression, without confining these to Italy or Nazi Germany.[39]

For several months following his outspoken statements in March and his constitutional equivocations in June, Pasternak took little part in literary events. He cooled considerably towards Tarasenkov, who disapproved of his friendship with Pilnyak and Selvinsky and high evaluation of Pavel Vasilyev's talent.[40] He was absent from an anniversary meeting of Paris Congress delegates held in the Gorky Park theatre in late June; as a Bureau member, he should have attended, and Aragon, Gide and others had come to Moscow specially to meet their Soviet colleagues. He was noted only as attending a Union Presidium meeting on 21 July devoted to the work of young authors.[41] Meanwhile a further series of sinister events engaged public attention.

Gorky's relations with the leadership had been in decline ever since the Congress of 1934; he was not sent to Paris in 1935, and since that time he and Stalin had only ceremonial dealings. With the connivance of his own secretary, Gorky was increasingly isolated, and evidence points to his having become a victim of the terror. At the time, however, elaborate stage-management presented his death as following on a grave illness.[42] The date of his demise on 18 June may have been so timed to prevent his meeting with André Gide, who had arrived in Moscow the previous day.

After Gorky's death Stavsky was appointed as Secretary of the Writers' Union, and Shcherbakov was suddenly shifted from literary affairs to the post of Secretary of the Leningrad Party Regional Committee. Quite apart from the silencing of Gorky, Shcherbakov's transfer was not in Pasternak's favour: Stavsky was a leading anti-formalist compaigner and in the autumn of 1936 he sharpened his tongue especially on Pasternak.

During the summer and autumn of 1936 relations between Pasternak and Zinaida began to cloud again. In early summer, while Zinaida supervised the removal of herself, sons and furniture to the Peredelkino villa, Boris stayed for a short time at the Tverskoi Boulevard home of Evgeniya and Evgenii, and there was a new warming of relations. Evgeniya later described Boris' behaviour to Raisa Lomonosova:

Over the summer he was very drawn to young Zhenya and to me. He lived a few days with us and entered our lives so naturally and easily, as though he had only been away by chance. But despite the fact that, in his words, he is sick to death of that life, he will never have courage enough to break with her. And it is pointless him tormenting me and reviving old thoughts and habits . . .[43]

In the sudden space and calm of the Peredelkino dacha, Pasternak's unhappiness intensified along with nostalgia for his first family and a glum sense of duty to the second. Some of this percolated through in family correspondence. Zinaida was described as a compulsive worker, 'never sparing herself in this respect and [. . .] bristling like a she-wolf on her children's behalf'. As he told his parents in an autumn letter, he needed to simplify his life which for a long time had been 'like nothing on earth: it is impossible to exist and work with hell in one's soul. [But] I could part with Z[inaida] only if I could leave her taken care of and if I could rest assured on her account.'[44]

Pasternak was thus left to live with the reality of Zinaida's matriarchy. In 1937 her priorities were immortalised in her phrase about her two sons loving Stalin first of all, and after that their mama. By contrast with this, Evgeniya's sensitive nature, devotion to art, and discipleship of now disapproved masters

130

were bound to arouse Boris' sympathy.[45] The solution was to devise a lifestyle and routine that allowed Pasternak breathing space: with her sons attending school in Moscow, Zinaida spent much of the autumn and winter of 1936–37 in town, while he himself stayed alone at Peredelkino.

The acquisition of the dacha was itself the cause of some mental discomfort, since Pasternak was aware that his new material wellbeing was a form of 'manipulative favour', particularly incongruous in light of his own and the authorities' mutual disenchantment. As he announced that autumn, 'they treat me undeservedly splendidly, and the whole disarray in my order really amounts to the fact that in the given situation this could, and should, be incomparably better and more enjoyable than I have arranged for myself so far'.[46]

The removal to Peredelkino was celebrated by production of a new cycle of twelve short poems titled 'From Summer Notes' ('Iz letnikh zapisok'), dedicated 'to friends in Tiflis' and printed in the October issue of *Novy mir*. Under the heading of 'Travel Notes' ('Putevye zapiski') seven items later formed a section of the book *On Early Trains*. The cycle combined impressions from visits to Georgia with insights gained from his association with Georgian poets. Specially featured was the 'raw splendour of this world', of rearing mountains and rivers in spate together with heliotropes, apricots, tubs of oleander, the quaint alleys and grubby courtyards of Tiflis, and nightscapes where 'Gilly-flowers and Milky Way / Are watered from one can'. (*III*, 10–11; *SP*, 388; *SS*, II, 14–15)

Also featured were elements of Georgian popular fantasy, and the life of 'folk born in chemises' and living on easy terms with the grandeur of their scenery. These figures were unmarked by any politicised illusions about the heroism of labour; the poet's ruminations on the people suggested a depth of empathy in which his own identity was refashioned, but in no way that fitted Marxist designs (see p. 121).

The poems of summer 1936 also included addresses to two close friends. Yashvili's ferocity at the formalist discussions and later enthusiasm for the trials and death penalty had revolted Pasternak. However, in these verses he now recalled their earlier comradeship and offered a reconciliation. The penultimate poem portrayed Tabidze as a figure redolent of Rodin's Honoré de Balzac caught in rhetorical flight at a lamp-lit nocturnal garden feast.[47]

The sincerity and occasional deft imagery of 'From Summer Notes' did not conceal a certain facile vacuity. After circulating the manuscript, Pasternak wrote to the Tabidzes in embarrassment at this chirruping iambic trimeter: 'I can guess [. . .] how Vitya Goltsev probably came to see you saying "Just imagine what untalented babble your Borya has descended to [. . .]" Zina and Evg[eniya] Vl[adimirovna] just shook their heads and refused to believe I would ever hand this to the printers.' However, Pasternak explained, he was now putting verse aside in order to 'master the prose that is liberating and unchaining me'. In this, he promised, 'there will emerge traces of a life that seemed to disappear after *Second Birth*'.[48]

'From Summer Notes' marked a farewell to poetry for the next five years. Lyric inspiration was in abeyance, and public events were soon to demonstrate that, given Pasternak's oblique idiom and attitudes, any original poetic expression was fraught with risks. From late September through the winter Pasternak lived alone at Peredelkino and wrote prose, though without hope of completing anything in the short term. Part of the time he also spent reading. Michelet's history of France had been bought for Evgenii, but Pasternak now borrowed it back to read volume by volume, before later turning to Macauley.[49]

The year 1936 saw Pasternak's translations printed in Tabidze's *Selected Verse* (*Izbrannye stikhi*), and miscellanies such as *Stalin in the Songs of the USSR Peoples* (*Stalin v pesnyakh narodov SSSR*) and *Verses and Songs about Stalin* (*Stikhi i pesni o Staline*); in 1937 the *Georgian Lyricists* were reprinted along with further items in a Tiflis edition of Georgian verse and song dedicated to Stalin. Thereafter Georgian reprints virtually petered out. Pasternak's interest in translating from interlinear versions was also exhausted, and his main hope of ready income lay in translation from more familiar languages. In spring of 1936 he had honed up his old version of Kleist's *Prince Friedrich of Homburg* and offered it to Vishnevsky for printing in *Znamya*. *Literaturnaya gazeta* also announced a Pasternak Kleist edition, but this failed to materialise owing to a new view of Kleist as the bard of Prussian militarism; it was only after the Molotov–Ribbentrop pact that *Prince Friedrich* reappeared in print. Nothing materialised at all from a July announcement of reprinted translations from Rilke.[50]

Income apart, Pasternak valued the return to Western European translations as a vicarious communion with countries that were by now almost inaccessible physically. As he told Lydia in April 1936, 'Unexpectedly [. . .] there has revived in me a feeling which gradually waned over the last five years, of connection with the West, with the historical earth, with the face of the world – a sense of irrepressible need for it and of totally uncompensated separation.' But as a contribution to such communion Pasternak regretted the paucity of his own translatable works. Apart from publication of individual translated poems, there had only been Czech editions of his poems and of *Safe Conduct*.

It is a sad comedy when they translate me, or want to do so [. . .] It turns out that really there is nothing to translate. There has been some activity, demonstrable as a process, but there are no books, separate books about this and that, no Bovarys or Idiots or Dombeys and Sons. But quite apart from the stupidity and immodesty of such comparisons, the fault is not mine. The times are such.[51]

The malignancy of the Stalinist regime finally shook Pasternak's resilience and confidence in any historical justice in 1936. As he recalled, 'When those dreadful trials began again – instead of the period of viciousness coming to an end, as it seemed to me in 1935 – everything in me snapped. My identification with the age turned into a resistance which I did not disguise. I took refuge in translation. My own creativity came to a halt . . .'

On 15 August, the central press gave notice of what became known as the 'trial of the sixteen', the first of three major show trials. In addition to this however, during the next two years there were successive waves of arrests, forced confessions and sentences (with or without trial) to exile, prison, labour camp or execution. The terror extended across the country and engulfed vast numbers of population in every walk of life and of every rank.[52]

At the 'trial of the sixteen' the accused included Kamenev, Mrachkovsky, Smirnov, Zinovyev and others, of whom several had been interned since December of 1934. Press headlines called for savage penalties, and were backed up by commentary, letters of support from individuals and organisations, and eventually, reports on the proceedings that began on 19 August. During the trial, presiding judge Vyshinsky announced on 21 August that Bukharin too was to be investigated on 'terrorist' charges along with Radek, Rykov, Pyatakov and Tomsky. This was a subtle form of sadism, however, for on 10 September the case against both him and Rykov was closed, although the latter was rearrested within the month. Relieved on hearing that Bukharin had been cleared, Pasternak on 12 September sent him a letter of congratulation and assurance that he had never considered him guilty of any crime.[53] Nominally Bukharin remained in charge of *Izvestiya* until mid January 1937, although he ceased in August to be *de facto* controller; his successor Boris Tal, promoted from the staff of *Pravda*, lasted barely a year before his own arrest and execution.[54]

Under the heading 'Wipe Them from the Face of the Earth!' a collective letter from sixteen members of the Writers' Union appeared in *Pravda* on 21 August, calling for the death sentence. Listed among the signatories was Pasternak; others included Afinogenov, Fedin, Kirpotin, Leonov, Panfyorov, Pavlenko, Stavsky and Vishnevsky. Although some of these doubtless signed with alacrity, Pasternak refused. The Union, however, went ahead and added his name. Under great pressure from Stavsky, Pasternak agreed not to remove his name at the proof stage; his attitude was noted, however, and semi-publicly criticised, including by Tarasenkov at a meeting of *Znamya* staff on 31 August. Pasternak heard of this via Asmus and his attitude to Tarasenkov chilled. Zinaida fully supported her husband's stand, however.[55]

In disfavour for his reluctance to play verbal executioner, Pasternak also lost credit with readers ill-versed in Stalinist bureaucratic practice. Tsvetaeva read and believed the printed evidence, and was aghast at Pasternak's apparent endorsement of the death sentence. His true position was never publicly clarified, but eventually the incident was effaced by more horrendous events.[56]

After mid August 1936, the wave of terror began claiming several literary victims. Slightly earlier, the poet Pavel Vasilyev had been drummed out of the Union and then arrested; he was executed in 1937.[57] Now the Writers' Union began its own purge, 'unmasking' alleged Trotskyites. Those accused included authors Ivan Kataev, Serebryakova and Tarasov-Rodionov, and orthodox former RAPP critics like Ekaterina Troshchenko and Selivanovsky. Only a month before, the latter had cut Pasternak and his 'vulgar apologist' Tarasenkov down to size. His arrest along with others named ensued shortly after the Union had made its own charges.[58]

Similar lashings were also meted out to selected victims from Academe and involved Pasternak's cousin Olga Freidenberg. Her book on *The Poetics of Subject and Genre (Poetika syuzheta i zhanra)* had appeared in May 1936 and was later slated as 'pernicious drivel' in *Izvestiya*.[59] Criticism in such a forum was tantamount to a political denunciation, and after the work's confiscation from bookshops, even direr consequences threatened. Pasternak wrote his cousin a consoling letter recalling recent events involving fellow writers, and invited her to Peredelkino where among his neighbours she could meet victims of similar treatment in the persons of Fedin, Pilnyak and others.[60] She did not take up the invitation (the cousins last met personally in Leningrad in summer 1935). After writing a protest letter to Stalin, she had an audience in November with Volin, the Assistant Commissar for Enlightenment. Volin assured her that no harm would come to her professionally or personally. When one further venomous attack hit the pages of *Izvestiya* on 14 November, Pasternak's letter of complaint to Bukharin probably landed in the waste basket; as it emerged, Bukharin was by that time under virtual house arrest.[61]

On 1 October, Pasternak wrote both to Olga Freidenberg and in similar vein to the Tabidzes staking his sole faith in the idealised spirit of revolution and its 'greatest personalities', as distinct from the craven literary bureaucracy.[62] There was nothing in Pasternak's real surroundings to encourage such optimism or identify 'great personalities' however. He was himself perceptibly under threat, although an ironic humour did not abandon him. Leonov recalled meeting him on a walk in Peredelkino and enquiring after his health. 'Oh, I'm very well', Pasternak answered. 'I still haven't been "unmasked" yet.'[63]

In late October, the critic Pertsov who in 1924 had dismissed Pasternak as a superfluous 'fictional presence' in Soviet literature, was detailed by *Literaturnaya gazeta* to work him over once again. He did so with practised rudeness, wheeling out old arguments, suggesting that the present cult of the author was the fault of Ehrenburg and a conspiracy of Pasternak-fanciers, and now claiming that his impenetrable complexity arose not from sophistication of thought and content, but from defective technique. The April poems in *Znamya* were cited as examples of his shoddy workmanship.[64] Pertsov's article set the tone for assessments of Pasternak over the next several years. The last positive Soviet notice of the 1930s – a strangely unaccountable 'erratic' – was an article by M. Gutner printed in *Literaturny Leningrad* in the month of October.[65]

In September, when *Novy mir* held an evening designed to demonstrate its ideological house was in order, some of Pilnyak's supposed offences was brought to light, but he and chief editor Gronsky tried to present a picture of remorseful good intent.[66] Then, on 28 October the Writers' Union continued its internal purgation by requiring Pilnyak to present an account of himself before the Presidium. As a Presidium member, Pasternak was obliged to attend, but realising the aim of the meeting, he warned Pilnyak against turning up in person.[67] Pilnyak ignored the warning. Encouraged maybe by Pasternak's example, he abandoned his recent complaisance and adopted an assertive stance, defending his artistic independence. Several Presidium members were indignant, and *Literaturnaya gazeta* reported accusatory speeches by Aseyev, Stavsky, Elena Usievich, Vishnevsky and others. Pasternak's speech was officially noted for its 'sincerity'. In reality, what he said was totally out of key with other speakers and bitterly antagonised Stavsky, who at a general Union meeting on 16 December upbraided him for condemning their jeering attitude to Pilnyak and for failing to 'recognise the correctness of opinion of our community'.[68]

Pasternak's standing suffered a further blow in December of 1936 when he again refused to echo officially orchestrated opinion.

André Gide had been an avowed friend of the USSR since the early 1930s, supporting an ideal of the Soviet system seemingly embodied in the personality and liberal views of Maksim Gorky. During his 1936 visit his enthusiasm was wavering however. Because of the constant presence of third parties, exchanges *à deux* were few and brief. But in conversation with Pasternak Gide commented on the obvious lack of personal freedom in the USSR and certain truths were imparted not just by Pasternak, but by others Gide met, including Tabidze. Pasternak was however evidently the main person who opened Gide's eyes to what was going on around him and warned him against being deceived by official pronouncements and Soviet Potemkin villages.[69]

Gide's account of his visit, *Retour de l'U.R.S.S.* , published in Paris in November, confirmed his total disenchantment. The book evinced several views that were anathema to the Stalinist leadership: support for a multi-party system, the notion of the autonomy of art, and dismay at the intelligentsia's supine toleration of dictatorship. Gide was not deluded by official conversations and diverting spectacles organised to impress him, and he also displayed sufficient understanding not to name the confidential sources of information entrusted to him.

Gide's *volte-face* unleashed a vilification campaign of unbridled fury in the Soviet press. It included damning editorial articles and statements by several public figures and writers. Officials also pinned special hope on a denunciation from Pasternak as Gide's known friend and sympathiser. Pasternak refused to comply, on grounds that he had not read or even set eyes on Gide's book.[70] Needless to say, the unavailability of *Retour de l'U.R.S.S.* did not inhibit other accusers, and Pasternak's refusal to join the chorus was remembered by Stavsky and held against him.

Unfortunately, *Novy mir*'s record of ideological error was not cleared by the purgatory meeting on 1 September. At the general gathering of Moscow writers on 16 December, Stavsky maintained that 'through an obvious oversight by the editors' the October issue had printed verses by Pasternak which slandered the Soviet people. The offending lines allegedly presented the writer as a 'victim' of the people, for

> [. . .] like their own possession
> They place beneath the chisel
> Your dreams and your intentions.

In a speech whose savagery went far beyond the anodyne report in *Literaturnaya gazeta*, Stavsky noted Pasternak's further offense in the fact that Bukharin approved such verses, and he sneered at his acknowledgement of Pasternak at the 1934 Congress as almost a pinnacle of socialist poetry. 'But what is there here that is poetic?' Stavsky queried. 'And why do we remain silent?' *À propos* of the Gide issue, he referred to Pasternak's 'corridor conversations' supporting a 'blatant low-down slander of our social life emanating from abroad'. The reference was to a verbal clash with Tarasenkov at a banquet to celebrate the new Constitution held in Writers' House in early December. Within earshot of Dolmatovsky and others, Tarasenkov had harshly attacked Gide while Pasternak (whose exact comments are not on record) appeared to defend him, or at least his own right not to condemn without having read the book. 'How', Stavsky asked, 'can we deal with tasks facing the Soviet Writers' Union when we have such people here, and also folk who take them seriously?'[71] In fact, a secret police report at the time established that several Union members including Ivanov, Antokolsky, Budantsev and Aleksandr Gatov had spoken in support of Pasternak.[72] But there was no public statement by, or defence of, this emergent oppositional Peredelkino clique.

One answer to Stavsky was offered by the paper *Vechernyaya Moskva* (Evening Moscow). In an editorial on 19 December it printed a survey of Pasternak's work which did little more than catalogue his offensive conference statements over the last two years and condemn his isolation from Soviet society; Stavsky's attack on the slanderous verses was paraphrased; and all Pasternak's work starting with *My Sister Life* was described as inimical to Soviet literature.[73] As Lazar Fleishman notes, the article had some ominous new features which could not have escaped Pasternak's notice. The blame for his failings was laid directly at his own door and not ascribed to misleading flatterers. Furthermore, the indulgence for his 'defects' was removed and his vagaries were now seen as arising from conscious malign intent. The offending verses were naturally of little consequence in themselves and might never have attracted attention, but the establishment was now thirsting for revenge and no peccadillos could escape them.[74]

Stavsky's charges were serious enough to prompt Pasternak to send *Litera-turnaya gazeta* a letter, which was published on 5 January 1937. In it he cited the last three quatrains of the poem to which Stavsky objected, and explained:

In the second stanza I am talking about language; in the third one, which attracted censure, I am saying that individuality without the people is illusory; that in its very manifestation the authorship and virtue of being a motivating prime cause reverts to them, the people. The people are the master-craftsman (the carpenter or turner) and you, the artist, are the material. That is my actual thought, and whatever its subsequent fate, I see nothing in it that is incompatible with the people. I can explain the misunderstanding that has occurred only by the weakness and failure of this passage, as of these verses of mine in general.

Pasternak asked the paper to print his statement and he sent his comradely greetings. His explanation in no way resembled the public confession that might have restored even a reputation for good intent. The paper printed his message along with a response 'From the Editors', stating that his explanation contradicted the sense of the verses in question. Stavsky's distorted reading was thus pronounced correct, and Pasternak was therefore guilty of slander. In fact, of course, it is obvious that the artist's self-portrayal in the poem closely matched the passive lyrical persona in Pasternak's other verse, and it differed strongly from the now approved Mayakovskian stereotype of the poet as tribune and placard-bearer.

Oh, what a great thing is history! Here I am reading the 20–volume *Histoire de France* by Jules Michelet. I am now engaged on the sixth volume dealing with the terrible period of Charles VI and VII, with Joan of Arc and her sentence and burning at the stake. Michelet quotes page after page of primary sources, from the Chronique de Charles VI, [and] a contemporary active in that period, the prévôt des marchands Juvénal des Ursins. Where is this Juvénal now, who can say? And here I am reading his chronicle, which is half a thousand years old, and my hair stands on end with horror.

This passage occurred in Pasternak's letter to his parents of 24 November 1936. An honest account of the horrors that year would never have passed the postal censor – or left the author at liberty. Pasternak's description of French history was an intentional allegory on present-day events in Russia. The pondering on Juvénal des Ursins' fate doubtless hinted at the recent arrest of Leonid Pasternak's friend and supporter Yuvenal Slavinsky. Whether Pasternak's parents immediately deciphered the message is uncertain; after 1936 Boris was the only family member in Russia who still risked corresponding with his parents.[75] The year 1937 provided further horrendous parallels with Michelet's history.

On 23 January 1937 began the public 'trial of the seventeen', with Pyatakov, Radek, Sokolnikov and Serebryakov as the principal accused. Pasternak was acquainted with three of them. Radek had been Larisa Reisner's second husband and Pasternak had met him and others ·in the 1920s at Narkompros.[76] Pasternak also recalled Sokolnikov as a politically active schoolboy at the Fifth Classical Gymnasium in 1905. Serebryakov he had met through his authoress wife Galina (volume I, 367). Although not initially indicted, Bukharin was implicated during the proceedings and confined in his Kremlin apartment under virtual house arrest, and his protest and hunger strike failed to prevent his eventual detention in late February.[77]

Shortly after Bukharin was indicted, Pasternak sent a short note affirming that 'No forces will convince me of your treachery'. Such a message, sent to that address, was manifestly risky for the sender and when Bukharin read it, tears sprang to his eyes and his comment was: 'He has written this against himself.'[78] In the event, perhaps through blind chance, Pasternak was never called to account for his daring support. Bukharin's fate, however, was a foregone conclusion.[79]

Even before Bukharin himself stepped into the dock, the trial had stirred literary reverberations. Unlike the previous year's collective statements, individual writers now produced articles vilifying the defendants at the very start of proceedings and calling for their execution. The fact that figures such as Babel, Fedin, Mirsky, Olesha, Platonov and Tikhonov all wrote such material indicates the degree of pressure on them.[80] Pasternak was not among them. Nor, more significantly, did he figure among twenty-five signatories to a resolution passed at a special session of the Writers' Union, which reviewed the crimes of the Trotskyite 'parallel centre' and called for execution of all defendants: the Soviet people, led by the Party, should stamp out this viperous body and champion the cause of socialism triumphant.[81] Although he later pleaded illness, Pasternak's absence from that meeting and failure to sign the document were vividly eloquent – even Pilnyak, a personal friend of Radek's, had spoken against him; Bezymensky, Selvinsky and Surkov had called for elimination of the 'capitulatory literary conceptions of Radek and Bukharin'; and Vishnevsky also claimed that the defendants had a literary 'tail' that should be docked, and he cited the names of Artem Vesyoly, Ivan Kataev, Pilnyak and Pasternak.[82]

In fact, on the day of the meeting, Pasternak was gathering kindling twigs in Peredelkino and expatiating to Afinogenov on his reasons for not attending. The trial defendants were mostly distasteful to him, he claimed, and at their meetings in the 1920s these men had despised him for being 'soft-bellied' and out of touch with life; he in turn had disliked them for their stereotyped thought and speech. However, while others loudly condemned the defendants, his own ideas were *mal à propos*, inexpressible publicly, and concerned 'a writer's moral environment, and [. . .] thoughts that live in us and set us writing poetry and drama'.[83]

Despite such compunctions, Pasternak quickly realised that his absence from the meeting constituted an immense personal risk with no tangible gain. He therefore quickly sent a letter to the Writers' Union, asking that his signature be appended. Although unpublished, the letter cleared his record. At the same time it also hinted at his sense of helplessness. He had been 'absent through illness' and 'to the words of the resolution there is nothing to add.' He nevertheless added a further paragraph that seemingly reinforced the sentiments of the resolution, which repeatedly referred to the country and its noble population. But there was a paradoxical Pasternakian subtext here which alluded to a crime perpetrated against the nation:

The word 'homeland' [*rodina*] – an ancient, childlike and eternal word – and our homeland in its new meaning, the homeland of modern thought, rise up and fuse together in one's soul, just as they will do so in history. And everything becomes clear, and one has no wish to expatiate on anything, but only to work more fervently and industriously at the expression of truth – a truth that is open and unblustering, and which precisely in this respect defies subversion by any disguised and fratricidal falsehood.[84]

Possibly officials who read this never registered the real sense of Pasternak's message. The document was consigned to the files, after which Andrei Sinyavsky and myself were probably the first to see and evaluate it in the archive of the Moscow Institute of World Literature in the spring of 1964.

As Pasternak reminded his parents in mid February of 1937, later that month there would be celebrations for the centenary of Pushkin's death. But after experience of recent writers' gatherings he had no intention of participating:

[. . .] there have recently been several misunderstandings – that is, the way I speak and think is not always properly understood. I find commonplaces physically intolerable, and it is possible to say something of one's own only at a time of calm. Were it not for Pushkin, the possibility of misinterpretations might not have restrained me. But against the background of that name, any roughness or slips of the tongue would strike me as unbearably vulgar and indecent.[85]

The Fourth ('Pushkin') Plenary Session of the Board of the Writers' Union opened on 22 February in the Hall of Columns, scene of the First Writers' Congress and of the recent show trial. Elements of both these events figured in this nominally festive meeting, which was designed to celebrate Pushkin and also reimpose conformity and eliminate the last vestige of Bukharin's liberal platform of 1934. The final toppling of Pasternak as the perceived acme of modern poetic culture was thus inevitable.

In pursuit of these goals, Eidelman's press report of Tikhonov's opening address on 'Pushkin and Soviet Poetry' took him to task for his too lenient critique of Pasternak, who 'least of all can claim to represent Pushkinian principles' in poetry.[86] Tikhonov's omission was filled, though, by Dzhek Altauzen who took some trouble to demolish Pasternak's false reputation created by Bukharin and critics such as Mirsky and Tarasenkov. The familiar drooping bouquet of quotations from 'About these Verses', 'To a Friend', et cetera, was produced, and the 'poet posing as holy fool' was told that his readership, the people, were perfectly able to identify their true friends and foes.[87]

The poet Dmitrii Petrovsky used the podium to reinstate himself after the previous year's charges of 'formalism'. He did so by the well-proven method of attacking others, including Pasternak, whose poetry and recent civic behaviour he described as alien and hostile. As one witness commented, a genuine poet's crudely demagogic assault on colleagues was understandable only in terms of the 'psychology of the times, sated with a fear and meanness'.[88] A similar stand was also taken by Bezymensky and Surkov, the latter inveighing against the 'celebrated refinement' established by Bukharin as a prime quality of the best Soviet verse.[89]

Pasternak did not attend the first few days of the plenary meeting, and other absentees included Aseyev, Selvinsky, and Iosif Utkin. On the 26th, however, the last day of the speeches, both Pasternak and Selvinsky put in an appearance, probably at the benevolent urging of Fadeyev. Selvinsky evidently made a speech full of indignation at the recent criticism heaped on him, and claimed incomprehension at what was happening around him.

However, the Union management was by now persuaded that instead of a celebration of Pushkin, their meeting was degenerating into a literary kangaroo court all too redolent of recent political trials. On the final day an attempt at conciliation was therefore made. Bezymensky claimed that the savage critical attacks were in no way intended to excommunicate Pasternak or Selvinsky or to limit their artistic endeavour. Ever adept at alternating the roles of executioner and admirer, Fadeyev sought at the concluding session to defuse the situation by expressing only mild dissent with Selvinsky and Pasternak, denying that any 'betrayal' or 'libel of the Soviet people' could be imputed to them. Selvinsky, he claimed, had wrongly applied the oppositional stance of Pushkin and other masters of the past to his own confrontation with the Soviet public. Pasternak he tried to cajole out of his eccentric corner, urging him to exercise Pushkinian wisdom and listen to 'the voice of life', even if some of its pronouncements were abrasively expressed. Fadeyev's only scornful remarks were directed against the Komsomol poets Altauzen and Zharov for their lack of taste and technical polish.[90]

Pasternak spoke on the last day of the meeting, immediately following Fadeyev and in a tone matching his moderation. His address, like Selvinsky's, was not printed but only summarised in *Izvestiya*. While Selvinsky had played the martyr, Pasternak reportedly disavowed the inferences drawn from his own speeches or writings, and denied that he was setting himself up against the masses. In all his designs he claimed to be 'with you, with the country, with the Party'. Though Fadeyev had made no charge of disloyalty, Pasternak chose the occasion to cover himself by protesting at Gide's attempts the previous year to solicit material from him and others for his libelous book.[91]

In his speech of 25 February, Stavsky had cited Pasternak's recent 'politically mistaken' verses, noting that the poet had evidently learned nothing from the Minsk conference, the anti-formalist compaign, or the current meeting.[92]

However, following Fadeyev's signal for appeasement, the press report of Stavsky's speech and ensuing discussion merely described Pasternak as an ivory tower poet, 'contemplating his own navel' and contenting himself with 'general declarations' instead of active engagement in real life.[93]

It is debatable to what extent Fadeyev genuinely protected Pasternak against the ferocity of Stavsky and others. Maybe, though, he unknowingly assumed some of the functions of Shcherbakov. In any event, after the conciliatory conclusion of the Pushkin meeting, Pasternak was left in relative peace; political accusations had been waived, and he had been dismissed as a lyrical eccentric out of touch with real life. The corollary of this was the lapse of any claim to be the premier poet, or the heir of Mayakovsky. A subsequent writers' meeting in Leningrad also declared that 'the vessel of Soviet poetry will not navigate by Pasternak's poetry', and Tarasenkov sent a letter to *Znamya* correcting his earlier estimation of Pasternak, for which he had been reproved in *Pravda*; his withdrawal of support led to a two-year break in his dealings with Pasternak.[94]

During the ensuing weeks and months a general view became established that Pasternak was a second-rate escapist litterateur, best ignored and left to his own devices. This proved a merciful fate. The Union inquisitors turned their attention elsewhere. Just as the 'Pushkin' conference was ending, the Party's Central Committee held a plenary meeting at which the cases of Bukharin and Rykov were discussed, and the two men were plucked out of the meeting on 27 February and transferred to the Lubyanka. Shortly after this at a Moscow writers' meeting on 2–5 April, Stavsky summarised the results of the Central Committee meeting and went on to detail how the Trotskyite pestilence had infected Soviet literature. In the weeks that followed, the Writers' Union held its own purgative meetings. At these several seemingly unassailable personalities, including former members of RAPP, were verbally annihilated, and their physical arrest usually ensued shortly afterwards. Some of the victims included RAPP critic Averbakh and Gorky's secretary Kryuchkov. In June Pasternak's friend and ally Dmitrii Mirsky was lambasted by the critic Kirpotin and later arrested; his *Anthology of New English Poetry* (*Antologiya novoi angliiskoi poezii*) appeared in print at the end of the year with his name removed. Further inquisition victims were the author Ivan Kataev, the Polish émigré Jasieński, and the dramatists Kirshon and Afinogenov, although the latter for some reason managed to avoid actual arrest.[95]

In the midst of this witch-hunt, Pasternak sustained no more than a few glancing blows in the literary press. The accusations were predictable and referred to offences of omission such as his failure to match up to A. Gurshtein's stereotype of 'The poet of socialism', or his preference for what Aleksandrov called 'A Private Life'.[96] Then, in the May issue of the journal *Oktyabr'* a final verdict was passed on Pasternak, ushering in a long period in which he was ignored by the press and untouched by any security or judicial organs.

N. Izgoev's article cleared Pasternak of guilt by association with Gide, and particularly with Bukharin who allegedly, for political ends, promoted a distorted view of him. Izgoev also removed any suggestion of political crime in Pasternak's aesthetic or civic position. The strictures were familiar from RAPP critiques, and in light of the current attacks on former RAPP-ists they were relatively innocuous. Pasternak was again characterised as a lyricist divorced from his age, a 'subjective idealist', 'holy fool', and 'cloud-dweller' (*nebo-zhitel'*), and this was all said without any malice. While noting a certain disingenuousness in Pasternak's 'campaign for his so-called creative individuality, originality and independence', Izgoev saw his main malady as anaemic enfeeblement. Symptomatically Pasternak was thus the master translator, sensitive to the power of other poets and able to convey this, yet incapable of creating works that reflected 'the greatness and elevation of our epoch'. Izgoev's words proved prophetic so far as professional income was concerned. Moroever, translation had the virtue of freeing the translator of responsibility for the content of his source text. The conclusion was reassuring: 'Pasternak is talented, and our epoch knows how to value, protect and nurture human beings.'[97]

Pasternak's fate in the 1930s was thus settled. Whether this was Fadeyev's doing, or whether Stalin himself gave orders not to touch this 'denizen of heaven'[98] cannot be verified. But the expression gained currency and was attributed to the Leader. In the recent past Pasternak's insular behaviour had attracted even Zinaida's condemnation, since 'sitting out' invited suspicion and arrest.[99] Now there was little option however. Izgoev's article was symptomatic rather than legislative, but it indicated the establishment had abandoned attempts to reforge Pasternak's personality and intended to leave him in peace and to 'preserve rather than destroy'. Pasternak's work, after all, was never nakedly political; as Fadeyev said some years before, comparing him to Mandelstam, 'With Pasternak it's much easier for us – in his work there is nature.'[100]

While untouched himself, in spring and summer of 1937 Pasternak was the helpless witness of other people's tragedies and was aware of his own vulnerability. As he commented two years later,

In those awful, bloody years, anyone could have been arrested. We were shuffled like a

pack of cards. I don't want to indulge in vulgar rejoicing that I survived while others failed to. It is necessary for someone to proudly lament, wear mourning, and experience
• life tragically. Here tragic attitudes are prohibited however, it is regarded like pessimism and moaning. How wrong it is! . : . A living person is still needed as a bearer of this tragedy![101]

One effect of the literary inquisitions was to forge new friendships through a common sense of distress. Afinogenov lost his friend and protector when Yagoda was arrested on 3 April; later that month, along with Kirshon, he was pilloried at a writers' meeting and branded in the press as a murderous bandit who deserved to be annihilated. Expulsion from the Party and the Union followed, and he sat alone in Peredelkino awaiting his arrest. Although never a close ally, Pasternak was always personally well disposed to him, and he saw no reason to alter this attitude. At a time when others shunned them, Boris and Zinaida continued visiting Afinogenov and his American communist wife Jenny. Zinaida recalled Pasternak's belief that an elemental process was in progress in which 'no one could know on whose head the rock would fall, and he therefore showed not an ounce of fear'.[102] Afinogenov was spared the rock; in February 1938 he was reinstated in the Party and Union, and later perished during the bombing of Moscow in October 1941. In his diary was a touching recollection of Pasternak during 1937, busily writing his prose, never idle, never reading the press, given to solitary walks and reading Macauley's *History of England*.[103]

In late May of 1937, Mandelstam's Voronezh exile ended. In the interim, in 1936, Akhmatova and Pasternak had both tried and failed to obtain remission of his sentence; Mandelstam sent a grateful and admiring New Year greeting to Pasternak on the 2nd January; Nadezhda also brought him her husband's 'Second Voronezh Notebook' to which Pasternak responded with a set of detailed notes that were couriered back to Voronezh. Written in appalling misery, Mandelstam's new verse had an authority and lucence that highlighted the ebb of Pasternak's poetic inspiration. Akhmatova and Pasternak now each contributed 500 roubles to send Mandelstam and his wife for a six-week dacha vacation near Zadonsk.[104] The Mandelstams had forfeited their Moscow residence permit and apartment and after Zadonsk were forced to settle some hundred kilometers away at Savelovo. From there they paid frequent visits to Moscow and also came several times to Peredelkino. While she tolerated Afinogenov, Zinaida feared the contagion of associating with the Mandelstams who, as she believed, compromised her husband. She refused to receive them at the dacha and Pasternak on one occasion ruefully explained that Zinaida 'seems to be baking pies'. Conversation generally took place while strolling in Peredelkino. Nadezhda Mandelstam recalled how once at the local station they talked continuously as trains went by, Pasternak seemed obsessed by Stalin and blamed his own recent sterility on his failure in 1934 to secure an audience with him.[105]

Pasternak's close family were untouched by the terror, but his brother Aleksandr was affected in slightly macabre fashion. As an architect he was deployed to assist with the design of locks on the Moscow–Volga Canal. Since the project used convict labour, the construction sites were controlled by the NKVD. Although not employed by the security organs, for site work Aleksandr was obliged as a formality to wear NKVD military uniform; moreover his design work earned him an official award which led to a tragic contretemps with Leningrad relatives.

In winter 1936–7, Musya, the wife of Olga Freidenberg's brother Aleksandr (Sasha), was arrested. In the summer of 1937 Boris' brother and his wife Irina visited the Freidenbergs at their rented quarters in Detskoye Selo (formerly Tsarskoye Selo) near Leningrad. There Sasha Freidenberg implored his cousin to try and intercede for Musya when he met Kalinin at the presentation ceremony. (Kalinin was the veteran chairman of the Council of Ministers, an office which failed to prevent the arrest and imprisonment of his own wife the following year.) As Olga Freidenberg realised, the request was absurd, but when Aleksandr Pasternak refused, Sasha and his mother were filled with hatred. Aunt Asya renounced her nephew and his family.[106] Sasha correctly guessed that his own arrest was imminent; he was detained on 3 August, and a typewriter and binoculars were confiscated as 'evidence' of his alleged espionage activity. In January 1938, he was dispatched to Chita with a five-year sentence and evidently perished in captivity.[107]

In consequence of all this, there was a long hiatus in the Pasternak–Freidenberg correspondence. In summer 1938 Irina Pasternak visited Leningrad and heard of Sasha's fate from cousin Olga. Boris wrote to Olga in November, corroborating his brother's initial response and confirming that 'appeals from bystanders yield nothing and only make matters worse'.[108] Later, in January 1939, Pasternak retailed the last eighteen months' worth of Freidenberg news to Lydia in Oxford, part of it in semi-coded form: 'From Olya Irina heard that Sasha Konfaind [i.e. from the English "confined"] is their greatest sorrow.'[109]

On 15 May 1937 Beria lectured the Tenth Georgian Party Congress,[110] warning of political betrayal among Georgia's intellectuals and suggesting that certain writers – Yashvili, Mitsishvili and others – should examine their activities and publicly recant. As secretary of the Georgian Writers' Union, Yashvili had in 1936 helped purge the organisation of alleged Trotskyites; in

March 1936, his militancy at the anti-formalist discussions had even impaired relations with Pasternak; at the 'Pushkin' plenum, too, he had excelled in calling for vigilance and the elimination of ideological enemies.[111] His behaviour in fact reflected the situation of Georgia's writers, who were more zealous, or under even greater pressure, than their Moscow counterparts.[112] Now, he discovered that fealty made vulnerable, and he was one of the prime offenders singled out by Beria.

In late May, the Georgian Writers' Union began a series of investigatory tribunal sessions. Yashvili's links with the corrupt hydroelectric tycoon Jikia, the bacteriologist 'saboteur' Eliava, and with other enemies of the people were publicly rehearsed. Later, in June and July, he and others were hauled before an inquisitorial series of Union Presidium meetings, which made clear that their lives as well as their professional standing were on the line. At one of these sessions on 22 July, Yashvili produced a hunting gun and shot himself dead. The meeting went on to pass a resolution stating that Yashvili posed as a litterateur while engaging in treason and espionage, and maintaining that his suicide during the course of their meeting was 'a provocative act that arouses loathing and indignation in every decent gathering of Soviet writers'.[113]

News of Yashvili's suicide filtered to Moscow at first only as rumour. Pasternak heard it finally confirmed only on 17 August during a trip into town, but it took him ten days to set down on paper a coherent message of condolence to Yashvili's widow:

My poor, dear, beloved Tamara Georgievna,
What is all this? For about a month I lived in blissful ignorance and knew nothing. Now I have known for about ten days, and all the time I keep writing to you, writing and tearing it up. My existence is now of no value. I myself need comfort and I don't know what to say to you that might not strike you as idealistic babbling or highflown Pharisaism [. . .] When I realise again and again that never again will I see that striking face with its lofty inspired forehead and laughing eyes, or hear that voice whose very sound was captivating with its flow of thoughts, I weep, I am racked by anguish and can find no place for myself. [. . .] How I would like to see you! I will ask Titsian and Nina to embrace you for me, to be there and weep together with you.[114]

Pasternak and Tabidze had last met in March at a poetry evening in Moscow, when Pasternak read his translations along with Antokolsky, and the Spanish poet Rafael Alberti had been among the contributors.[115] Tabidze's family were soon to weep on their own account. His arrest was engineered by the Union President Demetradze shortly before his own exposure and execution in the autumn. In August Demetradze wrote to Beria, denouncing Titsian's mismanagement of the Mtatsminda and Kazbek museums, which compounded his alleged misdeeds revealed at the June–July inquisition. On

10 October Tabidze was expelled from the Union and arrested the same day.[116] He was tortured, charged, and executed within two months, although no announcement of this was leaked. Hearing of his arrest, Pasternak again ignored the contagion of contact with public enemies and sent Nina Tabidze an anguished telegram. When Stavsky in December suggested he attend a Rustaveli plenary meeting in Tiflis, he turned the idea down. His excuse was Zinaida's pregnancy, but privately the thought of visiting a Georgia without Tabidze or Yashvili was unbearable. In 1938, Pasternak heard from Simon Chikovani of his last meeting with Titsian in the autumn as he sat distraught and merely awaiting arrest.[117] Like Tabidze's family Pasternak clung on to hopes based on ignorance and continued writing Nina Tabidze encouraging letters for several years. In 1940 he helped her draft a petition on Titsian's behalf to Beria; he assisted her and her daughter financially and often invited them to stay in his home.[118] The illusion that 'Titsian is alive and somewhere not too far away, and there is less and less time to wait,'[119] was nurtured vainly, and the awful truth only emerged in the mid 1950s after the death of Stalin. Pasternak's grief at the destruction of his Georgian friends was something he carried through life.

The Pasternaks also witnessed the abduction of Pilnyak. On 25 October 1937 they called on their neighbours to smooth over the fact of not inviting them to Zinaida's birthday celebration the day before. (Zinaida disliked Pilnyak largely for his changeable attitudes towards her husband.) As they sat with Pilnyak and Kira his wife, a car drew up and a figure in military uniform appeared. Pilnyak greeted him in familiar fashion; they had evidently met at the Soviet Embassy in Japan. The man said Pilnyak was required on urgent business for a couple of hours; as they left, the Pasternaks too departed. Early the following morning Kira announced that her husband had been arrested and the house had been searched all night. It was later learned that Pilnyak was charged with espionage and treason, and executed on 21 April 1938 along with the poet Sergei Budantsev. (Fearing her own arrest, Pilnyak's wife left for Georgia to deposit their young son with her mother; she herself was arrested at the film studios in November and spent nineteen years in the camps before being amnestied in 1956.)[120]

Pasternak was convinced that his own turn would come, and false rumour of his arrest and sentence reached certain foreign journalists at about that time.[121] However, although the town apartments and villas of neighbours such as the Kataevs, Gerasimovs, Bespalovs, Marchenkos and others were gradually vacated, in summer of 1937 there were indirect signals that he was in no immediate peril: in the manner of that period he was called upon again to approve the sentence of other public figures charged with treason. (Pilnyak correctly read his own failure to be approached as an ill omen.)[122] The reassurance was not one calculated to rejoice Pasternak's heart however.

On 11 June, a Special Board of the Supreme Court passed capital sentence on a group of alleged military conspirators, including army commanders Robert Eideman (Pasternak's opponent in Minsk), Tukhachevsky, Uborevich, Yakir, and others.[123] Following the sentence, public support for the verdict was drummed up, and one afternoon an official appeared at the dacha soliciting Pasternak's signature to a collective letter. Pasternak almost physically assaulted the man, shouting: 'To sign this, one would have to know these people and know what they have done. I know nothing about them, I didn't give them life and I have no right to take it away. The state, not private citizens, should deal with people's lives. This is not like signing complimentary theatre tickets, and I refuse to put my name to this!' Pasternak ignored Zinaida's pleas that he sign at least for the sake of the child she was carrying; she was outraged at his cruelty although later appreciated his moral stand.

The writer Pavlenko next paid Pasternak a visit, calling him a 'little Jesus' and urging him to sign. Pasternak was also summoned by Stavsky to a meeting at another writer's dacha, but he refused to bend to threats. It was evident that Stavsky feared for himself, lest he be shown incapable of marshalling the membership under his authority. Kaverin later commented on Pasternak's courage in resisting this pressure. He apparently left the meeting with Stavsky with head held high, although Zinaida was convinced his arrest was inevitable, and she packed a small suitcase for this emergency. Pasternak claimed then to have written a letter to Stalin: 'I wrote that I had grown up in a family where Tolstoyan convictions were very strong. I had imbibed them with my mother's milk, and he could dispose of my life, but I did not consider I was entitled to sit in judgement over the life and death of others.' The following day, *Izvestiya* carried a heading: 'No Quarter for the Soviet Union's Enemies. Letter by Soviet Writers' with Pasternak's name among the signatories to the statement. Devastated, Pasternak immediately set off to Moscow again to protest to Stavsky at the cynical abuse of his name and to demand a correction. Stavsky shouted at him and said that to admit the fabrication would put the whole Union management in danger; he then ordered a car and sent Pasternak back home, with a request to Zinaida to make sure her husband stayed in and kept quiet. Naturally, no correction was made, nor was Pasternak's name removed when the letter was reprinted in *Literaturnaya gazeta*.[124] Yet Stavsky's action served a dual and partly good purpose: while protecting his own administrative hide, he saved Pasternak's life with conscience intact. The role of Pasternak's letter to Stalin amid all this remains imponderable; it was not answered and has not been found in any archive; it must at least have reinforced his status as a denizen of heaven.[125]

The events of 1936–37 corroborated the official (and Pasternak's own) view that there was virtually no role for him in public literary life. In late June 1937 he refused an offer from *Literaturnaya gazeta* to compose banalities on Chkalov's flight from Moscow to America via the Pole.[126] His obituary note on the Daghestani bard Suleiman Stalsky in November contained a cryptic reminder of the euphoric 1934 Congress and the enviably modest figure cut by Stalsky (although Pasternak and he were hardly comparable or kindred figures).[127] The year 1937 also saw the appearance of Pasternak's last pre-war books, a Goslitizdat reprint of *Lieutenant Shmidt* and *The Year 1905*, and an edition of *Georgian Lyricists*. The only new works to appear were occasional poetic translations and an extract of his new prose in *Literaturnaya gazeta* in December.

Pasternak's exclusion from the public life of his profession with its commitments and moral compromises came as a partial relief. The night after refusing to endorse the execution order of army commanders, he allegedly slept soundly.[128] Shortly afterwards and still under the impact of this he wrote:

> I have never felt so cheery or known such mental clarity as these last one and a half years. Never in occasional compulsive moments have I so despised myself – so physically unrealisable and technically inachievable have honesty and faith to oneself become, even in reality, as a *fait accompli*. It is like writing on water or in the air. No trace remains.[129]

In the autumn of 1937, however, his uninvolvement gave Pasternak a new sense of liberation. Two years before he was 'offended at the inevitability of existing in the form of an inflated and incommensurate legend'. Now that was over. 'I heaved such a sigh, stood so straight and recognised myself so well again when they began hounding me!'[130]

The Second Congress of Writers in Defence of Culture took place during 4–17 July 1937, moving from Valencia via Madrid to Paris. The Soviet panel was dominated by Fadeyev, Koltsov, Stavsky, Aleksei Tolstoy, Vishnevsky and other stalwarts. And while liberals such as Agniya Barto and Ehrenburg were also fielded, Pasternak was by now deemed unsuited to represent the Soviet state.[131] Meanwhile the suspicion of any personal foreign contacts interrupted even correspondence with relatives. Breaking silence at last on 1st October, 1937, Pasternak told his parents:

> You ought to have guessed that [. . .] my protracted silence had to have another

explanation than staleness of spirit or dark indifference to the nearest and dearest that I have in life – yourselves.

In reality the times are disturbed not just by family events. The tension creates such suspicion all around, that the very fact of a perfectly innocent correspondence with relatives abroad leads sometimes to misunderstand-ings and forces people to refrain from it. But I cannot totally renounce getting news of you or sending you some signs of my existence.[132]

In addition, as Pasternak wrote, in Moscow 'anything material is absolutely unrealisable'. Inter alia, this meant no progress with arrangements for Leonid's return to Moscow. Ambassador Suritz who had offered help was transferred to Paris, and Leonid's pictures were left in crates at the Soviet Embassy in Berlin.

Pasternak was by 1937 thoroughly disenchanted with marriage to Zinaida, aware of having ruined the lives of Evgeniya and his son, and 'like someone under a spell, as though I have worked some sorcery on myself'. As he wrote to his parents in February 1937, 'what can I say of my own life with this feeling and awareness? [. . .] For the moment there is only one thing within and close to me that is healthy: nature and my work.'[133]

Since 1935 when Zinaida had wanted a child and was treated for infertility, Pasternak had been reconciled to having no more family. Her sudden pregnancy in 1937 was thus no source of delight. As of 1936 abortion had been declared illegal, and but for this fact, as Boris told his parents, 'the inadequacy of our joy on this account would have given us pause and she would have resorted to this operation'. By the autumn of 1937, however, Pasternak became resigned to the permanence of their relationship:

This woman, pregnant in the seventh month, flogging herself, doing the roughest of work from morn to night without domestic help, tormented by all her earlier life, and also by me, gives me no occasion to hate or condemn her [. . .] Of course, I love her, but maybe not as easily, smoothly or primordially as is possible in an undivided family . . .[134]

Apart from Zinaida's condition, a new medical concern also arose in the autumn of 1937. Two years prior to that, Adrian Neigauz, a boisterous, handsome and sport-loving youngster, had injured his back while practising ski-jumping from the roof of the garage. Now, suddenly, he became pale and began losing weight; he was diagnosed as having a tubercular condition of the spine, which was to torment him for eight years and led to his early death. His younger brother Stanislav, more introverted and with a handsome pathos of expression, meanwhile made rapid progress as a pianist, studying at the famous Gnesin Music School and appearing already in school concerts.[135]

In view of Zinaida's condition, the Pasternaks moved into town in autumn

1937 and took up residence in their newly completed top-floor apartment at 17/19 Lavrushinsky Lane. With Zinaida incapacitated, Boris packed up their property on the Volkhonka and supervised the removal operation, which lasted ten days. Because of the smaller rooms at Lavrushinsky, some of the bulkier furniture was deposited with neighbours and with Boris Zbarsky. Not long after their removal, the whole wing of the Volkhonka house where they had lived was demolished.[136]

To avoid leaving the Peredelkino dacha empty, Pasternak arranged that Evgeniya and their son should live there over the New Year holiday period. Dmitrii Lyaskovsky, a young relative of Genrikh Neigauz who had lodged with them, stayed on at the dacha. He and Evgeniya struck up a liaison and afterwards lived together as man and wife at her apartment on Tverskoi Boulevard. Their partnership lasted only about a year, however, and thereafter she formed no more close attachments.[137]

The Pasternaks planned to see in the New Year of 1938 with their apartment neighbours, Vsevolod Ivanov and his family. However, at 7 pm on 31 December Zinaida went into labour and Boris took her to the Klara Zetkin Hospital. Later, at the Ivanovs, he heard by phone that on the stroke of midnight she gave birth to a healthy boy. The child was named Leonid after his grandfather, and as Pasternak announced to Raisa Lomonosova, 'he came into this world and landed straight in a glass of champagne'.[138] The timing of his birth occasioned a short paragraph in the paper *Vechernyaya Moskva*.[139] Owing to Pasternak's error in registering the birth as occurring at zero hours midnight on 1 January *1937*, Leonid became permanently credited with an extra year of life.[140]

7

Prose, Obscurity and 'Hamlet'

One morning in late September, Tonya asked me to take Shura out for a walk . . . So I took him by the hand and set out with him into the forest.

The dankness and dark immediately resounded with his exclamations. It was the chatter of his age, the trilling of his species. Standing as he did not a yard above the earth, his way of thought was shared by all earth's creatures. Suddenly he ran off and then called me to come. A young jackdaw with a trailing wing was hopping through the grass and stumbling as it tried to flutter upwards. At first it evaded us. But finally I stood up holding it. I folded its wings back and allowed its little hooded head to poke out from my cupped hands. I stood bending there for a long while, showing it to my son, then clutching it to my breast. My eyes were fixed on my hands which were filled by a little heart which I could feel pounding there through the down and feathers. When I straightened up and looked around, my eye could not adjust to the sudden change of posture. And it was then, almost for the first time, that I was struck by autumn's greatest marvel: the harmonious isolation of deciduous woods and evergreens. The former stood among black conifers that disappeared aloft like rising smoke, in the same way as an ornate gilded city's streets, rooftops and belfries are enclosed by a rainswept sky.

Twenty years have passed since that time. Twenty years that have fallen on the Revolution, that major event which has eclipsed all others. A new state has been born, undescribed and unprecedented. And it is Russia that has given birth to it, the same Russia caught up and then abandoned in my recollections . . .

from *Before Parting*

Nadezhda Mandelstam's *Second Book* of memoirs recalled that her contemporaries firmly believed that a poet made do with verse until he was ripe enough for prose, at which point he immediately graduated to a higher rank. Tynyanov, Eikhenbaum and Shklovsky mentioned the example of Pushkin, Lermontov and Gogol whose attention shifted to prose writing after their earlier poetic experience, and it was Tynyanov who announced that, overall, the time of prose had now come because the age of poetry was over.[1] A widespread 'gigantomania' that favoured extended works in prose was also encouraged by the doctrine of socialist realism, and even Pasternak was not altogether immune to this. At the time of his divorcement from literary life in the later 1930s, as he strove to maintain an artistic identity after the flow of verse had ceased, the novel represented for him 'a hunt for time past in order to find his own place amid the shifting current of the days and to fathom the meaning of this movement'.[2]

Pasternak's turn to prose had been encouraged and approved publicly by colleagues, including Fedin speaking at the formalist discussions of 1936. His own confidence in this new project even prompted him to announce it to *Novy mir*, and in its subscription renewal publicity the journal advertised a 'new novel' by Pasternak as a forthcoming attraction for 1937.[3]

Living alone in Peredelkino during the winter of 1936–37, Pasternak found that writing in prose came with difficulty however. As he complained in a letter, 'in verse I am always master of the situation and I know approximately in advance what will emerge and when. But here I cannot foresee anything, and with prose I never believe that it will turn out. It is my curse, and I am drawn towards it ever more strongly.'[4] In the woodland bliss of spring 1937, however, the work moved on apace, and Pasternak reported to his parents in mid May:

I now possess the nucleus, the blinding nucleus of what can be called happiness. It lies in that amazing, gradually accumulating manuscript which once again after an interval of many years puts me in control of something voluminous that systematically expands and accrues in a vital way, as though the vegetative system whose disruption two years ago caused my sickness, is now gazing at me from its pages, full of health, and is returning to me from there.

Unlike the prose *Story*, which he now dismissed as a 'decadent fragment', the new work was a 'large whole with more modest but more stable resources' and 'a more transparent form'. 'The whole time I keep thinking of Chekhov, and the few people I have shown anything to are reminded of Tolstoy', Pasternak announced.[5]

Even by mid 1937, however, it was apparent that the novel was some way from completion. Living in rustic retreat, Pasternak allowed himself a fairly leisurely lifestyle. Indeed, as he told his parents, without gathering firewood for the winter, walking in the open air, bathing in the nearby river Setun even in the first October frosts, and reading Michelet and Macauley, he might have found it impossible to work at all.[6]

On the last day of the year 1937, *Literaturnaya gazeta* carried a first extract from Pasternak's recent prose, entitled 'From a New Novel about the Year 1905'.[7] It described various incidents at the time of the revolution in

December 1905 as recalled from the narrator's childhood. The happenings include a fall from a wardrobe by the mistress of the house, Anna Gromeko, an invasion of the Gromeko family's backyard by armed workers fleeing from the dragoons, and the exploits of Aunt Olya, a politically active female relative. The setting and events were evidently based on Pasternak's memories of 1905. This published episode, along with other chapters written over the next two years, emerged as similar in some respects to the early parts of *Doctor Zhivago*.

A short note to *Literaturnaya gazeta* along with Pasternak's manuscript now explained that 'This year [i.e. 1938] I shall write the first part of a novel [. . .] in three parts. I don't know what it will be called. Part one will be about children.' A further three extracts appeared in the literary press over the next two years, and they included two Moscow childhood sequences and an episode set in the Urals during the First World War.[8] The corrected typescript of all these episodes was submitted in 1939 to *Znamya* magazine, but no further printings ensued. Provisional titles Pasternak jotted on the folder containing the typescript were: 'When the Boys Grew Up', 'Notes of Zhivult', and 'Notes of Patrik'. There may have been a hint here of Rilke's *Notes of Malte Laurids Brigge*, but the material clearly stemmed from autobiographical sources; the name 'Zhivult' on the other hand seems to prefigure 'Zhivago'.

The *Znamya* typescript, which was returned to Pasternak in 1956 from the archive of Vishnevsky, the former chief editor,[9] gives an impression of the general shape of Pasternak's scheme. Two introductory chapters, 'A District Behind the Lines' and 'Before Parting' show the first-person narrator reviewing events of 1916 from the vantage point of the 1930s.[10] During World War 1, the narrator, one of the Moscow intelligentsia, is in the Urals, living with his wife Tonya and young son Shura at the isolated dacha of his father-in-law Aleksandr Gromeko. In the nearby town of Yuryatin he makes the acquaintance of Evgeniya Istomina (whose maiden name was evidently Luvers); she agrees to rent the Gromeko dacha while the owner's family return to Moscow. The narrator's proposal to remain behind to assist Istomina alarms his family, who sense some impending act of infidelity. Here this narrative strand (clearly related to similar events in part two of *Zhivago*) breaks off however. Instead, one night, the hero falls into a 'living dream' (like the hero of the prose *Story*) in which he recalls incidents from his Moscow boyhood. The remaining chapters from Vishnevsky's typescript deal with these recalled incidents of family history and the revolution of 1905.

The setting of these 'Notes of Patrick' obviously derived from Pasternak's childhood and wartime experiences in the Urals. The Gromeko family were evidently based on the Garkavi-Ugrimovs who were well known to the

Pasternaks in the 1900s; aspects of their later fate, including banishment from Russia in 1922, were also incorporated in *Doctor Zhivago*.[11]

Looking ahead to Pasternak's later novel, the opening two chapters of the 'Notes' are clearly related to the Varykino and Yuryatin episodes, while the 'childhood' sections are identifiable with the Moscow chapters. Like the *Story*, however, the 'Notes' run up against an impassable narrative barrier with the year 1917. Some basic themes of *Zhivago* were still missing too: there was no indication of the central hero's 'quarrel' with his age, or of the fact that he was a poet or creative artist. Also, as Pasternak explained to Olga Petrovskaya, the 'Notes' were 'entirely based on plot, without philosophy'.[12]

The novel chapters as they survived in typescript do not suggest that this was an unpublished masterpiece. Yet Afinogenov, who heard Pasernak read some extracts in summer of 1937, found them 'superb' and singled out their 'concise phraseology, unusual imagery, simplicity, and sweep of events and range'. Pasternak invoked the spirit of Dickens, Tolstoy and Chekhov as he set to work on his novel, and the latter two were certainly present in his claim to Afinogenov that countered any modern cult of socialist heroics: 'The artist must be able to stop and be surprised at what he has seen. For him one does not need to fly across the Pole or rush to see many things [. . .] One needs to develop one's inborn capacity to see.'[13] Yet the 'Notes' seem disappointingly lifeless after the narrative exuberance of *Safe Conduct* and earlier stories. This was, however, a cultivated quality. As Pasternak told Lomonosova in April 1938, reviewing his winter's work, 'the boredom of it did not frighten me off, and I derived pleasure from the work'.[14]

With the onset of Adrian's illness and return to Moscow in autumn 1937, Pasternak set his novel aside in order to raise funds by translation work, since his now reduced publications had shrunk his earnings. Late in the year, he wrote Lydia in England asking her to send him *The Albatross Book of Living Verse*, edited by Louis Undermeyer (London, 1933), which she duly did and which served as one of his main English poetic sources. In the same letter he also recalled his first acquaintance with the English poets on the eve of World War 1:

The influence, say, of even Byron on Pushkin, Lermontov and their time was revealed to me from a new and unexpected angle. As always with artists, there is here a far greater influence of language, phonetics, speech structure, et cetera, than the impact of their ideas or worldview [..] The fact of English poetry's physical influence on our classics [. . .] appeared so striking to me that I thought poetry as such was English poetry, and in European history since the Renaissance it has occupied the position that Greece had for the ancients.'[15]

Pasternak's alertness to the physical 'feel' of poetic language was evident in his early verse described by Mandelstam in the 1920s (volume 1, 286–7) and some of the English and other poets he now lighted on to translate shared a 'textural' rather than philosophical kinship with him. Thus Keats's ode 'To Autumn' and sonnets 'On the Grasshopper and the Cricket' and 'On the Sea', or various items from Verlaine's 'La Bonne Chanson', 'Romances sans paroles', 'Langueur' and his famous 'Art poétique' from 'Jadis et Naguère' reflect writings from a kindred sensory poetic world – more so than his rendering of Byron's 'Stanzas to Augusta'.[16] Reported plans and even a signed contract in 1938 to translate Byron's *Don Juan* were never realised.[17]

The turn to small-scale works in translation during 1938 caused Pasternak few regrets, 'since it is sometimes useful to forget and benumb oneself with some persistent, rapidly changing and almost journeyman's task'. His menu was very varied, and included Georgian and German revolutionary verse and Hans Sachs; and there were plans for various French *symbolistes*, Blake and Spenser.[18] During 1938–9 *Literaturnaya gazeta*, *Ogonyok*, *Krasnaya nov'*, *Novy mir* and other periodicals carried several of these translations as well as reworkings of earlier pieces. Original new versions were made from the Spanish of Rafael Alberti (whom Pasternak met along with María Teresa León at Tabidze's Moscow recital on 4 March 1937). With Tabidze, Mitsishvili and Yashvili now tainted and unpublishable, Pasternak concentrated on translating some of Simon Chikovani. Other poetic translations included work by Johannes Becher, Sándor Petöfi, Tychina and Shevchenko, and Shakespeare's Sonnet 73 and two other short poems. Evgenii Pasternak recalled that Shevchenko's 'Maria', executed in folkloric vein, was one of his father's favourites, which he read at a Poets' Section recital on 25 December 1938.[19]

Pasternak's choices of text for the most part reflected his own tastes and enthusiasms. As one reviewer noted, 'overcome by a love for the poets translated, he has succeeded in conveying to the reader this superb creative excitement'.[20] Moreover, some translations were not just from poets 'congenial' to Pasternak; the selection of texts 'Aesopically' reflected moods and observations that would be quite out of place – 'decadent' or even adversarial – coming directly from a Soviet poet. Thus, for example, the naked religiosity of the nineteenth-century Shevchenko's invocation to the Virgin Mary, which included lines that inevitably formed a commentary on current Soviet events:

> O grievous sorrow of my heart!
> Not you I pity, hapless ones –
> The blind and beggarly of soul –
> But those who see above them raised
> Retribution's axe – yet forge

New shackles still. These murtherers
Will slay and kill, slaking their dogs
From bloodied fount.   (*SS*, II, 301)

The reviewer Abram Evgenyev courageously volunteered that this translation in particular was 'bound to play an even more vital part in Boris Pasternak's work than all his other translations'.[21]

Shakespeare's Sonnet 73 (translated in *Novy mir* no. 8 for 1938) strikingly captured a mortal man's autumnal sense of time and the need to 'love that well which thou must leave 'ere long'. Pasternak slightly altered this to make it refer to specifically human contacts. The translated sonnet in fact concludes with an exhortation:

. . . And seeing this, remember: beyond all price
Are trysts whose days are numbered.

There was thus an 'added' hint at memories of precious friends now hidden in what Sonnet 30 called 'death's dateless night'.[22] Over the next few years, translations of Shakespeare became a regular projected vehicle for Pasternak's own unspeakable thoughts.

Apart from innumerable executions with and without trial, the years 1938–39 saw an epidemic of denunciation, arrest and internment that placed some eight million in prison or labour camp, and left scarcely a family in which someone was not sentenced. Ilya Ehrenburg claimed to recall an encounter during this period one snowy night in Lavrushinsky Lane when Pasternak raised his hands to the sky and exclaimed: 'If only someone would tell Stalin about this!'[23] Pasternak for long clung to a delusion that the Leader was uninformed of what was happening, and various of his immediate entourage in Peredelkino, although people of great integrity, had a similar trust in the wisdom of the leadership.[24] The regime as a whole, however, Pasternak plainly saw to be corrupt and evil as more and more manifestly innocent friends or colleagues were swallowed by the security and punitive systems.

On 2 March 1938, began the 'Great Trial' of twenty-one accused – with Bukharin, Krestinsky, Rakovsky and Rykov as chief political figures in the dock. Charged along with them were Yagoda, former head of the NKVD, and a variety of minor and patently non-political figures: Kryuchkov, the former secretary of Gorky, now branded as an accomplice to his killing, and three doctors. Among the latter was the Pasternaks' former family physician, Dr Lev Levin, who as a member of the Kremlin Medical Commission had attended several prominent political figures and between 1928 and 1934 travelled regularly to Italy as Gorky's doctor. Levin was charged with a barely credible series of medical murders, including Menzhinsky, Gorky's son Maksim Peshkov, Kuibyshev and Gorky himself. The verdict, announced on 13 March, was a foregone conclusion, and only Rakovsky and two other minor figures escaped execution. Levin's elder son Vladimir, who had tried to defend his father, was also arrested and perished.[25] During the trial, at a time when they were shunned by all others, Pasternak showed innocent boldness in visiting Levin's other doctor son Georgii and his family in Mamonovsky Lane. There he told them of a meeting at the Writers' Union where a paper was passed round demanding death for the 'killer doctors' and 'anti-Soviet rightist Trotskyite bloc'. Everyone present apart from himself had signed.[26]

After two heart attacks in the autumn of 1937, Mandelstam managed via Stavsky's offices to go with his wife for a two-month stay at a sanatorium in Samatikha. They arrived there in March 1938, but before the end of their stay, on 2 May secret police arrested him and transported him away in a lorry. It was his final internment. In 1940 his brother received notification that he had died of heart failure in the GULag on 27 December 1938.[27]

In similar manner and at various times during 1937–8 many of Pasternak's literary and intelligentsia acquaintances disappeared. To find expression for this, not to mention the agony of a whole nation, was evidently beyond his powers, and he fought shy of this even in his later autobiography of the mid 1950s.[28] Akhmatova, however, did not tremble at the task, and she said as much to another woman waiting in line at one of the Leningrad prisons. In November 1939, on a visit to Moscow she read Pasternak some of her new verse (including, conjecturally, parts of her 'Requiem'). His response was: 'Now even dying holds no terrors . . .'[29]

There was barely a hint of public events in correspondence with friends or family. Sasha Freidenberg's arrest was alluded to in semi-code in a family letter, and when Sergei Spassky's wife was interned in 1938 Pasternak dared write only enquiring about his 'sick patient'.[30]

Meanwhile, after his final marginalisation in 1937, Pasternak's own position remained unchanged and, in that sense, secure. He still figured as signatory on various innocuous collective letters. His name appeared alongside others in celebrating Malyshkin's memory and in protest at Germany's annexation of Sudetenland. Fadeyev's protective eloquence also continued in the literary press, particularly after 1938 when he succeeded Stavsky as Union Secretary. At a November 1938 meeting of Moscow poets, for instance, he called for a halt to adulatory prancing before 'proletarians' such as Altauzen, Surkov and Zharov, and he named Pasternak along with Aseyev, Selvinsky and Lebedev-Kumach(!) as 'major poets who are able to help our young people to grow and who are bound to assist in forming poetic opinion'.[31] Similarly, in April 1939, at a Writers' Union Presidium meeting concerned with literary criticism Fadeyev stated in his speech:

It is not enough to condemn, praise and encourage. In each able and talented writer, in each work, one must be able to find a special, new individual element [. . .] Vsevolod Ivanov, Aseyev, Pasternak, Olesha, Babel, Kirsanov, Selvinsky, Leonov, Tvardovsky – each of them is a total and complete phenomenon in the field of literature.[32]

This statement was made only three weeks before the arrest of Babel himself, on 15 May. Of that, however, probably even Fadeyev had no inkling: Babel was evidently eliminated through having been too close to Ezhov whose period as head of the NKVD ended with his arrest and execution. This complection of events illustrated the limits of Fadeyev's power. While he could protect or damage reputations, and approve arrests, he was unable to prevent them if higher authority required them.

Owing to the risk of any links with abroad, Pasternak's foreign correspondence languished during the later 1930s. With Lomonosova he had no communication from spring of 1938 until after World War 2. Family letters to parents and sisters also became extremely rare, especially because of the suspicious link with Germany, and Pasternak wrote only one letter directly to his parents in 1938. More frequent messages to Lydia in England contained news that was of course relayed to Josephine and their parents.

By late 1938 Josephine and her husband and children had also moved to Britain. There they were later joined also by her parents who planned a last family visit before departing for Russia; all their belongings, including Leonid's pictures which had been stored at the Berlin Embassy, were therefore shipped to England. Although still not under direct threat from the Nazi regime, their position as Soviet citizens was increasingly uncomfortable, and they left Germany several months before the Molotov-Ribbentrop pact temporarily turned Nazi Germany and Soviet Russia into friendly powers.[33]

Josephine Pasternak's position was slightly different. As an Austrian citizen, her husband together with his Jewish family only came under threat after the Anschluß. Forced to sell off their house in Munich to the first-comer, Frederick and Josephine Pasternak in summer 1938 fled to join Lydia in England, as their nearest and most obvious refuge. (Impressions of this departure, of a Kristallnacht victim, and of arrival in England were later included in Josephine's second book *To Pedro's Memory* [*Pamyati Pedro*]).[34] Prior to leaving Munich, Frederick had flown to America to investigate the chances of employment and a home for himself and his family. The idea of leaving Europe was repugnant to Josephine, but Frederick insisted for their children's sake. However, their departure from Britain planned for August 1939 was delayed because of the American immigrant quota system and then prevented altogether by the outbreak of war. They thus stayed on in England where, for the second time in his life, Frederick was classified as a potential 'enemy alien' and spent a period in internment.[35]

Boris Pasternak's letter to Lydia of late October 1938 contained various family news – of Evgeniya's seemingly happy partnership with Lyaskovsky and summer holiday at Voloshin's old estate in Koktebel; Evgenii's academic successes, maturity and physical prowess; and the death of Genrikh Neigauz's very elderly father. Pasternak also made one of his ritual mentions of hoping shortly to obtain permission to visit his parents. Nothing of course emerged from this, and in less than a year world events removed all chance of family reunions.

After spending the spring and summer of 1938 at Peredelkino, in late September Zinaida and the children returned to town while Pasternak stayed on 'absolutely alone, without a house-help or even the dog' (the latter having been hit by a lorry and dispatched to the vet). At the end of October he wrote to Lydia reporting on his own life in the mouse-infested woodland villa, which was badly built, dilapidated and rotting after only three years. His activities consisted of a daily walk and bathe in the River Setun, collecting twigs for the kitchen stove, and writing – all in all a spartan lifestyle that Zinaida never relished, but which appealed to him and reminded him of family summers at Karzinkino during the Civil War. Just once a week, he travelled into Moscow by train for an overnight stay to see the family, collect mail, purchase supplies, and so forth.[36]

Apart from a love of country life and a sense of distance from Moscow public life with all its unpleasantness, Pasternak was able in winter 1938–9 to turn again to his interrupted prose novel. By January he reported 'seven or eight chapters copied out, three or four written in draft and requiring further working, several more in my head; the whole plot has been thought out, and although I cannot even formulate my chief difficulties, it's a disgrace that there is still no novel there (only talk) – that is, despite everything it has not been written down.' In early November, Pasternak was forced to down tools again, and moved back to Moscow. Nevertheless, several chapters were now finished and had been read to friends; a public reading of extracts formed his contribution to a Poets' Section evening on 25 December 1938, and two episodes found their way into print in December and January. Five chapters offered to *Krasnaya nov'*, however, were not published.[37]

The winter of 1938–39 was a period of near-total eclipse of Pasternak's official fame. This was driven home when in February the Supreme Soviet announced medal awards to no less than 172 writers. Akhmatova, Bulgakov, Platonov and Pasternak were not among them. Although Pasternak had sought to escape the laureate's limelight, to be passed over when so many nonentities were honoured was a slap in the face.[38] Protest was pointless of course, and it was not difficult to see this slight as a reprisal for his earlier protection by Bukharin and refusal to endorse various execution orders.[39] To drive home the point, Pasternak was snubbed a second time in February 1939 when the 25th anniversary of Aseyev's literary début was celebrated with official fanfare. He attended the ceremony and printed his congratulations 'To a Friend and Splendid Comrade'. Pasternak's own anniversary that same year was passed over in silence however, but as on other occasions he preferred a show of cordiality to Aseyev rather than exposure of his own hard feelings.[40]

In December 1937 Meyerhold's theatrical work was denounced in *Pravda* as ideologically bankrupt and as a slanderous distortion of Soviet life, and in January 1938 his theatre in Moscow was closed down.[41] Following this, Meyerhold moved to Leningrad to mount Lermontov's *Masquerade* at the Pushkin (former Aleksandrinsky) Theatre; a further Leningrad project he had in prospect was Shakespeare's *Hamlet*. Pasternak was approached for a new translation of this and he gladly accepted, part of the attraction being a renewed artistic link with Leningrad.

In order to familiarise Pasternak with his latest work, Meyerhold several times in winter 1938–9 proposed a joint trip to Leningrad to see *Masquerade* which opened in December. Pasternak each time declined, however, uncertain of the practical purpose.[42] Nevertheless, in the early New Year of 1939 he began work on the *Hamlet* translation and by late March had drafted two and a half acts (i.e. half of the whole), and an extract from the drama presentation at court (Act III, scene ii) appeared in an issue of *Ogonyok*.[43]

As Pasternak realised, there were probably already at least fifteen translations of Shakespeare, and of *Hamlet* in particular, and he perceived little necessity for a new version. On the other hand, as he told his parents in a letter of April 1939, 'if out of snobbery, or for some other reason, I am repeatedly approached with such an offer, why shouldn't I take advantage of this theatrical caprice, even if there is no hope of rivalling my predecessors? After all it is a pretext for me to go off and bury myself in Shakespeare, and this absorption – i.e. even slow reading – is in itself an incomparable treasure.'[44]

However, in translations 'there [were] trifles and major things'. In April 1939 Pasternak was forced to resort to the former in order to boost income again, since he had no major publications since 1937. To swell their earnings,

Zinaida also took on various music copying work, and Pasternak was observed forever wearing the same old tattered jacket (although even in more opulent periods he had a 'Tolstoyan' penchant for dilapidated clothing). Among the Peredelkino community the dramatist Pogodin, who at that time was prospering, also assisted with a cash loan,[45] and in a further effort to raise funds rapidly, Pasternak used German versions as a medium to produce a bouquet of translations from the Hungarian Romantic poet Sándor Petőfi, which were published in a June issue of *Literaturnaya gazeta*.[46] This he initially saw as a journeyman task, but he warmed to Petőfi as he recognised a kinship with the German Sturm und Drang poet Lenau and, through this, a common poetic heritage.[47]

In spring of 1939, the family move to Peredelkino was delayed. Their villa had originally been acquired with the return of Boris' parents in mind. Since this was no longer in immediate prospect, such ample accommodation was unnecessary. Zinaida had never liked the cavernous rooms; the damp and shaded site, hemmed in by trees, was also ill-suited for the vegetable garden that Boris longed to cultivate; furthermore, the whole location aroused painful memories of friends and neighbours recently arrested. Through the good offices of Pogodin who was then head of Litfond, Pasternak therefore arranged their removal to a smaller villa with a sunny setting, backing onto woods but with a southern view across ploughed fields towards the river Setun, church and cemetery. The new house – number 3 on what was later called Pavlenko Street – had been the home of author Aleksandr Malyshkin who had died in 1938. However it was in need of repair and redecoration.[48]

Zinaida went out to Peredelkino on 15 May to supervise the removal and organise the new household. Boris stayed on in town, partly, as he told his father, in order to investigate his chances of being permitted to visit his parents. Their letters over many years contained increasingly anguished requests for Boris to visit them. Now, with their removal to London (where they celebrated their golden wedding) and the seemingly imminent departure of Josephine and family for America, they once more implored Boris to visit them. His approaches were in vain however. As he told Leonid in May, 'You should not express doubt about my devotion and desire to see you – this torments me. I cannot provide an intelligent or exhaustive answer to these suspicions of yours. But if you are yourself unaware, ask other people and they'll tell you that it isn't in my power to prove such things.'[49] A further letter explained that without extraordinary petitions at highest level (unthinkable in the conditions of the time) there was no prospect of his being allowed to travel to Britain. Yet 'if some miracle like a foreign delegation descended on me, or a prize award, or some even crazier smile of fortune, no Hamlet would stop me and I would be ready in a trice.' In the absence of this, however, Pasternak suggested his parents reconsider the idea of returning to Russia – maybe at first without heavy baggage, and travelling by steamer through the Baltic.[50]

After a further few days in town, during which Evgenii stayed with his father while decorating went on at Evgeniya's, Pasternak joined his family at the new dacha in early July.[51] The bliss of this comfortable permanent home was described to his father:

I can tell you that this is what one might have dreamed of all one's life. Even seen from a distance [. . .] the views, the freedom, convenience, tranquillity and organisation of the place used to put one in a poetic frame of mind. The slopes stretching across the whole horizon like the course of some river, amid birch wood and with gardens and little wooden houses with mezzanines in Swedish-Tyrolean cottage style, which one could glimpse at sunset from a railcarriage window, used to make you lean out and gaze back at this settlement with its atmosphere of unreal and enviable splendour. And suddenly life has turned out in such a way that in my decline I too have been plunged into this gentle, eloquent colourful setting which I once used to view from a distance.[52]

All this, plus flexible arrangements for paying a very nominal rent, made the move to the new Peredelkino villa highly gratifying. In addition Peredelkino had an attractive sense of community, with congenial neighbours in the persons of Konstantin Fedin and Vsevolod Ivanov. As the latter's son recounted, although their lifestyle had a certain quality of 'Feast in Time of Plague', his parents, the Afinogenovs, Fedins, Leonovs, and the Selvinskys who in those years exchanged notes and met at one another's villas for discussion and reading formed something akin to the literary circles of olden days. These people now framed Pasternak's existence, replacing his now vanishing reading public and the tainted official entourage of the Writers' Union. Indeed, while shunning the trappings of popular fame, Pasternak still relied on a congenial group of literary people as his public, 'audience', 'resonator', and moral support.[53]

Despite life's pleasant setting, various events – both distant and close at hand – made the summer of 1939 one of tragedy in more than one sense. Translation work was resumed in May at Lavrushinsky Lane and continued at Peredelkino. Although interrupted at various points and absorbed by sporadic gardening activity, Pasternak steeped himself in Shakespeare and completed a draft of *Hamlet* in August. He had finally given up smoking altogether, but the narcotic effect of physical and mental exertion helped innure him to the summer's bitter news.[54]

On 20 June 1939 came report of the arrest of Meyerhold; this followed the

All-Union Conference of Stage Directors, at which he came under blistering attack and replied with a caustic dismissal of the achievements of the Soviet socialist theatre.[55] Subsequently, less than a month later, his actress wife Zinaida Raikh was found murdered and horribly mutilated in their Moscow apartment. Details of the crime, committed with NKVD connivance, emerged only when files were opened in the later 1980s. Meyerhold himself was tortured, tried *in camera* on 1 February 1940, and executed next day. Subsequently it emerged that Fadeyev was party to his denunciation as a 'foreign agent', just as he personally approved the arrest of Spassky and many others.[56] Under savage torture Meyerhold apparently admitted to a series of non-existent crimes that implicated other innocents. Pasternak at the time knew nothing of this, but his own name was deeply involved; when in 1955 the military procurator Boris Ryazhsky, who dealt with posthumous rehabilitations, examined the Meyerhold and Babel files, he was amazed that Pasternak had remained at liberty.[57] Quite apart from the Meyerhold affair, however, by 1939 it was generally perceived that he was a marked man and dangerous to associate with; it was at this stage that Tarasenkov abandoned making diary notes of his meetings and conversations with Pasternak.[58]

At Streatham Hill in London, England, Rozaliya Pasternak died on 23 August, two days after suffering a stroke. Four bouts of influenza the previous winter had left her considerably weakened, although shortly before her death she played in Schumann's Piano Quintet at a house concert arranged by one of the directors of the British Museum.[59] The Moscow Pasternaks learned of her death via a postcard sent by Lydia. Boris himself was devastated, although his first response to the family in England was written only on 10 October, delayed as he explained by 'bitter and strange circumstances' surrounding him about which he could not write (an allusion to recent arrests and other tragedies). Unlike Boris, who never celebrated family members in verse, Josephine Pasternak wrote a moving lament on 'Mother's Death' ('Smert' materi'), which was followed by over ten years of poetic silence.[60]

The outbreak of war resolved various questions about the Pasternaks' fate in Britain. Leonid could not now return to Russia; all thought of exhibitions or transporting his works to Moscow was abandoned, and he eventually arranged for his legacy of pictures to be shared among his children. When Rozaliya died, Lydia and family were planning to move to Oxford, and space had been set aside for her parents in the large terrace house at 20 Park Town, which was where Leonid spent the last six years of his life. Frederick and Josephine too resolved in early August to remain in Britain. They moved to a rented apartment in Oxford close to Lydia, eventually purchasing a house at 18 Carey Close, not far from the Woodstock roundabout. Rozaliya's ashes were meanwhile brought to Oxford and the urn deposited in the columbarium of a local crematorium.[61]

Although frank exchanges were impossible, Boris' ominously evasive letters and report of Russian events from other sources had given his parents pause over returning to Moscow. Others were less warned, more credulous or else persuaded by patriotic nostalgia. One such innocent was Marina Tsvetaeva. She arrived in Moscow with her son on 18 June 1939, to be greeted by news that her sister Anastasia was in prison. Her husband Sergei Efron and daughter Ariadna who returned in 1937 had kept the news from her, lest she be dissuaded from returnng. Efron himself was ill but drew a small salary for services rendered to the NKVD while in France and he was maintained under a cover name at Bolshevo near Moscow. Ariadna stayed with him and worked as an interpreter for VOKS. It was in Bolshevo that Marina and her son were now reunited with their family.

The inadvisability of Tsvetaeva's return at such a juncture tempered whatever pleasure Pasternak felt at her appearance. In fact they met only once during summer of 1939, when she called bringing him her latest verse; in order not to blow Efron's cover she explained that she had been instructed to live incognito and avoid seeking any literary prominence.[62] Then, on the night of 27 August, Ariadna Efron was arrested. Tortured and charged with espionage, she was sentenced to eight years' hard labour. Following this, Sergei Efron was arrested on 10 October and, as later emerged, he was shot on 16 October 1941.[63] The need for the incognito was thus removed. Pasternak visited Tsvetaeva at Bolshevo in early November, and shortly after that she came to Moscow and lodged for a time with her sister-in-law. In Moscow, Pasternak introduced her to Evgeniya and Evgenii, when she behaved with well-bred restraint and modesty. He arranged meetings with Kruchenykh, Maria Yudina and various other literary contacts, and also took her to Goslit publishers, introduced her to Chagin and Ryabinina, and some translation work was promised. In addition, Pasternak appealed on Tsvetaeva's behalf to Fadeyev, requesting she be admitted to Litfond so as to guarantee some material security. The suggestion was angrily rejected, and her own personal approach to Fadeyev for help with her archive and accommodation was answered only by a suggestion that she rent quarters out of town at Golitsyno and try earning her way by translations.[64]

On 1 September 1939, Nazi Germany invaded Poland, leading to the declaration of war by Britain and France. With a German alliance that freed his hand, Stalin in November invaded Finland. During spring and summer of 1940,

Soviet forces occupied and annexed the Baltic countries and incorporated the eastern part of Poland and Romania. Hitler in the West meanwhile invaded Denmark, Norway, Holland, Belgium and began the invasion of France.

Although disquieted by these events, which spelled danger to his own relatives, Pasternak kept track of developments only in a general way. He neither read the press nor listened to the radio, but picked up the essentials from others, including the ten-year-old son of his neighbours the Ivanovs. Because of prolonged sickness as a child, Vyacheslav (or 'Koma') Ivanov read widely and was unusually well informed on a multitude of subjects; his precocious intelligence made him an early confidant of Pasternak's and later took him on to a scholarly career of high distinction.[65]

Pasternak's removal from foreign, family, and even local events was assisted by the location of Peredelkino and by his absorption with *Hamlet*, despite the fact that all chance of a Leningrad performance vanished with Meyerhold's arrest, and Pasternak admitted to Olya Freidenberg his own fear that 'some accident could prevent my bringing the translation to completion'.[66] To his father he described the work as a rendering of 'thoughts, situations, pages and scenes of the original, not individual words and lines. The translation is utterly simple, smooth, comprehensible at first hearing and natural. In a period of false rhetorical bombast the need for ardent, direct and independent speech is great, and without thinking I have yielded to this need.'[67]

By the autumn of 1939, Pasternak completed and polished his *Hamlet* and gave various readings from it to friends and interested theatre people. On the upper floor of the Ivanovs' villa next door lived the dramatist Trenyov. In his quarters Pasternak gave one of the first of these readings. Vsevolod Ivanov recalled that everyone was rivetted by its poetry and power, and by Pasternak's seeming transformation into an embodiment of the tragic hero as he sat there reading. Leonidov from the Moscow Arts Theatre recalled: 'And do you know, he himself is Hamlet! *He* should do the acting, and I'll do the producing.'[68] This identification of hero and translator was more than just a felicitous chance remark. For the next two decades the figure of Hamlet came to symbolise Pasternak's own predicament in real life.

Vsevolod Ivanov reported on Pasternak's translation to friends at the Moscow Arts Theatre where a production of *Hamlet* had been in prospect since the previous year, and Anna Radlova had been commissioned to produce a new translation. In November Pasternak gave a reading of his version in two installments for members of the company. At the first of these, veteran producer Nemirovich-Danchenko was so overwhelmed that while insisting Radlova should receive her full fee, he decided against using her version in production.[69] Writing to appease her, he explained that Pasternak's version was 'exceptional in its poetic qualities' and undoubtedly 'a literary event', and this being the case, the Arts Theatre could not pass up the opportunity.[70]

Pasternak's second reading session on 18 November, when the final three acts were presented, reinforced the original impression. The entire company were gripped by Pasternak's air of detached concentration, and he himself relived that 'supreme, incomparable pleasure of reading even half of it aloud and without cuts. For three hours one feels human in the highest sense'.[71] Nemirovich-Danchenko, who recalled earlier meetings with Leonid Pasternak, struck Boris as a sprightly '84-year-old scamp in boots and gaiters, with rounded beard and face without a wrinkle'.[72] He supervised the drawing up of a contract, which was signed up on 27 November 1939. The foundation was thus laid for several years of collaboration between Pasternak and the Moscow Arts Theatre. In particular he became friends with the secretary and head of the literary section Vitalii Vilenkin, whom he met at Neigauz's Beethoven recital on 13 November, and with Boris Livanov who was slated for the role of Hamlet.[73]

Although the translation was substantially ready, some fine-tuning and polishing were necessary. Nemirovich-Danchenko had some minor reservations and comments, for instance, about the need for an equilinear version and the lowering of the register in Pasternak's reading of certain dialogue passages. Such details were ironed out during the winter of 1940 with Vilenkin acting as courier between the theatre and translator. Although standing firm on some issues, Pasternak agreed with alacrity to most of Nemirovich's suggestions and incorporated them. This process became part of the final polishing of a book edition of *Hamlet* which was published by Goslit in 1941.[74]

8

World War and Evacuation

'False Alarm'

From early dawn – confusion
With buckets, troughs and pails,
Then onset of dank evenings
And sunset through the rain,

And after nightfall – choked-
Back tears and heaving sighs,
A locomotive signal
From sixteen versts up-line.

And over yard and garden
An early dusk draws in;
A host of small calamities . . .
September time again.

The autumn's noontide vastness
Is rent by howls of grief
And keening from the graveyard
That lies beyond the stream.

And when across the knoll
A widow's sobbing carries,
I'm with her heart and soul
And stare death in the face.

And from the hallway window
I see, as every year,
The long delayed approach
Of my own final hour.

Its pathway cleared, the winter
Through yellow stricken leaves
Now stares down from the hilltop.
Its gaze is fixed on me

(1941)

Despite Pasternak's literary marginalisation, his approaching fiftieth birthday in 1940 was officially noted. He accidentally discovered that the Writers' Union was planning a celebration, but the memory of the previous year's snub had not faded, and with some effort he managed to dissuade them from their plan. He had no intention of holding a private celebration either, and arranged to be out all day from the Lavrushinsky Lane apartment.[1] With the deadline approaching for delivery of the revised version of *Hamlet*, he spent 10 February working at the Arts Theatre in Kamergersky Lane, and that evening attended a Chopin recital by Vladimir Sofronitsky. The *Hamlet* manuscript was handed over on the 14th.[2]

In early 1940 Pasternak also paid hommage to another unappreciated literary celebrity. Along with many from the Arts Theatre he was grieved by news of Bulgakov's terminal illness. He had visited him on his sickbed, although their long private conversation went unrecorded. Later, after Bulgakov's death on 10 March, Pasternak was one of several actors, artists and writers in the guard of honour as his coffin stood in the Union of Writers.[3]

Much of the year 1940 passed under the sign of Hamlet. Pasternak gave a reading of his translation at the Writers' Club on 19 April. Tsvetaeva arrived for this slightly late, and garbed in a full black dress like Agnessa Kun and other 'camp widows'; as she appeared, Pasternak stopped reading and went down to kiss her hand and usher her to a seat before continuing. His translation was rapturously received both on that occasion and at a later reading at Moscow University.[4]

There were also discussions and plans for readings in the Georgian capital and Leningrad, although these failed to take place. The Leningrad date on 30 May and a long-awaited reunion with the Freidenbergs were cancelled a few days beforehand when Pasternak was hospitalised with an attack of radiculitis; hopes of rescheduling the visit for the autumn fell through.[5] Meanwhile, an offer came from Radio Moscow for a fifteen-minute broadcast in English in which Pasternak would discuss his personal view of Shakespeare and recent translation. In 1939 he had taken English conversation lessons, but later gave them up through lack of time; now, in fear of showing up his defective English he turned down the broadcast offer.[6]

Pasternak became acutely concerned in the spring and early summer of 1940 at news of the Nazi advance into Belgium, France and Holland, with an increasing threat to Britain where his family were. As he told cousin Olya Freidenberg, he had 'mentally said farewell to all that I loved and all that was lovable in Western Europe's traditions and aspirations. I mourned for this and buried it, and my own family along with it.'[7] A pungent reflection on this funereal motif occurred in one of the new items included in the edition of

Pasternak's *Selected Translations* that appeared in autumn of 1940. Along with Kleist's *Prince Friedrich of Homburg* (now approved after the the Molotov–Ribbentrop pact),[8] Shrovetide playlets by Hans Sachs, and various short poetic translations from Becher, Byron, Keats, Walter Raleigh, Petöfi, Verlaine, and Shakespeare, there was a new version of the latter's Sonnet 66.[9] The poem's relevance to the Russian situation was eloquently apparent, opening with a line: "Tir'd of all these, for restful death I cry', and enumerating woes that include 'right perfection wrongfully disgrac'd, / And strength by limping sway disabled, / And art made tongue-tied by authority, / And folly (doctor-like) controlling skill, / And simple truth miscall'd simplicity'. In Pasternak's version, this sonnet acquired a richly emblematic significance for Russian readers with their suffocated sensibilities. A sign of this was Shostakovich's choice of this text for one of his *Six Romances on Verses by English Poets*, Opus 62, composed and premiered in 1942.[10]

Pasternak's main ambition in 1940 was to see public performance of 'his' *Hamlet*. As he told cousin Olga, the work would start to pay dividends only eighteen months after it went on stage.[11] The first production, in 1940, was in fact by the Red Torch Theatre of Novosibirsk. Work on Moscow Arts Theatre productions rarely moved rapidly however. Further revisions were requested in winter 1940–41; rehearsals were then halted on Russia's entry into the war in summer 1941; work was resumed in 1943, and after Nemirovich-Danchenko's death in April of that year they continued under Sakhnovsky.[12] Meanwhile, stage production was overtaken by publications of Pasternak's *Hamlet*, which themselves were literary events.

A printing of the 'arras' scene, no. 4 of Act III, in the monthly *Tridtsat' dnei*, in spring 1940 was followed by a complete version in *Molodaya gvardiya*.[13] The latter was prefaced by Pasternak's own note 'From the Translator' which described how his first drafts frequently coincided with earlier versions by Kroneberg, K. R. (Grand Prince Konstantin Romanov) and others. Pasternak praised Radlova's version of 1937 for its lively authentic dialogue and Lozinsky's, of 1933, for its accuracy and discipline.[14] His own method, however, instead of translating 'words and metaphors' was a 'rendering of thoughts and scenes':

The work should be judged as an original Russian dramatic work because apart from its accuracy, equilinearity with the original, etc., it contains more of that intentional liberty without which there can be no approach to great things. (*III*, 191; *SS*, IV, 386)

This first journal version of the play was essentially the text Pasternak prepared at the request of Meyerhold, and it differed substantially from all later book versions. It was also the redaction Pasternak preferred, and the one to which (as he wrote in a drafted note) he referred 'readers with taste and under-standing, able to distinguish truth from illusion'.[15] Shortly after the *Molodaya gvardiya* edition came out, in spring of 1940, Pasternak handed in to Goslitizdat the manuscript he had prepared 'under pressure of necessity' – that is, belletrised and 'purified' of lower-register expressions and nineteenth-century elements in line with Nemirovich-Danchenko's recommendations. This 'theatrical' version appeared in book format in May 1941 and served as the basis for all subsequent editions, which were variously modified in defer-ence to recommendations from various Shakespeare scholars and editors.[16]

Pasternak's suggestion that his *Hamlet* translation be viewed as an original Russian dramatic work hinted faintly at the play's problematic role in Russian culture. For a century and a half, performances of it had subversively implied a challenge to autocracy. Vilyam-Vilmont's review of Pasternak's version recalled how Catherine the Great banned performance of Sumarokov's version because the hero's predicament was too redolent of the heir and future Tsar Paul's situation.[17] Undesirable allusions were also discovered in the play during the early reign of Alexander I,[18] and more recently a subversive undercurrent in Akimov's production with music by Shostakovich at the Vakhtangov Theatre in 1932 had been transparently obvious to Stalinist cultural vigilantes.[19]

Aside from any political implications, the phenomenon of Hamletism figured in Russian nineteenth- and early twentieth-century letters, as in other European countries.[20] Despite what Sollertinsky described as the 'de-ideologi-sation' of European Hamletism,[21] Shakespeare's archetype of the brooding, frustrated idealist was at variance with the standard buoyantly combative image of Soviet socialist heroism. It also had some common features with acquired traits of Pasternak's personality and his cast of literary characters. His empathy and enthusiasm for *Hamlet* had emerged in 1924 when he first contemplated translating the play (volume 1, 336). Fifteen years later, under his hand the image was re-ideologised. Although a printed version of his ideas on the Shakespeare plays appeared only in 1946, it seems probable that his perception of a hidden strength and religious motivation in the character and role of Hamlet occurred at the time of his first work on the translation:

From the moment of the ghost's appearance, Hamlet renounces himself in order to 'do the will of him who sent him'. *Hamlet* is not a drama of characterlessness, but one of duty and self-sacrifice. When it emerges that appearance and reality do not coincide but are divided by a gulf, it is of no import that the reminder of this world's falsehood comes in supernatural form and that a ghost demands Hamlet's revenge. It is far more important that the will of fate elects Hamlet to be the judge of his own time and the servant of a more distant one. *Hamlet* is a drama of exalted calling, imposed heroic task, entrusted destiny.[22]

A view of this religious motivation was later expounded also in the poem 'Hamlet' from *Doctor Zhivago*. Already, though, the coincidence of this interpretation with Pasternak's stance in the late 1930s and on the eve of war was eloquent enough.

Although there were private critics of Pasternak's *Hamlet*, such as Kornei Chukovsky,[23] there were repeated public plaudits from authoritative readers such as Shakespeare scholar Mikhail Morozov and Nikolai Vilyam-Vilmont. Some of Nemirovich-Danchenko's reservations about the use of substandard language were reflected in a critique by Reztsov, while B. Solovyov regarded Pasternak's *Hamlet* as less suited to the realistic Moscow Arts tradition than to the Vakhtangov Theatre.[24] Even negative observations, however, detracted little from Pasternak's perceived achievement with his Russian *Hamlet*, which continued to be regularly reissued with only minor modifications.

During the winter 1939–40 Marina Tsvetaeva lived out of town, at Golitsyno where the Writers' Union had a resort and restaurant facilities she and her son could use. For the summer of 1940 she was able to move to the Herzen Street apartment of art expert and scholar Aleksandr Gabrichevsky while he and his wife were on holiday in the south.[25] The latter arrangement was negotiated by Nikolai Vilyam, who was one of many new friends she acquired via Pasternak, including Genrikh Neigauz, the Asmuses, Elena and Evgenii Tager. Pasternak cajoled Vilyam into doing much of the footwork, while he himself was available with practical advice, moral support, and a financial lifeline. However, there was no day-to-day close communion of brother and sister poets; even more remote were Tsvetaeva's earlier friendships with Antokolsky, Ehrenburg, and after her return she became closer with her new set of friends.[26]

Pasternak's introduction of Tsvetaeva to Goltsev produced some welcome translation work from Georgian, Spanish and Yiddish, which helped maintain her during the Golitsyno winter.[27] When she complained of her laborious progress, Pasternak advised a less 'committed' and more pragmatic approach so as to maintain the hundred lines or more per day that justified such activity; his counsel was not well accepted by one used to perfection.[28]

Despite Pasternak's fruitless initial approach to the Writers' Union, Fadeyev later called 'by chance' at his villa where Tsvetaeva was able to put her case again informally. Following this, she wrote an official letter to Union secretary Pavlenko taking special care to avoid her habit of using *ancien régime* orthography, and Pasternak appended his own supportive note; Pavlenko received her courteously but refused to assist.[29] Thereupon Zinaida Pasternak herself went the rounds of various neighbours collecting funds to assist Tsvetaeva rent accommodation. In September, after half a year of 'squatting', she found an affordable but cramped and dingy flatlet on Pokrovsky Boulevard.[30]

In July 1940 Nina Tabidze came to stay as a house guest at Peredelkino while making attempts to file an appeal on behalf of her husband. Pasternak took an active part in this and evidently wrote to petition Beria. Later in the year, he himself framed a further letter of appeal which Nina signed. Well practised in this genre, he also supported Tsvetaeva's resolve to appeal to Beria for her husband and daughter. Needless to say, nothing came of any of these approaches.[31]

The year 1940 saw more frequent contacts between Pasternak and Akhmatova. She shared with Tsvetaeva the predicament of being an unpublished poetic master as well as that of mother and spouse of innocent purge victims. Later, through Pasternak's intermediacy Tsvetaeva met Akhmatova on the latter's trip to Moscow in June of 1941; despite their common ground and two days of intense communion, however, this was yet another of Tsvetaeva's 'non-meetings'.[32] In later 1940, however, there were hints of an improvement in both women's professional standing. Encouraged by friends, Tsvetaeva put together a collection of verse and offered it to Gosizdat publishers, but its prospects were killed by a savage reader's report, in the spirit of the times, by Kornelii Zelinsky.[33]

After the start of World War 2, there were unexpected and unaccountable liberal events in literature, including publications such as Shklovsky's book on Mayakovsky,[34] and a new retrospective volume of Akhmatova's collected verse *From Six Books (Iz shesti knig)* released in May of 1940, as well as individual poems published in the journals *Zvezda* and *Leningrad*. This gladdening news of Akhmatova reached Pasternak while he lay in hospital; later he borrowed a copy of her book from Fedin his neighbour. In July he wrote Akhmatova a letter expressing admiration and gratitude for 'this embodied miracle', and indignation at Pertsov's panning of the book; he also sent a list of page references to personal favourite passages.[35] Akhmatova was touched, but mistakenly saw his concentration on her early 'classical' pieces as proof of his own self-absorption and as evidence that he had only just read her work properly for the first time: 'Dear, naive, adorable Boris Leonidovich!' In fact Pasternak had merely re-expressed the thrill of rereading what had delighted him back in 1915.[36]

In August 1940 Akhmatova turned up again in Moscow for five days, two of which she spent as Pasternak's guest. In Peredelkino she spoke with Fadeyev soliciting support in what proved a vain suit to release her son Lev Gumilyov. That autumn Pasternak wrote her a touching letter of sympathy in her sorrow:

Can I do anything at all to cheer you even a little and interest you, in this newly encroaching darkness, whose shadow I also tremulously feel on myself each day? How can I adequately remind you that to live and want to live (not anyhow, but in your own way) is your duty to those who are alive, because ideas of life are easily ruined and rarely supported by anyone, and you are their chief creator . . .

Urging her never to cease hoping, Pasternak observed that 'As a true Christian, you are bound to know this. [. . .] Do you know the value of your hope and how you must preserve it?'[37] This emphasis on the comforts of Christianity was another sign of his own evident move towards active religious belief during the war period,[38] and it came close in time to recognition of features in *Hamlet* indicating a Christian sense of mission.

Akhmatova shared Mandelstam's view of translation. In 1940, and despite Pasternak's intoxication with the success of *Hamlet*, she observed that 'nothing destroys one's own verse like translating someone else's'. She also regarded Pasternak's marital and domestic scene as inimical to creativity, and her August impression was that things were now even worse than on her last visit: 'Now he is sullen. He says he was getting set to write some verse but didn't manage to. "First of all Zina was getting ready to leave for the Crimea [. . .] and then the cucumbers ripened . . . I had to lay in a store of barrels . . . then steam the barrels . . ."'[39]

As the epitomy of non-domesticity and an admirer of gardens rather than of gardening, Akhmatova little understood the importance of such activities to Pasternak – not just therapeutically, but as an active stimulus to creativity. Before Zinaida left for Feodosiya to bring the boys back from summer camp, Boris and she had both enthusiastically tilled their plot of land. She had watched as Boris 'dug the earth with rapture and worked in the kitchen garden. As he worked he shed his clothes and acquired a suntan wearing only his shorts. Before dinner he would take a cold shower, afterwards he would relax for an hour then sit down to his translations.'[40] In 1940–41 the results of this labour were huge crops of potatoes, cucumbers, cabbage and other staple vegetables that largely fed the family for two winters. Furthermore, in the summer setting of Peredelkino Pasternak enjoyed what Olya Freidenberg described as his 'seventh youth': after a long fallow period of translation, he now began drafting new original work.[41]

In summer of 1940 Pasternak returned again to his novel. As he told Evgeniya in July:

In the first instance I was struck by how I had forgotten how to write, but then I was drawn to it, and now with my usual former passion I tremble over every hour devoted to my work. It's the same novel again, and at best I'll either finish it, or push it forward or to one side.[42]

In fact, again, nothing was finished, and the following year Pasternak took part of the incomplete manuscript away with him when he was evacuated.[43]

The most important product of the summer was a new flow of lyric verse that continued for the next three years. The first two poems appeared as a pair in the January 1941 issue of *Molodaya gvardiya* . Entitled 'Summer' ('Leto') and 'The City' ('Gorod'), in revised form they composed the nucleus of the 'Peredelkino' cycle completed the following spring. 'Summer' (later renamed 'Summer's Day') describes the luxurious fulfilment of the poet's day in the garden with the sun firing his tanned body covered in a potter's glaze, followed by a night when the mezzanine window 'will fill me like a ladle / With water and with flowers' (III, 233; *SP*, 608; *SS*, II, 147.) The poem reinstates nature as a central thematic axis. 'The City' too offers a poet's view of the metropolis from a snow- and ice-bound countryside, where winter represents 'not a season of the year / But ruin and the end of time'. The poem rehearses a familiar Pasternakian theme of the city as an incarnation of history and human activity. Marked by a sense of eternity in contrast to nature's changeability, the city 'seems immortal to these thickets: / Here – spruce and fir-cones; there – whole eras' (III, 235; *SS*, II, 152.) Recent bitter happenings in the city are unmentioned, but this is not a form of silent acceptance. As in the 'Space' or 'Expanse' viewed from Khotkovo in 1927, the poet contemplates a general historical vista greater than the sum of particular tragic events (volume I, 414–15).

In summer of 1940 Adrian's health became a new source of concern, especially to his mother. While at the Young Pioneers' camp in Koktebel he was hospitalised with pleurisy and Zinaida travelled down to bring both boys back; subsequently Adrian spent a further month in the Kremlin section of the Botkin Hospital. Doctors advised several months' convalescence, but he was allowed back to school in autumn and Zinaida and her two sons lived at the Lavrushinsky apartment. Adrian however continued running a temperature and suffering fatigue, which eluded diagnosis until examination of a purulent swelling on his left foot established that he had osseous tuberculosis. It took another six months of effort to get him admitted to the 'Red Rose' tubercular clinic at Balashikha near Moscow.[44]

Pasternak meanwhile wintered in Peredelkino and a nursemaid Marusya helped look after three-year-old Leonid. It was a time of happiness and fulfilment in tune with nature and the minute particulars of a careful and laborious routine. Slip up for an hour and the house gets so cold that no furnace will warm it. If you stand gaping, the potatoes start to freeze or the cucumbers go mouldy. All this has its own breath and aroma, it is all alive [. . .] And the trips into town, waking before six in the morning and walking over three kilometers through the nightbound field and woods, and the wintery rail track [. . .] and the flare of the morning train for which you arrive late and which overtakes you as you emerge from the woodland clearing to cross the line. Oh, how relishing the life is here . . .[45]

The predawn visions of countryside, trains and people found their way into several new poems of spring 1941. Pasternak's winter sorties into Moscow in late 1940 were usually for his twice weekly meetings with Vilenkin at the Moscow Arts Theatre. As production work on *Hamlet* continued, there were further requests for minor changes and revisions.[46]

The enjoyment of solitary life, absorbed in work and living close to nature was intensified during the winter. Details of the Pasternaks' new round of marital difficulties were never spelled out, but the incompatibilities noted already were the probable cause. In February, after a quarrel, Pasternak parted from Zinaida. As he told his cousin, 'I was tormented a little, but then I was again struck by the noise and numbing quality of freedom, its liveliness, movement and variety. This world right next to us – where does it vanish to when we are not alone? I was transformed and I believed again in the future. I was surrounded by friends. Unexpected things began happening.' Maybe matters would have long remained like that but for news of Adrian's worsening condition. A sense of duty again took Pasternak back to Zinaida and relations were patched together.[47]

When Akhmatova next visited Moscow, in June of 1941, Pasternak read her an almost complete new cycle of poems. It seemed to her that his reunion with nature had helped him overcome a long poetic silence.[48] What Pasternak produced was not pure landscape poetry, but a celebration of the healthy interaction between nature and human life. The poet takes his example from thrushes ('Drozdy') who fill the landscape with music and live there in the copse as performing artistes should live; lying on their backs beneath the trees, the poet and his companion are 'counted among the pines' assembly' ('Sosny'); later on the winter's stare through 'yellow stricken leaves' is a reminder of delayed autumn in the poet's own life. ('Lozhnaya trevoga')[49]

Most of the poems in the cycle were about nature, or human activity in a frame of nature, and only indirectly about public issues. In some ways this was a return to a pre-*Second Birth*. To his cousin Pasternak explained in May 1941 that 'after fifteen or more years I again feel as I did then, my everyday work is on the boil in all its former spontaneity, when it is totally natural, without the feeling of being focussed on the whole country'.[50] Broader, 'national' issues were not excluded however. Indeed a new patriotic sense emerged in 'On Early Trains' ('Na rannikh poezdakh'), which later gave its title to an entire book in 1943. With boots squeaking in the snow, and surveyed by starry constellations from the cold pit of January, the poet makes his way to catch the 6.25 am Moscow-bound commuter train. Once on board, he observes his fellow passengers, and 'through many past vicissitudes and years of war and poverty' he silently recognises the 'incomparable traits of Russia'. These features are incarnate in peasantwomen, suburban dwellers, students, and workmen, for all of whom the poet stops just short of outright adoration.[51]

After the emotional and intellectual tautness of his early verse, the new poems revealed a disappointingly relaxed Betjeman-esque quality belying their graver philosophical underlay. In the wartime setting in which they were published, the lines on the Russian landscape and people acquired a new poignancy however. The signs of this 'populism' were evident in the 1930s to Pasternak's close friends, and were encouraged by the Peredelkino setting and proximity to the rural population. Quite apart from his literary talents, Pasternak's neighbour Vsevolod Ivanov, who was of Siberian origins, appealed to him partly as a 'man of the people', although he found some of Pasternak's own views on 'the people' to be quite mistaken. Subjectively, though, Pasternak now saw himself as one who, in the words of his poem, 'became the kith and kinsman' of commoners. This was consistent with his lifelong preference for a simple lifestyle and with his desire, fulfilled in Peredelkino, to combine literary pursuits with physical work in field or garden. Some of these Tolstoyan features appeared in the hero of his unfinished novel drafts and later in Yurii Zhivago's enjoyment of rural pursuits, his return on foot from Siberia and marriage to the local gatekeeper's daughter. Despite its sincerity, Pasternak's attraction to the simple life and common people was perhaps marked initially by sentimental rapture. The war, however, created a greater sense of their common cause and a multitude of witnesses could testify to the reality of this bond.[52]

In the 1950s Pasternak expressed a dislike of his own style prior to 1940,[53] and in later years he was dismissive about most of his early work. Whether or not one accepts his own 'Zhivago-telic' view of his career, 1940 was undoubtedly a turning-point no less radical than that of *Second Birth*. In the autumn of that year a new fount of inspiration was tapped, and in the verse that began emerging the following spring the poet discovered the 'unprecedented simplicity' first sought a decade earlier. Apart from any natural gravitation towards a simpler profundity, the process was doubtless assisted by his recent 'bath in

Shakespeare' recommended by Rolland, as well as other translating experience. To Simon Chikovani he later identified the disappearance of dazzling tropes as a sign of maturity. Plain formulation and metaphor marked 'different stages of thought: early thought, born of the moment and still unclarified in metaphor, and thought that has settled, determined its meaning and merely perfects its expression in non-metaphoric statement'.[54]

That this purified style appeared to satisfy the socialist realist code of 'popularity' was coincidental. What Pasternak sought, and found, was a directness of vision and primary feeling rather than the blandness of expression and 'typicality' of official literature. Indeed, as identified by *Safe Conduct* in relation to Scriabin, simplicity of underlying concept did not preclude a convolute idiom.[55] However, his new transparency secured a positive critical response when the new verses were published. As Pasternak told his cousin, the poems were 'a sample of how I would write in general if I were able to engage in free original work'. However, financial necessity and the dictates of history (as distinct from Party directive) were soon to rechannel his activities yet again.

At the beginning of 1941, Pasternak secured a new major translation assignment for Shakespeare's *Romeo and Juliet*. To obtain such a contract was not easy, as he explained to his cousin:

> The new enthusiasm openly confessed is for Ivan the Terrible, the *oprichnina* and cruelty. It is on these themes that new operas, dramas and scenarios are being written [. . .] I scarcely succeeded in arranging that my non-independent labour, which is all I have left, be devoted to something worthwhile like *Romeo and Juliet*, since they kept offering me second-rate dramatists from the national republics to translate.[56]

With morale high at his newfound poetic fertility and success with the Shakespeare contract, Pasternak made rapid progress in spring 1941 with *Romeo and Juliet*. Two excerpts from the Prologue and Act I, scene 1, appeared in magazines that year, and only the advent of war delayed the work's completion.[57]

The Nazi invasion of Western Europe abruptly reduced exchanges between the Pasternak brothers in Moscow and their family in England. An occasional postcard from Russia got through, with expressions of concern and alarm after news of the July 1940 air raids on Britain. Then, after almost a year's silence, Pasternak sent his father in Oxford some photographs and a letter on 19 June 1941. To avoid delays with wartime postal censorship he wrote in an English that revealed him as a Shakespeare reader and more habitual user of German. The uncorrected text reads:

Dear Papa!

I sufficiently imagine, how suspectable a letter, not to speak of a photograph or of a book in foreign language must be in such times as ours. Yet I try to send you the newappeared Hamlet-tragedy in my version and the card here inclosed. Perhaps after the examinations it must necessarily undergo both on our and your side, it will happily reach your eyes.

The represented is your grandson and namesake Leonid, the most coward, fantastical and sliest creature, ever seen, whose chief passion is drawing, and who, being asked: 'Who is painting better than anybody' points at your admirable chalk-and-oil studies on the wall and replies 'My grandfather'.

I spent with him this winter in this postofficeless village, the very reason why I asked (and it remains for the future) to use for telegraphs and letters Shurah's [i.e. Aleksandr Pasternak's] town-address. Our country house is my blessing. God helping I hope to dwell my lifetime not in the town. Last year we got of our spacious kitchen garden, – the fruit of our own, esp. Zenaida's labours – half a cellar of potatoes, two casks of sourcrout, 4000 tomatoes and a great deal of peas, french beans, carrots and other vegetables not to be consumed in a year.

Eugene has brilliantly made his school abiturium. After our new rules be must turn soldier this autumn. Eugenie was newly in Leningrad. All the people are living and at health. Mamma's death is kept secret from the aunts Anne and Claudia. On the contrary I esteem you strong enough as to learn without farther harm, than the calm and inevitable sorrow the late deaths of uncle Joseph [i.e. Dr. Osip Kofman] and your niece Sophy [i.e. Sofia Aleksandrovna Genikes].

After all you know of me it is needless to say what grief I have to suffer at the incessant events in the West. As it will seem the feelings are here generally for the english cause. Among other intentions I am occupied with 'Romeo and Juliet', half of which I have already made in russian.

Judge my 'Hamlet' not too severely. Accustomed to good old translations you will never like it. Excuse the vignets, which are partly tolerable but for the most helpless and childish. And the abominable paper!

And now, farewell! Never make you torments with letterwriting of to day. We shall content ourselves with your telegraphs as before. Pardon me if my lines will bring you any annoyance.

Farewell once more. Except the war I might say myself overhappy with my life, save that I never understood nor will ever comprehend that I and you will die some day.

Commend me to your sons in law and their wives and children, my dear sisters and nephews and nieces. How are Lydia and her baby?

I embrace you endlessly.

Your Boris.

The Soviet leadership evidently believed implicitly in the Ribbentrop-Molotov pact and intelligence warnings of an imminent attack on the Soviet Union were ignored. Rumours of a threatened German invasion circulated in

Moscow in June 1941 and caused alarm and disbelief among the literary community. Fedin's wife Dora called on the Pasternaks on the afternoon of Saturday the 21st in a state of distress. Pasternak did not listen to radio, but news of Molotov's repeated broadcast announcing the German invasion was brought by both the Fedins and Koma Ivanov. Later that day Zinaida returned to Peredelkino after visiting Adrian together with his father. On the way back she had heard the news in town and seen the public chaos and signs of panic buying. Pasternak was evidently calm and consoling; their kitchen garden would ensure they did not starve, and he was confident that the Soviet Army would quickly repel and defeat the invaders.[58]

The German army made rapid advances however, and by July air attacks on Moscow were expected. The first suspected air-raid roused the Pasternaks and forced them to spend the night under the pine-trees behind the house; later this was announced as a rehearsal. Shortly afterwards, blackout instructions were imposed, and every household in Peredelkino had to dig a trench in the garden as a makeshift shelter. The Pasternaks dug a joint one with the Fedins. Every night there was an alert and they usually went round to sit in the Fedins' house, but there was no actual air-raid and nobody used the trench.[59]

As the German advance continued, measures for defence and partial evacuation of population were introduced. Those evacuated were usually persons perceived as vital to the country's interests. They included Boris Zbarsky, who was detailed to take Lenin's embalmed body to safety in Tyumen in Siberia – a personal enactment of the slogan that 'Lenin is always with us'![60] The Writers' Union also arranged for members and their families to be moved eastward – initially to the Kazan area in the Tatar Republic; later other safe locations were designated in the Caucasus and at Tashkent in Uzbekistan. A special Litfond commission handled the evacuation of wives and children, and Pasternak was insistant that his family leave. There was much grief and divided feeling over this, since Adrian was still in the clinic after a bone operation on 18 June. Boris undertook to visit him regularly, and there was assurance that staff and patients would also be evacuated. After various changes of plan they were eventually moved to the Nizhnii Ufalei hospital near Chelyabinsk in the Urals. Meanwhile, Zinaida persuaded the Litfond commission to let her accompany and help supervise the other children. On Tuesday 9 July, together with Leonid and Stanislav she joined one of the first parties leaving by train for Bersut on the river Kama, where a residential school was to receive the children. They were allowed little in the way of luggage. Zinaida took some special treasures wrapped up in Leonid's fur coat, including the manuscript of part two of *Safe Conduct*, thus ensuring its preservation when much else was lost. Boris' letters to her were left in the safekeeping of a woman friend who returned them to her in 1943.[61]

Boris' parting from his small son was particularly heart-rending as Zinaida recalled, although he remained confident and encouraging.[62] Two weeks earlier Pasternak also bade farewell to his elder son. On the outbreak of war, Evgenii was not quite eighteen and had just completed the tenth class when he was sent off with a detachment of schoolboys to help dig anti-tank trenches near Smolensk. After being strafed by German fighter-bombers they escaped on foot to Vyazma and were evacuated back to Moscow in mid-July.[63]

After Zinaida and the children left, Boris divided his time between the town apartment and Peredelkino. Assisted be Elena Petrovna, Evgeniya's house-keeper, he tidied, weeded and watered the sun-baked and neglected vegetable garden; Marusya, young Leonid's nurse, also stayed on to help in the house in return for free meals. Intermittently, apart from day-to-day contacts with Chukovsky, Fedin, Ivanov, Leonov and other neighbours, Pasternak was also visited by his brother and sister-in-law, Evgeniya and Evgenii, Tusya Blumen-feld and her sister Olga, and by Genrikh and Militsa Neigauz together with his favourite pupil Svyatoslav Richter.[64]

On the night of 21–22 July and for several weeks following, there was heavy bombing of Moscow. On the second night Pasternak began regular duties with a firewatching squad on the house roof in Lavrushinsky Lane. During most of the time till mid August he lived in Peredelkino and came into town for these duties when required. Spells on watch were shared with playwright Anatolii Glebov, Vsevolod Ivanov, Selvinsky and others, under the intrepid leadership of editor Ivan Khalturin. Armed only with shovels their task was to dislodge incendiary bombs from the roofing and throw them out of harm's way into the road. Letters to Zinaida during this time described intense bombing with the men on the roof often surrounded by a sea of flame and deafened by explosions and anti-aircraft fire. The house was extensively damaged by two bombs on the night of 11–12 August, and well before that date most of the windows had been blown out by the shockwave from nearby explosions. Pasternak's letters conveyed his clear sense of being close to death. He and his comrades were unhurt however; witnesses reported how both he and Ivanov preserved a bold and imperturbable mien throughout the attacks.[65]

During the bombing, the evacuation operation continued. Neigauz and Fedin were offered a refuge down in Nalchik in the Caucasus but declined because of the expense. Pasternak too was short of money; contracts were hard to secure; rates per line of verse were reduced, and quick and substantial fees could be earned only with topical press articles. At a time when Pasternak was inspired by a need 'to express the whole of oneself, to the very depths,' he was loath to emulate colleagues with ready pens who were ready to 'fib fervently and receive money for printed banalities'.[66] This was not readily understood by Zinaida however. Moreover, in answer to his tender and concerned messages, he harvested regular complaints about the delay in delivery of his letters.

Towards the end of August there was a new prospect of regular earnings, but none of Pasternak's articles written for VOKS were printed. To earn a living by literary work for an establishment with blinkered vision and on a wartime budget was hard indeed. As the enemy advance continued, his comment in September was that 'Before the Germans get interested in me, I'll have been starved to death by my own people'.[67] Further distressing news in mid September reported the deportation of Volga Germans to Kazakhstan. In addition, all ethnic Germans were removed from Moscow. This was a tragedy for various inhabitants of Peredelkino, all of them fugitives from Nazism and 'clean, honest working folk'. Also affected was the sister-in-law of Aleksandr Pasternak, while an absurd bureaucratic paradox appointed Nikolai Vilyam, her brother, as an interpreter with the NKVD counter-espionage service. All this and the 'unbearable spiritual non-freedom' were openly mentioned in Pasternak's correspondence with Zinaida together with the remark: 'I cannot say how I long for Russia's victory and I know no other desires. But can I wish victory to stupidity, and a long life to vulgarity and falsehood?'[68]

In *Doctor Zhivago* one of the characters was to state: 'When war broke out, its real horrors, real danger, and threat of real death were a blessing compared with the inhuman domination of the lie, and they brought relief because they broke the magic spell of the dead letter.'[69] In fact that relief was only partial. In battle or when bombs were falling there was indeed a sense of shared reality and common cause. Behind the battle lines, in official public life, including that of literature and the media the rule of the lie was still in force.

Opportunities for writing of whatever sort were further reduced after 28 August when Pasternak along with Fedin, Leonov, Panfyorov and others was summoned for special military training. (Pasternak's childhood leg injury prevented his actual conscription.) This involved attendance at 4 pm each day on the shooting range at Moscow's Krasnaya Presnya Gate. Pasternak evidently excelled at this particular exercise and showed the skills of a born marksman.[70]

In the remaining time Pasternak managed to strike other short-range literary targets. Verse translations from Chikovani and the Latvian Jānis Šudrabkalns found an easy outlet in newspaper publications.[71] On 4 September he succeeded in landing a contract with Chagin at Gosizdat for a translated selection of verse by the Polish Romantic Słowacki. More importantly, the same day he talked to Khrapchenko of the All-Union Arts Committee and on the 18th submitted the contractual proposal and outline of an original theatrical drama.[72]

The idea for Pasternak's drama sprang indirectly from his recent work on Shakespeare and collaboration with the Arts Theatre company on *Hamlet*. With them in mind he proposed a new four-act play called 'In a Soviet City' and based on topical material dealing with the defence of Moscow. The setting was to be: 'a large Soviet town in winter in increasing proximity to the battle-front, and then under siege from the enemy, with frequent bombings, raids and hostile diversions, amidst hardships, dangers and a sense of spirit that increasingly becomes a matter of habit'.[73] Describing the project, Pasternak invoked the example of Ibsen and Chekhov; the play's characters would embody 'primary features of the new historical type'. These, so went the claim, were as yet imperfectly captured by Soviet literature, although no explanation was offered as exactly what this meant. The work would be written 'in a new free style' and would also show what Pasternak called 'the identicality of the Russian and socialist element as the chief and most substantial fact of the first half of the twentieth century in world history'.[74] The scheme as described sounded impressive but not particularly Pasternakian; the work in question was never completed, but like the 'Dramatic Fragments' of 1917, it helped mark a bold turning-point in Pasternak's evolution.

Despite his theatrical plans Pasternak's first works on the war theme were a series of short lyrics written in the wake of the 'Peredelkino' cycle. The journal *Krasnaya nov'* requested some new war poems and published 'On Early Trains' and 'The Loner' ('Bobyl'') in issues 9–10 for 1941. The second of these was a vignette self-portrait of a lonely man whose land is invaded and who has sent his family to safety; he awaits news of victory and alone in the garden, he gazes west to Smolensk (where Evgenii had dug trenches in July) and ponders his own vitality and prowess as a marksman. Two further items appeared in *Ogonyok* on 14 September. A late September issue of *Literaturnaya gazeta* then printed 'Daring' ('Smelost'') an elevated, but rhythmically monotonous address to the 'nameless heroes of towns under siege'. This was followed two weeks later by an apostrophe 'To the Russian Genius' ('Russkomu geniyu'), in which despite its patriotic theme, the editors identified a dissident trace and demanded removal of an offending second stanza:

> However loud the din about you
> Proudly maintain your silence.
> Do not complete another's falsehood
> By the shame of explanations. (*SS*, II, 153)

Explanations were indeed unnecessary to confirm that the din and falsehood were qualities of *Soviet* propaganda no less than the enemy's.[75] Another poem of 1941 in patriotic key was 'The Old Park'('Staryi park'), published later in 1943. In it Pasternak pictured one of the injured patients of the military sanatorium set up in Peredelkino; the young man's thoughts turned to his future plans, which closely resembled Pasternak's own artistic project:

> He himself would write a drama
> Inspired by the events of war [. . .]
>
> In it, in provincial language,
> Clarity and order he'd contrive
> To bring to the unimagined course
> Of an unprecedented life.   (III, 38; *SP*, 413–14; *SS*, II, 46)

While in town on 7 August, Pasternak learned that Evgeniya and Evgenii had the previous day left for Tashkent with another evacuation party.[76]

Pasternak had advised Tsvetaeva against leaving the capital where there were still sources of literary income. However, after her sixteen-year-old son Georgii was conscripted with other menfolk to serve in a rooftop fire-prevention squad, she resolved to leave, even though her son himself was sullenly reluctant. On 8 August mother and son left from the Southern River Station heading by steamer on the ten-day journey to Elabuga on the river Kama. It was here that the Writers' Union agreed to evacuate her, rather than Chistopol, further downstream, where more prestigious writers were accommodated. Pasternak travelled in from Peredelkino together with the young poet Viktor Bokov to see Tsvetaeva off. Still unadjusted to the privations of Soviet life, she had expected a buffet saloon on the boat and turned up without any food for the journey. Bokov and Pasternak came to the rescue by purchasing some bread, sausage and cheese for her at a nearby foodstore. It was Pasternak's last favour and farewell to her.[77]

Despite her depressed state, neither Pasternak nor other friends suspected she would be dead before the month was out. In despair at the prospect of staying in Elabuga, where she rented a room with an elderly local couple, she made the river trip to Chistopol, petitioning for a transfer there. Yet although she was successful and also found Lidiya Chukovskaya and friends ready to help, she returned unexpectedly to Elabuga, and for three days hesitated between staying put or moving to Chistopol. Then on 31 August, while 'Mur' and her hosts were out, she hanged herself.[78]

It took just over a week for Pasternak to hear the news – in the form of unconfirmed report from Fedin. To Zinaida, who had now moved from Bersut to Chistopol, he wrote an anguished letter, telling her to make enquiries and at least concern herself with the fate of Tsvetaeva's son. Pasternak himself was overcome by remorse and self-reproach:

If this is true, what guilt rests on me! No use talking about 'other concerns' after this! It will never be forgiven me. This last year I ceased to take an interest in her. She was in high regard in intelligentsia society and among people of understanding. She became fashionable and concern was shown for her by my personal friends [. . .] Since it was flattering to be counted her best friend, for several reasons, I moved away from her and didn't force myself on her, and this last year I almost completely forgot her. And now look what has happened! How terrible![79]

Although Pasternak spoke of the lame excuses and collective guilt of Aseyev, Fedin, Fadeyev and others who failed to help Tsvetaeva,[80] he was haunted by a sense of responsibility for her fate. These feelings emerged in the later poetic memorial he wrote to her, as well as in the 'Three Shades' section of his autobiographical essay. He described her there as 'a woman with an active masculine soul, decisive, militant, untamable' and possessing an 'impetuous, greedy and almost rapacious drive towards finality and definition' – hardly therefore a character whose destiny could have been moulded by Pasternak.[81] His guilt-ridden grief was nevertheless genuine, and after her death he remained one of her most resolute champions. In early October 1941 he briefly saw her son, who returned to Moscow after his mother's suicide; eventually, in 1944, the young man was called for military service and perished in action in July of that year.[82]

With Leningrad now blockaded, and as German troops closed in on Moscow, the Soviet Government and diplomatic corps in October 1941 transferred to Kuibyshev on the Volga. Fadeyev drew up a further party of writers to be evacuated, including Fedin, Leonov and Pasternak. All three had stayed on at Peredelkino without their families, imagining they might pay a short visit to Chistopol, after which they would hole up for the winter in one of their dachas. Vsevolod Ivanov had meanwhile joined the Sovinformburo at Kuibyshev while his family travelled with the evacuation party to Tashkent. At the end of September Akhmatova flew in, rescued from the Leningrad blockade. (When they met at Olga Berggolts' sister's, she pronounced the words of Firs at the end of *The Cherry Orchard*: 'They've forgotten someone,' – as if to say: 'Here I am, friends, take me with you.') Pasternak had thought of settling Akhmatova in Evgeniya's flat on Tverskoi Boulevard, but in the event she too was put on Fadeyev's evacuation list and headed for Tashkent.[83]

The order to leave was now almost mandatory. Official attitudes to those who stayed varied unpredictably. Pasternak's friend Valentin Asmus was of German extraction but he was established among the communist professoriate and not forcibly evacuated. Genrikh Neigauz delayed leaving and was arrested by the NKVD on 4 November; accused of waiting in Moscow for 'his' Germans to arrive, he was held in the Lubyanka and withstood eight months of interrogation without breaking. Eventually, on 19 July 1942 he was released, but exiled to the Urals near Sverdlovsk and only allowed to return to Moscow in October 1944.[84]

Suddenly faced with a departure order, Pasternak experienced a few days of panic as he tried to arrange accommodation for various treasured possessions. The Tretyakov Gallery turned down a request to take Leonid Pasternak's pictures and folios; the Tolstoy Museum agreed but was far away and unable to assist with transport. Sadly, many drawings, etudes and canvases were therefore left in Peredelkino and Lavrushinsky Lane and were damaged or destroyed not by enemy action but by vandals in the Soviet military.[85] Pasternak handed valuable documents like Tsvetaeva's letters and a few letters from Gorky, his parents and Rolland to a friend working at the Scriabin Museum where there was a safe. However the Tsvetaeva letters were lost when the woman, who lived out of town, accidentally left them by the roadside after alighting from a suburban train. The text of eighteen letters survived however; copies of these plus three originals had been kept by Kruchenykh, who was engaged in editing them. Thus the tripartite correspondence of Tsvetaeva, Pasternak and Rilke was preserved and later published.[86]

On the early morning of 14 October – the day that German troops seized Mozhaisk, not far to the west of Moscow – the party of writers left Moscow by train for Kazan. Fellow passengers from the Maly and Vakhtangov Theatres stayed on board and continued to Siberia. The writers however transferred to river steamer for the journey to Chistopol, where they arrived in the late evening of Saturday 18 October.[87]

9

Chistopol Translation

'Hamlet'

A hush descends. I step out on the boards,
And leaning on the door-frame, I endeavour
To perceive what the future holds in store,
Devining it amidst the distant echoes.

Darkness, thousandfold, is focussed on me
Down the axis of each opera-glass.
If it may be, I pray Thee, Abba, Father,
Grant it: let this chalice from me pass.

I love and cherish it, Thy stubborn purpose,
And am content to play the allotted role.
But now another drama is in progress.
I beg Thee, leave me this time uninvolved.

But alas, there is no turning from the road.
The order of the action has been settled.
The Pharisee claims all, and I'm alone.
This life is not a stroll across the meadow.

(1946)

On the train and river journey to Chistopol Pasternak travelled light while several writers brought large consignments of supplies. The dramatist Trenyov was accompanied by his huge Great Dane and another lively canine midget whose defaecations on board aroused general disgust. After one such performance emptied the whole promenade deck, Vadim the young son of playwright Bill-Belotserkovsky watched as Pasternak discreetly returned to sweep the offensive litter overboard.

On arrival in Chistopol, Pasternak assisted with unloading the cargo of luggage. As a devotee of physical exercise he was also later drafted into a team which for three days unloaded a barge full of firelogs that arrived for use by the writers' community.[1]

The provincial town of Chistopol founded in 1781 had a population of 25,000 before the war. After its designation as a receiving area for evacuees in June 1941, however, the figure swelled to over 40, 000. It was the second largest such centre after Kazan, capital of the Tatar Autonomous Republic, and received people of fifty different nationalities. Among them were sixty writers and their families.[2] The *literati* from the capital evidently cut quaint figures and raised smiles from many of the locals. Dramatist Aleksandr Gladkov provided some neat vignettes of leading personalities among the company. They included Shklovsky, talking with everyone but thinking his own thoughts; Leonov, with whiskers, looking like a foreigner; Glebov, calm and cheerful, always busy; Aseyev, diminutive and resembling a pike-fish; Fedin, with pipe and posing as provincial squire; Trenyov, frowning and unwelcoming (he spoke out strongly against letting Tsvetaeva reside in Chistopol), and many others, 'among them as a sort of merry contrast – the harmonious, benevolent, confiding figure of Boris Leonidovich Pasternak, absorbed with himself and his own work'.[3]

An event that galvanised the official life in the literary community was the arrival of Fadeyev in November 1941, and several Union activities were now centred in Chistopol rather than Moscow. A local 'ruling quintet' was set up consisting of Aseyev, Fedin, Leonov, Trenyov and Pasternak. In this capacity Pasternak attended board meetings on 4 December 1941, and 5 January 1942, and he enjoyed the intimacy of these functions after the impersonality of the Moscow organisation.[4] Administrative work involved no heavy time commitment, and despite a nostalgia for their Moscow haunts, the informality encouraged by the genial pace of life and provincial setting created a new warmth of fellow-feeling among writers and a sense of belonging again to a cohesive literary community.[5]

In particular, the warmth of Pasternak's earlier relations with Aseyev was restored. Although they had gone different ways, both men treasured memories of their earlier closeness and now again enjoyed frequent cordial meetings. Aseyev was genuinely thrilled by Pasternak's new verse, and in the early months of 1943 after Aseyev's return to Moscow, affectionate letters were exchanged.[6]

It was Aseyev who introduced Pasternak to the Avdeyev family. Their home at 74 Karl Marx Street was known among the local intelligentsia and became a frequent meeting place for evacuated writers. Dmitrii Avdeyev was an educated and cultivated doctor; his sons Arsenii and Valerii were respectively a specialist in theatre and a biologist. With the latter Pasternak became specially close and for many years afterwards corresponded and occasionally met with him. At the Avdeyevs Pasternak also got to know Maria Petrovykh; familiar already as a translator, she now emerged as an impressive original poet.[7]

While some writers rented luxurious accommodation, Pasternak lodged and worked in a badly heated little room which Zinaida had rented for him at 75 Volodarsky Street, in the house of the Vavilov family. Some impressions of life in Chistopol were well caught in Pasternak's letter to his cousin in July 1942:

It is Sunday, seven in the morning, and a day of rest. This means that since yesterday evening Zina has been here, and at ten in the morning Lyonechka [Leonid] will come. The rest of the week they are both at the children's home, where Zina works as nurse and housekeeper. It is a fresh, rainy morning – my good fortune, since because of the deep continental location there would otherwise be an equatorial heat [. . .] I got up at six a.m. because the pipes to the pump in our region where I fetch water are often out of commission; apart from which it is only available twice a day at certain set hours. You have to seize the opportunity. While half asleep I heard the entire street filled with the clank of buckets. Every housewife here has her own yoke, and the town is full of them.

One of my windows looks onto the road, beyond which there is a large garden designated as the 'Culture and Recreation Park'. The other window looks into the daisy-covered courtyard of the public court, where they often bring teams of emaciated prisoners who have been evacuated to the local jail from other towns, and where their are shrieks and yells whenever any locals are put on trial.

The road is covered in a thick layer of black mud that oozes out from under the cobbles. They have exquisite soil here, black earth of such quality it seems as if coal-dust has been added. And if you gave such soil to an industrious and disciplined population who knew what they were capable of, what they wanted and what they were entitled to demand, social and economic problems would have been solved, and in this New Burgundy an art would have flourished like that of Rabelais or Hoffmann's 'Nut-cracker'.[8]

Zinaida Pasternak left an extensive housewife's memoir of their stay in Chistopol. Apart from work at the school, she also shopped for Boris' dinner and eventually fixed for him to eat at the school kitchens which she controlled. Stanislav became so caught up with school work and with helping at a local collective farm that he temporarily gave up the piano, although he later resumed practising and gave some concerts at the school hostel, sometimes playing duets with his mother.[9]

Adrian Neigauz remained confined in the tubercular clinic at Nizhnii Ufalei, near Sverdlovsk, and his condition deteriorated. In late spring 1942, in a vain attempt to prevent the disease from spreading, one of his legs was amputated. The psychological impact of this on a handsome and active youth was disastrous. Zinaida was allowed two weeks' leave to visit him. Adrian knew nothing of his father's arrest, but the problem of breaking this news was averted when Neigauz himself wrote to him after his release, on 19 July. Given a choice of exile in Alma-Ata, Tbilisi or Sverdlovsk, he had chosen the latter so as to be near his son.[10]

Pasternak's first wife and son Evgenii were meanwhile in Tashkent where correspondence sometimes took two months to reach them. In Tashkent, Evgenii enrolled at the Central Asian State University to study maths and physics, but in early 1942 he was mobilised and transferred to the local Military Academy. He and his mother lived in the same house as the Ivanovs and Pogodins. Other friends and acquaintances were also in town, including Akhmatova, and for prolonged periods during 1941–3 the families of Chukovsky, Marshak, and Aleksei Tolstoy resided in Tashkent. Nadezhda Mandelstam later spent the period 1943–6 there. At one point in early 1942 Pasternak too considered moving there. He also had hopes that the Freidenbergs might be able to flee the Leningrad blockade, from where reports and letters were appalling in their content, and either join Evgeniya in Tashkent, or stay in her Moscow apartment. Nothing came of these proposals however. Pasternak stayed on in Chistopol and the Freidenbergs lived through and survived the blockade; Aunt Asya died in April 1944.[11]

Although taking time off in Chistopol for walks, socialising and cultural activities, Pasternak impressed onlookers by his industry. At lunchtime in the writers' canteen on Volodarsky Street, while others sat in their coats idly chattering, he normally sat with sheets of paper by his plate of cabbage soup and after courteous greetings or invitations to join him usually apologised and continued working.[12]

Pasternak attended most of the regular Wednesday meetings when writers read and recited to one another during the winter of 1941–2. In addition to his own readings, he heard Fedin's presentation of his recollections of Gorky.[13] He was raptly attentive at Elizaveta Loiter's piano recital in a frozen auditorium lit by kerosene lamps, and in January 1942 he took the chair at Aseyev's evening of readings in Teachers' House. At various times during the year he also attended evening recitals by Nikolai Nikitin, Leningrad poetess Vera Inber and others, while he himself contributed to various programmes including a literary and musical concert organised by Valerii Avdeyev.[14]

A first literary task in Chistopol during winter 1941–2 was to complete the translation of *Romeo and Juliet*. While engaged on it Pasternak continued reading around his subject, including Victor Hugo's writings on Shakespeare.[15] The translation was substantially ready by February 1942, although it cost him more pains than *Hamlet* 'in view of the comparative paleness and mannerism' of several episodes. Yet although prepared for failure, as he told Evgeniya, he 'avoided disgrace' with the final result.[16] Pasternak's translation technique, as outlined to Gladkov, was simpler than with *Hamlet*. Unlike his predecessors, he attempted to find 'sense equivalents' rather than trying to register every untranslatable image and locution.[17] In doing so, as he discovered, he initially produced a rendering of Romeo's speeches so redolent of Mayakovsky's diction that he deliberately changed certain passages.[18] Once he had his own version, he then consulted other available translations by such as Grigoryev, Mikhalovsky, Radlova and Sokolovsky; these were procured for him from a local school library by Valerii Avdeyev. He also used Avdeyev as audience to try out the sound of various renderings and discussed the whole translation with him.[19]

Pasternak celebrated the completion of his work by reading it publicly at Teachers' House in Chistopol on Thursday 26 February. Tickets cost four and five roubles, and the event was held as a benefit performance for soldiers of the Red Army. The start of the presentation was delayed half an hour, and because of a power failure the stage was lit by two kerosene lamps. Pasternak appeared quaintly clad in black suit, a parti-coloured knitwear tie and with white felt boots on his feet. The manuscript text was unfurled from a roll of newspaper, and he began with some introductory remarks.[20] As for the performance, Gladkov recorded that Pasternak 'read not exactly well, but pleasingly, loudly and clearly', although his attempts to 'perform' struck Gladkov as naive. Most successful was his rendering of Romeo and Friar Lawrence. A few days later, a second reading was given for the Chistopol town theatre company.[21]

In summer of 1942, Pasternak had to defend his whole Shakespeare translation method once more against convention-bound editors and scholars. First of all, a new edition of *Hamlet* was being prepared by the children's publisher Detgiz. Having seen various recommendations by Shakespeare scholar Mikhail Morozov, Pasternak's first reaction was despair: Morozov seemingly failed to understand the basis of his method; his strictures were essentially scholarly and concerned the tonal and semantic accuracy of certain details in the text. As Pasternak told the Detgiz editor Anna Naumova, he altogether rejected contemporary views on translation and found the work of Lozinsky, Radlova, Marshak and Chukovsky artificial, soulless and superficial. 'My position is that of the nineteenth century', he explained, 'when translation was viewed as a literary problem so loftily conceived that it left no room for philological enthusiasms.' Pasternak was quite unperplexed, however, by the prospect of having to bowdlerise certain indecent passages for the benefit of a junior edition, and saw this as 'a five-minute job'.[22] Learned opinion was not

191

rejected out of hand, however, and Pasternak did re-examine the text and removed some 'rough passages' noted by Morozov.

Pasternak explained to Morozov that his approach to *Romeo and Juliet* was more radical than to *Hamlet*, 'since *Romeo* is a young, spoiled and headstrong tragedy which had to be translated on a short rein.' Nevertheless, he claimed he had 'nowhere indulged in whims and fancies or tried to be original for the sake of it'. Morozov was in fact deeply impressed by the new version; his quibbles were far fewer than with *Hamlet* and they centred around the tone of individual words and phrases, and the fact that Pasternak had occasionally slightly condensed the original.[23] For all his strictures, Morozov's scholarly review placed a stamp of enthusiastic approval on Pasternak's work as a whole.[24] The first edition of *Romeo and Juliet* appeared in 1943 with the All-Union Authors' Copyright Board, and both Detgiz and GIKhL published editions of it the following year. Although deemed successful, however, the work generally failed to attract the same critical attention as *Hamlet* three years earlier.[25]

In the spring of 1942 Pasternak turned to his next money-raising project and rapidly translated the Polish poems by Słowacki commissioned from Goslitizdat. The complete set was mailed at the end of May and was in Chagin's hands by mid-June. Unfortunately no edition materialised, although two items were printed in *Krasnaya nov'* and *Ogonyok* in 1942. Pasternak left his own copy of the translation with Avdeyev when he finally left Chistopol in 1943, and these versions were published in book form only in 1975.[26] Following this Pasternak planned 'to work on something of my own, for myself . . . I want to write a play and a story, a *poèma* in verse and various small poems'. Such was his report, after a long mail silence, to Evgeniya in Tashkent on 12 March 1942.[27]

In fulfilment of this ambition, a small number of poems was produced during the winter of 1941–2. During a walk and conversation with Gladkov on the 20 February, Pasternak observed several barges frozen in the ice of the Kama. The sight reminded him of Tsvetaeva, who had claimed she would herself freeze into the ice at Chistopol rather than leave . . . 'Some time', Pasternak commented, 'I shall write about her [. . .] But I am holding back in order to gather strength worthy of the subject – worthy of Marina, that is.'[28] The ice-bound barges and other winter impressions figured in the memorial poem that Pasternak completed at Kruchenykh's prompting in December 1943.[29]

The plan to write a story came to nothing. Nor was there any progress with the novel fragments. As Pasternak told Gladkov, its composition had been constantly impeded by shifting official attitudes towards the 'imperialist' First World War.[30] He was also dismayed by the effect of the Stalinist 'literary process' as a whole, which he likened to the 'blind, mechanical, uni-directional motion' of hair-clippers – 'the mysterious distribution of cutters that pull and jerk forwards regardless of whether one's personal observations confirm or reject this'.[31] Press evidence of Bolshevik revisions of Russian history also aroused Pasternak's dismay – particularly certain trends in the theatre. In search of precedents legitimising Stalin's rule, various historical images of tyranny were now promoted. Stalin Prize winner Aleksei Tolstoy was announced as being at work on a drama about Ivan the Terrible; this was also the title (*Ivan Groznyi*) of a trilogy by V. I. Kostylev, published in 1943–7 and awarded a Stalin Prize in 1948; Sergei Eisenstein's film of the same title was also shot during the war at a studio near Alma-Ata. Not surprisingly, the official mind-set had made it hard in 1941 for Pasternak to justify retranslation of an anodyne old classic such as *Romeo and Juliet*.[32] His view of Stalin's rule had by now thoroughly soured, and in frank conversation he referred to the leader as a 'giant of the prechristian era of humanity'. If prewar terror was resumed, he saw every chance of joining his many friends in the camps of the Soviet north.[33]

Despite his distaste for recent trends in the theatre, some of Pasternak's close contacts in Chistopol were with established dramatists such as Pavlenko, Trenyov and Aleksandr Gladkov. Gladkov, who had for five years worked in Meyerhold's studio, made a name just before the war with his play *Long, Long Ago (Davnym-davno)* and was in 1942 working jointly with Arbuzov on the drama *The Immortal One (Bessmertnyi)*.[34] Pasternak took a special interest in Gladkov, praised his work and promoted his candidature for the Writers' Union; Gladkov for his part kept a careful account of their many meetings and was heartened by Pasternak's own current interest in the theatre. In Chistopol even the novelists Fedin and Leonov were busy writing dramatic works. Leonov's *Invasion (Nashestvie)* in particular had a concept and setting similar to the drama Pasternak was planning, but its conclusion seemed to him as if written by a committee, and he later described it as a 'talented and brilliant piece of untruth' – this, by comparison with Trenyov's feeble effort *Towards a Meeting (Navstrechu)* and Fedin's *The Ordeal (Ispytanie)*, a play of 'dead words and passions whose content would fit into a matchbox'.[35] Nevertheless, the Chistopol thespians encouraged Pasternak's interest in the theatre, and in precarious financial times, such works potentially offered good returns if once accepted for production and in repertoire.[36]

Although he did not secure a firm contract for his projected play before leaving Moscow, a new proposal to the RSFSR Arts Committee was accepted on 10 February and an advance paid. Ten days later Pasternak also signed an agreement with the Red Torch Theatre in Novosibirsk, where his *Hamlet* was in production, for delivery by July of a play 'on a theme and subject topical today'.[37] His recorded conversations and letters of the time throw further light on his intentions.

Among the titles considered for the drama were: 'This World' ('Etot svet') or 'In this world' ('Na etom svete') (perhaps more idiomatically rendered as 'The Here and Now'), and 'In a Soviet Town'('V sovetskom gorode'), which described the actual setting of the action.

Only two scenes of Pasternak's manuscript survived, designated as scenes three and four from the first act of 'a complex four- or five-act tragedy'. The first two scenes, Pasternak told his first wife, were to be set respectively on a station square and in the room of a seamstress near the station; more we do not know, and he gave no indication of the overall sequence of the action.[38] Scene 3 of the first act is set in a bomb-shelter in a house basement in the town of Pushchinsk. Soviet troops are in retreat, and a German occupation force is expected any moment. General conversation introduces a variety of characters in the shelter, including a one-time political prisoner, a former priest who resigned his calling and has been in exile, a couple of looters one of whom recognises the priest, an injured civilian, and others. Amidst all this, a young woman called Druzyakina recounts her life story and recent escape from danger; this theatrically static episode later formed the basis for Tanya Bezocheredeva's story in the prose epilogue of *Doctor Zhivago*. Two male protagonists, Gordon and Dudorov, also have names recurring in Pasternak's novel although apart from being articulate and educated they are not obviously prototypes.[39]

The second surviving scene is set in a forest clearing with Dudorov's house in the background, and the edge of a potato field with benches and a path. Barely realisable stage directions prescribe: 'A day with changeable weather at the end of October. There was snow, but now it is windy and clear, but the snow could start again at any minute . . .' The Germans are expected and Innokentii Dudorov attempts to rally the locals to organise themselves and their households for the ordeal ahead. Dudorov now begins to emerge as a character recognisably doubling for the author and prefiguring Yurii Zhivago. In the face of calamity, he urges Gordon to appreciate this moment of existential patriotism:

Quickly, Gordon, old chap, down on your knees and kiss this earth. Use the chance, before it passes from one set of imposters to another. Right now the minutes are numbered, but there it is on its own – just the land of our amazing birth and childhood, just Russia, just our immeasurable pride, just the place of our revolution that gave this world a new Golgotha and a new god.[40]

Dudorov recollects the loneliness of Hamlet and laments for the wife and children he may never see again. Then he addresses a prayer:

O Lord, o Lord, why do I so love Your order? Lord, You will tear my heart with immensity of its capacity! I thank Thee, Lord, for making me a man and teaching me to say farewell. Farewell, my life. Farewell, my recent past, my yesterday, my foolish offensive twenty years . . .

Darkness gathers and the snow begins to fall, distant funeral music is heard for Ptitsyna, a local teacher who has been killed. Dudorov stands silent, then resumes his prayer:

. . . I thank Thee, Lord for giving me eyes to see, and to shed tears when it is too late to see. Lead my soul out of the prison to confess Thy name. Here we think that life means home, work and rest. Yet when some shock strikes us, how this catastrophe floods us with something familiar and close! Ruination is more in our nature than order. Birth, love, and death – all these are separate devastating shocks, each step in life is an exile, a loss of heaven, the breakup of paradise . . .[41]

The scene ends in a discussion with Dudorov about how to conceal a German soldier who has surrendered to the locals after getting separated from his unit.

This was Pasternak's first attempt since *Aerial Ways* (1923) to deal with Soviet subject matter, and it was clearly based on his own recent experience or direct reports. Some features were literally from Pasternak's own back garden: the potato crop, the benches, the path to the station, the impending invasion and the reaction of local residents. Pasternak's interest in 'the people' is reflected in his cast of characters and plentiful use of substandard colloquial speech (in Chistopol he made a collection of local folk phraseology, and this philological interest emerged again in the speech of Kubarikha in *Doctor Zhivago*).[42] The thoughts and phraseology of Dudorov's last soliloquy also anticipated the Zhivago poem 'Hamlet', with its strong motif of life as sacrifice illuminated by Christian religious belief (above, p. 187). The setting of the play – a no-man's land between the lines of two militant regimes – is reminiscent of the 'hermetic' location of the Varykino episode in *Doctor Zhivago*. Situational detail also coincided, including the departure of the hero's family, and the hint of an incipient illicit relationship.

The most striking feature of Pasternak's drama sketches was the Christian religious philosophy illuminating the fate of the main hero. While the deeper motivation for this cannot be documented, it is evident that at this stage Pasternak underwent not so much a religious conversion as the activation of a religiosity what was potentially there in *Lieutenant Shmidt* and even in some lyrics of the 1910s and 1920s.[43] Conjecturally the cause of this could be any man's sudden midlife realisation of his own mortality; but in this case it had been reinforced by the experience of massive fatalities under the terror and by an apocalyptic perception of war.

Quite apart from the play's theatrical ineptness, the religious element and other features made it unstageable in any Soviet theatre. Pasternak himself realised this and in June 1942 told Chagin he was 'writing a contemporary realistic play [. . .] absolutely for myself'.[44] The producer Tairov, who wrote from evacuation in Barnaul enquiring about the work, was also told that it was 'so independently conceived that unless there are serious changes in our literary and theatrical attitudes, it can hardly be suitable for staging or printing'.[45]

Pasternak's Shakespearian experience was also in evidence notably in the cast of characters and free juxtaposition of the lofty and the low (a quality which he had especially observed in *Romeo and Juliet*).[46] In addition, the dramatic model of Chekhov was also present in the drama's conception. As Pasternak told Mikhail Morozov, apart from the example of Shakespeare, 'this is a Russian Faust in the sense in which a Russian Faust must contain Gorbunov and Chekhov'.[47] Peredelkino was in some sense a perpetuation of Chekhov's nineteenth-century genteel drama settings; and in the poem 'The Old Park' located there, a fictional scion of the Samarins contemplated writing his own theatrical drama – an imaginary model for Pasternak's own dramatic scenes.[48]

In summer of 1942, Pasternak laid his play aside, although some of its motifs and themes continued to incubate. In the autumn, he ran into Gladkov at the Writers' Club in Moscow and told him he 'had not finished, and maybe not even started it, but would return to this idea again'.[49] But prior to that he had read the manuscript to his brother and the Asmuses and a few other friends, who were even frightened by its freedom and independent tone. Since it was unperformable and unprintable and could compromise author or audience if were ever seized and produced in evidence, Pasternak was persuaded to destroy it. The two manuscript scenes that survived among his papers do not persuade one that this was a masterpiece in the making.[50] The destroyed pages joined many more such items that were scrapped, lost or destroyed during Pasternak's career. Apart from which, the mutilation or destruction of compromising papers and other items was by this time common practice. Aleksandr Pasternak arranged for an inkblot to obscure the face of Dr Levin on a family photograph; Vyacheslav Ivanov and Aleksandr Gladkov kept notes of meetings and conversations with Pasternak in abbreviated and partly coded form; and Tarasenkov ceased this activity altogether in 1939.[51]

By the spring of 1942 Pasternak was anxious to return to Moscow, partly out of curiosity, and partly in order to contact his editors, since he had now completed Słowacki, *Romeo and Juliet*, and the *Hamlet* revisions and was now merely killing time. Return to Moscow required a government summons and permit however. Pasternak applied in June, but received permission only in late September. On 2 October he was back in the capital.

There was considerable bomb damage in the city, but Pasternak's town and country homes had been wrecked by his own people. The Lavrushinsky apartment was taken over by anti-aircraft gunners who turned the upper floor into a thoroughfare with doors wide open. Items of clothing and other valuables had been stolen; pictures had been taken from walls; gaps in windows were stuffed with drawings by Leonid Pasternak, and the whole apartment had been vandalised. Some property which had been left with Evgeniya's home-help Elena Petrovna was safe, and together with what was salvaged from the town flat it was packed up in two suitcases and sent via Litfond to Chistopol.[52]

Although warned in advance by the Ivanovs who had returned earlier, Pasternak was appalled by the devastation at the Peredelkino dacha. The house had been requisitioned for army use, and troops had been stationed there. The Pasternaks' property had been removed next door to the Ivanovs'. This included all Pasternak's papers (among them the drafts for his novel) and a large chest containing works by his father. Some of Leonid's canvases had been used, though, to patch up holes in shattered windows. Worse than that, through the recklessness or vandalism of army staff, a fire during the winter had destroyed the Ivanovs' entire house and contents. Pasternak had heard of this in March and sent his brother in Moscow a horrified letter surmising that all their possessions had been destroyed 'in the simpleton hands of humanity's liberators, illuminated by an oriflamme of even greater genius'.[53] For Pasternak the worst loss was his father's paintings and other relics bound up with memories of the past. The Ivanovs had lost a magnificent and irreplaceable library; they were infuriated by the behaviour and attitude of the Soviet military, and temporarily moved in with Lidiya Seifullina, their neighbour further along the street.

After seeing the wreckage of his homes, Pasternak could not bring himself to revisit either Lavrushinsky Lane or Peredelkino. Instead he lodged part of the time with his brother, but lived mainly with the Asmuses on Zubovsky Boulevard.[54] The lack of any habitable dwelling ruled out the family's speedy return to Moscow, and after three months of nomadic existence Pasternak himself was forced to leave again.

While in the capital Pasternak reestablished contact with relatives in Britain. He had not attempted to correspond from Chistopol as this was described as 'too complicated an enterprise'. From Moscow, however, in November he sent several postcards with greetings in English (for the military censor's benefit) and various family news. In answer came a wire from Oxford reassuring him that all were alive and well.

In October 1942, a new contract was signed for Pasternak's translation of *Antony and Cleopatra*, and Nemirovich-Danchenko expressed keenness to produce it at the Arts Theatre. In autumn Pasternak also wrote a note 'On Shakespeare' for the Sovinformburo. Its printed title in no. 47 of *Ogonyok* was 'My New Translations' ('Moi novye perevody'). Although nominally just an announcement of the writer's present activities and interests, there was an implicit polemic against certain of the literary fraternity (including Fadeyev) who claimed translation work was an unpatriotic act of ideological retreat in time of war. Pasternak had this to say:

Shakespeare will always be the favourite of generations who are historically mature and have experienced much. Numerous ordeals teach men to value the voice of fact, active cognition, and the grave and ample art of realism.

Shakespeare remains the ideal and pinnacle of this trend [. . .] When in his works there is talk of good and evil, falsehood and truth, we see before us an image that would be inconceivable in a situation of cringing and servility. We hear the voice of a genius, a king among kings, and judge of gods, the voice of later western democracies [. . .] His people are with us. Working at this one never forgets it for a moment. We and his cause are destined to triumph over the dark forces of fascist obscurantism.

Pasternak went on to express an interest in Shakespeare's historical chronicle plays, for 'our time prompts a new interest in them' (*III*, 192–3). While the author of the sonnets or the figure of Hamlet were spokesmen for the poet as individual, Shakespeare's major dramatic opus (and the act of translating it) constituted a form of commentary on current history. This was not Pasternak's own sudden discovery of course. Hugo's comments on Shakespeare, the theme of the regicide ruler, Hamlet's feigned madness as a ploy to avenge this, and Meyerhold's awareness of the topicality of *Macbeth*, had all figured in Chistopol conversations with Gladkov.[55] While in Chistopol the following June, Pasternak also discovered and copied out on the fly-leaf of his Everyman edition of the tragedies a passage from *Henry IV Part 2* that seemed to confirm Shakespeare's relevance to modern times:

> There is a history in all men's lives
> Figuring the nature of the times deceas'd;
> The which observed a man may prophesy,
> With a near aim of the main chance of things
> As yet not come to life, which in their seeds

And weak beginnings, lie intreasured;
Such things become the hatch and brood of times.[56]

Disliking the idea of literary heroics produced far from the battlefield, Pasternak shared with several other writers a desire to visit the Soviet front line. In early November 1942 he asked Fadeyev to arrange this; the idea was welcomed but nothing resulted. He then approached the military journal *Krasnaya zvezda* which responded belatedly and offered a trip to the Bryansk front line just when Pasternak was on the point of returning to Chistopol; the idea was therefore shelved until the spring.[57]

While in Moscow, Pasternak submitted to Sovetsky Pisatel publishers his new verse collection. *On Early Trains* consisted of four sections: 'Months of War' containing five war poems of late 1941; 'The Artist' (four poems of 1936); the 'Travel Notes' of 1936; and twelve poems of early 1941 under the heading 'The Year in Peredelkino'.[58] The book eventually appeared to much acclaim, although artistically it was unsatisfactory. Despite refreshing nature depiction, and a new injection of colloquial syntax and lexicon, the collection lacked an organic unity and Pasternak himself recognised it was divided by an internal rift.[59]

Along with many confrères, Pasternak was asked to respond to the 25th anniversary of the October Revolution. His offering, sent to the paper *Komsomol'skaya pravda*, was not printed. He copied it out, though, for Kruchenykh's album, adding a note that 'it is is a piece of good fortune that it was not printed. It is very pale rubbish, in this case especially stupid in its incongruous intimacy.'[60] The poem was no worse than some of Pasternak's other circumstancial verse, although it remained a pedestrian utterance despite its bright sentiments, which were later better expressed in Pasternak's prose reportage from the front.[61]

December was a month of gentle snow and optimism. The encirclement of Nazi occupied Stalingrad was complete; in Moscow the curfew hours were extended; a more liberal atmosphere pervaded the Writers' Union, and there was a sense that the time of repressions was over. On the 15th Pasternak recited from his new verse collection in the large hall (nowadays the restaurant) of Writers' House. As a friendly gesture to Nikolai Aseyev, the start was delayed specially in order to await his arrival. The recital drew a large and appreciative audience, and the later comments and discussion ended in an ·ovation in Pasternak's honour. Among the audience was the young Balkarian poet Kaisyn Kuliev whom he had met as a drama student in 1939 through Maria Petrovykh. Pasternak's liking for both the man and his poetry blossomed in a warm, though mainly epistolary friendship.[62]

Pasternak had already presented his new translation of *Romeo and Juliet* on 23 October at the All-Russian Theatrical Society. In December this was now repeated by special request of the Maly Theatre company, and at the end of the month it was announced that the translation had been accepted for production there.[63]

On 26 December Pasternak finally left for Chistopol by train. The last lap of the journey, from Kazan, was by air however. It was Pasternak's first flight, evidently in a plane that did little more than hedge-hop, 'flying as if at the tip of a telegraph pole', as he told Fedin's daughter on arrival.[64]

Back in Chistopol in early 1943, Pasternak considered composing a further two chapters as continuation of *Safe Conduct*. This was reported in a letter of 19 January to Aseyev, who was staying on in Moscow.[65] Nothing materialised however. Instead he concentrated almost exclusively on *Antony and Cleopatra*. In mid January a telegram from Vilenkin informed him of Nemirovich-Danchenko's interest and asked to be notified of its completion. After reading earlier versions by Minsky and Radlova, Nemirovich realised again the 'murderous compromise' he would be forced to accept, unless he could secure a translation from Pasternak.[66] In February Nemirovich-Danchenko also resumed working in earnest on the production of *Hamlet*. Despite the disappointing delays over this, Pasternak was excited by the prospect of seeing *Antony and Cleopatra* on stage. Knowledge of Nemirovich-Danchenko's interest was a great stimulus. Writing from Chistopol, Pasternak reported that half of the play was already translated in draft, and that he was working on it day and night. Not having met up with him while in Moscow, Pasternak was interested to hear his ideas about the play.[67] The veteran producer replied on 18 February with a set of notes summarised at the end in a series of antinomies: male versus female; Rome versus Egypt; marble and iron versus femininity and tenderness; duty versus passion – 'and all this clothed in poetry that is austere and richly coloured'.[68] Inspired by the concept, Pasternak completed the work in time to read it to a gathering at the Avdeyevs' in Chistopol, and he brought it to Moscow ready for printing at the end of June 1943.[69] Alas, Nemirovich-Danchenko did not survive to read the work; he died on 25 April, which stalled further production plans for both *Hamlet* and *Antony and Cleopatra*.

Back in Moscow, on 8 July, Pasternak read his new translation at the All-Russian Theatrical Society where it received a rapturous reception.[70] Shortly afterwards, the presentation was repeated at the Moscow Writers' Club. One witness noted down some of Pasternak's preliminary remarks which referred to literary heroines such as Anna Karenina and Madame Bovary, and described Cleopatra as 'the Nastasya Filippovna of antiquity'.[71] His ideas on the play were shortly afterwards developed in his translator's notes. He maintained that the deep inherent realism of Shakespeare's work was at its strongest in the Roman plays, enhanced by the very remoteness of the time and place of action. These plays, especially *Antony and Cleopatra* were 'the fruits of studying unadorned everyday life', a study which 'led to the "physiological novel" of the nineteenth century and constituted the even more indisputable splendour of Chekhov, Flaubert and Lev Tolstoy'.[72] On its publication the following year, the play was greeted by Morozov as 'the most successful' of Pasternak's translations. 'It is more than a translation. It is the meeting of poet with poet.'[73]

Before this critical accolade, in the spring of 1943, on the strength of his first two Shakespeare translations and the poems of *On Early Trains*, still awaiting publication, Pasternak was nominated for a Stalin Prize, the highest national award for literature. Despite this evidence of a certain lobby of official supporters, Pasternak's candidature was rejected – both now and two years later when it was again proposed. Conjecturally, this must have been partly due to the adverse effect of an admiring article in the Western press by Pasternak's future translator Stefan Schimanski. Writing in the February 1943 issue of *Life and Letters Today*, Schimanski singled Pasternak out along with various younger Western artists who by their very abstention from propaganda and political statements, even in time of war, were upholding the freedom of spirit and lofty cultural and moral principle in whose name the war was being fought. This allegedly distinguished Pasternak from lesser Soviet writers, such as Sholokhov, who engaged in what was maybe good war journalism but failed to qualify as art.[74] As Fleishman notes, Schimanski was doubtless responding to Pasternak's own note 'On Shakespeare' published as 'My New Translations' in *Ogonyok* in late 1942; yet he also showed an intuitive understanding of what had also been Pasternak's position in Paris in 1935. However, such favourable publicity damaged his position at home by articulating his dissident stance, and it frustrated any attempts to repair his reputation with officialdom. This was by no means the last occasion when foreign approval worked to Pasternak's disadvantage back in Russia.[75]

10

War and Peace in Moscow

'Spring'

Everything this spring is special.
Much livelier the sparrows' clamour.
I even try not to express it –
How radiant my soul and tranquil!

I think and write not as before.
Like resonating choral octaves
The powerful voice of earth will sound
In every liberated province.

Our homeland's breath and waft of spring
Will rinse away all winter's traces,
Remove dark stains and rings around
The tear-worn eyes of Slavic nations.

Grass everywhere will start to thrust.
Though silent now, Prague's ancient alleys,
Each more winding than the last,
Will echo like ravines and valleys.

The lore of Czech, Morave and Serb
In springtime luxuriance stirring,
Will tear away the lawless shroud.
From under snow they'll sprout and burgeon.

A haze of legend will be cast
Over all, like scroll and spiral
Bedecking gilded boyar chambers
And the cathedral of St Basil.

By midnight denizens and dreamers
Moscow most of all is cherished.
Here is their home, the fount of all
With which this century will flourish.

(1944)

On the 25 June 1943 Boris, Zinaida, and the two boys boarded the steamer *Mikhail Sholokhov* along with other Writers' Union members and left Chistopol bound for Moscow. Many of the evacuee community had by this time returned to the capital, but the Pasternaks' own departure had been delayed by Zinaida's bout of pleurisy and her duties at the children's home.[1]

Pasternak tried vainly to persuade his wife that they should live in a hotel while attempting to secure another apartment in Lavrushinsky Lane, but she insisted on going to Peredelkino. The nursemaid Marusya was still there, but apart from the kitchen table, a samovar and young Leonid's bicycle, the house was bare and uninhabitable. The few items that had not been lost when the Ivanovs' villa burnt down had been deposited with the Fedins, Vishnevskys and others, and could not be retrieved immediately.[2]

Despite the spartan conditions, Leonid was left in Marusya's care while the rest of the family found temporary lodging elsewhere. Zinaida and Stanislav went to stay with the Pogodins. She and Anna Pogodina were on close terms, although Pasternak now steered clear of her husband who he realised was a cynical time-server. He himself lodged with the Asmuses in town, and for the next several months stayed either with them or at his brother's apartment. The occupation force in Lavrushinsky Lane could only be dislodged in October.[3]

It was a year however before the dacha could be reoccupied. Meanwhile, in autumn of 1943 steps were taken to reunite the family and organise Adrian's return to Moscow. His overall condition had deteriorated further. He was immobilised through loss of his leg, the disease had spread to his lower spine and he was feverish and in constant pain. Zinaida went to fetch him home in early September; Genrikh Neigauz was still exiled in Sverdlovsk and helped her collect Adrian from Nizhnii Ufalei and saw them off on the Moscow train. On arrival Adrian was placed in the Yauza tubercular clinic, but after a contretemps with the doctor over conditions there, he was transfered to the Sokolniki clinic under a specialist who was a personal friend of Militsa Neigauz. The family's worst fears were now confirmed: Adrian was incurably ill, and he too unfortunately realised this. The years of mental anguish and hard work in Chistopol had also left their mark on Zinaida, who had lost weight and aged considerably.[4]

When the Freidenbergs were blockaded in Leningrad, contacts almost ceased, and Pasternak assumed they had either perished or been evacuated. However, in late October 1943 pianist Maria Yudina returned from there with reassuring news that cousin Olga and her mother were both safe.[5]

By autumn of 1943 Evgeniya and Evgenii Pasternak had also returned to Moscow. Evgenii was now aged twenty and he enrolled in the second year at the Moscow tank construction academy to continue training started at the

Tashkent Military Academy.[6] Shortly after returning Evgenii was able to save some of his father's earliest work from destruction. Clearing out the town apartment Pasternak discovered large amounts of old manuscript material. Since the apartment block had central heating and no stoves, a large bundle of papers was handed over for use as kindling in the Tverskoi Boulevard apartment; among them Evgenii discovered the manuscripts of war poetry, translations from Hans Sachs, the early *Suboctave Story (Istoriya odnoi kontroktavy)*, and letters from Nadezhda Sinyakova and Elena Vinograd. As a habitual destroyer of old manuscripts, Pasternak was not pleased at his son's archivist instinct and no further consignments of fuel were offered; what else was lost or discarded at that time we cannot know.[7]

The poetry collection *On Early Trains* appeared in bookshops in mid June 1943 and was favourably though not widely reviewed. Konstantin Simonov, a younger-generation poet and dramatist who enjoyed official favour, described Pasternak as having pursued 'The Correct Path'. Allegedly he had rightly ignored his didactically-minded critics of the 1930s; the war events had helped him realise a need to write accessibly, and while retaining his boldness of imagery, Pasternak had 'discovered a miraculous simplicity that goes right to the heart'. Some of his new work, Simonov maintained, deserved a place in the golden treasury of Russian war poetry and should be recited as inspiration to Soviet front-line troops.[8]

The new book was a public success, although some readers expecting stentorian tones rather than *mezza voce* lyrics in a book of war poetry were disappointed. Pasternak was also dissatisfied. The book contained some items he was proud of, though little of recent vintage. As he told Nadezhda Mandelstam, 'there are about fifteen quality poems here when there ought to be a hundred and fifty. In this lies the embarrassing insignificance of the book.'[9] However, he was under contract with GIKhL to assemble another general poetic *Selected Works (Izbrannoe)* in which he planned to include 'everything descriptive'.[10] For all their simplicity, his war and other lyrics were hardly remarkable in theme or sentiment, and the lyric poem now generally seemed to dissatisfy Pasternak as a vehicle for developed personal statement. A sense of malaise and unfulfilled promise was detected in Antokolsky's review in *Znamya*,[11] and Pasternak was relieved when Akhmatova told him in spring of 1944 that she had not yet seen *On Early Trains*.[12]

Pasternak gave another reading of *Antony and Cleopatra* at the Writers' Union on 20 July, where the audience included Loks, Fedin, Tomashevsky and Vilenkin. The latter thought it Pasternak's best translation to date.[13] On the other hand, as Pasternak told Gladkov, 'at such a time as this one cannot subsist on translations [. . .] After all, it is a surrogate for real activity'.[14] Moreover, a series of mishaps interfered with various Shakespeare production plans and royalties were very limited. Nemirovich-Danchenko's death in 1943 was followed by that of associate producer Sakhnovsky, and prospects for *Antony and Cleopatra* at the Moscow Arts Theatre foundered. *Hamlet* suffered even worse setbacks. After many delays, the Theatre's artistic commission watched a private 'dry run' performance in 1945, which was adjudged unsuccessful and the work was abandoned, which was a blow to Pasternak and to Boris Livanov, who played the title role.[15] A rumour circulated for many years that production was cancelled after Livanov asked Stalin at a Kremlin reception about his opinion of how to play Hamlet, to which the Leader responded with a disparaging remark about the play as a whole.[16] The story was later disavowed by Livanov, but it nevertheless reflected an awareness that the times were not propitious for such a play. Probably Stalin liked it no more than *Macbeth* or *Boris Godunov*, which also depicted a tyrant's bloodstained path to power.[17]

Shuttling between the Asmuses and his brother, Pasternak in summer and autumn 1943 busied himself with small-scale tasks. In August he wrote a short review of Akhmatova's poetic collection that had appeared in Tashkent, edited by Zelinsky. Identifying Akhmatova's major place in Russian poetry, Pasternak described these 'headlong and gripping poems by a great human being recording a great subject [. . .] the life and work of an unbendable, direct and dedicated daughter of her people and her age, accustomed and hardened to losses, and courageously prepared for the ordeals of immortality'.[18] The review was commissioned by *Ogonyok*, but did not appear. A similar fate befell a somewhat longer article for *Literatura i iskusstvo* (Literature and Art) on Akhmatova's *Selected Works (Izbrannoe)*.[19] The quota of liberalism and page space that allowed her reemergence in print was evidently exhausted.

Pasternak had better success with the exiled Lachian poet Óndra Łysohorsky. They had met in Moscow before their respective evacuations to Chistopol and Tashkent, and discovered 'a communality of poetic attachments and experienced influences', including the verse of Rilke. Pasternak liked Łysohorsky's original thought and 'indestructible pictorial taste'. Then, in July 1943 they met again, and their mutual sympathy was reinforced by a shared sense of frustration in the current political environment. Łysohorsky provided interlinear glosses, and five poems translated by Pasternak together with a short article on 'A Slavonic Poet' appeared on 21 August in *Literatura i iskusstvo*.[20] A volume of Łysohorsky's work with ten of Pasternak's translations later appeared in 1946 but without the introductory article he had hoped to write. Łysohorsky left Moscow for home in mid 1946 but remained ever grateful for Pasternak's inspiration and moral support.[21]

During summer 1943 Pasternak renewed his efforts to visit the fighting front. On 5 August Soviet troops recaptured Oryol and Belgorod, an event marked two days later in Pasternak's 'Hasty Lines' ('Speshnye stroki') of jubilant doggerel.[22] Two weeks later, on Monday 23 August, the recapture of Kharkov was celebrated in Moscow with huge public gatherings, victory salutes, fireworks and churchbells. Several writers including Ehrenburg, Fedin, Vsevolod Ivanov, Leonov, Tikhonov and Aleksei Tolstoy marked the occasion with articles in the central press. Although no admirer of war reportage, Pasternak accepted an invitation from the chief editor of *Krasnaya zvezda* and joined a group of writers on a two-week visit to the Third Army to collect material for a projected book 'In the Battles for Oryol'.

Leaving Moscow by army lorry on the morning of Friday 27 August, the literary brigade included veteran novelist Serafimovich, Pasternak's friends Antokolsky, Fedin and Ivanov, Konstantin Simonov, and the widow of the deceased revolutionary classic Nikolai Ostrovsky. Travelling south through Tula, Chern, Mtsensk, to Oryol itself and the local military headquarters at Pesochnya, their progress was marked by meetings, formal and spontaneous, with army commanders and soldiers, readings to gatherings of servicemen and wounded soldiers, and numerous contacts with the population of newly liberated areas.

Pasternak kept a detailed diary and notes which later formed the basis of articles and various war poems. As he told Valerii Avdeyev, his trip to the front 'did not so much show me what I could not have expected or guessed, as it liberated me inwardly. Suddenly everything was near at hand, natural and accessible, much more in keeping with my usual thoughts than with generally accepted depictions'. By his own account, Pasternak felt quite at home with the senior military who received them,[23] and Ivanov recounted how he 'charmed everyone in the army, from soldiers to generals. He captivated them by his bravery, unpretentiousness and fascinating speeches' which contrasted with the tedious performances of several other writers. After a supper with General Gorbatov, for instance, Pasternak 'spoke vividly, patriotically, in elevated fashion and with humour [. . .] The officers and generals were pale, moved, and listened in total silence. They perhaps understood Pasternak better than all the rest of us.' Simonov and Gorbatov himself confirmed Ivanov's impressions. Later Pasternak was proud to be chosen as the one to compose the writers' collective address to the Third Army.[24]

The people who most impressed Pasternak were those with qualities now cultivated in his own life and work. He was specially struck by General Gorbatov's intelligence, sincerity and lack of affectation. Accounts of the slain war hero General Gurtyev and a visit to his grave also made a deep mark. To Gurtyev's memory Pasternak later dedicated his poem 'Reanimated Fresco' ('Ozhivshaya freska').[25]

Some of what Pasternak saw, particularly the war-shattered city of Oryol, figured in chapter sixteen in *Doctor Zhivago* in which his heroes Dudorov and Gordon also serve in the Soviet army in precisely that area in summer 1943. Pasternak's notebooks and his two articles suggest that the most telling experiences were not so much the scenes of devastation but the human contacts and conversations. His impressions were manifestly those of a 'literary patriot' with sharp aural perception as well as a keen eye. Entering Oryol revived memories of Turgenev, Leskov and Bunin's descriptions; Colonel Kustov sparked memories of the heroes of 1812. Visiting one location and hearing the speech of the locals, Pasternak realised suddenly:

We were at the primary source of our greatest national treasure. In these districts arose the speech that formed our literary language and about which Turgenev made his famous pronouncement. Nowhere has the spirit of Russian authenticity – our noblest possession – expressed itself so exhaustively and freely. And our friends here were natives of this region. They bore the mark of our supreme Russian gift. They are of one flesh and blood with Liza Kalitina and Natasha Rostova.[26]

The writers' brigade returned to Moscow on Friday 10 September, just a week before Soviet forces recaptured the city of Bryansk. Pasternak was full of creative impetus. He had ideas for a series of articles, and he was anxious to press ahead with the narrative war poem first conceived the previous year, after which he hoped to pay a return visit to the front.[27] Some of these hopes were frustrated however.

He had little success with his belated interest in war reporting. Only two poems were included in the book to which he was supposed to contribute. Only one of the two articles he wrote – *A Visit to the Army* ('Poezdka v armiyu') – appeared in a heavily cut version in the newspaper *Trud* (Labour) on 20 November. What went into print was a series of descriptive passages. Omitted were a lengthy concluding address to the warriors of the Third Army, and an Aesopic passage purportedly contrasting fascist Germany and communist Russia but concealing a deeper parallel. The pure revolutionary ideal, admired as a product of the Russian national genius, was contrasted with Germany's now forfeited cultural primacy. The hidden term, however, which made an equation from two contrasting elements was the distortion and degeneration that over- take any ideal that is debased by mediocrity and violence:

Anyone guilty of villainy to others also commits a crime against himself. Evil is universal. He who violates the commandment to love his neighbour betrays himself first of all [. . .] If revolutionary Russia ever required a crooked mirror to distort her own features with a grimace of hate and incomprehension, then here it is: Germany has set about producing it . . .

'The element of genius that prepared our revolution', Pasternak claimed, was a 'phenomenon of national morality', manifest as 'a deeply felt right to measure everything in this world by one's own yardstick, a sense of oneness with the universe, the enjoyment of one's close blood-tie with history, a feeling of access to all things living'. Yet inevitably, 'the carefree generosity of natural talent is always followed by something envious, commonplace and mediocre [. . .] The ignoramus starts with sermonising and ends with bloodshed.' (*SS*, IV, 664–5.) Probably editorial staff failed to draw the damning implied parallels between Nazism and the Stalinist regime. But as with tsarist censorship, complex argumentation or theoretical passages aroused a morbid distrust among ideologues, and for safety' sake these passages were excised from Pasternak's text.[28]

Despite his shaky journalistic start, Pasternak still hoped to 'get into the papers' as he told Olga Freidenberg.[29] He benefited by wartime liberalisation that in 1942 permitted even Akhmatova to publish alongside other women authors in the Party newspaper *Pravda*.[30] The same paper now approached Pasternak for contributions on topical themes.[31] One work that qualified was his projected narrative poem on a wartime theme. *Nightglow* (*Zarevo*) took its title from the salutes and firework displays over Moscow that greeted the liberation of Oryol. Pasternak submitted to *Pravda* what he had written so far, and thirteen quatrains of introduction presenting a common soldier inspired by the victory flares and evidently destined for future heroism, duly appeared on 15 October. However, when 'Chapter One' was submitted, it was turned down outright, and with a vehemence that killed any prospect of a published sequel. Hopes of the poem's publication in *Znamya* were also dashed, and Fadeyev personally advised Pasternak against continuing work on it.[32]

The reason for *Pravda*'s decision was understandable in its own terms. The story lacked any conventional heroics, depicted quite unheroic 'naturalistic' detail, and contained uncomplimentary hints at modern literary moral standards. In the winter of 1943–44 Pasternak expressed a particular interest in Simonov and Tvardovsky's work and wanted to understand the 'mechanism' of their celebrity. *Nightglow* was evidently an essay in emulation, an attempt to write something akin to Tvardovsky's popular epic with its soldier-hero *Vasilii Tyorkin*, which began appearing serially in 1942. Pasternak's enthusiasm for Tvardovsky evidently endeared him to General Gorbatov and his men, and he described the poem as 'the miracle of a poet's total dissolvement in the element of popular speech'.[33] Probably some of *Tyorkin's* intonations sounded in the opening of *Nightglow*, as Volodya the infantryman returned to Moscow after the battle for Oryol, thinking:

> [. . .] 'I'll find things there
> Which so far I've never dreamed of
> – What victory and blood have bought.
>
> 'And we'll not stop at empty phrases,
> But like in some great dreamed-of vision
> We'll build still grander than before,
> And brighter than before we'll glisten.'   (*SS*, II, 51)

With these thoughts Volodya made his exit from *Pravda*. Manuscript copies retained by Pasternak's friends Yakov Chernyak and Lev Ozerov subsequently helped reconstruct the poem's continuation. Uplifted and transformed by battle experiences, Volodya dreamed of a better future, of 'horizons with prospects' and the 'novelty of the people's role'. Meanwhile, though, his sluttish wife had been unfaithful and was evidently embedded in her unsavoury past. More offensive than the story, though, was Pasternak's contrast of modern authors with writers of the past who were not seekers after blandishments and whose heroes suffered from epilepsy (like Dostoevsky's 'Idiot') and were burned up and radiant with suffering. Implicitly, modern authors did not match up to their predecessors and Pasternak claimed that without an ability to 'embroider harmless thoughts', he and his contemporaries would write no differently and no better than Hemingway and Priestley (authors of whom Pasternak had no high opinion, with the exception of Hemingway's *For Whom the Bell Tolls*).[34]

Pasternak was indignant at the rejection of his poem and he turned down the *Pravda* editors' counter-proposal for a translation of Leonidze's 'Childhood of the Leader'. He had rejected a similar commission in 1941, and such a task would by now have been even more repugnant.[35] Pasternak's only further collaboration with *Pravda* was the publication of one victory poem in May of 1944. As he told his cousin in mid November, 'It is very hard for me to battle against the tone dominating in the press. Nothing is successful; probably I shall surrender again and go back to Shakespeare.'[36]

The one product of Pasternak's trip to the front which secured publication was a handful of war poems that appeared in the press between November 1943 and April 1944. However, by no means every submission was accepted. In winter of 1944, the Yiddish partisan writer Abraham Sutskever visited the offices of *Literatura i iskusstvo* and saw the enthusiasm of editorial staff for

Pasternak's work overruled by Surkov the chief editor; the poem in question, 'Winter Holidays', was published in *Literaturnaya gazeta* however.[37]

Pasternak's war poems varied greatly in quality and were sometimes slightly pedestrian efforts, written just for their earning capacity. One such example was 'The Victor' ('Pobeditel'') marking the end of the Leningrad blockade and published in *Trud* on 28 January 1944, and two items commissioned by the paper *Krasny flot* (The Red Fleet) in spring of 1944. Elsewhere the artistry lagged far behind the poems' situational poignancy. Some discomfort was evident in Tarasenkov's review of these verses when they were collected and published under one cover in 1945. As Boris Thomson later commented, the simplicity of some of these poems has 'more simplification than new wisdom' and Pasternak had little to add to established and well-worn martial and patriotic themes.[38]

The best of Pasternak's wartime poems were maybe those such as 'Winter is Coming' ('Zima priblizhaetsya') that combined martial and patriotic with rural motifs, or else those deriving from incidents Pasternak heard of first-hand on his journey to the front. In the latter category, Pasternak's notes on the feat of a soldier who was fatally wounded and died in silence so as not to betray his comrades served as the basis for 'The Sapper's Death' ('Smert' sapera'),[39] which climaxed in a statement of his philosophy of sacrifice:

> To live and burn out is the custom.
> But only then is life immortal
> When you by act of sacrifice
> Have blazed the path to light and glory.
> (III, 48; *SP*, 417; *SS*, II, 59)

With his poems on martial and political subjects, Pasternak had to contend also with the military editorial mind at work, and he was infuriated, for instance, when *Krasnaya zvezda* published 'The Sapper's Death' on 10 December 1943 with one stanza omitted and with several assonance rhymes 'corrected'. As he told his friend Daniil Danin, this was a poem with 'serious intentions', originally linked in his mind with the idea behind *Nightglow* and some other poems in similar style and meter.[40] Another incident of the same sort occurred in spring 1944. After the poem 'Spring' appeared in *Trud* on 1 May, *Pravda* also claimed it and printed it on 17 May with a politically enhanced concluding prophecy:

> Here is *my* home, the fount of all
> With which the *centuries* will flourish.

This political speculation with his verse, about which Pasternak complained to

Kruchenykh and others, was typical of utilitarian press attitudes to the arts in general.[41]

The last recorded thoughts and words of General Gurtyev as reported by Gorbatov, in whose arms he died, formed a basis for 'The Reanimated Fresco', the best and most sophisticated of Pasternak's war poems. It was drafted in late March of 1944 and published in *Literatura i iskusstvo* on 15 April 1944.[42] The dying man's thoughts conflated memories of the defence of Stalingrad with childhood recollections of a monastery and its fresco of St George fighting the dragon, which in turn led back to thoughts of recent battle. There were two further complete manuscript variants of the poem. The first, entitled 'Stalingrad', concentrated on Gurtyev's imagined recollection of the battle of Stalingrad; the second, with the title 'Resurrection' ('Voskresenie') had religious overtones that made it unprintable in the Soviet press; it linked the hero's posthumous memory with the idea of Christ's resurrection, prefiguring the philosophy of *Zhivago*.[43]

Also unpublishable for similar reasons were the religiously coloured memorial verses to Tsvetaeva, conceived at Chistopol and set down in Kruchenykh's album on 25–26 December 1943. Pasternak recited them publicly several times during the 1940s, but they were never printed during his lifetime.[44]

As the literary community returned to Moscow in autumn of 1943, Pasternak's coterie resumed their meetings, but now in Lavrushinsky Lane. Pasternak, Vsevolod Ivanov and others shared a sense of optimism when once the course of the war turned in Russia's favour. As Ivanov's son records, there was a resurgence of spiritual forces of a sort that flourished at the start of the century and in early 1917. 'After so many years of complete spiritual stagnation and despair, the few who survived both physically and inwardly sensed again a hint of the return of a general Russian spiritual uplift [. . .] a hope that the blood shed in the war had not been in vain'. Some of that mood that owed its impetus to the latter war years was captured in the final prose chapter of *Doctor Zhivago*.[45]

The optimism of this period was of an embattled sort however, based objectively on no more than an awareness of the German retreat and a memory of ideological relaxation in the early phase of the war. In late 1943 the atmosphere seemed to be reverting to its former oppressiveness however. Among the barometric signs of this was the mood of stark tragedy in Shostakovich's Eighth Symphony, a public rehearsal of which Pasternak attended on Wednesday, 3 November in the Large Hall of Moscow Conservatoire. Premiered next day in the aftermath of Russia's triumph over German troops at Kursk and the liberation of Kiev and Smolensk, its brooding sense of catastrophe, as one commentator put it, 'rang a very dissonant – not to say dissident – note'. Well attuned to such non-verbal signals, Pasternak was heard to comment after another performance at that time of Shostakovich's Fifth Symphony: 'Just imagine, he said everything – and they didn't do anything to him.'[46]

In the final days of 1943, Pasternak's relations with literary officialdom began to deteriorate, and a series of unpleasant incidents affected several writers of liberal persuasion. On 6 December a Writers' Union Presidium meeting heavily censured the journal *Oktyabr'* for its publication of the opening of Zoshchenko's story 'Before Sunrise' ('Pered voskhodom solntsa'). At another Union meeting on 30 December Fadeyev severely berated Zoshchenko again and a group of other writers including Aseyev, Fedin, Selvinsky, and Pasternak for various sins of 'ideological distortion'. In Pasternak's case this involved elements of 'great-power chauvinism' in his poem 'Winter's Approach' ('Zima priblizhaetsya')![47] As Pasternak told Danin on the last day of the year:

I no longer believe in the success of my present efforts. [. . .] But the general tone of literature, and the fate of individual exceptions marked by any kind of thought, is discouraging. They have given Zoshchenko a working-over; they have leaned on Aseyev who after many years of chill vacuity has started writing in a human way; and now Selvinsky's turn has come, it seems. It's all the same. I have no liking for anyone now. [And] I have started exploding for other reasons, and with such ferocity that some day this will be my undoing.[48]

Pasternak's sense that he and his generation would be caught up in some final Apocalyptic disaster was captured in his birthday toast proposed on 24 February 1944 to Vsevolod Ivanov: 'I never believed in either the fourth dimension or in devils. But by 1950 there will be both devils and a fourth dimension. Questions important for man have been raised but not solved, although it appears that they have been. Just now we have the rolling wave between their rising and their solution. We are like fragments in a maelstrom.'[49] Later that year in a postcard message to poetess Anna Lebedinskaya who was interned in a labour camp in the northern Urals, Pasternak wrote that 'Many of my friends are in the same situation as yourself, and the fact that I am here in Moscow and not with you is a matter of pure chance . . .'[50]

Meanwhile, in the winter of 1943–44 Pasternak began work again on theatrical translations which occupied him for the next three years. On the 18 January 1944 he gave a reading of *Antony and Cleopatra* to the Moscow Arts Theatre company in the presence of theatre celebrities such as the Kachalovs,

Knipper and Tarasova. Vilenkin had canvassed senior members of the company in support of Pasternak, and Khmelyov the general artistic director accepted the play for production. Another pleasant consequence of the recital was Pasternak's new friendship with the elderly actor Kachalov.[51]

Pasternak's repute as *the* Shakespeare translator was now beyond challenge, and this provided several years of steady income. As he told Valerii Avdeyev the following year, 'Shakespeare, the old man of Chistopol, is feeding me as before'.[52] In autumn of 1943 the British Embassy had written to him with compliments and thanks for his Shakespeare translation work; now, in 1944, he received a publisher's proposal for a 'collected Shakespeare', to consist of *King Lear*, *Macbeth* or *The Tempest*, and two chronicles, *Richard II* and *Henry IV*.

Before attending to this project, Pasternak first worked on a new *Othello* for the Maly Theatre.[53] The play was never one of his favourites and he claimed in June 1944 to be translating only 'half-consciously'.[54] Part of his dislike was a purely technical objection later explained in his translator's notes. Unlike the lively introductory and final scenes, he found the centre of the play and its deployment of event and counter-event contrived.[55] On the other hand, aspects of *Othello* seemed like an oblique comment on Soviet public life. In his prefatory note to Act IV scene 3, published separately in December 1944, Pasternak contrasted the Iago's absolute and unlimited freedom of evil with the non-freedom of Othello and Desdemona who were human beings constrained by moral compunctions.[56] As the 1946 translator's 'Notes' commented, for Shakespeare Othello was 'a man of history and a Christian'; Iago was 'unconverted, prehistoric, and bestial' – epithets almost identical to those Pasternak applied in conversation to the rule of Stalin.[57]

As he completed *Othello* in August 1944, Pasternak swore that he would never do any more translations,[58] and he dreamed of returning to his own dramatic project. However, as he told his cousin, although he had literary ideas to express, 'we have no literature and under present conditions there will not, and cannot, be any. Last winter I signed a contract with two theatres for an independent tragedy about our day, on a war theme, with a setting in the future (which I reckoned on situating in this autumn). I thought that circumstances by this time would change and things become slightly freer. But the situation doesn't change.'[59]

This was Pasternak' last mention of his wartime drama project, which was now shelved and forgotten. Also abandoned was the resolve to give up translation in favour of original work. In autumn of 1944 the Maly Theatre's planned staging of his *Romeo and Juliet* was cancelled after a vicious attack in *Pravda* led to dismissal of the director Sudakov.[60] However, *Othello* was quickly printed; it appeared twice in 1945–6 – with GIKhL and in an edition by the All-Union Board of Authors' Copyright. At the same time Pasternak produced more short poetic translations, published in the literary press and in editions of Isaakyan, Rylsky, and Shevchenko. There was more poetry by Chikovani, and translated material in an *Anthology of Georgian Patriotic Poetry (Antologiya gruzinskoi patrioticheskoi poezii)*. January of 1945 saw a new contract signed for the translation of both parts of Shakespeare's *Henry IV*.[61]

Apart from translation work, the spring of 1944 found Pasternak elaborating new ideas that advanced his artistic horizon and philosophy as prolegomena to some future major artistic project at present unwritten, and in present conditions unprintable. One of his manuscripts for the Tsvetaeva memorial verses carried a note that linked this poetry with ideas for an article about Blok and the young Mayakovsky.[62] Nothing on Mayakovsky was committed to paper, but the intention to write on Blok remained a serious one, and two years later Pasternak drafted some notes 'Towards a Characterisation of Blok'.[63] But first to emerge from the ganglion of new ideas was an article on Paul-Marie Verlaine designed for the French poet's centenary, and printed in the 1st April issue of *Literatura i iskusstvo* for 1944.

Pasternak saw in Verlaine a spiritual and stylistic kinship with Rilke, Ibsen, Chekhov, the later Blok, and the Impressionist art of France, Russia and Scandinavia. The essence of his art was recognised in its 'realism' – not that of nineteenth-century prose fiction, but of Impressionist or Symbolist depiction, showing a 'reality totally caught up in transition and ferment'. In this sense Verlaine was akin to 'Blok the realist [who] provided the most sublime, uniquely intimate picture of St Petersburg in this flashing of portentous happenings'. This view of Blok as a prime exemplar of a personally refracted realism remained with Pasternak and was developed in his autobiographical essay of the mid 1950s. Verlaine's call for 'de la musique avant toute chose' was in Pasternak's view not a cult of musicality at the expense of semantics, but part of poetry's attempt to capture 'real experience', a record of the sound of bells, the scent of flora, birdlife, and 'all the modulations of silence, both inward and external, from winter's starlit hush to the summer torpor of a heated noonday'. In doing this, Verlaine 'imparted to the language in which he wrote that boundless freedom which was his discovery in lyric verse, and which is encountered only in masters of prose dialogue in the novel and in drama'.[64]

The 'correctness' of this interpretation of Verlaine was less important than its demonstration of Pasternak's own artistic priorities which were elaborated further in his other writings of the time. For instance, he descried in the

English verse of Shelley certain further links with the world of Verlaine, Shelley himself being a 'precursor and prophet of the urbanistic mysticism subsequently breathed by Russian and European Symbolism'. In his apostrophe of the elements in his 'Ode to the West Wind' Pasternak identified the 'future voices of Blok, Verhaeren and Rilke'.[65]

Some further ideas on artistic realism were featured in another article of 1945, which enshrined the composer Chopin in Pasternak's 'realist pantheon'. The article *Chopin* ('Shopen') was originally commissioned by the newspaper *Sovetskoe iskusstvo* (Soviet Art) for the 135th anniversary of the composer's birth, although it was printed only in abbreviated form in issues 15–16 of the journal *Leningrad*.[66] While talking nominally about music, Pasternak stated his overall view of artistic realism which was 'seen not to represent a separate trend, but to constitute a particular level of art, the highest degree of authorial precision'. Realism in this sense was counterposed to mere romanticism with its 'stilted pathos, false profundity, and affected sweetness', and exploitation of 'every form of artificiality'. Pasternak perceived Chopin as a 'realist in just the same way as Lev Tolstoy'; his work was *'original'* because of a close resemblance to a real-life model, and *biographical* because, 'like all great realists, Chopin regarded his own life as an instrument for experiencing all life upon earth'.[67]

Retrospectively the foundations of this personally understood realist aesthetic can be observed in Pasternak's verse and prose of the early 1930s. But his antagonism towards romanticism – understood not as a movement, but as an authorial habit of over-indulgence in fantasy, inflated rhetoric, or self-dramatisation – dated back to his early liberation from Scriabinism and Mayakovsky, and it continued to preoccupy him in the 1940s as a programme of resistance to the rhetorical and utopian misrepresentations of socialist realism.

Pasternak's view of Chopin was of course eccentric, controversial and partly self-contradictory. (While rejecting 'programme music', his article suggested depictive associations in several musical compositions that seemed to counter his own propositions.) However, as with Verlaine, the value of Pasternak's ideas lay not in their truth about Chopin. That same year of 1945 in a note to the paper *Zarya Vostoka* (Dawn of the Orient) he also claimed a place in his realist hall of fame for the Georgian Romantic Baratashvili. The principles Pasternak elaborated in these publications were valid essentially for his own creative aesthetic. Meanwhile the term 'realist' as applied to other artists was a form of honorific title conferred in later life on his favourite writers and composers irrespective of any realist hallmarks of a traditional sort.[68]

Pasternak's fullest embodiment of the ideas expounded in these articles of

215

1944–45 still lay ahead, in the novel *Doctor Zhivago* and his later verse. For the moment they largely remained a theoretical statement, applied, at most, in a few dozen lyric poems.

On 15 May 1944, Akhmatova flew in from Tashkent and spent two weeks in the capital before returning to Leningrad. In Moscow she gave a poetry recital at the Polytechnic Museum, where she received a standing ovation so ecstatic that she feared its consequences in light of official attitudes towards her.[69] In Moscow she also met up with Pasternak and, among other news, brought greetings from Nadezhda Mandelstam who had remained in Tashkent, where she taught English at the Central Asian State University. Akhmatova also brought from her a letter that Mandelstam had written and intended sending to Pasternak back in the New Year of 1937. As Evgenii Pasternak comments, there was a special poignance in this message from beyond the grave, and in its prophetic wish that Pasternak's poetry 'which has spoiled and undeservedly endowed us, should strain ever onward, to the world, to the people and to children . . . Just once in life let me say to you: thank you for everything, and for the fact that this "everything" is still "not yet everything".'[70]

Part of Mandelstam's wish was by 1945 already coming true, of course. Pasternak's trip to the front in 1943 had proved to him and to others that he had a popular readership and audience, and as he told Nadezhda Mandelstam in a letter of 1945, 'A discovery for me was the quantity and sort of public at my evenings this year; I had not imagined this, and it was a surprise to everyone.'[71] The success of these frequent readings continued until 1946, and they included solo recitals and contributions to joint programmes, where he figured sometimes in combination with officially approved figures such as Sofronov, Surkov, or Aleksandr Zharov.[72]

Pasternak's sense of contact with 'his' public partly reduced his reliance on – or desire for – the support of professional colleagues. Relations with the literary establishment took a further downturn when Tikhonov in 1944 for two years succeeded Fadeyev as chairman of the Board of the Writers' Union. Supposedly an old friend, and in principle more liberal than Fadeyev, once in post Tikhonov was reluctant to jeopardise his standing by any display of independent-mindedness. Pasternak made little secret of his disappointment in him.[73] As he admitted the following year:

Nothing is left of my former peaceableness and sociability. Not only do the Tikhonovs and the majority of the Union not exist for me, and not only do I reject them, but I lose no opportunity of stating this openly and publicly. And naturally, they are right to settle accounts with me. Of course this distribution of forces is unequal, but my fate has been determined and I have no choice.[74]

Pasternak spent the summer of 1944 in Moscow at the Lavrushinsky Lane apartment along with his younger stepson. Stanislav had that summer graduated from the Music College attached to Moscow Conservatoire, and was about to enter the Conservatoire itself, studying under his own father's assistant Vladimir Belov.[75] Genrikh Neigauz was still in exile in Sverdlovsk and directed his son's career moves by letter and he had Pasternak arrange Stanislav's admission via Shebalin, the new Conservatoire director.[76] Genrikh Neigauz himself was able to return to Moscow only in October 1944.

Zinaida Pasternak meanwhile lived at the Peredelkino dacha with Leonid, where she tended the garden and worked to make the villa habitable again. Twice a week she visited Adrian at Sokolniki. That summer the Asmuses also lived at the Pasternaks' dacha, and in late July Boris wrote to Olga Freidenberg (who in April had lost her mother), inviting her to join them, in which event he himself would temporarily move to Peredelkino. Olga did not come however, and the cousins' contacts remained limited to correspondence.[77]

In July Pasternak delivered to Sovetsky Pisatel publishers a new poetic collection entitled 'Free Perspective' ('Svobodny krugozor') and containing ten poems from *On Early Trains* and thirteen reprinted war poems. For the edition, which appeared in late January 1945, the title was changed to *Earthly Expanse* (*Zemnoi prostor*), and some alterations were imposed by the censor in the wake of Fadeyev's outburst against national chauvinism and other ideological sins. 'Waltz with Devilry' ('Val's s chertovshchinoi') and 'To the Russian Genius' were omitted; 'Winter's Approach' had some lines replaced;[78] and some verses in 'The Scouts' and 'Pursuit' that notionally tarnished the image of Soviet soldiery – swearing 'ornately' like brigands in their lair, and bursting into a village 'insolently, like thieves or pedlars' – were excised.[79] Quite apart from this interference, the book was a mediocre, 'make-weight' publication, and Pasternak felt a 'physical antipathy' towards its flimsy production on cheap and nasty paper of pocket diary proportions, held together by a single staple.[80]

Reviewing *Earthly Expanse* in the journal *Znamya*, Tarasenkov, and the poet Sergei Spassky writing in *Leningrad* both contrasted the beauty of the landscape lyrics in part one with the sententious placard-like rhetoric and dryness of the war poetry. The only successful item in the war cycle, Tarasenkov maintained, was the final poem 'Spring', but he missed the voice that created *Second Birth* and earlier masterpieces, and looked in vain for the 'organic unity' that once linked civic and lyrical elements in Pasternak. Tarasenkov concluded:

Yes, the poet should be a dreamer and midnight denizen,[81] but not a rhetorician, nor a battlefield reporter [. . .] Pasternak used to have too many individualist faults [. . .] too much intimacy and complexity. [. . .] But let them be replaced by genuine, not illusory, values. Let there sound again [. . .] the ardent word of the patriot and lyricist, the master and heartfelt dreamer, which always excited the hearts of readers.[82]

While some commentators found Pasternak was 'wiser and simpler' than his earlier ornate style, and although he avoided the rhetoric cliché of some wartime bards, his verse in this genre was not viewed as a pinnacle of his achievement.[83] One of Tarasenkov's wishes was granted, however, when *Selected Verses and Poems (Izbrannye stikhi i poemy)* appeared in the summer of 1945. The proofs had been corrected in summer of 1944, and the book appeared with Goslitizdat shortly after *Earthly Expense*. This was his first such general miscellany of verse since the reprint of *Poems in One Volume* in 1936. It included 'The Year 1905' and 'Lieutenant Shmidt', and while omitting 'Malady Sublime', 'Spektorsky', and the lyrics of socialistic consensus from the 1930s, it contained an ample selection of his finest work. The book's appearance was a product of the liberal wartime interval whose promises were about to fade. Symptomatic maybe were the placement of 'Spring' as the very last item in the book and the appearance of only three short anonymous reviews.[84]

During the winter of 1944–45 Pasternak lived mainly in the newly habitable Peredelkino dacha and worked intensively on *Henry IV*. For two weeks around New Year time, he suffered an attack of periostitis,[85] followed by a four-month bout of nervous inflammation in the shoulder. In consequence the Shake-speare manuscript was written mainly with his left hand – a result of 'clerk's rather than writer's exhaustion', as he told Nina Tabidze. In spring of 1945 Pasternak was also afflicted by conjunctivitis and by enlargement of the liver, but as he told Olga, he had 'neither the time nor the will to get treatment; through all the suffering and tears I have had a surge of incomprehensible humour, indestructible faith and a certain fervour'.[86]

On Sunday 29 April, Adrian Neigauz died. The last weeks of his life were clouded by the death of his wardmate from tubercular meningitis, and he himself succumbed and died of this disease. As he neared the end, his mother was allowed to live in the sanatorium along with him; the only means of saving him would have been treatment with streptomycin, but there was no way of ordering this from America in time. Zinaida was devastated at her son's death, and Boris too was distraught and tearful.[87]

Zinaida was opposed to cremation, but assented since she could then take home Adrian's ashes. Three days later, Stanislav brought the urn to Pere-delkino and it was buried in the garden by the currant bush that Adrian planted as a little boy. The Asmuses who were staying at the dacha were evidently of great support, and Boris too did his utmost to comfort Zinaida's almost suicidal grief. His homily on the idea of there being no death, since the dead continue living in the memory of those dear to them, was probably lost on Zinaida. But evidently his thoughts closely prefigured Yurii Zhivago's words of comfort to his sick mother-in-law in the novel *Doctor Zhivago*.[88]

Barely a month after Adrian's death, news arrived that Leonid Pasternak had died of heart failure in Oxford on 31 May, at the age of 83. In his last years he had led a semi-reclusive life at Lydia's home in Park Town. Apart from painting and enjoyment of his family, his main pleasure was in visiting the Ashmolean Museum. The only publicity he attracted was on his eightieth birthday, which was noted in the British press. He was also visited by Soviet ambassador Ivan Maisky, but plans for an exhibition in aid of the Soviet war effort fell through.[89] During the war period Leonid was saddened by the rare contact with his sons in Moscow; he received only one of the dozen or so books that Boris sent him, and a letter passed through diplomatic channels and Ambassador Maisky never reached him.[90] He was cremated in Oxford and his urn placed alongside that of his wife. His passing was noted in Russia, and an obituary article by the art expert Igor Grabar appeared in the paper *Sovetskoe iskusstvo* (Soviet Art).[91]

A foreboding of Nazi Germany's defeat was apparent even in 1943, and 'A Visit to the Army' had opened with a tribute to the 'progress and logic of our wondrous victory'. Pasternak also assumed that there could be no return to the grey uniformity and suppression of the 1930s, and his essay hinted at this in proclaiming that 'diversity has triumphed' and that 'a new supreme period in our historical life is opening up'.[92] The same sentiment also animated the poem 'Odessa' of 1944, which promised the avengement of evil and the pronouncement of 'some new word' to alleviate the sorrow of relatives and widows of victims.[93]

Prior to the victory of May 1945, Pasternak's own behaviour conveyed a sense of buoyancy that reflected not the oppressive official attitudes toward him, but his delighted discovery of a personal following in Russia and signs of his appreciation abroad. In light of this, his acceptability to the Fadeyevs and Tikhonovs concerned him less.

Particularly significant was an increasing number of English contacts, mostly arising from the fame of his Shakespeare translations. Following a letter of appreciation in 1943, the British Embassy in 1945 published in its Russian-language newspaper *Britansky soyuznik* (British Ally) an article by Christopher Wrenn surveying his Shakespeare translations.[94] One of the embassy staff now in charge of producing *Britansky soyuznik* in Moscow was Pasternak's own first

English translator and champion George Reavey. That same year, Pasternak had also written to the English actor John Gielgud. Three years previously, some of Pasternak's verse had appeared in Gerard Shelley's translation of *Modern Poets from Russia* (London, Allen & Unwin, 1942); in 1943 more translated work figured in Oxford Professor Maurice Bowra's *A Book of Russian Verse* (London, 1943); and in 1944 the magazine *Horizon* carried an article by J. M. Cohen on Pasternak's 'individualist' poetry which was later disputed in the Soviet press.[95] More important, however, was Stefan Schimanski's translated anthology of Pasternak's collected prose published by Lindsay Drummond in 1945. Containing *Safe Conduct* and the early completed stories, it presented a lengthy and perceptive introduction by Schimanski with illustrations from work by Leonid Pasternak. The introduction not only emphasised the link between Pasternak and his father's example, but also traced a spiritual descent from Pushkin in his singular personal integrity.[96]

Pasternak was embarrassed at seeing translations of his very earliest prose and disowned all except *Zhenya Luvers' Childhood*. He also disliked the Kukryniksy cartoon portraying him as a sphinx, and a retouched photo of himself with Mayakovsky. But he was generally delighted with Schimanski's book, which forged a symbolic link with his own past as well as with his family and with sympathisers in British literary circles.

As Pasternak also told Schimanski in a letter at the year end, he had read various articles in the journal *Transformations* edited by him together with Henry Treece. (Probably these were shown to Pasternak by George Reavey who also contributed.) The London journal was the platform for a new philosophy of 'personalism' that struck a common chord with Pasternak, and which, as he told Schimanski, was a source of encouragement in his own endeavours.[97] In June of 1945 he had given Sergei Durylin a sympathetic account of the movement and of his own adoption by the personalist group after 'The Childhood of Luvers' appeared in the first issue of *Transformations*.[98]

Pasternak's first significant translated début in English seemed to sound an optimistic note that harmonised with his own mood after the defeat of Nazism. Yet in 1945 even the signs of a return of prewar oppression barely indicated how cruelly his hopes would soon be dashed.

11

'From Immortality's Archive': The Birth of a Novel

'Winter Night'

Snow on snow the blizzard blew,
All frontiers enswirling.
A candle on the table stood,
A tallow candle burning.

Like summer midges' swarming flight
Towards the candle chasing,
The snowflakes eddied to the light,
Converging on the casement.

And on the pane the blizzard hewed
Its arrows, darts and circles.
A candle on the table stood,
A tallow candle burning.

And shadows settled overhead
Upon the illumined ceiling,
Dim forms of crossing arms and legs,
Fate's shadows interlacing.

A pair of shoes slid to the floor
And raised a sudden clatter.
And on her gown the waxen flare
Shed tears that oozed and spattered.

And all was lost in snowy murk,
A pallid grey-white blurring.
The candle on the table stirred,
A tallow candle burning.

A sudden draught breathed on the flame,
Seductive fires enkindling,
With arms outspread in cruciform
Like two wings of an angel.

All February the blizzard raved,
Yet ever and anon, unchanging,
The candle, table still remained,
A candle ever flaming.

(1946)

The decay of Pasternak's relations with the literary establishment by the end of the war was matched by a plumetting assessment of several (though not all) officially approved poets. As he told poet and critic Igor Postupalsky in a letter of November 1945, ever since Mayakovsky, Soviet literature had been stuck in a state of 'obsolete cowardliness and mendacity'. In current poetry he recognised genuine 'paired' talents such as Selvinsky and Surkov, Aseyev and Simonov, and Tvardovsky and Isakovsky. But Antokolsky, Tikhonov, the Leningrad group and others showed only 'an illusory "mastery", a forced "jauntiness", a vacuous rhetoric devoid of personality, imagery, and even versifying competence'. Postupalsky had written to Pasternak from a Kolyma labour camp, and Pasternak's advice to him, if he wished to make something of his own writing, was to 'turn to your own arduous, hellish life of hard labour. [...] Draw from it some real, even if forbidden words. Write prose that is genuine and seizes one with its content. Forget all this Lefist-Acmeist, un-Blok-like, anti-Christian garbage, and may God help you.'[1]

Pasternak himself strove to follow this injunction, and while aware of his own incongruity on the poetic scene, some events and circumstances provided encouragement. It was probably from George Reavey or Isaiah Berlin, who joined the British Embassy staff in autumn of 1945, that he heard of approval of his Shakespeare translations in British university circles.[2] Meanwhile, at home his successful public recitations continued, at Moscow University, the House of Scholars, and the Polytechnic Museum. As he told Durylin, 'I expected only failure and a stage fiasco. But just imagine, it brought only pleasure. In my modest way, I realised how many people are favourably disposed towards everything worthwhile and serious. The existence of this unknown corner here at home was a revelation to me.'[3]

Another form of address to this public was of course the Shakespeare translations themselves. Both parts of *Henry IV* were ready in early August 1945, and that month a contract was drawn up with Goslitizdat. The volume was to be edited by Sergei Durylin, and Pasternak sent his friend a long letter with suggestions for how to approach the introduction.[4] *Macbeth* and *King*

Lear (the latter already started) still remained on the agenda and were also planned for inclusion.

In August 1945, however, Shakespeare was laid aside in favour of other translation work. Pasternak was again suffering severe pains in his right arm and had chronic conjunctivitis, and he considered going to the Georgian spa of Tskhaltubo to recuperate. As he told Chikovani, 'a trip to Georgia is tantamount to an immense creative release for me; a journey to see you is a journey into myself, my cherished dream as an artist'. Unfortunately the plan for such recreation fell through because, as he told Nina Tabidze, 'one has to earn in proportion to the amount of ink used, and not the role and quality of what one has done'. Professional frustrations were intensified when it became clear that any Moscow productions of Pasternak's translations had to have special sanction from the Arts Section of the Party Central Committee. Pasternak's autumn letter to Stalin protesting this was delivered to the Kremlin postbox by Evgenii his son. There was no response, however,[5] and Pasternak's ailments and depression eventually passed off amid a new artistic preoccupation with Georgia: Chikovani, now secretary of the Georgian Writers' Union, commissioned from him a translation of the complete verse of Nikoloz Baratashvili, the centenary of whose death was to be celebrated in October.

Pasternak saw the project as a chance to apply his now well-honed translation method. The verbal accuracy of earlier versions by Antokolsky, Lozinsky, Spassky and others removed any need to repeat their achievement. 'As I understand my task,' Pasternak wrote, 'Russian verses have to be made out of this, as I did with Shakespeare, Shevchenko, Verlaine and others [. . .] If possible, one has to provide something light, fresh and direct. This may strike many people as arguable, and they'll claim this Baratashvili is too free. But that does not frighten me.' Pasternak detailed Chikovani to draw up an agreement with Zakgiz publishers, insisting at the same time that 25 per cent of any advance should be paid out to Nina Tabidze.[6]

Translation work progressed with great fluency and by October Russian versions of almost the whole of Baratashvili were ready. They included some of Pasternak's finest work, which became widely read, recited and anthologised. During the autumn of 1945 and early 1946 various poems appeared in the journals *Leningrad*, *Ogonyok*, *Oktyabr'* and *Zvezda*, and Pasternak's complete Baratashvili anthology eventually appeared as part of the 'Ogonyok Library' series in Moscow in summer 1946. (In 1948 'Merani', an apostrophe of the Georgian Pegasus, was included in the *Oxford Book of Russian Verse*.)[7]

Although Pasternak was minded to postpone travel plans yet again, he was prevailed upon by his Georgian friends to come to Tbilisi for the Baratashvili centenary in mid October. He was met at the airport by Chikovani and insisted on driving directly to Nina Tabidze's home before checking in at the hotel. The three of them then sat together yarning for several hours. When Pasternak finally arrived at his hotel, the room reserved had been taken; he therefore stayed at Chikovani's and enjoyed its clean, bright rooms and panoramic view of the town.[8] Apart from official ceremonial, Pasternak's fortnight in Tbilisi was marked by meetings with old friends and new contacts, such as the artist Gudiashvili. In addition to various public readings of his translations, he also printed a short article on Baratashvili in the Tbilisi paper *Zarya Vostoka* on 21 October.[9]

During his stay Pasternak showed special attention to Nina Tabidze and her family. Since Titsian's arrest she had never attended any literary functions, but her resistance was broken when Chikovani sent a special car to fetch her and Pasternak made his own participation conditional on her attendance. As she recalled, he personally led her into the auditorium and seated her next to him, and when called on to recite, he did so demonstratively turning to face her. Pasternak also persuaded her to accompany him to the Paliashvili Opera and Ballet Theatre for further ceremonies. His demonstration of friendship for Nina Tabidze was an act of personal respect; at the same time such a show of sympathy to the wife of a condemned man was an unambiguous political gesture which placed Pasternak at risk. By this time such conduct could no longer be regarded as a sign of naïveté; it was a calculated act of defiance.[10] Despite this, Pasternak was fêted in Tbilisi in a way that contrasted sharply with the official indifference or interference he endured in Moscow.

On the return flight on 30 October, the critic Stepanov and Pasternak both found themselves without seats and spent the whole flight sitting on their own suitcases. It was a preparation for the anticlimax back in Moscow. As Pasternak confessed to Nina Tabidze, 'I am connected up to real life by three forces: Georgia, England and my Russian future, but not my life in Moscow today, not my present relations here.'[11] The life of the capital left its dreary trace on an introduction composed for the Russian book edition of Baratashvili. As Pasternak shamefully explained, 'From bitter experience with my articles I know that the presence of any thought raises objections, discussions and prohibitions. So to avoid delaying the edition I decided to relieve them of any disappointment and wrote an utterly banal biography devoid of personality or content.'[12] The essay incorporated Baratashvili in Pasternak's recognised cohort of realists,[13] but it was omitted from the published volume. Also unprinted were 'A few Words about Modern Georgian Poetry' written in December for a volume of *Georgian Poets (Gruzinskie poety)* to be published by Zarya Vostoka.[14] No room was found for such literary reflections, which included a view of Symbolism as the progenitor of all subsequent poetic culture. Renewed contacts with Georgia led to a further series of translations, however, and in the later 1940s there appeared new versions of Gaprindashvili, Grishashvili, Kaladze, Leonidze, Pshavela, Tsereteli, and Chikovani. In 1946 Sovetsky Pisatel also brought out a new volume of selected Georgian poets, with yet another miscellany published in Tbilisi the following year.[15]

Pasternak's record of defending victims of the regime went back to the early 1920s and the cases of Nikolai Vilyam and musicologist Iosif Kunin;[16] later he had refused to ostracise the families of purge victims, and offered both material and moral support to several prisoners, including Ariadna Efron, Anastasia Tsvetaeva, Ilya Postupalsky, and Nikolai Smirnov, a former editor with *Krasnaya nov'*.[17] In the postwar period, though, Pasternak made a public show of his attitudes which worried many of those close to him. This included one occasion when he held forth passionately to Aleksandr Gladkov in a crowded Moscow tramcar after hearing how Gladkov's brother interned in Kolyma had received a book of his verse from fellow prisoner Ilya Postupalsky.[18] In the short postwar interval before police state conformity was reimposed, these vagaries were still condoned or ignored however.

During the interval before the Cold War began, Pasternak also had several meetings with the Russian-speaking British diplomat and scholar Isaiah Berlin. Berlin was acquainted with the poet's sisters in Oxford and in early autumn of 1945 came to Peredelkino bringing letters and gifts including some boots that had belonged to Leonid Pasternak, and examples of Lydia's own verse in English. Some of her poems particularly impressed her brother, who was struck by the vitality of her earliest Moscow impressions, and by the 'traces of art' and of an emotional life even less joyful than his own.[19]

After a first encounter in Peredelkino, Pasternak was visited by Berlin several more times in Lavrushinsky Lane where they met almost weekly during the later months of 1945. Berlin got to know Pasternak fairly closely and on two trips to Leningrad also met and befriended Akhmatova.[20] Pasternak's conversation and personality made a deep impression, revealing 'a poetic genius in everything he did and was'. Yet Berlin was no more able than other memoirists to capture his intonations on paper, with their grand leisurely periods punctuated by surges of speech, passages of precision interlaced with bizarre and brilliant imagery, all delivered in a characteristic nasal boom.[21] Apart from recollections, the two men's discourse covered other issues that absorbed Pasternak at that juncture – his curiosity about Herbert Read and the personalists, his current immersion in Proust, his apparent ignorance of Sartre and Camus, and his interest in the fate of H. G. Wells, James Joyce, Bunin and Khodasevich.[22]

Berlin was struck by Pasternak's patriotism, his desire to be seen as a specifically Russian writer, and his negative attitude to his own Jewish origins. His view of the Jewish nation, later elaborated in *Doctor Zhivago*, was that their historical mission lay in being assimilated; any mention by Berlin of recent events concerning Palestine aroused only pained indifference. Pasternak came over as a maybe unorthodox but believing Christian who also 'believed that he was in direct communion with the inner life of the Russian people', and shared their hopes, fears and dreams. He 'felt that he had something which he needed to say to the rulers of Russia – something infinitely important, which only he and he alone could say.' The exact nature of this remained unclear, and Akhmatova too failed to comprehend whenever Pasternak was gripped by vatic urges.[23] It was plain, however, that Pasternak in late 1945 still hoped for some great 'renewal of Russian life resulting from the cleansing storm which in his view the war had been'; the vileness of events in the 1930s followed by a terrifying war appeared as a 'necessary prelude to some future inevitable and unprecedented triumph of the spirit'.[24] This hope – maybe utopian in its timing – illuminated the prose epilogue of *Doctor Zhivago*. Pasternak re-counted some ideas for this forthcoming prose narrative, and when he left Russia in early January Berlin took back to Britain an extended letter to Pasternak's sisters containing an appreciation of their father, an account of his own wartime doings, and of new plans for a major work in prose. Pasternak also asked Berlin to relay back to Oxford some manuscript material including, probably, his recent article on Chopin.[25] Later, in June 1946, he wrote asking him to pass copies of the Shakespeare 'Notes' to Bowra and Schimanski, requesting assistance in publishing them somewhere neutral like the *TLS* (rather than *Horizon*, which he believed was 'too special and distinctive').[26]

Thanks to several months freed up by paid translation work, Pasternak was able to resume writing his novel in the winter of 1945–6. He did so using a block of superb writing paper that Nina Tabidze had given him from Titsian's legacy in October 1945. Pasternak saw this as a symbolic challenge to his own creative mastery.[27]

During New Year's Eve a chance meeting with Aleksandr Gladkov on Mokhovaya Street led to further remarks about the novel. Gladkov recollected Pasternak's emphasis on its strong confessional element and 'collective' authorial subjectivity. 'I am writing this novel about people who might have become representatives of my school – if I had ever had such a thing . . .'[28] Traces of this eventually emerged in the partly 'collective' personality of Zhivago, Lara, and Vedenyapin.

In mid January 1946, after a visit from Eduard Babaev, a young Tashkent poet friend of Nadezhda Mandelstam, Pasternak wrote to her further elaborating his artistic plans:

I now have the chance of working for about three months on something totally my own and without thinking about our daily bread. I want to write some prose about the whole of our life from Blok up till the recent war, if possible in ten to twelve chapters, no more. You can imagine with what haste I am working and how afraid I am lest something happen before I finish my work!

Despite some conceptual overlap with the prose fragments of the thirties, Pasternak's intention to embrace the whole period up to recent times was new. His letter talked of how, regardless of his will, 'matters of great moment are entering the circle of my fate', and of the challenge of this attempt to 'embrace a broader circle [. . .] now I cannot even remain what I am, and how I miss Osip Emilyevich [Mandelstam]. He, who was consumed in this fire, understood these things all too well!'[29]

Olga Freidenberg was told in February 1946 that Pasternak hoped to finish this major prose work by summer. He did not hold to this schedule however,[30] although certain thematic embryos of the novel now began developing. One of them was contained in a first draft of the poem 'Hamlet', written in February (above, 187). It consisted of two quatrains – variants of the eventual first and last stanzas – and was probably linked in Pasternak's mind with the Hamlet motif in Blok; its use of a proverb in the final line was also identical with Zabolotsky's 'On New Year's Eve', written at the same time while living in Peredelkino.[31]

In the summer of 1946 Pasternak also worked on some drafts 'Towards a Characterisation of Blok' ('K kharakteristike Bloka') prompted by the forthcoming anniversary of his death; he also marked out several passages and made notes on Blok's verse, starting with a disquisition on Hamletism. Eventually, the idea and impetus for these were incorporated in the novel and autobiographical essay of the mid 1950s.[32]

The refraction of Shakespeare in Pasternak's novel also came directly from translation work. Although absent in the first draft of the poem, the figure of Christ was yoked with that of Hamlet in another work of spring 1946. Pasternak spent the month of June in town in order to write an introduction to his projected two-volume Shakespeare. For this edition Pasternak kept his options open with Goslitizdat but also offered the book to Iskusstvo, the Moscow-Leningrad publisher who eventually produced the work.[33] The edition ultimately appeared without any preface, but *Notes on Translations of Shakespeare's Dramas* ('Zametki k perevodam shekspirovskikh dram') before then acquired a separate published life of their own. As Pasternak told his cousin in autumn 1946, 'In thirty pages I have managed to say what I wanted about poetry in general, about the style of Shakespeare, about each of five translated plays and various questions linked with Shakespeare: the state of education at that time, and the authenticity of Shakespeare's biography.'[34]

In the *Notes* Pasternak adopts some classic attitudes probably derived from a reading of English Shakespeare critics, including Dr Johnson who was the source for a vivid image of Shakespeare 'so brazenly unashamed of his own mistakes that he yawned in the face of history'. Pasternak's idea of the central acts of Shakespearian drama as weaker than the openings and endings reversed the commonly held view. His critique of repetitions in *Hamlet* and *Romeo and Juliet* (in his own translations such imagery was dropped) was consonant with his view of Shakespeare as the 'father of realism', who used metaphor only as a 'shorthand of genius, the speedwriting of the spirit' in contrast to his more distilled and finished prose.[35]

Pasternak sent his 'Notes' to Vissarion Sayanov in Leningrad in the hope that his journal *Zvezda* or else *Leningrad* would print them. Owing to changes in the cultural climate in August, no publication took place, and only an anonymous abbreviated English translation appeared in the journal *Soviet Literature*.[36] The manuscript sent to his sisters in Oxford was not translated or printed immediately. Meanwhile a most eloquent response to the Shakespeare notes came in the form of a letter from Olga Freidenberg. After retrieving the manuscript from Sayanov, she wrote Boris an enthralled appreciation of this 'document from the archive of immortality' whose remarks on *Hamlet* and *Othello* reflected some of her own thinking.[37]

In the summer of 1946 Pasternak also worked on generally improving his English. He regularly practised speaking with his Peredelkino neighbour, the American-born widow of Afinogenov, and also listened for an hour or so each day to the BBC's English-language broadcasts, all of which was technically and ideologically possible before the Cold War began.

The spring of 1946 saw continuation of Pasternak's platform appearances. Akhmatova came to Moscow with a company of Leningrad poets. Since the almost frightening success of her Moscow reading in spring 1944,[38] she had performed several times, earning rapturous responses and official disapproval of such a bourgeois literary sensation. A further volume of her verse was also in preparation, plus a book of her notes and essays on Pushkin. On her new visit to Moscow, apart from private readings at the Ardovs', she and Pasternak gave a joint recital at the Moscow Writers' Club on 2 April, and next day they contributed to a general programme of Moscow and Leningrad poets in the Hall of Columns. According to her, Pasternak showed total mastery of stage

1 Boris Pasternak and Anna Akhmatova (April 1946)

technique and audience manipulation, starting with a belated surreptitious
arrival on the platform which aroused spontaneous applause and forced Surkov
to interrupt his own reading.[39] The incident was a fair indication of popular
enthusiasm for Pasternak and probably further antagonised Surkov. On 4 April
a similar programme was performed at Moscow University and the audience
refused to let Pasternak leave the stage; he took up twice his allocated time,
and by popular request recited his verses 'To the Memory of Marina Tsvetaeva'.[40]

On 27 May Pasternak even surpassed this success in his solo recital at the
Polytechnic Museum which was followed by a spate of encores with 'The
Death of the Poet' in its original version as a telling coda to the programme.[41]
Thanks to British Embassy staff in the audience, report of this performance
acquired resonance in Western Europe. Despite these successes, however, as
Pasternak told his sister Lydia, their everyday life remained almost indescrib-
able:

[. . .] There are no comparisons in normal terms. But in general everyone in your
country has already seen through it and has a fairly exact picture of how things are –
obscurity, silence, and a terrible, monstrous thirteenth century. Amidst all this I am

poised on a knife-edge, and I have no choice. [. . .] It is interesting, absorbing, and probably dangerous.[42]

This situation was still not readily understood in Britain: Josephine and Lydia had hopes of shipping all their father's works back to Russia where they believed he would achieve his due posthumous recognition. In June Pasternak drafted a telegram forbidding any such plan: 'Never think sent off fathers work pictures till definitive securing postwar ways and betterment our life conditions spare damages losses embrace heartily you all – Boris Pasternak.' In fact the message was delivered personally by a Mrs Halcroft, the second of two friends of Raisa Lomonosova, who came to Moscow bringing gifts of clothing for the ladies of the Pasternak family. Leonid Pasternak's works thus remained in Oxford.[43]

After completing the Shakespeare notes, Pasternak joined his family in Peredelkino where he resumed work on the novel. The urgency of this task emerged in a letter of late June to Raisa Lomonosova – his first message to her since before the war and one whose frankness reflected the mood of that epoch:

At one time it was impossible to write anything because political conditions prevented this. Now I pay no attention to them. Now one can communicate nothing essential in one's life, conversation or letters because the time has come to state the main thing of all, and this has not yet been said, and failing that everything else is non-essential and uninteresting.

But it will be said. I feel well, I am entirely caught up with the future and I live by this.[44]

The 'main thing of all' was the message of Pasternak's novel, and Olga Freidenberg later received a report on his summer's achievement. The novel was to be called 'Boys and Girls' ('Mal'chiki i devochki'); its planned ten chapters were to embrace the period 1902–1946, and nearly a quarter of the project had been written up by October. The work was an urgent statement of ideas denied expression for long decades. Now, though, after decades of living on a 'forcibly restrained programme' the moment of truth had come. It was no longer possible to exist 'on the passive tokens of one's abilities and on other people's favourable attitude'.[45]

'Boys and Girls' was evidently related in some way to some of the 'childhood' novel fragments of the 1930s and to those chapters of *Doctor Zhivago* that sketched the boyhood of the main hero and his companions. Pasternak gave several readings of the start of his new work to friends – one at the Ardovs' home on the Ordynka in the presence of Akhmatova and Olga

Berggolts, when it apparently produced no special impression.[46] On 3 August, the still incomplete first chapter, supplied with a nominal 'cardboard ending', was given a private reading in Peredelkino to Zinaida, the Asmuses, and Fedin. Without detailed or critical comment, Fedin later made a note of the work's title, the fact that chapter one dealt with events of 1903, carried an epigraph from Blok, and had some connection with the Volga area of central Russia.[47] Absorbed by the summer's narrative impulse, Pasternak in late August sent off pleading letters to Chagin and Fadeyev requesting that Goslitizdat go ahead and publish his collected Shakespeare translations to date, without requiring him to drop everything in order to complete *King Lear* and *Macbeth*.[48]

Fifteen months of relative postwar liberalism came to a rude end in late summer of 1946. On 14 August the Party Central Committee passed a resolution 'On the Magazines *Zvezda* and *Leningrad*', which denounced their publication of material hostile and alien to the interests of Soviet literature. The concerns of 'the world's most progressive literature' were defined as identical with those of the state and people, and its function was to assist in providing correct ideological education. Any lack of ideology, apoliticality, or 'art for art's sake' was thus alien to Soviet literature and should not be permitted in Soviet journals. The specific crime of *Zvezda* and *Leningrad* lay in printing work by Zoshchenko and Akhmatova. *Zvezda* was consequently instructed to reform itself, while *Leningrad* was closed down altogether.[49] (Both journals had also recently carried translations by Pasternak, and the Chopin essay appeared in *Zvezda*.)

One week later the Central Committee resolution was reinforced personally by the Secretary responsible for ideology, Andrei Zhdanov, who addressed the Leningrad Party organisation and Leningrad branch of the Writers' Union with abusive speeches containing violent personal attacks on Akhmatova and Zoshchenko.[50] In the wake of this, on 4 September the two writers were expelled from the Writers' Union, which meant a ban on publication of their work and effectively deprived them of their livelihood. Thus began the policy of cultural repression known as 'Zhdanovism', whose effects lasted until the death of Stalin in 1953.[51]

The selection of Akhmatova as victim, she believed, was partly due to her meetings with Isaiah Berlin; but probably more offensive had been the wave of public enthusiasm attending her re-emergence on the literary scene, including the ovation that greeted her in Moscow that spring.[52] However, after the sacrifice of two scapegoats, a state-wide campaign began with public meetings to endorse the Central Committee resolution as a binding general cultural policy. During August and September further Party decrees on the Soviet theatre and cinema followed,[53] and the world of Academe was also affected. At Leningrad University for instance, the Rector appeared before a meeting of staff, sporting a Russian peasant shirt under his jacket, and denounced the infection of Soviet scholarship by Western culture, calling for the 'unmasking' of any staff members who purveyed incorrect views.[54] In due course the nation's entire cultural life was affected by Zhdanov's policies, and the artistic and scientific intelligentsia were stunned into a paralytic conformity.

Although Pasternak was not cited in the initial resolution or speeches, he was a likely potential target for criticism, and a group of orthodox colleagues were busy undermining his reputation. In June of 1946 Tarasenkov received a scurrilous letter from Vishnevsky insinuating that Pasternak treasonably 'preserved letters from Germany' and 'fled' from Moscow at the start of the war.[55] Pasternak was jeopardised by his known closeness to Akhmatova. Furthermore, as the first draughts of the Cold War began to blow, an aggressive Soviet-style patriotism became *de rigueur*, and the establishment lashed out against any obsequious reverence for 'bourgeois' (i.e. Western) culture, past or present. If Pasternak's translation work had earlier been a place of refuge from culpable originality, now the fact of indulging in translation of Western literature as well his known following in the West laid him open to censure. This was further aggravated when his candidature for the Nobel Prize was mooted in the autumn, although a proposal of Sholokhov's candidature was approvingly noted in *Literaturnaya gazeta* on 19 October.[56]

The same meeting that stripped Akhmatova and Zoshchenko of Union membership also reappointed Fadeyev as General Secretary of the Writers' Union replacing Tikhonov.[57] Fadeyev marked the occasion by abandoning his enthusiasm for Pasternak and raising new political accusations against him. Now, allegedly, Pasternak was an alien element who refused to acknowledge 'our ideology'. Indeed, instead of writing topical poetry during the war he had sought refuge in translation work. Forgotten totally was the fact that not so long ago Fadeyev had berated Pasternak for his 'great-power chauvinism', which was too patriotic for literary hacks who were busy flaunting their 'internationalism'! (above, p. 217) The new accusation was also absurdly at variance with the certificate and medal Pasternak was awarded by the Supreme Soviet in January 1946 with a citation 'For Valiant Labour in the Great Patriotic War 1941–1945'.[58] (In fact the honour was conferred on virtually all Union members, and Pasternak hardly treasured it: when he innocently suggested to Polikarpov on the phone that his son might come to collect the award, the official was furious and told him he was not being asked to pick up just a can of kerosene!)[59] Now, however, Fadeyev identified Pasternak's stance as suspiciously antagonistic, and he rehearsed his accusations twice within a fortnight – first in a speech to the Board of the Writers' Union on 4 September, and thirteen days later at a gathering of Moscow writers in the House of Scholars.[60]

Pasternak was thus marked as permitted quarry in a new hunting season. In the ensuing months not only he was attacked, but individuals and journals that had favourable things to say about him were taken to task. His first reaction was to answer back, and a drafted response was later found among his papers, although it seems unlikely that the message was sent:

According to information from the Union of Writers, in certain literary circles in the West an improper significance is ascribed to my activity, out of keeping in its modesty and unproductiveness . . . It is futile to set me up against a reality that is in every respect loftier and stronger than I am. Along with all ordinary folk with vital and natural feelings, I am bound by an unanimity of soul and thought to my age and my country.

And I would be a blind nonentity if behind certain ephemeral and unavoidable severities of our time I did not perceive the moral beauty and greatness towards which modern Russia has strode and which were announced by our great predecessors.[61]

Pasternak's comportment, however, was eloquent enough. In fact he repeated his earlier tactic and before Fadeyev opened the case against him, simply stayed away from meetings designed to reinforce Zhdanov's policy. When a courier arrived to summon him to a Union Board meeting on 31 August, he begged off on grounds of radiculitis but was told: 'Better think of something else. Fedin already has radiculitis.' He then wrote on the back of the summons: 'I will try to be there if I am well enough and if nothing prevents me.' He did not attend.[62]

To conformist colleagues who advised that Pasternak's own statement on Akhmatova was called for, he retorted that this was impossible, since he was fond of her and had reason to think she returned his feelings. Rumour also recounted that when officials warned him that his own offence was scarcely less grave than Akhmatova's, his outrageous reply was: 'Yes, yes, [out of touch with] the people, modern times . . . You know, your Trotsky once told me the same thing . . .'[63]

Immersed in chapter 3 of his novel, Pasternak therefore sat out the summer in Peredelkino and even joked in a letter to Gudiashvili about the irritation caused by his 'sojourn in the bosom of nature, like in pictures by Manet and Renoir, at such a time(!)'.[64] Zinaida Pasternak heard the latest developments in the campaign each time she travelled into town, and her distress on Boris' behalf evidently even exceeded his own. Friends also voiced concern: on 3 September Leonov, recently appointed to the Union secretariat, incredulously asked Chukovsky why Pasternak prevented his friends from interceding for him and instead kept 'babbling God knows what'.[65] In fact, on 9 September, the very same day *Pravda* reported the Union's proclamation of Pasternak as 'an author lacking in ideology and remote from Soviet reality', a large company was invited to the Peredelkino dacha to hear Pasternak read the opening chapters of his novel; the guests included Chukovsky and his son and daughter-in-law, Kornelii Zelinsky, Nikolai Vilyam and some ten others. Evidently Pasternak had not heard of the Union attack, and Zinaida kept news of the press article from him. But the truth leaked out over dinner following the reading. Pasternak appeared shocked. Chukovsky hurried back home, believing that to throw such a feast had the unfortunate appearance of bravado.[66]

By the time the family moved into town in late September, Pasternak's mood had changed from disquiet to one of boredom and irritation, and in a letter to his cousin he seemed confident of riding out the unpleasantness.[67] However, his attitudes and disdainful absence from meetings seriously angered the Union management, and in the autumn he was removed from the Union Board. Two projected publications also fell victim to the campaign against foreign bourgeois and Decadent literature: the *Notes on Translations of Shakespeare's Dramas* were rejected by the new editors of *Zvezda*, and the planned article on Blok foundered when the August celebration of the 25th anniversary of his death was soft-pedalled.[68]

Although excesses in the style of the 1930s continued, Akhmatova and Zoshchenko were not arrested, nor was Pasternak personally touched. In his case his prominence abroad played some part in this. But the abortion of all liberal hopes after the war was deeply traumatising, and after his earlier readiness to accept and accommodate to tyranny, the year 1946 marked a crucial and irreversible turning-point in Pasternak's attitudes. An unpublished memoir note of 1956 recalled that after the sense of community during the '*live* period' of the war and the hard-won victory, 'when they reverted to the cruelty and sophistries of the dullest and darkest prewar years, for the second time (since 1936) I felt a sense of dumbfounded abhorrence at the established system – a feeling even stronger and more categoric than the first time'.

After an earlier flexibility of response, Pasternak now adopted a more stable political stance.[69] Without extending to declared and open opposition, this involved an eloquent non-participation in public cultural affairs. In this sense, Fadeyev and literary officialdom correctly understood and interpreted him. So, too, did Agnessa Kun who called on him at Lavrushinsky Lane in late 1946 to discuss their collaboration on a translated edition of the Hungarian poet Sándor Petöfi; at the start of the conversation Pasternak produced a copy of his recently printed *Selected Verse* and slapped it down on the table saying, 'Here there never was and never will be mention of the name of Stalin'. (In fact the *Selected Verse* had even been proposed for a Stalin Prize by Antokolsky, Aseyev, Kirsanov and Tarasenkov, but Polikarpov, Organizing Secretary at the Writers' Union, had scotched the idea at committee level.)[70]

Another result of events in August 1946 was the virtual cessation of Pasternak's correspondence with abroad, even with close relatives. After November, when Pasternak sent a cable to his sisters with greetings and enquiring about the fate of his Shakespeare article, regular communication on his part ceased for almost ten years. From time to time verbal greetings were conveyed, as when Simonov visited the United Kingdom and Oxford in spring of 1947 and reported meeting with Lydia and her two handsome Russian-speaking sons Michael and Nicolas.[71] Pasternak broke silence extremely rarely however – with a greetings telegram of January 1948 and a letter of astounding frankness at the end of that year to Frederick and the Pasternak sisters which was smuggled out of Russia together with part of the *Zhivago* manuscript.

12

Faustian Pursuits in Life and Letters

'Daybreak'

You it was who shaped my fate,
But then came times of war and ruin,
And for many a long day
There was no word of you, no sign.

Then, after many moons, again
Your rousing voice once more has called me.
All night I read your Testament
And woke as from a swoon next morning.

And now I long to join the crowd
And morning bustle. I'm prepared
To render the entire world down,
Set everyone upon their knees in prayer.

Quickly down the stairs I go,
As though for the first time hasting
Into streets all clad with snow,
To walk the deadened pavements.

People arise to light and warmth,
Drink tea and hurry to the tramway.
All the city is transformed
In minutes, and in every aspect.

A blizzard in the gateways knits
Thick gusting flakes into a tissue.
And making haste, folk leave their homes
With plates of food and drink unfinished,

I feel for all of them as though
I'm in their skin and share their fortune.
Like melting snow, I also thaw
And clench my eyebrows like the morning.

With me there are no names for folk,
For stay-at-homes, and trees, and youngsters.
By each and all I'm overwhelmed.
Herein alone thus lies my conquest.

(1947)

Despite Zinaida's musical training, she showed little evidence of sensitivity or refined taste. Although a staunch defender of her husband's privacy and work regime, she was an inadequate partner in his artistic pursuits; her favourite spare-time occupation was playing cards with the wives of Selvinsky and Trenyov.[1] Moreover, for all her domestic efficiency, Pasternak was upset by her frequent grumpiness and felt increasingly lonely within his own home. The death of Adrian in 1945 placed a further barrier between them. Zinaida regarded it as fate's punishment for her abandonment of his father whom she still seemed to revere more than Pasternak. As a consequence, the physical and emotional basis of marital relations with Boris ceased to be. Nevertheless, surprisingly, the framework of their marriage remained strong. Zinaida had a proprietorial view of her husband and family, and neither heart nor conscience persuaded Pasternak to go against this. He continued to live and work at home, and on a day-to-day basis remained on good and civil terms with his wife.

Zinaida herself emphasised that Boris continued to be considerate and supportive; he maintained his family generously and was even angry when Zinaida made to accept Neigauz's contribution towards a new piano for Stanislav. Additionally, they entertained frequently and had several house guests especially in summer. Over and above this, Pasternak made regular payments towards Evgeniya's upkeep; routine Sunday dinner parties continued; and there were numerous acts of generosity to victims of the regime – sometimes total strangers, such as the tattered and unshaven schoolmaster who arrived at the dacha in 1947, having made the pilgrimage to see Pasternak immediately on release from a labour camp.[2]

In the early postwar years Zinaida Pasternak and Pogodin's wife became involved with a Writers' Union commission to help children orphaned by the war. Pasternak approved of this commitment, to which she brought both talent and dedication. However, her work involved prolonged absences from home, which encouraged Pasternak's already wandering attention. Yet as one observer noted, only a woman more egotistical and self-assured than Zinaida could challenge and dispute with her.[3] One such woman did, however, appear.

Pasternak's last great love affair acquired a melodramatic notoriety exceeding even the one with Zinaida fifteen years before. He met Olga Ivinskaya in October 1946 at the Pushkin Square offices of the journal *Novy mir*, where she was junior assistant to the recently appointed chief editor Konstantin Simonov. Ivinskaya was aged thirty-four, sociable and vivacious, and described by one acqaintance as 'an attractive but slightly faded' blonde.[4] She apparently never concealed her relishment of amorous conquests and adventures, including her relations with Pasternak, and she was known to be ambitious and manipulative. Early in their acquaintance, she told Pasternak how her first husband Ivan Emelyanov had hanged himself because of her, leaving her with an infant daughter Irina. She then married his rival Aleksandr Vinogradov, by whom she had a son Dmitrii (Mitya). Soon afterwards Vinogradov died however, and when she met Pasternak, she was sharing an apartment in Potapovsky Lane with her mother, stepfather, and her children.[5]

Evidently there was a noticeable postwar tendency for some writers to cast off old wives in favour of younger women, and Zinaida claimed to have fended off several young admirers who threatened Boris' matrimonial and artistic equilibrium. The seriousness of Pasternak's involvement with Ivinskaya was thus not immediately apparent, and it was some months before Zinaida discovered a letter from her on his desk, which further impaired their relationship.

On his own admission, Pasternak had a 'sweet tooth' where female company was concerned and he responded readily to Ivinskaya's saccharine flirtation. Unlike Zinaida, she also had some literary enthusiasm and discernment, although her behaviour, minor publications and later memoirs revealed no incisive intelligence or taste. Her veneration for Pasternak was quite genuine though, and she had long been an admirer at the time of their introduction. The sophomore gush of her response to the appearance of 'God' at her office desk was well captured in her memoirs, which registered the deity's tanned features, eyes of 'aquiline amber', virile jaw and uneven equine teeth.[6]

Pasternak's response to Ivinskaya's admiring interest was undisguised. After their introduction, he produced copies of his verse for her, telephoned frequently, and sometimes of an afternoon called at the office to escort her home. He made no secret of his enthusiasm, and the two of them were seen together at literary readings and other events. To Lyusya Popova, an artist acquaintance who sometimes functioned as go-between, he spoke of Ivinskaya as 'so charming, so bright, so golden. And now this golden sun has entered my life, it is so splendid, so splendid'. Several of his retailed confessions to Ivinskaya indeed suggest that his occasional talent for amorous fatuity had not dimmed with age.[7]

In early 1947 Pasternak was also introduced to Ivinskaya's mother and stepfather and her children, and she later recognised Irina in the portrait of Katenka, Lara's daughter in the novel.[8] Eventually, in early April while Ivinskaya's mother and stepfather took the children on a day's outing, Pasternak and she spent the day at her Potapovsky Lane apartment 'as newly-weds spend their first night together'. Her account continued with masterly laconicism: 'I ironed his crumpled trousers. He was animated and ecstatic at this victory. Truly, "There are marriages more mysterious than man and wife".' Impressions of subsequent passionate trysts in Lavrushinsky or Pota-povsky Lane were later immortalised in the Zhivago poem 'Summer in Town' ('Leto v gorode').[9]

For all its ecstasy, the relationship was at the same time a tormented and tragic one. Pasternak was haunted by guilt feelings over the family he felt unable to abandon. Meanwhile Zinaida at one point turned up personally to assure Olga that she 'couldn't give a damn' for their relationship and would not permit her family to be broken up. Though not minded to oppose this, Pasternak nevertheless vowed to assume responsibility and take care of Ivins-kaya and her family.[10] However, while he had no plans for a change of status, Ivinskaya was plagued by her mother who was critical of Pasternak's age and the fact that he remained married with children. Olga herself was prone to alternating bouts of jealous fury and tenderness.[11] As Evgenii Pasternak summarised their situation in 1946–47, 'an awareness of the sinfulness and obvious doomed nature of their relations imparted a particular glow to them at that time. Pangs of conscience on the one hand, and lighthearted egoism on the other, often faced them with the need to part, but pity and a thirst for emotional warmth drew him towards her again.'[12] Some of this torment was captured in the poem 'Explanation' ('Ob"yasnenie'):

> [. . .] Don't weep. Don't purse your swollen lips.
> Don't knit your lips together.
> You'll crack apart the dried-up scab
> Of our last springtime's fever.
>
> So take your hand from off my breast.
> We're cables at high tension.
> Watch out, for we'll be reunited,
> Whatever our intentions.
> [. . .]
> However strongly I am bound
> By nighttime's anguished fetters,
> Repulsion's power is stronger yet,
> The passion to escape still beckons. (*DZh*, 538–9; *SS*, III, 516–17)

The affair with Ivinskaya was fruitful in artistic terms. The next decade's worth of love lyrics, some of them attributed to Yurii Zhivago, recorded the peripeteia of their romance. Yet, as in Pasternak's earlier love poetry, few specific features of his partner's character or appearance were registered; both personality and situations were highly poeticised. Her appeal lay in her entrancing femininity rather than in any individual virtues (which, compared with Evgeniya or Zinaida, were few). Nevertheless, in her memoirs Ivinskaya claimed to find many personal details of their dealings. Aspects of Pasternak's translation work (especially the characterisation of Gretchen in Goethe's *Faust*) were also coloured by their liaison. Even more so the novel: several passages reflected the lyrical warmth as well as the doomed nature of their illicit love, and although based partly on Zinaida's early life, the figure of Lara acquired some of Ivinskaya's attributes.

The autumn and winter of 1946 were marked by significant events among family and friends. In late December, Olga Serova, the eldest daughter of Leonid Pasternak's artist friend and Boris' own close contemporary, died. During the summer of 1946 Irina Asmus was diagnosed with leukemia; her husband took her for a rest cure in the Crimea in the autumn; however, back in Moscow in late December she passed away.[13]

In summer of 1946, Evgenii Pasternak graduated triumphantly from the military academy, but stayed on as an advanced student (*ad"yunkt*) with the rank of senior lieutenant.[14] During 1946 Stanislav Neigauz married his childhood sweetheart Galina Yarzhemskaya and went to live with her parents, where they had more ample living space. For the next fourteen years, however, they and their children spent summers at the Peredelkino dacha, and Galina later wrote her own reminiscences of Pasternak.[15]

After the war, there was no revival of Pasternak's Peredelkino 'cénacle' in which he had felt at home. Some individual friendships survived with Fedin, the Ivanovs and Chukovsky, but these could not compensate for a growing sense of artistic isolation. In the city, however, there were private and even semi-public gathering grounds for liberal-minded intellectuals. A regular company gathered for concerts and talks in the Scriabin Museum, and for recitals by Neigauz, Sofronitsky, Maria Yudina and the young Svyatoslav Richter, or symphony concerts with works by Shostakovich at the Conservatoire, where a certain 'club atmosphere' reigned in the foyer. Pasternak was often seen at these functions; as his friend Polivanov recalled, that music 'tacitly but firmly opposed the deadening spirit of the time'. The faint postwar auguries of freedom described in *Doctor Zhivago* were perhaps most apparent around the Conservatoire.[16]

It was in these circles that the first drafts of Pasternak's novel were introduced. By the end of 1946 the first two chapters introducing the main hero and Lara were written and Pasternak gave private readings of them, usually at the home of friends. One such event took place on 27 December in the flat of Marina Baranovich who lived on Granovsky Street, just opposite the impressive block of government apartments. A former actress, she first met Pasternak at poetry evenings organised by 'Uzel' in the 1920s, where she had recited verse by Tsvetaeva and others. Now, in the postwar years she became Pasternak's regular copy-typist for his new verse and novel. Others present included Andrei Bely's widow Klavdiya Bugaeva, and Baranovich's poet friends Kochetkov and Maria Petrovykh.[17]

Another reading from the novel took place on 6 February 1947 in the overheated, bug-ridden apartment of pianist Maria Yudina. The company, which included Ivinskaya, Lidiya Chukovskaya and art historian Mikhail Alpatov, made their way by car through a heavy blizzard to Yudina's home somewhere in the north-west of Moscow. The evening began with Yudina playing Chopin. Later, Pasternak read his chapters and some of the poems, including the newly composed 'Christmas Star' ('Rozhdestvenskaya zvezda'). In Ivinskaya's mind the snowblown setting of that evening was later linked with the poem 'Winter Night', although in fact it was written somewhat earlier.[18]

Ivinskaya herself arranged another private reading session on 5 April 1947, when the first three chapters were presented. The venue was the Nastasyinsky Lane apartment of literary scholar Pyotr Kuzko and his wife. The company of nearly a score of listeners included Kuzko's former wife who was Simonov's secretary, Boris Agapov from the board of *Novy mir*, Chukovskaya and Emma Gershtein. Pasternak explained beforehand that he regarded his poetry as a form of preliminary sketch towards prose writing, while the novel itself constituted a 'powerful forward surge at the level of ideas'. Stylistically, it was meant not just to be descriptive, but to 'present feelings, dialogues and characters in *dramatic* embodiment. This is the prose of my time, of our time, and very much my own.' This draft version included a piquantly erotic sequence between Lara and Antipov which was excised from later versions; Lara at this stage was a brunette; and poems such as 'Winter Night' and 'The Christmas Star' were also at this stage contained within the actual prose text.[19]

Encouraged by Chukovskaya, Emma Gershtein later personally delivered an eager handwritten appreciation of what she heard to Pasternak's home at Lavrushinsky Lane. Many of the company, though, were unenthusiastic. In the corridor afterwards the literary scholar Ilya Zilbershtein was heard to comment: 'How sorry I am for him [Pasternak]. He's so fond of his work.'[20] Vsevolod Ivanov was also critical. On the 11 May, he and his son Vyacheslav heard Pasternak read his chapters again at the home of the artist Pyotr Konchalovsky. As the three of them later returned home, Ivanov remarked on the work's evidently unfinished state and heterogeneous style. Pasternak out of modesty tended to disparage his own work and later talked of its 'home-spun', unprofessional quality and naïveté.[21] But he was miffed to hear criticism from others, and he was probably also right in believing Ivanov had missed some innovatory elements, in light of which a few stylistic rough edges were considered unimportant.[22]

Another reading was given a few days later at an evening in memory of Olga Serova. It took place at the Serovs' home on the corner of Serebryany Lane and Molchanovka, a spot in Yurii Zhivago's 'enchanted lane' where several significant events in the novel would take place.[23] Among the guests were Genrikh Neigauz, Dmitrii Zhuravlyov, Olga Berggolts, and Sofia Andreyevna, a granddaughter of Lev Tolstoy. Pasternak himself turned up with Ivinskaya. Also present was Ninel (or Nina) Muravina, a recent graduate who had introduced herself to Pasternak a short time before at Neigauz's concert in the Small Hall of the Conservatoire.[24]

Pasternak's prefatory comments continued the dialogue with his informal critics and commentators. He claimed to have abandoned any sophisticated stylistic pretensions, and pointed out that the conversations and philosophy expounded in the novel's early pages were not 'memorised' (although relatable to Tolstoy), but pure artistic invention. A final title had not yet been decided. He had rejected his own first idea – 'At the Turning-Point' ('Na rubezhe'), and meanwhile had only a subheading in mind: 'Scenes from Half a Century of Life' ('Kartiny iz poluvekovogo obikhoda'). The version of chapter 2 concerned with the 1905 revolution was at that time called 'Boys with Guns' ('Mal'chiki strelyayut') – controversially based on personal reminiscence rather than on official history books.[25]

Pasternak's remarks at the Kuzkos' and Serovs' highlighted the principles of his concept. In addition to pursuing a transparent 'realistic' idiom, he had already talked to Gladkov and others of his admiration for the honest simplicity of Pushkin and Chekhov by contrast with the didacticism and 'fussy restlessness of Gogol, Dostoevsky and Tolstoy'. Later in the novel he also had Yurii Zhivago pay tribute to these Pushkinian and Chekhovian virtues in his Varykino notebooks.[26] Nevertheless, the work was to emerge as a 'novel of ideas', a Christian *roman à thèse* dealing with 'ultimate questions' in the manner of Tolstoy and Dostoevsky, and preaching a philosophy of sacrificial acceptance of a God-imposed fate, with echoes of a Tolstoyan non-violent resistance to evil. Indeed, conventional realism was occasionally suspended for 'epistemological' reasons. The long disquisition by Vedenyapin in chapter 1 laid the foundation of a philosophy that was to be elaborated and collectively enacted by the central characters.

In spring of 1947 Akhmatova visited Moscow, staying again with her friends the Ardovs; it was probably then that Pasternak slipped a thousand roubles under her pillow to help her after the Zhdanov decree took away her livelihood.[27] He also staged a reading of his chapters at the Ardovs. Akhmatova, though guarded in his presence, was not impressed. (Her view in fact became increasingly negative as work on the novel progressed. She was irritated by the figure of Lara, partly no doubt due to similarities with Zinaida and Ivinskaya, whom she disliked in fiction no less than in real life. Later she described the novel as a 'brilliant failure' and denied any similarity between its fictional world and the one she had lived in and clearly recalled.)[28]

Pasternak later joked to Gladkov that he had tormented Akhmatova with his novel and almost given her an angina attack, but he was pained by her response and took some of it to heart.[29] Probably with this in mind, he eliminated some details of character and incident involving Lara in the early draft chapters. Zinaida for her part also disliked the early Lara episodes and denied her cousin was the blackguard he became in the person of Komarovsky. Pasternak and his hero's 'Komarovsky complex' in fact became one of the growing points from which the novel developed.[30]

In May of 1948 Pasternak sent Valerii Avdeyev a letter outlining the general plot and scheme of the novel as it later emerged. The doctor-hero was his own contemporary, destined to die in 1929. His archive was later to be sorted out by a step-brother who lived in Siberia and whom Zhivago himself had never known. Among the dead man's papers would be notes, diaries and many poems, which would be collected to form a chapter in the second part of the book. Pasternak's current verse-writing was 'a contribution to the poetic inventory of this character' – 'something in between Blok, Mayakovsky, Esenin and myself – not a mixture, not a synthesis, but a slightly more composed and objectified version of myself'.[31]

For Pasternak the interlacement of verse with prose – and its subservience to prose – was now a point of doctrine. To Agnessa Kun in 1947 he once quoted Goethe to the effect that 'the essential thing in poetry is what remains when it is transferred into prose'; and to another correspondent in 1948 he claimed he had '*never liked nor recognised verses as an aim in themselves*'.[32] In chapter 3 of the novel, in fact, Zhivago is described as having since his schooldays 'dreamed of writing in prose, of a book of life's impressions in which he would place, like buried clusters of explosive, the most striking things he had seen and thought about. But he was too young to write such a book, and instead settled for

243

writing poetry, like a painter who spends his whole life producing sketches for a large picture he has in mind.'(*DZh*, 65–6; *SS*, III, 67) Unlike his hero, Pasternak survived to fulfil his greater plan.

The complection of verse and prose made Pasternak's novel one of the great *Künstlerromane* of European literature, exemplifying what it described and thus transcending Thomas Mann's achievement in *Doktor Faustus* (a work that dissatisfied Pasternak, and he was later irritated by Genrikh Neigauz's enthusiasm for it). By the winter of 1946–47 several of the Zhivago poems were ready, including 'Hamlet', 'Winter Night' and 'Indian Summer'. The last of these was sketched in the autumn of 1946, a period whose events left their mark on the rueful statement that 'everything has its appointed end', and that it is 'senseless to stare / When all you behold is burnt up'.[33]

The novel's religious message sounded strongest of all in the poems of Yurii Zhivago. The religious thematic strand was described by Pasternak already in the autumn of 1946 in a letter to his cousin:

I want to provide a historical image of Russia over the last 45 years. And at the same time, in all aspects of its subject, which is grave, sad and, ideally, worked out in detail as in Dickens and Dostoevsky, this work will be an expression of my views on art, the Gospel, the life of man in history and many other things. In it I am settling accounts with Judaeism, with all forms of nationalism (included even in internationalism) with every shade of anti-Christianity [. . .]

The atmosphere of the work is my Christianity, slightly different in its breadth from Quaker or Tolstoyan belief, deriving from other aspects of the Gospel in addition to the moral.[34]

The spiritual yeast on which this new dispensation of Christianity grew was described in one of Pasternak's pencil drafts for the novel as a mixture of Dostoevsky, Solovyov, socialism, Tolstoyanism, Nietzscheanism, and of *modern poetry*. 'Our time,' Pasternak claimed, 'has understood anew that aspect of the Gospel [. . .] which of old has been best sensed and expressed by artists. [. . .] It is that spirit of the Gospel in whose name Christ speaks through parables from daily life, explaining truth in the light of everyday things. It is the idea that communion between mortals is immortal and that life is symbolic because it is significant.' (*SS*, III, 575) In this sense, creativity for Pasternak became a religious act, and his whole novel was thus designed to show human life suffused by a spirituality best perceived and expressed by a Christian artist.

The religious element in Pasternak's prose and verse sketches for the novel was symptomatic of his increasingly active religious belief in the postwar years. Ekaterina Krasheninnikova (one of the Scriabin Museum circle) obtained a Bible for him, and several close friends confirmed Zinaida's observation that

Pasternak 'loved to read the Bible, learned psalms off by heart, and admired their high moral content and poetic quality'. Zinaida also claimed, however, that 'in the generally accepted sense he was not religious'. Doubtless, this was true, although not quite in Zinaida's sovietised understanding of the term. While no great sinner, Pasternak was selective in observing the Commandments; furthermore, Zhivago's convictions that earthly life in itself constituted a form of resurrection, and that immortality resided largely in human *memory*, were not marks of conventional Christianity.[35] In the postwar years Pasternak also resumed at least sporadic church attendance, and the Ivanovs observed that he knew and could join in singing all the services. He occasionally attended the little church in Peredelkino visible from the upper floor of the dacha; it had remained open throughout the Soviet period and was frequented by local believers although the literary community scarcely ever showed their faces there.

In early 1947 several of the typed-up Zhivago poems including 'Hamlet', 'Holy Week', 'The Christmas Star' and 'Explanation' were hand-bound and distributed to friends under the title 'Verses from a Novel in Prose'.[36] And by the end of the year autograph copies of further items, including 'Daybreak', 'The Miracle' and 'Earth' were in the hands of people such as Boris Kuzin, Chikovani, Vera Zvyagintseva; they were further copied and distributed among Pasternak's sympathisers, and during 1948 new poems were added.

At Simonov's suggestion, and with the advocacy of Ivinskaya and Chukovskaya (then a literary adviser to *Novy mir*), some of the less overtly religious poems including 'March', 'Indian Summer' and 'Winter Night' were submitted to the journal in January 1947. At more or less the same time a contract was signed with the journal for a novel titled 'Innokentii Dudorov'; due for delivery in August, it was to consist of roughly 150 pages.[37] Simonov was deeply impressed, especially with 'Winter Night', but nothing was printed. The effective manager of the journal was in fact the deputy editor Krivitsky, who was extremely hostile to Pasternak and angrily read crude political messages into the innocent nature lyrics. Simonov reluctantly backed down and telephoned Pasternak to break the news. Pasternak responded with humorous aggressiveness and demanded that as 'one of our country's most prominent and influential public figures', Simonov should publicly unmask the wreckers who interfered with his work![38]

Ivinskaya also had various contretemps with Krivitsky. He was clearly infuriated at her friendship with Pasternak, and after she went ahead, against Chukovskaya's advice, with the reading at Kuzko's in April, he made threatening remarks in the office about her promotion of 'underground readings of a counter-revolutionary novel'.[39]

Novy mir's refusal to print verse from Pasternak's novel coincided with other publishing setbacks. In January 1947 his collected Shakespeare was put on hold at Iskusstvo because of an adverse opinion by their internal reviewer A. A. Smirnov who was a colleague of Olga Freidenberg's. The latter gave a damning account of Smirnov's academic and moral qualities. But private indignation achieved nothing, and the edition finally came out only in 1949, after Fadeyev's intervention.[40]

Amid his attacks on Pasternak, Fadeyev hypocritically continued conferring personal favours. In the run-up to the thirtieth anniversary of the Revolution, Sovetsky Pisatel publishers announced a new series of editions by leading authors, and Pasternak wrote in requesting to be included. Fadeyev put this to the secretariat of the Writers' Union Board, a contract was drawn up, and Fyodor Levin was detailed to compile a volume in collaboration with the poet. Their joint work began in February, and Pasternak even assented to make some minor revisions. But after the *Selection (Izbrannoe)* was printed, its publication was halted, and the whole edition lay gathering dust and awaiting a go-ahead from on high before it could be marketed.[41]

During autumn and winter 1946–47 the theatre and cinema came under violent attack by the authorities. One of the victims was Eisenstein, whose health soon after gave way and he died within two years. And although in 1947 Zhdanov switched his attention to the sciences, the campaign against the arts continued. Pasternak fully expected to be indicted and he was observed to be in a nervous and dejected state.[42] The attack was launched by literary colleagues at the All-Union Conference of Young Writers, which opened on 3 March 1947. The critic Pertsov delivered one of his routine damning statements on Pasternak's verse.[43] Fadeyev also declared that Pasternak had not fulfilled earlier revolutionary promise, remained closeted in his private world and exercised a pernicious influence on young poets.[44] The main assault however came from Surkov whose speech combined Party duty with personal animus, and was later followed up by his vicious editorial in the paper *Kul'tura i zhizn'* (Culture and Life) on 21 March. Using a traditional array of quotations, taken out of context and misread, he contrived to demonstrate Pasternak's 'scanty spiritual resources' which were supposedly incapable of 'generating great poetry'.[45]

During the spring and summer of 1947, further critical attacks against Pasternak by Fadeyev, Sofronov, and others continued,[46] and one critic even dug up his old offence of failing to welcome the Party Resolution on literature back in 1925.[47] Although no measures were taken of the severity applied against Akhmatova and Zoshchenko, Pasternak was on edge and occasionally even rounded on people who expressed sympathy with him. One of these was the recently repatriated entertainer Aleksandr Vertinsky.[48] However, Pasternak took the March attack and all that followed with bitter stoicism, aware that short of some gross moral compromise, there was little he could do to alter his fate. As he told his cousin at the end of the month, 'I am in my usual cheerful mood despite the attacks on me which have got more frequent'. There was hope that things might simply pass off, but as he now observed, 'although in the past I was surrounded by a lot of stupid confusion, this present clarity is even less acceptable'.[49]

Potentially, the ongoing campaign had grave implications for Pasternak's status and profession. The authorities were bent on expunging all manifestations of Western influence, printed or broadcast. The British Embassy was obliged to cease publishing its Russian-language paper *Britansky soyuznik*, and the Anglican church in Chernyshevsky Lane was closed, later to be used as a 'Melodiya' gramophone studio. Neither they nor Pasternak could control foreign publications, however, and he remained embarrassingly prominent in the West after the appearance in 1947 of J. M. Cohen's translation of *Selected Poems* in London, lengthy samplings of his verse in a Czech miscellany compiled by Josef Hora, a Polish anthology, and two French collections. In 1948 Maurice Bowra included seventeen poems in his *A Second Book of Russian Verse*, and in various Western textbooks Pasternak was regularly identified as the most significant living Russian poet.[50] None of this prominence was mentioned in the Soviet literary press; officialdom was displeased but preferred to rake up the less embarrassing sins of Pasternak's earlier celebrity, such as Schimanski's eulogy of 1943.[51] All this created an ambience so unpleasant that Pasternak eventually even forbade Zinaida to talk or tell him about all the slander. Some things, though, could not be ignored, such as Viktor Goltsev's springtime letter following the attacks by Surkov and Pertsov, in which he assured Pasternak:

You are a profoundly Soviet person, and [. . .] I am fond of you. But you have given our enemies grounds for praising you. You have given me some verses from a novel which can be interpreted as a reaction to the modern situation – and therefore you have to make a statement with your usual characteristic sincerity.[52]

Goltsev's letter was symptomatic of the professional milieu. Colleagues were privately amiable – Fadeyev remained chummy, and Simonov socialised with Lydia on a visit to Oxford – but nobody allowed friendship to interfere with a public readiness to condemn. Even during the war Pasternak had sized up Fadeyev as 'personally well disposed to me, but if he is ordered to hang, draw and quarter me, he will conscientiously carry this out and cheerfully report it.

Although later, when he gets drunk again, he'll tell me he pities me and that I was a good man.'[53]

Amid the hostility however, there was some half-reassuring news in April of 1947. As Pasternak ruefully reported to Gladkov, 'they have decided not to let me starve to death after all: they've sent me a contract to translate *Faust*.'[54] With no original publications in prospect, translation commissions could not be refused, although they left little time for original creativity.[55] The situation was aggravated further in the late 1940s when rates were reduced, which meant increased exertion to produce the same earnings. The contract with *Novy mir* for a novel to be delivered by August 1947 thus became unfulfillable. Furthermore, even translated publications came under fire. Pertsov maintained that Pasternak's ideological shortcomings had deprived his rendering of Baratashvili's 'Merani' of its proper defiance and energy,[56] and over the next few years there were hardly any unequivocally positive reviews of his translations. *Henry IV* was virtually ignored by the critics in 1948; the Iskusstvo Shakespeare edition was shelved; and later in 1948 an entire translated anthology was cancelled and broken up.

In May of 1947 Pasternak reported to his cousin that although he thought he had passed the 'age of translation', circumstances had forced him to accede to a whole series of tentative proposals . . . 'until suddenly all of them were accepted'. He was thus faced with having to translate *Faust*, *King Lear* and 'The Brave Hero János' by Petőfi during the summer. Nevertheless, he vowed, 'I will continue writing my novel in the twenty-fifth hour of the day'.[57] Sheer inability to carry this through, however, had a depressive effect. As he told Chukovskaya in June, 'When writing the novel, I felt around me a special tribe of folk akin to me and with whom I felt no pain. But now all this is left far behind as though it had never been.'[58]

Translations brought material security however. They enabled Pasternak both to provide amply for all his dependents and to assist friends incarcerated, exiled or impoverished by the regime. Among his surviving papers of the postwar period was a vast quantity of counterfoils from money orders sent to many different addresses in the USSR. Additionally, after Ivinskaya's ongoing contretemps with Krivitsky and others at *Novy mir*, Pasternak insisted that she leave her job in early 1948, and he undertook to help subsidise her and her family. He also began instructing her in the art of verse translation and arranged with Gosizdat for her to translate the Uzbek poet Gafur Guliam. On her admission, she made a poor job of it and handed over to him; the work was never published however. Later, Ivinskaya apparently took over some translations from Pasternak in order to help free up his time for work on the novel; it is hard to establish the exact degree of her input into various short translations that appeared in the late 1940s, although renditions known to be by her are pedestrian compared with Pasternak's own.[59] Yet even without Ivinskaya's help, Pasternak's ample earnings from translation enabled him to divide up his work over the next few years: spells of concentrated translation freed up and financed further periods of several months for original creative work.

In early 1947 Pasternak revised his *Hamlet* for the children's publisher Detgiz, which involved 'going through it at a run', lightening, simplifying and occasionally bowdlerising.[60] That spring he also revived his old contract with Detgiz for a new version of *King Lear*. In September he wrote Morozov a typically modest letter, ceding primacy still to the nineteenth-century version by Aleksandr Druzhinin, or the modern one by Shchepkina-Kupernik. His reserve arose partly from a more pragmatic view of translation: 'Maybe the tragic confusion of all this lies in the fact that I am a translator not by good fortune but through misprision, and if conditions were better I ought not to be translating at all'.[61] The whole of *Lear* was completed and typed in little over two months, and as he neared the end of the task, in September Pasternak was aware of working in almost slapdash fashion simply in order to get back to his novel.[62]

On 6 January 1947 a contract was also signed with Goslitizdat for a translated anthology of Polish poetry. Pasternak was at work on this when the Polish writer Jan Kott visited him in great secrecy at Peredelkino. Hearing Kott exult at the new freedom enjoyed by Polish writers, Pasternak urged caution; indeed, within a very short time, as Czesław Miłosz put it, 'the world of Orwell ceased to be a literary fiction in Poland'.[63]

Pasternak had started translating verse by the Hungarian Romantic Sándor Petöfi in 1946, using German versions and Russian glosses furnished by Antal Hidas and his wife Agnessa Kun. In 1947 a large collected edition was projected, which Pasternak took on, like his other translations, as a penance. In the early summer he translated 2,500 lines of Petöfi inside five weeks. As he told Kun on 3 July, 'You'll kill me with your Petöfi, and you will answer before history.'[64] Thanks to her, however, Pasternak was able to command the top translator's rate, and the work was done partly with Ivinskaya's assistance. It was completed, in fact, at the high tide of his affection for her, and there often seemed a correspondence between Petöfi and his translator's sentiment. His inscription to her on the published volume read: 'In May and June of 1947 the word "Petöfi" was a coded sign, and my close translations of his lyrics are an expression of my feelings and thoughts for and about you, adapted to the demands of the text.' As Ivinskaya herself recalled, 'Petöfi was our first declaration of love'.[65]

During summer 1947 Pasternak's brother and sister-in-law, his son Evgenii, Stanislav and his wife, and Nina Tabidze were among the many house guests. Between bouts of translation, he and Zinaida worked in the garden. In September, once the potatoes had been dug, the whole family moved back into town and Pasternak continued with his novel.[66] The fourth chapter of the narrative dealt with the First World War, and he began reading up on the subject. But he quickly found the available literature boring, deceptive and exasperating, and as Chukovskaya recalled, he conceived his novel partly as a form of protest against them.[67]

Implicitly Pasternak also saw his novel as contrasting with other contemporary works more 'factological' than his own. (A notable feature of *Doctor Zhivago* was it almost total failure even to name or allude accurately to figures and events of the period in which it was set.) In July 1947, after reading Ehrenburg's war novel *The Storm (Burya)*, he commented on the 'strange population' and 'edifying events' in it: 'I cannot check whether there are Martians existing on Mars – maybe there are! – but *these* people certainly don't exist.' The same infection was also detected in the theatre. On a recent production of *Uncle Vanya* he commented that 'Everything is covered in lacquer. This is a show for modern generals and their wives. It bears no relation to Chekhov.'[68]

The distortion of cultural life in the later 1940s eventually affected even the most faithful of the faithful. The vulnerability of even the most favoured was underlined in Pasternak's chance meeting with Fadeyev in Peredelkino in late 1947. The two of them chaffed one another about reversals of fortune they had both suffered, for Fadeyev had been reprimanded for defects in his war novel *The Young Guard (Molodaya gvardiya)*, especially its failure to highlight the leading role of the Party in a depiction of the underground resistance movement, and for its (accurate) picture of Soviet disarray in the face of the German advance. Fadeyev obligingly confessed, rewrote the book and retained his celebrity; Pasternak continued in disfavour but with integrity intact.[69]

In January of 1948 Pasternak confessed to having almost strangled the poet Sergei Vasilyev at a New Year party for claiming he was unknown except to a few of the older generation.[70] In fact, there was convincing (if rarely available) evidence of a substantial following. On 6 January 1948 at the Union of Writers, Tikhonov presided over a special evening celebration of Petöfi at which Hidas gave an introduction and Nikolai Chukovsky, Vera Inber, Martynov, Obradovich and Pasternak read translations. On stage Pasternak seemed a tragic, aged figure with grey and sunken features, but each of his readings was greeted with thunderous applause and, according to one witness, 'from an evening of Petőfi it turned into a Pasternak evening'.[71]

On 30 January, at Gladkov's instigation, Pasternak gave a reading in the chief producer's office at one of the Moscow theatres where he was warmly received by the actors. There was less interest, though, in his translation of *Antony and Cleopatra* than in his original work, and the evening ended with a talk about his novel and a recital of mainly religious poems, with 'Winter Night' repeated as an encore.[72] The season of public fêting ended, however, on Saturday 7 February. Despite recent criticism of him, Pasternak was suddenly scheduled to appear with nineteen other poets at the Polytechnic Museum in a 'Poets' Evening. For Peace. For Democracy', which was staged as part of an official campaign against NATO. Pasternak was clearly out of place in the company of official bards such as Bezymensky, Mikhalkov, Narovchatov, Sofronov and Surkov. His inclusion may have been a way of drawing a larger audience, although unintentionally it virtually sabotaged the political impact of the meeting.

Pasternak did not appear with the main platform party, and the programme began without him. Surkov opened the proceedings with a verbal assault on NATO, Winston Churchill and other cold-warriors, but towards the end of his speech he was suddenly drowned out by thunderous applause, manifestly not addressed to him. A glance over his shoulder revealed Pasternak slipping into his place from the wings. Several subsequent performers were applauded half-heartedly. However, when Pasternak was called to recite, there was an eruption of applause which he himself tried to quell, maybe recalling the damage done by Akhmatova's accolade in 1946. Pasternak then shunned the microphone and instead stepped down and addressed the audience from the floor, declining as it were to share even the same platform as other speakers. He announced that 'Unfortunately, I have no poem on the theme of the evening, but will read you some things I wrote before the war.' A selection of poems from *Earthly Expanse* followed. Each item was applauded loud and long, and several voices prompted sympathetically whenever he seemed to falter. (In fact by now he was an experienced recitalist and prepared himself thoroughly; Vyacheslav Ivanov suggests that his memory lapses were maybe a calculated ploy for 'testing' his audience.) Then came public appeals for encores, which Pasternak obliged, although requests for Shakespeare's Sonnet 66 were declined – perhaps wisely: such lines might have been an excessive provocation (see above, p. 170). Instead, Pasternak read some recent verse, including 'Winter Night' and 'Daybreak'. It seems barely credible that such religious poetry could be recited publicly at that time; yet many listeners, especially the officials, simply failed to identify the divine addressee to whose 'testament' the poem 'Daybreak' referred.[73] The applause for Pasternak eventually turned into a form of demonstration. The chairman, Boris Gorbatov, was visibly unnerved, and Pasternak smiled in embarrased but triumphant appreciation. Gorbatov repeatedly rang his bell and finally restored order, after which an intermission was announced.

Despite his provocative public accolade Pasternak suffered no reprisals. However, apart from a more staid repetition of the evening in the Hall of Columns, this was his last public recitation of the 1940s.[74]

Meanwhile some darker clouds were gathering on the cultural horizon. After discussions in mid January 1948 of 'formalism in music' at which Zhdanov repeated his boorish attacks on literature, theatre and the sciences, the Central Committee passed a decree on 10 February condemning the opera *The Great Friendship* by the Georgian Vano Muradeli for its political errors and formalist tendencies. Following this, at the Soviet Composers' Congress, a general witch-hunt began against formalist abuses by the major figures of Khachaturyan, Myaskovsky, Prokofiev, Shebalin, and Shostakovich. To support Shostakovich after his initial prevarications, Pasternak sent him a message of encouragement, only to hear that next day the composer read out a craven prepared confessional statement, promising to obey Party directives and write for the people. Pasternak was desolated and privately exclaimed: 'O Lord, if only they knew at least how to keep silent! Even that would be a feat of courage!'[75]

The 'historic' February Resolution reverberated in literary quarters too. At a Moscow writers' meeting to discuss it on the 1st March, Surkov picked on Pasternak as an example of 'individualistic artistry' eulogised by 'foreign aesthetes',[76] and a further series of attacks followed.

In the April issue of *Oktyabr'*, an article referred to the campaign against formalism in music and found similar deviations in the work of certain writers. An extreme case was Pasternak, whose aesthetism, incomprehensibility, subjectivism and antisocial worldview all offended against the legacy of Mayakovsky, and had set a bad example to other poets and 'inflicted serious damage on Soviet poetry'.[77] In the May issue of *Novy mir* Pasternak was again targeted as one of several 'formalist poets' responsible for creating a cult of Futurist Velemir Khlebnikov though his 'impressionistic randomness', fetish of 'external acoustic form' and 'militant lack of ideology'.[78]

Under the critical onslaught, Pasternak's *Selection* of poetic works was finally cancelled and almost all the 25,000 copies were destroyed. By an oversight, though, after its initial approval, two copies of the book were deposited in the Lenin Library, and a few enterprising readers thus contrived to read it. The book contained an author's afterword that challenged orthodox positions, omitting mention of the Revolution, identifying his own father, Tolstoy, Blok and Mayakovsky as major formative influences, and citing his own banned book *Safe Conduct*.[79] Later in 1948, Sovetsky Pisatel also cancelled a complete miscellany of Pasternak's translations that had already been set up in print. Again, however, just one copy survived in the Lenin Library manuscript department.[80]

As earlier, Pasternak's recent 'working-over' by the literary authorities left him with many sincere but pusillanimous well-wishers who urged him to make some gesture of compromise. Children's authoress Agniya Barto who lived on the same staircase in Lavrushinsky Lane and idolised her neighbour, quizzed Chukovskaya in October 1948 as to why Pasternak did not write two or three poems about the Komsomol in order to make his peace: 'After all, it's so easy for him, it would cost him nothing!'[81]

Quite apart from the moral cost of such a gesture, Pasternak was uninterested in commissioned *vers de circonstances*. A summer note to Zinaida out at Peredelkino reported: 'My mood [. . .] is splendid: I firmly know what I want, what I like and what I cannot tolerate, and this urban summer I regard as a period of enforced and increased resistance in this struggle of mine with my despicable contemporaries – and consequently I'm enjoying both the heat and the bedbugs, and I just keep whistling.'[82] Pasternak's ability to remain elated in adversity was genuine and emerged in several letters of the later 1940s. Banishment from official literary life simplified his existence and freed him from an irksome 'profession'; beyond translating as a livelihood, he could work at his novel; and the possibility of being arraigned for some fictional offence was beyond his control and concern. He had virtually achieved the earlier 'enviable' freedom of Mandelstam, and in a letter to Chikovani he thanked the Creator for 'such a generous and unusual literary fate [. . .] still gapingly empty, like Noah's ark before the Flood. But now I do have hope of filling this space with works and achievements.'

After a winter's work on the First World War sequences of the novel, the early summer of 1948 was spent on touching up *Henry IV* for Detgiz publishers and on further adjustments to the delayed edition of Shakespeare. In early June Akhmatova was again in Moscow, and despite her proud refusal to sign a grant application, Litfond promised her a subsidy of three thousand roubles. Also, after representations by Pasternak the Central Committee and Union sanctioned her engagement as translator, and this for several years became her staple income, although Pasternak had to do battle by phone to convince the director of Goslitizdat that she was actually capable of translating![83]

For June and part of July Pasternak stayed on alone in Lavrushinsky Lane, where he was visited and photographed by his friend Lev Gornung.[84] Meanwhile Zinaida stayed with Leonid at the Peredelkino writers' holiday home. Without any request or permission from the Pasternaks, the dacha was under repair and temporarily commandeered to house some Union employees. Out of favour as he was, Pasternak saw this as a reminder of how tenuous was his claim to the property he occupied. In mid July, however, they were able to reoccupy the dacha.[85]

The contract signed with Goslitizdat for a Russian version of part I of Goethe's *Faust* required delivery of a manuscript by 1 May 1948. After delays and extensions, however, the translation of its 4,700 lines was basically carried out in the six-month period starting August 1948,[86] and for this purpose Pasternak stayed on in Peredelkino in September after Zinaida and their son returned to town. Finances were tight again, and *Novy mir* was demanding return of the advance issued in 1947 for the unwritten novel 'Innokentii Dudorov'. This project he regarded as 'a totally selfless and unprofitable enterprise', and none of the chapters so far written were ready for printing.[87] Fortunately, though, the Goethe translation was delivered and payment released in February 1949, just in time to avert legal proceedings by *Novy mir*.[88]

Pasternak had for years communed with the world and work of Goethe. Faustian motifs figured in some of his earliest verse;[89] the idea for a joint translation of *Faust* with Tsvetaeva was discussed in the mid 1920s; and a letter of 1929 mentioned a plan to translate *Faust* or to revise the older versions by Fet and Bryusov. Re-examining their work, Pasternak was now struck by its lack of spontaneity – a quality he hoped to restore in his own new version.[90]

Although not as subversive as Shakespeare's *Hamlet*, some of Pasternak's *Faust* became a form of politically charged lyric confession, and some lines acquired a further disturbing piquancy through translation.[91] Inevitably, work on Goethe also had some effect on the novel. In it, as Lev Kopelev observed, both Zhivago and Antipov offered 'variants of a Faustian fate',[92] although it was Antipov who was guilty of more obvious submission to a Mephistofelian philosophy. Possibly the unwritten 'Innokentii Dudorov' had a Faustian hero who became a secondary character in the completed novel, and it was perhaps with this in mind that Pasternak at one point considered subtitling his novel an 'Attempt at a Russian Faust' ('Opyt russkogo Fausta').[93] (When his ideas were still in flux, in 1947 he told Emma Gershtein that the novel's main hero would emerge as the Jewish apostate Misha Gordon.)[94] This very fluidity of conception, however, was germane to the Faustian world and was described by Valentin Asmus as a primary sense of 'the infinite openness of this world, its inexhaustible plenitude of ideas and images, poetic ánd philosophic, scientific and artistic'.[95]

Although the translation of *Faust I* was quickly finished, Pasternak was to have a longer-term involvement with Goethe's drama as a whole, and his eventual work on part II again ran concurrently with composition of the novel. Not surprisingly, Faustian associations and reflections figured frequently in Pasternak's thoughts, correspondence and conversations of the late 1940s and 1950s.[96]

In summer of 1948 Pasternak revised his completed novel chapters, and Baranovich produced a dozen copies and carbons for distribution. Akhmatova took one of these back to Leningrad, where it was read by Pasternak's friend Sergei Spassky. Unlike Akhmatova, his response was overwhelmingly positive, discovering a new source of 'patent, unconcealed energy' in the work. 'Quite simply, your entire poetic arsenal is now in play, ' he assured the auther.[97]

In October 1948 a second version of the novel's first four chapters was ready; Pasternak regarded this section as now complete, and he had settled on the final title of 'Doctor Zhivago'.[98] Copies were circulated to interested friends in Moscow, and also sent on a postal round of distant addressees. Ariadna Efron, exiled in Ryazan after release from labour camp in 1947,[99] sent Pasternak a lengthy opinion on his chapters in late November. She found the various connective episodes between tableaux to be over-schematic, but the secondary characters and evocations of feeling, thought and lyric detail seemed to have a special 'limpidité' which typified for her all that was best in Pasternak.[100] At the author's request Efron sent the chapters on to his correspondents Elena Orlovskaya and the exiled Balkarian poet Kaisyn Kuliev in Frunze, Kirghizia. Later the typescript was mailèd to Anastasia Tsvetaeva who was in exile near Novosibirsk, and who was harshly critical of the novel's pale characterisation and Pasternak's seeming 'loss of himself'.[101]

Pasternak's chapters also circulated among Leningrad relations. Olga Freidenberg's letter of late November demonstrated that she was well attuned to the message of her cousin's novel, which for her almost effaced any technical considerations:

Your book stands above any judgement. One can only apply to it what one says about history, as a second universe. What breathes from it is something immense. Its peculiarity [. . .] lies not in the genre, not in the plot construction, even less in the characters [. . .] This is a peculiar variant of the book of Genesis.

255

Freidenberg's final thought however had a more terrible and topical pungency: 'It seems to me that you are afraid of death, and that this explains everything – your passionate immortality which you construct as a cherished personal issue.[102]

At the time of his literary debut in 1913, Pasternak had talked about immortality in the context of artistic creativity. (volume I, 149–52) In the opening of his novel, however, he now developed a 'general immortality theory' applied to all humanity and expounded in chapter 3 in Yurii Zhivago's sickbed homily to Anna Gromeko.[103] Meanwhile Olga Freidenberg was not in error. In Pasternak's life there were intimations of a very cruel mortality that lent a special urgency to the message of his novel and the task of completing it.

13

The Darkness Before Dawn

'The Soul'

My grieving soul, weep and lament
For dear ones laid to rest.
You have become a sepulchre
For all those done to death.

Interring and embalming them,
Enshrining them in verse,
In mournful tones bemoaning those
Committed to the earth,

In this our age of selfishness
For conscience, come what may,
You are the funerary urn
That bears their last remains.

The sum of all their suffering
Has bowed you to the floor.
You breath the tainted dust of death,
Of cemetery and morgue.

My soul, o columbarium,
Your millstones ground and crushed
All that you witnessed and endured,
Converting it to mulch.

And all that has befallen me
Grind down and mince and knead
To graveyard humus, as you did
For well nigh forty years.

(1956)

In December of 1948 Pasternak was able to send an uncensored letter to relatives in Oxford, together with four completed chapters of his novel. The unidentified courier was probably someone from the British Embassy with diplomatic coverage. Although letters and photographs reached him sporadically, Pasternak himself had not written abroad for nearly two years. His new message contained family news and greetings, and reassurances that, materially at least, the Moscow Pasternaks were provided for. Half of the letter, however, was concerned with the novel. He urged his relatives to duplicate and hand copies of his chapters to people such as Berlin, Bowra, Schimanski and others. But he emphasised that the material should not be printed either in Russian or in translation – first of all because it was unfinished, but principally because any foreign publication 'would threaten me with disastrous, not to say fatal, consequences, since the spirit in which it is written and my situation here make its appearance impossible'.

Pasternak also described the banning of his work on orders 'from the spheres', and the fact that he was now officially 'conceived of only as translator'. Nevertheless, he claimed, his situation made him psychologically independent, and no matter what lay in store, his mood was not altogether dismal:

Even if you hear that they have hung, drawn and quartered me, you should know that I have lived a very happy life [. . .] Recently and at present I have enjoyed my most settled spell of constant happiness, because I have at last learned the art of expressing my thoughts and am master of this ability to the degree that I require, which was not the case before.[1]

At the time when this letter was written, however, events were brewing which further limited the realm of Pasternak's contentment. The Zhdanov decree and ensuing campaigns were followed in late 1948 by a drive against so-called 'cosmopolitanism'. After a critique of recent drama and Fadeyev's mid-December speech lambasting certain theatre critics, *Pravda* printed an editorial on 28 January 1949 which signalled a new campaign against harmful anti-patriotic attitudes in 'aesthetic-formalist' disguise.[2] The article intensified the already continuing pogrom among the intelligentsia. Furthermore, although not explicitly anti-semitic, the campaign unfolded with a sharply anti-Jewish bias. The Jewish actor and public leader Mikhoels had been murdered in early 1948; the Jewish Anti-Fascist Committee was dismantled; and Stalin was infuriated by a Jewish show of spontaneous enthusiasm at Golda Meir's Moscow visit and at the arrival of a new Israeli diplomatic mission in October. Now a nationwide process of dismissal, public vilification, arrest, confinement and execution began, striking specially at the traditionally Jewish professions of medicine, science, the arts and Academe. Jews accounted for 70 per cent of all intellectuals and artists attacked in the media, [3] and even when they avoided dismissal and arrest, many honest professional men and women were driven to despair, sickness and an early grave.[4]

In the literary field, apart from closure of the Jewish section of the Writers' Union, the effect of the campaign was to paralyse any signs of talent and originality. In February 1949 various poets and authors were pilloried, including Aliger and Antokolsky, and even non-Jewish figures of impeccable loyalty such as Simonov and Tvardovsky were not immune to attack. Pasternak's poetic collection, suppressed the previous year, was cited as a malicious breach of the ideological front and Fyodor Levin, the compiler, was taken to task for abetting it.[5] On 19 March in the Union Poets' Section, Mikhail Lukonin, the head of *Novy mir*'s poetry section, gave a résumé of the previous year's poetry, observing that Pasternak was unknown to 'our people' and supported only by 'bourgeois aesthetes' and 'rootless cosmopolitans' (i.e. Jews).[6] Similar hostile remarks were made in the literary press, and Tarasenkov who before 1946 had been Pasternak's ardent admirer cleared his record between 1949 and 1952 by becoming his most frequent detractor.[7]

Amid the inquisitorial atmosphere, repeated *ad hominem* attacks in the literary press seemed to indicate that Pasternak was in imminent danger of arrest. Although he was hardly indictable as a Zionist in view of his 'assimilationist' views, any evidence could have been fabricated if required. It was rumoured, for example, that on 27 January, when Yiddish author Peretz Markish was arrested, MGB agents confiscated a copy of Pasternak's translation of his threnody on the death of Mikhoels.[8] To Nina Muravina and Yulii Daniel in early March Pasternak reported he had been called up by Akhmatova and Olga Berggolts from Leningrad, where rumour of his arrest was rife; and in Moscow, Neigauz and Lili Brik even visited his house in person to reassure themselves of his safety.[9] Some years later prosecutor Lev Sheinin confirmed that the security organs had been preparing to arrest Pasternak when Stalin himself intervened with orders to leave the 'cloud-dweller' in peace.[10] The decision not to arraign Pasternak certainly made political sense and avoided the negative publicity this would have aroused in the West. Other unfortunates were not so protected however; several literary figures involved in the now disbanded Jewish Antifascist Committee were sacrificed, and cases of arrest and official harrassment became everyday events.

Pasternak meanwhile contrived to live an outwardly normal life; he followed his usual work routine, and in March and April he was seen at concerts by Neigauz and Richter. However, he was haunted by a sense of time running out for his main creative project. At the end of March he explained to Maria Yudina that now *Faust I* was complete, he intended resuming work on the novel and would accept no further delays since 'everything is in such a state of unclarity!'[11]

On 1 April 1949, Pasternak gave a first reading of *Faust I* to a private audience of about fifteen people, and Neigauz next day wrote an enthralled account of the occasion.[12] The Detgiz edition appeared later that year, and the translation was also included in a Goethe miscellany with an introduction and commentary by Nikolai Vilyam.[13]

In September, thanks to the personal intervention of Fadeyev, the two-volume Iskusstvo edition of Pasternak's Shakespeare also finally appeared. Although Fadeyev's repeated private and public double-dealing in regard to him by now left little room for actual friendship, Pasternak wrote specially to thank 'Dear Sasha' for his help. He also used the pretext to remind his benefactor how genuine 'cosmopolitan' fame was perfectly compatible with patriotism:

This is the achievement of our revolution in its most general, most primary sense; this is the achievement of the recent victory of Russian arms, but it is also the achievement of Russian literature . . . And in some part, somewhere between Blok and Esenin and yourself and others, I too have assisted in this – unimaginable, amazing and undeservedly improbable though this seems even to me. And this is the source of my patriotic feelings.[14]

The note of slight self-deprecation here reflected Pasternak's increasing concern at failure to justify his own self-expectations – no matter how understandable the causes. Among these causes he specially resented the fact that his own reluctant Jewishness worked against him. In a letter of summer 1949 to Olga Freidenberg, he mentioned his recognition abroad, which only emphasised 'the disgrace of my failure here'.

In the final analysis, what am I worth if the obstacle of blood and origin has not been overcome (the only thing that needed to be overcome)? [. . .] And really, what sort of a pretentious nonentity am I if I end up with some narrow unofficial popularity among the most hounded and wretched of Jewish intellectuals? Well, if that's the case, then I'd rather have nothing. And what sort of person can I be and what mention do I deserve when I am so easily and totally abandoned by heaven?[15]

Pasternak apologised to his cousin for this self-preoccupied tirade. Nevertheless, it demonstrated his sense of vulnerability, and of shame – maybe partly at the evident failure of his philosophy of assimilation expounded most recently in chapter 4 of his novel.[16]

Relations with Ivinskaya had been regularly punctuated by jealous scenes arising from her desire for a formal legalised relationship and Pasternak's unwillingness to break with his family and plunge everyone's life into chaos. In the spring of 1948 she had come to Evgeniya Pasternak, weeping and imploring her – of all people – to reconcile them. Evgenii Pasternak disliked this misplaced hysterical familiarity, and his mother categorically refused to abet the break-up of Boris' second family.[17]

Subsequent months were marked by continuing scenes and mutual disenchantment. Probably part of her suit to 'possess' Pasternak was her announcement that she was expecting his child; but friends were later told that she had had a miscarriage following a jolting taxi ride.[18] The reliability of part or all of this story is impaired by the fact that all obstetric information stemmed from Ivinskaya herself. In any event, no child was born, and in spring Pasternak finally decided to break with her. Life became immediately more tranquil. But it was also more lonely, and there was no improvement in relations with Zinaida. By agreement with her, Pasternak had never mentioned his affair with Ivinskaya to other family members. In August, however, he broke this moratorium and reported to his cousin that the earlier mirage of happiness with Zinaida now filled him with gloom, and he was left contemplating a state of 'loneliness and walking along a knife-edge in literature, the ultimate aimlessness of my efforts to write, and the strange ambiguity of my fate "here" and "there"'.[19] It was in this mood that Pasternak spent the summer at Peredelkino, where he worked on his novel and on various translations, and during the holiday months entertained the Chikovanis and Leonidze as house guests.

Ivinskaya's memoirs characteristically made no mention of her estrangement from Pasternak and instead talked of the late summer and early autumn 1949 as a 'surprising phase of tenderness, love and understanding'.[20] These 'reminiscences' were symptomatic of their author and served a private agenda of justifying her behaviour and enhancing the picture of her affair with Pasternak. A corpus of testimony from family and friends in fact confirmed the fact of their broken relations.[21]

Also well substantiated was Ivinskaya's talent for embroilment in other misadventures. In 1948 an extensive criminal investigation began into irregularities in the offices of *Ogonyok* magazine, involving misuse of unattributed manuscript copy and embezzlement of funds. The principal accused was Osipov, a deputy editor and an obvious scapegoat for his superior, Surkov. Ivinskaya was marginally implicated through her link with Osipov, and in the autumn of 1949 she was repeatedly hauled in along with other witnesses for questioning. Though no longer on an intimate footing with her, Pasternak almost certainly knew of her involvement in the affair.[22]

What Pasternak could not know in summer 1949 was the extent to which Ivinskaya was already under scrutiny by the security police. In 1948, he had given her money to engage an English teacher for her daughter. The instructor emerged as Yurii Krotkov, a dramatist and film writer brought up in Georgia, who regularly worked 'free-lance' for the MGB, and had a long record of suborning foreign officials, journalists and diplomats. One of his assignments was to penetrate Pasternak's circle, which he did partly via Ivinskaya, and later through Zinaida's passion for cards, and also by delivering messages to and from Pasternak's friends in Tbilisi. (Later, in 1963, he fled to the West and *inter alia* wrote memoirs of the Pasternaks and a belletrised version of the Nobel Prize story.)[23] The degree to which Pasternak's affairs had been penetrated was partly revealed at Ivinskaya's interrogation by the MGB in winter of 1949–50. Pasternak probably never suspected, however, what was evident to the security police: that Ivinskaya was tractable if not actually corrupt, and that his concern for her was a weakness in his own otherwise strong moral armour.

On 9 October, security police arrested Ivinskaya at her apartment in Potapovsky Lane. In their search of her home, they laid aside all books and documents connected with Pasternak, together with her own personal papers. She was taken to the Lubyanka, where she was held in a cell with fourteen other women pending interrogation.[24] Pasternak evidently discounted any connection with the *Ogonyok* peculations, and immediately guessed that the reason was her link with himself. The decision to arrest her was doubtless taken after plans to arrest Pasternak himself were abandoned. Her internment was a means of both punishing and manipulating him. Naturally he felt acutely responsible for her fate. Similar considerations probably governed the treatment of Akhmatova at almost the same time. She herself remained free while her second husband Nikolai Punin was re-arrested on 30 September (he died in a labour camp in 1953), and her son Lev Gumilyov's third arrest followed on 6 November (he was released in May 1956).[25]

Ivinskaya's investigation lasted over half a year. Her file was opened on 12 October 1949, and the importance of her case was underlined by the fact that Abakumov the Security Minister personally conducted her preliminary interrogation. Both he and the official interrogator Semyonov concentrated almost entirely on her links with Pasternak, emphasising the inappropriateness of her liaison with 'this old Jew', his allegedly anti-Soviet attitudes, supposed espionage connections with Britain, and a ludicrous plan supposedly hatched by the two of them to flee abroad with the complicity of some (unidentified) Russian aviator! The investigation was also highly interested in the anti-Soviet novel Pasternak was allegedly working on.[26]

Ivinskaya's memoir account suggests that she was spared the very worst conditions of cell confinement and physical torture. The sadistic climax probably came when instead of a promised meeting with Pasternak, she was locked for a time in the Lubyanka prison morgue. (This experience, she maintained, induced premature labour and another miscarriage.[27] Her known proneness to fabrication, however, raises questions about the generality and detail of this story; her prolonged estrangement from Pasternak prior to arrest casts especial doubt on the report of a *premature* birth of a child by *him*; to have Pasternak and posterity believe this story, true or not, certainly served her own double aim – of manipulating their relations, and enhancing her later embellished account of them.)[28] To her credit, however, Ivinskaya appears not to have broken under the pressure to indict Pasternak. He himself was later convinced she had saved him from a similar fate, and told a correspondent, 'It is to her heroism and endurance that I owe my life, and the fact that I was left untouched in those years.'[29]

Whatever Pasternak's gratitude and Ivinskaya's heroism, the fact is that had the authorities seriously intended sentencing him, false witnesses and evidence could have been produced with ease.[30] The decision to strike at her rather than him suggests a high-level resolve not to make a public martyr of an international celebrity and Nobel Prize candidate. However, if Ivinskaya's internment was intended as a means of breaking his morale, it showed little understanding of Pasternak, whose imagination and creativity were stirred by nothing so powerfully as by the real or imagined spectacle of suffering womanhood.

Although greatly perturbed after Ivinskaya's arrest, Pasternak did not advertise his concerns. During the November Revolution anniversary holidays he turned up with Zinaida to see the Asmuses and confidentially told Valentin what had happened. From day to day, however, he continued hard at work on 'everything at once – original writing and translation, in verse and prose'. In the final months of the year he was also observed in public, evidently in the best of moods and talking buoyantly of artistic plans. However, as he admitted to his cousin, with all this work he was, at best, attempting to 'benumb' himself.[31]

As he corrected the proofs of *Faust I* a few days after Ivinskaya's arrest, he was stunned by the confluence of literature and life. As he wrote to Nina Tabidze:

Real life has quite literally repeated the final scene of Faust, 'Margarete in the Cell'. My poor Olya has gone the way of our dear Titsian. [. . .] How much she has suffered because of me! And now this! Don't write to me of this, of course. Don't measure the degree of her trouble and that of my suffering.[32]

The voice of nostalgia, guilty conscience, or merely Pasternakian paradox, was also evident in this letter, for he then went on to maintain that he still had at heart Zinaida's interests and their life together, and would allow nothing to sadden or offend her. In view of his wife's organic grumpiness, that vow was hard to sustain, and Pasternak was evidently miserable. Although perfectly sociable, he looked fatigued and aged at Stanislav Neigauz's January concert in the Conservatoire.[33]

In spring of 1950, after going through Ivinskaya's papers and other evidence, her investigator ruled that various books with Pasternak's personal inscriptions to her should be returned to him. Pasternak was duly summoned to the Lubyanka and handed a wad of his own letters to her, manuscript material including a version of 'Hamlet', and several books bearing his dedications. His reaction was to refuse the items, saying 'Return them to the person from whom you took them.' He evidently remonstrated loudly with the investigator, then demanded writing materials and immediately wrote a letter of protest to Abakumov. Its tenor was that if Ivinskaya had done wrong, then he too was guilty, and if his status as a writer had any value, they should believe him and imprison him instead. Nothing came of the protest except that Semyonov later showed Ivinskaya the first few lines of his message and taunted her that even Pasternak seemed ready to believe in her guilt.[34]

Pasternak was also summoned on a second occasion to the Lubyanka, this time for questioning on the subject of a manuscript by Nina Muravina about his work, which was confiscated from Ivinskaya. But no charges arose from this.[35] Then, on 5 July 1950, without any conclusive admissions or proofs, Ivinskaya's case was wound up. An official resolution dated 29 July cited Article 58-10, part 1, of the Criminal Code and stated that she had 'manifested anti-Soviet attitudes and also attitudes of a terrorist nature', and she received a sentence of five years' hard labour for 'association with persons suspected of espionage'.[36] After a brief respite in the transit jail of Butyrki, she was transferred to a labour camp in Potma, Mordovia, where she remained until amnestied in spring of 1953.

In addition to continued work on the novel and the *Faust* proofs, Pasternak wrote a handful of poems in November and December 1949 under the impact of Ivinskaya's arrest. Among them were four poems on Gospel themes, later included in the novel – 'Evil Days' ('Durnye dni'), two items under the heading of 'The Magdalene' ('Magdalina'), and 'The Garden of Gethsemane' ('Gefsimanskii sad'). These verses eventually concluded the Zhivago poetic cycle. Pasternak made no mention of Rilke in this context, but the religious poems sustained obvious parallels with *The Life of Mary* (*Das Marienleben*) and certain of the *New Poems* (*Neue Gedichte*). Rilke's 'Der Oelbaum-Garten', in particular, seemed to find an answer in Pasternak's 'Garden of Gethsemane' and, as Donald Rayfield observes, 'disseminate[d] its imagery into other poems of *Doctor Zhivago*'.[37] Collectively the religious poems offered an illumination of Zhivago's (and of any) human biography, while 'Evil Days' seemed a more specific comment on the current trials of Pasternak's own life.

In the last two months of 1949 Pasternak also wrote some of Zhivago's 'biographical' lyrics: 'Autumn' ('Osen''), 'Parting' ('Razluka') and 'Meeting' ('Svidanie'), celebrating bitter-sweet memories of a tragic former romance. The poems circulated among friends in manuscript and along with others inevitably found their way into the hands of the security organs. The investigator quizzed Ivinskaya about 'The Magdalene' in particular, clumsily though correctly suspecting that it had some bearing on her character and relations with Pasternak.[38] To Ariadna Efron Pasternak described the biographical poems as 'unstriking and too (unartistically) personal',[39] a view endorsed also by Akhmatova. Quite apart from disliking Ivinskaya, she disapproved of the juvenile eroticism in some of the poems. 'That stuff about Olga . . .' she commented, 'I can't stand it. He shouldn't be writing that sort of thing at the age of sixty.'[40]

Such verse was indeed frivolous compared with Akhmatova's enforced response to the events that shattered her life in 1949. In a desperate attempt to secure her son's release, she sacrificed her art and honesty and produced a eulogistic lyric cycle entitled 'Glory to Peace' ('Slava miru'). Praising the Soviet peace campaign and stigmatising foreign warmongers, the poems were published in *Ogonyok* in 1950 and may well have helped save Lev Gumilyov's life.[41] In an April 1950 letter to Nina Tabidze, Pasternak recognised Akhmatova's noble sacrifice and hoped this would now rehabilitate her as a publishing poet. At the same time he was uncomfortably aware that now 'everyone has started looking expectantly in my direction'. But his own poetic concession to the regime, he realised, had been too freely and prematurely made in the 1930s, without any mitigating tragic coercion, when he compromised himself with topical addresses to Stalin. As he now admitted, 'Such things are not repeated several times. They either mean something or else have no meaning, and in the latter instance no repetition can put matters right.'[42]

Olga Ivinskaya's memoirs give a condensed but graphic account of her years in the Potma labour camp. Her experiences duplicated many similar stories of such confinement. During that time Pasternak wrote to her and also sent a notebook of recent verse which she was allowed to read under supervision before surrendering it. His first letters evidently failed to reach her since prisoners were allowed no correspondence except with close relatives. Eventually though, in 1951, he began sending postcards signed as if by her mother, but the handwriting and effusive idiom were recognisably his own. The first such message was dated 31 May 1951:

My dear Olya, my joy! You are quite right to be displeased with us. Our letters to you ought to flow straight from the heart in streams of tenderness and sorrow. But it is not always possible to give way to this most natural urge. An admixture of caution and concern are involved in all this. A few days ago B. saw you in a dream, dressed in something long and white. He was constantly going places and landing in various situations, and each time you appeared on his right hand, airy and encouraging [. . .] He sent you a long letter and some verses, in addition to which I have sent you several books. Evidently all this has got lost. God be with you, my darling. All this is like a dream. I send you endless kisses. Your Mama.[43]

This and similar messages suggested an inspired and inspiring devotion to Ivinskaya, and as she laboured in the scorching fields or shivered in the bitter Mordovian winter, such reassurance was doubtless just what she needed, along with letters from her family and children. However, she clearly discounted how readily Pasternak delivered effusive endearments. She also overrated the uniqueness of her role in his life, and she later even dreamed up a heart attack he supposedly suffered on her account in 1950.[44]

Ivinskaya was not the first or only friend of Pasternak to suffer a similar fate. The emotional break with her had occurred early in 1949, and his concern and commitment were revived only by the knowledge of her suffering as a scapegoat for himself. Yet Pasternak's postal sentiments never amounted to a renewal of earlier amorous feeling, and when she was released in 1953 he felt no urge to renew relations with her.[45] Throughout her internment Pasternak gave repeated evidence of being in buoyant mood and 'very happy with my fate, with the chance to earn a living by honest labour, and by the clarity of my mental condition'.[46] There was no mention of Ivinskaya even in his letter of January 1953 to her mother, in which he thanked Providence for a happy life and capped this by telling her it was to Zinaida that he owed his life – a life in which everything he had seen and experienced was 'so good and simple'.[47]

During Ivinskaya's sentence, Pasternak continued to help support her family who were particularly hard pressed after her stepfather's death in January 1952, when they lacked even the money to bury his ashes. Until late 1952, when his own heart condition prevented the climb to their sixth-floor apartment, Pasternak visited the family, showed an interest in the children (particularly Irina who had begun writing poetry), and in early 1953 arranged for Ivinskaya's mother to draw funds directly from fees payable to him by Goslitizdat publishers.[48] Zinaida was of course not told of these arrangements, and colleagues and friends who telephoned or wrote were asked to refrain from mentioning Ivinskaya, although it was not hard to guess that her family were among those that Boris was assisting.

Pasternak's material support was of solace to Ivinskaya, although Irina her daughter later dismissed it as mere swabbing of his own guilty conscience.[49] Whatever his private motivations, as a charge raised by a third party her opinion (strangely shared by Ariadna Efron) seems grossly unfair. The self-castigation and charity of those who remained free while others were innocently punished did not constitute any objective guilt; indeed Pasternak assisted many people well beyond the call of conscience. Ivinskaya herself recalled that after being offered an additional royalty by Goslitizdat for his Shakespeare translations, he announced to Kotov the director that 'people are being locked up and I've no means of helping them. I'm going to send the money to those who have been arrested.' Ivinskaya's memoirs contained a whole chapter about Pasternak's assistance to the victims of Stalinism. She also quoted his poem written in 1956 – an apostrophe of the poet's own soul as a reliquary for all those who suffered and perished.[50]

In 1950 Stanislav Neigauz graduated from Moscow Conservatoire, after six years of study, latterly in his father's pianoforte class; he then stayed on for three more years of graduate study during which time he laid the basis of a successful concert career, including recital and concerto appearances and a duo partnership with his father. An essentially romantic player, he became specially famed for his Chopin and Scriabin interpretations. Pasternak keenly followed his stepson's career and rarely missed his concerts in Moscow. For reasons probably connected partly with Pasternak as well as his non-Russian descent, Stanislav was removed at the last minute from the Soviet team sent to the 1949 Chopin competition in Warsaw. But in the 1950s he went on to build an international career.[51]

The success of Evgenii Pasternak was also a source of pride to his father, as early postwar correspondence confirmed. Unfortunately, in April 1950 his graduate studies at the military academy in Moscow were curtailed when he failed to complete his dissertation on time, and he was sent for garrison duty, first at Cherkassy in the Eastern Ukraine and later, after 1952, in the Chita region. This depressing interlude came to an end only in 1954 when he was demobilised and resumed a successful academic career.[52]

2 Boris Pasternak with Olga Ivinskaya (1959)

Pasternak's younger son Leonid was still at school in 1949. Like Stanislav, he was a quiet and amiable introvert, slow to make friends but very close to his stepbrother and Galina his wife. Artistic talent was evident, but Zinaida felt unequal to supervising yet another child musician and Leonid later reproached his parents for not encouraging his musical studies; he subsequently studied physics at Moscow University, but his specialisation in crystallography remained a *pis aller* for the piano.[53]

The multi-valency of Pasternak's feelings towards women in the absence of one consuming passion became apparent again in the early 1950s. After Ivinskaya's arrest an outward semblance of normal family relations was restored, and Zinaida and various friends evidently closed ranks intending to thwart any further distraction of her husband. Pasternak however meanwhile suffered in the emotional vacuum in which he found himself. As he later commented, 'I have a well developed technique for rejoicing. But I lack a moral approach towards suffering. I don't know how to deal with such things.'[54]

Pasternak first met Nina Muravina shortly before his reading in the Serov household in summer 1947, and she became part of the circle among whom new poems and novel chapters were circulated. She had started to establish herself as a literary critic and Pasternak approved her manuscript article about his work. After its confiscation and his interrogation on the subject (above, 264), Pasternak met her at a Conservatoire concert and advised her what had happened. However, despite some problems she had in publishing her work, which were probably ascribable to MGB interference, she suffered no worse reprisals.[55]

Most of Muravina's meetings with Pasternak were on semi-formal occasions, at concerts, or when she called at Lavrushinsky Lane to bring or collect manuscripts, birthday greetings, etc. Maybe she had hoped for more, and was upset by Pasternak's lack of interest beyond minor favours and courtesies. She later claimed to recognise herself in the demure 'touch-me-not' of a love poem 'Without Title' published in *Znamya* in 1956. But while certainly not a portrait of Ivinskaya, the image of the addressee seems to be a generalised romantic one, defying precise identification.[56] Certainly, by the time Muravina met Pasternak again, at the Conservatoire in December 1951, relations seemed neutral, and their subsequent contacts, though cordial, were infrequent and somewhat distant.[57]

The years 1949–50 marked a climax in Pasternak's published translation career. Apart from the two-volume Shakespeare edition in September, the year 1949 also saw publication of *The Poetry of Georgia (Poeziya Gruzii)*, containing eight different translated poets, *Faust* part one, two separate editions of *King Lear*, and contributions to anthologies of Chikovani, Leonidze and Petöfi. In 1950 there was a separate edition of Petöfi's *The Bold Knight János*, contributions to volumes of Chikovani, Navoi, Rylsky, Śudrabkalns and Tychina, and a large 'selected works' of Goethe with introduction and commentary by Nikolai Vilyam which included *Faust I* and various poems.

The need for a 'modern' Russian *Faust* was emphasised in 1949 when volume five of a complete Goethe edition, begun in 1932, included the outmoded nineteenth-century Kholodkovsky translation. Reviewing Pasternak's translation in *Novy mir*, the critic Motylyova found even this version unsatisfactory as a Soviet *Faust*. Pasternak, she claimed, 'blatantly distorts Goethe's thought' by following a reactionary theory of 'pure art', giving the text an 'aesthetic-individualistic tinge' and distorting the play's 'socio-philosophical meaning'.[58] Later in 1950, a review by Aleksandr Dymshits in *Literaturnaya gazeta* spared all compliments and talked only of the 'ideologically defective quality' of Pasternak's translation.[59]

As Pasternak told Ariadna Efron, 'There was some alarm when my *Faust* was torn to pieces in *Novy mir* on the basis that supposedly the gods, angels, witches, spirits, the madness of poor Gretchen and everything "irrational" was rendered too well, whereas Goethe's progressive ideas (which ones?) were left in the shade and unattended.'[60] Fortunately, though, despite this critical buffetting, the contract for part two, signed in April, was not revoked; Pasternak resumed work in the autumn of 1950 and submitted the complete manuscript by mid August 1951.[61]

In June 1950, Pasternak also completed a translation of *Macbeth* inside a single month and with this rounded off his monumental sequence of Shakespeare's dramas.[62] By this time however he regarded translating even such masterpieces as a commercial task rather than a creative form of self-expression. His versions of the later tragedies thus adhered more closely to the original with less evidence of 'artistic transformation'. On the other hand *Macbeth*, like *Hamlet*, required no special enhancement in order to be read as a commentary on political tyranny. It was not published under separate cover, but only included in a Detgiz volume of *Tragedies (Tragedii)* printed in 1951 and in a Shakespeare *Selected Works (Izbrannye proizvedeniya)* published in 1953.

Between translations Pasternak continued work on chapters 5 and 6 of his novel, set in the First World War. At this stage he regarded his work as three-quarters complete, with maybe just two more chapters required – as in the cursory account in *Safe Conduct* – to cover the decade prior to Zhivago's death in 1929.[63] Drawing on personal memories of the revolutionary summer of 1917, chapter 5 described Zhivago's work alongside Lara Antipova in an army field hospital, the outbreak of revolutionary chaos and killing of a Provisional Government commissar (based on the death of the historical Commissar Linde),[64] and the hero's return, to Moscow, haunted by two contrasting visions of revolution – that based on liberal student memories of 1905, and the bloody militarised Bolshevik affair.

Chapter 6 showed Zhivago and his family's fate amid the revolutionary chaos in Moscow, with the events of February and October perceived as part of a single elemental impetus, and the Bolshevik uprising viewed as an unique manifestation of the Russian national genius. Pasternak's own experience of ruination, hunger and disease in revolution-torn Moscow was relived by Zhivago, before his enigmatic half-brother Evgraf appeared and urged the family 'back to the land' in a replay of Pasternak's own visits to Karzinkino and Kasimov, now fictionally transferred to the Urals (volume I, 245, 276).

Each new episode of Pasternak's novel was probably seen first of all by Vsevolod Ivanov and his family. [65] In autumn and winter 1950–51 informal readings were given for family, neighbours and friends including Fedin, the Ivanovs and Livanovs. Another presentation was given at Marina Baranovich's in the presence of her daughter, son-in-law, and family. Pasternak vocally dramatised his reading and was apparently amused at his own imitation of the simpleton janitor Markel and other characters. Mikhail Polivanov recalled his disappointment, and Nadezhda Mandelstam also later claimed no janitor ever spoke like Markel; Pasternak, like Akhmatova, wrote essentially in 'one voice'. Other readers, too, found the new material written at half-strength and confused in its account of revolutionary events after an earlier clarity; Gordon and Dudorov had for some reason faded into the background; other characters seemed imperfectly controlled, and the religious thinker Vedenyapin reappeared unaccountably transformed as an armchair Bolshevik. The author's own seeming disorientation was projected onto his hero. As Mikhail Polivanov recalled, 'Something had fallen apart. Something had died [. . .] The weird, undecoded mention of his diary with the title "Playing at People" cast a deathly light over the whole faded picture of life.'[66]

Another early reader observed to Pasternak that his picture of revolutionary chaos was more typical of the Civil War than the winter of 1917–18; Pasternak subsequently motivated this and other disruptions of chronology by including remarks such as: 'maybe it was indeed so, or maybe the doctor's impressions were overlaid by the experience of later years . . .'[67] However, as he later explained, and as one gathers from other sources, this confused sense of time reflected a widespread subjective view of events at that time as links in a single revolutionary process.[68] For Pasternak, the subjective rendering of the spirit of an epoch seemed to require or condone the sacrifice of historical precision. His letter to the Georgian sculptress Raisa Mikadze also suggested that by abandoning the features of traditional novelistic 'professionalism' his novel was more 'adequate' to their age. He admitted, however, that several relatives and trusted friends 'view my most recent interests and present simplicity, achieved with such difficulty, as a decline, loss of my own identity and lapse into banality. Well [. . .] if there is to be suffering somewhere, why should my art not suffer, and I myself along with it? My friends may be right, or they may be wrong.'[69]

It was significant that 1917 marked the point where Pasternak's depiction and chronology begin to disturb readers and to diverge from nineteenth-century or socialist-realist expectations. Almost all his earlier narratives, including *Spektorsky*, the *Tale* and the novel sketches of the 1930s, were set in the pre-1917 period and seemed to draw back from crossing the revolutionary Rubicon; Gorky's epic novel of Klim Samgin also tailed off with the February revolution, all of which reinforced a general view of 1917 as a historical watershed. Pasternak's pursuit of his plot through to Zhivago's death in 1929 was thus, for him, an innovatory feature. Meanwhile, however, as he started work on chapter 7, creative impetus was interrupted by the demands of translation and health problems.

Early in 1951 Pasternak suffered acute pains in his left shoulder, neck and back. Swinging his arms made walking painfully laboured. More seriously, all writing became a physical ordeal, and while he still coped with essential translation work, correspondence was much reduced. Particularly excruciating were the twisting motions of the neck required in looking back and forth between an original text and translated manuscript. A doctor diagnosed degenerative changes of the neck vertebra, but Pasternak himself suspected cancer of the spine, and he was in a valedictory frame of mind as he visited Agnessa Kun to deliver his final contributions to the three-volume *Collected Works* of Petöfi and an *Anthology of Hungarian Poetry (Antologiya vengerskoi poezii*, 1952).[70]

Pasternak continued working while Zinaida, Stanislav and his wife visited Georgia in early April. Later, in July, Nina Tabidze came with her grandson Giviko to stay in Peredelkino. During their visit Pasternak continued revising his Shakespeare versions for the Detgiz edition of *Tragedies (Tragedii)*, and he finally completed part II of Goethe's *Faust*. He found this harder going than part I, and in winter had made heavy weather of this 'clumsy mixture of embryonic and suppressed brilliance and triumphant twaddle'. Overall, he saw it as 'a piece of work that nobody needs. But since it is required that I do something unrequired, then I had best get on with it,' he told Ariadna Efron.[71] With time, however, Pasternak became absorbed by his task in a way comparable even with the writing of *My Sister Life*. Unlike *Hamlet*, for which he consulted other versions for comparison, *Faust II* was translated without any guides or reference to other editions. Once under way, the work moved rapidly and it was complete and ready by mid August of 1951.[72]

With Goethe behind him, Pasternak spent six weeks in the open air at Peredelkino, digging over the whole vegetable plot in front of the house and replanting trees. It was in a garden-stained condition that he greeted Boris Orlov, a young poet with whom he had earlier corresponded and who brought news from Kuliev and other exiled friends in Kirghizia.[73] Pasternak stayed on alone at the dacha for all of September while Zinaida redecorated the lower floor of the Lavrushinsky apartment, and he moved back to town only on 3 October.[74]

Pasternak's correspondence and communion with a small circle of friends replaced participation in Moscow literary life. 'I do not now exist in literature,' he told Elena Orlovskaya, 'just as K[uliev] does not exist in it, and I have long ceased to be concerned whether this is fair or not'. It was also perfectly clear that Pasternak's forthcoming *chef d'oeuvre* would also be unpublishable: 'when they print it, in ten months or fifty years, is unknown to me and just as immaterial'.[75] In fact, however, he was not always so nonchalant about his isolation. To Tatyana Tankhilevich, who had read the Zhivago chapters and returned them to Lavrushinsky Lane on 4 May 1952, he remarked on feeling 'so out of tune, out of touch with life [. . .] Maybe all of them out there are writing badly [. . .] But it's better to be wrong all together than for one person to be wrong. I've now been left completely on my own.'[76] Yet there remained the advantage of being unmolested and virtually ignored even by former ill-wishers. As he reported in summer of 1952, 'We have been living well and have not been in need, there have been no particular attacks on me, and if there were any, I haven't known about them.'[77]

While ties with Moscow literati atrophied, the warmth of Georgian contacts still glowed. Apart from letters, there were regular visits during these years from Chikovani, Leonidze, and of course Nina Tabidze. Chikovani's public fortunes, like Pasternak's, had also waned: in 1951 after seven years as Secretary of the Georgian Writers' Union, he was removed from office. For Pasternak, Chikovani's situation was a proof of his integrity, highlighting the contrast between a poetic artist who was 'genuine, pure and gifted' and 'the whole pack of petty, untalented nonentities who are created and nurtured by squabbles, embittered by defects in their own nature and ready to wreak vengeance on anyone that lacks them'. The only advice Pasternak could offer in this unequal struggle was: 'Agree with everything that you hear, and the more absurd it is, the more uncomplainingly. The Gospel's message of offering the other cheek is not a miracle of sanctity or a heroic feat, but the only practical way out of a situation, when appearances are judged by reality.'[78]

The vicarious company of insulted and injured with whom Pasternak communed was joined in 1952 by a major new literary talent. Varlam Shalamov had been condemned to perpetual exile in Yakutia after serving a camp sentence, and in mid June 1952 his wife passed to Pasternak a letter and two books of unpublished verse as 'a modest testimony of my eternal esteem and love for a poet whose verse has kept me alive for twenty years'.[79] Pasternak's answering letter commented on his own earlier work and present position, and offered detailed comments on Shalamov's poems.[80] Correspondence and eventual meetings with him continued for the next four years.

Closer to home was the small 'masonic lodge' of young friends who attended Pasternak's last public recitals and continued to read and circulate his verse and prose manuscripts. Among them the one who enjoyed closest long-term contact with him was Vyacheslav Ivanov.[81] Another intimate, until his arrest in 1951, was Konstantin (Kostya) Bogatyryov, son of the eminent folklorist. Bogatyryov was charged with fictional terrorist offences although he was also interrogated about Pasternak; he survived torture in Sukhanovka prison, was sentenced to death and reprieved, then served a camp sentence until liberated in 1956. He eventually achieved fame as a translator of Rilke and other German authors and became a prominent and colourful enlightenment personality until his murder in 1976.[82]

During Pasternak's worst years of isolation, a small 'inner circle' of longstanding intelligentsia friends and neighbours remained intact. Some vignettes of this company, which often appeared at Sunday dinners, were recorded by Andrei Voznesensky with the incisive eye and memory of a student architect. (Voznesensky himself had sent Pasternak some of his verse as a teenager in the late 1940s; Pasternak approved his talent, and subsequently he became a protégé and regular visitor.)[83] Apart from the host and Zinaida, recalled as an *art nouveau* figure with short haircut and lips pouted in a Cupid's bow, the guests included, first of all, the Pasternaks' nextdoor neighbours – the ample ursine figure of Vsevolod Ivanov and the 'gothic' Fedin. Frequent habitués and summer guests were Valentin Asmus, usually to be found plunged in thought, and Genrikh Neigauz, screwing up his eyes, 'diminutive and silent, with a grey aura of intellect and a tousled granite-like head of hair'. Neigauz's pupil and friend Svyatoslav Richter was at that time in his thirties; he would sit at the table, 'distrait, with slightly closed eyelids, drinking in the colours and sounds'. Richter's regular companion who later became his wife was the singer Nina Dorliak, 'elegant, triste, graphic, like black lace'. The actor Livanov appeared like the inevitable samovar at these gatherings, 'in stature like Peter the Great, noisy and coruscating, consuming probably several buckets of drink'. Dmitrii Zhuravlyov from the theatre was 'like a may bug in a brown suit, his large eyes peering in benign confusion'. Once Voznesensky sat next to Akhmatova, who was 'remembered forever in semi-profile' like a figure from antiquity, 'august in her poetry and age', speaking little and dressed in a broad tunic-like garment. Also memorable was the majestic figure of Iraklii Andronikov who once reduced the company to Homeric groaning with his imitation of Samuil Marshak. (He was famed socially, *inter alia*, for his take-off of Pasternak' ecstatic nasal booming.)[84]

Dinner with some of the above company, together with occasional visitors from Georgia and elsewhere, was sometimes preceded by the host's reading of his own new work. Guests would then assemble in the upper-floor study with its semi-circle of windows looking across the field and grove of trees towards the distant cemetery and church. At such reading sessions which normally lasted about two hours, guests had a chance to pre-hear almost the whole of Pasternak's novel and its attendant verse as well as other poetry. Afterwards, everyone repaired down to the dining room. At the table there was normally a shortage of chairs, and stools were brought in. The table ritual with food and drink was presided over by Pasternak with a rhetorical gusto learned from his Georgian friends. Most of the company described were also invited to the Pasternaks' town residence for the New Year of 1952.[85]

In early spring of 1952, while revising *Faust* and a few Shakespeare items for re-edition, Pasternak was asked to produce Russian versions for three new projected Georgian collections. He accepted without evident pleasure and volumes of Leonidze, Tsereteli, and Georgian Soviet poetry appeared in 1953–55, but an earlier delight in Georgian translation failed to rekindle. 'Evidently I ought not to translate any more from cribs,' he told Chikovani, 'but only from languages that I know.'[86]

In late April Pasternak returned to his novel and promised a private reading of new material before the move to Peredelkino for the summer. Scrambling to meet his own deadline, he assembled the next episode from an array of sketches, and on the evening of 2nd June presented chapter 7, 'The Journey', to listeners at the Lavrushinsky apartment. Apart from Akhmatova, Scriabin's daughters and Zhuravlyov and his wife, fourteen-year-old Leonid for the first time listened to his father reading; the boy evidently liked what he heard, and Boris was delighted.[87]

Chapter 7 completed the first part of the novel and centred on the rail journey of Zhivago and his family in spring of 1918 to the Urals. The location described as they neared their destination was familiar from the novel fragments of the 1930s, all deriving from First World War experiences. With memorable nature descriptions and colourful incidents, the chapter also brought focus to the 'quarrel with history' of Zhivago and his father-in-law, describing how the casuistry of politics had subverted idealism and revolutionary *élan*. Zhivago's confrontation *en route* with the Bolshevik Antipov-Strelnikov was a quasi continuation of Spektorsky's brush with Lemokh at the end of the *Tale*, and there was premonition of a further more menacing encounter. An embodiment of revolutionary willpower, moral and logical purity, and deaf to the dictates of emotion or intuition, Strelnikov cast himself as one of history's judges. An avatar of Pasternak's earlier Lemokh, Kovalevsky, Polivanov and similar characters, he was perhaps initially more familiar to listeners and readers in 1952 as another of the 'iron men' who populated early Soviet novels by communist writers such as Fadeyev, Furmanov and others.

Despite its increased ideological acuity, Pasternak's seventh chapter aroused an equivocal reaction from his first listeners. Used as he was to unappreciative comment on his novelistic efforts, he was by now almost blasé about this. As he told the Chikovanis in a letter soon after his reading, 'Most people that have read the novel are dissatisfied [. . .] they tell me they expected more, and that the work is pale and unworthy of me. And when I hear all this, I melt in a smile, as though this abuse and condemnation were words of praise.'[88] Pasternak was also ruefully self-dismissive in conversation with fellow author Venyamin Kaverin, and he virtually guaranteed he would be disappointed at the unoriginality of this new work, and its failure to address the (unspecified) 'main problem that everyone else takes on their shoulders'.[89]

During the summer, the Livanovs invited Boris and Zinaida to accompany them to Leningrad for guest performances by the Moscow Arts Theatre troupe. Pasternak declined and stayed on at Peredelkino to continue working, and in August chapter 7 was typed up by Marina Baranovich.[90] In the event, Zinaida took Leonid and went to Leningrad independently. Later in the summer Nina Tabidze came for a short stay, followed in September by her daughter Nita who took a copy of chapter 7 back with her to Tiflis. A quiet summer's industry and family routine were soon followed however by personal and public events that reshaped the rest of Pasternak's life.

14

Creations of the Thaw

'August'

As promised and without deceit,
From curtain to the sofa spanning,
The early morning sunray cast
Its penetrating slash of saffron.

A blazing ochre was outspread
Over nearby copse and homestead,
My tear-stained pillow and the bed,
The stretch of wall beyond the bookshelf.

And I recalled the reason why
My pillow-slip was lightly dampened:
I dreamed you'd come to say goodbye,
Wending your way amid the woodland.

You filed in ones and twos, in streams,
Then suddenly came recollection:
This was the ancient August feast,
This was our Lord's Transfiguration.

This day a flameless radiant light
Is said to issue from Mount Tabor,
And autumn, like a portent bright,
Commands enraptured observation.

You made your way amid the sere
And starkly shimmering alder thicket,
Then through the graveyard's russet leaves,
A blaze of glowing ginger biscuit.

Aloft, the trees' quiescent crowns
Had solemn heavens for their neighbour,
And distance echoed back the sound
Of roosters' long-drawn ululation.

And there among the trees and graves
Stood death, to make official survey
And look into my lifeless face
And size the limbs for my interment.

Then, near at hand and heard by all,
A voice spoke, calm and reassuring –
My own prophetic voice of yore,
Intact, untainted by corruption:

'Farewell, Transfiguration's azure
And gold of Saviour's Day the second.
Let gentle female hands caress
Me as the bitter ending beckons.

'Farewell to those uncounted years.
We fain must say goodbye, o woman,
Who braved indignity's abyss!
My heart was witness to your striving.

'Farewell, o span of outstretched wing,
Free flight forever soaring onwards,
World's image manifest in speech,
And artistry, the work of wonders!'

(1953)

In the autumn of 1952, after harvesting a bumper crop of potatoes, the Pasternaks moved back into town. Pressing on with the novel Pasternak quickly completed chapter 8, and by mid October it was handed to Marina Baranovich for typing.[1] A few days afterwards, while in town on 20 October, Pasternak began feeling unwell and after struggling home he suffered a severe heart attack. He was rushed to the Botkin Hospital in a critical condition and remained there for eleven weeks. The 'farewell clarity' of his impressions at the time of his admission was imprinted on his memory, and he later recounted it all to Akhmatova who visited him in December, and also described it in letters to Olga Freidenberg and Nina Tabidze. Subsequently the whole experience gave rise to the eloquent religious poem 'In Hospital' ('V bol'nitse'). These verses, some of Akhmatova's favourites, recalled Pasternak's sense of blissful calm and gratitude to God 'for laying on colours so densely and for making life and death such that your language is majesty and music [. . .] for making me an artist, for the creativity that schooled me, and for preparing me all my life for this night.'[2]

After a week in the emergency ward, when his life hung in the balance, Pasternak was moved to the eighth block of the Botkin Hospital. There he was treated initially by the eminent cardiologist ·Dr Miron Vovsi, and later by another well-known specialist, Dr Boris Votchal. Gradually, as his condition improved, he was visited by a few selected friends. Akhmatova's impressions of her visit extended to approval of the patient's new dentures: after removal of his awesome mastodon incisors, he now had a new 'classical' look – 'pale, handsome, and with a head of great nobility'.[3]

Zinaida monitored her husband's visitors with almost excessive zeal and saw fit to rebuke Nina Muravina for sending an unsolicited letter and chrysanthemums; Pasternak later apologised for this.[4] However, as he well realised, Zinaida's attentions were largely responsible for nursing him back to health over the coming months, and she also meanwhile assisted by making fair copies of some chapters of the novel.

Pasternak had his own thoughts on the cause of his near fatal cardiac attack. Olga Freidenberg's condolatory letter referred to his 'fashionable misfortune',[5] and in the novel Yurii Zhivago in the late 1920s diagnosed his own 'sclerosis of the cardiac vessels' and noted increasingly frequent cardiac haemorrhages as a common illness of the time:

'I think its causes are of a moral order. The vast majority of us are required to indulge in a constant duplicity that has been elevated into a system. Your health cannot be unaffected if day after day you have to declare the opposite of what you feel, grovel before what you dislike, and rejoice at what brings you misery. Our nervous system isn't just an empty phrase or an invention. It's made up of the fibres of our physical being. Our soul occupies a place in space and has its seat within us like the teeth in our head. You cannot continuously violate it with impunity.' (*DZh*, 494–5; *SS*, III, 476)

Of course, Pasternak was hardly guilty of such spiritual self-destruction, but years of living under threat of arrest and of dealing with the security organs had taken their toll. As he himself recalled, his heart trouble had started immediately following his various summons to the Lubyanka.

Pasternak was discharged from hospital on the 6 January, and a month later, on 4 February, he went for a two-month convalescent stay in the sanatorium at Bolshevo. For the first few weeks Zinaida stayed with him but later left for Moscow. The stay in Bolshevo was marked by a new sense of uplift and happy productivity.[6] His recuperation at home and in the sanatorium also took him out of circulation and maybe saved him from involvement in unpleasant events in the dying days of Stalin's regime. A number of Jewish doctors had been arrested over the previous year or more, including Vovsi, who after treating Pasternak was interned in November 1952. A cousin of Mikhoels, he was savagely tortured and although released, his health was broken and he eventually died in consequence. Before that, however, on 13 January came a press announcement of an alleged 'Doctors' Plot' in which leading doctors, as in 1937, were accused of 'medical murders' and of planning crimes against the state. Among their alleged victims were two former scourges of the literary community – Shcherbakov (who had died in May 1945 of liver cirrhosis, exacerbated by overindulgence at Kremlin banquets) and Zhdanov (who died of heart failure in August 1948, also due to alcoholic excess).[7]

The January accusations started a ferocious new antisemitic campaign in which official plans were laid to deport all Jews from Moscow and other major cities. Pasternak's condition and location probably prevented his being asked to sign a 'Jewish Statement' appealing to Stalin and the Government after revelations about renegade Jewish involvement in medical crimes and in an American-Zionist plot to destabilise the government; to protect Soviet Jews at large from the supposed wrath of the people, it was requested that for their own safety they be resettled in 'developing territories in the East'. (There was evidence that new labour camps in Siberia, Kazakhstan and Birobidzhan were being prepared partly for this purpose.) Publication of the appeal was forestalled by Stalin's death, but not before various prominent Jews had been prevailed on to sign. They included musicians David Oistrakh and Matvei Blanter, the physicist Landau, and writers Dolmatovsky, Marshak and Vasilii Grossman. The very few who refused to sign, including Ehrenburg and Kaverin, Major General Kreiser, and Bolshoi Opera soloist Mark Reizen, probably owed their lives to Stalin's demise.[8]

Pasternak missed out on all these events as he enjoyed the the restful atmosphere of Bolshevo, surrounded by attention and pleasant company.[9] Moreover, as he told Valentin Asmus, in his position of disgrace and obscurity, he was now 'happy and free, healthy, gay and jaunty', and working away at his 'Zhivago, which nobody needs and yet is inseparable from me'.[10] The status of his novel, as he joked in a letter to Aseyev, appeared symptomatic of all Soviet (as distinct from earlier) literature, which seemed to be 'consolidated on firm foundations irrespective of whether it is read or not [. . .] a proud and self-sufficient phenomenon with an unshakeability and infallibility shared with other things established by the state'.[11] After smoothing out a few passages in chapter 8 of Zinaida's handwritten copy, Pasternak pressed on further, and his buoyant productivity was apparent to his visitors and various correspondents.[12]

Pasternak was still in the sanatorium when the death of Stalin was announced on 5 March. While Moscow life was dislocated by arrangements for the lying in state and funeral, the serenity of Bolshevo was hardly disturbed. In a letter written two days later, Pasternak observed laconically that 'yesterday morning, far off beyond the birch trees some rolled-up banners with black borders were carried past, and I realised what had happened. It is quiet all around. All words have been filled to the brim with meaning and truth. And it is quiet in the forest.'[13] Pasternak had no illusions about the Stalinist regime now ended. But from long observation of colleagues, individuals and organisations, he was aware that its malignancy resided not just in the character of the Leader. A faint residue of Stalin's former charisma was perhaps revealed in his observation to Shalamov's wife that 'the present tragic event' had caught him away from Moscow and that 'my state of health will not permit me to go into town during the days of leave-taking'.[14] Had he been healthy, he would no doubt have observed the ceremonial as he had the funeral of Lenin – without paying obeisance, but fascinated by a monumental event of the age. On 14 March Pasternak wrote to Fadeyev, the devoted literary Stalinist. His letter passed no verdict on Stalin's regime. Instead it dwelt enigmatically on the tragic grandeur of human death, on the public disarray and bereavement, on nature's seeming involvement in the solemn obsequies, and on Russia's chosen destiny to right historical injustices.[15]

As he later reflected on the Stalin regime, Pasternak found it 'surprising how I survived those terrible years. The mind boggles at what liberties I took!!'[16] Yet, as he told his cousin, the main significant change in his own life was in witnessing 'the daily, massive disappearance of names and personalities' and the return of survivors from the camps.[17] The changes after Stalin's death were rapid and unmistakeable. Apart from Party and government demotions and promotions, on March 27 an amnesty for various prisoners was declared. Regardless of their offence, all mothers with children, sick and old people, and minors under eighteen were released; so too were all with less than five-year sentences, while sentences in excess of that were reduced by half, except in the cases of specially grave offences. Further, in early April, the whole 'Doctors' Plot' was announced to have been a criminal fraud, and among other changes the powers of the secret police were now radically curtailed.

The amnesty inevitably released many common criminals, and for several months Muscovites bolted their doors as hoards of embittered, foul-mouthed, louse-ridden trouble-makers arrived in town. Former political prisoners also began returning in the course of the year, although by no means all exiles were immediately allowed to reside in Moscow. Shalamov, however, called to see Pasternak at Lavrushinsky Lane on 13 November, the day after his first return to the capital in seventeen years.[18] One of Pasternak's first thoughts in spring of 1953 was that Tabidze's release must be imminent, and it was July before hope gave way to realisation that he had perished.[19] (Later, in 1954, false rumours that Babel and others were still alive also encouraged further brief flickers of hope for Tabidze, Pilnyak and others.)[20] The bitterness of Tabidze's loss was to haunt Pasternak for the rest of his days. Meanwhile, though, there were prospects of return for many others in camp, prison or exile. From Pasternak's circle these included Shalamov, Spassky, Konstantin Bogatyryov, Aleksandr Gladkov, Anastasia Tsvetaeva, Ariadna Efron, as well as Ivinskaya. In some cases, prisoners and exilees had months to wait for release; Efron returned to Moscow only in 1955; Bogatyryov and many others were only freed in 1956.

Doctors' orders on discharging Pasternak from Bolshevo in early April were that he should exercise caution, avoid strain and official activities, and live out of town if possible. In fact, apart from sorties into Moscow, he now lived permanently in Peredelkino, as he had before the war. The one exception was in winter of 1953–54, when major plumbing and reconstruction were carried out in the dacha, rendering it so 'palatial', Pasternak told his cousin, that he even felt ill at ease. However, his work-room was furnished as before, with the bare essentials necessary for writing – bookshelves, a simple pine table and a bed, which contrasted starkly, for instance, with Vsevolod Ivanov's study with its sumptuous oriental furnishings, Buddhas, elephants and Chinese caskets.[21]

Despite doctors' orders, from February onward Pasternak worked intensively on his novel. But his illness left him more uncertain than before as to how much time was left to him. As he told Fedin in an April letter of condolence on the death of his wife Dora, and which closely echoed Zhivago's advice to his mother-in-law: 'our salvation lies in our labour, which is threaded through with reflections on these mysteries and their laws'.[22] After the truth of her husband's fate had dawned, Pasternak also recommended to Nina Tabidze the tranquillising and sometimes uplifting effect of a demanding work routine as a means of coping with despair and preserving sanity.[23]

A sense that his time on earth may now be limited led Pasternak to reduce his correspondence and socialising. He still entertained however, and Zabolotsky who came to dinner with Chikovani in August later recorded a poetic vision of a 'grey-haired youth' on the verandah, 'like a portrait in an antique medallion'.[24] Pasternak apologised to his cousin for not writing, and explained that he was now 'even more than before excluding and sacrificing everything for the sake of two or three tasks and pieces of work that have become unpostponable after my heart attack'.[25] The tasks he had in mind were the readying of *Faust* for the printer and completion of the novel. For this reason even an approach from Goslitizdat to republish his *Selected Verses and Poems* of 1945 was rejected – partly because this would have been a mere reprint that failed to reflect the new state of his art.[26]

During the summer Pasternak received *Faust* back from the publisher, copy-edited, and at this stage he rewrote almost a tenth of the whole 600–page work. Some changes were made under duress. Nikolai Vilyam had been detailed to comment on the translation, and his overzealous (in Pasternak's view, craven) desire for 'accuracy' at the expense of rounded expression or interpretative freedom occasioned several changes including, for instance, a reworking of Gretchen's spinning song.[27] Pasternak was irked by such editorial carping, but this was overridden by his desire to communicate a new understanding of Goethe's masterpiece; at this stage once again translation work became an inspired act of creativity – or re-creation. Pasternak wrote several lengthy letters on the subject, and as he told the Zhuravlyovs, 'conversations about Faust became a sickness of this last summer'.[28] Thoughts on *Faust* also figured in the Varykino notebook ponderings of Yurii Zhivago. To Marina Baranovich Pasternak claimed that a cardinal feature of Goethe's work was its demonstration of the power of the lyric imagination:

Faust has conquered and added to the spiritual territories of humanity those potentialities that have been discovered and captured by the lyric power of this work. One cannot say that these areas do not exist independently, without *Faust*. But they arise here warmed by the breath of this lyricism, they come to life and exist thanks to it, and they are present while the effect of *Faust* lasts, i.e. while it grows and is created line by line and scene by scene, just as (in a figurative non-real sense) spirits that have been summoned up are there while the effect of the spell remains in force.

Yet, as he explained to Baranovich, Pasternak saw the lyric force of *Faust* as bearing directly on the real empirical world. Herein lay the miraculous power of artistic expression – akin to the power of the Gospel's religious text to illuminate earthly existence. At about the same time Pasternak yoked these ideas together with the image of his own Faustian strivings, describing them in the final verse of the poem 'August' as:

> '[. . . the] span of outstretched wing,
> Free flight forever soaring onwards,
> World's image manifest in speech,
> And artistry, the work of wonders!'   (*DZh*, 549; *SS*, III, 526)

Goethe's play thus emerged for Pasternak as a 'realist' work of art in the sense that he defined back in the 1940s, and as he now described to Baranovich:

The area whose spirit is expressed by *Faust* is the realm of the organic, the world of life. This world lives by the same laws that animate the idea of *Faust* and make up the secret of its brilliance. And here there is nothing until you strongly desire that it should be; but once you have a burning wholehearted desire, then as if to order new creations are brought to life, children are born, new epochs begin with their faces turned towards the sun of truth, journeys are made, discoveries occur [. . .] Goethe touched on the nerve of this element in *Faust* so fully and closely that his language in this work appears as the natural voice of this force itself.[29]

Pasternak's *Faust* translation bore strongly upon specifically Soviet realities in another respect. *Pace* local scholarly attempts to 'assimilate' the work, its whole spirit was incompatible with either Marxist-Leninist theory or Soviet reality. Yet Pasternak's version was an acknowledged attempt to 'read "Faust" with the eyes of a contemporary', such that even *Faust II*, which he earlier dismissed as 'a pedantic accumulation of fantastic allegories', emerged as a poetic masterpiece.[30] Changes of tonality arising from Pasternak's translation method included a consistent clarification of thought, reinforcement of Christian religious elements and pronouncements of a personal confessional sort.[31] Additionally the work was made to reverberate with political-ideological overtones, including commentary on Stalin's notorious canal-building projects. Goethe's Baucis tells of an ornamental canal built by forced labour, recounting how

> Menschenopfer mußten bluten,
> Nachts erscholl des Jammers Qual;
> Meerab flossen Feuergluten,
> Morgens war es ein Kanal.
> Gottlos ist er, ihn gelüstet
> Unsre Hütte, unser Hain . . .   (*Faust II*, V, 11127–11132)

(Literally: Human victims had to bleed, /At night sounded the torment of grief; /Fiery glowing flowed from the sea, /On the morrow there was a canal./He is godless, he wanted/Our cottage and our grove . . .)

Pasternak in 1953 made of this a text that translated:

> Are human sacrifices
> Justified by a canal?
> He is an atheist, your engineer,
> And what power he has gained!
> He desperately needed
> Our house and heights.

After transmuting Goethe's images, Pasternak in his last couplet even encoded the name of the author of the dreaded canal projects:

> *Stali* muzhny dozarezu
> Dom emu i nasha vys'.[32]

In later *Faust* editions of 1955, 1957 and 1960, this passage was toned down, presumably after some editor spotted its non-congruence with the Russian.[33]

After its appearance in December, Pasternak's *Faust* became acknowledged along with Shakespeare, as his finest translated achievement, although it was not widely reviewed in the literary press.[34] And even if he seemed dubious whether in his translation, 'as a system of thought, something new, something immediately revealed and apparent, was achieved', he was well pleased with *Faust*'s 'fluidity and naturalness of language and form, the sole condition that makes it possible to read about 600 pages of lyric verse'.[35]

Pasternak's chief regret was that he was not allowed to write his own introduction for the *Faust* edition. 'But of course', he snorted to his cousin, 'how could some uninitiated non-Party member be entrusted with such a responsible ideological preserve?' Instead of his own 'piece of light and concentrated prose' giving 'a lively and accessible account of the contents',[36] there was a preface by Nikolai Vilyam, the professional Germanist. Using the requisite bouquet of quotations from Marx, Engels and Stalin, Vilyam 'prepared' Goethe's work for the modern age, demonstrating that the feudal or bourgeois tragedy of Faust, where ideal and reality inevitably diverged, was overcome by Goethe's visionary optimism and 'boundless faith in the better future of humanity', all of which endeared him to 'builders of the new democratic Germany' and to 'Soviet people erecting the structure of communism'.[37]

With Goethe finally dispatched in late July of 1953, Pasternak worked single-mindedly on the novel and by the year end had completed sketches and an outline narrative for the whole of part two except for the epilogue.[38] In the spring he had also noted down various further subjects for the poems to be attributed to Yurii Zhivago, and a dozen or more of these were composed in the summer and autumn.

Of these poems, a couple of brief amorous ponderings – 'Sleeplessness' ('Bessonnitsa') and 'Under Open Sky' ('Pod otkrytym nebom') – were later excluded from the cycle and published posthumously. In August Pasternak sent a letter with 'two poems about nightingales' – 'White Night' ('Belaya noch'') and 'Bad Roads in Spring' ('Vesennyaya rasputitsa') – to Marina Baranovich for her and her family to read at their summer dacha.[39] 'White Night' with its images of Petersburg, nightingale's trilling in the thickets, and an urban summer night was linked fairly obviously with Ivinskaya, but only tenuously with Zhivago's fictional biography;[40] 'Bad Roads in Spring' was related to Zhivago's equestrian outings in part two of the novel, which had also figured in the 1930s novel fragments.[41]

'August', one of the most magnificent Zhivago poems (above, pp. 277–8), incorporated still fresh memories of Pasternak's grave illness and dream visions of his demise in a Peredelkino setting with impressions of the August feast of the Transfiguration.[42]

In the autumn of 1953 Pasternak put together and showed to friends a short sequence of Zhivago poems under the title 'Cradle Songs' ('Kolybel'nye pesni'), containing poems which, though later 'claimed' by Ivinskaya, conveyed an almost abstract amorous nostalgia. In 'Sleeplessness' for instance:

> What time is it? It's dark. Most likely, after two.
> Again, it seems it's not intended that I sleep.
> At dawn I'll hear the village shepherd snap his whip.
> And from the window on the yard
> A waft of chill will blow.
>
> I am alone.
> Not so,
> By your whole wave of whiteness
> I'm enfolded. (*SP*, 569; *SS*, II, 163)

Similarly, in chapter 14 of the novel, after Lara's final departure, the woman of Zhivago's poems grew away from her living prototype in response to 'an inner reticence that forbade him to expose too openly his personal experience and real events, so as not to injure or offend those directly involved' (*DZh*, 464–5; *SS*, III, 447).

In addition to poetic miniatures, the 'Cradle Song' sequence included 'August', and the 'Fairytale' ('Skazka') whose composition was actually described in chapter 14. The original poem had a fourth part with repeated refrains of 'Lullaby' (*Bayushki-bayu*), but Pasternak later removed this coda, aware of a similarity with Chukovsky's children's poem 'The Crocodile'! The poem referred of course to the relations of Zhivago and Lara; Ivinskaya's later claim that it was an intentional allegory of her release from labour camp seems unconvincing.[43]

If friends and colleagues were sceptical about Pasternak's prose narrative, the Zhivago verses produced a quite different reaction. When he read several of them to the Livanovs and Fedin in September 1953, they were reduced to tears, and he himself wrote that: 'Sometimes I feel as if I am not in control of myself, but in the creative hands of the Lord which make of me something unknown, and I am afraid.'[44] By autumn the poetic cycle forming chapter 17 of the novel was complete, and on 8 December Marina Baranovich typed up the last poems. The final order of items in Zhivago's poetic notebook was established only in the autumn of 1955 however.[45]

If creativity was divinely guided, human situations were less well controlled. When the amnesty of prisoners was announced, Pasternak was happy and relieved that Ivinskaya would be among their number. But he saw little prospect of resuming relations with her. Apart from the inertia of a life without her, he believed he owed his recovery to Zinaida and had no wish to deceive her again or to endure the tormenting sense of shame before his family and friends. (Ivinskaya's own view that he feared to return to her because her looks had suffered after four years of forced labour was a piece of fanciful conceit.[46]) Since 1949, if not totally fulfilled, his life had not been empty. He and Zinaida had developed a *modus vivendi*, and if there was no inspiring romance, he retained many female friends and allies including Akhmatova and Olga Berggolts, and warm epistolary relationships with Ariadna Efron, Olga Freidenberg and others.

When Ivinskaya's release was imminent, in April of 1953, Pasternak arranged to meet her daughter Irina on Chistoprudny Boulevard. He charged her to tell her mother that despite his goodwill and readiness to help as before, he had no intention of resuming relations. Irina saw Pasternak's message as a typical blend of 'candour, splendid naïveté and downright cruelty', and she in fact told her mother about it only after his death.[47]

In her memoirs Ivinskaya aimed to represent herself as Pasternak's chief confidante and spiritual heir, and also as the main prototype of Lara in the novel. (In fact, this figure was a composite and partly fictionalised portrait. According to Irina Emelyanova, Pasternak was attracted by some qualities of Lara in her mother – her recklessness, faith in life and sense of pity. But as he told her on another occasion, she also reminded him of Vysotskaya, his first love described in *Safe Conduct*.[48]) On her return to Moscow, Ivinskaya claimed there was a sudden rush of tenderness and a mutual resolve to remain together.[49] In fact, however, Pasternak was in no mood to be pressured, and it was several months before they became intimate again. Meanwhile he assented to occasional meetings and continued providing material support and performing various acts of kindness.

Anticipating her return, he arranged with Ryabinina at Goslitizdat for her to take on various translation work. One of her first assignments was some verse by Chikovani originally intended for Pasternak's attention, and he asked Ryabinina (as well as Nina Tabidze, who was also kept *au courant*) not to tell Chikovani the nature of his new translator's link with him.[50]

Probably the chief reason for Pasternak's continuing sense of obligation towards Ivinskaya (and for their eventual rapprochement) was a feeling of responsibility for what she had endured. She for her own reasons did nothing to counter these feelings, and consciously or unconsciously played upon them.[51]

The resumption of even nominal contacts with Ivinskaya was initially concealed from Pasternak's family and friends. One of the few to enjoy his confidence, Nina Tabidze, was asked to assure Genrikh Neigauz on holiday in Georgia that the inspiration for his recent amorous lyrics was indeed Zinaida; he moreover claimed that 'Zina is a god for me and apart from her nobody has existed, nor ever will. This is what everybody should believe.'[52] However, Pasternak was no master of such situations. Racked by 'self-flagellation and discontent at what is happening to me and at what I am doing', he evidently received some sound advice from Nina Tabidze. In view of her firm friendship with Zinaida, she most probably cautioned him – though too late – against having further dealings with Ivinskaya.[53]

Pasternak's sensitivity about Neigauz's view of his relations with Zinaida was somewhat hypocritical in view of his quarrel with his musician friend over the latter's attitude to women. Neigauz's relations with his wife had run into the ground, and during summer of 1953 he cheerfully abandoned her to conduct an affair on the side. Writing to Nina Tabidze, Pasternak contrasted his own 'compassion and awe' and 'shy adoration of women' with Neigauz's 'masculine glitter', his 'perfection of skirt technique, enviable and inaccessible to me[!], and this cheerful advertising of trousered virtuosity'.

Pasternak's other quarrel with Neigauz was maybe less specious. While Pasternak worked relentlessly on *Faust* and *Zhivago*, Neigauz's summer plans for practising and writing a book were postponed on the flimsy excuse of inclement weather. Unlike his friend, Pasternak believed in self-discipline as much as inspirational moods, and he was irritated at this 'lordly, amateurish, lazy involvement with the whole world of self-sacrifice and labour' which reminded him of Tolstoy's aristocratic dilettantes Nekhlyudov or Vronsky.[54] After giving Neigauz a piece of his mind, however, Pasternak regretted doing so, and obeyed Nina Tabidze's exhortation to make peace with his friend. Relations were repaired back in town in December at a cordial dinner party which Maria Yudina also attended.[55]

Pasternak eventually suppressed the onrush of poetic inspiration that overtook him in summer and early autumn. He told various friends that the poems he had sent them were '*merely* tender and musical, but [that] apart from music verses have to contain painting and meaning'. Indeed, 'to such an extent is my concern exclusively with prose and the novel, that I won't allow myself to get distracted and spend myself on verses.'[56]

He was as good as his word. A progress report on the draft of part two of the novel in mid November announced that 'The hero has already parted from the main heroine and will never see her again. In first rough draft I have yet to describe the doctor's sojourn in Moscow from 1922 to 1929, how he went downhill and forgot everything and then died; then I have to write the epilogue that relates to the end of the Patriotic War [i.e. World War 2]. Only once before in life – in "Zhenya Luvers' Childhood" – have I written in this continuous manner, without pausing over details and leaving them to the final polishing.'[57]

With the change of regime, there was a noticeable relaxation in cultural policies. One of the beneficiaries was Stanislav Neigauz who in summer 1953 was allowed to travel to Paris to take part in the Marguérite Long Piano Competition. Although unplaced he made a strong impression and won various broadcasting and concert engagements. Among the gifts he brought back was a grey jacket which Pasternak wore every day for the rest of his life.[58]

In Soviet literature the ice also began to break in spring 1953. One month after Stalin's death an article by Olga Berggolts deplored the disappearance of lyric feeling from modern verse and called for its revival. In *Znamya* magazine, Ehrenburg described the prime concern of the writer as being the 'inner world' of human psychology rather than humanity seen as a mere function of economic, political and social forces. In the December issue of *Novy mir* Vladimir Pomerantsev published a challenging article 'On Sincerity in Literature' calling for writing that would be truthful to real life rather than politically embellished mirages.[59] At the same time works gradually began to appear that embodied a new veracity and honesty – Viktor Nekrasov's *In One's Native City (V rodnom gorode)*, Panova's *Seasons of the Year (Vremena goda)*, and Ehrenburg's novel *The Thaw (Ottepel')* which gave its name to this whole period of cultural liberation. The spirit of the time was wrily summed up in Pasternak's greeting over the garden fence to Chukovsky on 20 October: 'A new era is starting. They want to publish *me*!'[60]

Pasternak was cautious in evaluating the changes however. As he told Olga Freidenberg after *Faust* appeared in December, 'in order for all this (Faust, me myself, my work, the joys of life) to exist, have meaning and movement, one needs air. It is unthinkable in an airless space. But there is no air yet. Yet I am happy even without it.'[61] In fact, by the year end Pasternak saw only few signs of a free and vital literature. Mark Volynsky, well known later as a physicist, sent some verse for his approval and was told there was no point in knocking on literary doors, which could be entered only by reiterating one single hypocritical idea – 'and the outrageously monotonous repetition of this idea has served as the background and cover for so many crimes. So why knock at this door if you still have [. . .] the chance to forget about its existence?'[62]

Pasternak's advice to Volynsky was in effect to follow his own example and the one he was fictionally creating for Yurii Zhivago in the 1920s in his novel. After his return to Moscow following the Civil War, Zhivago's total non-participation in the 'literary process' and failure to have dealings with, or even mention, a single literary personality of the time was a reflection not of Pasternak's own experience in the 1920s, but of his current withdrawal from official literature.

Pasternak regarded his novel as a sole potential source of satisfaction and of his claim on the attention of his age. As he told his cousin, 'My time has not yet come. I refuse to write nonsense just for the sake of being published. And what I am writing – which corresponds ever more closely to what I think and feel – is not yet suitable for printing.'[63] The environment still seemed inhospitable to a work like *Doctor Zhivago*. Liberalisation was modest and partial, and the Second Congress of Soviet Writers in December 1954 was to show the strength of the conservative camp and the new leadership's limited understanding of artistic freedom. The religious verses of Zhivago were thus unacceptable, although ten of the 'biographical' lyrics from the cycle were printed in the April 1954 issue of *Znamya*.[64] Along with them appeared a first printed announcement of the forthcoming novel and an explanation of the period covered by the work, together with a brief portrait of the character whose poetic legacy formed the book's final chapter.

Now that he was printable again, Pasternak resumed public reading, although his appearances were few in number and on a limited scale. On 16 April 1954 he presented parts of *Faust* at the All-Russian Theatrical Society with Morozov presiding.[65] Shortly after that he recited Petöfi at a poorly advertised evening of Hungarian verse on the outskirts of Moscow before an audience of technical college students. But some intelligentsia friends and literary guests attended, including Antal Hidas, who had just been released from labour camp and who exclaimed as Pasternak mounted the rostrum: 'O Lord, o Lord, it's all true! Geniuses do not grow old!'[66]

For all his doubts and reservations, Pasternak noted a perceptible change in human relations in spring of 1953. 'Acquaintances began speaking in more lively fashion and with greater meaning; it has become more interesting to visit and see people.' In addition 'fate has been approached, surrounded and endowed with an outline by something approximating to an organic atmosphere, filled with life. It has become easier to work.'[67] During the winter of 1953–54, after a long hiatus, the Aseyevs invited Pasternak, and the three of them spent an evening together at which he recited all his recent poems by heart; some tears were shed, and as Oksana commented, it was just as if *My Sister Life* had been taken from under wraps![68] During the winter, Pasternak also attended events such as the obsequies for the author Mikhail Prishvin, at which Yudina's piano playing made a deep impression.[69] On the family front, there were also changes. Evgenii Pasternak was demobilised in 1954 and able to resume his academic career. Teaching first at a technical college, he later joined the staff of the Moscow Energy Institute, received his *kandidat* (PhD) degree and remained in post until 1974; later in the 1970s he joined the research staff of the Institute of World Literature which recognised his expertise in his father's work, his research and publishing activities.

One highlight of the 'Thaw' in the theatre was Kozintsev's production of Pasternak's *Hamlet* at the Pushkin Theatre in Leningrad. With designs by Natan Altman and Shostakovich's music from the bold Akimov production of 1932, such a production of *Hamlet* would have been unthinkable under the *ancien régime*. Kozintsev sought to underscore the play's inherent protest against tyranny: instead of ending with Shakespeare's scene of the arrival of Fortinbras and the English Ambassadors, the production ended with a reading of his Sonnet 74. Pasternak was asked to translate this, and he was miffed when Kozintsev eventually used an older published version by Marshak.[70]

Kozintsev wrote to Pasternak about the production in May and later in October of 1953, hoping he would travel to Leningrad to advise on the production and attend the première. In the event, Pasternak pleaded he was 'maniacally un-free' because of work on the novel, and he also turned down an invitation to stay at Olga Freidenberg's.[71] However, he wrote Kozintsev letters of a general nature allowing him a free choice between the various Iskusstvo and Detgiz redactions and the 1953 Goslitizdat anthology, and also giving him *carte blanche* to cut the text wherever artistically necessary.[72]

From afar Pasternak took a keen interest in the Leningrad *Hamlet* production, including a special request to his cousin and Kozintsev to ensure that his surname on any reprint of the poster was correctly declined as a Russian word and not left uninflected.[73] Several Moscow friends and acquaintances, including Lili Brik, made the trip to Leningrad specially for the première, and Pasternak received a detailed report by letter from his cousin[74] as well as from Kozintsev's sister, who was married to Ehrenburg. Subsequently there were further *Hamlet* performances and readings, including a solo rendition at the 'Theatre of One Actor' by Sergei Balashov, which Ivinskaya and her daughter attended on Pasternak's tickets.[75]

On 16 April Pasternak's *Faust* was discussed at the Union of Writers, with Vilyam, Ivinskaya and other friends in attendance. In a dismally conformist atmosphere, criticisms were offered and Motylyova repeated her negative opinions of 1950. The mood was relieved only after spontaneous applause greeted a speech from the floor by a student of the Bauman Institute, who enthusiastically proclaimed what a revelation Pasternak's rendering of Goethe had been. After this the discussion took a much more positive turn.[76]

As if to prove the student's point, in spring of 1954 Pasternak received an intriguing new theatrical commission from the director Nikolai Okhlopkov, and for several days in May he laid the novel aside and worked on producing a shortened performing version of Goethe's complete *Faust*. Unfortunately, the project never reached the stage however.[77]

In summer of 1954, Pasternak was hard at work again on the previous year's draft chapters. As he told his cousin, he found them and his more recent sketches disappointingly boring and incompetent.[78] Sections of the Civil War episode were now rewritten using various reference materials on history and folklore, borrowed from libraries and friends. These included Afanasyev's *Russian Folktales*, Bazhov's *Malachite Casket*, and Propp's *Historical Roots of the Magical Tale*, and Pasternak also read through his own notes made in Chistopol in 1942.[79] This menu of reading had a direct bearing on the already unconventional character of part two of the novel. As Pasternak explained in a letter, 'Its greater unusualness, as I see it, lies in the fact that [. . .] the totality of its action is set even farther from the generally accepted dimension than in the first, almost on the border with fairy tale.' In this Pasternak perceived a 'philosophy frequently hidden even from the author: [. . .] the narrower, mysterious and little-known *reality of life* amid the broader, everyday, social, accepted and usual reality'.[80]

The less conventionally 'realistic' atmosphere of the novel's second part was signalled at the very outset of 'Arrival'. Zhivago's family found themselves 'in a different territory, in another provincial world that had its own different centre of gravity' (*DZh*, 263; *SS*, III, 253). This location provided a setting and perception of events that challenged the traditional sense of literary realism prevailing in the pre-revolutionary 'European' chapters. Life was here characterised by its political-ideological ambiguities and by a proximity to myth, legend and folk culture; this was apparent in the florid chatter of Vakkh (Bacchus) the carter, Samdevyatov whose name and appearance seemed straight out of an old Russian ballad, Lara's residence in a house girded by disturbing caryatid figures, and the quaint incantations of Kubarikha that unhinged even the logic and sequence of Zhivago's own thoughts.[81] Later on, the mysterious arrival of Zhivago's half-brother Evgraf – 'like my good genius and rescuer' – reminded the hero that 'every lifestory requires the involvement of some secret, unknown force, an almost symbolic figure who comes to the rescue unsummoned' (*DZh*, 297; *SS*, III, 285). The effect of these unknown forces – both described, and motivating plot and incident – became increasingly evident as part two of *Doctor Zhivago* progressed.

Pasternak's depictive and narrative method, designed to capture the elusive 'reality of life' was expounded in a letter of 1959 to the poet Stephen Spender, contrasted his own 'life perception' with the causality of the nineteenth-century novel. As he explained:

I would pretend (metaphorically) to have seen nature and the universe themselves not as a picture made or fastened on an immovable wall, but as a sort of painted canvas roof or curtain in the air, incessantly pulled and blown and flapped by something of an immaterial, unknown aand unknowable wind [. . .] There is an effort in the novel to represent the whole sequence of facts and beings and happenings like some moving entireness, like a developing, passing by, rolling and rushing inspiration, as if reality itself had freedom and choice and was composing itself out of numberless variants and versions.[82]

The effects of this were strongly felt in part two of the novel. After earlier small disruptions of chronology, ascribed to the subjectivity of the hero's memory, there were now major subversions of sequence: compression of recounted happenings into a shorter spell than history allowed and the failure of foreground events to coincide with the known history of the Civil War.[83] Symptomatically, experiences on Yurii's return journey to Yuryatin 'produced the impression of something unearthly and transcendental [. . .] like particles of some unknown lives on other planets [. . .] Only nature had remained faithful to history and appeared to the gaze as contemporary artists portrayed it' (*DZh*, 388; *SS*, III, 373).

The 'superimposing' of events from a different age onto a described present had featured in Pasternak's *Safe Conduct*, and a similar technique was also applied in the novel. Zhivago's diary included thoughts on nature, creativity, the sterility of political rhetoric, Faust, the pursuit of 'Pushkinian' simplicity – all drawn from different periods of the author's own development. Lara's analysis of Antipov's replacement of life by arbitrary schemes and quest for some 'Roman civic valour'(*DZh*, 309; *SS*, III, 297) had hints of Vedenyapin's historical speculations on the savagery of the prechristian Roman empire – thoughts which Pasternak enunciated during World War 2 after witnessing the Stalinist terror.[84] Yet the intimidation and hounding of 'enemies of the people', Zhivago's later fear for his life and cardiac illness, were features of the 1930s and postwar era, as also was the 'loss of faith in the value of personal opinion', the negation of morality, and the urge to 'sing in unison and live by other people's ideas that had been forced on everyone' (*DZh*, 414; *SS*, III, 398). But as Isaac Deutscher observed in an early critique of Pasternak's novel, this was hardly true of the time when Lara was speaking.[85] Three and a half decades of Pasternak's Soviet historical experience were thus compressed into the minds of his fictional heroes of the 1910s and 1920s.

Among other character traits in common, Pasternak shared Yurii Zhivago's intelligence and talent, which in some sense replaced an atrophied willpower,[86] making both of them victims to physical manipulation by persons or situations, even while retaining a spiritual independence. In Pasternak's private life this was most obvious in his return to Ivinskaya. Probably at some point in the early summer of 1954 she managed to cajole or pressure him into resuming their earlier intimacy. Her children and mother spent the summer with an aunt at Sukhinichi, and she meanwhile paid regular visits to Peredelkino. Their meetings were facilitated in July and early August by Zinaida and Leonid's absence on holiday in Yalta together with the widow of Trenyov.[87] Ivinskaya later claimed that she again became pregnant by Pasternak during that summer, but in late August allegedly suffered yet another miscarriage because of a rough car ride. Pasternak, she claimed, was distraught and wept bitterly.[88]

If this was not another lurid invention, and if a child had been born, one can only conjecture how Pasternak might have dealt with that situation. Under the circumstances, Zinaida was merely grieved and offended at Ivinskaya's reappearance, and he once again nursed his pained conscience. But as before he declared himself unready to make major changes in his life, and was content to live from one amorous tryst to another. The fact that both women's consequent suffering might conflict with his own philosophy of pity for offended womanhood seemed to escape him. The renewed situation was reflected in the 'Varykino' chapter of *Doctor Zhivago*, when the hero began deceiving his wife with Lara, and when he later took up with her again after escaping from the partisans.

Amid the first 'Thaw' period, there were many reminders of the continuing strength of literary conservatives and their low tolerance of heterodoxy. After publishing several 'progressive' items in *Novy mir*, the editor Tvardovsky was replaced in 1954 by 'yesterday's liberal', Simonov. A private admirer of Pasternak, Simonov officially maintained that his Zhivago poems 'demonstrated no advance in his understanding of people and of the times'.[89] Writing in *Pravda* in June 1954 to condemn persisting harmful artistic trends, the orthodox critic Ermilov cited Pasternak's recent lyrics, especially 'The Wedding' ('Svad'ba'), as a pernicious instance of passivity and decadence, and of a *false* 'sincerity' in literature.[90]

While preparations for the Second Soviet Writers' Congress were under way, there was news that Pasternak had again been balloted for the Nobel Prize. These reports were confirmed by BBC broadcasts and rumours of announcements in the foreign press.[91]

His celebrity overseas was in stark contrast to Pasternak's standing locally. At that juncture, too, it conflicted with his own desire to live in peace and privacy and finish his novel instead of being dragged into the public eye. However, 'evidently God had mercy, and the danger passed,' he told his cousin. The story as he heard it was that in his place the Soviet authorities tried to press the candidature of Sholokhov, but this was turned down and the Nobel award went instead to Ernest Hemingway. Nevertheless, 'it was a joy to be placed alongside Hamsun and Bunin, and to be ranked next to Hemingway, even if it was a misunderstanding'.[92] Needless to say, the Nobel candidature did nothing to raise Pasternak's reputation with the establishment. 'You cannot imagine how strained my relations are with the official scene,' he told Olga Freidenberg, 'and how frightening it is for me to issue reminders of myself. As soon as I make a move, they are entitled to quizz me about my most basic views. And there is no power on earth that would make me answer them in the way that everybody else does.'[93]

Pursuing his desire to live 'far away and secretly', Pasternak spent the winter 1954–55 at Peredelkino, and although officially delegated, he did not attend the Second Congress of Writers that opened in the Large Kremlin Palace on 15 December. In Kaverin's expression, the whole event passed off 'Sholokhov-ishly' (*sholokhovato*), and Paustovsky and other liberal writers were not invited to speak. Akhmatova, now reinstated, was also absent. Characteristically, whereas the Congress of 1934 had fêted Pasternak, the Second one virtually ignored him. Surkov, who succeeded Fadeyev as Union Secretary, continued his vendetta by leaving him totally unmentioned in his keynote speech 'On the State of Soviet Literature and Its Tasks', and only one speaker made passing but negative mention of his failure to rise to the epoch's inspiring ideas.[94]

Pasternak stayed at his desk throughout the winter of 1954–55. After hearing of Ivinskaya's reappearance, Zinaida evidently reinforced his industry by keeping him under virtual house arrest, and she was openly rude to him in front of guests. Pasternak himself seemed downcast, suddenly aged and unwell, and out of touch with events in town. In May he had not heard of the death of Lozinsky which occurred in early February.[95]

Confinement to Peredelkino was good for productivity however. During the winter the later chapters of the novel were revised and polished, and various new material was inserted.[96] Although the later chapters were designed to support Pasternak's vision of a 'moving entireness', some of the sketchy narrative manner criticised earlier by Ariadna Efron was not easily distinguished from mere hastiness in composition. To be sure, in his concern not to overload and lengthen the work unnecessarily, Pasternak was aware of artistic lapses as he hurried to complete it. His friend Ivanov, a remorseless craftsman, compared the immaculate precision of Pasternak's early prose and of *Safe Conduct* with this seeming amateurishness.[97] In sending a few chapters to his literary scholar friend Nikolai Smirnov in early April 1955, Pasternak admitted to having 'lost my artistic coherence and inwardly let go, like a slackened violin or bowstring. I have written this prose unprofessionally, without a consciously sustained creative aim, in a homespun way (in the bad sense), and with a certain dullness and naïveté which I allowed and forgave myself.'[98]

For all this self-indulgence, Pasternak had little patience with interruptions and distractions. Evgeniya Kunina caught him in such a mood when she asked him to call on his old friend Konstantin Loks, who was now sick and aged. Pasternak refused: 'There is work to do, things that I have to do . . . Are you trying to say I am a scoundrel?'[99] Similarly when Bertold Brecht came to collect a Stalin prize in late May 1955, he expressly asked that his speech of thanks be translated by Pasternak. Irked by the honour, Pasternak obliged. But when the Writers' Union suggested he might translate more of Brecht's work, he let rip to secretary Mikhail Apletin: 'Surely Brecht realises that engaging in translations is a disgrace. I am busy with important work, for which the time has not yet come – unlike Brecht's old junk [*star'ë*].' Two years later, after seeing the Berliner Ensemble with Helene Weigel perform *The Caucasian Chalk Circle (Der kaukasische Kreidekreis)*, Pasternak modified his opinion.[100]

In early summer of 1955, Ivinskaya together with her mother and children moved out to stay in Peredelkino where, at Pasternak's expense, they rented half of a rambling villa on the lake shore at Izmalkovo. This was conveniently close to Pasternak, who could walk through the wood and reach Ivinskaya's villa by crossing a long plank bridge over the water. Some cinefilm footage survives which was taken at that time by Ivinskaya's daughter; during the summer Pasternak tried unsuccessfully to help her gain entry to the Moscow Film Institute.[101]

After a summer of heat, thunderstorms and luxuriant wildrose blossoms, Ivinskaya decided to stay on instead of returning to Moscow. She accordingly moved to other, more cramped but cosy all-season quarters, which she rented until 1959 before moving once again. She later recalled the period starting 1956 as the most truly happy one of her life. However, her account of regular and prolonged 'daily communion with a man I loved' and with mutual friends was, again, embellished with romance. In fact Pasternak lived and worked all the time at home, and visited her mainly on afternoon walks.[102]

Ivinskaya nevertheless played an important and active part in Pasternak's life. She did various copy-typing and proof-reading for him. Also since he himself was disinclined to interrupt his work and travel into town on business, she eventually undertook many of these errands for him, conducting literary and financial dealings with editors and publishers. All this saved time and energy, although it also unfortunately advertised the extent to which he was beholden to her.

Pasternak's Leningrad cousin Olga Freidenberg had throughout the years remained in contact with him, exchanging news, ideas and feelings, despite postal censorship. But in her letter of 6 January 1954 she wrote that 'for several years I have not been speaking with you because of Shpekin' (her name for the anonymous plurality of spies surrounding eveyone's life in Stalinist times).[103] After an unfulfilled and frustrated academic career she had finally retired in the summer of 1951. She was in poor health, suffered various stomach disorders, and for long nursed vain fears of having cancer. Her last letter to Boris was dated 17 November 1954, a message of encouragement and faith, celebrating his 'vicarious coronation' after rumours of his Nobel candidature.[104] On 26 June 1955 Pasternak heard from their other Leningrad cousin Maria that Olga had been hospitalised. With two urgent commissions on his hands from the Maly and Arts Theatres (a condensed performing version of *Henry IV*, and a translation of Schiller's *Maria Stuart*), he postponed immediately travelling to Leningrad.[105] He sent an apologetic explanatory letter to Maria on 6 July, only to receive next day a telegram announcing Olga had died – as he later learned, from chronic hepatitis and dystrophy of the liver.[106] The blow of her death and Pasternak's belief in her (and his own) immortal achievement amid setbacks and tragedy probably imparted a special note of poignancy to the epilogue chapter of *Doctor Zhivago*.[107]

On 5 August Pasternak informed Marina Baranovich that the Zhivago manuscript in its 'second redaction' was ready for typing. The work consisted of five notebooks containing a total of some 600 manuscript pages. Despite the fact that she was diagnosed as suffering from throat cancer, Baranovich finished the task inside two weeks.[108] Pasternak too continued polishing the text, and trysts with Ivinskaya and other summer activities did not disturb the intensive work routine. There was however the usual series of house guests, and visitors from further afield such as Ettore lo Gatto from Italy and his Spanish 'translatee' Rafael Alberti. In August, Pasternak was also contacted from the Lubyanka by Lieutenant Boris Ryazhsky who was handling Meyerhold's posthumous rehabilitation; his testimonial exonerating Meyerhold of

3 Zinaida and Boris Pasternak, their son Leonid, and Aleksei Kruchenykh
(Peredelkino, 1948)

any crime was filed in a dossier of similar statements by Ehrenburg, Ivanov, Olesha, the puppeteer Obraztsov, Okhlopkov, Shostakovich and Sofronitsky. In a similar role he also vouched for the widow of Prokofiev on her rehabilitation. During September Zinaida and Leonid went on holiday to Georgia as guests of the Tabidzes and Leonidzes.[109]

During September Pasternak carefully checked Baranovich's typescript, discovering several 'heavy and complicated passages which will have to be simplified and lightened'. He abandoned some of his extrapolated images after noting a number of 'long sentences with a lot of subordinate clauses that come from excessive thoroughness, and from a desire to imbue every single perception with all its accompanying details'.[110] With some sections, though, he was well satisfied. 'I have just read the end of the first binder', he told Baranovich a few days later. 'Praise God, it is good rather than bad. Probably its main virtue [. . .] is something which, as I recall in retrospect, seemed to me a shortcoming and unfinished: the *unliterary* calmness of expression and absence of glitter in the most important, powerful or dreadful passages.'[111]

After revising the typescript, Pasternak in early October intended asking Baranovich to produce one more complete 'clean' version. There were friendly but pressing demands from the Zhuravlyovs, Ariadna Efron and others to let them read his work. But although ready to circulate the completed work, he decided on one final revision of the text, which occupied the whole of November. Baranovich's throat cancer had worsened (although, happily, she was to recover and lived another twenty years). Retyping of part two was thus completed by a sister of the poet Stefanovich and another professional typist engaged by Ivinskaya; the two of them finished their task on 22 December.[112]

Although Pasternak foresaw making a further few minor changes, the manuscript was essentially ready on the 10 December. On that day he announced completion of his major work in letters to three friends – Shalamov, Nina Tabidze, and Zelma Ruoff who corresponded with him from her place of exile in Vorkuta.[113] To Nina Tabidze he wrote:

You cannot imagine what an achievement this is! Names have been found and given to the whole of that sorcery which tormented, evoked debates and disbelief, and which astounded and created so many decades of misery. Everything has been disentangled, everything has been named, simply, transparently and sadly. Once again, freshly and in a new manner, definitions have been given to the dearest and most important things, earth and heaven, great and ardent feeling, the spirit of creativity, life and death.[114]

Pasternak's sense of achievement was darkened only by awareness of his continuing isolation and the fact that his work was 'completely unfit for publishing', as he told Shalamov.

At the year end a hired typist was engaged to produce another complete text with carbons. These copies, bound in brown covers, were hand-delivered by Ivinskaya to the journal *Znamya* and to Goslitizdat for inspection, with a further unbound copy sent to *Novy mir*. After this, Pasternak made some further fine adjustments on two of Baranovich's earlier texts; one of these 'title copies' he handed to Baranovich and he himself retained the other one. Differences between these various 'final' versions were to cause confusion and conflict between publishers and editors for almost twenty years.[115]

15

The Skies Clear . . . and Darken

'When Weather Clears'

The spreading saucer of a lake.
Beyond it rainclouds seeth and gather
In stern, forbidding white array,
Like a mountain glacier.

Gradually the shifting light
Transforms the forest trees' complexion.
Now they're aflame, now plunged in night
As sooted shadows settle.

Then with the passing of the rains,
The clouds are pierced by cobalt flashes.
How festive shines the open sky!
How jubilant the grasses!

And sunlight floods the earth. With skyline
Cleared, the winds diminuendo.
Foliage starts to glow and shimmer
Like figures in church windows.

Thus, in their glinting sleepless crowns
The watchful stained-glass saints and hermits
Gaze outward from their mullion panes
And ponder the eternal . . .

As though terrestrial expanse
Were like some great serene cathedral,
And from afar I sometimes catch
An echoed anthem pealing.

O nature, world, creation's sanctum,
Weeping tears of exaltation,
Inwardly I thrill and quiver,
Standing through your longdrawn celebration.

(1956)

300

Pasternak's differences with literary confrères were highlighted in late 1955, when invitations came to participate in the new almanac series *Literaturnaya Moskva* (Literary Moscow) edited by a group of talented liberals, including Fedin, Ivanov, Kaverin, Kazakevich and Paustovsky. Although nominally independent, such publications were still ideologically inhibited and bridled by the censor, and Pasternak disdained them as a poorer forum than the official journals, since they were over-cautious and fraudulently substituted 'what was required' for truly free expression.[1] To Nina Tabidze he confessed:

There is so little in common between me and the people who respect or like me and believe that I am theirs because of the times [. . .] I desire something quite different from what they want, and something immeasurably greater [. . .] Every time I run into them, I begin to feel that I am ungrateful, an apostate, traitor, a bad colleague, friend and comrade . . .[2]

For all his reservations, when Kaverin and Kazakevich came asking for material, Pasternak nevertheless offered them his *Notes on Translations of Shakespeare's Dramas*, a condensed version of them was printed in the first issue of *Literaturnaya Moskva*, which was timed to appear for the Twentieth Party Congress in February 1956.[3] However, he was reluctant to contribute further. As Kazakevich commented, for Pasternak '*Literaturnaya Moskva* is a compromise. He would like them to declare freedom of the press tomorrow.'[4] In fact, the touchstone of literary freedom for him was the publishability of his novel, which at present seemed a dim prospect. As he told Paustovsky, 'I think you will all be stopped short by the unacceptibility of the novel. Yet you ought to be printing only unacceptable things. Everything acceptable was written and printed long ago.' Kazakevich did eventually read Pasternak's manuscript and disliked it; according to Kaverin he was, like many readers, put off by certain technical infelicities and missed the work's deeper spiritual message.[5]

The reformist Twentieth Party Congress signaled the start of a new and more extensive 'Thaw'. Although little was said of the slaughter, starvation and enslavement of millions, Khrushchev's 'Secret Speech' to the Congress denounced some of Stalin's crimes and his 'personality cult'. Yet even a partial revelation of historical truth brought dramatic changes in the social and cultural climate, and encouraged writers to take a new view of honesty in literature. New stories and novels contained disturbing reminders of the gulf between propaganda and truth, between the life of the elite and the common population. A major uproar occurred over *Novy mir*'s serialisation of Dudintsev's *Not by Bread Alone (Ne khlebom edinym)*, which handled this theme with unprecedented frankness. Additionally, the fresh voices of a new generation of lyricists could be heard, led by Evtushenko and Voznesensky, and works by suppressed or forgotten poets such as Akhmatova, Tsvetaeva, Martynov and Zabolotsky, were revived and republished. Many such writings implicitly questioned the very foundations of official socialist art.

The restoration of literary reputations occurred partly with Pasternak's help. There were plans to republish Tabidze, whose 'unlawful repression' was acknowledged in October 1955. Although Pasternak was by now engrossed in his novel, some Tabidze translations appeared in the July 1956 edition of *Novy mir* and in a rehabilitatory *Selected Works (Izbrannoe)* published in Moscow the following year.[6] Further Georgian verse renderings also appeared during 1957–8 in volumes of Baratashvili, Vazha Pshavela, Gaprindashvili, and two anthologies.[7]

With Mandelstam's fate no longer threatening, Pasternak resumed an old habit of writing *vers de circonstances* as a means of privately airing moods and opinions. One such poem was composed after a meeting with Lieutenant Ryazhsky *à propos* of Meyerhold's posthumous rehabilitation.[8] Another set of jaundiced quatrains written in summer of 1956 complained how little had changed following the denunciation of Stalin's crimes. The 'cult of personality' had gone, but an evil monotony still held sway, as demonstrated by press photographs of 'nothing but porcine snouts' and by epidemics of slander and philistinism such that 'Folk shoot themselves from drunkenness, / Because they cannot stand it any more.'[9] The allusion to Khrushchev's appearance was not lost on Pasternak's private audience, and while crediting the new premier for relaxing an earlier tyranny, he shared a common contempt for his crudity and boorishness. One of his remarks was that after being ruled over by a madman and murderer, they were now governed by a fool and a pig – 'yet the murderer did have occasional *élan* and an intuitive flair for some things; but now we are ruled by mediocrities . . .'[10]

The allusion to drunken suicides transparently referred to Fadeyev, who had shot himself at his Peredelkino dacha on 13 May. Official reports referring to an alcoholic fit conflicted with current rumour and with Fadeyev's suicide note which was addressed to the Central Committee and, when published in 1990, more or less confirmed Pasternak's diagnosis. Despite occasional favours to the regime's victims and moments of inebriate honesty such as the one in which he wrote his final message, Fadeyev had blighted many careers and helped to mutilate Russian literary culture. Now he suddenly saw the results of his activities: 'Literature – the holy of holies – [had] been handed over to be savaged by bureaucrats and the most backward popular elements.' Fadeyev claimed his life had lost all meaning; he was now fleeing from an existence beset by 'lowdown trickery, lies and slander', and his one regret was not having told all this to the country's new rulers (over the last three years his requests for an audience had been ignored).[11] Pasternak was reported as being in the guard of honour by Fadeyev's coffin in the Hall of Columns. His comment as he gazed at the body was: 'Aleksandr Aleksandrovich has rehabilitated himself' – a phrase not unlike his remark on being told of Tarasenkov's death that same year: 'His heart got tired of telling lies.'[12]

Revelations arising from the Twentieth Congress were embarrassing not just to former Stalinists. In spring of 1956 Chukovskaya's authoress-friend Nadezhda Adolf-Nadezhdina was released from the same camp where Ivinskaya was interned. She revealed that she had received none of the goods and money which Ivinskaya had collected over the last three years from friends and colleagues and claimed to have been sending to her. Chukovskaya's assumption that she had simply appropriated these items concurred with earlier memories of Ivinskaya as 'slovenly, pathologically duplicitous, and given to petty intrigues'. Various parties defended Ivinskaya against false charges brought by the state under Stalin and Khrushchev, but Chukovskaya's story was never refuted or disavowed. (Ivinskaya herself remained silent, claiming only that Chukovskaya had picked up slander originating with Surkov and his associates.) Chukovskaya spared Pasternak these revelations. There was no material proof; she had no wish to upset him, and was in any case certain that he would believe the fibs of his mistress against any other allegations.[13]

Pasternak's admiration for Ivinskaya seemed to be a function of his general poor ability to read female character. Or if aware of her faults, he never publicly conceded this. Whatever his real view of her professional skills, he went to some length to further her literary career, securing translation contracts nominally or partially carried out by himself, but which contained sections of her own work. Surviving papers include a number of drafted opening lines in Pasternak's hand with a note to an assistant to 'continue in the same vein'. Some of these openings, however, seem to have been pitched at Ivinskaya's pedestrian level rather than his own.[14]

Ivinskaya's name thus appeared along with Pasternak's among the listed translators in Abasheli's *Selected Works* and in volume seven of Tagore's *Works*, both published in 1957; and thirty-two of her renderings also appeared in Galaktion Tabidze's translated verse published the following year. Their collaboration was distasteful to Zinaida and her friends, but when Nina Tabidze objected to Ivinskaya's participation in Titsian's *Selected Works*, Pasternak was able to insist by threatening to withdraw all his own contributions.[15]

In the spring of 1955, Goslitizdat had again approached Pasternak about a new 250–page volume of his verse, to contain work from all periods of his career. Pasternak did not refuse, although he now had little interest in his own past and had doubts about his present acceptability. As he told Nikolai Smirnov, 'so little am I in tune with modern times, and so [. . .] out of place among the rest. I am not saying at all that they are bad, or that modern Soviet literature is colourless; on the contrary, probably it is very good [. . .] But I cannot follow its course: with my inborn and former democratism and revolutionary approach to life, my norms of behaviour and actions, quite other forces rule over me when I approach my art . . .'[16]

Furthermore, since he was absorbed by his novel, poetry as such had little interest for Pasternak. His son Evgenii had sent him some of his own poems in 1954, and although conceding that he liked their language – 'more natural and free than usual with beginners, amateurs, and non-professionals' – Pasternak's answering letter revealed an undercurrent of displeasure at this proliferation of poetry in the family. On comparing some verse by Arsenii Tarkovsky with work by his own son, he told Evgenii: 'You and I can do better than that. But you can indulge in literature after my death!' Moreover: 'I have never liked poetry lovers and connoisseurs. I lacked their erudition and faith that the realm of their predilections actually existed.'[17] The translator Mark Vatagin who sent Pasternak some work in 1955 was told even more categorically: 'I do not like "verses in general", I don't understand poetry in the accepted way of comprehending it'; and the very word 'poet' Pasternak described as 'a term more suitable for the wrapping on toilet soap'.[18]

With *Zhivago* virtually complete, however, Pasternak did not rule out the idea of returning to poetry. But, just as once before in 1928, he alarmed friends by announcing a desire to touch up and 'improve' his early work. In May 1955, when Chukovskaya reported his intention to alter even some of *My Sister Life*, Akhmatova threw up her hands in horror at such vandalism. However, Ivinskaya and the editor apparently managed to prevent at least some of Pasternak's intended 'improvements'; subsequent opinion has also tended to prefer earlier inspirations to the revised versions of his old age.[19]

Actual compilation of the new poetry volume began in winter of 1955–56. A young editor, Nikolai Bannikov, was put in charge, while Ivinskaya assumed the task of seeking out earlier publications in journals and elsewhere. Bannikov also commissioned a new author's preface for the volume. Pasternak cast it in the form of an autobiographical essay, and he wrote it before actually composing any new poetry. Provisionally titled 'In Lieu of a Preface' ('Vmesto predisloviya'), it was substantially ready by the end of June 1956; on mid-summer's day Pasternak sat on the terrace and read several episodes from it to his dinner guests, who included Asmus, Genrikh Neigauz and his wife, Olga Berggolts, Shalamov, the poet Lugovskoi and his wife, and Ruben Simonov, producer of the Vakhtangov *Romeo and Juliet*.[20]

The essay began with a stated intention to avoid the 'affected manner' that spoiled *Safe Conduct*. Instead of the earlier work's florid exuberance, the new essay took a distant and almost serene look at the author's past life. Pasternak again dealt with events and personalities perceived as having shaped him as an artist, but he avoided mere rephrasing of an already familiar story. In the new work the emphases fell differently, and figures came to the fore with qualities shared or sought by Pasternak in the 1950s: Blok was shown as possessing the hallmarks of greatness and as a model of 'realism' in whose confessional verse a whole age appeared mirrored;[21] Scriabin was now viewed as an artist who used the inherited medium of predecessors in order to say something astonishing and revitalising; Tolstoy was regarded as an exemplar of moral and inspirational authority; Rilke was represented by two translations to illustrate his diction, and the kindred shades of Tsvetaeva, Tabidze and Yashvili were also invoked.

As in Pasternak's other narratives, a settled and coherent account of life breaks down with the advent of the revolutionary period, and virtually ceases after 1930. The twenties are reduced almost to a description of Pasternak's changing perception of Mayakovsky, with reflections on the decay of his artistry and the nature of suicide. A whole epoch lies hidden behind a phrase describing the late 1920s as a time when 'literature came to an end'; and in three notes on Tsvetaeva, Yashvili and Tabidze, readers are left merely to infer that these poets were victims of the Stalinist system. A further afterword added in 1957 explained that to continue the narrative further would have involved 'years, circumstances, people and destinies framed by the revolution' and presenting an insurmountable challenge. Any account of such things, Pasternak claimed, should make hearts falter and hair stand on end – a task requiring talent of the calibre of Gogol or Dostoevsky, to which he laid no claim.[22]

Yet even within the frame of Pasternak's declared purview, certain lacunae occurred partly from his readiness to sacrifice many memories:

In this life it is more essential to lose than to acquire. The seed brings forth no fruit unless it dies. One must live untiringly, looking ahead and feeding on those vital reserves created by oblivion as well as memory. (II, 34; *VP*, 448; *SS*, IV, 328)

Essentially, the essay offered an account of some elements that shaped the author of *Doctor Zhivago* and the fictional mentality of its hero. Here both oblivion and faulty memory played a part, as well as controversial judgement.

Critical readers of Pasternak's manuscript included several people with an active recall of earlier events. For instance, Bobrov was aggrieved at Pasternak's totally negative account of Futurism and their early collaborations. Ariadna Efron also took umbrage at her mother's juxtaposition with Aseyev, both epitomising a classical clarity of poetic diction. Aseyev in turn was offended at Pasternak's dismissal of Mayakovsky's entourage and his post-revolutionary achievement, and he had virtually no contact with Pasternak thereafter.[23] Several names and dates were also inaccurately given, including a confusion of Akhmatova's *Evening (Vecher)* collection with her later *Plantain (Podorozhnik)*, which mortally offended her and contributed to a slight curdling of relations in the late 1950s. However, contrary to her claim, Pasternak had read, memorised, and could recite much of her work.[24]

Apart from the exclusion of entire historical periods, for censorship reasons Pasternak's essay made no mention of religion. While the novel notionally filled this gap, the essay dealt with the subject metonymically, by referring to near-contemporary poets such as Blok, Mayakovsky, and Esenin, who 'valued passages from church anthems and readings in their literal sense, as fragments of real life, on a par with the street and their home and phrases of colloquial speech' (II, 41; *VP*, 454; *SS*, IV, 335).

Also missing – as in *Safe Conduct* – was any picture of Pasternak's domestic, family and emotional life, although some aspects of it were closely bound up with his creativity. Shortly before writing the essay, he had mounted and hung up several of his father's sketches, and he now recalled these pictures and his father's work as part of the background to his early life. But Leonid Pasternak's shining perennial example of artistry, and the tragedy of his mother's sacrificed career, which Pasternak freely talked of in letters and conversation, went unmentioned. Evidently he had not yet rid himself of a complex over his father and still seemed to be struggling to prove himself worthy. Symptomatically, both Patrik in the 1930s novel fragments and Yurii Zhivago were depicted as fatherless orphans who eventually parted with their own children; for Pasternak autobiography was apparently not a genre for discussing filial or parental relations.

On reading the essay manuscript, Bannikov evidently foresaw problems with a text that failed to pay even token attention to the Bolshevik revolution. At his request Pasternak then sketched out a further section called 'My Sister Life'. In it he described the 1917 revolution as an elemental outbreak of pent-up popular moral outrage, of which Lenin emerged as the conscience, guiding spirit and spokesman.[25] But this too was deemed unsatisfactory (not least to the author); it was never printed, and remained in Bannikov's archive. The sketch was congruent with the account given in *Doctor Zhivago*, which made no actual mention of Lenin. Totally at variance with the official view of Lenin as leader of a political vanguard, Pasternak's novel took a 'Tolstoyan' view of history as a natural, supra-human process in which revolutionaries and leaders acted merely as history's 'organic catalysers and yeast'.[26]

The autobiographical essay was first printed in late 1956 in a Georgian translation by Margvelashvili in the Tbilisi journal *Mnatobi*.[27] During that year Pasternak also tried for an independent Moscow publication and detailed Ivinskaya to approach *Novy mir* on his behalf. His final choice of title was *People and Situations* ('Lyudi i polozheniya') and it was scheduled for publication in the December 1956 issue together with four verse fragments on Blok entitled 'The Wind' ('Veter'). Other events upstaged this plan however, publication was cancelled, and the essay was published in Russia only after Pasternak's death, in *Novy mir* in 1967, when it appeared with slight cuts.[28]

While composing his autobiography and new verse in summer of 1956, Pasternak reiterated to the visiting Italian scholar Angelo Ripellino his view of poetry in the hierarchy of human creative activities, emphasising that:

Poetry never began of itself, never defined states of mind, moods and views of any age [. . .] but on the contrary served to express these views when once they had been formed by scientific achievements, publicism, belletristic prose, and a new circle of state interests and aspirations.

These latter elements Pasternak likened to the major structure of an entire house and home, in which poetry appeared as a mere item of interior decoration.[29] In this scheme, the 'house' had now been constructed in the form of *Doctor Zhivago*, and this alone now justified a reversion to poetry and the creation of a new volume of verse in 1956–59.

In the draft conclusion of *People and Situations*, Pasternak recorded his ambivalent view of his own and other people's poetic past. He claimed he would happily consign three quarters of his work to oblivion, and the publication of a few grains of felicitous poetic discovery from all the regrettable chaff was justified only now, as a preamble to the appearance of his 'most significant work'.[30] ,

Pasternak's criteria for preserving earlier verses were their simplicity, brevity, and clarity – i.e. qualities integral to the 'realism' expounded in *People and Situations*. This justified retention of early pieces such as 'Venice' and 'The Station' – because of a 'realistic' pictorial content.[31] The touchstone for grading poetry was thus strikingly similar to what Pasternak expected of prose writing. In a conversation with the Ivanovs in the late 1950s, he developed his simplistic heresy even further and considered a reprint of all his early verse with a 'parallel text' of prose explanations![32]

In deference to new requirements, selected earlier poems thus had their metaphor simplified or eliminated, and items such as 'Marburg', 'The Mirror' and 'The Replacement' lost several stanzas; others such as 'With Oars at Rest' were radically rewritten, and even some commonly perceived masterpieces were discarded.[33] Later poems were less interfered with or mutilated. 'From Summer Notes' of 1936 reinstated the verses dedicated to Tabidze and Yashvili and incorporated 'To the Memory of Marina Tsvetaeva'. Most of the wartime verse and *Zhivago* poems were planned for inclusion in the new collection, and as Pasternak told Chikovani, by way of 'rearguard cover' at Bannikov's request the book was to conclude with eighteen new poems written in 1956.[34]

Pasternak began composing his new poems in the second half of July, immediately after finishing the essay. To Marina Baranovich he reported he was 'writing them unprofoundly, without strain, as I did once long ago before the Revolution. I am utterly unaware, and have no sense of their quality.'[35] In fact, an impression of ease and lightness was reflected in their final tone, although the surviving drafts bear evidence of intensive work, with many changes and variants, and some fine lines were eventually cut. Some of the poems were written so as to form a group for publication in *Novy mir* or *Znamya* in the autumn.[36]

The two new poems that later headed the final verse cycle *When Weather Clears* (*Kogda razgulyaetsya*) had a general programmatic significance for Pasternak's latter years. The first began:

> In everything I want to probe
> Into the kernel.
> In work, in searching for the way,
> In heartfelt turmoil.   (III, 61; *SP*, 446; *SS*, II, 72)

It is consciously a 'late poem' in its affirmation of a striving after global fathoming and summation. The poet seeks to encompass all experience – 'To live, think, feel, and love, / To make discoveries', and seize upon the 'qualities of passion'. Verses should be laid out like a garden and have breathed into them 'the breath of roses, / Breath of mint, / Meadows, sedges, mowing hay'. Although some images may seem familiar from earlier, here no 'God of details' is at work, but a poetic seeker after all-embracing essences and generalities. Nor is language now searching and hinting impressionistically at a world seen as though for the first time. Now, as poetry claims to 'contain' its object,

Pasternak proceeds to enumerate and display objects for enraptured appreciation.

'It is not fitting to be famous . . .' ('Byt' znamenitym nekrasivo . . .') was drafted in May and also had the status of a 'creed' that validated the entire cycle of late verse. One manuscript sketch was actually entitled 'I believe' ('Veruyu').[37] This was one of Pasternak's first new lyrics to become well known – Tamara Ivanova memorised it from one hearing just before leaving for Czechoslovakia with her husband and in Prague she recited it to Nezval who immediately translated it.[38]

> It is not fitting to be famous.
> It is not this that elevates.
> One should not bother keeping papers
> Or fussing over manuscripts.

The principle described here was not new to Pasternak. Nor was his view of self-renunciation (*samootdacha*) as the aim of creativity. This was a summative artistic statement of what Hingley called Pasternak's 'choreography of self-effacement' – a sacrifice of past and present (and of any painstaking literary record of them) in order to 'engage the love of open spaces', hear the 'summons of the future', retain one's personality, and remain 'alive and nothing more, / Alive and vital to the end'.[39]

Not all the verse written in 1956 was intended for inclusion in the new Goslitizdat volume. 'The Soul', written as a threnody for victims of recent history, was not catered for by any revelations of the Twentieth Party Congress and was printed in Russia only several years after Pasternak's death. Equally unpublishable at that time was 'Change' ('Peremena'), one copy of which was kept by Kornei Chukovsky. Pasternak's Congress speech of 1934 had warned against the temptation to become a 'literary overlord', and this poem now recalled youthful ideals of modesty and fellow-feeling allegedly betrayed when poets became infected with the taint of an age when 'grief was held up to shame' and people 'played vulgarians and optimists'.[40]

Items selected for the new collection suggest that Pasternak tried to avoid any obvious topical piquancy. One exception however was the poem prompted by the recent centenary of Mickiewicz's death in November 1955, 'Grass and Stones' ('Trava i kamni'), which praises the free nature and culture of Georgia and Poland. The Georgians brought out Pasternak's *People and Situations* just at the time when *Novy mir* rejected the work, and the mention of Poland was a partial allusion to the anti-communist fermentation there in the summer and autumn of 1956.[41] That autumn the literary scholar Seweryn Pollak visited and talked to Pasternak about Polish editions of his work, and Pasternak later sent a New Year message to the paper *Tribuna Ljudu* in which he expressed faith in the recent 'breath of renewal' in Poland; however, his courier decided not to pass on the message, so as to avoid trouble for its author.[42] An image of Poland as a torchbearer of freedom was later enhanced when the journal *Opinie* ignored the Soviet ban and printed excerpts from *Doctor Zhivago* in the summer of 1957.

The only love lyric in Pasternak's new collection was 'Without Title', a poem of subdued feeling and uncertain attribution. The poem 'Eve'('Eva') also lacked a personal addressee and instead paid tribute to half a dozen incarnations of the eternal feminine wringing out their bathing suits at the lakeside. However, the finest of the 1956 lyrics were those celebrating land-scape, weather and human activities of Peredelkino – a quasi-continuation of the cycle so titled. Most striking was the imagery capturing nature's freshness at moments of sudden illumination, as in the title piece 'When Weather Clears' (above, p. 300).

Equally memorable were some philosophical passages springing from natural imagery, such as the famous quatrain that later suggested the title of Ivinskaya's memoirs and summed up the poet's nocturnal ruminations:

> Sleep not, sleep not, o artist,
> To sleep never resign
> You hostage of Eternity
> Held prisoner in time.   (III, 82; *SP*, 463; *SS*, II, 97)

'In Hospital' was the only poem of 1956 to invoke very explicit religious feeling and, as Chukovskaya remarked, it worked miracles out of 'rubbish' as the final prayerful stanzas climaxed from prosaic enumerations of pavements, entrances, militiamen, faces, and a nurse with a phial of smelling-salts.[43]

And yet, for all their rapt and exultant attentiveness and luminous clarity, these poems seem to have lost something intrinsic in Pasternak's early manner and which has not been fully compensated. Was it the result of translation and prose writing? Or a misplaced pursuit of wrong ideals? Instead of detailed perceptions, enacting and arousing rapture, there are slack moments of moralising or abstract conclusion, or mere statements of a resolution to rapturise, to remain vital and responsive, and to live on by faith with thanksgiving. Too often this verse arises from such a faith (and relies on similar belief in the reader), which is evidently stronger than any faith which the poetry itself can arouse. Maybe for this reason the New Testament poems of *Doctor Zhivago*, which exploit the powerful existing valencies of religious belief, formed the apex of Pasternak's late achievement. After that landmark, this final cycle as a whole is disappointing, even though some items were admired by critical readers such as Akhmatova. Comparing 'The Christmas Star' with the technical glitter of the early lyrics, Vladimir Weidlé wrote that in reading these lines 'we do not pour diamonds from palm to palm, we merely listen, and in the distance through their gentle shimmer we glimpse the entire rainbow of the world: gold, purple and azure'.[44] Turning to the final lyrics, though, Angela Livingstone observes 'the poet is seeing the world for the last time. He sees it at a distance – sees more of it than before, but much less of it in sharp detail; he loves it and finds truth and faith in it, but cannot really smell or taste it. He adds it up, recognises its sum as right and good, and then leaves it: it is not any more his world.'[45]

By the end of the year, twenty-one new poems were written, all but three of which were scheduled for inclusion in Pasternak's new collection. Several copies of these poems circulated in Moscow in the form of twenty-four typescript pages bound and headed 'From the Blue Notebook' ('Iz sinei tetradi').[46] Apart from the contracted volume, Pasternak sought other forums for this verse and opted again for the official journals rather than any semi-independent editions;[47] this emerged as a wise choice in view of the clamp-down on unofficial publications later in the year. In September 1956 *Znamya* printed a bouquet of eight 'New Verses', including the first two programmatic items and several nature lyrics; the *Den' poezii* (Poetry Day) almanac, recently founded by Lugovskoi, printed 'Daybreak' and 'Winter Night', and 'Bread' ('Khleb') appeared in the October issue of *Novy mir*.

Despite the moratorium on *Zhivago*, *Novy mir* in September endorsed Pasternak's poetic artistry as being at a new height. Calling for a dogma-free revaluation of current literature, the critic Sarra Shtut emphasised his indubitable 'bold sincerity' and the 'tragedy of his lyric hero': 'One's attitude to B. Pasternak may vary, but not even his bitterest opponent would call him a minor poet.' In the climate of the day this was praise indeed, although in such conditions Shtut's evaluation did not go unchallenged by more orthodox commentators.[48] By this stage, however, as his most recent verses on Blok ('Veter' – 'The Wind') made clear, Pasternak had little regard for critical opinion.

Despite evidence of his successful collaboration with Bannikov and his publishers' enthusiasm for the poetry volume, there was a long silence over *Doctor Zhivago*, which indicated problems. However, there was rumour of its planned publication both in Russia and abroad, and in early May 1956 a foreign broadcast by Moscow Radio mentioned this. The Milan communist publisher Giangiacomo Feltrinelli, who two years later brought out Lampedusa's novel *The Leopard*, (*Il Gattopardo*) to considerable acclaim, had detailed Sergio

D'Angelo, a young correspondent working in the Italian section of Radio Moscow, to look out for Russian authors and works of potential interest. To secure the rights to *Doctor Zhivago* would be a particular prize.[49]

D'Angelo went to see Pasternak and found him working in the garden. He was given a cordial reception, and the two of them sat for a long time talking on the verandah. Bringing conversation round to *Zhivago*, D'Angelo inquired about the book and was told the situation. Assuming, however, that in the new political climate a foreign publication would present no problems, d'Angelo suggested that should Feltrinelli wish to publish, any announcement could be so phrased as to avoid problems or objections on the Soviet side. Pasternak had never considered direct dealings with a foreign publisher, but he allowed himself to be talked into handing d'Angelo a typescript copy for Feltrinelli's inspection. It was one of the unproofread typescripts, and no one then appreciated the consequences of this. Pasternak believed he was offering a sample copy, not an immaculate manuscript, and he expected its return. His parting quip as he saw d'Angelo off at the gate was: 'You're now invited to attend my own execution.'[50]

Despite later appearances, Pasternak had no considered plan of campaign. He had taken a risk and acted more or less spontaneously, as he was to continue doing. Yet despite the Soviet publishers' silence, in the relaxed atmosphere following the Twentieth Congress, there was a reasonable hope of the novel's appearance, even if in abridged form. (Pasternak told the American journalist Henry Shapiro that the removal of some politically explicit passages might allow the censor his pound of flesh without impairing the essential message of the work.[51]) Alternatively, even failing a Soviet edition, Pasternak may have decided the risk of official wrath was worth taking: at a time of worse suppression after 1929, Pilnyak had successfully managed to resume his professional career. But nobody since then had broken the prohibition on foreign publication, and although heterodox writings found their way abroad in the 1960s, Pasternak's action in May 1956 was an unprecedented feat of boldness which, as Kaverin commented, with one blow broke through the psychological barrier separating Russia from the West.[52]

Later in the day, after d'Angelo left, Pasternak greeted Stanislav and Galina Neigauz with news of his action and showed mischievous relish at their anxiety; however he asked them not to tell Zinaida.[53] The same evening Ivinskaya also heard the news and reacted with alarm. Though slightly uneasy, Pasternak was on the whole pleased with his decision and reassured by the fact that both d'Angelo and Feltrinelli were Italian communist party members.

Apart from any other reprisals, Ivinskaya correctly guessed that Pasternak's action would cause cancellation of his poetry volume. But having made his decision, he remained resolute; as he told the visiting Italian litterateur Ettore Lo Gatto shortly afterwards, so long as the novel appeared, he was prepared to 'face the music' and he impatiently swept aside Zinaida's apprehensions.[54] However, over the next several months, to protect his wife's sanity and avoid domestic scenes, Pasternak told her very little about his problems and subsequent ugly confrontations with the authorities.

Pasternak made no effort to conceal his action from the Soviet bureacracy, although for some time he played the slightly bemused innocent. In a letter of July, for example, he told Paustovsky that 'by the way, during the springtime influx of delegations when the manuscript was being passed around, I'm afraid it was taken abroad somewhere without my knowledge [. . .] In that case it'll be my death – though maybe these fears are unfounded.'[55]

A day or two after hearing Pasternak's news, Ivinskaya told Bannikov, who confirmed that their publishing project was in jeopardy. She then went to see d'Angelo hoping to retrieve the manuscript, but learned that without telling Pasternak he had meanwhile flown to Berlin and handed it to Feltrinelli, who had had it read and was now bent on going ahead with publication. To help avoid an international incident, however, d'Angelo agreed to try and persuade Feltrinelli to delay until the novel appeared in the USSR.

Ivinskaya then revealed a new aspect of her character. Her previous punishment had left her nervous to the point of cowardice, and much of her seeming concern for Pasternak emerged as a concern for *his concern* for *her*. I. e. she expected him to protect her and not expose her to new danger. To this end she began taking her own action to square matters with the authorities. The effects of this were indistinguishable from the cynical 'comradely concern' displayed by officialdom to impose their will and supposedly save errant citizens from their own improvidence. In fact, rather than serving Pasternak's interests, she became a tool in the hands of the authorities.

Symptomatic was Ivinskaya's first errand to the unenlightened and oppressive figure of Kozhevnikov, the chief editor of *Znamya* magazine. He undertook to contact Polikarpov, head of the Central Committee's Cultural Section, with the object of finding a solution. Anxious to avoid a damaging scandal, Polikarpov summoned Ivinskaya and urged her to keep talking to d'Angelo and to try and secure return of the manuscript by offering Feltrinelli first option on a revised text which would be released in the USSR. Communicating via d'Angelo, however, Feltrinelli remained resolute; he doubted the likelihood of any Soviet edition, and claimed that he could not deprive the world of such a masterpiece.[56]

Polikarpov changed tack. If foreign publication was inevitable, a face-saving operation must be mounted – to assist domestic publication or, better, obtain

legal rights to control the manuscript. In Ivinskaya's presence he called up
Kotov, the director of Goslizdat, and announced that she and Pasternak would
be coming to see him and requesting him to draw up a contract. Shortly
thereafter, Pasternak and Ivinskaya met with Kotov who congratulated him on
his work and assured him that publication would go ahead with a few minor
alterations, to which Pasternak agreed in principle. Kotov placed in charge of
the edition Anatolii Starostin, a devotee of Pasternak's work, who in good
faith foresaw the work as 'an apotheosis of the Russian people'.[57]

Starostin and Puzikov, the Goslitizdat chief editor, discussed details with
Pasternak in Peredelkino, and a contract was eventually drawn up and signed
on 7 January 1957. While the publishers remained enthusiastic, the state
authorities however viewed the contract purely as a means of acquiring a legal
basis for demanding alterations to the novel and for recalling the manuscript.

Meanwhile, via d'Angelo Feltrinelli had confirmed to Pasternak his wish to
publish and sent an eight-clause contract drawn up in French. Pasternak
discussed the document with his sons Evgenii and Leonid, and with their
approval signed it on 13 June 1956. The contract entitled Feltrinelli to
proceed with an Italian edition of *Doctor Zhivago*. It also ceded to him various
other rights which Pasternak in his ignorance of international copyright law
failed to comprehend. Feltrinelli's rapid and thrusting exploitation of these
rights without consultation of his author's wishes would cause brainracking
problems for other Western friends who had Pasternak's interests at heart.[58]
At the time of signature, though, none of this was foreseen. The only
precaution taken in anticipation of difficulties was an understanding with
Feltrinelli that the latter would heed messages from Pasternak only in French
or German, and ignore instructions in Russian. This agreement was to be
significant.

Pasternak was delighted at the prospect of publishing his work and had but
one concern: in his letter to Feltrinelli of the 30 June he warned that 'if its
publication here, which is promised by several of our journals, is delayed and
forestalled by you, this will create a tragically difficult situation for me'. His
overriding belief, though, often expressed over the next few months, was that
'thoughts are not born in order to be hidden away or inwardly suppressed, but
in order to be spoken.'[59] Shortly after releasing his manuscript to Feltrinelli,
he presented another copy to a Polish friend, Ziemowit Fedecki, who visited
Peredelkino, and a further copy went to a Czech publisher via the Foreign
Commission of the Writers' Union. Meanwhile the novel was also under
consideration by *Literaturnaya Moskva*, although its length precluded publication in toto, apart from which Kazakevich was unenthusiastic. Yet as
Pasternak told Paustovsky, it was precisely the work's unacceptability which in

his eyes made publication so necessary and which distinguished it from work by such as Dudintsev, a journeyman writer who offered no more than a permitted simulation of protest against incidental shortcomings rather than against basic principles of the Soviet system.[60]

Meanwhile, on 25 August, a KGB communiqué on Pasternak was passed to the Central Committee, and at the end of the month Polikarpov sent a lengthy statement to the Central Committee Presidium describing the novel as a 'heinous calumny' of the Revolution and of Soviet life; the *Zhivago* issue thus became a major affair of state.[61] Shortly afterwards, in mid September, *Novy mir* turned the novel down. The decision was summarised in a collective letter addressed to Pasternak which, when published in 1958, was signed by five members of the editorial board – Agapov, Lavrenyov, Fedin, Simonov and Krivitsky. (In 1956 there was report of twenty signatures, but the number in itself was not significant.[62])

The editorial letter followed on Simonov's discussion with Surkov and Polikarpov.[63] It was a document of considerable length, with detailed discussion and extended quotation. The position adopted in the letter was an orthodox socialist-realist one, which in a novel presupposed a central hero linked closely with the authorial persona, a 'dialectical' presentation of political issues, and a conclusion reinforcing Party philosophy. The letter explained that the novel's untenable features could not be corrected by editorial cuts or alterations, since the whole tenor of the work amounted to a rejection of the October Revolution. Pasternak's fault allegedly lay not so much in distorting the truth as in having selected a series of Russian intelligentsia heroes who were manifestly self-centred, uninterested in the revolutionary cause, and whose egocentric philosophy – a blend of Tolstoyanism and Christianity – was neither justified by the main hero's own behaviour nor successfully countered by a spokesman for the opposition.[64]

As Simonov later recollected, he himself composed the main body of the letter, various panel members fine-tuned the text, and Fedin added a lengthy episode berating Pasternak and his hero for their grossly inflated individualism.[65] Fedin saw a direct parallel between Christ's words to the apostles in the final poem of the Zhivago cycle – 'The Lord deemed you worthy / Of living in my day' – and Zhivago's opinion of his intellectual companions in the 1920s, which was taken (in fact correctly) as Pasternak's own verdict on his contemporaries:

'Dear friends, how hopelessly ordinary you are, you and the circle that you represent, and the splendour and the art of your favourite names and authorities. The only bright and vital thing about you is the fact that you are living at the same time as myself and have known me.'   (*DZh*, 565, 493; *SS*, V, 539, 474)

Interestingly, although the letter claimed that Pasternak saw the October Revolution as having brought nothing but misery and evil, the authors did not verbalise the work's most heretical insinuation: by artistically conflating the Stalinist period with early revolutionary history, Pasternak implied (many years before Solzhenitsyn's *GULag Archipelago*) that the tyranny of the last twenty-five years was a direct outcome of Bolshevism, whereas the Twentieth Party Congress had maintained that its excesses were an alien distortion of Marxist ideals.[66]

On receiving the letter, Pasternak did not advertise the fact or respond.[67] Rumour of it spread in literary circles however, and Akhmatova heard the story confirmed by Pasternak in person. A 'master of ominous forebodings', she infected Chukovskaya and all her friends with alarm and predicted a 'grandiose scandal' if the novel was totally banned in the USSR and appeared in Italy.[68]

Fedin's help in suppressing the novel came as a sore blow. For decades Pasternak had admired his artistry and seen him as an ally, friend, and kindred spirit. As recently as the 31 August, Fedin had given their neighbour Chukovsky an inspired description of *Doctor Zhivago* as a work of genius, 'extremely egocentric, proud, satanically haughty, studiously simple, and at the same time utterly literary – an autobiography of the great Pasternak'.[69] For all that, however, Fedin was affronted at Pasternak-Zhivago's proud egocentrism and dismissal of his contemporaries. And unlike Pasternak, while no unprincipled careerist, Fedin had always in a quiet way attached some importance to official status, or what he saw as public duty. This was highlighted by an uncomfortable incident in Pasternak's house at Easter time in 1955. Alluding to Fedin's recent appointment as First Secretary of the Moscow Writers' organisation, Andronikov proposed a toast to the 'new management' in terms somewhat offensive to Fedin, who replied by drawing a contrast between writers who sacrificed their talents for the common good and those who cultivated them in a self-centred manner, avoiding social responsibilities. Picking up the hint, Evgenii Pasternak wanted to reply on his father's behalf, but Boris restrained him with a gesture and quickly changed the subject.[70] In effect the reply was given in *Zhivago*: the novel amply demonstrated that for Pasternak and his hero artistic integrity took precedence over any conscientious administrative service.

As the rejection letter showed, if required, Fedin was ready to ignore personal opinion and to betray a friend. But as with Aseyev and Fadeyev, Pasternak preferred to seeth inwardly while maintaining courteous relations. He invited Fedin to dinner on Sunday 23 September, as if nothing had happened; the note of invitation merely asked him not to bring up the subject of the editorial letter.[71] Also invited were the Ivanovs, Akhmatova, and Richter and Yudina who played before and after the meal. Akhmatova found the occasion heavy going: she privately suspected someone present could be reporting their conversations; she was uncomfortable amid such 'opulence' (which was negligible compared with that of the real literary grandees); and she disliked Pasternak's 'naughty boy' behaviour towards Zinaida whom he constantly addressed as 'mamochka' (mummy dear) while consorting with the 'thief' Ivinskaya.[72]

When the letter of rejection was delivered, Pasternak merely noted its message without examining it closely. Later, on 26 September, he sent Tamara Ivanova a nicely nuanced ironic assessment of it, describing it as 'composed very courteously and gently, painstakingly thought out from a viewpoint that has become traditional and seemingly irrefutable'. In its own terms, indeed, the letter seemed 'perfectly fair', and Pasternak claimed to be 'pained and regretful at having caused my comrades such work'.[73]

The *Novy mir* refusal backed up by a Central Committee decision was an ill omen. Nevertheless, plans for publication with Goslitizdat were still in place, and there seemed no grounds yet for grave alarm. However, advice came from several quarters to stop the Italian edition. When Isaiah Berlin revisited Moscow in late summer, he was urged by Genrikh Neigauz and by Zinaida to try and persuade Pasternak for his own and his family's sake to halt Feltrinelli's scheme. This he did with sufficient vehemence to anger Pasternak, who remained determined and assured Berlin that his sons at least were totally behind him.[74]

When he returned in September, Berlin took back with him a copy of the *Zhivago* manuscript and Pasternak's first detailed letter to his Oxford relatives for nearly eight years. From now on until his death, there was animated family correspondence. An earlier letter had been postponed at Zinaida's request, so as not to damage Leonid's chances of university entry. (The previous year he had been rejected by the Higher Technical Institute because of his father and 'because in certain organs my life is known in even finer detail than to me myself'! Now Leonid was accepted by the Moscow University Faculty of Physics and thus avoided immediate military service.) Apart from basic family news, Pasternak's letter talked mainly of his own work. The novel manuscript was to be retyped and circulated among his family's Oxford University friends – Professors Katkov, Konovalov, Obolensky, and Maurice Bowra. Isaiah Berlin knew the publishing arrangements, and when the time came Pasternak wanted his sisters to help secure the best possible translators for the English version. A suggestion from Berlin that he visit Britain was meanwhile put on hold.[75]

In the wake of the *Zhivago* manuscript Pasternak also couriered to his sisters typescript copies of *People and Situations* and of his latest poetry. Still anticipating an imminent Soviet edition of these, in their autumn correspondence he asked his sisters to place the essay with *Encounter* magazine or elsewhere, and he showed rather unrealistic impatience that little progress was made by early November. (It was published in 1959 by Collins and Harvill, who the following year brought out an edition of the new poetry.)[76] Following his visit to Peredelkino Isaiah Berlin sent Pasternak a gift of the twenty-one-volume edition of Virginia Woolf, an author with whom he saw stylistic similiarities with Pasternak. Then, in mid September, George Katkov, the Moscow-born émigré Oxford historian, returned to Russia, met Pasternak and armed with a further copy of the novel later set up the English translating team of Manya Harari and Max Hayward.[77]

Despite the *Novy mir* rejection, there was rumour in literary circles in autumn that a limited edition of *Zhivago* – maybe three thousand copies – might be sanctioned in order to prevent mass distribution and to refute foreign claims that the work had been suppressed. Hopes of *Literaturnaya Moskva* had fallen through, but in summer 1956 there was talk of various liberal writers setting up their own independent publishing enterprise called 'Sovremennik' (Contemporary), and Vsevolod Ivanov offered Pasternak his personal services as editor. Nothing came of this venture however.[78]

In the latter half of the year, the literary climate again cooled rapidly. In August came reminders that the old 'Zhdanov' resolutions of 1946 had not been rescinded.[79] Then, in the autumn, as the leadership took fright at the continuing unrest in Poland and October rebellion in Hungary, the 1956 Thaw was brought to a halt. Liberal authors such as Dudintsev, Evtushenko and Voznesensky came under attack; editorial boards were restaffed; independent publications, such as *Literaturnaya Moskva*, were closed down (the second volume had been 'frozen' by the censor for ten weeks, and issue number three was cancelled); an official campaign against the heresy of 'revisionism' began, conservative forces regained an upper hand, and with slight variations in temperature, this new ideological freeze continued for another six years. Pasternak remained no more than a dismayed witness as the climate changed and became totally inhospitable to his work. Some editor friends' attempt to bolster his position by printing a comment on the British intervention in Suez and the Hungarian events produced a dismissive response: 'I know you would like me to say that blood is being spilt in Egypt, and in Hungary only water, but . . .'[80]

Despite these inauspicious developments, during the winter months Pasternak took further steps to strengthen his ties with the Western literary world.

Copies of his new poems and the novel circulated among devotees in Moscow, and one reader was the Moscow correspondent of *France-Soir*, Dmitrii Ivanov (son of the émigré Symbolist poet and known professionally as Jean Neuve-celle). Ivanov was able to see a typescript copy of *Zhivago* at the Scriabin House-Museum in Vakhtangov Street, where a cultural cénacle gathered, including young literary enthusiasts as well as musical celebrities such as Sofronitsky.[81]

In December 1956 Pasternak also re-established contact with the French philosopher Brice Parain, who had been cultural attaché at the French Embassy in the mid 1920s; through Parain, who now worked as a 'reader' for Éditions Gallimard, he hoped to pass on a copy of *Zhivago* for publication in France.[82] Similarly, he planned for his sisters in Oxford to release the manu-script for translation and publication in English. The fourth clause of his contract with Feltrinelli had stipulated that 'the sole person authorised to negotiate the concession of foreign rights' was 'the Publisher' (i.e. Feltrinelli) and that the 'Owner' (i.e. Pasternak) was 'bound by the contract accepted by the Publisher'.[83] Feltrinelli was acting accordingly. But Pasternak meanwhile believed it was up to himself to arrange further foreign editions, and a saga of international legal complications was about to unfold because of this misun-derstanding.

Pasternak's expanding French contacts in winter 1957 were to become specially important to him. He had held his usual New Year dinner party with Akhmatova, Efron, the Livanovs, Neigauzes, Fedin and Voznesensky,[84] and later on the evening of 1st January he was visited by the young poet Nikolai Shatrov and two friends from the 'Scriabin cénacle'; they brought with them the young French scholar Jacqueline de Proyart, a Radcliffe-Harvard PhD graduate, who was attending courses at Moscow University. Pasternak was evidently impressed by her personality, practical suggestions and eagerness to assist, and during her subsequent visits over the next few weeks he accepted her suggestion that together with Michel Aucouturier, Hélène Peltier (who had both met him the previous year) and Louis Martinez, she prepare a translation of *Zhivago* for Gallimard.[85]

In addition to the translation, Pasternak also decided to place in Proyart's hands the authority to handle all his other rights and publications abroad. This included production of a Russian-language edition, for which he accepted her suggestion of Mouton publishers in Holland. He also undertook to cede to his new French assistants the profits from these publications (an offer which, honourably, neither of these ladies used to their advantage).[86] When Jacque-line de Proyart left Russia in early February, Pasternak accordingly gave her a written power of literary attorney, and sent with her letters to Hélène Peltier and to Gallimard entitling Proyart to represent him in 'all matters literary, juridical and pecuniary'. Another letter of the same date was directed to Feltrinelli, in no way suspending or revoking their contract, but notifying him in general terms that Pasternak had appointed Proyart as his attorney and approved a team of French translators which whom he should communicate *à propos* of the French edition. The path to confusion was thus prepared.[87]

16

The Printing and the Prize

'The Evil Days'

Not more than one week had passed
Since Jesus rode into the city,
And palm branches were strewn in his path.
Hosannas resounded in greeting.

Yet each day brought new gloom and fresh menace.
Hearts untouched by love were unmelted,
And eyebrows were clenched in contempt.
And then came the postlude, the ending.

And the yards of the town were oppressed
By skies filled with leaden foreboding,
While Pharisees sought for their proofs
And fawned like vixen before him.

And sinister powers of the temple
Deferred to the judgement of scoundrels,
And now he was damned with a fervour
No less than the praise that resounded.

And there in the neighbouring gateway
A throng of spectators now crowded,
And they heaved and surged back and forth
And jostled, awaiting the outcome.

And whispers passed down the streets
And rumours invaded the precincts,
And his childhood now seemed like some dream –
All those tales of his flight into Egypt . . .

He remembered the grand elevation
Of the wilderness scarp and the mountain
Where he quelled the satanic temptation
And renounced earthly might and a kingdom.

And the feast at a wedding in Cana,
Where the throng were amazed by that wonder,
And the time when, in mist, as though walking
On land, he had trodden the waters.

And the hovel where paupers were gathered,
And the candle-lit stairs he descended,
When the flame in its fright was extinguished
As a dead man was resurrected.

(1949)

Production of Pasternak's theatrical translations was unaffected by the new stringencies of late 1956. Early that year he was delighted by the production of his *Macbeth* at the Maly Theatre, and he now felt happier with this company than with the Arts Theatre, contacts with which had 'gone to sleep'.[1] Later, in the autumn, Ruben Simonov's production of *Romeo and Juliet* opened at the Vakhtangov Theatre with Yurii Lyubimov and Lyudmila Tselikovskaya in the title roles. At the première which Pasternak attended with Andrei Voznesensky an intriguing and ominous incident had occurred. During a sword fight the tip of Romeo's weapon snapped off, flew into the stalls and struck the armrest of Pasternak's seat. His comment after this narrow escape was: 'Just look at that! There has to be a reason for that sort of thing!'[2] Events of the next two years perhaps confirmed a belief in such auguries.

In the autumn of 1955, the Moscow Arts Theatre had commissioned a translation of Schiller's *Maria Stuart* from Pasternak after rejecting one by Nikolai Vilyam. Pasternak delivered his version within six weeks, and it was accepted for production. Vilyam was mortally offended, and the incident permanently blighted his relations with Pasternak.[3]

Playing Maria Stuart was the distinguished Alla Tarasova, who began work on the role almost immediately; serious rehearsals started only in November 1956 however, and a première date was set for 23 March 1957. Pasternak regularly travelled in from Peredelkino to assist at rehearsals, and impressions of these journeys through the snow were described in letters and figured in 'Bacchanalia' ('Vakkhanaliya') and other poems.[4] During this period he was also invited to the Arts Theatre for the sixtieth birthday of actress Anastasia Zueva; instead of attending he sent a congratulatory poem which was then printed in the journal *Teatr* (The Theatre). Later, in 1958, while on tour in London with the Moscow Arts Theatre, Zueva met Pasternak's sisters and brought back messages from them.[5]

During the winter, in January and February, Zinaida spent a few weeks on holiday with Nina Tabidze and Leonidze's wife at Tskhaltubo in Georgia. During this time Pasternak revised and polished his Schiller translation, and he had his final meetings with Jacqueline de Proyart who was heading back to France. He was also visited by Dmitrii Ivanov and his French press colleague Michel Gorday, and he also entertained his son Evgenii with his new wife Elena, a granddaughter of Gustav Shpet.[6]

In the winter weeks Pasternak continued producing seasonal poetry, some of which was included in the new cycle *When Weather Clears*. At the same time a more ambitious 'winter poem' was planned, drawing together impressions of the season's meteorological, theatrical and social events. The result was 'Bacchanalia', eventually completed in August of 1957.[7] One of the events recorded in it was the joint birthday party of Ivanov and Fedin held on 24 February. Their celebration, at which Pasternak contributed versified impromptu toasts, was later described by Ivanov's wife.[8] From Fedin, however, as Evgenii Pasternak later recalled, Pasternak experienced a growing sense of alienation after his part in the suppression of the novel. He did his best to conceal his pain, but every now and then bitter feelings found an outlet – in some of the drafts of 'Bacchanalia' and other unpublished 'occasional' lines:

> Dearest trash, kinsmen and friends,
> Well you suit the present hour!
> Oh, how shall I betray you yet,
> You dolts, nonentities and cowards!
>
> Perhaps this is a sign from God
> That life for you holds little promise
> Apart from hovering in the doorway
> Of some ministerial office.[9]

Work on Schiller's *Maria Stuart* and its subsequent production and mention in 'Bacchanalia' marked Pasternak's return to a theme he had first handled thirty years before, when he translated Swinburne's *Chastelard*. Both these works played on his perennial preoccupation with the suffering and sacrifice of women. He had once compared Zinaida to Mary Queen of Scots in a letter to his parents; overtones of Mary Stuart reverberated in the figure of Lara in the novel, and Ivinskaya's sufferings in the GULag had made her an object of pity and inspiration that identified her with the heroine of Schiller's play. An episode of 'Bacchanalia' captured another vision of the Scottish queen, immortalised in Tarasova's stage realisation.[10]

Pasternak's poetic account of the première of *Maria Stuart* in late March was a construct of his imagination however. On leaving the Peredelkino dacha to attend a rehearsal on 12 March, he was suddenly racked by an excruciating pain in the right knee.[11] Totally handicapped, he was taken to hospital and immobilised for almost four months. The official diagnosis of an inflamed meniscus came only after he had privately considered arthritis, radiculitis, cancer of the lumbar region and other horrors commensurate with his agony. A legacy of his childhood riding accident and crippled right leg, the condition eventually forced him to stand for lengthy periods while working, and Zinaida managed to find an impressive lectern for him at a second-hand shop.[12]

Later, in early summer, during June and July, when the worst was over, Pasternak went to recuperate at the Uzkoye sanatorium in the south-east of Moscow, on the former estate of the Trubetskoi family. The philosopher Vladimir Solovyov died here in 1900, and while walking in the grounds Pasternak showed Evgenii and Elena his wife the room where this occurred.[13] Impressions of Uzkoye were shortly afterwards gathered in several poetic sketches including 'The Linden Avenue' ('Lipovaya alleya') with its picture of meadows, wheatfields, hills and woods, gates and archway, and the fine house set amid green parkland.

Even during his worst suffering in March and April, Pasternak managed to write letters and instructions to Ivinskaya regarding the planned poetry volume. The edition had been typeset in the second week of January and the proofs were received on schedule for a publication date in spring. However, circumstances conspired to prevent all this. After rejecting *Zhivago*, Simonov refused to publish even extracts from the autobiographical essay.[14] Official measures to prevent the novel's appearance in Italy and elsewhere had so far been unsuccessful, and the KGB and Polikarpov were in no mood to condone editions of Pasternak's other writings. This was sufficient to arrest all his publications, and supporters in Goslitizdat were powerless to break this ban. The publication date of the poetry collection was not kept, and at this point Kotov suddenly collapsed and died while on business in Leningrad; then, in June, it was announced that the volume had been cancelled.[15] Thereafter, apart from a verse selection in volume one of an *Anthology of Russian Soviet Poetry 1917–1957 (Antologiya russkoi sovetskoi poezii 1917–1957)*, the only lifetime Soviet editions of Pasternak were a scattering of poems published that year in an October issue of *Literaturnaya gazeta*, in the Moscow *Den' poezii* annual, and a collection of *Verses of 1956 (Stikhi 1956 goda)*; a few poems also appeared in Georgia, in the fourth issues of *Literaturnaya Gruziya* for 1957 and 1958, and in a miscellany called *Tbilisi in Poetry (Tbisili v poezii)* (Tbilisi, 1958), but nothing more.[16]

Despite cancellation of the poetry volume, however, Goslitizdat did not

4 Boris Pasternak with Nikolai Bannikov (Uzkoye, June 1957)

break up the plates and retained them for several years. Pasternak also kept copies of the proofs, and after news of the cancellation eventually sent them to Jacqueline de Proyart in January 1958; these redactions were incorporated in the Michigan University Press edition of Pasternak's *Works (Sochineniya)* which appeared in 1961 and for many years remained the most complete and authoritative edition.[17]

Using the Goslitizdat contract for *Zhivago*, the Central Committee's Cultural Section began acting independently of Pasternak to halt Feltrinelli's Italian edition, and in early 1957 attempted to recover the manuscript via pro-Soviet channels in Italy. Among others, the communist leader Togliatti tried persuading Feltrinelli to cancel publication plans and return the text. Feltrinelli replied that he would sooner leave the Party than break his agreement with Pasternak.[18] In February Goslitizdat then sent Feltrinelli a letter requesting a deferment until September, supposedly to give time for an amended edition to appear in the USSR. In his letter to Feltrinelli of 6 February which was brought out of Russia by Jacqueline de Proyart, Pasternak mentioned the pressure on him to send a telegram requesting the deferment, and he asked Feltrinelli to respond directly to Goslitizdat. He also urged that whatever abridgements a Soviet edition might contain, the Italian text should adhere strictly to the original manuscript.[19]

Feltrinelli did not let his author down, and Pasternak remained eternally grateful for his staunch resistance to Soviet pressure. However, Feltrinelli also stood up for his own rights against each and all, including the author and his attorney. He failed to appreciate Pasternak's personal wishes and the peculiar complexity and delicacy of his predicament, and he was bent on extracting maximum business advantage from the situation. Pasternak never fully understood this and remained indulgent towards Feltrinelli's desire to reward himself for his efforts. Unlike other Western publishers, Feltrinelli for long refused to recognise de Proyart's power of attorney; to have done so would have immediately limited his control over all foreign editions of *Doctor Zhivago*. He therefore continued to bypass Proyart and communicated with Pasternak through Ivinskaya and via d'Angelo and other intermediaries. Pasternak was thus in some sense left in a vacuum: while de Proyart tried to use her attorney's rights in his own best interests, Ivinskaya and Feltrinelli ran his affairs in line with their own.

Feltrinelli's answer to Goslitizdat was dated 10 June 1957. He refused to return the manuscript but was ready to defer publication till September as requested. Reaffirming his admiration for the novel, he assured the Soviet side of his readiness to settle matters amicably and without scandal. The authorities probably found little consolation in this reply.[20] Thanks partly to Feltrinelli's marketing initiatives, international interest increased, and by August Pasternak wrote enthusiastically to Chikovani about the proliferation of translations in preparation – in English, French, German, Italian, Czech and Polish.[21]

The intricate high-level machinations to delay or quash publication of *Doctor Zhivago* are hard to fathom or reconstruct, and as Pasternak realised, they went on 'in spheres inaccessible'. However, in early August, he was summoned to a meeting of the Union of Writers' Secretariat to examine the whole matter.

Pasternak probably recalled his advice to Pilnyak and others to stay away from such events. As he later heard, it was 'a meeting of the 1937 type, with furious wailing about this being an unprecedented occurrence, and demands for retribution'.[22] Fearing he could suffer another heart attack if over-excited, Ivinskaya persuaded him to wait at her town apartment while she and Starostin went to the Union on Vorovsky Street as his representatives. At a preliminary discussion Surkov comported himself in civil fashion and listened to Ivinskaya's account of events. Inside the meeting, however, he gave a distorted and passionately aggressive report of the affair, accusing Pasternak of deception, treachery and scheming to obtain money from foreigners. Ivinskaya's attempts to correct and contradict were ignored. When she was eventually allowed to speak, some listeners such as Tvardovsky tried to get her a fair hearing, but she was repeatedly and rudely interrupted by Sobolev, Kataev and other hecklers. Starostin was also allowed to make a statement in which he calmly vindicated Pasternak's work and his actions and laid the blame for what had happened on the hostility and intransigence of Surkov and the Union. Thereupon, Surkov announced that the meeting would continue *in camera*, and Ivinskaya and Starostin were asked to leave. Without their or Pasternak's presence, however, the meeting fulfilled its function: a form of inquiry took place and a form of judgement was passed.[23]

The day after the Union meeting, Ivinskaya continued her contacts with the authorities and arranged for Pasternak to talk with Polikarpov. Again, though, instead of attending in person, he sent her with a letter which he wrote early that morning:

People without moral discrimination are never content with themselves; there are many things they regret and repent. The one thing in my life that I have no grounds to repent is my novel. I wrote what I thought, and to this day I stand by these thoughts. Perhaps it is a mistake I did not conceal it from other people. I can assure you that had it been written feebly, I would have hidden it away. But it proved stronger than I ever dreamed, and strength comes from on high, and thus its subsequent fate is not in my hands and I am not going to interfere in it. If the truth that I know has to be bought by suffering, there is nothing new in that and I am ready to accept any such suffering.[24]

Polikarpov was irate at Pasternak's defiance and made Ivinskaya tear up the letter in his presence. After that, on 19 August, Pasternak went personally to confront him and the following day also met with Surkov. There is no exact record of their conversations, but Pasternak was upset and angered at being so humiliated. By his own account he must have addressed Polikarpov with brazen frankness. To the question: 'What do you mean? You are against the October Revolution?' his answer was: 'You guessed it, Dmitrii Alekseyevich! How well you've understood everything!' Yet despite their superficial politeness, neither official addressed what for him was the main issue – his right to act and think as he saw fit. They did, however, demand his compliance in preventing the book's appearance, which involved his ceding to Goslitizdat the right of further negotiation and sending a further message to Feltrinelli requiring return of the manuscript. He was granted a few days in which to think matters over.[25]

Pasternak later put a bold interpretation on this episode and talked of his 'happy and elevating sense of calm and inner rectitude'.[26] But despite the agreement with Feltrinelli to ignore messages in Russian, he was at first reluctant to endorse any telegram text, and he reacted with proud and bitter anger to Ivinskaya's and d'Angelo's attempts to persuade him to sign.[27] In this Ivinskaya's wishes entirely reflected her general compliance with officialdom. She was unwilling to mount the pyre to defend Pasternak's principles; and even if her pusillanimity shielded him from official wrath, in artistic and moral terms it was a betrayal. Polikarpov doubtless realised they had successfully found the key to controlling Pasternak, who found it hard to say no to her. At the same time her readiness to continue running errands, to minister to him, and handle unpleasant interviews, was entirely to his taste, and it left him to the calm pursuit of his artistic routine. It was shortly after these events that Chukovskaya heard Akhmatova report various *obiter dicta* from Zinaida Pasternak, one of which was: 'Boris Leonidovich no longer exists. There is only Olga Vsevolodovna'; to which Akhmatova added: 'I'm afraid Zina is right on that point. That woman has gobbled him up. Swallowed him alive.'[28]

The required telegram was sent on 21 August, which Polikarpov confirmed to the Central Committee. Meanwhile Pasternak was secretly confident that it would be ignored, since it was couched in Russian. Just to make sure, though, in September he also sent a verbal message to his family in Britain via the American scholar Miriam Berlin who visited him. This was to confirm that any message purporting to emanate from him and cancelling publication of the novel should be ignored.[29]

During summer 1957, despite these disruptions, Pasternak completed more translations from Chikovani's Georgian which were printed in the January 1958 issue of *Literaturnaya Gruziya*. Further Russian renderings of Georgian verse also continued appearing, although they gave little personal satisfaction. As he told the editor Bebutov in February – and Chikovani later that year – translations had deprived him of his best working years, now he had to concentrate on his own writings and not waste time on other people's.[30]

The summer also saw a modest output of new verse, with several sketches and nine complete lyrics which were included in Pasternak's last poetic cycle.[31] In November a new typewritten album was prepared and bound, forming the so-called 'Green Notebook'; copies of it were distributed to friends in Moscow and also sent abroad to de Proyart and others. Under the title 'In the Interlude' ('V pereryve'), the Notebook contained all the *Zhivago* poems and 31 other recent compositions.

In the 'Green Notebook' the new poems figured for the first time under their final title: 'When Weather Clears' and were headed by an epigraph from

Proust's *Le temps retrouvé*: 'Un livre est un grand cimetière, où sur la plupart des tombes on ne peut plus lire les noms effacés.' The quotation reflected Pasternak's long-standing enthusiasm, resurrected after completing *Doctor Zhivago* when he no longer feared Proust's infectious influence. At this time Evgenii Pasternak and other witnesses recalled Pasternak's discussions of Proustian 'time past' that lingered and organically fused with images of the present. A sense of this in fact imbued the entire new poetic cycle, just as temporal 'overlapping' characterised his autobiographies and novel. Proust's graveyard image also gave special resonance to 'The Soul', which was the third item in the sequence.[32]

In the later summer of 1957, official anger with Pasternak was fuelled by foreign publication of excerpts from the novel. This included a printing of the religious poems in *Grani* (Facets), the Russian émigré journal published in Frankfurt am Main. The poems appeared anonymously as 'Verses from Russia', but the link with Pasternak was not hard to establish.[33] In late August Polikarpov also took action via 'Polish comrades' to censure and suppress the review *Opinie*, which had printed extracts from *Doctor Zhivago*.[34] On 28 August Tvardovsky warned Fedin in a note that Polikarpov expected him to talk to Pasternak and discover how the *Zhivago* manuscript found its way to Poland. Fedin was told it depended largely on him whether Pasternak would 'find the strength to admit he has got in a tangle and wants to extricate himself and save his civic honour'; Surkov and Tvardovsky both telephoned Fedin and put him under heavy pressure to inform on Pasternak. Fedin's diary for August recorded he was 'tormented by the inescapability of the case', but that he had refused to probe Pasternak about the Polish connection.[35]

The September dateline for a Soviet edition of *Zhivago* came and went. On 23 October Pasternak was prevailed upon to send yet another letter to Feltrinelli – in Russian – cancelling the Italian edition.[36] That same month Surkov attached himself to a group of Soviet poets visiting Rome. At their conference the Italian Angelo-Maria Ripellino eulogised Pasternak, while Zelinsky played down his significance and cautioned against politically inflating his importance.[37] Surkov also gave a press conference condemning Pasternak's novel and stating that its publication contravened the author's own wishes. Particularly sinister was his recollection that this affair seemed to repeat the case of Pilnyak's *Mahogany*, which was rightly understood as warning of an impending witchhunt.[38]

Surkov's statement was also clear evidence of the souring spirit of the times, and there were other signs of growing official intolerance. In late November, Khrushchev personally admonished a large gathering of Moscow writers and

329

artists to observe the tenets of socialist realism, and reminded them that they were all servants of the Party. At the same meeting Surkov condemned a fashionable recent tendency to rehabilitate suppressed or unorthodox figures such as Babel, Bulgakov, Pilnyak, and Tsvetaeva, as well as attempts to 'canonize' the work of Pasternak.[39] At some point during this period Khrushchev himself was evidently shown some extracts from *Doctor Zhivago*, supposedly demonstrating its pernicious character. Subsequently, however, he claimed not to have read the book at the time; he considered he had been wrongly advised, and regretted the work was not published.[40]

Feltrinelli in October sharply rebuffed Surkov's intimidating remarks and maintained that Pasternak's messages were fabricated and that he intended going ahead with publication plans.[41] Meanwhile Surkov travelled on to Paris and there tried vainly to persuade Gallimard to cancel publication. The Soviet commercial attaché in London also reported failure in his attempt to get Collins & Harvill to return the manuscript, which Manya Harari and Max Hayward were already busy translating.[42]

Finally, on 22 November 1957, the Italian translation of *Doctor Zhivago* appeared to much fanfare in Milan. The first imprint of six thousand copies sold out the same day, and several reprints followed. There was a flurry of articles and press notices in Europe and America. In Moscow meanwhile, foreign journalists, mainly from Britain and America, began asking for interviews with Pasternak. Hoping to manipulate opinion, Polikarpov organised a press conference at which Pasternak would adopt the same disapproving line as in his letters to Feltrinelli.[43] Meetings took place with two groups of foreign journalists in Peredelkino in December, and gritting his teeth and full of disgust Pasternak mouthed a version of official opinion, although his later private conversations with some reporters established a truer picture of his thoughts,[44] and in correspondence he vehemently disavowed his public statements and urged that they be disregarded. As he assured Jacqueline de Proyart, no matter what the consequences to himself, '*mon propre sort est moins important pour moi que celui de mes idées*'.[45] There was no consideration of Pasternak's own suggestion that, even at this late stage, the situation could be defused if an abridged version of the novel were published in Russia – just as in its day Tolstoy's *Resurrection* had appeared in differing Russian and translated versions.[46]

Any such possibility was altogether ruled out by public response to the Italian *Zhivago*, and by Western press commentary on the story of its publication and of Soviet attempts to prevent its appearance. The novel was generally greeted as a major artistic triumph and as a sign of the survival of Russian spiritual values despite decades of oppression. Pasternak's ties with European culture and literary tradition were also rehearsed in many reports and commentaries. During the winter of 1957–58 Polikarpov's department was kept *au courant* with extracted copies of Western press coverage. Attempts to stem further publications petered out amid awareness that they would fail and merely discredit the Soviet government.[47] Some hopes that the official version of the story might be confirmed by 'progressive' French writers such as Louis Aragon and others were also disappointed. Meanwhile, the Soviet press maintained a stony silence. In Party circles Pasternak's success was played down. To disguise his own failure, Polikarpov reported to the Central Committee that the book had attracted no special attention in Italy, and that the would-be orchestrators of an anti-Soviet campaign had failed in their plan.[48]

Despite presentiments of 'a terribly serious winter, full of ordeals and blows',[49] Pasternak found himself surprisingly untroubled. In public he certainly never acted like someone aware of being in disgrace. In this spirit he resubmitted the autobiographical essay to *Novy mir* with a few minor amendments and a different conclusion omitting mention of his recently completed novel. Just before the year end the literary scholar Andrei Sinyavsky spent a day with Pasternak, discussing *inter alia* his own critical essay that later formed a preface to the 1965 'Biblioteka poeta' edition of his verse.[50]

A sense of complacent wellbeing animated Pasternak's New Year's address in prose 'To Friends in East and West', which was dated 20 December 1957 but was published posthumously. In an appeal for peace and reconciliation, he reminded readers of his country's recent historical ordeals, and of the changed nature of modern humanity both in Russia and abroad. Rehearsing an existential thought recently expressed in the novel and elsewhere, he wrote that man 'comes as a guest to the feast of existence and realises the important thing is not how much he inherits, but how he behaves while visiting, what people love and remember him for'.[51]

In December 1957 Hélène Peltier-Zamoyska visited Moscow and saw Pasternak several times over the Christmas holiday period, finding him 'just as young and ardent' as the previous year.[52] Pasternak was impatient to hear of progress with various publication projects, and also discussed plans for a possible preface to the French *Zhivago*; the idea was later abandoned however, because of his health, and so as not to court further official displeasure.[53] During January he wrote to his sister Lydia in coded form of his recent pleasure at welcoming 'Elena from distant Tula' (i.e. Hélène from Toulouse) as a guest, and also of his impatience for 'Yura to reach Galya and Kolya' (i.e. for *Zhivago* to appear with Gallimard and Collins publishers).[54]

In January of 1958 a further official attempt to get Pasternak to write directly to Gallimard and stop the French edition of *Zhivago* foundered on a technicality: as Pasternak pointed out, Gallimard were bound by their contract with Feltrinelli and thus not juridically answerable to himself. Nevertheless, unaware that Soviet blocking tactics were on the point of failure, he sent a private letter to the French translation team urging them not to despond.[55]

Unlike translations of *Doctor Zhivago*, the Russian-language edition was fraught with problems unforeseen and not fully understood by Pasternak owing to a lack of open communication with his attorney and others. The whole episode also showed Feltrinelli's concern for Pasternak's wishes as secondary to his monopolistic instincts.

Having ignored de Proyart's mandate of 5 February, Feltrinelli's attitude to her at a meeting in Paris became positively aggressive once it became clear that the Soviet edition of *Doctor Zhivago* was finally cancelled. Effectively this untied his hands as sole controlling publisher of the novel. To achieve his aim he now performed a volte-face. Having courted Soviet wrath by publishing the novel, he now blocked Pasternak's approved plan for a Russian edition with Mouton, claiming that this would anger the Soviets and harm the author's interests. In October 1957 he wrote to the Michigan University Press forbidding their plan to publish a Russian text as part of the projected multi-volume Pasternak edition, and in November he wrote warning all Western publishers of *Zhivago* against breaching his interdict on a Russian-language edition. Ranged against him were de Proyart with her author's mandate to publish a Russian text, and various 'pirate' émigré publishers who acquired one of the texts circulating in Moscow and had their own publication schemes.[56]

Through a court order in the Hague, Feltrinelli stopped Mouton's publication plans. Pasternak was much vexed at this but maintained his continuing gratitude to Feltrinelli as a supposed reason for not interfering.[57] In March 1958, however, Feltrinelli changed position again. A factor behind this was Pasternak's renewed candidature for the Nobel Prize, which would be considerably enhanced by publication of his novel in Russian. To qualify as part of his achievement, however, a Russian-language edition had to be published by no later than August 1958. Feltrinelli then allowed Mouton to run off a limited Russian edition, but insisted on its release under his own imprint. Anxious to avoid conflict, the Mouton director gave way, and a title page was affixed, advertising 'Feltrinelli Milan 1958'. Several hundred copies of this, reprinted photomechanically and bound in blue cloth, were released on 24 August 1958. Further copies, printed in the same type, but without Feltrinelli's imprint (and to his alleged puzzlement) were evidently available to Soviet visitors and other inquirers at the Vatican Pavilion of the Brussels World Fair in late summer and autumn of 1958. This was evidently the same Russian text which the NTS (Popular Labour Union) émigré organisation planned to issue in pocket format for distribution in Russia.[58] Rumours of CIA connivance and financing for this 'unofficial' edition were of course impossible to prove. Within the next half-year, Feltrinelli then released a market edition of *Doctor Zhivago* in Russian, using a 1957 dateline and the copyright purportedly secured by his *Italian* translation; thus the Feltrinelli house confirmed its status as publisher of the Nobel candidate.[59] What was not apparent to Mouton or Feltrinelli was that they had printed from a defective uncorrected typescript, very different from the best 'clean' copy held by Jacqueline de Proyart; Pasternak was annoyed by the many blemishes, and it took years of pressure by de Proyart before Feltrinelli brought out a corrected text.[60] (Ironically, since the USSR in 1973 subscribed to the international copyright convention, it also required assent from Feltrinelli's heirs before a clean text, verified and collated with de Proyart's manuscript, could be released in Russia in 1988.)

After the *Zhivago* success, Feltrinelli's ambitions extended to a world monopoly on all Pasternak's writings, and he was furious in summer 1958 when de Proyart's French edition of the autobiographical essay appeared, pre-empting his own. Without authorial sanction, he in December 1958 released a lavish bilingual Russian-Italian edition of all the verse from the 'Green Notebook' and the autobiography, including Pasternak's cancelled concluding note that mentioned the novel and also named (and thus compromised) the editor Nikolai Bannikov. This was a characteristic instance of Feltrinelli's failure to heed advice or appreciate Pasternak's and his friends' precarious situation.[61]

Owing to the lack of regular open communication with Western Europe, Pasternak was only partially aware of the peripeteia of his various foreign editions. Apart from which, he was *hors de combat* during the first three months of 1958. At the end of January, he suffered a recurrence of his previous year's illness, with urological complications, acute pain and a high temperature. A catheter could not be found locally and one was eventually purchased in town by Kaverin's wife and fitted by a visiting consultant. But there was no precise diagnosis; a blood analysis suggested cancer, but this was not confirmed, and attention finally concentrated on a trapped spinal nerve. Hospitalisation was called for, but nothing suitable was available. The previous year someone in the Writers' Union had ruled that he was 'unworthy' of treatment at the Kremlin hospital. For a week he therefore languished at home, reading Henry James and listening to the radio between bouts of pain. Once, while

Chukovsky was at his bedside, the pain returned and with eyes full of horror Pasternak said: 'I keep thinking it would be so good to. . . [the sentence trailed off] After all, I have already done everything I wanted. It would be good that way.' It took a week of concerted efforts by family, neighbours and friends, medical visits by a neuropathologist and Dr Vovsi's assistant, rounds of various hospitals, and Chukovsky's approaches to the Central Trade Union Council, to Mikoyan's assistant and the Council of Ministers, before a bed was found in the Kremlin clinic. Finally, on 8 February the patient was borne out on a stretcher through the snow to a waiting ambulance, blowing kisses to his friends and family.[62]

Hearing of this albeit belated VIP treatment, Akhmatova tartly commented that someone who wrote what Pasternak wrote should not expect a private ward in the Central Committee hospital; but as Chukovskaya objected, Pasternak never *had* expected it – his family and friends had wished it and obtained it by persistent effort.[63]

After hospital treatment, Pasternak was transferred to recuperate at the suburban hospital in Davydkovo near Peredelkino and returned home only in April. During the enforced inactivity he ran his affairs as best he could. But serious work was ruled out when his requests to be placed in a private ward where he could spread out his books and papers went unheeded. Aware of an impending financial crisis, despite vast intangible royalties accumulating abroad, in early March he wrote Puzikov of Goslitizdat proposing a re-edition of his 1953 Shakespeare collection.

Another letter, to Ivinskaya, reported on a proposal from Panfyorov, editor of the journal *Oktyabr'*, who was determined not to 'surrender' Pasternak to the 'foreigners' and had recommended that he go off to Baku and seek fresh socialist inspiration among the oil rigs! No help was offered with relocation in a private ward. However, as Pasternak family correspondence later revealed, Panfyorov that summer visited Britain for medical treatment and combined this with a visit to Lydia in Oxford, where he presented himself as Boris' friend and repeated his Baku scheme, and with a last-ditch attempt to dissuade Collins from publishing *Zhivago*.[64]

Among the post that reached him in hospital and at Davydkovo, Pasternak read and approved some translations of the *Zhivago* poems and other recent lyrics, by his sister Lydia. He was also delighted at news of a successful display of their father's work at the Ashmolean Museum, and of a further exhibition at London's Pushkin Club.[65] Later, in May, he recorded some impressions of extracts from their father's notes and papers which Josephine sent, and also reflected on the tragic eclipse of their mother's talent, which now seemed echoed by his own present fate.[66]

It became increasingly clear that many letters sent to and by Pasternak through the official mail were being interfered with, lost or confiscated. Postcards emerged as less vulnerable, however, and in July he took to writing in English and without signature even to relatives. Whenever possible, messages were sent with friends as couriers however. The Oxford sisters gleaned additional news and details of Boris' life from the French student Georges Nivat, who was studying in Moscow and had befriended the daughter of Ivinskaya. That summer, Ivinskaya pursued her own mischief in letters to the Pasternak family, and Boris had to write specially to confirm to his sisters that he had not abandoned Zinaida and was not actually living with Olga.[67] Another aspect of Ivinskaya's deviousness was more serious and hinted at her later conspirative alliance with Feltrinelli: she was supposed to mail an important letter of 28 September from Pasternak to his Oxford relatives explaining details of his legal mandate to Jacqueline de Proyart; the letter was not sent however, and it was later found among Ivinskaya's papers with various other items of mail which she failed to dispatch.

As *Zhivago*'s foreign success gained momentum, Pasternak was increasingly deluged by mail from abroad containing readers' responses, congratulations, press cuttings and reports. In hospital he bitterly regretted his inability to respond, but later he tried manfully to answer most letters. By the autumn, the Peredelkino postwoman sometimes brought up to fifty items per day. Dealing with such correspondence became a heavy burden, and friends were surprised that Pasternak squandered so much time on this. Many of his answers were repetitious, and correspondence now ceased to be the extension of original creativity it had once been. But after years of enforced isolation, Pasternak felt exhilarated by these contacts, and a poem of early 1959 celebrated his joyful communion with 'God's World' ('Bozhii mir'). Also, as he told one correspondent, this proved an ideal way of brushing up his foreign languages![68] Some of these correspondences however acquired a confessional and affectionate momentum of their own – notably the exchanges with Jacqueline de Proyart, Hélène Peltier-Zamoyska, and Renate Schweitzer. Other significant (and later published) correspondence began in 1958 with the American Trappist monk Thomas Merton and with Kurt Wolff of Pantheon Books.[69]

Some letters came from would-be translators. In 1957 Eugene Kayden, an American scholar, wrote outlining plans for a volume of Pasternak's hundred best poems. Pasternak was polite but unenthusiastic (and openly critical in family correspondence). He also disliked the inaccuracies in Kayden's draft and objected to translations of earlier verse which he had now discarded (this argument was raised repeatedly in correspondence over the next two years).[70]

Several old friends and admirers from abroad also now resumed contact with Pasternak, including Boris Zaitsev, Fyodor Stepun, and Pierre (Pyotr) Souvchinsky. Pasternak particularly valued professional testimonials by prominent authors and scholars. A letter in June of 1958 from Albert Camus specially delighted him; Camus sent a copy of his own previous year's Nobel Prize speech in which he spoke of 'the great Pasternak', and reiterated his admiration. In answer Pasternak wrote two characteristically exuberant postcard messages, the first clouded only by realisation that Valentin Kataev, one of his 'executioners', had recently represented himself to Camus as his friend.[71]

Correspondence also brought Pasternak some minor unpaid writing commissions. In May 1958 a London-based biographer of Tagore asked him to write something on this subject for publication in India, and another short piece on *Faust* was composed for the Faust Memorial Museum near Stuttgart.[72]

The French translation of *Doctor Zhivago* was released on the 23 June 1958. The translators were not named, and their anonimity assisted Aucouturier and Peltier-Zamoyska to return to Russia and visit Pasternak during a Slavists' conference in September and over the coming year. On August 18 Gérard Frémy, Neigauz's French piano student, brought to Peredelkino both the translated novel and autobiography. It was an experience that Pasternak wrote and talked of with great emotion.[73] In August, too, the English *Zhivago* appeared with Pantheon Books and with Collins & Harvill in London. Pasternak received a copy in September and was equally delighted, although disconcerted by the garish dust-jacket and disappointed that the verses were rendered in prose instead of poetic versions by Stephen Spender that he had hoped for.[74]

In spring and summer Pasternak had many visitors, some invited, some unexpected, from Russia and abroad. One of these was Zoya Maslenikova, an amateur sculptor who in spring persuaded him to let her model him in clay. Exasperated at the waste of time, Pasternak agreed out of politeness, but their wide-ranging conversations during these sessions were noted down and later published by her, forming a valuable source of anecdote and of Pasternak's opinion on a wide variety of topics.[75]

Pasternak was visited by various Western Slavists attending an international conference in Moscow in September. Oxford don Ronald Hingley was one of several who later described their visits to Pasternak. At the dining table Zinaida, elderly and clad in black, presided with silent courtesy, but tacitly conveyed her unease at these foreign contacts which simultaneously compromised and protected her husband. Observers within the family also observed the tensions that arose over visitors and foreign mail. In the presence of visitors, however, doubts and anxieties were usually masked by Pasternak's vigour and cascading loquacity. Certainly, Hingley and most other visitors that summer – including Vadim Andreyev, Evtushenko, Nils Nilsson, Angelo Ripellino – observed a figure with handsome suntan offset by white hair and radiating ebullience and good humour. Pasternak also behaved with striking nonchalance over the likelihood of being under constant surveillance. However, Hingley observed his host occasionally stiffen as a black limousine of the type used by the security police passed slowly down the narrow lane, almost halting by the gate of dacha no. 3.[76]

For several months after returning from hospital in spring 1958, Pasternak did not feel 'master of [his] own future' and feared a relapse; he was forced to keep exercising his leg, daily walks sometimes lasted two to three hours, and he now tended to work standing at his lectern to avoid long periods of sitting.[77] With huge consignments of mail, posing for Maslenikova, frequent scheduled and impromptu visitors, reading Proust, Faulkner and Camus, and examining verse sent for his opinion by Evtushenko, Berestov, Slutsky and others, the summer months of 1958 had many distractions. Creative ambition burned brightly however, and Pasternak felt ready for some new major undertaking. To Marina Baranovich in early May, he mentioned starting on some new prose work. Disappointingly, though, he found his 'awakening thought functions begin, as always, with verses'. And despite a wish to address serious, profound and significant themes, 'all around there is mud, springtime, empty woodland, lonely birds twittering – and all this comes to mind first of all, postponing more worthwhile intentions'![78]

Some friends, including Bannikov and Ivinskaya, thought Pasternak should continue writing poems on such subjects, in his latest manner. But in mid June he was still complaining at the assertive flow of poetical trivia. In his view, *Doctor Zhivago* had in some way cleared a space for further major works, and to Vyacheslav Ivanov that summer he expressed a belief that the novel fulfilled a 'desire to start saying everything to the end and to evaluate life in the spirit of an earlier absoluteness [*bezuslovnost'*]', thus barring the road back to mere 'iambics'.[79]

Of seven complete new poems eventually included in *When Weather Clears*, six items circulated in typescript as 'Additions of July 1958' ('Iul'skie dopolne-niya 1958 g.'). Two of them appeared in *Literaturnaya Gruziya*, and over the next year a handful also found their way into the émigré journals *Grani* and *Mosty* (Bridges).[80]

Most of the new verse of 1958 went through many drafts and revisions.

Some early sketches originated in those spring nature images that obtruded on the poet's attention. Rather than forming mere landscapes, though, they provided settings or metonymies for reflection on the noble tragedy of Pasternak's predicament – on the threshold of world fame, yet unprintable in his home country. Some drafted lines came close to a pamphleteering genre, combining indignation at his slightment with invective against the 'masks and puppets', 'flatterers and spongers' whose company he eschewed.[81] Other poems meanwhile offered a confident summation of life and an embracement of the future and eternity; it was only these positive sentiments which distilled out in the finished poems, affirming the title of the cycle. This symbolic 'clearing of weather' with a pledge of the poet's survival occurred in several of the 1958 drafts and poems.[82] A recurring image was that of the singing bird, emblematic of the artist. In 'Around the Turning' ('Za povorotom') the bird, encircled by unfriendly nature, sings away among the conifers, trusting in its own roulades as in some charm, while just round the bend, in the depth of a woodland gully, 'The future awaits me, / More sure than any pledge'.[83] 'After the Thunderstorm' ('Posle grozy') celebrates the all-powerful transforming hand of the artist; it is time to make way for the future after the storms of half a century; yet it is not shocks and revolts that clear the way for new life, but the 'Revelations, storms and lavishness / Of some man's blazing heart' (III, 105–6; *SS*, II, 125).

During the exuberant summer of 1958, Pasternak's darker moods that were filtered out of poetic manuscripts were observed only by those close to him. There was no obvious campaign of persecution, and after the winter of Polikarpov's discontent, even the Central Committee and Politburo files on him were quiescent between February and September.[84] Nevertheless, Pasternak wrote in May to Josephine of 'a constant, though temporarily alleviated *political* threat to my position, in which any sense of terra firma beneath one's feet is unthinkable'. Occasionally these feelings surfaced in other correspondence, and a letter of 6 September to Jacqueline de Proyart mentioned vague threats and rumours of his alleged offence against the order.[85]

These anxieties were not just the product of frightened imagination. In June Chukovsky as well as his wife headed Pasternak off from accepting an invitation to contribute to a literary evening at the Arts House in Peredelkino, which might have been an occasion for local hacks to voice their disapproval.[86] Dark premonitions were also confirmed by various events as the summer drew to an end. Practically all Pasternak's and Ivinskaya's translation contracts were by that time suspended. By autumn, Ivinskaya was virtually out of work, and was evidently the first to react and 'conjure up demons' at each breath of rumour concerning Pasternak's purported crime.[87] On 9 September, *Literaturnaya gazeta* published an article by Pertsov referring to Pasternak's 'epigone religious verses with their stench of mothballs from the Symbolist suitcase'.[88] Then, in mid September, during a congress of Italian and Soviet poets, Aleksei Surkov answered a question from the floor about Pasternak's absence by explaining that he had written an anti-Soviet novel against the spirit of the Russian revolution and had sent it abroad for publication. Although only in verbal form, this was a first public statement of accusation.[89]

The late summer of 1958 brought new rumours of Pasternak's likely candidature for the Nobel Prize in Literature. Fearing the complications this could cause, Pasternak hoped hard that he might be bypassed in favour of, say, Alberto Moravia – another name cited as a likely candidate.[90] On the other hand, as he reasoned to Josephine in one of his English messages, if the Prize were his, then he would have to go to Sweden, and 'I can seen no means not to try, and not to want to take with me O. [Ivinskaya] in the voyage, if the permission only is to be obtained, not to say about the probability of my own travel.' His more fundamental hopes were different, though: 'I wish this 1958–59 winter (or year) fraught with such unexpected prospects should be quicker over, I long for the renewings of my quiet daily work.'[91]

The Soviet literary management were also apprised of the likely award. Amazingly, in October Surkov and Polevoi secretly proposed to the Central Committee the very idea that occurred to Pasternak earlier – to defuse the situation by quickly publishing an edition of *Doctor Zhivago* of, say, 5,000– 10,000 thousand copies for private distribution. This was of course proposed merely as a damage containment exercise, but in view of the perceived anti-Soviet character of the work, the Central Committee's Cultural Section rejected the idea.[92]

Shortly afterwards, on 21 October, Polikarpov and Propaganda Chief Ilyichev worked out contingency measures in case Pasternak received the Nobel award: the *Novy mir* rejection letter, a further writers' letter condemning the award, and Pasternak's correspondence with Feltrinelli cancelling publication of *Zhivago* should all be published; if the award were shared by Pasternak and Sholokhov, then the latter must demonstratively refuse it; if Pasternak were sole winner, then his friends Fedin and Ivanov must be persuaded to prevail on him to reject the Prize.[93]

Pasternak's hopes and wishes to be left to work in peace were all in vain. On the 23 October the Nobel Prize was awarded to him. This came after six earlier nominations – every year from 1946 to 1950, and then again in 1957;[94] it was one of a series of awards during 1946–60 that went to various innovatory figures in modern literature such as Hermann Hesse, André Gide, T. S. Eliot,

William Faulkner, and Saint-John Perse.[95] Needless to say, the Swedish Academy never tailored its awards to political considerations, and rumours of behind-the-scenes enquiries about the appropriateness of this or any other award have been vigorously denied. Nor was there evidence in 1958 that the Swedish Academy foresaw the Soviet reaction; *Zhivago*'s unavailability in Russia was seemingly regarded as a temporary circumstance.[96] The citation for the award was based on Pasternak's 'important achievement both in contemporary lyrical poetry, and in the field of the great Russian epic tradition'.

17

'Other new goals': the final year

'The Nobel Prize'

I'm chased and driven, run to earth.
Out there is liberty and light,
Behind – the noise of the pursuit,
No escaping from my plight.

Bank of pond and darkened wood,
Athwart the road felled trunks of spruce,
The way is blocked on every side.
Come what may, I have no choice.

Did I commit a heinous crime?
A murder, or some evil deed?
At the beauty of my land
I merely made the whole world weep.

Yet on the threshold of the tomb
I still believe: there'll come a time
When power of good will overrule
The force of evil and of spite.

(1959)

On the evening of Wednesday 22 October, Pasternak was visited by NYT correspondent Max Frankel to whom he repeated his concern about the problems any Nobel award would cause for him.[1] However, the next day, Anders Österling of the Swedish Academy dispatched a telegram to Pasternak and announced the new award to waiting pressmen. Within hours the news had flashed round the world.[2]

On his usual afternoon walk on 23 October, wearing wellington boots, cap and mackintosh, Pasternak was met by expectant foreign newsmen. At this point he had had no personal notification, and beyond thanks for their congratulations and a show of obvious pleasure, he made no special comment.

At about 11 o'clock that night, the Ivanovs were telephoned by the wife of Union secretary Tikhonov with news of the award. Since Pasternak had no telephone, she asked them to inform him, but opined that any rejoicing was premature. Wearing a dressing-gown and coat over his pyjamas, Vsevolod Ivanov and his wife Tamara went round to the Pasternaks. Zinaida had heard the news in town that day and had already told Boris, but she expected nothing good of the announcement and had retired. Boris therefore sat and celebrated over a bottle of wine with the Ivanovs and Nina Tabidze.[3]

Next morning, Ivanov (the only one in their row of villas with a telephone) was asked to warn his neighbour Fedin that Polikarpov was on his way to visit him. Ivanov himself had refused to be used as a means of influencing Pasternak, but Fedin shortly afterwards turned up while Zinaida was baking. On being shown up to the study, he announced that this was not a social but an official visit in order to urge Pasternak to reject his Nobel award. Failing this, he must expect the Union's displeasure and a campaign of public condemnation. Initially, Pasternak was incensed and stubbornly refused, but it was agreed he should have a couple of hours to consider. Polikarpov would be waiting at Fedin's house to hear his decision.[4]

As Fedin left, Pasternak was at first literally prostrated, then angry and upset. After walking round and consulting the Ivanovs however, he resolved to accept the prize. But he felt deeply injured by Fedin's behaviour and did not call back to see him; Polikarpov angrily drove back into town.[5]

Friday 24 October was Zinaida's name day. In addition to the usual well-wishers, Western reporters and cameramen turned up in the forenoon. There were congratulations, questions and answers, photographs, and a festive atmosphere. In the early afternoon Chukovsky turned up with his granddaughter Elena. Apart from the Ivanovs he was the only Soviet literary figure to congratulate Pasternak. Several telegrams had come from abroad, but nothing from within the USSR. Zinaida seemed preoccupied with whether she would accompany her husband to the ceremony in Stockholm on 10 December, and what to wear. Later in the afternoon Pasternak composed his message of acceptance to the Swedish Academy, stating simply: 'Immensely grateful, touched, proud, astonished, abashed. Pasternak.'[6]

Chukovsky meanwhile called on Fedin and found him miserable at the role he had been obliged to play despite his initial refusal to be 'set up against Pasternak'.[7] Later that afternoon, Pasternak walked over to Ivinskaya's and sat for a long time, reassuring himself of his decision to accept the prize.

In the evening, apart from family members and Nina Tabidze, many friends gathered at the Pasternak dacha, including the Asmuses and Neigauzes and Anna Pogodina, wife of the writer. (Pogodin himself cultivated a carefully 'official' stance, and during the period of Pasternak's ideologically leperous condition never compromised himself by visiting or socialising.) Also among Pasternak's guests that day were the Likhotals, a Soviet press photographer and his wife who came with the foreign newsmen and stayed on. The company discussed Chukovsky's idea that Pasternak write to Furtseva the Minister of Culture, and he immediately drafted a message, stating his dismay at the reaction to his award and recalling his earlier candidature before the novel was written. Couched in elevated terms, the letter ended by stating Pasternak's faith in protection by 'higher powers not just on this earth but in heaven'. Some thought the theological element inappropriate, but the letter was written and Likhotal volunteered to deliver it (although for some reason he later had second thoughts and handed it back; delivered or not, it would have scarcely affected the outcome.)[8]

The Soviet media maintained two days of silence. An initial restrained and surprised official response by Mikhailov, an assistant Minister of Culture, seemed to suggest that the establishment might grit their teeth and ride out the episode.[9] However, this preceded Pasternak's acceptance of the prize and the international reaction. As Suslov and Gromyko maintained to the Central Committee, Western press emphasis on the political rather than literary aspects of Pasternak's novel identified the Nobel award as an aggressive political act, and Pasternak's offence lay in refusing to distance himself from this. The vehement measures against him in fact reflected not his own misdemeanour but the scale of its international political resonance, and of official Soviet paranoia at that time.[10]

On Saturday 25 October the storm broke. Early morning crowds that bought up *Literaturnaya gazeta* from the kiosks read report of a 'Provocative Sally by International Reactionary Forces', together with the text of the 1956 *Novy mir* letter of rejection. A prefatory note explained the general tenor of the letter and expressed disgust and contempt at Pasternak's 'shameful, unpatriotic attitude'. The Nobel award was described as 'a hostile political act' instigated by 'Swedish "literary" conservatives'. The novel for which the prize was allegedly presented was characterised as 'an artistically poverty-stricken and malicious work' filled with 'hatred of socialism' and 'contempt and hatred for the people', and its hero was as alien to the Soviet people as that 'spiteful literary snob, Pasternak himself'.[11] That same day there was a 'spontaneous' demonstration by students of Moscow's Literary Institute who handed a collective letter denouncing Pasternak to Voronkov at the Writers' Union. Radio Moscow also broke silence and echoed the printed reports.[12] Next day, on 26 October, the campaign continued and extended to the provincial press and radio. *Pravda* employed the notorious veteran pamphleteer Zaslavsky to compose a vitriolic personal assault on Pasternak.[13] Following on all this came shoals of letters to the press, largely from benighted non-literary folk who had of course never read Pasternak's novel, or anything else by him. But there were some more shameful responses. After first sending his friend a congratulatory telegram, Selvinsky saw the hostile press response and wrote him a letter saying he should refuse the prize; then, together with Shklovsky and two others on holiday with him in Yalta he licked himself clean by publicly condemning Pasternak.[14]

Copies of the papers were brought to the house and Zinaida was horrified by what she read; but it was not Pasternak's custom to follow the media, and he was spared from seeing himself vilified in print. Alarmed by the attacks, Evgenii Pasternak hurried to Peredelkino but found his father in buoyant spirits, and there was amusement that, in publishing the rejection letter, *Literaturnaya gazeta* had inadvertently regaled the public with all the novel's most offensive passages. Pasternak was now at work on a translation of Polish Romantic dramatist Juliusz Słowacki's *Maria Stuart*; it was the one contract work he had managed to retain, after Polish friends rejected any alternative translator. He eventually completed the work in spring of 1959.[15]

On Monday 27 October, a special extended meeting of the Union of Writers' Presidium was called, with representatives also from the Moscow Section of the RSFSR Writers' Union. Pasternak too had received a summons and travelled into town to Ivinskaya's apartment where they were joined by Koma Ivanov. Collectively with friends it was agreed that Pasternak himself should not attend personally. Instead he drafted a letter to the meeting which Ivanov delivered to Vorovsky Street by taxi. His message pleaded sudden indisposition as a reason for absence; his novel, he believed, was quite compatible with his status as a Soviet writer; he rehearsed the history of the *Zhivago* manuscript and the missed opportunities to publish an amended or censored version; he considered the Nobel award as an honour both to him and to Russian literature; and he stated his willingness to surrender the prize money to the Peace Fund set up at Soviet instigation in 1950. In conclusion, Pasternak cautioned against taking any extreme measures that might later have to be revoked: 'This will add nothing to your glory or your happiness.' The warning proved correct: it was not long before he was invited to apply for readmission, and he was posthumously reinstated in February 1987. The Union destroyed the allegedly 'Jesuitical' letter, and a copy was only recently discovered in the Russian Presidential library. On the way home, Pasternak called on his son Evgenii to tell him of the meeting and his message to it.[16]

Two days prior to the Union meeting there had been a conclave of its Party members when there was criticism of Surkov and of the secretariat's tardy and too liberal handling of the case; the idea that Pasternak should be exiled was also mooted.[17] Polikarpov attended both this meeting and the general Union gathering. At the latter Tikhonov was in the chair; forty-two members were present, with twenty-six absent on grounds of health, vacation or foreign travel. With a knowledge of *Doctor Zhivago* based on the published letter of rejection, twenty-nine speakers rehearsed the points of Pasternak's offence. There was no vocal opposition, but several, including Aliger, Arbuzov and Tvardovsky left the hall without voting; when sounded out by Polikarpov in the corridor, they frankly stated their dissenting view. Nevertheless, a 'unanimous' meeting, including some surprising liberal names such as Panova and Nikolai Chukovsky, noted Pasternak's 'political and moral downfall, his betrayal of the Soviet Union, of socialism, peace and progress' and proceeded to expel him from the Union. The implications of this were clear from the earlier fate of Akhmatova and Zoshchenko. It meant being ostracised and deprived of income and of pension rights, although Pasternak remained a member of Litfond, which allowed use of medical facilities and the right to reside in the Peredelkino dacha.[18] The blemish on those fourteen members who spoke advocating Pasternak's expulsion was not forgotten in the literary community. Slutsky was tormented by guilt for the rest of his days.[19]

Pasternak's expulsion from the Union was announced in *Literaturnaya gazeta* on Tuesday 28 October.[20] Chukovskaya, who called to see him that morning, observed a Pobeda saloon car parked nearby with four agents evidently watching the residence, and a radio-equipped jeep standing opposite the house remained in position for the next 2–3 days.[21] Pasternak himself seemed unusually tense and untalkative. That afternoon he walked over to Ivinskaya's lodging with a double dose of Nembutal and proposed that the two of them commit suicide, as an escape from further suffering and in revenge against the authorities. His suggestion was possibly connected with the recent double suicide of scholar Evgenii Lann and his wife, which caused a sensation in literary circles. Though deeply upset, Ivinskaya managed to persuade Pasternak to take no rash action. He left again, promising to come and see her in town next day. Now, once again, she ran to consult the authorities – this time in the person of Fedin.

Pasternak's neighbour opined that the suicide threat was an act of blackmail; if carried out, it would be a second 'stab in the back' to his country, and it must be prevented. He arranged for Ivinskaya to see Polikarpov next day (Wednesday 29 October) at the Writers' Union. Her appeal to Fedin meanwhile came as a timely reminder of her influence on Pasternak; despite their distrust of her, the authorities now used her directly and openly, and Fedin faded from the picture, much to his relief. Polikarpov's message was that Ivinskaya must help Pasternak find his way 'back to the people', and it was time for him to make a statement; meanwhile she would be held responsible for preventing any more of his absurd ideas. By the time this was reported back, Pasternak's mental state had slightly improved, and he was disposed at least to bide his time.[22]

Family tactics were in disarray however. On the morning of the 29th a *Pravda* reporter who turned up to collect Pasternak's signature on a statement renouncing the Nobel Prize was seen off by Zinaida, who angrily bristled in her husband's defence. Meanwhile Pasternak drove into town by car with his brother and without consulting anyone went to the Central Telegraph Building and in slightly idiosyncratic French sent a telegram to the Swedish Academy renouncing the prize: 'En vue du sens que cette distinction subit dans la société que je partage je dois renoncer au prix immérité qui m'a été attribué. Ne prenez pas en offense mon refus volontaire. Pasternak.'[23]

Pasternak's motives were clearly bound up with his other telegram to the Central Committee, to the effect that he had given up the Nobel Prize, and Ivinskaya should therefore be allowed to work again. To what extent Ivinskaya actively abetted Pasternak's refusal of the prize is unknown. Whatever its motives, Pasternak's refusal appeared almost deliberately to exacerbate his situation by drawing attention to the clamorous publicity and threat of reprisals against him. Indeed, two days later a Moscow Writers' meeting viewed his message as a calculated slap in the face, and the news of his refusal unleashed a chorus of international protest from several bodies and individuals, including the International PEN Club and a group of prominent British authors.[24]

When Pasternak returned from town, the approach to the dacha was surrounded by Western press vehicles, but he made no comment to reporters. Morale was at an observable all-time low. *Pravda* that day carried an article on the Soviet physicists Cherenkov, Frank and Tamm, who had gained the Nobel Prize for physics, and it contrasted this deserved award with the machinations behind the literary prize.[25] The article was written by a respected group of Academicians, and the invidious remarks were editorially inserted without their assent; the scientist Leontovich was sufficiently upset that he motored out to Peredelkino together with Evgenii Pasternak to reassure Pasternak about the support for him.

On arrival Evgenii Pasternak barely recognised his father, who was grey in the face and disorientated.[26] To add to his distress, later that day a female doctor with First Aid impedimenta arrived, announcing she had been detailed by the Central Committee to stay at his home and keep a 24–hour watch over him. Resistant to all protest, she was accommodated in the drawing room where she spent three monotonous weeks, causing inconvenience and serving as the butt of Pasternak's mockery. Nevertheless, she performed two useful functions. When Pasternak suffered pains in his right arm and shoulder, she applied a sling and for the next few days he contrived to write with his left hand. That same evening she also administered a camphor injection when Pasternak came out in a cold sweat after receiving another summons to a Moscow Writers' meeting. She confirmed there was no question of his attendance, and as Zinaida commented, the outcome was predictable anyway. After receiving his summons, Vsevolod Ivanov suffered a cerebral stroke and was also unable to attend.[27]

The campaign against Pasternak was almost unaffected by his rejection of the Prize. On Thursday 30 October, the media carried an abusive diatribe delivered by Komsomol leader Semichastny the previous day at a mass rally in the presence of Khrushchev. In metaphoric fury Semichastny described Pasternak as a mangy sheep in the flock and as worse than a pig, which would never foul its own sty, and he claimed the Soviet government would scarcely object if Pasternak were to leave the country.[28] On hearing of this, Pasternak discussed with Zinaida the question of emigrating. Anxious that he spend his final years in honour and serenity, she was happy to countenance his departure if he so wished; but she was unwilling to leave herself, and Pasternak was adamant that he would not go without his family. The same subject was also ventilated with Ivinskaya and he allegedly drafted but then tore up a letter announcing his intention to emigrate. Unlike Zinaida, she feared for her own fate in the event of his departure, and it was probably her persuasion that convinced him to remain and endure his fate.[29]

Seeking ways of protecting Pasternak's and her own interests, on the morning of 30 October, Ivinskaya approached the head of the Authors' Rights Department in Lavrushinsky Lane, but was cold-shouldered. In the corridor as she left however, she was addressed by Isidor Gringolts, a young specialist in copyright law and a devoted admirer of Pasternak.[30] Gringolts urged that in order to avoid being exiled, Pasternak should address a personal plea to Khrushchev. Later, at Ivinskaya's apartment Gringolts drafted a letter which she and Irina edited together with Ariadna Efron and other friends. In her later memoirs, Ivinskaya branded Gringolts as an agent provocateur responsible for coercing Pasternak into a shameful act of self-abasement. The text and tone of the letter were not specially penitential however; it was she, not Gringolts, who was the prime persuader, and her view that Pasternak should sign the letter was not shared by her own daughter.[31]

Irina Emelyanova and Vyacheslav Ivanov took the letter to Peredelkino and Pasternak signed almost without demurring. The letter mentioned his rejection of the prize (the first public mention of this fact) and stated that he was tied to Russia by his life and work; he never imagined himself involved in a political campaign; exile would be tantamount to death for him and he pleaded to be spared this extreme measure. It was not the penitential statement the authorities hoped for, and it ended with a 'hand on heart' statement that 'I have done something for Soviet literature and may yet be of benefit to it.'[32] Emelyanova and another friend delivered the letter next day to Central Committee headquarters on Old Square. The letter slightly eased but did not totally resolve the problem: when Tass released the text on 2 November, a note of comment stated that Pasternak had never requested or been refused an exit visa, but should he wish to emigrate, the state would raise no objection.[33]

On Friday 31 October, in Cinema House, just across the street from the Writers' Union, a meeting of Moscow writers endorsed the Union resolution. Among those who stepped up under prose-writer Sergei Smirnov's chairmanship to vilify Pasternak were some old enemies and friends, among them Pertsov, Bezymensky, Martynov, Slutsky, Sofronov, Soloukhin, and Zelinsky. (The latter was until recently a would-be editor of Pasternak's novel. Now he not only attacked Pasternak, but also denounced Vyacheslav Ivanov in a manner that resulted in his dismissal from the staff of Moscow University.)[34] The meeting passed a further motion proposed from the floor by Vera Inber, calling for Pasternak to be deprived of his citizenship. The meeting's decision was registered as unanimous, although many left without voting, and at the end one elderly woman shouted out her opposition and the chairman was forced to take note: it was the sister of Nadezhda Allilueva, recently released from the camps. The results of the meeting were published in *Literaturnaya gazeta*.[35] Some of those who defamed Pasternak did so evidently in a fit of cowardly moral inertia, and Slutsky was afterwards distraught at the blot on his reputation. Several, like Kaverin, 'boldly' stayed out of reach of Voronkov's three-line whip, and many others disapproved in silence. There were similar writers' meetings in other parts of the USSR, and some saddening betrayals – as when Chikovani expressed to the Georgian Writers' Union his pride that 'Georgia has no writer like Pasternak'. The issue became an effective litmus test of the integrity of many literary figures, although as in the past with Aseyev and Fedin, Pasternak preferred to overlook the conduct of Selvinsky, Chikovani and others.[36]

The same day, while writers debated, Pasternak and Ivinskaya were unexpectedly whisked away by government limousine and taken for a further meeting with Polikarpov and an official who remained silent throughout, but

who Ivinskaya claimed was Suslov, the Party's 'grey cardinal'.[37] Polikarpov
announced that Pasternak would not be exiled, but he must find a way of
making his peace with the Russian people, whose righteous anger would
express itself next day in *Literaturnaya gazeta*. Pasternak upbraided Polikarpov for making free with the word 'people' and almost walked out in fury at
his over-familiar tone. After tempers were restored, Pasternak was told he must
make a further public statement which Ivinskaya would assist in preparing.
Typically, she did not refuse. Later on, the official limousine that took
Pasternak home became stuck in the mud in front of the dacha and had to be
dislodged with assistance from Leonid Pasternak and their domestic help. The
farcical symbolism of this did not escape those involved.[38]

On 4 November, Polikarpov called Ivinskaya's apartment while Pasternak
was visiting, and announced it was time for an open letter to the people.
Pasternak drafted a message that laid bare the motive for his recent action: he
believed the Nobel award should have been an honour for his people, and his
rejection was not from a sense of guilt but out of fear for those close to him.
This was not at all what Polikarpov required, and he ordered Ivinskaya to help
refashion the text. The promised reward for collaboration would be the
restoration of mail deliveries which had been cut off, a reprinting of *Faust* and
a go-ahead for professional translation work.[39]

Pasternak was by now tired and wanted to end his suspension in limbo. He
signed the revised letter and it was printed in *Pravda* on 6 November. The
ideas and phraseology were patently not his own. The letter claimed that all his
recent actions were made of his own free will – a point so laboured and
repeated as to prompt disbelief. The request to publish this letter arose, so it
was claimed, from Pasternak's respect for the truth; he was dismayed at the
political abuse of the Nobel award and therefore renounced it voluntarily; he
had a deep faith in the country and its people and never intended to harm the
state; he regretted that his novel cast doubt on the Revolution, and that
publication had not been stopped as he requested; the letter emphasised that
Pasternak had not been persecuted or threatened, and ended with a statement
of belief in his ability to restore his good name and his comrades' trust.[40]

Lacking any gesture of apology, the letter was not so much a capitulation as
a concesssion – primarily to Ivinskaya. By signing Pasternak got the authorities
off his back, while the letter did not significantly compromise his artistic
integrity. As Fleishman comments, it was an example of what *Safe Conduct*
described as the 'inessentials bearing witness to [a poet's] concessions to pity
and coercion'.[41]

Polikarpov's 'popular wrath' hit the pages of *Literaturnaya gazeta* on 1st

November. An editorial note stated the paper had been inundated with letters from citizens in all walks of life condemning Pasternak, and a double-page selection of these followed. None of the accusers had read *Doctor Zhivago*, and some letters were from folk with only basic literacy. One distressing indictment came from Pasternak's Georgian translatee Iraklii Abashidze.[42] The theme of his treachery was also rehearsed in the national and provincial media. The wave of printed and broadcast abuse lasted several days and faded only gradually.

Although none was printed, *Literaturnaya gazeta* is known to have received some letters from within the country supporting Pasternak. The very next day after reaching agreement with Polikarpov, Pasternak was deluged with mail. Some letters condemned, and some were gratuitously wounding. But there were many that offered praise, support and sympathy, and they came not just from Russians (some of whom had read one of the circulating typescripts of *Zhivago*) but from hosts of foreign readers. As Pasternak told a correspondent in December, 'The local storms and anathematisation are nothing compared to what comes and reaches out to me from the world as a whole.'[43]

There was also vocal resistance from some Soviet citizens to the authorities' treatment of Pasternak. In November 1958 Ehrenburg stood up to a publisher who wanted to censor a passage extolling Pasternak's virtues as a poet, and in an interview with the *Saturday Review* in 1959 he described Pasternak as an unfortunate victim of Cold War tensions, and maintained the public should have had chance to read and evaluate his novel.[44] Even Sholokhov defended a similar view in Paris in April 1959, although he spoke disparagingly of the novel itself. Such liberal pronouncements by establishment figures aroused disquiet at Central Committee level.[45] In summer of 1959, clearly implying Pasternak though without naming him, Margarita Aliger published an eloquent poetic address to any generalised author urging him to write no matter what the cost, and to have faith in his work.[46]

Apart from thousands of supporting messages, Pasternak's mail also contained various exotica – chain letters, American parents arranging 'showers' for their daughters, money requests from individuals and charities, invitations to lecture, a professorship offered at Florida State University, and a New York Jew reviling Pasternak in the wake of David Ben-Gurion's own condemnation of *Doctor Zhivago* for its disloyalty to the Jewish nation.[47]

By various routes Pasternak heard of other tributes to his work. The British *Sunday Times* voted *Zhivago* the novel of the year, in Italy it won the 1958 Bancarella Prize, and other tributes came from Poland and elsewhere.[48] The post also contained several foreign press clippings, newspapers and magazines, with reactions both to the novel and to the recent campaign. Round the world, there was public support even from such bodies as the Austrian

Communist Party. Powerful advocacy came from celebrities such as Camus, Alberto Moravia, Henri Troyat and the Icelandic socialist writer Halldór Laxness; Ernest Hemingway offered Pasternak a home if he were driven from his native land; Słonimski, the chairman of the Polish Writers' Union, also publicly defended him in early December. At state level, Queen Elisabeth of Belgium wrote to Voroshilov,[49] and Prime Minister Nehru of India criticised Pasternak's treatment at a press conference on 7 November and, according to Ehrenburg, personally telephoned Khrushchev. It was Pasternak's considered view that these various pressures from abroad were what saved him from exile.[50]

During November the storm of public abuse abated, giving way to a suffocating silence and isolation. In town, Pasternak's name as translator was removed from posters at the Maly and Arts Theatres. Microphone and personal surveillance of Ivinskaya and her contacts in Peredelkino was intensified. At one point drunken hooligans hurled stones at the dacha windows and shouted abuse.[51] It was a period when all but a few faithful friends dropped away. The reasons were apparent, Pasternak condemned no one and only occasionally commented – to the Ivanovs, for instance, he dropped an ironic remark that 'Andrei [Voznesensky] has evidently settled on another planet'. Meanwhile he enjoyed casual contact and banter with ordinary folk in Peredelkino, including the local militiaman, and also valued the company of Irina Emelyanova, and of Yurii Pankratov and Gennadii Aigi, two friends of hers who later made names with their own poetry,[52] as well as Koma Ivanov, Kostya Bogatyrev and others.

At the same time Pasternak also made the acquaintance of some foreign newsmen. The German correspondent Gerd Ruge first visited him in 1957; while writing a short book about Pasternak, he was introduced to Ivinskaya; in February of 1959 he also brought 12,000 roubles from Kurt Wolff, part of the accumulating royalties from Pantheon Books.[53]

Ruge subsequently introduced Ivinskaya and Pasternak to Heinz Schewe, correspondent for *Die Welt*, who first visited the dacha at the height of the Nobel affair. Schewe became a valued friend of Ivinskaya and the people around her, and performed favours that included ferrying letters back and forth to Western Europe in his red Volkswagen.[54] He was also a friend of Feltrinelli's and acted as his courier and agent. Via him, Feltrinelli eventually warned Pasternak against further contact with d'Angelo. The latter had left Moscow in autumn 1958, and after his translation of the autobiographical essay appeared with Feltrinelli in December 1958, he broke with his publisher, claiming a share in the *Zhivago* profits. D'Angelo had meanwhile been authorised by Pasternak to transfer funds from Feltrinelli to Moscow, but as Jacqueline de Proyart later realised, d'Angelo was a 'free cannon' whose dare-devil currency operations jeopardised everyone involved. Schewe also warned both Pasternak and Ivinskaya of risks that could arise from Feltrinelli's misunderstanding of the Soviet situation. (A typical 'Western' communist, Feltrinelli continued to believe Pasternak's problems arose entirely because of a factional struggle within the Soviet leadership.) Ivinskaya was to pay dearly for not heading Schewe's advice, and as events proved, the KGB were well aware of all the gifts and money transfers from d'Angelo and others.[55]

Bruised and exhausted as the campaign against him receded, Pasternak resumed contact with Oxford on 10 November and sent a cable: 'Tempest not yet over do not grieve be firm and quiet tired loving believing in the future – Boris.' However, his actual mood was maybe better reflected in a letter next day to his Leningrad cousin Maria Markova: 'This is a very difficult time for me. It would be best of all to die right now, but probably I shall not lay hands on myself.' He also later tried to relieve his sisters of responsibility for any of their own initiatives, since whether or not they protested on his behalf this would change little in his overall fate.[56]

Amid the general diminuendo of abuse, there were still occasional salvoes of invective, sometimes spontaneous, sometimes provoked. In early December at the first Constituent Congress of Writers of the RSFSR there were virulent attacks on Pasternak by Surkov and other conservatives, and Sergei Smirnov added a new charge of corrupting the youth. He cited especially the young poets Kharabarov and Pankratov who allegedly led a cult of Pasternak at the Literary Institute, for which they were eventually expelled from Komsomol and exiled to Kazakhstan.[57]

Another explosion of official wrath was provoked by an interview with British journalist Alan Moray Williams. In the *News Chronicle* of 19 January 1959, Pasternak was recorded as defending the modern artist's independence in an 'Age of Technocracy'. The artist was described as 'the Faust of modern society', an isolated individualist who must inevitably strike conformist minds as a 'semi-madman'. Pasternak went on to state that 'The Union of Soviet Writers would like me to go on my knees to them – but they will never make me.' Broadcast back to Russia by Western radio, this statement nullified the effect of his two penitential letters and publicly confirmed that they were written under duress.[58]

At about the same time Pasternak privately drafted another letter in a resentful and aggressive tone: 'I realise [. . .] that I have no rights. That [. . .] I can be crushed like a midge, and nobody will say a word. But [. . .] before that

5 and 6 Boris Pasternak in his study at Peredelkino during the last year of his life

stage, someone somewhere will take pity on me [. . .] I was stupid to expect signs of generosity and largesse in response to those two letters.'[59] The message was never sent, and it somehow – maybe through Ivinskaya's carelessness – fell into the hands of the KGB and was placed in Pasternak's dossier.

Finally, in January 1959, giving way to a fit of despair, Pasternak considered the idea of going with Ivinskaya to Tarusa, to stay as guests of Paustovsky. But on 20 January, their scheduled departure date, he announced that he could not go through with a plan that would cause his innocent family to suffer. Ivinskaya left in fury and returned to Potapovsky Lane. There she was called up by Polikarpov, who was livid at the newspaper interview and demanded that she halt any further acts of folly by Pasternak. The official thus found himself in the odd role of peacemaker. Pasternak was not required to retract his remarks to the *News Chronicle*, and relations with Ivinskaya were later repaired by a telephone call made from the Peredelkino writers' club.[60]

During the last ten days of the month Pasternak composed four 'January additions of 1959' that were added to the manuscript of *When Weather Clears*. Among them, 'God's World' was a cheery reflection on the writer's postal exchanges with half the globe, while 'Days One and Only' ('Edinstvennye dni') bathed the cycle in the warm light of happy reconcilement:

> And half-dozing clock-hands are too idle
> To circle round the dial.
> One day last longer than an age.
> Embraces never tire.   (III, 110; *SP*, 488; *SS*, II, 130)

The best-known poem of the group – 'The Nobel Prize' ('Nobelevskaya premiya') – was probably written on or soon after 20 January, at a moment of darkest gloom after parting from Ivinskaya. It was the pained protest of a poet trapped like some wild creature and with no way of escape. Soon afterward, the poem was reworked; allusions to his paramour as his 'right hand' were removed, and it thus remained with a more positive ending, stating a belief in the powers of good.[61] Even with such an ending and after removal of personal specifics, the poem eloquently confirmed Pasternak's dismal mood and reluctant rejection of the Nobel Prize. It was in this frame of mind that he on 26 January wrote a further letter to Khrushchev. Unlike his earlier messages, it had a more genuine personal tone and merely requested that, despite any other forfeits, he be allowed still to earn his living by translation work. There was no direct response, but over the next few months there were signs that his request had been heeded. Another concern which did not abate, however, was Pasternak's fear that Ivinskaya rather than he himself might yet be arrested; in this event he arranged with Jacqueline de Proyart to send a telegram announcing that someone in the family was sick with scarlet fever.[62]

Through his own insouciance, or naïveté, and a journalist's indiscretion, 'The

Nobel Prize' poem further aggravated Pasternak's troubles. On the 30 January he was visited by Anthony Brown of the *Daily Mail,* and by A. Echeparri, a Uruguayan journalist, who was accompanied by an official from the Ministry of Foreign Affairs. The latter knew no English and could not follow the details of the conversation, but he later reported that Pasternak seemed relaxed and natural, and also concerned to be reassured that there was no offence in his receiving foreigners. In the official's presence Pasternak handed Brown a copy of one of his allegedly 'old poems' for sending to a friend in Paris. The work in question was 'The Nobel Prize', and although Brown eventually mailed it to Jacqueline de Proyart, on returning he also published a translation of the poem in his paper on 11 February, together with a crude political commentary.[63]

Pasternak heard of Brown's misdeed the same day, from the *Daily Express* correspondent who arrived at the dacha hoping to collect material for a report. Pasternak was dismayed and later told Henry Shapiro, the United Press correspondent, he would have no more dealings with meddlesome newsmen, and he signed a statement denouncing Brown's action. In Shapiro's presence Zinaida also upbraided her husband for his Western press contacts, although as she later realised, this merely encouraged correspondents to go to Ivinskaya and also drew Boris away from hearth and home.[64]

The authorities regarded the episode as a deliberate act of defiance, and immediately cut off Pasternak's mail again. Polikarpov phoned Ivinskaya and instructed that Pasternak cease all contact with the press. Furthermore, since a British parliamentary delegation headed by Harold Macmillan was to visit Russia from 21 February to 3 March, with risk of a cohort of foreign newsmen descending on Peredelkino, or of a delegation member requesting a meeting with the disgraced author, Pasternak was advised to remove himself from the Moscow area, for his own good. He at first angrily objected. But with Zinaida it was then decided to take up a standing invitation to visit Nina Tabidze in Tbilisi. Pasternak chose this in preference to travelling with Ivinskaya, and after a bitter quarrel, she departed in a huff to visit Leningrad relatives. On 20 February Pasternak and Zinaida left by air for Tbilisi.[65]

Nina Tabidze's apartment in the Georgian capital commanded a fine view of the city, with the Daryal Gorge and Mount Kazbek in the distance. She lived with her daughter Nita, son-in-law and grandson, and despite shortage of space they freed up one room so that Pasternak could maintain something of his normal routine. Abashidze had warned Nina against seeking any publicity, and official literary circles had been primed to arrange nothing in his honour. Pasternak spent most of the time reading Proust and Faulkner and roaming the streets of Tbilisi together with Nita Tabidze. In the evenings he happily joined the company of young friends – an assortment of mainly actors, poets and artists – whom she invited home.[66]

With time on his hands, Pasternak also attended to correspondence and wrote several conciliatory letters to Ivinskaya. In them, *inter alia*, he repeatedly talked of a need to live more slowly and simply, and he also recalled a suggestion from Polikarpov that 'I should draw my horns in, calm down and write for the future'.[67]

Despite his incognito, news spread of Pasternak's visit, and there were several festive reunions with the families of Leonidze and Chikovani. Friendship also blossomed with the artist Gudiashvili who arranged a gathering at his home in Pasternak's honour, and the conversation and candlelit recitations among the pictures made an indelible impression. Pasternak also struck up a tender friendship with Gudiashvili's ballerina daughter Chukurtma, with whom he afterwards corresponded.[68]

One tragic event occurred as a result of the Georgian visit however. The elderly poet Galaktion Tabidze, already mentally disturbed after a life of persecution, was harrassed by the authorities to write a letter to the press condemning Pasternak during his visit, and in a fit of despair he committed suicide by throwing himself from the balcony of a mental hospital. It was a horrifying reminder of the actor Yakhontov's suicide in 1945 after attempts to recruit him to inform on Pasternak. All of which emphasised that while Pasternak was himself untouched, those who associated with him were endangered.[69]

While in the south, Pasternak had the idea for a new novel about Georgia. In it modern geologists unearthing relics of the third century AD and of early Christianity in Georgia would discover their fates to be closely interlinked with a distant past. For a few weeks after returning to Moscow, Pasternak pursued the idea; he had Asmus bring books from the University library and wrote asking Margvelashvili for further literature on Georgian saints and archaeology. Eventually, however, the idea was abandoned in favour of other projects.[70]

After two and a half weeks in Georgia, Pasternak appeared healthier, stronger and more buoyant. He returned however to face the aftermath of the incident of 'The Nobel Prize' poem. In the late morning of 14 March, an official black Volga arrived at the dacha and Pasternak was escorted into town to the office of Chief Prosecutor Rudenko. In preparation, Rudenko had actually drafted arrangements for stripping him of his citizenship, although he stopped short of that extreme measure.[71] The 'man without a neck' told him his actions rendered him liable under article 64 of the USSR Penal Code, and he was threatened with arrest if he continued his duplicitous anti-patriotic activities. Pasternak refused to sign any undertaking not to receive foreign visitors, but gave Rudenko a verbal assurance and said it was up to the authorities to impose a tighter cordon if they saw fit. After signing a protocol recording his answers to Rudenko's questions, he was then delivered back to Peredelkino by an official car in mid-afternoon. Shortly afterwards, Ivinskaya was also summoned to the Lubyanka and in similar wise ordered to avoid foreigners.[72]

In his report, Rudenko stated that during the interview Pasternak 'behaved like a coward' but evidently drew 'the obvious conclusions' from the threat of arrest. On the latter point Rudenko was correct. Aware of his lucky escape, Pasternak wrote next day to his sisters of his 'fatal imprudence with the poor poem', and for the postal censor's benefit paid tribute to 'the meekness and humanity of our powers towards me'.[73]

In Peredelkino a notice appeared on the front door of the dacha stating in English, French and German that 'Pasternak does not receive. He is forbidden to receive foreigners'. Notes to this effect remained posted for the next several months, although their wording varied as would-be visitors kept removing them as mementoes. However, not all visitors were so repelled, and the rule was not rigorously enforced. The authorities took their own measures to 'frustrate Pasternak's contacts however. On 27 April Professor Nils Nilsson of Stockholm was intercepted at Peredelkino station and told to return to town. Pasternak was barely able to have any contact with his old friend Brice Parain who visited Moscow in spring. American journalist Patricia Blake was merely greeted from the top step of the porch, where Pasternak read the letter she had brought and apologised for not inviting her in; a few others who turned up were also regaled with nothing more than a walk and talk in the garden. In early May, after an invitation to visit the Swedish Embassy, Pasternak was warned via Ivinskaya not to attend. The proferred reward for this compliance – release of payment for the 'frozen' Słowacki translation – was not forthcoming however.[74]

There was meanwhile blatant and continued surveillance of the dacha. Vehicles with electronic equipment were regularly stationed nearby. Possibly, at their own level of competence, domestic helpers informed on what they heard and saw, and in February 1959 KGB chief Shelepin reported to the Central Committee details such as Pasternak's birthday guest list and his various foreign press contacts and other visitors. Ivinskaya herself was described as 'very anti-Soviet', a 'bad influence' on Pasternak, and 'could be qualified as intelligent, but is morally corrupt' – a view shared, incidentally, by several of Pasternak's friends and family.[75]

Although the January letter to Khrushchev was evidently heeded, the economic blockade around Pasternak was not immediately lifted. However, from various quarters came proposals that he request to be reinstated in the Writers' Union – 'which inevitably involves the renunciation of my book. But that shall never be,' he told Nina Tabidze. There were also 'comradely' suggestions that he assist his rehabilitation by writing a poem in praise of the Soviet 'sputnik' programme, or an open 'Peace Letter' to Mr Nehru. Such humiliating gestures were of course rejected out of hand.[76]

During early summer, however, some of the clouds began to lift. The Third Congress of Soviet Writers in May was a humdrum affair but marked by a note of liberalism. Khrushchev's address to the meeting emphasised tolerance, writers' freedom to err, and the need to handle literary matters in a comradely fashion without appeal to the Party. 'Revisionists' were given a freer rein and old-guard dogmatists were restrained. Symptomatic was the removal of Surkov as Union Secretary – allegedly due partly to his mismanagement of the *Zhivago* affair. He was replaced by Fedin. (On 23 April Pasternak had met Fedin in the road and shaken him by the hand, aware that by 'forgiving' his co-executioner he had also managed to put one over him.) Other encouraging changes were the liberal Tvardovsky's appointment to the Union secretariat, and the reactionary Kochetov's replacement by poet Sergei Vasilyevich Smirnov as editor of *Literaturnaya gazeta*.[77]

Though uninvolved in these events, Pasternak benefitted indirectly from the improved atmosphere: his name reappeared on the Arts Theatre notices where *Maria Stuart* was playing. Also, despite Polevoi's charge that poems such as 'The Soul', 'Change' and 'The Wind', recently published in Feltrinelli's edition of *Autobiografia e nuovi versi*, were continuing examples of Pasternak's infamy, Polikarpov on 29 May recommended that no action be taken. Later, in August, *Kazakhstanskaya pravda* made favourable note of Pankratov and Kharabarov, who in 1958 had been drummed out of Komsomol on Pasternak's account.[78] These and other circumstances suggested an official decision to palliate the Pasternak problem by simply ignoring him. And indeed the Central Committee dossier on him remained virtually inactive for the remaining months of his life.

None of this denoted an official pardon and reprieve however, Pasternak remained unsure about the liberties he could take, and he continued to regard his situation with misgiving and uncertainty.

Domestic neglect contrasted with Pasternak's awareness of his celebrity overseas, and he relished and enthused over his foreign correspondence and vicarious fame. He evidently did this at his last meeting with Akhmatova at Koma Ivanov's thirtieth birthday party on 21 August, when there seemed to be a latent psychological duel beneath her queenly dignity and his vivacious loquacity. She was irritated by trifling details of his behaviour and later contrasted Shostakovich's fame, worn like a hunch on his back, with Pasternak, who wore his like a crown that was hastily crammed on his head and kept slipping. Clearly, though, Akhmatova had problems with her own shameful neglect, for which Pasternak was not guilty.[79]

Apart from daily shoals of routine 'fan mail', requests for pictures and autographs, several significant new correspondences arose. Walter Philipp, whom Pasternak had tutored before the Revolution, wrote to him from Berlin in January 1959. Correspondence continued with Boris Zaitsev in Paris, who sent copies of his own recent writings. There were also exchanges with poets Stephen Spender and T. S. Eliot. In answer to letters from Bengali poet and Harvard Professor Amiya Chakravarty, Pasternak wrote something on Tagore and via Chakravarty also sent thanks to Mr Nehru for the support he had shown. In December 1959, Chakravarty travelled to Moscow and met Pasternak.[80]

Pasternak's mail brought several invitations to travel. However, official reaction was uncertain and there were no guarantees of an unhindered return passage. Apart from which, he was loath to disrupt his work schedule and turned all offers down, which included lecture programmes in the USA and Britain, and invitations to a Dostoevsky memorial dinner in Chicago in December 1959, Chekhov celebrations in Stuttgart in January 1960, and a Tolstoy commemoration in Venice in July.[81]

Correspondence and visitors from abroad also became a source of extended foreign reading in Pasternak's final years. Letters and the books on his shelves indicated an interest in, or new awareness of, Camus, Claudel, Teilhard de Chardin (sent by Jacqueline de Proyart), Kafka, Kierkegaard (who struck a specially sympathetic note), Nietzsche's letters, Virginia Woolf, various works by D. H. Lawrence, Lawrence Durrell, Pär Lagerkvist, and some modern American novels. In December 1959 Renate Schweitzer sent him poems by Li Tai-Po, with whom she perceived a certain kinship. On the other hand, Mallac is probably right in believing that little of what Pasternak read in his later years genuinely excited him.[82]

It is true that not much of his known reading matter related closely to his current creative endeavours. While still working on the novel he had told Valentin Berestov, 'Don't get upset. It's not just you I haven't read. I haven't read Slutsky, Evtushenko, Vinokurov, and someone else they say is very good [. . .] I cannot get worked up about the microscopic differences between you all.' Although personally well disposed, he felt little artistic sympathy with Zabolotsky. He did, however, like the work of the young Viktor Bokov, later appreciated the somewhat similar talent of Voznesensky, and approved the original poetic work of Gennadii Aigi. Evtushenko believed Pasternak probably liked his own youth and energy more than his actual verse, despite speaking favourably of his work. In the mid 1950s, despite the sensation caused by Dudintsev's *Not By Bread Alone*, Pasternak admitted to not having read it, although he was enthusiastic about Yashin's artistically mediocre story 'The Levers' ('Rychagi').[83]

Inevitably, Pasternak took a keen interest in his own foreign publications. While he was happy to see editions of the novel, autobiography and recent verse, and approved 'the token of a free developing vital future, and evidence of its obvious germs', some translators' and publishers' interest in earlier works consigned to oblivion was something he described to Lydia as 'an objectionable disorder'.[84] He had strong private reservations therefore about George Reavey and Eugene Kayden's translation plans. He also disliked the versions by Henry Kamen, despite their endorsement by Oxford cognoscenti. As he told his elder sister, he liked 'only translations of great rhythmical might and precipitation, masterly rhymed and precise'.[85] Thus, for instance, he approved the English versions produced by his sister Lydia (although professional translators such as Chukovsky were sharply critical). Other versions of his work which he specially admired were the French and German renderings by Michel Aucouturier and Rolf-Dietrich Keil.[86]

In early summer of 1959, after reassurance by Polikarpov, Pasternak resumed professional translation work. The previous autumn he had been introduced to translator Nikolai Lyubimov by Koma Ivanov. In spring a contract was signed with Iskusstvo publishers for a version of *The Steadfast Prince (Il principe constante)* from the Spanish of Calderón, and Ivinskaya assisted by delivering various draft episodes to Lyubimov and returning them with his notes and corrections.[87] Working from a French translation and Schlegel's German, Pasternak's first impression was that Calderón paled at the side of Shakespeare. He complained to his visitor Yurii Glazov in August that it was 'difficult, complicated' and 'a mass of borrowed Mediterranean words'. Later, though, quite apart from the financial incentive, he warmed to the Spanish dramatist's world, and in autumn reported he was 'translating Calderón from morn till night, as once I did with *Faust* [. . .] it was pleasant to come upon a totally unknown phenomenon [. . .] a quite special world, very highly developed, brilliant and profound.' The translation was reported complete after three weeks' intensive work, on 3 November, and it was published in a Calderón collection in 1961.[88]

In various responses to press cuttings and articles sent from abroad Pasternak set a finer focus on his approach to the Russian novel and *Doctor Zhivago* in particular. In a negative review in the *Anglo-Soviet Journal*, left-wing author Jack Lindsay criticised *Zhivago*'s weak characterisation, diffuseness and poor motivation, all of which Pasternak refuted in a letter of 18 April to Lydia. As he realised, the journal's ideological slant precluded any eulogy. Yet Lindsay seemed blind even to the distinction between tradition and innovation. Indeed, while 'incoherence, inaction, lack of movement, of plot and consistency' were qualities that Tolstoy criticised in Chekhov's plays, the 'replacement and effacing of lines and limits' were qualities that captivated him in Chekhov's prose.[89]

Pasternak had strong reservations about the American critic Edmund Wilson's interpretations based on a detailed symbolic 'decoding' of his novel. While acknowledging the presence of a few obvious 'symbols' – e.g. in the surname of the central hero, or in certain reverberative images such as the burning candle or the rowan tree – Pasternak dismissed 'false idiotic attempts' to read the novel as a labyrinthine cryptogram.[90] Hearing of these objections, which were spelt out to several correspondents, the *Encounter* editor Stephen Spender invited Pasternak to send an article elaborating his views. So as to avoid trouble over unsanctioned foreign publications, Pasternak responded in the form of a letter that was subsequently much cited, and in which he justified the novel's seeming lack of causal motivation, its coincidences and pale characterisation.[91] All in all, however, Pasternak saw too few of the perceptive foreign articles on *Zhivago*, and this was the probable reason why he turned down Kurt Wolff's idea for a published 'Monument to Zhivago' consisting of the best critical essays and reviews.[92]

It was partly to elucidate his own view of 'realism' in the novel and his condemnation of self-indulgent or fantasy-ridden 'romanticism', that Pasternak tried to engage publishers' attention with his essay of 1945 on Chopin. Stephen Spender showed some interest from *Encounter*, and it was translated by Keil in *Die Zeit* in November 1959 after Pasternak discussed it at some length in a letter to Renate Schweitzer.[93] The theses of the article also figured in several letters and conversations of the late 1950s.

Apart from the Georgian novel project, during winter and spring of 1959, Pasternak apparently briefly considered another narrative, reminiscent of Nabokov's *Glory* (*Podvig*, 1932), – about the clandestine return to Soviet Russia of an émigré patriot. The story never got beyond the vague planning stage, however, and its theme obviously excluded any prospect of publication in the USSR.[94] By mid 1959, however, a more promising concept began to germinate, and Pasternak became sufficiently absorbed to abandon his letter-writing. He stayed in Peredelkino and worked at it all summer, while Leonid took Zinaida and Nina Tabidze by car to the Baltic coast, and Evgenii, his wife and infant son Pyotr ('Petya') came to stay at the dacha. (That summer, Josephine Pasternak and her husband visited Jacqueline de Proyart in Paris.)[95]

The new work was for the stage, a genre that usually excited Pasternak each time he engaged in extensive translation of other dramatists (in this case Schiller, Słowacki and Calderón). Laborious but exhilarating, the work became a test of his own 'blessed, unheard, thrilling, Goethe-like, strenuous and fruitful sort of existence'. The project acquired for him the same stature as his novel, and as he informed Zaitsev in the autumn, after an initial piece of lighthearted 'tomfoolery or mere endeavour' it had become 'a cherished activity and a matter of passion'.[96]

Pasternak's drama trilogy was on a Russian historical subject. Its title, *Blind Beauty (Slepaya krasavitsa)*, denoted a composite image of Russia derived from Blok's poem *Retribution (Vozmezdie)* and from Bely's reading of Gogol's *The Terrible Vengeance*, in which an evil sorcerer captures the soul of the sleeping heroine Katerina.[97] The trilogy was set in three different periods and illustrated the spiritual awakening and 'un-blinding' of Russia as it emerged from a tyrannical serf-owning society to the enlightenment of the late nineteenth century; all this was symbolically represented by the fate of a peasant girl Lyusha, blinded in an accident caused by her master's fury, but later restored to sight. Evidently, this was an intended parallel with Russia's modern-day emergence from the dark age of Stalinism, and it thus reinforced the message in the epilogue of *Doctor Zhivago*.

In January of 1960, when the trilogy was still far from completion, Pasternak gave a detailed synopsis of the proposed action to Olga Carlisle, the granddaughter of novelist Leonid Andreyev who visited him from America.[98] For all their interest, however, Pasternak's outline and the completed scenes from the Prologue and Act 1 confirmed an earlier impression that, despite his enthusiasm, Pasternak had little aptitude for stage writing. After suppressing an onrush of poetic inspiration in the mid 1950s, Pasternak never found his way to the 'further new goals' and the 'grandeur avant toute chose' which he declared as a prime quest in the last year of his life.[99] However, he was absorbed by his play, and several times during the winter give spirited readings of it to Ivinskaya and other friends. Some of the *dramatis personae* almost acquired a life of their own – the former nihilist and future populist Vetkhopeshchernikov, and Prokhor the peasant who rose to be a merchant and entrepreneur.[100] As gestures of recognition to new friends in France and Sweden, Pasternak also introduced the real-life figure of Dumas (père) who visited Russia in 1858, and a Swedish Lieutenant Rimmars.

In his play Pasternak evidently attempted to recreate an impression of 'perceived reality' similar to the one pursued in *Doctor Zhivago*. As preparation he read extensively on the history of the Russian serf theatre and reforms of the 1860s. Eventually, though, he abandoned these researches. 'After all,' as he told Olga Carlisle, 'what is important is not the historical accuracy of the work, but the successful recreation of an era. It is not the object described that matters, but the light that falls on it – like that from a lamp in the distant room'.[101]

First rumours of *Blind Beauty* immediately aroused interest abroad. There were enquiries in autumn 1959 from the Swedish publisher of *Zhivago* Georg Svensson and from London publisher Paul Elek, and Lydia Pasternak Slater was approached to translate it by the New York agent Kurt Hellmer. British producer Basil Ashmore showed interest in mounting it, and there was talk of a production by the Royal Drama Theatre in Stockholm and in various German theatres. All this was somewhat premature however. The project progressed slowly despite a 'sprout of reality' in the manuscript which Lydia was told about in the winter.[102]

While the work was still in embryonic state, in November 1959 Pasternak wrote to Feltrinelli via Heinz Schewe, suggesting that he might eventually wish to publish the play, and he commissioned Jacqueline de Proyart in due course to sign it up with Feltrinelli, or failing that with Gallimard or Collins. He also asked Lydia to urge patience on all enquirers, although he realised that once the play was finished, Feltrinelli would most likely bid to snap it up and control its translation and distribution. Privately, Pasternak by now had few illusions about the acquisitiveness of Feltrinelli; in practice and from afar, however, it was easier to continue accommodating him than to engage in combat.[103]

Earning immense wealth to which he had no access and with his artistic fate controlled from Milan, Pasternak's relationship with Feltrinelli became strangely similar to that of Y-3 and his rich patron in the prose *Story* (above, p. 10). This maybe provoked one of his more humorously bizarre suggestions to de Proyart in late 1959 – that when he died, Feltrinelli should purchase his body from the Soviets and bury it in Milan, where Ivinskaya should be permitted to come as guardian of the tomb! By the end of 1958, according to one source, Feltrinelli had deposited $900,000 to Pasternak's credit in a Swiss bank account; other sources suggest more modest, though still considerable sums. Fearing these funds could be used for nefarious anti-Soviet purposes, Polikarpov proposed that Pasternak should contribute them to the International Peace Fund.[104]

Despite a trickle of royalties from theatre performances and the receipt of small converted rouble sums from abroad, in his last two years Pasternak was in financial straits and wondered incredulously that at the age of seventy he still seemed unable to feed his family. In early 1959, Chukovsky lent him 5,000 roubles, and Gerd Ruge in March loaned the equivalent of another five thousand dollars.[105] On 11 January 1959 Pasternak wrote to Grigorii Khesin, the director of Authors' Rights, complaining that promises to lift the embargo on his translations had not been honoured; *Faust* had not been republished; Słowacki's *Maria Stuart* lay gathering dust; and verse translations published in *Verses about Georgia (Stikhi o Gruzii)* were still unpaid for. As a way out of the impasse, he even suggested 'swapping' fees with various Western authors such as Hemingway and Laxness who were owed rouble royalties for Soviet editions of their work. Eventually, on 1 April Pasternak applied for leave to draw the cash deposited by foreign publishers in a Norwegian bank. Despite his offer to contribute part of the sum to Litfond to assist aged writers, Polikarpov and Furtseva ruled that the funds should not be touched. At their meeting, however, Polikarpov hinted that so long as Pasternak quietened down, 'it wouldn't be so bad if they even brought you your money in a bag'.[106] This, according to Ivinskaya, was taken as an implicit go-ahead to make private arrangements to acquire the funds.

Through various couriers Pasternak had in fact already received some payments. In January 1959, Kurt Wolff sent 12,000 roubles (the approximate average annual earnings of a Soviet citizen), and Feltrinelli sent another 80,000 via Schewe in May. After this there seemed to be a prospect of earning via translation again, although de Proyart continued arranging for various amounts to be delivered in converted rouble sums in August and November, and a further 6,000 roubles from Gallimard were brought by Georges Nivat in December 1959.[107]

In more difficult times Pasternak had been generous with family and friends. (His first wife and son used to receive a thousand roubles monthly.) Accumulating foreign credits now untied his hands further and he detailed de Proyart to have Feltrinelli dispatch gifts to various friends abroad. Owing to Feltrinelli's reluctance to collaborate, it was some time before payment was made. But handouts of $5,000 eventually went to a few of his more valued correspondents, and to each of the English, French, Danish, German and Italian translators of the novel, with sums of twice this amount to his assistants in France and various German and Italian couriers.[108]

The contretemps between Feltrinelli and de Proyart was part of what

Schewe called the 'unholy mess' arising from contradictory letters, contracts and mandates, and Pasternak's inability to resolve from afar the problems these created. But matters were exacerbated by Feltrinelli's view of every action by de Proyart as a challenge to his own monopolistic ambitions. (His desperado maximalism in all things was ultimately best exemplified by the manner of his death – blown up while engaging in left-wing sabotage activity in 1972.) Feltrinelli thus shared none of her aesthetic reservations regarding the sale of film rights to *Doctor Zhivago*, and he sent a stream of bitter complaints about her lack of cooperation. Deeply alarmed by this rebellion against his 'French guardian angel' and aware that Feltrinelli was little better than other capitalist sharks, Pasternak refused to let emotions boil over in his correspondence and still protested gratitude to the 'true and noble friend' who had defended his novel.[109]

True to character, in the summer of 1959 Feltrinelli began sending verbal requests for a new, backdated contract that would give him control over all Pasternak's past and future publications. Pasternak did not refuse, but insisted that only de Proyart was entitled to negotiate and sign this. Meanwhile the discord between publisher and attorney extended to the former's threat of legal action against both de Proyart and Gallimard. The publicity arising from this could have seriously compromised Pasternak with the Soviet authorities, and this risk (which typically aroused most panic in Ivinskaya) caused Pasternak to back down and urge de Proyart to appease Feltrinelli and allow him to dictate terms. Eventually, in January 1960 he himself signed a new contract backdated to 30 June 1956, and wrote to de Proyart hoping that she might remain as his counsellor and representative, but in a 'passive role'. The absurdity of such an arrangement, and the risk of being held responsible for actions she was unable to control, led inevitably to her request, on the advice of her lawyer husband, to be relieved of her duties as Pasternak's attorney. In a document dated 12 April 1960, Pasternak complied, but with considerable regret and well aware that she had amply fulfilled all his expectations of her.[110]

Pasternak's further business decisions continued in a similar vein. In April 1959 he had given d'Angelo a signed authority to transfer $100,000 to him in Moscow,[111] and the manner in which Feltrinelli and his associates implemented this was doubtless a factor that aggravated Ivinskaya's fate after Pasternak's death.

Describing his situation to Bely's widow in autumn of 1959, Pasternak wrote:

I can hardly cope with the strange, half-real, fabulous fate that has fallen to me. On the one hand, it is made extremely difficult, continuously threatened, barely tolerable. On the other, it is undeservedly bright and somehow [. . .] more freed of inessential and random elements and borne to a loftier level than I ever dared hope.[112]

It was in this 'airborne' state that Pasternak spoke with the American conductor Leonard Bernstein. Anxious for a meeting, Bernstein had cabled from Leningrad in advance, and he and his wife were invited to Peredelkino and later met Pasternak again after the New York Philharmonic Orchestra concert on 11 September. To his complaint at the outrageous behaviour of officials from the Ministry of Culture, Pasternak's repost was: 'What have ministers got to do with it? The artist communes with God, and God puts on various performances so that he has something to write about. This can be a farce, as in your case; or it can be a tragedy – but that is a secondary matter.' Bernstein was evidently delighted at this formulation of their problem.[113]

At an earthly level, however, Pasternak took heed of ministerial and Party prohibitions, which included avoiding any provocative or unsanctioned activities. He therefore turned down Oleg Prokofiev's invitation to contribute to *Sintaksis*, a new dissident journal.[114] He also declined an invitation from India to write something on Quasimodo, the new Nobel Laureate who the previous year had spoken out against Pasternak's own award![115] However, after the liberalisation of May 1959 Pasternak was slightly bolder in some of his communications. For the Cologne magazine *Magnum* he wrote a note in German in answer to an editorial questionnaire on the subject 'Was ist der Mensch?' (What is Man?) to which others, such as Karl Barth, Le Corbusier, Doderer, Robbe-Grillet and Pierre Emmanuel, also responded. In his answer Pasternak offered a new rejection of Nietzscheanism which he saw embodied in the communist cult of the 'proud sound' of man's name. His stated preference was for Kierkegaard, whom he had recently discovered, and his advocacy of the Gospel message of self-sacrifice carried strong echoes of Vedenyapin's disquisition in chapter one of the novel, announcing that 'Man is real and true when he is active, when he is a craftsman, a farmer, or a great – unforgettably great – artist, or a creative scholar, a discoverer of truths.'[116]

Despite the liberalisation, there were still irksome reminders of official disfavour. In September, Lydia's son, Nicolas Pasternak Slater, was denied a visa for postgraduate study in Russia under the Anglo-Soviet Cultural Agreement, and initial hopes that this decision would be rescinded proved in vain.[117]

In late 1959 a further overture came from the Writers' Union suggesting Pasternak should apply for readmission. Pasternak refused categorically. As he remarked to family members, 'they all showed themselves up at that time, and now they think that everything can be forgotten.'[118]

In September Pasternak showed his face in public for the first time since his troubles. Apart from the New York Philharmonic concert on the 11th, he attended Stanislav Neigauz's recital in the House of Scholars on Sunday 20th. In the autumn he also ventured out to the theatre. With Ivinskaya he saw Hauptmann's *Before Sundown (Vor Sonnenuntergang)* at the Vakhtangov Theatre with Astangov and Tselikovskaya. Centred on the tragic love of a man of seventy for a young girl and the havoc caused by this, the play depressingly reminded him of his own involvement with Ivinskaya.[119]

Pasternak last appeared in public in mid December at guest performances by the Hamburg Drama Theater. Heinz Schewe obtained three tickets in the front stalls for Goethe's *Faust*, and Pasternak attended with Zinaida and Leonid. He was enthralled by the performance, which included Gustaf Gründgens as Mephisto and vividly incarnated a work so close to his heart for many years. Later, together with Ivinskaya, he saw the company's production of Kleist's *The Broken Pitcher (Der zerbrochene Krug)* and afterwards went backstage again and spent several hours talking with the cast. An invitation to the company to visit him in Peredelkino was cancelled however, owing to concern about the reaction of Zinaida and of even higher authority.[120]

The last two years of Pasternak's life were marked by changes in many old friendships and a discovery of several new ones. One factor was doubtless his awareness of aging, and an energetic desire to stay young and cultivate young company. This was evident in his friendships with Chukurtma Gudiashvili and Nita Tabidze and her friends in Tbilisi, and in correspondence with Renate Schweitzer, which had a tender and passionate Platonism.

Pasternak was also drawn towards the young people that gathered around Ivinskaya thanks to her daughter's student colleagues and friends.[121] Ivinskaya for her own reasons encouraged these connections. She drew Ariadna Efron into her own circle, which slightly irked Pasternak, and attempted to ween Bogatyryov into their company. It was also partly due to her engineering that Pasternak cooled towards the old company he traditionally entertained at home, most of whom refused to acknowledge her. She was largely responsible for Akhmatova's distance in the late 1950s. Moreover, following her emotional entanglement with Shalamov which he then ended, she avenged herself by breaking his friendship with Pasternak; the two men hardly met after 1956.[122]

Independently, however, Pasternak became increasingly tetchy and demanding with some old friends. Some acquaintances, such as Aseyev, were abandoned altogether. Contacts with the Asmus and Neigauz families became rarer and were jolted by a contretemps with Livanov whose excesses under intoxication had long caused irritation. On 13 September 1959, he turned up late to the Pasternaks' Sunday dinner, horribly inebriated and with some male drinking companions in tow. Their gross behaviour, which included toasting Pasternak's artistic genealogy and skill as a translator ended in their being shown the door. A letter from Pasternak followed next day and concluded: 'I do not believe in you. And you will lose nothing by going your own way. I am a faithless friend. I have always said such nice things to you, to Neigauz and Asmus, and may well go on doing so. But of course, what I would most like to do is hang the lot of you.' Some time later, relations were repaired; Livanov returned the letter, and Pasternak apologised to Asmus for his remarks. The Livanovs were later vexed when Ivinskaya abused their privacy and reprinted the letter in her memoirs.[123]

Pasternak's letter of 5 February 1960 to Lydia was the last he wrote to his family abroad. A letter to Chukurtma Gudiashvili of the same date also had a valedictory note:

Some benign forces have brought me close to that world where there are no circles, no fidelity to youthful reminiscences, no distaff points of view – a world of serene, unprejudiced reality, a world where at length and for the first time you are appraised and tested, almost as if at the Last Judgement, judged and measured and relegated or preserved; a world which the artist prepares himself all his life to enter, and to which he is born only after death, a world of posthumous existence for those forces and ideas for which you have found expression.[124]

Pasternak had not quite rung down the curtain however. On 10 February, his seventieth birthday, the weather was cold and snowy, and he seemed youthful and energetic as he arrived for a celebration at Ivinskaya's with Schewe in attendance. There were even jokes over their recent anxieties. 'I could live forever like this', he claimed. 'I am ashamed only of those Polikarpov letters. It's a pity you made me sign them [. . .] But you must admit, we took fright only out of politeness!' (More accurately, of course, it was Ivinskaya who had taken fright.) Among the gifts Pasternak brought home was an alarm clock in a leather case sent by Mr Nehru. Later on, there was a small birthday celebration at the dacha, with the Ivanovs, Elena and Evgenii Tager, family members and a few other guests.[125]

Pasternak's sisters cabled greetings for his birthday, and Lydia sent a lengthy epistle via a forwarding address in France arranged by Georges Nivat. But in the weeks before the spring of his final illness, Pasternak was increasingly aware of time running out. He was preoccupied with his play and radically reduced his letter writing.

On 17 April, apart from family members, the Pasternaks' Easter Sunday dinner party included their perennial house guest Nina Tabidze, the Chikovanis and Leonidze, Genrich Neigauz and his new wife Silvia Eichinger (a Swiss violinist who settled in Russia and played with the Moiseyev Ensemble), and Renate Schweitzer visiting from West Berlin. There were the usual toasts and speeches and Pasternak appeared in good health, though afterwards he looked pale and exhausted.[126]

Pasternak had wanted Schweitzer to postpone her visit, but his message had not reached her in time. Both his health and concern about appearing in public with foreigners led to cancellation of a planned theatre outing. Schweitzer came to Peredelkino a second time on 20 April, before finally departing. Her visit was an emotional occasion for her, although perhaps an anticlimax following their exalted correspondence. After they called on Ivinskaya, Pasternak regretted his affection for Schweitzer had aroused Olga's jealousy. He felt physically drained after seeing off his German guest. Under oath that she reveal nothing to Zinaida, he told Nina Tabidze of his fear that the pains in his back and shoulder were a sign of lung cancer.[127]

The final weeks of Pasternak' life added further confusion to his financial and publishing affairs, with consequences extending long beyond his own lifetime, and raising general doubts about his sound judgement at this juncture. At the centre of this were his relations with Ivinskaya and with his family whom he left totally unprovided for in any testamentary papers.

Three days after freeing Proyart of her duties as attorney, on 15 April he was pressured by Ivinskaya into giving her a letter of authority which was to be dispatched to Feltrinelli. This document, set out in French and Russian, established her as his sole literary heiress with unique control of his rights and estate abroad. She had already been acting as receiver for his foreign royalty payments; in February 40,000 roubles were brought by Italian journalist Leo Palladini, and in March 180,000 roubles in a suitcase were handed over by another Italian visitor to Ivinskaya's daughter.[128] In her letter to Feltrinelli on 5 June, after Pasternak's death, Ivinskaya recommended that he find ways of accommodating Jacqueline de Proyart's counsels, but pointed out that none of Pasternak's family in Russia held any rights to his publications, and she offered assurance that in the event of claims or challenges arising from his relatives abroad, Feltrinelli could rely on her total support. Urgent self-interest thus underlay her vow to 'carry out the wishes and will of Boris after his death as fastidiously as if he were still alive.' Feltrinelli's answering letter of 8 July stated that copies of the old and new contracts 'should not fall into the hands of the state authorities or the Pasternak family'.[129] He and Ivinskaya thus conspired to deprive Pasternak's family of any share in his wealth, and the way was clear for them to exercise virtually complete control over his posthumous financial destiny. There was an element of poetic justice in the fact that they were eventually thwarted – partly by the devil-may-care incaution of Feltrinelli and his Italian associates, partly through Ivinskaya's vain stupidity, and partly by the vindictiveness of the Soviet state.

Pasternak was already ill when he saw Ivinskaya for the last time on Saturday 23 April, at her lodgings in Peredelkino. He was anticipating another delivery of royalties from abroad and left a note with her, should Schewe or one of the Italians turn up. He also produced from his briefcase a copy of the incomplete manuscript of *Blind Beauty*, for her safekeeping until his recovery. She had the fortunate presence of mind to have several typescripts made immediately. One copy was intended for Goslitizdat, and another went to Feltrinelli with a view to eventual publication; the original manuscript was later seized by the KGB.[130]

Pasternak overcame the first symptoms of his final illness by sheer willpower. He ignored bouts of cardiac arhythmia and pains in his shoulder-blade, and during his working day he occasionally lay down until the pain subsided, then resumed writing. Meanwhile he refrained from mentioning his ailments so as to avoid doctors, sanatoriums, and the 'slavery of compassion'.[131]

On Saturday 23 April, he began keeping a diary of his illness, noting pains in his left arm, heart and back, general exhaustion and difficulty in standing at his work desk. Finally, on the 25th he was forced to take to his bed completely; he was examined by Dr Samsonov and, despite his own suspicions, the diagnosis was angina and complete rest was ordered.

Wednesday 27 April saw signs of improvement. Pasternak planned to get up and go to make some phone calls. He was re-examined by one of Dr Votchal's assistants from the Botkin Hospital, and a cardiogram showed no cause for alarm. On the 30th, however, he found he could no longer climb the stairs and a bed was made up for him on a couch in the music room. Between bouts of pain, he continued working on the play, completing a fair copy of act one and making sketches for the continuation. Samsonov's second examination meanwhile confirmed his earlier diagnosis. Conscious of the end approaching, Pasternak on 1 May had Ekaterina Krasheninnikova go over the Orthodox confession service with him.[132]

By 5 May Pasternak recorded feeling 'markedly better'. But that was his last diary entry. The next day he got up and sent a telegram to Renate Schweizer, and also wrote his last letter to Fyodor Stepun, thanking him for his article in

Die Neue Rundschau, and describing his illness as 'extremely painful, even if not threateningly dangerous'.[133] Later on the 6th, however, after deciding to wash his hair, Pasternak suddenly felt very unwell and the doctor was called. In a quavering hand he managed to write a note for delivery to Ivinskaya; on receiving it she went into Moscow to muster some of her own medical contacts. Zinaida too became alarmed and called Pasternak's brother and his wife, who came and stayed on at the dacha for several weeks.[134]

In the night of 7–8 May Pasternak suffered a heart attack. Another consultant, Dr Fogelson, confirmed this, and from now on Dr Anna Golodets from Litfond remained in attendance together with two nurses from the Kremlin Hospital. One of them, Marina Rassokhina, called regularly to report the patient's condition to Ivinskaya each time she came off duty; Vyacheslav Ivanov and the other nurse also delivered various messages and reported on Pasternak's courage in his sufferings. At this point Leonid took leave from the University and stayed at home, helping to shave his father and performing other services. At Boris' request, Nina Tabidze also delayed plans to return to Tbilisi and stayed on to assist.[135]

News of Pasternak's illness reached the foreign press; Western newsmen turned up almost every day, and Aleksandr Pasternak spoke to them out in the lane and updated the reports. On 17 May Boris' sisters in Oxford sent an anxious telegram inquiring details. Aleksandr's wife replied on the 19th saying they were still expecting a favourable outcome. Subsequent cables however charted the hopeless nature of his illness.

Hearing of Pasternak's state, many friends came to visit, including Evgeniya Pasternak, Akhmatova, the Asmuses, Ivanovs, Neigauzes, the Selvinskys and several younger poets; each day Zoya Maslenikova came bringing fruit and flowers. But apart from nurses and doctors, Pasternak allowed only Zinaida and his brother to see him. His message to his visitors was that he loved them all but was no longer there, and there was something in his lungs and stomach that could love no one.[136]

At that stage, despite her animosity, Zinaida said she was willing to countenance a visit from Ivinskaya, but Pasternak rejected this outright, stating that 'Even as it is I have a lot to answer for before God!' He also forbade Nina Tabidze and his brother to connive at any visit, although Ivinskaya kept turning up in tears in the lane. In some of his last conversations with son Evgenii and Koma Ivanov, Pasternak blamed her for the spoiling of many of his old friendships. Also, apart from a desire to die at home in his own bed, he was adamant about not being hospitalised since this could lay him open to visits from Ivinskaya.[137]

The cardiologist Dolgoplossk who had helped treat Pasternak in 1952 came at Ivinskaya's summons on the 14 May, but his pronouncement of an apparent recovery from the heart attack proved over-encouraging. The following day, a consilium of Doctors Fogelson, Petrov, Popov and Shpirt confirmed miocardiac infarctation, thrombosis of the stomach blood vessels and stomach cancer. Approached in his official capacity, Fedin arranged for delivery of an oxygen tent. On 25 May a mobile X-ray apparatus was also brought to the dacha and pictures were made by Elena Tager's radiographer brother. The final diagnosis was widespread cancer of the lungs, with secondaries in the heart, liver and bowel. The patient was getting weaker due to internal bleeding, and a transfusion was carried out on the 27 May, but it was clear that there was no hope of recovery. By this stage, although Ivinskaya retained cash reserves, Zinaida had spent almost all the family savings on doctors' consultation fees and expenses.[138]

As Pasternak neared the end, Zoya Maslenikova brought him communion from the Patriarchal church in Peredelkino. Despite occasional moments of confusion, Pasternak's faculties in general remained clear. He urged Vyacheslav Ivanov to destroy his unfinished manuscripts; he expressed a repeated desire that his sisters be called, and uttered a special wish to see Lydia before he died. A telegram was duly sent by Aleksandr Pasternak on Friday 27 May. Lydia rushed to the Soviet Embassy in London, and Sir Isaiah Berlin tried to use his diplomatic contacts. On the 28th another cable was sent by Pasternak's sons: 'Cable immediately possibility flying inform if help needed acquire visa. Lenya. Zhenya.' On Sunday 29 May, Pasternak's sons also sent a telegram to Khrushchev via the Central Committee, asking that Lydia be allowed to see her dying brother. (All in vain. Lydia spent a week waiting in London while the Soviet authorities prevaricated; she was finally granted a visa two days after the funeral on 2 June.) Aleksandr meanwhile assured Boris that Lydia was on her way, and Evgeniya Pasternak and Mikhail Polivanov twice went to Vnukovo Airport hoping to meet her from a London–Moscow flight.[139]

Towards the end of the day on 30 May, after a further blood transfusion, it was evident that the end was near. At 9.30 in the evening Pasternak called Zinaida and bade her farewell. His last words to her were: 'I loved this life and I loved you greatly. But I am leaving without any regrets: all around there is too much vulgarity, not just here but throughout the world. That is something I cannot reconcile myself to.' He thanked her for everything, kissed her and had her call Evgenii and Leonid.[140]

Pasternak's words to his sons were very laboured, with increasing pauses between phrases. His remarks as recalled by Evgenii were to the effect that everything had been taken care of and looked after by the law, and that apart from any pain and sorrow his death may cause them, there was no threat to them. Out of concern for them he wished not to involve them in that part of his legacy that lay abroad and uncontrolled by law. Supposedly this would all be looked after by Lydia when she came.

Pasternak died at 11.20 on the night of 30 May 1960.

Shortly before the end, Pasternak talked of his life as spent in a duel between the forces of vulgarity and the free play of human talent.[141] Even if the latter had triumphed, however, his last words to his sons expressed a simplicity that was perhaps more easily achieved in art than in real life. The splendour of Pasternak's artistic achievement stood in contrast to the world's malign complexities and all the uncertainties that he himself bequeathed. Although these were not strictly part of Pasternak's biography, it would tantalising to say nothing of that legacy:

There was no church funeral, but a local priest celebrated Orthodox requiem in the dacha for family and closest friends on 1st June. Although officially ignored and boycotted, the funeral on 2 June was attended by many hundreds – apart from family and friends, there were many students, intelligentsia, foreign newsmen, local inhabitants, and anonymous admirers who had learned of his death by word of mouth. Richter and Yudina played as mourners filed through the drawing room past the flower-decked coffin. Official transport for the burial was ignored, and the coffin was borne out along the road to the cemetery by a group of young men including Pasternak's sons, the two sons of Vsevolod Ivanov, Stanislav Neigauz and Mikhail Polivanov. The coffin lid was carried by Yulii Daniel and Andrei Sinyavsky. Pasternak was buried beneath three pines at the edge of the Peredelkino cemetery. At the graveside Valentin Asmus gave a short, restrained but courageous speech of appreciation, and Golubentsev recited 'Hamlet'. After the formalities, many people ignored official attempts to end the meeting, and for hours continued to recite Pasternak's poetry – beloved early pieces and some still unpublished masterpieces.

Among the absentees was Pasternak's neighbour and former friend Fedin, who was thought to be hiding behind closed curtains; as it later emerged, he was seriously ill at the time of Pasternak's death. Although Asmus declared his intention to speak at the funeral to the University authorities, the fact was unfavourably noted, and Furtseva herself later described Livanov's presence as a political demonstration. KGB photographs also identified many others who took the risk of attending.

On 30 May each year, Pasternak's grave has remained a place of pilgrimage where poetry is recited, and surviving relatives, friends, and admirers of a later generation come to pay tribute. There are now only two pines, and young birches have sprung up around the grave plot on what was once an open hillside.

When Lydia Pasternak Slater flew to Moscow with her younger daughter Ann, the funeral was over. After meeting with Ivinskaya, she realised there was little she could do to sort out her brother's affairs. Pasternak died leaving no will and testament. His estate, such as it was, was legally divided three ways – between Zinaida and his sons Evgenii and Leonid. There were no savings or great valuables to bequeath. After Pasternak's death, Zinaida lived on at the Litfond-owned dacha, although she was unable to cover all the costs of rental and repair and running the house. She had virtually no income, and applications by Chukovsky and other friends to secure her a pension were for a long time ignored. During her remaining years (she died in June of 1966) she worked on ordering her husband's archive and produced some memoirs with Zoya Maslenikova as amanuensis.

Evgeniya Pasternak died in 1965.

Immediately after Pasternak's funeral, KGB agents confiscated Ivinskaya's manuscript copy of *Blind Beauty* in order to thwart any attempt at foreign publication. They were doubtless aware of Feltrinelli's ambition to bring all Pasternak's unpublished works out of Russia, and of Ivinskaya's appointment as literary executor. In August 1960 Ivinskaya was arrested shortly after receiving an instalment of foreign royalties to the tune of half a million roubles, brought by an Italian tourist couple. Shortly afterwards, her daughter Irina Emelyanova was also arrested as an accomplice. Mother and daughter were accused of illegal currency operations and received labor camp sentences of eight and three years respectively. The prosecution's case and the conduct of the trial were manifestly rigged, and the charges were revoked in the late 1980s. As far as one knows, however, the money confiscated, which should have been shared among Pasternak's family heirs, was not restored. The sentence of Ivinskaya and her daughter, which raised an international protest, were part of an (unsuccessful) scheme to impound and establish state control over Pasternak's literary legacy. Whatever the corruption of legality and technical injustice, however, many people close to Pasternak and his family regarded Ivinskaya as having earned her punishment.

Feltrinelli held to his commitment to Ivinskaya as Pasternak's sole executor, but eventually, in the later 1960s, began making royalty payments to Pasternak's sons and Stanislav Neigauz (as Zinaida's heir). As Kosachevsky, Ivinskaya's defence lawyer, explained in an article, although she was named as Pasternak's 'sole heiress', she 'considered it impossible to accept all payments for the novel and voluntarily ceded two thirds of the inheritance to his "legal heirs"'.[142]

After her release, Irina Emelyanova married Vadim Kozodoi, whom she met in the camps, and they eventually emigrated to Paris, where she teaches Russian at the Sorbonne. Olga Ivinskaya published her memoirs in Paris in 1972. She died in Moscow in 1995.

In November 1997 the newspaper *Moskovsky komsomolets* published extracts from Ivinskaya's letters recently released from the KGB archives. After Pasternak's death she attempted to blame the publication of *Doctor Zhivago* on him and his family, whereas she – allegedly on orders from the authorities – had worked to intercept his many contacts with foreigners. Had Pasternak suspected the degree of her collaboration with the Soviet security police, the story of their relations might have ended very differently.

In retirement Pasternak's brother Aleksandr produced some finely written memoirs recalling the earlier years of his family and life in pre-revolutionary Russia; these were translated into English by his niece Ann Pasternak Slater. Aleksandr Pasternak died in 1982. Lydia Pasternak Slater continued for many years to translate verse both by her brother and other Russian poets; together with her children and other advisers she set up the Pasternak Trust, which continues to promote mainly the work of Leonid Pasternak. Apart from writing and publishing her own verse in Russian, Josephine Pasternak also edited her father's notes and memoirs which were published in Moscow in 1975. Lydia died in 1989, and her sister Josephine in 1992.

Evgenii Borisovich Pasternak taught at the Moscow Energy Institute until 1974, when he was asked to leave owing to his association with the exiled family of Solzhenitsyn. Prior to that, and especially after his election to the research staff of the Institute of World Literature, he and his wife Elena have been the principal collectors, curators and publishers of Pasternak's archives. Their authority and energy in preserving and propagating his legacy are reflected in innumerable public lectures, conference appearances, and in publications, many under their own names, but many more with other named authors who, like the present one, have been assisted, encouraged and spiritually enriched by their association. *Doctor Zhivago* was published in Russia in 1988. A symbolic reward for devotion to his father's achievement was offered in Stockholm in 1989, when Evgenii Pasternak was able to collect the Nobel medal and certificate that Boris should have received thirty-one years earlier.

For several years following Pasternak's death, his family were allowed by Litfond to retain use of the dacha. In the inhospitable early 1980s the premises were forcibly reclaimed. But before any other would-be residents could move in (Chingiz Aitmatov was the prime candidate), the forces of Gorbachev's *perestroika* encouraged creation of a Pasternak House-Museum. Its curator is the widow of Leonid Pasternak junior, whose own tragic death was described in the opening of this volume.

The Pasternak dacha and its surroundings have changed since my own first visits in the early 1960s. The distant high-rise buildings of an expanding city can be seen over the tree-tops. Birch trees have sprung up along Pavlenko Street and overshadow the drive leading up to the dacha; Pasternak's elderly dog Tobik and his kennel have gone; Fedin no longer lives in the nextdoor dacha, to grouse when the Pasternak grandsons' football flies over the fence; the grandsons and a granddaughter have grown up and have their own families; long-term neighbours Vsevolod and Tamara Ivanov are dead; Vyacheslav their son holds the Moscow University Chair of the History of World Culture and is visiting professor at UCLA; Zinaida no longer sits wreathed in cigarette smoke and playing patience; like Evgeniya Pasternak, she lies in the same grave plot as her husband. The dacha, garden and woodland no more echo to the sound of Stanislav Neigauz practising (he died in 1980). Boris Pasternak's greatest legacy and fame still resound however.

Notes

The following notes provide reference to published or documentary sources. With letters, rather than indicating multiple and/or reprinted sources, the most complete and authoritative text for any one particular correspondence is given. Certain information in the text has been derived from relatives and acquaintances of Pasternak, most of whom are identified and acknowledged in the preface rather than in endnotes. Full references are given only for those works not in the bibliography. The following abbreviations are used in the notes:

APT	Archive of the Pasternak Trust, Oxford.
BPZNP	*Pis'ma B. L. Pasternaka k zhene Z. N. Neigauz-Pasternak.* Moscow, 1993.
Dossier	*Le dossier de l'affaire Pasternak.* Paris, 1994.
DZh	*Doktor Zhivago.* Milan, 1957.
EBP	E. Pasternak. *Boris Pasternak: Materialy dlya biografii.* Moscow, 1989.
EPIV	E. Pasternak, 'Iz vospominanii', *Zvezda*, 7 (1996), 125–91.
FBP20	L. Fleishman. *Boris Pasternak v dvadtsatye gody.* Munich, 1981.
FBP30	L. Fleishman. *Boris Pasternak v tridtsatye gody.* Jerusalem, 1984.
FBPPP	L. Fleishman. *Boris Pasternak: The Poet and His Politics.* Cambridge MA-London, 1990.
Lettres	*Lettres à mes amies françaises 1956–1960.* Paris, 1994.
LG	*Literaturnaya gazeta.*
LN	*Literaturnoe nasledstvo*
NNVV	N. N. Vil'mont. *O Borise Pasternake. Vospominaniya i mysli.* Moscow, 1989.
PBP	*Perepiska Borisa Pasternaka.* Moscow, 1990.
Perepiska	*Perepiska s Ol'goi Freidenberg.* New York, 1981.
PFA	Pasternak Family Archive, Moscow.

PPL	' "Neotsenimyi podarok". Perepiska Pasternakov i Lo-monosovykh (1925–1979)'. *Minuvshee*: 15 (1993); 16 (1994); 17 (1995).
PVSSP	*Pervyi vsesoyuznyi s"ezd sovetskikh pisatelei. 1934. Steno-graficheskii otchet.* Moscow, 1934.
*Soch.*I/II/III	*Sochineniya.* Ann Arbor, 1961. Volumes I/II/III.
SP	*Stikhotvoreniya i poemy.* Moscow-Leningrad, 1965.
SS, I/II/III/IV/V	*Sobranie sochinenii v pyati tomakh.* Moscow, 1989–92. Volumes I/II/III/IV/V.
Vek Pasternaka	*Literaturnaya gazeta. Dos'e 'Vek Pasternaka'. February 1990.*
Vospominaniya	*Vospominaniya o Borise Pasternake.* Moscow, 1993.
VP	*Vozdushnye puti. Proza raznykh let.* Moscow, 1982.
ZRL	L. Pasternak. *Zapisi raznykh let.* Moscow, 1975.

1 THE CRISIS OF THE LYRIC

1 Zhuravlev, *Zhizn'*, 343. *DZh*, 501–4; *SS*, III, 482–5.

2 Letter of 3 February 1929 to L. O. Pasternak (APT).

3 'Est' li krizis v sovremennoi poezii?', *Molodaya gvardiya*, 12 (1928), 191–201. V. Zhak, 'Na lozhnom puti (k voprosu o "krizise" v nashei poezii)', *Na litera-turnom postu*, 10 (1929), 61.

4 See I. Serman, ' "Vysokaya bolezn'" i problema eposa v 1920–e gody', in Loseff (ed.) *Boris Pasternak 1890–1960*, 75–94.

5 Comment on A. E. Kruchenykh's presentation copy of *Poverkh bar'erov* (1931), *Vospominaniya*, 460.

6 See L. Fleishman, 'Iz perepiski B. Pasternaka', *Russian Literature Triquarterly*, 13 (1976), 543–4.

7 E. g., Sergievsky, 'Boris Pasternak'; Lezhnev, 'Boris Pasternak'.

8 Aleksandrov, 'Nashe poèticheskoe segodnya'; Manfred, 'Boris Pasternak'.

9 Loks, 'Boris Pasternak'; Tynyanov, *Arkhaisty i novatory*, 563–8, 579–80; Bragin, 'Boris Pasternak'. On *Poverkh bar'erov* (1929), see above, vol. I, 508–15, and *FBP20*, 92–112; also (see Bibliography): E. V. Pasternak, 'Rabota Borisa Paster-naka nad tsiklom *Nachal'naya pora*'; Frolovskaya, 'Nekotorye nablyudeniya nad obraznoi sistemoi stikhotvornogo tsikla B. Pasternaka *Poverkh bar'erov*'; Gasparov, ' "Bliznets v tuchakh" i "nachal'naya pora" B. Pasternaka'. See also Zakharenko (ed.) *Russkie pisateli*, 354.

10 *FBPPP*, 150. See vol. I, 408–15.

11 Letter of 29 September 1930 to S. D. Spassky, *SS*, V, 310; see vol. I, 320.

12 Letter of 31 May 1929 to N. A. Tikhonov, *PBP*, 469.

13 Letter of 22 December 1928 to S. D. Spassky, *SS*, V, 257.

14 Letter of 30 March 1929 to S. D. Spassky, *SS*, V, 266.

15 Geller, *Andrei Platonov*, 155–7. On Pasternak and Platonov, see Nagibin, 'Bliz chelovecheskogo serdtsa', 9–11.

16 Wright, *Mikhail Bulgakov*, 143–7.

17 Letter of 14 June 1929 to N. A. Tikhonov, *PBP*, 471–3. See also 'Iz perepiski s pisatelyami', *LN*, 93 (1983), 679–80.

18 'Zametki o peresechenii biografii Osipa Mandel'shtama i Borisa Pasternaka', *Pamyat'*, 4 (1981), 306–11. O. Mandel'shtam, 'Chetvertaya proza', in *Sobranie sochinenii*, vol. 2, 227–9.

19 Letter of 6 April 1928 to R. I. Pasternak (APT).

20 Letter of 12 January 1929 to L. O. and R. I. Pasternak (APT).

21 Letter of 28 February 1929 to R. N. Lomonosova, *PPL, Minuvshee*, 16 (1994), 152; similarly in letter of 3 April 1929 to L. O. Pasternak (APT).

22 Gornung, 'Vstrecha za vstrechei', 77.

23 Letter of 11 June 1930 to O. M. Freidenberg, *Perepiska*, 132.

24 On 'Tri glavy iz povesti', see vol. I, 284–5. M. Gor'ky, letter of 4 October 1929 to B. L. Pasternak, 'Gor'ky – B. L. Pasternak', *LN*, 70 (1963), 296.

25 Letter of 28 January 1929 to P. N. Medvedev, *SS*, V, 261. 'Pisateli o sebe', *SS*, IV, 628–9.

26 See vol. I, 412. Letter of 6 March 1929 to A. A. Akhmatova, *SS*, V, 265.

27 *Perepiska*, 126–7.

28 Letter of 23 May 1929 to O. M. Freidenberg, *Perepiska*, 128–9.

29 Letter of 3 April 1929 to L. O. Pasternak (APT). On *Povest'* and Pasternak's own life, see vol. I, 16, 99, 141, 185–7, 204, 226.

30 See vol. I, 328, 364–5, 411–12.

31 See vol. I, chapters 8 and 9. Shtein, ' "I ne tol'ko o nem. . ." ', *Teatr*, 1 (1988), 171–90.

32 *NNVV*, 192.

33 Letter of 4 December 1929 to R. N. Lomonosova, *PPL, Minuvshee*, 16 (1994), 165.

34 G. Yakubovsky, ' "Krasnaya nov'" i "Novyi mir" v 1929 g.', *Proletarskii avangard*, 6 (1930), col. 125. Adamovich, 'Literaturnye zametki'.

35 See L. O. Pasternak, letter of 21 May 1929 to B. L. Pasternak (PFA).

36 Salys, 'Love, Death and Creation', 265 ff.

37 Letter of 30–31 October 1928 to A. Bely, *SS*, V, 251. Letter of 19 November 1928 to N. A. Tikhonov, *ibid.*, 252–3. *Perepiska*, 118.

38 *EBP*, 469. Letter of 1 January 1930 to L. O. and R. I. Pasternak (APT). 'Boris Pasternak et Romain Rolland: Correspondance (1930)', publ. M. Aucouturier, *Europe*, 767 (March 1993), 104–5, 115. On M. Kudasheva, see *ibid.*, 116.

39 Letter of 9 October 1930 to R. N. Lomonosova, *PPL, Minuvshee*, 16 (1994), 172. See 'Boris Pasternak et Romain Rolland', 106–11.

40 'Anketa izdaniya "Nashi sovremenniki" ', *SS*, IV, 625.

41 *PBP*, 403–4.

42 *PPL, Minuvshee*, 15 (1994), 237–8; *ibid.*, 16 (1994), 173.

43 *Soch.*I, 137; *SP*, 552; *SS*, I, 551.
44 Letter of 20 June 1928 to E. V. Pasternak, quoted in *EBP*, 440.
45 Letter of 31 May 1929 to L. O. and R. I. Pasternak (APT).
46 Letter of 15 December 1929 to L. O. and R. I. Pasternak (APT).
47 L. O. Pasternak, letter of 13 December 1929 to B. L. Pasternak and family (PFA).
48 Letter of 4 December 1929 to R. N. Lomonosova, *PPL, Minuvshee*, 16 (1994), 163.
49 *Perepiska*, 127.
50 E. V. Pasternak (ed. and publ.), 'Boris Pasternak: ankety, zayavleniya, khodataistva 1920–kh godov, 42, 47–9. *EBP*, 455. *EPIV*, 127.
51 E. V. Pasternak, letter of 17 January 1928 to L. O. and R. I. Pasternak (APT).
52 Letter of 20 May 1928 to O. M. Freidenberg, *Perepiska*, 110.
53 Letter of 20 August 1959 to J. de Proyart, *Lettres*, 194–5.
54 Letter of 15 July 1929 to L. O. Pasternak (APT).
55 *EBP*, 458.
56 *Ibid.*, 456–9. 'Perepiska s Evgeniei Pasternak', *Znamya*, 2 (1996), 169. *EPIV*, 138.
57 See vol. I, 403. *EBP*, 456.
58 Letter of 15 December 1929 to L. O. and R. I. Pasternak (APT).
59 Letter of 23 January 1928 to L. O. Pasternak (APT).
60 See Salys, 'Love, Death and Creation', 273–8.
61 Letter of 31 May 1929 to L. O. Pasternak (APT).
62 Letter of 14 June 1929 to N. S. Tikhonov, *SS*, V, 276.
63 Letter of 30 June to L. O. and R. I. Pasternak (APT).
64 *EBP*, 458.
65 'Pis'ma k V. M. Sayanovu', publ. A. V. Lavrov, *Ezhegodnik Rukopisnogo otdela Pushkinskogo doma na 1977 god* (Leningrad, 1979), 195–6. Letter of 20 August 1929 to P. Medvedev, *SS*, V, 278–9.
66 See Superfin (publ.), 'B. L. Pasternak.' *FBP20*, 134–6. Letter of 24 July 1929 to R. I. and Zh.L. Pasternak (APT). *EBP*, 458.
67 'Pis'ma k V. M. Sayanovu', 194–6.
68 Letter of 3 December 1929 to L. O. and R. I. Pasternak (APT). See vol. I, 84.
69 'Iz poemy "1905 god" ', *Volya Rossii*, 2 (1927).
70 On this episode, see M. Hayward, 'Pilnyak and Zamyatin', 85–9. *FBP20*, 123–9. Andronikashvili-Pil'nyak, 'Dva izgoya', 143 ff.
71 E. Zamyatin, *Litsa* (New York, 1955), 96–7, 277–82. *FBP20*, 128–30.
72 Letter of 1 May 1929 to V. S. Pozner, *SS*, V, 270.
73 'Dvor', *Krasnaya nov'*, 7 (1928), 153–9. Letter of 14 June 1929 to N. A. Tikhonov, *SS*, V, 276. B. Pil'nyak, 'Gorod vetrov', *Zhurnal dlya vsekh*, 2 (1928).
74 Letter n.d. (spring 1929) to Zh. L. Pasternak (APT).
75 See *LG*, 16 September 1929. E. I. Zamyatin letter of 21 September 1929 to K. A. Fedin, cited in Andronikashvili-Pil'nyak, 'Dva izgoya', 145, and 'Moi otets', 153.
76 'Borisu Pil'nyaku', *SS*, V, 226, 682–3.
77 Andronikashvili-Pil'nyak, 'Moi otets', 150–1.

78 *Na literaturnom postu*, 24 (December 1929), 1.
79 Letter of 5 December 1929 to N. S. Tikhonov, *SS*, V, 288–9.
80 Gornung, 'Vstrecha za vstrechei', 77.
81 Cf. the hero's dream in *Povest'* of ransoming exploited women.
82 See vol. I, 407–8. Cf. a similar motif in M. Tsvetaeva, 'Dvoe' (1924), *Sobranie sochinenii v semi tomakh* (Moscow, 1994), II, 235–8, 512.
83 See *Soch.*I, 314–16; *SP*, 341–2; *SS*, *I*, 371–3. For discussion of the poem, see *FBP20, 134–70.*
84 Letter of 9 December 1929 to I. S. Postupal'sky, *Russkie novosti* (Paris), 7 February 1969.
85 Letter of 6 November 1929 to P. N. Medvedev, *SS*, V, 283–4.
86 Letter of 3 December 1929 to L. O. and R. I. Pasternak (APT).
87 Letter of 28 November 1929 and postcard of 5 December 1929 to P. N. Medvedev, *SS*, V, 285–8.
88 Letter of 30 December 1929 to P. N. Medvedev, *SS*, V, 295.
89 Letter of 29 December 1929 to Zh. L. Pasternak and family (APT).

2 TIME OF PLAGUE

1 G. Neigauz, 'Avtobiograficheskie zapiski', in Mil'shtein (ed.), *G. G. Neigauz*, 19 ff.
2 V. Asmus, 'I prelesti tvoei sekret Razgadke zhizni ravnosilen', *Vek Pasternaka*, 10–11. L. Ozerov, preface to Z. Pasternak, 'Vospominaniya', *Neva*, 2 (1990), 130. T. G. Suvorova, 'V 1922 godu . . .', in Zimyanina (ed.), *Stanislav Neigauz*, 13–14.
3 L. Stolovich, Preface to V. Asmus, 'Pasternak ob iskusstve', *Raduga*, 8 (1987), 60–1.
4 Z. Pasternak, 'Vospominaniya', *Vospominaniya*, 175.
5 'Godami kogda-nibud' v zale kontsertnoi . . .', *SS*, II, 392.
6 Letter of 6 March 1930 to L. O. and R. I. Pasternak, *EBP*, 460. Letter of 16 January 1929 to Zh. L. Pasternak (APT).
7 Z. Pasternak, 'Vospominaniya', 175. *EPIV*, 129. Letter of 23 March 1931 to R. N. Lomonosova, *PPL, Minuvshee*, 16 (1994), 177.
8 See E. J. Brown, 'The Year of Acquiescence', in Hayward and Labedz (eds.), *Literature and Revolution in Soviet Russia 1917–62*, 44–61. N. Mandel'shtam, *Vospominaniya*, 277.
9 'Ruki proch' ot M. Gor'kogo!', *LG*, 14 January 1931. See *FBP30*, 29.
10 Letter of 12 November 1930 to Andrei Bely, *SS*, V, 314.
11 Letter of 30 March 1930 to L. O. Pasternak (APT). On the Hosiassons, see Salys, 'Leonid Pasternak's *Moi proizvedenija*', 196–7.
12 Petrovskaya, 'Vospominaniya o Borise Leonidoviche Pasternake', *Vospominaniya*, 90–105, 702. See also *FBP30*, 15–18. On Pasternak's resignation from Lef, see vol. I, 383–91.
13 Letter of 1 April 1930 to N. K. Chukovsky, *SS*, V, 298.
14 Letter of 31 December 1928 to Zh. L. Pasternak (APT).
15 See *Izbrannoe* (Moscow, 1985), vol. I, 539. See vol. I, 408, 412–13.

16 Letter of 13 May 1929 to V. S. Pozner, *SS*, V, 273.

17 Letter of 14 June 1929 to N. A. Tikhonov, *SS*, V, 276–7. On Pasternak's dealings with Aseev, see: Barnes, 'Boris Pasternak: A Review of Nikolaj Aseev'; A. M. Kryukova, ' "Razgovor s neizvestnym drugom" ', 516–30; *EBP*, 452–3.

18 A. Gladkov, *Vstrechi s Pasternakom* (Paris, 1973), 57. E. V. Pasternak, ' "Ty – tsar': zhivi odin . . ." (Boris Pasternak i Vladimir Mayakovsky)', *Scandoslavica*, 38 (1992), 75–6.

19 See Brown, *Mayakovsky*, 362–3. Katanyan, *Mayakovsky*, 387. V. Mayakovsky, 'Nashe otnoshenie', *LG*, 2 September 1929; also in his *Polnoe sobranie sochinenii*, vol. 12, 196.

20 P. Kerzhentsev, 'O Mayakovskom', *LG*, 17 April 1930.

21 On Mayakovsky and Pasternak in 1929, see *FBP20*, 116–33.

22 Letter of 31 May 1929 to A. N. Tikhonov, *PBP*, 469.

23 Krotkov, 'Pasternaki', *Grani*, 63 (1967), 67.

24 Dolmatovsky, *Bylo*, 284.

25 *NNVV*, 146

26 *EBP*, 453. Katanyan, 'O Mayakovskom i Pasternake', 512–13. Kassil', *Mayakovsky*, 196. See also Pertsov, *Mayakovsky. Zhizn' i tvorchestvo*, 331.

27 'Perepiska s Evgeniei Pasternak', *Znamya*, 2 (1996), 169–70. 'Okhrannaya gramota', *SS*, IV, 237. O. Petrovskaya, 'Vospominaniya', 100. M. K. Rozenfel'd, 'Iz stenogrammy vospominanii o V. V. Mayakovskom', in Reformatskaya (ed.), *V. Mayakovsky*, 600–1.

28 See vol. I, 397–9; *FBP20*, 171 ff., esp. 187–8.

29 See above, ch. 1; *EBP*, 463 ff.; *FBP20*, 194 ff.; *FBPPP*, 159.

30 Letter of 28 February 1930 to L. L. Pasternak (APT).

31 *SS*, I, 47. See vol. I, 147.

32 Letter of 9 April 1930 to L. O. and R. I. Pasternak (APT).

33 *Soch*.II, 261; *VP*, 249; *SS*, IV, 206. See Aucouturier, 'Ob odnom klyuche k *Okhrannoi gramote*', in Aucouturier (ed.), *Boris Pasternak 1890–1960*, 345–6.

34 See *SS*, IV, 164. Rashkovskaya, 'Dve sud'by', in Podgaetskaya (ed.), *Pasternakovskie chteniya*, 238–9. Durylin, *V svoem uglu*, 304–9. See also vol. I, 282; G. Pomerantseva, 'O Sergee Nikolaeviche Duryline', in Durylin, *V svoem uglu*, 3–42.

35 See *Soch*.II, 268, 280; *VP*, 259, 271; *SS*, IV, 214, 226.

36 See M. Djurčinov, 'Pasternak i Majakovski', *Godishen zbornik na filosofskiot fakultet na Universitetot vo Skopje*, 22 (1970), 432–6. See *SS*, I, 390–1.

37 Vysheslavsky, *Naizust'*, 59–60.

38 *SS*, IV, 220. On polemics with Aseyev, see also *FBP20*, 177–84, 251.

39 Letter of 9 April 1930 to L. O. and R. I. Pasternak (APT).

40 Letter of 31 May 1930 to A. M. Gor'ky, 'Boris Pasternak v perepiske s Maksimom Gor'kim', publ. E. B. and E. V. Pasternak, *Izvestiya Akademii Nauk SSSR (Seriya literatury i yazyka)*, 45 no. 3 (1986), 279–80. See similarly letter of 9 January 1930 to L. L. Pasternak (APT).

41 A. M. Gor'ky, letter (n.d.) to B. L. Pasternak, 'Boris Pasternak v perepiske s Maksimom Gor'kim', 280–1.

42 Letter of 20 June 1930 to L. L. Pasternak, quoted in *EBP*, 462.

43 M. I. Tsvetaeva, letter of 12 October 1930 to R. N. Lomonosova. R. Devis (Davies) (publ.), 'Pis'ma Mariny Tsvetaevoi k R. N. Lomonosovoi', *Minuvshee*, 8 (1989), 231–2.

44 Letter of 4 November 1930 to R. N. Lomonosova, *PPL, Minuvshee*, 16 (1994), 172.

45 R. N. Lomonosova, letter of 18 November 1930 to B. L. Pasternak, *ibid.*, 174.

46 R. Rolland, letter of 28 November 1930 to B. L. Pasternak, 'Boris Pasternak et Romain Rolland', 114.

47 R. Rolland, letter of 4 December 1930 to B. L. Pasternak, *ibid.*, 115.

48 *EBP*, 467.

49 Z. Pasternak, 'Vospominaniya', 176.

50 *EBP*, 468.

51 Letter of 11 June 1930 to O. M. Freidenberg, *Perepiska*, 132. *NNVV*, 169.

52 *EBP*, 468. Letter of 15 July 1930 to Zh. L. Pasternak (APT).

53 Z. Pasternak, 'Vospominaniya', 176–7.

54 *NNVV*, 169. Z. Pasternak, 'Vospominaniya', 176.

55 'Godami kogda-nibud' v zale kontsertnoi . . .' *SS*, I, 392.

56 'Perepiska s Evgeniei Pasternak', *Znamya*, 2 (1996), 170.

57 *NNVV*, 172–3, 175–6. *EBP*, 468. Z. Pasternak, 'Vospominaniya', 178.

58 Vysheslavsky, *Naizust'*, 26 ff. Z. Pasternak, 'Vospominaniya', 177. *EBP*, 469. *NNVV*, 167

59 Letter of 20 October 1930 to O. M. Freidenberg, *Perepiska*, 136.

60 Letter of 29 September 1930 to S. D. Spassky, *SS*, V, 311.

61 Letter of 15 July 1930 to Zh. L. Pasternak (APT).

62 On Proust and Pasternak, see V. Baevsky, 'Preliminarii k teme "Marsel' Prust i Boris Pasternak"', in *Stilisticheskii analiz khudozhestvennogo teksta* (Smolensk, 1988), 100–8; M. Aucouturier, 'Pasternak and Proust', in Barnes (ed.), *Pasternak and European Literature*, 342–51; A. D. Mikhailov, 'Pasternak i Prust', *Russkaya mysl'*, 6 July 1990.

63 Letter of 20 October 1930 to O. M. Freidenberg, *Perepiska*, 136.

64 *EBP*, 469.

65 *NNVV*, 181–2. On 'Leto', see also Vysheslavsky, *Naizust'*, 35–8; G. Gutsche, 'Sound and Significance in Pasternak's "Leto"', *Slavic and East European Journal*, 25 no. 3 (1981), 83–93.

66 Z. Pasternak, 'Vospominaniya', 177.

67 *Ibid.*

68 *SS*, II, 133. *EBP*, 470.

69 Letter of 5 November 1930 to L. O. and R. I. Pasternak (APT).

70 Z. Pasternak, 'Vospominaniya', 179.

71 Letter of 24 May 1932 to Zh. L. Pasternak (APT). Z. N. Pasternak, *Vospomina-niya*, ed. M. Feinberg (Moscow, 1993), 240–4.
72 Letter of 30 July/1 August 1931 to Zh. L. Pasternak (APT).

3 NEW LOVE AND SECOND BIRTH

1 Letter of 20 October 1930 to O. M. Freidenberg, *Perepiska*, 136.
2 M. Gonta, 'Martirik', *Vospominaniya*, 232.
3 *ZRL*, 152.
4 'Iz perepiski s pisatelyami', *LN*, 93 (1983), 728–35.
5 Letter of 9 November to L. O. and R. I. Pasternak (APT). L. O. Pasternak, letter of 26 November 1930 to B. L. Pasternak (PFA).
6 *EBP*, 471. *EPIV*, 132. 'Perepiska s Evgeniei Pasternak', *Znamya*, 2 (1996), 171.
7 Z. Pasternak, 'Vospominaniya', 179–80.
8 Letter of 8 March 1931 to L. O. and R. I. Pasternak (APT). Letter of 15 February 1931 to S. D. Spassky, *SS*, V, 317.
9 Letter of 26 December 1930 to Z. N. Neigauz, *BPZNP*, 16–17. 'Uprek ne uspel potusknet'. . .', *SS*, I, 417. On Blumenfeld and his family, see Anastas'eva, 'Boris Leonidovich Pasternak', 364 ff.
10 Letter of 30 April 1931 to Z. N. Neigauz, *BPZNP*, 23.
11 Z. Pasternak, 'Vospominaniya', 180; faulty dating here has been corrected from external evidence.
12 Krotkov, 'Pasternaki', *Grani*, 60 (1966), 68; oral testimony of Irma Yudina.
13 Letter of 8–23 March to L. O. and R. I. Pasternak (APT).
14 Gornung, 'Vstrecha za vstrechei', 78. *BPZNP*, 29, 224.
15 *NNVV*, 201. Letter of 12 May 1931 to Z. N. Neigauz, *BPZNP*, 27.
16 'Pis'ma k I. A. Gruzdevu', *Zvezda*, 9 (1994), 105.
17 L. Chukovskaya, *Zapiski ob Anne Akhmatovoi*, I, 134; see similarly Ginzburg, *Chelovek za pis'mennym stolom*, 142.
18 D. Kal'm, ' "Spektorsky" B. Pasternaka', *LG*, 19 March 1931.
19 Gladkov, *Vstrechi s Pasternakom*, 12. Vilenkin, 'O Borise Leonidoviche Pasternake', 467.
20 Prozorov, 'Tragediya sub"ektivnogo idealista', 26–35. Selivanovsky, 'Poeziya opasna?', and 'Poet i revolyutsiya'.
21 Tarasenkov, 'Boris Pasternak', *Zvezda*, 5 (1931), 228–35. *FBP30*, 39–41; *EBP*, 473.
22 See inscription of 6 April 1931, *Vospominaniya*, 181. See *FBP20*, 321–2, for detailed discussion.
23 B. Pasternak, 'Pervye vstrechi s Mayakovskim', *LG*, 14 April 1931.
24 *EBP*, 474.
25 *FBP20*, 205, 326–9.
26 Letter of 30 April 1931 to Z. N. Neigauz, *BPZNP*, 24.
27 *Ibid*.
28 See *FBP30*, 98–9; *EBP*, 477.

29 Oral testimony of E. B. Pasternak.
30 'Vesennii den' tridtsatogo aprelya . . .', 'Kogda ya ustayu ot pustozvonstva . . .'; on these poems, see *EBP*, 477–8.
31 'Ne volnuisya, ne plach', ne trudi . . .'. See E. B. Pasternak, 'Rasskaz o khudozhnitse Evgenii Pasternak', 7.
32 E. V. Pasternak, letter of 2 August 1931 to R. N. Lomonosova, *PPL, Minuvshee*, 16 (1994), 181. *EBP*, 478.
33 *EBP*, 479.
34 Letter of 30 July–6 August 1930 to Zh. L. Pasternak, 'Perepiska s Evgeniei Pasternak', *Znamya*, 2 (1996), 172–3.
35 L. O. Pasternak, letter of 18 December 1931 to B. L. Pasternak (PFA). For the complete correspondence of 1931, see 'Perepiska s Evgeniei Pasternak', *Znamya*, 2 (1996), 171–80.
36 *EPIV*, 133–4.
37 Z. Pasternak, 'Vospominaniya', 180. Ozerov, 'Sestra moya – zhizn'', *Vospominaniya*, 444–5.
38 Z. Pasternak, 'Vospominaniya', 180.
39 *Ibid.* Letter of 14 May 1931 to Z. N. Neigauz, *BPZNP*, 32.
40 *Ibid.*, 32–3, 35.
41 *Ibid.*, 228.
42 *FBP30*, 44.
43 Letter (n.d.) of early June 1931 to Z. N. Neigauz, *BPZNP*, 52.
44 *Ibid.*, 53.
45 *EBP*, 480–1. A. I. Aleksandrov, 'B. L. Pasternak na "Chelyabtraktorstroe" v 1931 g.', ms., quoted *ibid.*, 480.
46 Letter of 26 June 1931 to Z. N. Neigauz, *BPZNP*, 71.
47 Letters of 9 June and 13 June 1931 to Z. N. Neigauz, *ibid.*, 55–6, 61.
48 Letter of 12 November 1930 to A. Bely, *SS*, V, 314. Letter of 19 February 1931 to Z. N. Neigauz, *BPZNP*, 19.
49 Letter of 13 June 1931 to Z. N. Neigauz, *BPZNP*, 62.
50 Letters of 18 June and 26 June 1931 to Z. N. Neigauz, *BPZNP*, 65, 71–2. 'Krugom semenyashcheisya vatoi . . .', *SS*, II, 403.
51 Letter of 26 June 1931 to Z. N. Neigauz, *BPZNP*, 67.
52 Letter (n.d.) of late June 1931 to Z. N. Neigauz, *BPZNP*, 75–6.
53 Letter of 30 July 1932 to P. D. Yashvili, *SS*, V, 326.
54 Quoted in D. M. Lang, *A Modern History of Georgia* (London, 1962), 63.
55 'Poka my po Kavkazu lazaem . . .', *SS*, V, 134–5. On this poem's link with Lermontov and Tabidze, see Rayfield, 'Unicorns and Gazelles', in Barnes (ed.), *Pasternak and European literature*, 379–80.
56 Letter (n.d.) from P. D. Yashvili to B. L. Pasternak, *Vospominaniya*, 183.
57 N. Tabidze, 'Raduga na rassvete', *Vospominaniya*, 289.
58 *SS*, IV, 343–4. See Rayfield, 'Pasternak and the Georgians', 39–45, and 'Unicorns and Gazelles', 576–81.

59 N. Tabidze, 'Raduga', 292.
60 A. Bely, letter of 12 July 1928 to B. L. Pasternak, cited in Nivat, 'Une lettre', 90–1.
61 *SS*, IV, 345; *SS*, II, 20. N. Tabidze, 'Raduga', 291–2.
62 *SS*, IV, 345.
63 Z. Pasternak, 'Vospominaniya', 182. Chikovani, 'Svyashchennye uzy bratstva', 93.
64 Z. Pasternak, 'Vospominaniya', 182.
65 Letter to Zh. L. Pasternak of 30 July–6 August 1930 (APT).
66 'Poka my po Kavkazu lazaem . . .', *SS*, II, 410–11.
67 Letter of 6 October 1933 to B. D. Zhgenti, ' "Krai, stavshii mne vtoroi rodinoi" ', *Voprosy literatury*, I (1996), 175.
68 Bebutov, 'Po stranitsam odnoi perepiski', 70–2.
69 See 'B. L. Pasternak. Pis'ma k G. E. Sorokinu', 199–200.
70 Hingley, *Pasternak*, 106.
71 'Lyubimaya, molvy slashchavoi . . .', *SS*, II, 400.
72 See vol. I, 348, 413.
73 Letter of 11 February 1932 to Zh. L. Pasternak (APT). See translation of the poem 'O znal by ya, chto tak byvaet . . .', below, p. 59.
74 'Kogda ya ustayu ot pustozvonstva . . .' *SS*, I, 413.
75 'Vesenneyu poroyu l'da . . .', *SS*, I, 422–4.
76 *EBP*, 493.
77 'Volny', *SS*, I, 381.
78 On the critical reception of *Vtoroe rozhdenie*, see below pp. 73–74.

4 A PRISONER OF TIME

1 Letter of 21 February 1932 to Zh. L. Pasternak (APT). Z. Pasternak, 'Vospomina-niya', 182, 184.
2 Letter of 11 February 1932 to Zh. L. Pasternak (APT).
3 'Iz perepiski Borisa Pasternaka s Andreem Belym', *Andrei Belyi: problemy tvorch-estva* (Moscow, 1988), 692. Baluashvili, 'Vdokhnovennyi póet-patriot', 86. G. P. Struve (pub.), 'K biografii Andreya Belogo: tri dokumenta', *Novyi zhurnal*, 124 (1976), 158–61.
4 *FBP30*, 48–9.
5 Letter of 13 December 1931 to T. and N. A. Tabidze, 'Pis'ma druz'yam', *Literaturnaya Gruziya*, 1 (1966), 80.
6 Kal'm, 'Na tvorcheskoi diskussii'. Kryukova, ' "Razgovor s neizvestnym drugom" ', 520–2. *EBP*, 500–1. Gonta, 'Martirik', 232–3.
7 Kal'm, 'Na tvorcheskoi diskussii'.
8 Selivanovsky, 'O burzhuaznom', 156–7 (A. S.'s emphasis). On Pasternak's speeches at this event, see *FBP30*, 49–54; *EBP*, 500–1.
9 Tarasenkov, 'Okhrannaya gramota idealizma'. For other reviews, see Zakharenko (ed.), *Russkie Pisateli-Poety*, 353.

10 'Pis′ma k I. A. Gruzdevu', 105–6. Letter of 20 November 1932 to G. Reavey, *SS*, V, 332.

11 'Pis′ma k I. A. Gruzdevu', 95. Letter of 14 June 1931 to Z. N. Neigauz, *BPZNP*, 64.

12 *BPZNP*, 222.

13 'Pis′ma k I. A. Gruzdevu', 105.

14 *FBP30*, 55.

15 'Iskusstvo sotsializma i burzhuaznoe restavratorstvo', *LG*, 18 December 1931. See also, P. Berezov, 'Pod maskoi', *Proletarskii avangard*, 1 (1932), col. 177 and Tarasenkov, 'Okhrannaya gramota idealizma'.

16 Miller-Budnitskaya, 'O "filosofii iskusstva" ', 160–8.

17 Selivanovsky, 'Poeziya opasna?'; Inge, 'Otkrytoe pis′mo poetu Borisu Pasternaku', 84–6; Miller-Budnitskaya, 'O "filosofii iskusstva" ', 166.

18 E. V. Pasternak, letters of 28 August 1931, 17 September 1931, 6 October 1931 to R. N. Lomonosova; B. L. Pasternak, letter of 20 October 1931 to R. N. Lomonosova; R. N. Lomonosova, letters of 21 October 1931 and 7 December 1931 to B. L. Pasternak, *PPL, Minuvshee*, 16 (1994), 181–9.

19 E. V. Pasternak, letter of 28 August 1931 to R. N. Lomonosova, in *ibid.*, 182–3.

20 Letter of 20 October 1931 to R. N. Lomonosova, in *ibid.*, 186. *EPIV*, 135.

21 E. V. Pasternak, letter of 14 December 1931 to R. N. Lomonosova, *PPL, Minuvshee*, 16 (1994), 190. L. O. Pasternak, letter of 18 December 1931 to B. L. Pasternak (PFA).

22 Letter of 27 May 1932 to R. N. Lomonosova, *PPL, Minuvshee*, 16 (1994), 194.

23 Ivanova, 'Boris Leonidovich Pasternak', 239. Letter of 1 February 1932 to S. D. Spassky, *SS*, V, 321.

24 Letter of 11 February 1932 to Zh. L. Pasternak (APT). Z. Pasternak, 'Vospominaniya', 184.

25 Z. Pasternak, 'Vospominaniya', 184.

26 *Ibid.*, 185.

27 Letter of 11 February 1932 to Zh. L. Pasternak (APT).

28 Letter of 21 February 1932 to Zh. L. Pasternak (APT).

29 Z. Pasternak, 'Vospominaniya', 185.

30 Letter of 11 February 1932 to Zh. L. Pasternak (APT).

31 Krotkov, 'Pasternaki', *Grani*, 60 (1966), 68. Z. Pasternak, 'Vospominaniya', 185. The private motivation for Pasternak's suicide attempt was confirmed in his letter of 11 February 1932 to Zh. L. Pasternak. Cf. the interpretation in *FBP30*, 57–8. See also Barnes, 'Suitsidal′nye motivy v poetike i zhizni', 286–90.

32 E. Pasternak, 'Rasskaz o khudozhnitse', 7. T. M. Levina, 'Energiya kholsta', *ibid.* Chernyak, 'Pasternak', 137.

33 Chernyak, 'Pasternak', 137.

34 Chukovsky, 'Iz dnevnika (o B. L. Pasternake)', 266.

35 Gornung, 'Vstrecha za vstrechei', 79.

36 *EBP*, 493. *EPIV*, 138.

37 Z. Pasternak, 'Vospominaniya', 185. Letter of 27 May 1932 to R. N. Lomonosova, *PPL, Minuvshee*, 16 (1994), 195.
38 Letter of 24 May 1932 to Zh. L. Pasternak (APT). V. A. Sletova, 'Tverskaya 25, 1932g.', ms. (PFA)
39 Letter of 24 May 1932 to Zh. L. Pasternak (APT).
40 Letter of 18 October 1932 to L. O. Pasternak (APT).
41 Cf. letter of 24 November 1932 to L. O. and R. I. Pasternak (APT), and E. B. Pasternak's oral testimony.
42 Z. Pasternak, 'Vospominaniya', 186.
43 Letter of 11 February 1932 to Zh. L. Pasternak (APT).
44 *FBP30*, 59–65. *EBP*, 502–3.
45 B. N. , 'Poet i ego okruzhenie. Na vechere B. Pasternaka', *LG*, 11 April 1932. IMLI RO, fund 120, item 1, No.17.
46 Baevsky, '. . . Chestnost′ privetstvovat′ prezhde vsego', 144–9.
47 See *EBP*, 502–3.
48 'Proletarskaya poeziya na pod″eme', *LG*, 23 April 1932. *FBP30*, 67. *EBP*, 503.
49 *Letopis′ zhizni i tvorchestva A. M. Gor′kogo*, vypusk 4, 1930–1936 (Moscow, 1960), 197–8.
50 *EBP*, 504.
51 *FBP30*, 92–4. On the history of socialist realism, see Ermolaev, *Soviet Literary Theories 1917–1934*.
52 Letter of January (n.d.) 1933 to A. Bely, *SS*, V, 334.
53 K. , 'O Pasternake', *LG*, 29 May 1932. See *FBP30*, 73–6.
54 Selivanovsky, 'Razgovor o poezii'. See *FBP30*, 90–91.
55 *FBP30*, 89–90. 'Pis′ma k G. E. Sorokinu', 206–8.
56 *FBP30*, 77–8.
57 Letter of 10 July 1932 to I. V. Evdokimov, quoted in *FBP30*, 78–9. Letter of 30 July 1932 to P. D. Yashvili, *SS*, V, 325–7.
58 G. Nivat, 'Pasternak dans l'Oural en 1932', in Aucouturier (ed.), *Boris Pasternek 1890–1960*, 521.
59 Z. Pasternak, 'Vospominaniya', 186–7. Ivinskaya, *V plenu vremeni*, 87. Ozerov, 'Sestra moya – zhizn″', 449.
60 Z. Pasternak, 'Vospominaniya', 187–8.
61 *Ibid.*, 187–8. Nivat, 'Pasternak dans l'Oural', 322. See also *FBP30*, 76–83.
62 Letters of 10 April 1932 to Zh. L. Pasternak, and 18 October 1932 to L. O. Pasternak (APT). See also *ZRL*, 93–5; Buckman, *Leonid Pasternak*, 75–6.
63 Letter (n.d.) of April 1932 to L. O. and R. I. Pasternak (APT).
64 L. O. Pasternak, letter of 28 April 1932 to B. L. Pasternak (PFA).
65 Letter of 27 December 1932 to L. O. Pasternak (APT).
66 Letter of 18 October 1932 to L. O. Pasternak (APT). *EBP*, 494.
67 Letter of 18 October 1932 to L. O. Pasternak (APT). Z. Pasternak, 'Vospominaniya', 186.

68 Letter of 24 November 1932 to L. O. and R. I. Pasternak (APT). Z. Pasternak, 'Vospominaniya', 186.
69 L. Chukovskaya, *Zapiski ob Anne Akhmatovoi*, I, 134; II, 358. Hingley, *Pasternak*, 109.
70 Letter of 22 October 1932 to S. D. and S. G. Spassky, *SS*, V, 329–30. 'Pis'ma k G. E. Sorokinu', 209.
71 Letter of 18 October 1932 to L. O. Pasternak (APT).
72 Letter of 27 December 1932 to L. O. Pasternak (APT). Letter of 19 October 1932 to N. N. Punin and A. A. Akhmatova, *SS*, V, 328–9, 635. Haight, *Anna Akhmatova*, 88–9.
73 'Zametki o peresechenii', 312–13. N. Mandel'shtam, *Vospominaniya*, 158. See also *FBP30*, 102.
74 Brown, *Mandelstam*, 129.
75 Cf. *FBP30*, 100.
76 'Zametki o peresechenii', 314. Z. Pasternak, 'Vospominaniya', 195.
77 Prozorov, 'Tezisy dushi', 5–7. Cf. also Smol'yakov, 'Zametki o poezii', 25.
78 Tarasenkov, 'Vtoroe rozhdenie'.
79 N. I. Khardzhiev, V. V. Trenin, 'O Borise Pasternake', in Nilsson (ed.), *Pasternak*, 7–8. E. B. Pasternak, 'Reading Pasternak', 39–41.
80 'Pis'ma k G. E. Sorokinu', 208.
81 Selivanovsky, 'Poet i revolyutsiya'.
82 Selivanovsky, 'Boris Pasternak', *Krasnaya nov'*, 1 (1933), 210–19; *Poeziya i poety*, 155–78; and 'Pasternak', *Literaturnaya entsiklopediya*, VIII, 465–71.
83 Miller-Budnitskaya, 'B. Pasternak. "Stikhotvoreniya"', *Literaturnyi sovremennik*, 11 (1933), 159–61.
84 Nusinov, 'Masterskaya starykh obraztsov', 7–9.
85 *FBP30*, 104–5.
86 Zelinsky, 'Liricheskaya tetrad'', 383–407. See also Zelinsky, *Kriticheskie pis'ma, Kniga vtoraya*, 228–82. Zholkovsky, 'Mekhanizmy vtorogo rozhdeniya', 36.
87 See A. Barmine, *One Who Survived* (New York, 1945), 264. Vasil'eva, *Kremlevskie zheny*, 204ff. For a belletrised account, see also V. D. Uspensky, 'Tainyi sovetnik vozhdya', *Roman-gazeta*, 7 (1991), 107–10.
88 Meilakh, 'Vnutrennyaya svoboda'.
89 *Ibid.* There is, however no evidence to confirm Fleishmen's more elaborate conjectures in *FBP30*, 98, and *FBPPP*, 172.
90 On this, see Barnes, 'Boris Pasternak and Mary Queen of Scots', 25–38.
91 On this feature in Shostakovich, see MacDonald, *The New Shostakovich*, 106–7.
92 V. Krymov, 'A. N. Tolstoi bez retushi', *Mosty*, 7 (1961), 370; quoted and discussed *FBP20*, 323.
93 Letter of 22 November 1932 to R. N. Lomonosova, *PPL, Minuvshee*, 16 (1994), 199.

94 Anastas'eva, 'Boris Leonidovich Pasternak', 365–7. See *Vospominaniya*, 704–5; 'A za mnoyu shum pogoni . . .', *Istochnik*, 4 (1993), 101–3.
95 Letter of 22 April 1933 to L. O. Pasternak. Postcard of 22 April 1933 to L. O. and R. I. Pasternak (APT).
96 Letter of 8 May 1933 to L. O. Pasternak (APT).
97 Letters of 1 June 1933 and 30 August 1933 to O. M. Freidenberg, *Perepiska*, 148.
98 Letter of early October (n.d.) 1933 to L. O. Pasternak (APT).
99 Letter of 18 October 1933 to O. M. Freidenberg, *Perepiska*, 150.
100 Letters of 5 March 1933 to R. I. and L. O. Pasternak; of 6 August 1933 to R. I. Pasternak; of October 1933 (n.d.) to L. O. Pasternak (APT).
101 Letter of October 1933 (n.d.) to L. L. Pasternak (APT).
102 Letter of 6 March 1933 to George Reavey, 'Iz perepiski s pisatelyami', 734–5. 'Pis'ma k G. E. Sorokinu', 210–14.
103 Letter of 4 March 1933 to A. M. Gor'ky, *SS*, V, 335.
104 A. M. Gor'ky, letter of 18 March 1933 to P. P. Kryuchkov, *M. Gor'ky. Neizdannaya perepiska*. Arkhiv A. M. Gor'kogo, vol. 14 (Moscow, 1976), 504. *EBP*, 502. *FBP30*, 330. 'Pis'ma k I. A. Gruzdevu', 105.
105 Ermolaev, *Soviet Literary Theories 1917–1934*, 162.
106 *FBP30*, 120–1.
107 Letter of 5 March 1933 to L. O. and R. I. Pasternak (APT). Lunacharsky died in December of 1933. On probably his last meeting with Pasternak, see V. Kirpotin, *Nachalo. Avtobiograficheskie stranitsy* (Moscow, 1986), 115–16.
108 Letter of 30 April 1933 to S. D. Spassky, *SS*, V, 339.
109 'Literaturnyi put'' Pavla Vasil'eva. Iz stenogrammy vechera, posvyashchennogo tvorchestvu P. Vasil'eva', *Novyi mir*, 6 (1934), 224. *Vospominaniya*, 716. See also *FBP30*, 123–8.
110 'Mayakovsky v moei zhizni', *LG*, 4 October 1989.
111 *FBP30*, 131–5.
112 Letter of 6 August 1933 to R. I. Pasternak (APT).
113 *SS*, V, 628. *FBP30*, 137 ff.
114 Letter of 6 October 1933 to B. D. Zhgenti, ' "Krai, stavshii mne vtoroi rodinoi" ', 175.
115 Letter of October 1933 (n.d.) to L. L. Pasternak (APT). See also letter of 5 November 1933 to G. E. Sorokin, 'Pis'ma k G. E. Sorokinu', 220–1.
116 Letter of 23 October 1933 to T. Tabidze, in T. Tabidze, *Stat'i, ocherki, perepiska*, 246–7.
117 Letter of 4 January 1934 to N. S. Tikhonov, *SS*, V, 345–7.
118 N. Tabidze, 'Raduga', 293.
119 Letter of 17 November 1933 to Z. N. Pasternak, *BPZNP*, 78.
120 Chikovani, 'Svyashchennye uzy bratstva', 96. Letter of 23 November 1933 to Z. N. Pasternak, *BPZNP*, 81.
121 See *FBP30*, 149–51.

122 Letter of 6 October 1933 to B. D. Zhgenti, ' "Krai, stavshii mne vtoroi rodinoi" ', 175.
123 Letter of 20 October 1933 to R. I. and L. O. Pasternak (APT).
124 A. Akhmatova, 'Mandel'shtam (listki iz dnevnika)', *Sochineniya*, (New York, 1968),II, 179.
125 N. Mandel'shtam, *Vospominaniya*, 157.
126 On this episode, see *FBP30*, 141–6.
127 Letter of 18 October 1934 to A. O. Freidenberg, *Perepiska*, 151.
128 N. Mandel'shtam, *Vospominaniya*, 133.
129 O. E. Mandel'shtam, 'My zhivem, pod soboyu ne chuya strany . . .' *Sobranie sochinenii*, I, 202.
130 'Zametki o peresechenii' 316. Cf. a wordier variant in Ivinskaya, 76.
131 N. Mandel'shtam, *Vospominaniya*, 168–9.

5 CONGRESS, CONSENSUS AND CONFRONTATION

1 Letter of 4 January 1934 to N. S. Tikhonov, *SS*, V, 345–6.
2 'Iz perepiski Borisa Pasternaka s Andreem Belym', 692. Letter of 14 February 1934 to P. M. Folyan, 'Pis'ma druz'yam', *Literaturnaya Gruziya*, 1 (1966), 81. 'Pis'ma k G. E. Sorokinu', 226–7. Tarasenkov, 'Pasternak', 151.
3 'Andrei Bely (nekrolog)', *Izvestiya*, 9 January 1934.
4 L. Kamenev, 'Andrei Bely', *Izvestiya*, 10 January 1934. A. Bolotnikov, 'Andrei Bely', *LG*, 16 January 1934. See *FBP30*, 154–8, on this episode.
5 E. Gershtein, 'O Pasternake', 92.
6 *Ibid.*
7 Letter of 27 February 1934 to L. O. and R. I. Pasternak (APT). 'Ruki proch' ot geroicheskogo rabochego klassa Avstrii!', *LG*, 22 February 1934. 'Vchera vecherom v Moskvu prileteli tovarishchi Dmitrov, Popov i Tanev', *LG*, 28 February 1934.
8 L. O. Pasternak, letter of 15 March 1934 to B. L. Pasternak (PFA).
9 Letter of 7 November 1934 to Zh. L. Pasternak (APT).
10 Letter of 27 February 1934 to L. O. and R. I. Pasternak (APT).
11 Letter of 4 January 1934 to G. E. Sorokin, 'Pis'ma k G. E. Sorokinu', 223.
12 Letter of 14 February 1934 to P. M. Folyan, 'Pis'ma druz'yam', *loc. cit.*, 81.
13 L. Gornung, 'Vstrecha za vstrechei', 78. Letter of 11 February 1934 to G. E. Sorokin, 'Pis'ma k G. E. Sorokinu', 225, 227.
14 Letter of 14 February 1934 to P. M. Folyan, 'Pis'ma druz'yam', *loc. cit.*, 81.
15 Letter of 24 October 1934 to R. N. Lomonosova, *PPL, Minuvshee*, 17 (1995), 364–5.
16 Letter of 23 June 1934 to L. O. and R. I. Pasternak (APT).
17 Letter of 4 October 1934 to S. D. Spassky, *SS*, V, 350–1. See S. Spassky, *Moya Gruziya* (Moscow, 1935).

18 Letter of 8 December 1934 to T. and N. A. Tabidze, *SS*, V, 352.
19 N. Mandel'shtam, *Vospominaniya*, 158.
20 'Priem v Soyuz sovetskikh pisatelei', *LG*, 16 May 1934.
21 Letter of 16 August 1934 to Z. N. Pasternak, *BPZNP*, 83.
22 Kal'm, 'Poeticheskoe tvorchestvo'.
23 'Sovetskaya poeziya pered s"ezdom. Na vsesoyuznom poeticheskom soveshchanii', *LG*, 24 May 1934.
24 Tarasenkov, 'Polden' liriki', and 'Pasternak', 153–4. On this episode, see *FBP30*, 168–75; *EBP*, 505–6.
25 'Zametki o peresechenii', 316.
26 Akhmatova, 'Mandel'shtam (listki iz dnevnika)', 182; N. Selyutsky, 'Eshche odna versiya zvonka Stalina Pasternaku', *Pamyat'*, 2 (1979), 438.
27 'Zametki o peresechenii', 316–17.
28 N. Mandel'shtam, *Vospominaniya*, 7ff. Brown, *Mandelstam*, 127–31.
29 See *FBP30*, 160–3. 'Iz gruzinskikh poetov', *Izvestiya*, 6 March 1934.
30 'Zametki o peresechenii', 317.
31 *Ibid.*, 318.
32 Chudakova, *Zhizneopisanie Mikhaila Bulgakova*, 340–1. Milne, *Mikhail Bulgakov*, 187, 244.
33 Akhmatova, 'Mandel'shtam (listki iz dnevnika)', 182. Maslenikova, *Portret Borisa Pasternaka*, 54–5. For some recent varying interpretations, see: 'Zametki o peresechenii', 316–19; Selyutsky, 'Eshche odna versiya', 438–41; *FBP30*, 175ff.; Solov'ev, 'Telefonnyi razgovor'; A. Aloits, 'Podvig ili predatel'stvo?'.
34 'Zametki o peresechenii', 317. Ivinskaya, *V plenu vremeni*, 77ff. Berlin, 'Vstrechi s russkimi pisatelyami', 527. Maslenikova, *Portret*, 54–5. *EPIV*, 176.
35 *NNVV*, 217–18.
36 N. Mandel'shtam, *Vospominaniya*, 153–4. Akhmatova, 'Mandel'shtam', 182–3. Z. Pasternak, 'Vospominaniya', 195–6. 'Zametki o peresechenii', 317–19.
37 'Zametki i peresechenii', 319. N. Mandel'shtam, *Vospominaniya*, 155–6. Chukovskaya, *Zapiski*, II, 351.
38 Chudakova, *Zhizneopisanie*, 408, 411.
39 Z. Pasternak, 'Vospominaniya', 196–7.
40 *FBP30*, 176.
41 Letter of 23 June 1934 to L. O. and R. I. Pasternak (APT).
42 'Zametki o peresechenii', 317, 319. *SS*, I, 717.
43 Letter of 23 October 1934 to R. N. Lomonosova, *PPL, Minuvshee*, 17 (1995), 362.
44 Letter of 3 September 1934 to L. O. and R. I. Pasternak (APT). N. Tabidze, 'Raduga', 294.
45 See *PVSSP, passim*; R. Mathewson, 'The First Writers' Congress. A Second Look', in Hayward and Labedz (eds.), *Literature and Revolution*, 62–73. On aspects of this relating to Pasternak, see *FBP30*, 197–219.

46 *SS*, IV, 631. Gladkov, *Vstrechi s Pasternakom*, 22.
47 Letter of 22 August 1934 to Z. N. Pasternak, *BPZNP*, 84.
48 *Ibid.*
49 M. Shugal, 'Pervaya vstrecha s gruzinskoi poeziei', ms. (PFA). Graf, *Reise in die Sowjetunion, 1934*, 93.
50 'Vecher gruzinskoi poezii', *LG*, 24 August 1934. See also S. M. Tret'yakov's Congress speech, *PVSSP*, 345.
51 *Ibid.*, 184–5.
52 *Ibid.*, 495.
53 *Ibid.*, 497.
54 Koen, *Bukharin*, 423–4.
55 *PVSSP*, 512.
56 *FBP30*, 212–14. Koen, *Bukharin*, 424.
57 *PVSSP*, 548–9. *SS*, IV, 632. The Soviet printed version replaced 'socialist overlord' by 'literary overlord'. See IMLI, fond 4, op.1, No.199, pp.76–8; *EBP*, 508.
58 *FBP30*, 214. *EBP*, 508.
59 Erenburg, *Lyudi, gody, zhizn'*, bks. 3–4, 420. Ivinskaya, *V plenu vremeni*, 83.
60 *PVSSP*, 208, 234–6, 279.
61 Mindlin, *Neobyknovennye sobesedniki*, 429.
62 Ivinskaya, *V plenu vremeni*, 85. *EBP*, 510.
63 Letter of 27 September 1934 to S. D. Spassky, *SS*, V, 349.
64 *EBP*, 510–11. Tarasenkov, 'Pasternak', 155–8.
65 Letter of 30 October 1934 to O. M and A. O. Freidenberg, *Perepiska*, 152.
66 Letter of 24 October 1934 to R. N. Lomonosova, *PPL, Minuvshee*, 17 (1995), 364.
67 L. O. Pasternak, letter of 8 January 1935 to B. L. Pasternak (PFA).
68 Letter of 7 November 1934 to Zh. L. Pasternak (APT).
69 Letter of 27 November 1934 to Zh. L. Pasternak (APT).
70 Josephine Pasternak's second verse collection was *Pamyati Pedro* (Paris, 1981). See I. Erenburg, *Lyubov' Zhanny Nei* (Riga, 1925).
71 Letter of 5 December 1932 to R. N. Lomonosova, *PPL, Minuvshee*, 16 (1994), 202.
72 Shtein, ' "I ne tol'ko o nem . . ." ', *Teatr*, 2 (1988), 197.
73 Letter of 23 March 1931 to R. N. Lomonosova, *PPL, Minuvshee*, 16 (1994), 178.
74 *NNVV*, 191.
75 Letter of May (n.d.) 1932 to L. O. and R. I. Pasternak; letter of 24 May 1932 to Zh. L. Pasternak (APT).
76 Letter of 4 March 1933 to A. M. Gor'ky, 'Boris Pasternak v perepiske s Maksimom Gor'kim', 281–2.
77 Letter of 25 December 1934 to L. O. and R. I. Pasternak (APT).
78 Barnes, 'Pasternak, Dickens and the Novel Tradition', 326–41. Salys, 'A Tale of Two Artists', 84–6.

79 Letter of 11 January 1935 to Z. N. Pasternak, *BPZNP*, 91–3.
80 Letter of autumn (n.d.) 1935 to L. O. and R. I. Pasternak (APT).
81 'Nakanune plenuma'. See also *FBP30*, 230.
82 Letters of 4 January and 11 January 1935 to Z. N. Pasternak, *BPZNP*, 86, 91.
83 *FBP30*, 222. Letter of 11 January to Z. N. Pasternak, *BPZNP*, 92. Mikulich, 'Povest' dlya sebya', 82.
84 Ya. E. [idel'man], 'Na vechere Dm.Petrovskogo', *LG*, 30 January 1935.
85 N. N., 'Poety sovetskoi Gruzii'. Chukovsky, 'Iz dnevnika', 266; and *Dnevnik 1930–1969*, 122. N. Tabidze, 'Raduga', 292.
86 Z. Pasternak, 'Vospominaniya', 188.
87 Letter of 14 March 1935 to L. O. Pasternak (APT), contradicting *EBP*, 513, over the fact of Pasternak's attendance.
88 Letter of 14 March 1935 to L. O. and R. I. Pasternak (APT). Letter of 10 March 1935 to T. Tabidze, 'Pis'ma druz'yam', *Literaturnaya Gruziya*, 1 (1966), 82. *EPIV*, 143.
89 Letter of 12 April 1935 to L. O. and R. I. Pasternak (APT).
90 Chudakova, *Zhizneopisanie*, 419, and 'Pasternak and Bulgakov', 88.
91 *FBP30*, 218–19.
92 'Skorb' i gnev', *Izvestiya*, 2 December 1934. 'Ponesem ego znamya vpered!', *Novyi mir*, 12 (1934), 5.
93 *FBP30*, 224ff.
94 Letter of 14 April 1935 to S. D. Spassky, *SS*, V, 356; 'Iz pisem B. Pasternaka k S. Spasskomu', *Voprosy literatury*, 9 (1969), 177–8.
95 Letter of 3 April 1935 to O. M. Freidenberg, *Perepiska*, 153.
96 Krotkov, 'Pasternaki', *Grani*, 60 (1966), 65.
97 J. Pasternak, 'Patior', 47; translated in *Vospominaniya*, 27–8.
98 Letters of July (n.d.) 1935 and of 12 July 1935 to Z. N. Pasternak, *BPZNP*, 96, 98.
99 *Stikhi pesni narodov Vostoka o Staline* (Moscow, 1935); *Molodaya Gruziya* (Moscow, 1935); *Sbornik proizvedenii molodykh pisatelei Sovetskoi Sotsialisticheskoi Respubliki Gruzii* (Moscow, 1935); also verse in *Literaturnoe Zakavkaz'e*, 4–5 (1935), etc.
100 Z. Pasternak, 'Vospominaniya', 186. *EBP*, 513. E. V. Pasternak, letter of 24 April 1935 to R. N. Lomonosova, *PPL, Minuvshee*, 17 (1995), 368–9.
101 *Pravda*, 11 May 1935; *LG*, 15 May 1935. Polivanov, 'Zametki i materialy', 72.
102 *EBP*, 513. Anastas'eva, 'Boris Leonidovich Pasternak v zhizni nashei sem'i', 369–70.
103 T. Tabidze, letter of 17 June 1935 to B. L. Pasternak, in his *Stat'i, ocherki, perepiska*, 245. Letter of 11 June 1935 to R. N. Lomonosova, *LLP, Minuvshee*, 17 (1995), 372.
104 Letter of 3 March 1953 to V. F. Asmus, *SS*, V, 510.
105 See *Mezhdunarodnyi kongress pisatelei v zashchitu kul'tury. Parizh, iyun' 1935. Doklady i vystupleniya* (Moscow, 1936); Erenburg, *Lyudi, gody, zhizn'*, bks. 3–4, 466ff. On Pasternak, see: *FBP30*, 236ff.; Struve (publ.), 'Boris Pasternak. Slovo', 9–15.

106 *FBP30*, 288ff.
107 Struve, 'Boris Pasternak', 10. *FBP30*, 242–3.
108 Berlin, 'Vstrechi', 520. Z. Pasternak, 'Vospominaniya', 188, 190.
109 A. N. Pirozhkova, 710. 'Babel' v 1932–1939 godakh (iz vospominanii)', *I. Babel. Vospominaniya sovremennikov* (Moscow, 1972), 333.
110 J. Pasternak, 'Patior', 45.
111 *Ibid.*, 45–8. Letter of 3 July 1935 to L. O. and R. I. Pasternak (APT). Letter of July (n.d.) 1935 to Z. N. Pasternak, *BPZNP*, 96.
112 Erenburg, 'Pis'mo s kongressa', and *Lyudi, gody, zhizn'*, bks 3–4, 471.
113 Goldberg, *Ilya Ehrenburg*, 152–3.
114 Regler, *The Owl of Minerva*, 231.
115 Erenburg, *Lyudi, gody, zhizn'*, bks 3–4, 470–1. *EBP*, 513. Pirozhkova, 'Years at His Side', 190. See vol. I, 1.
116 Berlin, 'Vstrechi', 520–1. *Mezhdunarodnyi kongress pisatelei*, 375. Struve, 'Boris Pasternak', 9. *EBP*, 514.
117 *EBP*, 513.
118 Letter of 18 May 1936 to L. O. and R. I. Pasternak (APT).
119 Annenkov, *Dnevnik moikh vstrech*, II, 163–4.
120 Letter of July (n.d.) 1935 to Z. N. Pasternak, *BPZNP*, 96, 231–2. Letter of 3 July 1935 to L. O. and R. I. Pasternak (APT). J. de Proyart, 'Une amitié d'enfance', in Aucouturier (ed.), *Boris Pasternak 1890–1960*, 519. Bakhrakh, *Po pamyati, po zapisyam*, 65.
121 Polyanina, 'Neopublikovannoe pis'mo M. I. Tsvetaevoi k N. S. Tikhonovu', 209–10. *EBP*, 514.
122 M. I. Tsvetaeva, letter of 2 July 1935 to A. Tesková, in her *Pis'ma k A. Teskovoi*, 126.
123 Berberova, *Kursiv moi. Avtobiografiya*, I, 236. Gershtein, 'O Pasternake i ob Akhmatovoi', 396. M. I. Tsvetaeva, letter of 6 July 1935 to N. S. Tikhonov, *Pis'ma k A. Teskovoi*, 210.
124 M. Tsvetaeva, letter of 15 February 1936 to A. Tesková, *Pis'ma k A. Teskovoi*, 134. Efron, *O Marine Tsvetaevoi*, 162, 164.
125 Karlinsky, *Marina Cvetaeva: Her Life and Art*, 89, 95–6, and *Marina Tsvetaeva*, 213–15. NKVD – National Commissariat of Internal Affairs, the post-1934 title of OGPU.
126 Letter of July (n.d.) 1935 to Z. N. Pasternak, *BPZNP*, 95–6. A. Efron, letter of 1 August 1948 to B. L. Pasternak, in Efron, *Pis'ma iz ssylki (1948–1957)*, 6.
127 Ivinskaya, *V plenu vremeni*, 65.
128 Letter of 25 May 1950 to A. S. Efron, in *Pis'ma iz ssylki*, 63.
129 R. N. Lomonosova, letter of 7 July 1935 to B. L. Pasternak, *LLP, Minuvshee*, 17 (1995), 378.
130 Letter of 5 August 1935 to R. N. Lomonosova, *ibid.*, 379–81.
131 On Schcherbakov, see Conquest, *The Great Terror*, 237. N. Mandel'shtam, *Vospominaniya*, 147. *FBP30*, 262.
132 Katanyan, 'O Mayakovskom i Pasternake', 510–11.

133 Chernyak, 'Pasternak. Iz vospominanii', 138. Ya. Z. Chernyak, letter of 11 July 1935 to B. L. Pasternak, *Vospominaniya*, 710.
134 Berlin, 'Vstrechi', 521. K. M. Polivanov, 'Zametki i materialy', 72–3.
135 Z. Pasternak, 'Vospominaniya', 190–1.
136 Letter of 16 July 1935 to L. O. and R. I. Pasternak (APT). L. Chukovskaya, *Zapiski*, II, 358.
137 Z. Pasternak, 'Vospominaniya', 191.
138 Letter (n.d.) of October 1935 to M. I. Tsvetaeva, A. Efron, *O Marine Tsvetaevoi*, 162; also her 'Stranitsy bylogo', *Zvezda*, 6 (1975), 169. Letter of 15 December 1955 to M. G. Vatagin, *SS*, V, 543. E. B. Pasternak's verbal evidence contradicts *FBP30*, 264–5, based on *Pravda*, 31 July 1935, which names invitees, not participants.
139 Letter (n.d.) 1935 to Z. N. Pasternak, *BPZNP*, 101.
140 Letter of autumn (n.d.) 1935 to Z. N. Pasternak, *ibid.*, 100.
141 Letter of 26 October 1935 to L. O. and R. I. Pasternak (APT). See also letter (n.d.) of October 1935 to M. I. Tsvetaeva, A. Efron, 'Stranitsy bylogo', 169.
142 Zhid (Gide), 'Novaya pishcha', 161–96. Tarasenkov, 'Pasternak', 161.
143 Boris Pasternak, *Liryka*, trans. J. Hora, afterword by A. Bem (Prague, 1935).
144 Letter of 15 November 1935 to J. Hora, 'Iozef Gora i Boris Pasternak', *Voprosy literatury*, 7 (1979), 184. G. Struve, 'Dnevnik chitatelya: Pasternak i ego cheshskii perevodchik', *Russkaya mysl'*, 29 April 1967. Frits Bryugel' [Fritz Brügel], 'Razgovor s Borisom Pasternakom', *Voprosy literatury*, 7 (1979), 179–80.
145 Boris Pasternak, *Glejt* (Prague, 1935).
146 Jakobson, 'Randbemerkungen zur Prosa des Dichters Pasternak', 357–74. On 'Vassermanova reaktsiya', see vol. I, 166–7. See also Jakobson, 'Kontury "Glejtu"', in Pasternak, *Glejt*, 149–62; translated as 'The Contours of *Safe Conduct*', in *Semiotics of Art* (Cambridge, MA, 1976), 188–96.
147 D. Oblomievsky, 'Boris Pasternak', *Literaturnyi sovremennik*, 4 (1935), 127–42.
148 Semenov, 'Boris Pasternak'.
149 Tarasenkov, 'Pasternak v krivom zerkale', 228–35, and 'Pasternak', 160.
150 Mirsky, 'Zametki o poezii', 231.
151 'Vstrechi s Il'ei Erenburgom', *LG*, 11 November 1935.
152 T. Tabidze, 'O knige B. Pasternaka "Gruzinskie liriki"', *Stat'i, ocherki, perepiska*, 132–3. Tarasenkov, 'O gruzinskikh perevodakh Pasternaka', 201–9. Mirsky, 'Pasternak i gruzinskie poety'. Tsybulevsky, *Vysokie uroki*, 90, 127.
153 Gaprindashvili, 'Perevod – dvoinik originala'.
154 K. Zelinsky, 'Voprosy postroeniya istorii sovetskoi literatury', *Literaturnyi kritik*, 2 (1935). See *FBP30*, 289–90.
155 'Rech' B. L. Pasternaka na pervom vsesoyuznom soveshchanii perevodchikov', *Literaturnaya Gruziya*, 8 (1968), 40.
156 Letter of 26 October 1935 to L. O. and R. I. Pasternak (APT).
157 Shtein, '"I ne tol'ko o nem"', *Teatr*, 2 (1988), 176–7.
158 Letter of 22 November 1935 to B. L. Pasternak (PFA).

159 Letter of April (n.d.) 1936 to L. O. and R. I. Pasternak (APT).
160 Letter of 28–9 December 1935 to L. O. and R. I. Pasternak (APT).
161 L. O. Pasternak, letter of 21 January 1936 to B. L. Pasternak (PFA).
162 Letter of 15 November 1935 to Josef Hora, 'Iozef Gora i Boris Pasternak', 183.
163 *SS*, IV, 338. *FBP30*, 269–73, 276–8. Fleishman, 'Pis′mo Pasternaka Stalinu'. Polivanov, 'Zametki i materialy', 73.
164 L. Chukovskaya, *Zapiski*, II, 594.
165 *FBP30*, 275–6. Gershtein, 'O Pasternake i ob Akhmatovoi', 392–4. Z. Pasternak, 'Vospominaniya', 194.
166 *FBP30*, 273–5.
167 Gutner, 'O putyakh liriki', 161.
168 Koen, *Bukharin*, 425, 429.
169 Ivinskaya, *V plenu vremeni*, 73. *SS*, II, 620.
170 Koen, *Bukharin*, 433–4.
171 Letter of 6 March 1936 to L. O. and R. I. Pasternak (APT).
172 A. Larina, memoirs of Pasternak, ms (PFA).
173 *SS*, II, 142–3, 642. Ivinskaya, *V plenu vremeni*, 73.
174 Tarasenkov, 'Pasternak', 162.
175 *SS*, *II*, 619–20. Ivinskaya, *V plenu vremeni*, 74.
176 *FBP30*, 283. Gornung, 'Vstrecha za vstrechei', 80.
177 *FBP20*, 118–19.
178 Geller, 'Poet i vozhd′', 227–40. D. Volkogonov, 'Triumf i tragediya. Politicheskii portret I. V. Stalina, *Roman-gazeta*, 19 (1990), 77–9.
179 Chudakova, 'Bez gneva i pristrastiya', 256–8, and *Zhizneopisanie*, 422, 465.
180 'Sumbur vmesto muzyki. Ob opere "Ledi Makbet Mtsenskogo uezda" ', *Pravda*, 28 January 1936. Shostakovich, *Testimony*, 113–14.
181 Letter of 1 October 1936 to O. M. Freidenberg, *Perepiska*, 158. *FBP30*, 295–302.
182 On this episode, see *FBP30*, 295–302.
183 Letter of 13 May 1936 to R. N. Lomonosova, *PPL, Minuvshee*, 17 (1995), 393–5.
184 Z. Pasternak, 'Vospominaniya', 191–2. Tarasenkov, 'Pasternak', 161–2.
185 *FBP30*, 305. *EBP*, 514–15.
186 'O sovetskoi poezii. Doklad A. Surkova na III plenume Pravleniya SP SSSR', *LG*, 16 February 1936.
187 ' "Za Mayakovskogo." Rech tov. Altauzena', *LG*, 16 February 1936. Barnes, 'The Original Text', 298. R. Eideman, 'Literatura i oborona', *LG*, 29 February 1936. 'Literatura i deistvitel′nost′. Rech′ tov.V. Inber', *ibid.*
188 Mirsky, 'Poeziya Gruzii'.
189 'Vershiny mirovoi poezii. Rech′ tov. Mustangovoi', *LG*, 24 February 1936.
190 Letter of 6 March 1936 to L. O. and R. I. Pasternak (APT). Mikulich, 'Povest′ dlya sebya', 82. Barnes, 'The Original Text', 294–303. B. Pasternak, ' "O skromnosti i smelosti". Rech′ na tret′em Plenume Pravleniya soyuza sovetskich, pisatelei SSSR', *LG*, 16 February 1936.

191 Barnes, 'The Original Text', 297.
192 *SS, IV,* 636–8. Barnes, 'The Original Text', 301.
193 'Nadmennyi nishchii', *SS, IV,* 261–2. Barnes, 'The Original Text', 301. Tarasenkov, 'Pasternak', 162.
194 *LG,* 12 February 1936. On the Minsk conference, see *FBP30,* 303–23; *EBP,* 514–16, 526.

6 PEREDELKINO AND THE PURGES

1 'Telegramma SP Gruzii, V. D. Zhgenti', ' "Krai, stavshii mne vtoroi rodinoi" ', 168.
2 'Otkrovennyi razgovor. O tvorchestve Borisa Pasternaka', *Komsomol'skaya pravda,* 23 February 1936.
3 Druzin, 'Na poeticheskie temy', 242–7.
4 Letter of 28 February 1936 to Fedin, 'Pis'ma B. L. Pasternaka – K. A. Fedinu', 167.
5 D. Osipov [i.e. D. O. Zaslavsky], 'Mechty i zvuki Marietty Shaginyan', *Pravda,* 28 February 1936. See also 'Ob advokatakh formalizma', *Komsomol'skaya pravda,* 28 February 1936.
6 Chudakova, *Zhizneopisanie,* 425 ff. Milne, *Mikhail Bulgakov,* 213–14.
7 Letter of 28 February 1936 to K. A. Fedin, 'Pis'ma B. L. Pasternaka – K. A. Fedinu'. Tarasenkov, 'Pasternak', 162.
8 Stavsky, 'O formalizme i naturalizme'.
9 Letter of 1 October 1936 to O. M. Freidenberg, *Perepiska,* 158.
10 ' "Namerennyi risk" ', 87–9. See also *EBP,* 517–18.
11 ' "Iskusstvo na kholostom khodu". Iz rechi tov.N. Aseeva', *LG* 20 March 1936. Dolmatovsky, 'Protiv ravnodushiya i khaltury', *ibid.* 'Vliyanie formalizma v poezii. Iz rechi tov.A. Surkova', *ibid.* 'Poeziya dlya millionov. Iz rechi tov.A. Gidash', *ibid.* Ya. Eidel'man, 'Dnevnik diskussii', *LG,* 15 March 1936. 'Za iskusstvo pobedivshego natroda. Rech' tov.Kirpotina na obshchemoskovskom sobranii pisatelei', *ibid.*
12 'Dve vynuzhdennye repliki', *Komsomol'skaya pravda,* 16 March 1936. 'S obshchemoskovskogo sobraniya pisatelei', *Pravda,* 16 March 1936. On this episode, see *FBP30,* 329 ff.
13 Tarasenkov, 'Pasternak', 164.
14 E. g. A. Adalis, 'Golos chitatelya', *LG,* 20 March 1936.
15 'Na obshchemoskovskom sobranii pisatelei 16 marta', *LG,* 20 March 1936. See also, Golodny, 'Partiinoe pristrastie v poezii'; Nikulin, 'Men'she pretenzii – bol'she knig', *ibid.*
16 Letter of 1 October 1936 to O. M. Freidenberg, *Perepiska,* 158.
17 Letter of April (n.d.) 1936 to L. O. and R. I. Pasternak (APT). Gladkov, *Vstrechi s Pasternakom,* 9–10.
18 *FBP30,* 337–8.

19 M. Gor'ky, 'O formalizme', *Pravda*, 3 April 1936, reprinted in his *Sobranie sochinenii v 30 tomakh*, vol. 27 (Moscow, 1953), 521–8.
20 N. Bukharin, 'Marshruty istorii – mysli vslukh', *Izvestiya*, 6 July 1936. Koen, *Bukharin*, 435.
21 Chukovsky, *Dnevnik 1930–1969*, 141.
22 Letter of 8 April 1936 to T. Yu. and N. A. Tabidze, *SS*, V, 358. On these poems, see also Tarasenkov, 'Pasternak', 165.
23 'Vse naklonen'ya i zalogi . . .' *SS*, *II*, 144–6. *FBP30*, 287–8. Levin, 'Zametki k stikhotvoreniyu B. Pasternaka' in Podgaetskaya (ed.), *Pasternakovskie chteniya*, 67–75. On a subtextual dialogue with Mandelstam, see 'Zametki o peresechenii', 321–2.
24 'Nemye individy . . .', *SS*, *II*, 12–13.
25 'Skromnyi dom, no ryumka romu . . .' *Soch*.III, 5–6; *SP*, 383–4; *SS*, *II*, 9–10. Letter of 8 April 1936 to T. Yu. and Tabidze, ' "Krai, stavshii mne vtoroi rodinoi" ', 179.
26 'On vstaet. Veka, Gelaty . . .' *SS*, *II*, 621–2.
27 Letter of 8 April 1936 to T. Yu and N. A. Tabidze, *SS*, V, 357–8.
28 Letter of 1 October 1936 to O. M. Freidenberg, *Perepiska*, 161–2.
29 See vol. I, 226–8, 348–9.
30 Letter of 25 April 1936 to L. L. Pasternak, quoted in *EBP*, 526–7.
31 L. O. Pasternak, letter of 7 April 1936 to B. L. Pasternak (PFA).
32 Letter of 1 October 1936 to O. M. Freidenberg, *Perepiska*, 160.
33 Letter of 13 May 1936 to L. O. and R. I. Pasternak, quoted in *EBP*, 528.
34 Letter of summer (n.d.) 1936 to L. O. and R. I. Pasternak (APT).
35 A. P. Ryabinina, memoirs, ms (PFA).
36 Z. Pasternak, 'Vospominaniya', 192–4. Letter of 24 November 1936 to L. O. and R. I. Pasternak (APT).
37 L. O. Pasternak, letter of 24 December 1936 to B. L. Pasternak (PFA).
38 'Novoe sovershennolet'e', *Izvestiya*, 15 June 1936; *SS*, IV, 639–40. See *FBP30*, 356–62.
39 T. Tabidze, 'Druzhba narodov – osnova Stalinskoi konstitutsii', *Izvestiya*, 23 June 1936. Krotkov, 'Pasternaki', *Grani*, 63 (1967), 63.
40 Tarasenkov, 'Pasternak', 169–70.
41 *FBP30*, 363–5.
42 Ivanov, 'Pochemu Stalin', 91–134.
43 E. V. Pasternak, letter of 9 October 1936 to R. N. Lomonosova, *LLP, Minuvshee*, 17 (1995), 396.
44 Letter of autumn (n.d.) 1936 to L. O. and R. I. Pasternak (APT).
45 See L. Chukovskaya, *Zapiski*, II, 358.
46 Letter of autumn (n.d.) 1936 to L. O. and R. I. Pasternak (APT).
47 Letter of 1 October 1936 to T. Yu. and N. A. Tabidze, 'Pis'ma druz'yam', *Literaturnaya Gruziya*, 1 (1966), 83. Rayfield, *The Literature of Georgia*, 270. See below fn.107. *Soch*, III, 12–13, 16–17; *SP*, 389–90, 393–4; *SS*, *II*, 16–17, 20–1.

48 Letter of 1 October 1936 to T. Yu. and N. A. Tabidze, 'Pis'ma druz'yam', *Literaturnaya Gruziya*, 1 (1966), 83.
49 Letters of 24 November 1936 to L. O. and R. I. Pasternak, and late 1937 (n.d.) to L. L. Pasternak Slater (APT). *EBP*, 531. 'Perepiska s Evgeniei Pasternak', *Znamya*, 2 (1966), 182.
50 Tarasenkov, 'Pasternak', 165–6, 169–70. 'Perevody iz Kleista', *Literaturnaya gazeta*, 10 July 1936. *FBP30*, 372.
51 Letter of 25 April 1936 to L. L. Pasternak Slater (APT).
52 Conquest, *The Great Terror*, 151 ff.
53 Medvedev, *Nikolai Bukharin*, 138. Larina, *Nezabyvaemoe*, 309.
54 Koen, *Bukharin*, 436–7.
55 Tarasenkov, 'Pasternak', 169.
56 M. I. Tsvetaeva, letter of 14 November 1936 to A. Tesková, in *Pis'ma k A. Teskovoi*, 145. *FBP30*, 367–70. See also Vaksberg, *Stalin's Prosecutor*, 83.
57 See *Vospominaniya o Pavle Vasil'eve*, ed. F. Chernyshova (Alma-Ata, 1989), 201, 265, 284.
58 Selivanovsky, 'V zashchitu sovetskoi kul'tury'; 'U moskovskikh pisatelei'; Stavsky, 'Sdelat' vse prakticheskie vyvody', and various other speeches, in *LG*, 27 August 1936.
59 'Vrednaya galimat'ya', *Izvestiya*, 28 September 1936.
60 Letter of 1 October 1936 to O. M. Freidenberg, *Perepiska*, 159–61. N. Perlina, 'Olga Freidenberg's Works and Days', *Strumenti critici*, 2 (1990), 180ff.
61 On Volin, see *FBP30*, 125–6. *Perepiska*, 165–8.
62 Letter of 1 October 1936 to T. Yu. and N. A. Tabidze, 'Pis'ma druz'yam', *Literaturnaya Gruziya*, 1 (1966) 83.
63 Verbal testimony of R. D. B. Thomson from recollection by Leonov's daughter.
64 Pertsov, 'Literaturnye zapiski', *LG*, 27 October 1936. See also vol. I, 472.
65 Gutner, 'Tvorcheskaya deklaratsiya'.
66 P. Saratovsky, 'Na vechere v "Novom mire"', *Novyi mir*, 9 (1936), 242–52. See also FBP30, 376–7.
67 Polivanov, 'Zametki i materialy', 73.
68 'Na obshchemoskovskom sobranii pisatelei. Doklad V. P. Stavskogo o Chrezvychainom S"ezde Sovetov na obshchem sobranii chlenov SSP SSSR 16 dekabrya 1936 goda', *LG*, 20 December 1936.
69 Bakhrakh, 'Po pamyati', 364. *FBP30*, 362–3, 381. Muravina, *Vstrechi*, 24. Tarasenkov, 'Pasternak', 169.
70 Gladkov, *Vstrechi s Pasternakom*, 11.
71 'Na obshchemoskovskom sobranii pisatelei. Doklad V. P. Stavskogo'. Tarasenkov, 'Pasternak', 169. Polivanov, 'Zametki i materialy', 74–5.
72 'Spetsspravka o nastroeniyakh sredi pisatelei', ed. and commentary K. M. Polivanov, *De visu*, 0 (1992), 35–8.
73 'V storone ot zhizni. O tvorchestve Borisa Pasternaka', *Vechernyaya Moskva*, 19 December 1936.
74 *FBP30*, 385.

75 *EBIV*, 145.
76 Afinogenov, 'Iz dnevnika 1937 goda', *Vospominaniya*, 376.
77 Koen, *Bukharin*, 438.
78 Larina, *Nezabyvaemoe*, 309. *FBP30*, 406. Medvedev, *Nikolai Bukharin*, 138.
79 Koen, *Bukharin*, 438.
80 I. Babel', 'Lozh', predatel'stvo, smerdyakovshchina'; K. Fedin, 'Agenty mezhdunarodnoi kontrrevolyutsii'; D. Mirsky, 'Chuzherodnyi sor'; A. Platonov, 'Preodolenie zlodeistva'; Yu. Olesha, 'Fashisty pered sudom naroda', *LG*, 26 January 1937.
81 ' "Esli vrag ne sdaetsya – ego unichtozhayut." ' Rezolyutsiya prezidiuma Soyuza sovetskikh pisatelei ot 25 yanvarya 1937 goda', *LG*, 26 January 1937.
82 *FBP30*, 389–90. Andronikashvili-Pil'nyak, 'Dva izgoya', 152.
83 Afinogenov, 'Iz dnevnika', 376.
84 Polivanov, 'Zametki i materialy', 78–9.
85 Letter of 12 February 1937 to L. O. and R. I. Pasternak, 'Pozitsiya khudozhnika. Pis'ma Borisa Pasternaka', *Literaturnoe obozrenie*, 2 (1990), 5.
86 Ya. En. 'Zametki i vpechatleniya. Na chetvertom plenume pravleniya SSP', *LG*, 26 February 1937.
87 'Ne otstavat' ot zhizni. Rech' tov.Dzh.Altauzena', *LG*, 26 February 1937.
88 Gladkov *Vstrechi s Pasternakom*, 10–11.
89 A. Surkov, 'Lyubimyi narodnyi poet', *LG*, 26 February 1937. 'Nakanune velikoi godovshchiny. Rech' tov. A. Bezymenskogo', *ibid.*, 5 March 1937.
90 'Za podlinnuyu demokratiyu. Rech' tov. A. Fadeeva', *LG*, 10 March 1937. Gladkov, *Vstrechi s Pasternakom*, 50–1. Cockrell, 'Two Writers', 17.
91 *SS*, IV, 640–6. 'Na pushkinskom plenume pravleniya Soyuza sovetskikh pisatelei', *Izvestiya*, 28 February 1937. On this episode, see also *FBP30*, 394–406.
92 'Reshitel'no uluchshit' rabotu Soyuza pisatelei. Iz soobshcheniya tov.Stavskogo na IV plenume Pravleniya Soyuza pisatelei SSSR', *LG*, 20 March 1937.
93 Ya.E[idel'man]. 'Preniya po dokladu tov. V. Stavskogo', *LG*, 5 March 1937.
94 'Obshchee sobranie leningradskikh pisatelei', *LG*, 26 March 1937. 'O politicheskoi poezii', *Pravda*, 28 February 1937. Tarasenkov, 'V redaktsiyu zhurnala "Znamya" ', 284–5.
95 Conquest, *The Great Terror*, 329. G. Nekhoroshev, notes on D. S. Mirsky in *Pamyatnye knizhnye daty* (1990), 111.
96 A. Gurshtein, 'Poet sotsializma', *Pravda*, 12 April 1937. V. Aleksandrov, 'Chastnaya zhizn'', *Literaturnyi kritik*, 3 (1937), 55–81. See also negative appraisals in V. Lugovskoi, 'Byt' ekhom velikogo naroda', *Molodaya gvardiya*, 4 (1937), 185. E. Usievich, 'K sporam o politicheskoi poezii', *Literaturnyi kritik*, 5 (1937), 76. O. Voitinskaya, 'Vrazhdebnye vliyaniya v poezii', *LG*, 30 May 1937. Novikov, ' "Otzvuki i grimasy" ', 107–8.
97 Izgoev, 'Boris Pasternak'.
98 Ivinskaya, *V plenu vremeni*, 146.
99 Afinogenov, 'Iz dnevnika', 384.
100 N. Mandel'shtam, *Vospominaniya*, 159.

101 Tarasenkov, 'Pasternak', 173.
102 Z. Pasternak, 'Vospominaniya', 198.
103 Afinogenov, *Stat'i, dnevniki, pis'ma*, 150, 152–3; and 'Iz dnevnika 1937 goda', 378–87.
104 Mandel'shtam, *Vospominaniya*, 151. 'Zametki o peresechenii', 322–6. *EBP*, 575.
105 Akhmatova, 'Mandel'shtam', 183. Mandel'shtam, *Vospominaniya*, 318. 'Zametki o peresechenii', 326.
106 *Perepiska*, 172–3.
107 *Ibid.*, 174–5.
108 Letter of 1 November 1938 to O. M. Freidenberg, *Perepiska*, 178.
109 Letter of 12 January 1939 to L. L. Pasternak Slater (APT).
110 'Literatura i iskusstvo Gruzii. Iz doklada L. P. Beriya na X S"ezde KP(b) Gruzii', *LG*, 5 June 1937.
111 'Nablyudatel'nost', bditel'nost' i zorkost'. Rech' tov.Pavla Yashvili', *LG*, 5 March 1937.
112 Rayfield, 'The Killing of Paolo Iashvili', 9–14.
113 *Ibid.*, 14. Rayfield, *Literature of Georgia*, 269–70.
114 Letter of 28 August 1937 to T. G. Yashvili, in Baluashvili, 'Vdokhnovennyi poet-patriot', 88–9.
115 T. Tabidze, *Stat'i, ocherki, perepiska*, 189–90. V. Yanov, 'Vecher T. Tabidze, *LG*, 10 March 1937. M. Shugal, 'Pervaya vstrecha s gruzinskoi poeziei', ms (PFA).
116 Rayfield, *Literature of Georgia*, 275. See also *ibid.*, 297–310.
117 Tarasenkov, 'Pasternak', 172–3. Chikovani, 'Svyashchennye uzy bratstva', 100.
118 *EBP*, 535. Dadashidze, ' "Ya ni v maloi stepeni" '; Z. Pasternak, 'Vospominaniya', 198.
119 Letter of 27 December 1940 to N. A. Tabidze, 'Pis'ma druz'yam', *Literaturnaya Gruziya*, 1 (1966), 85–6.
120 Z. Pasternak, 'Vospominaniya', 197. Fedina, 'Iz istorii gorodka pisatelei v Peredelkine', 9.
121 *FBP30*, 416.
122 Berlin, 'Vstrechi', 528. *EPIV*, 145.
123 Conquest, *The Great Terror*, 223–4.
124 'Ne dadim zhit' vragam Sovetskogo Soyuza', *LG*, 15 June 1937.
125 On this episode, see Nilsson, 'Besuch bei Boris Pasternak', 108; Ivinskaya, *V plenu vremeni*, 145–6; Z. Pasternak, 'Vospominaniya', 198–9; *FBP30*, 421; *EBP*, 534; Polivanov, 'Zametki i materialy', 77.
126 *FBP30*, 424–6.
127 *Ibid.*, 426–8.
128 Z. Pasternak, 'Vospominaniya', 199.
129 Letter of 1 July 1937 to R. N. Lomonosova, *PPL, Minuvshee*, 17 (1995), 398–9.
130 Letter of 1 October 1937, to L. O. and R. I. Pasternak (APT).
131 Erenburg, *Lyudi, gody, zhizn'*, bks 3–4, 634ff.
132 Letter of 1 October 1937 to L. O. and R. I. Pasternak (APT).

133 Letter of 12 February 1937 to L. O. and R. I. Pasternak (APT).
134 Letter of 1 October 1937 to L. O. and R. I. Pasternak (APT).
135 Z. Pasternak, 'Vospominaniya', 199–200.
136 *EBP*, 536.
137 Letter (n.d.) of March 1938 to R. N. Lomonosova, *PPL, Minuvshee*, 17 (1995), 401.
138 *Ibid.*, 400.
139 'Moskovskaya khronika', *Vechernyaya Moskva*, 2 January 1938.
140 Z. Pasternak, 'Vospominaniya', 200.

7 PROSE, OBSCURITY AND 'HAMLET'

1 N. Mandel'shtam, *Vtoraya kniga*, 210, 387ff.
2 *Ibid.*, 389.
3 Fedin, 'Dva vida oruzhiya'. See *Vospominaniya*, 378.
4 Letter of 12 February 1937 to L. O. and R. I. Pasternak, quoted in *EBP*, 533.
5 Letter of 12 May 1937 to L. O. and R. I. Pasternak, quoted *EBP*, 533–4.
6 Letter of 1 October 1937 to L. O. and R. I. Pasternak, quoted *EBP*, 535. Afinogenov, 'Iz dnevnika', 379–81.
7 'Iz novogo romana o 1905 gode', *LG*, 31 December 1937. *SS*, IV, 271–86.
8 'Uezd v tylu', 'Nadmennyi nishchii', 'Tetya Olya', *SS*, IV, 240–51, 256–71.
9 *SS*, IV, 826.
10 See above, p. 162, for an extract from 'Pered razlukoi'.
11 Salys, 'From the Pale to the University', 447–8; and 'Leonid Pasternak's *Moi proizvedeniya*', 208–9, 261–2.
12 Letter of 22 February 1935 to O. Petrovskaya, in her 'Vospominaniya', *Vospominaniya*, 104.
13 Afinogenov, 'Iz dnevnika', 379.
14 Letter of 14 April 1938, to R. N. Lomonosova, *PPL, Minuvshee*, 17 (1995), 402.
15 Letter (n.d.) of late 1937 to L. L. Pasternak Slater (APT).
16 Etkind, *Poeziya i perevod*, 93–5. P. France, 'Pasternak and the English Romantics', in Barnes (ed.), *Pasternak and European Literature*, 315–25. Podgaetskaya, 'Pasternak i Verlen'. In his later years, Pasternak carried in his pocket a handwritten copy of two stanzas from Verlaine's 'Sagesse XXI': 'Va ton chemin sans plus t'inquiéter . . .' and 'Surtout il faut garder toute espérance . . .'
17 Letter of 5 November 1938 to N. K. Chukovsky, *SS*, *V*, 378. Letter of 5 November 1938 to L. K. Chukovskaya (PFA).
18 Letter of 14 April 1938 to R. N. Lomonosova, quoted *EBP*, 537.
19 *EBP*, 538.
20 Evgen'ev, 'Perevody B. Pasternaka', 14.
21 *Ibid.*, 15.
22 *SS*, II, 314.
23 Erenburg, *Lyudi, gody, zhizn'*, bks 3–4, 662.
24 Ivanov, 'Perevernutoe zerkalo', 200–201.

25 Conquest, *The Great Terror*, 367–426. *EPIV*, 136.
26 Salys, 'Leonid Pasternak's *Moi proizvedeniya*', 279. Belkina, *Skreshchenie sudeb*, 398–9. No collective letter was published but various articles and editorial material appeared in *LG*, 12 and 15 March 1937, and a statement from various artistic unions: 'Trebuem besposhchadnogo prigovora', *LG*, 5 March 1937.
27 Brown, *Mandelstam*, 133–4. N. Mandel'shtam, *Vospominaniya*, 386–416.
28 See vol. I, p. xi; below, p. 305.
29 Akhmatova, *Sochineniya*, I, 353. L. Chukovskaya, *Zapiski*, I, 53.
30 Letter of 18 April 1939 to S. D. Spassky, *SS*, V, 378.
31 'Vybory byuro poeticheskoi sektsii. Na obshchemoskovskom sobranii poetov', *LG*, 1 December 1938.
32 'Iz rechi tov. A. Fadeeva', *LG*, 6 May 1939.
33 *ZRL*, 95.
34 Zh. Pasternak, *Pamyati Pedro*, 85ff.
35 L. O. Pasternak, letters of 9 May 1939 and 14 August 1939 to B. L. Pasternak (PFA). See vol. I, 185.
36 Letter of 30 October 1938 to L. L. Pasternak Slater (APT).
37 Letter of 12 January 1939 to L. L. Pasternak Slater, quoted *EBP*, 539.
38 Belkina, *Skreshchenie sudeb*, 97–8. Ginzburg, *Chelovek za pis'mennym stolom*, 312. Fadeev had earlier stated in a memo to the Central Committee that Babel, Ehrenburg, Olesha and Pasternak were politically dubious personalities and thus unworthy of official distinction. See Babichenko (ed.), '*Literaturnyi front*', 38.
39 V. F. Khodasevich, 'Ordenonostsy', *Vozrozhdenie*, 17 February 1939. J. Malmstad, 'Binary Opposites', in Fleishman (ed.), *Boris Pasternak*, 112. Ivanov, 'Perevernutoe zerkalo', 201.
40 'Drugu, zamechatel'nomu tovarishchu', *LG*, 26 February 1939; *SS*, IV, 376–7. Molochko and Molova, *Tebe, moya zhizn'*, 11–14.
41 P. M. Kerzhentsev, 'Chuzhoi teatr', *Pravda*, 17 December 1937. Elagin, *Temnyi genii*, 380ff.
42 Letter of 12 January 1939 to L. L. Pasternak Slater (APT). Letter of 14 February 1940 to O. M. Freidenberg, *Perepiska*, 180.
43 'Gamlet. Predstavlenie vo dvortse', *Ogonek*, 18 (1939), 8.
44 Letter of 29 April 1939 to L. O. and R. I. Pasternak (APT).
45 Z. Pasternak, 'Vospominaniya', 200. Ivanov, 'Perevernutoe zerkalo', 201, 205–6.
46 Sh. Petefi, 'Pyat' stikhotvorenii', *LG*, 26 June 1939.
47 Letter of 22 June 1939 to L. O. Pasternak (APT).
48 Z. Pasternak, 'Vospominaniya', 192. Letter of 29 April 1939 to L. O. and R. I. Pasternak (APT).
49 Letter of 21 May 1939 to L. O. Pasternak (APT).
50 Letter of 12 June 1939 to L. O. Pasternak (APT).
51 Letter of 29 April 1939 to L. O. and R. I. Pasternak. Letters of 22 June 1939 and 15 July 1939 to L. O. Pasternak (APT). *EPIV*, 146.
52 Letter of 15 July 1939 to L. O. Pasternak, quoted in *EBP*, 540. On family and

Peredelkino dacha life in the 1930s, see Zimyanina (ed.), *Stanislav Neigauz*, items by M. V. Anastas'eva (pp. 36–40), Ts. A. Voskresenskaya (pp. 41–3), T. I. Sel'vinskaya (pp. 43–5).

53 Ivanov, 'Perevernutoe zerkalo', 202–4.
54 *EBP*, 541. Letter of 4 November 1939 to relatives in Britain (APT).
55 Elagin, *Temnyi genii*, 406–10.
56 Leach, *Vsevolod Meyerhold*, 29. Ivanov, 'Perevernutoe zerkalo', 204.
57 Gladkov, *Vstrechi s Pasternakom*, 135. Vaksberg, *Stalin's Prosecutor*, 181–6.
58 Danin, *Bremya styda*, 285.
59 L. O. Pasternak, letter of 14 August 1939 to B. L. Pasternak (PFA). *ZRL*, 96.
60 Zh. Pasternak, *Pamyati Pedro*, 105.
61 L. O. Pasternak, postcards of 30 November and 4 December 1939 to B. L. Pasternak (PFA).
62 Karlinsky, *Marina Tsvetaeva*, 229. *EBP*, 542. Belkina, *Skreshchenie sudeb*, 30, 80. Tarasenkov, 'Pasternak', 174.
63 'Da, v vechnosti – zhena, ne na bumage!' (publ. M. Feinberg and Yu. Klyukin) *Bolshevo. Literaturnyi istoriko-kraevedcheskii al'manakh*, 2 (1992), 180.
64 *EBP*, 542. *EPIV*, 147. Belkina, *Skreshchenie sudeb*, 98–101.
65 Ivanov, 'Perevernutoe zerkalo', 205. Ivanova, 'Boris Leonidovich Pasternak', 241–2.
66 Letter of 14 February 1940 to O. M. Freidenberg, *Perepiska*, 180. See also letter of same date to L. O. Pasternak (APT).
67 Letter of 14 February 1940 to L. O. Pasternak, quoted *EBP*, 543.
68 Ivanov, 'Perevernutoe zerkalo', 204–5. Vilenkin, *Vospominaniya s kommentariyami*, 83, and 'O Borise Leonidoviche Pasternake', *Vospominaniya*, 471.
69 *EBP*, 541. Vilenkin, *Vospominaniya s kommentariyami*, 82–3.
70 V. I. Nemirovich-Danchenko, letter of 6 November 1939 to B. L. Pasternak, in his *Izbrannye pis'ma v dvukh tomakh*, II, 672.
71 Letter of 14 February 1940 to O. M. Freidenberg, *Perepiska*, 180.
72 Letter of 14 February 1940 to L. O. Pasternak (APT).
73 *EBP*, 541–2. Vilenkin, *Vospominaniya s kommentariyami*, 82–5.
74 *Ibid.*, 85–6.

8 WORLD WAR AND EVACUATION

1 Ivanov, 'Perevernutoe zerkalo', 206. Ivanova, 'Boris Leonidovich Pasternak', 242.
2 Letter of 14 February 1940 to L. O. Pasternak (APT).
3 Milne, *Mikhail Bulgakov*, 234. A. Shvarts, 'Zhizn' i smert' Mikhaila Bulgakova', *Kontinent*, 54 (1987), 126. Vilenkin, 'O Borise Leonidoviche Pasternake', 478–9. Wright, *Mikhail Bulgakov*, 254.
4 A. Grishina, memoirs ms. (PFA). *EBP*, 544. Agnessa (Ágnes) Kun was the daughter of Hungarian communist Bela Kun, and wife of Antal Hidas who had been arrested.

5 Letters of 21 and 28 May, and 18 June 1940 to O. M. Freidenberg, *Perepiska*, 181–2.
6 Letter of 22 May 1940 to L. O. Pasternak (APT).
7 Letter of 15 November 1940 to O. M. Freidenberg, *Perepiska*, 185.
8 Tarasenkov, 'Pasternak', 169–70, 719. E. V. Pasternak (publ.), 'Boris Pasternak: Ankety, zayavleniya, khodataistva', 41.
9 *Izbrannye perevody* (Moscow, 1940), 112–14.
10 MacDonald, *The New Shostakovich*, 165–6.
11 Letter of 15 November 1940, to O. M. Freidenberg, *Perepiska*, 185.
12 *EBP*, 543. *EPIV*, 147–8.
13 *Tridtsat' dnei*, 3–4 (1930), 70–73. V. Shekspir, 'Gamlet, prints datskii', *Molodaya gvardiya*, 5–6 (1940), 15–131.
14 See letter of 1 March 1940 to M. L. Lozinsky, *SS*, V, 381–4.
15 *EBP*, 544. *SS*, IV, 846.
16 *EBP*, 544.
17 Vil'yam-Vil'mont, ' "Gamlet" ', 288.
18 Gorbunov, 'K istorii russkogo "Gamleta"', in Uil'yam Shekspir. *Gamlet. Izbrannye perevody*, 9.
19 MacDonald, *The New Shostakovich*, 81. Wilson, *Shostakovich*, 80–2, 86.
20 See Rowe, *Hamlet*.
21 Sollertinsky, ' "Gamlet" ', 230.
22 *SS*, IV, 416. See *Soch.*III, 261; *SS*, IV, 853–4. See France, 'Boris Pasternak's Interpretation', 219–22.
23 See L. Chukovskaya, *Zapiski*, I, 91.
24 Morozov, '*Gamlet*', 144–7. *NNVV*, 288–91. Reztsov, 'Prints datskii', 52–5. Solov'ev, 'V poiskakh *Gamleta*', 140–8. See also in Zakharenko (ed.), *Russkie Pisateli-Poety*, 286–7.
25 Belkina, *Skreshchenie sudeb*, 166.
26 *Ibid.*, 166, 212, 219.
27 Karlinsky, *Marina Tsvetaeva*, 231–2.
28 *EBP*, 545. Belkina, *Skreshchenie sudeb*, 115.
29 Belkina, *Skreshchenie sudeb*, 180–4. *EBP, Skreshchenie sudeb*, 545. *SS*, V, 387.
30 *EBP*, 555. Belkina, *Skreshchenie sudeb*, 194.
31 Dadashidze, ' "Ya ni v maloi stepeni" ' *EBP*, 545. Polivanov, 'Marina Tsvetaeva', 53.
32 Belkina, *Skreshchenie sudeb*, 266–71. Karlinsky, *Marina Tsvetaeva*, 237–8. Efron, *O Marine Tsvetaevoi*, 259–62. Gershtein, 'O Pasternake i ob Akhmatovoi', 395–7.
33 Karlinsky, *Marina Tsvetaeva*, 236.
34 Shklovsky, *O Mayakovskom* (Moscow, 1940).
35 Letter of 28 July 1940 to Akhmatova, *SS*, V, 384–6.
36 L. Chukovskaya, *Zapiski*, I, 146–7. See vol. I, 186–7.
37 Letter of 1 November 1940 to A. A. Akhmatova, *SS*, V, 388–9.
38 Hingley, *Pasternak*, 138.

39 L. Chukovskaya, *Zapiski*, I, 89, 164.
40 Z. Pasternak, 'Vospominaniya', 213. See also 'Letnii den'', *SS*, II, 22.
41 Letter of 15 November 1940 to O. M. Freidenberg, *Perepiska*, 184.
42 Letter of 3 July 1940 to E. V. Pasternak, quoted *EBP*, 547.
43 See 'Iz prozy kontsa 1930–kh godov', *SS*, IV, 507–12; *ibid.*, 826.
44 Z. Pasternak, 'Vospominaniya', 201.
45 Letter of 15 November 1940 to O. M. Freidenberg, *Perepiska*, 184.
46 *EBP*, 543.
47 Letter of 8 April 1941 to O. M. Freidenberg, *Perepiska*, 191.
48 *EBP*, 548.
49 *Soch.*III, 20–2, 31–2; *SP*, 396–8, 407–8; *SS*, II, 23–5, 38–9.
50 Letter of 8 May 1941 to O. M. Freidenberg, *Perepiska*, 193.
51 'Na rannikh poezdakh', *SS*, II, 35–6.
52 Ivanov, 'Perevernutoe zerkalo', 200. See E. V. Pasternak, 'Znachenie nravstvennoi propovedi L. Tolstogo', 154–63. *EBP*, 554.
53 *Soch.*II, 34; *VP*, 448; *SS*, IV, 328.
54 Letter of 6 October 1957 to S. I. Chikovani, *SS*, V, 555. See also *EBP*, 548–50.
55 *Soch.*II, 210; *VP*, 198; *SS*, IV, 146.
56 Letter of 4 February 1941 to O. M. Freidenberg, *Perepiska*, 187. On the *oprichnina*, see vol. I, 62.
57 *Tridtsat' dnei*, 4 (1941), 41–2. *Internatsional'naya literatura*, 5 (1941), 147–51.
58 Z. Pasternak, 'Vospominaniya', 202. Ivanov, 'Perevernutoe zerkalo', 206.
59 Z. Pasternak, 'Vospominaniya', 202–3.
60 A. Shtein, ' "I ne tol' ko o nem . . ." ', *Teatr*, 2 (1988), 182ff.
61 Z. Pasternak, 'Vospominaniya', 203; the entry regarding the letters is at fault. *EBP*, 550–1.
62 Z. Pasternak, 'Vospominaniya', 203.
63 *EBP*, 551. *EPIV*, 149.
64 Letters of 12, 20, 21 July and 17 August 1941 to Z. N. Pasternak, *BPZNP*, 104–9, 116.
65 Letters of 24 July, 17 August and 8 September 1941 to Z. N. Pasternak, *BPZNP*, 110, 117, 133. Letter of 14 September 1941 to O. M. Freidenberg, *Perepiska*, 202. Ivanov, 'Perevernutoe zerkalo', 206.
66 Letters of 26 and 11 August 1941 to Z. N. Pasternak, *BPZNP*, 120–1, 115.
67 Letter of 1st September 1941 to Z. N. Pasternak, *ibid.*, 128.
68 Letter of 12 September 1941 to Z. N. Pasternak, *ibid.*, 137–8.
69 *DZh*, 519; *SS*, III, 499.
70 Letter of 2 September 1941, to Z. N. Pasternak, *BPZNP*, 129–31.
71 *EBP*, 553. Ya. Sudrabkaln, 'Russkomu narodu', *LG*, 17 September 1941. S. Chikovani, 'Tbilisskii rybak', *ibid.*, 15 October 1941.
72 Letter of 4 September 1941 to Z. N. Pasternak, *BPZNP*, 131.
73 Lekić, 'Pasternak's "Na etom svete" ', 17.

74 *Ibid.*, 18.
75 *EBP*, 553.
76 Letter of 7 August 1940 to Z. N. Pasternak, *BPZNP*, 113.
77 Belkina, *Skreshchenie sudeb*, 303 ff. *EBP*, 552. Bokov, 'Sobesednik roshch', *Vospo-minaniya*, 350–2, 753.
78 Karlinsky, *Marina Tsvetaeva*, 241–5. Belkina, *Skreshchenie sudeb*, 310–29.
79 Letter of 10 September 1940 to Z. N. Pasternak, *BPZNP*, 135.
80 Gladkov, *Vstrechi s Pasternakom*, 53.
81 See *Soch.*III, 45–8; *VP*, 459–63; *SS*, IV, 338–42.
82 *EBP*, 556. On Georgii Efron's fate, see Belkina, *Skreshchenie sudeb*, 332–82.
83 Gershtein, 'O Pasternake i ob Akhmatovoi', 397.
84 Z. Pasternak, 'Vospominaniya', 206, 722.
85 Letter of 5 November 1943 to O. M. Freidenberg, *Perepiska*, 222.
86 'Lyudi i polozheniya', *Soch.*II, 48; *VP*, 463; *SS*, IV, 342 (in *Soch.*II, 48) See R. M. Rilke, B. Pasternak, M. Tsvetaeva, *Pis'ma 1926 goda* (Moscow, 1990), 36, 235. On Pasternak's letters to Tsvetaeva, see *ibid.*, 35–6, 234; Belkina, *Skreshchenie sudeb*, 508–9.
87 *EBP*, 556. Ivanov, 'Perevernutoe zerkalo', 207.

9 CHISTOPOL TRANSLATION

1 Z. Pasternak, 'Vospominaniya', 206. V. Avdeev, 'Vspominaya Pasternaka', *Vospo-minaniya*, 342.
2 Mukhanov, 'V dolgu pered temoi', in Mukhanov (ed.), *Chistopol'skie stranitsy*, 3ff.
3 Gladkov, *Vstrechi s Pasternakom*, 26. On the writers' wartime stay in Chistopol, see Mukhanov (ed.), *Chistopol'skie stranitsy*; V. A. Klimentovsky, *Russkie pisateli v Tatarskoi ASSR* (Kazan, 1960), 116–49. On Pasternak in Chistopol, see Porman, 'B. L. Pasternak v Chistopole', 193–5.
4 Letter of 22 March 1942 to A. L. Pasternak, *SS*, *V*, 413.
5 Letter of 12 March 1942 to E. V. Pasternak, 'Perepiska s Evgeniei Pasternak', *Znamya*, 2 (1996), 183.
6 Kryukova, ' "Razgovor s neizvestnym drugom" ', 524–5, 529. *EBP*, 562–3.
7 Avdeyev, 'Vspominaya Pasternaka', 342–6.
8 Letter of 18 July 1942 to O. M. Freidenberg, *Perepiska*, 210–11.
9 Z. Pasternak, 'Vospominaniya', 207.
10 *Ibid.*, 208–9.
11 *EPIV*, 150–1. Ivanov, 'Perevernutoe zerkalo', 207. Letters of 8 October 1941 and 18 March 1942 to O. M. Freidenberg, *Perepiska*, 204–6.
12 Gladkov, *Vstrechi s Pasternakom*, 28.
13 Letter of 12 March 1942 to V. V. and T. V. Ivanov, in Ivanova, 'Boris Leonidovich Pasternak', 244. Gladkov, *Vstrechi s Pasternakom*, 28–9.
14 Gladkov, *Vstrechi s Pasternakom*, 31, 41–2. Mukhanov (ed.), *Chistopol'skie stra-nitsy, passim.*

15 Gladkov, *Vstrechi s Pasternakom*, 39–40.
16 Letter of 12 March 1942 to E. V. Pasternak, quoted in *EBP*, 557.
17 Gladkov, *Vstrechi s Pasternakom*, 47.
18 *Ibid.*, 51.
19 Avdeev, 'Vspominaya Pasternaka', 344.
20 Cf. 'Zametki o Shekspire', *SS*, IV, 687–94.
21 Gladkov, *Vstrechi s Pasternakom*, 55–6. O. Dzyubinskaya, 'Gorod serdtsa moego
   . . .', Mukhanov (ed.), *Chistopol'skie stranitsy*, 174–5.
22 Letter of 23 May 1942 to A. O. Naumova, 'K perevodam shekspirovskikh dram',
   Masterstvo perevoda 1969, 6 (1970), 342–3.
23 Letter of M. M. Morozov to B. L. Pasternak of 1 October 1942, *ibid.*, 359–61.
24 Letter of 15 July 1942 to M. M. Morozov, *ibid.*, 344–6.
25 Morozov, 'Novyi perevod "Romeo i Dzhul'etty"'. Lozinskaya, 'Novyi perevod
   "Romeo i Dzhul'etty"', 13.
26 E. Pasternak, 'Posleslovie' in Yu. Slovatsky (J. Słowacki), *Stikhi. Mariya Styuart*
   (Moscow, 1975), 171. *EBP*, 558.
27 'Perepiska s Evgeniei Pasternak', *Znamya*, 2 (1996), 183.
28 Gladkov, *Vstrechi s Pasternakom*, 52–3.
29 *EBP*, 556–7. See *Soch*.III, 39–40; *SP*, 567–8, 703–5; *SS*, II, 48–9, 628.
30 Gladkov, *Vstrechi s Pasternakom*, 52.
31 Letter of 8 April 1942 to T. V. and V. V. Ivanov, *SS*, V, 414.
32 Letter of 4 February 1941 to O. M. Freidenberg, *Perepiska*, 187. T. Ivanova, 'Boris
   Leonidovich Pasternak', 245–6; *SS*, *V*, 414, 651. M. Levin, 'Neskol'ko vstrech',
   Vospominaniya, 354.
33 Gladkov, *Vstrechi s Pasternakom*, 32, 54.
34 On Gladkov, see V. P. Korshunova, ' "Protokolist svoego vremeni" (Pis'ma A. K.
   Gladkova k bratu)', *Vstrechi s proshlym*, 4 (1982), 289–311.
35 *EBP*, 560. Letter of 16 September 1942 to E. V. Pasternak, *SS*, V, 419.
36 P. Antokol'sky, letter of 9 July 1942 to B. L. Pasternak, 'K perevodam shekspirovskikh dram', 351.
37 Gladkov, *Vstrechi s Pasternakom*, 68. *EBP*, 558.
38 Letter of 16 September 1942 to E. V. Pasternak, *SS*, *V*, 419.
39 *SS*, *IV*, 513–22.
40 *Ibid.*, 526–7.
41 *Ibid.*, 528–9.
42 Smolitsky, 'B. Pasternak', 23–8. On Pasternak's wartime drama, see Lekić,
   'Pasternak's "Na etom svete"'; E. [V.] Pasternak, 'O chistopol'skoi p'ese Borisa
   Pasternaka', 22–3.
43 On this, see Bodin, 'Boris Pasternak and the Christian Tradition', in Barnes (ed.),
   Pasternak and European Literature, 388–90; and 'The Count and His Lackey. An
   Analysis of Pasternak's Poem "Ballada"', *Zeszyty Naukowe Wyższej Szkoły Pedago-
   gicznej w Bydgoszczy. Studia Filologiczne*, 31 (12), 1990. *Filologia Rosyjska. Poetika
   Pasternaka – Pasternak's poetics*, 37–63.

44 Letter of 14 June 1942 to P. I. Chagin, quoted *EBP*, 558. See also letter of 18 July 1942 to O. M. Freidenberg, *Perepiska*, 212.
45 Letter of 9 August 1942 to A. Ya. Tairov, quoted E. V. Pasternak, 'O chistopol'skoi p'ese', 23. See also letter of 16 September 1942 to E. V. Pasternak, *SS, V*, 419.
46 'Zametki k perevodam shekspirovskikh tragedii', *Soch*.III, 198–9; see also *SS, IV*, 418.
47 Letter of 15 July 1942 to M. M. Morozov, *Masterstvo perevoda 1969*, 347. Gorbunov, an actor of the Maly and, later, Aleksandrinsky Theatres, specialised in 'folk' and character roles.
48 Zingerman, *Teatr Chekhova*, 145ff.
49 Gladkov, *Vstrechi s Pasternakom*, 74.
50 *EBP*, 561. Lekić, 'Pasternak's "Na etom svete"', 19. See *SS, IV*, 513–30.
51 Danin, 'Vospominaniya o nevernom druge', 132. Ann Pasternak Slater, 'Introduction', in A. Pasternak, *A Vanished Present*, xxii. Ivanov, 'Perevernutoe zerkalo', *passim*. Gladkov, *Vstrechi s Pasternakom*, 54.
52 Letters of October (n.d.) and 29 November 1942, to Z. Pasternak, *BPZNP*, 142, 150.
53 Letter of 22 March 1942 to A. L. Pasternak, *SS, V*, 411.
54 Ivanov, 'Perevernutoe zerkalo', 207–8. Letter of 5 November 1943 to O. M. Freidenberg, *Perepiska*, 222–3.
55 Gladkov, *Vstrechi s Pasternakom*, 39–41.
56 *The Chronicle of Henry the Fourth Part 2*, III, i, 80. This material observed by Ann Pasternak Slater was cited in C. Barnes, 'Introduction', in Boris Pasternak, *People and Propositions* (Edinburgh, 1990), 22.
57 Letters of 29 November, 6 December, 12 December 1942 to Z. N. Pasternak, *BPZNP*, 150, 153–6.
58 These poems are discussed above, pp. 115–16, 131–2, 175, 176–7, 183–4.
59 Gladkov, *Vstrechi s Pasternakom*, 77. Girzheva, 'Nekotorye osobennosti pozdnei liriki Borisa Pasternaka', 57ff.
60 *EBP*, 562.
61 See below, pp. 206–8. 'Russkomu geniyu', *SS, II*, 153.
62 Vysheslavsky, *Naizust': Vospominaniya*, 41ff. 'Boris Pasternak i Kaisyn Kuliev', 259. Gladkov, *Vstrechi s Pasternakom*, 76.
63 Gladkov, *Vstrechi s Pasternakom*, 74–5, *EBP*, 561.
64 Fedina, 'Dom oknami na Kamu', in Mukhanov (ed.), *Chistopol'skie stranitsy*, 222.
65 Kryukova, ' "Razgovor s neizvestnym drugom" ', 525.
66 Vilenkin, *Vospominaniya s kommentariyami*, 96, and 'O Borise Leonidoviche Pasternake', 477.
67 Vilenkin, *Vospominaniya s kommentariyami*, 87, 97. Letter of 29 January 1943 to V. I. Nemirovich-Danchenko, 'Novye pis'ma Vl. I. Nemirovicha-Danchenko', publ. V. Vilenkin and S. Vasil'eva, *Teatr*, 1 (1976), 80.
68 V. I. Nemirovich-Danchenko, letter of 18 February 1943 to B. L. Pasternak, *ibid.*, 79–80.

69 Avdeyev, 'Vspominaya Pasternaka', 345.
70 Gladkov, *Vstrechi s Pasternakom*, 82–4.
71 *EBP*, 563.
72 'Zamechaniya k perevodam iz Shekspira', *SS, IV*, 421.
73 Morozov, 'Novyi perevod "Antoniya i Kleopatry" Shekspira'.
74 Schimanski, 'The Duty of the Younger Writer'.
75 *FBPPP*, 233–5.

10 WAR AND PEACE IN MOSCOW

1 *EBP*, 563. Z. Pasternak, 'Vospominaniya', 210.
2 Z. Pasternak, 'Vospominaniya', 210. Letter of 16 July 1943 to A. S. Shcherbakov, Babichenko (ed.), '*Literaturnyi front*', 79–80.
3 Letter of 21 October 1943 to V. D. Avdeev, Mukhanov (ed.), *Chistopol'skie stranitsy*, 256–7.
4 Z. Pasternak, 'Vospominaniya', 210–12. Letter of 5 November 1943 to O. M. Freidenberg, *Perepiska*, 224.
5 Letter of 5 November 1943 to O. M. Freidenberg, *Perepiska*, 221.
6 *Ibid.*, 224.
7 E. B. Pasternak, preface to B. Pasternak, 'Istoriya odnoi kontroktavy', 252.
8 Simonov, 'Pravil'nyi put'', 13.
9 N. V. , 'O novykh stikhotvoreniyakh Borisa Pasternaka', 159–60. Letter of 10 June 1943 to N. Ya. Mandel'shtam, 'Zametki o peresechenii', 328.
10 Gladkov, *Vstrechi s Pasternakom*, 86.
11 Antokol'sky, 'Boris Pasternak', 312–16; also in his *Izpytanie vremenem* (Moscow, 1945), 99–107. For other reviews of *Na rannikh poezdakh*, see Zakharenko (ed.), *Russkie Pisateli-Poety*, 359.
12 Berlin, 'Vstrechi', 530.
13 Vilenkin, 'O Borise Leonidoviche Pasternake', *Vospominaniya*, 480.
14 Gladkov, *Vstrechi s Pasternakom*, 80.
15 Vilenkin, 'O Borise Leonide Pasternake', 477–8.
16 Ivinskaya, *V plenu vremeni*, 324. Berlin, 'Vstrechi', 533–4. Voznesensky, 'Mne chetyrnadtsat' let', *Vospominaniya*, 577.
17 Gladkov, *Vstrechi s Pasternakom*, 81. V. Livanov, 'Nevydumannyi Boris Pasternak: vospominaniya i vpechatleniya', *Moskva*, 10 (1993), 183–4.
18 'Novyi sbornik Anny Akhmatovoi', *SS, IV*, 389–90.
19 ' "Izbrannoe" Anny Akhmatovoi', *ibid.*, 390–2.
20 'Slavyanskii poet', *SS, IV*, 388–9.
21 On Pasternak and Łysohorsky, see *SS, IV*, 847; Shugrin, 'Takoi nastoyashchii, talantlivyi i neozhidannyi', 14.
22 *SS, II*, 157–8.
23 Letter of 21 October 1943 to V. D. Avdeev, Mukhanov (ed.), *Chistopol'skie stranitsy*, 257.

24 Khelemsky, 'Ozhivshaya freska', 138. Ivanova, 'Boris Leonidovich Pasternak', 247. *EPIV*, 152.

25 'Ozhivshaya freska', *Soch*.III, 55–6; *SP*, 423–4; *SS*, II, 68–9.

26 Turgenev spoke of the 'great, mighty, free and truthful' Russian language; Kalitina and Rostova are heroines of his *Dvoryanskoe gnezdo* and Tolstoy's *Voina i mir*. On Pasternak's trip to the front, see Tregub, *Sputniki serdtsa*, 200–203; Khelemsky, 'Ozhivshaya freska', 123–41; *EBP*, 564–8; *FBPPP*, 235–8.

27 Letter of 21 October 1943 to V. D. Avdeev, Mukhanov (ed.), *Chistopol'skie stranitsy*, 257.

28 For discussion of 'Poezdka v armiyu', see *FBPPP*, 236–8.

29 Letter of 5 November 1943 to O. M. Freidenberg, *Perepiska*, 224.

30 A. Akhmatova, 'Muzhestvo', *Pravda*, 8 March 1942. See also V. Vasil'evskaya, 'Sovetskaya zhenshchina'; L. Seifullina, 'Zhenshchina na strazhe', *ibid.*

31 Shugrin, 'Takoi nastoyashchii'.

32 Gladkov, *Vstrechi s Pasternakom*, 91–3. *EBP*, 568. *FBPPP*, 237–8.

33 *EBP*, 568. Khelemsky, 'Ozhivshaya freska', 138. Gladkov, *Vstrechi s Pasternakom*, 95.

34 *SS*, II, 52. Berlin, 'Vstrechi', 522. *EPIV*, 154.

35 *FBPPP*, 238. Letter of 9 May 1941 to S. D. Spassky, *SS*, V, 401.

36 Letter of 12 November 1943 to O. M. Freidenberg, *Perepiska*, 225.

37 Leneman, 'Begegnung mit Boris Pasternak', 96–8. (This article contained many errors; see letter of 27 July 1958 to Hélène Peltier, *Lettres*, 109.) 'Zimnie prazdniki', *LG*, 11 November 1944.

38 Zhdanov, 'Boris Pasternak', 268–9. Thomson, *The Premature Revolution*, 274.

39 *SS*, II, 57–9, 547–9, 629–70. Khelemsky, 'Ozhivshaya freska', 132.

40 Letter of 31 December 1943 to D. S. Danin, *SS*, V, 424. *EBP*, 570.

41 *EBP*, 572.

42 Khelemsky, 'Ozhivshaya freska', 128, 132–5. *EBP*, 568.

43 *SS*, II, 68–9, 553–6.

44 *SS*, II, 48–9, 628. Rannit (publ.), 'Neizvestnyi Boris Pasternak', 13–17.

45 Ivanov, 'Perevernutoe zerkalo', 210–11.

46 Gladkov, *Vstrechi s Pasternakom*, 99. MacDonald, *The New Shostakovich*, 167. Polivanova, 'Iz razgovorov Pasternaka', *Vospominaniya*, 488.

47 EBP, 570, 573. ' "Eto tramplin, doping, zaryadka . . ." (Iz dnevnikov A. M. Faiko)', *Vstrechi s proshlym*, 5 (1984), 305.

48 Letter of 31 December 1943 to D. S. Danin, *SS*, V, 424.

49 Ivanov, 'Perevernutoe zerkalo', 211.

50 Quoted in Betser, 'Neskol'ko shtrikhov k portretu B. L. Pasternaka'.

51 Vilenkin, 'O Borise Leonidoviche Pasternake', 480–4.

52 Letter of 3 December 1944 to V. D. Avdeev, in Mukhanov (ed.), *Chistapol'skie stranitsy*, 258.

53 Letter of 5 November 1943 to O. M. Freidenberg, *Perepiska*, 223. Letter of 31 December 1943 to D. A. Danin, *SS*, V, 425.

54 Letter of 16 June 1944 to O. M. Freidenberg, *Perepiska*, 231.
55 'Zametki k perevodam iz Shekspira', *SS*, IV, 419–20.
56 'Novyi perevod "Otello" Shekspira', *LG*, 9 December 1944. *SS*, IV, 401.
57 *SS*, IV, 421. Cf. *DZh*, 10; *SS*, III, 14. Ivanov, 'Sestra moya – zhizn'’.
58 Gladkov, *Vstrechi s Pasternakom*, 100.
59 Letter of 30 July 1944 to O. M. Freidenberg, *Perepiska*, 232.
60 Gladkov, *Vstrechi s Pasternakom*, 101.
61 *EBP*, 574.
62 *SS*, IV, 628.
63 *SS*, IV, 703–8. Letter (n.d.) of late 1945 to N. Ya. Mandel'shtam, 'Zametki o peresechenii', 330.
64 'Pol' Mari Verlen', *SS*, IV, 395–9.
65 'Zametki perevodchika', *Znamya*, 1–2 (1944). *SS*, IV, 395.
66 *EBP*, 575.
67 'Shopen', *SS*, IV, 403–4.
68 'Velikii realist', *SS*, IV, 407. On Pasternak and romanticism, see P. France, 'Pasternak et le romantisme', in Aucouturier (ed.), *Boris Pasternak 1890–1960*, 83–91; Djurčinov, 'Antonimiya "romantizm – realizm" v poetike Pasternaka', *ibid.*, 95–102; *SS*, IV, 850–51. On Pasternak's 'realism', see MacKinnon, 'Boris Pasternak's Conception of Realism'.
69 Haight, *Anna Akhmatova*, 136.
70 O. E. Mandelstam, letter of 2 January 1937 to B. L. Pasternak, 'Zametki o peresechenii', 322. See *EBP*, 573; letter (n.d.) of late 1945 to N. Ya. Mandel'shtam, 'Zametki o peresechenii', 330.
71 Letter to N. Ya. Mandel'shtam (n.d.) of late 1945, 'Zametki o peresechenii', 330; *SS*, V, 435.
72 *FBPPP*, 240.
73 *FBPPP*, 241. Letter of 5 May 1944 to A. S. Shcherbakov, Babichenko (ed.), '*Literaturnyi front*', 131–2; see also *ibid.*, 135–6.
74 Letter (n.d.) of November 1945 to N. Ya. Mandel'shtam, 'Zametki o peresechenii', 330; *SS*, V, 434.
75 Neigauz, 'Avtobiografiya', in Zimyanina (ed.), *Stanislav Neigauz*, 9. V. S. Belov, *ibid.*, 69–71.
76 G. Pasternak, 'Vospominaniya' in Rikhter (ed.), *Genrikh Neigauz*, 102. G. G. Neigauz, letter of 24 May 1943 to Z. N. Pasternak, *ibid.*, 207.
77 Letter of 30 July 1944 to O. M. Freidenberg, *Perepiska*, 232. *EBP*, 573.
78 *Zemnoi prostor* (Moscow, 1945), 30. Letter of January 1944 (n.d.) to D. S. Danin, in D. Danin, 'Eto prebudet s nami', *Vospominaniya*, 317. *EBP*, 572–3.
79 *EBP*, 573.
80 Gladkov, *Vstrechi s Pasternakom*, 101.
81 See 'Spring', above p. 202.
82 Tarasenkov, 'Novye stikhi Borisa Pasternaka', 138–9. Spassky, 'B. Pasternak', 31–2.

83 Gromov, 'Boris Pasternak', 157–9. Hingley, *Pasternak*, 149. *EBP*, 576. On Pasternak's war poetry, see also Zelinsky, 'O lirike', 183–4.

84 Zakharenko (ed.), *Russkie Pisateli-Poety*, 360.

85 Letter of 22 January 1945 to O. M. Freidenberg, *Perepiska*, 233.

86 Letter of 14 August 1945 to N. A. Tabidze, quoted in *EBP*, 575. Letter of 21 June 1945 to O. M. Freidenberg, *Perepiska*, 236.

87 Z. Pasternak, 'Vospominaniya', 212.

88 Ibid., 212–13. *SS*, III, 69–70; *DZh*, 67–9.

89 Buckman, *Leonid Pasternak*, 79–80. J. Pasternak, 'Introduction' in *The Memoirs of Leonid Pasternak* (London-Melbourne-New York, 1982), 13–14. S. Schimanski, 'Introduction' in Boris Pasternak, *The Collected Prose Works* (London 1945), 11–12.

90 Letter of 21 June 1945 to O. M. Freidenberg, *Perepiska*, 235.

91 I. Grabar', 'Pamyati Leonida Pasternaka', *Sovetskoe iskusstvo*, 13 July 1945.

92 *SS*, IV, 653.

93 *SP*, 568–9; *SS*, II, 160.

94 Wrenn, 'Shekspir'.

95 Livanov, 'Ne vydumannyi Boris Pasternak', *Moskva*, 10 (1993), 168. Cohen, 'The Poetry of Boris Pasternak', 23–36. Leites, 'Malen'kie nedorazumeniya', 163–5.

96 Schimanski, 'Introduction', 16–17. On this episode, see *FBPPP*, 244–6.

97 Letter of 25 December 1945 to S. Schimanski (unpublished); I am grateful to Dr George Simmons (Schimanski's brother) and to Mr Jeff Schaire of New York for sending me this text and for background information.

98 Letter of 29 June 1945 to S. N. Durylin, *SS*, V, 433. On Pasternak and the personalists, see Berlin, 'Vstrechi', 522; also: letter of December 1945 (n.d.) to Zh. L. and L. L. Pasternak, *SS*, V, 439–46.

11 'FROM IMMORTALITY'S ARCHIVE': THE BIRTH OF A NOVEL

1 Letter of 10 November 1945 to I. S. Postupal'sky, *SS*, V, 436.

2 Letter of November 1945 (n.d.) to N. Ya. Mandel'shtam, *SS*, V, 435.

3 E.g., on an 'Evening of Soviet Poetry' in the Hall of Columns on 24 April 1945, 'V neskol'ko strok', *LG*, 1 May 1945. Letter of 29 June 1945 to S. N. Durylin, *SS*, V, 433.

4 *Ibid.*, 430–2. 'Pis'ma k V. M. Sayanovu', 200.

5 Letter of 3 August 1945 to S. I. Chikovani, ' "Krai, stavshii mne vtoroi rodinoi" ', 181. Letter (n.d.) to N. A. Tabidze (PFA). *EPIV*, 155.

6 Letters of 3 August and 9 September 1945 to S. I. Chikovani, ' "Krai, stavshii mne vtoroi rodinoi" ', 181–2.

7 *The Oxford Book of Russian Verse*, ed. M. Baring (Oxford, 1948), 238–9.

8 N. Tabidze, 'Raduga', 303. Letter of 5 November 1945 to S. I. and M. N. Chikovani, 'Pis'ma druz'yam', *Literaturnaya Gruziya*, 2 (1966), 84.

9 'Velikii realist', *SS*, IV, 407. L. Gudiashvili, *Ya – khudozhnik. Kniga vospominanii* (Moscow, 1987), 112–13.
10 N. Tabidze, 'Raduga', 303. *EBP*, 581–2.
11 Letter of 1 November 1945 to N. A. Tabidze, 'Pis'ma druz'yam', *Literaturnaya Gruziya*, 1 (1966), 90–1.
12 Letter of 24 January 1946 to N. A. Tabidze, *SS*, V, 447.
13 See 'Nikolai Baratashvili', *SS*, IV, 407–10.
14 'Neskol'ko slov o novoi gruzinskoi poezii', *SS*, IV, 410–12.
15 *Gruzinskie poety v perevodakh Borisa Pasternaka* (Moscow, 1946); *Gruzinskie poety* (Tbilisi, 1947).
16 See vol. I, 329. 'A za mnoyu shum pogoni. . .', publ.M. Rashkovskaya, *Istochnik*, 4 (1993), 101–3. Kunina, 'O vstrechakh s Borisom Pasternakom', *Vospominaniya*, 112–13, 703.
17 E. A. Novikova, 'Iz proshlogo', ms.(PFA).
18 Gladkov, *Vstrechi s Pasternakom*, 100.
19 Letter of 10 December 1945 to Zh. L. and L. L. Pasternak, *SS*, V, 439. L. Pasternak Slater, *Before Sunrise*, 11–14, 21.
20 Berlin, 'Vstrechi', 519 ff. Haight, *Anna Akhmatova*, 140–3. Letter of 10 December 1945 to Zh. L. and L. L. Pasternak, *SS*, V, 439–46.
21 Berlin, 'Vstrechi', 523.
22 *Ibid.*, 522. On Pasternak and the personalists, see above p. 220; also *FBPPP*, 258–9.
23 Berlin, 'Vstrechi', 526–7.
24 *Ibid.*, 530–1.
25 *Ibid.*, 743. *EBP*, 582. At this stage (*pace* Berlin) there was no novel manuscript ready for circulation.
26 Letter of 26 June 1946 to I. Berlin, cited with thanks to Sir Isaiah Berlin.
27 Letter of 24 January 1946 to N. A. Tabidze, *SS*, V, 446–7.
28 Gladkov, *Vstrechi s Pasternakom*, 104.
29 Babaev, 'Gde vozdukh sin'. . .', *Vospominaniya*, 536–47. Letter of 26 January 1946 to N. Ya. Mandel'shtam, *SS*, V, 448.
30 Letter of 1 February 1946 to O. M. Freidenberg, *Perepiska*, 239.
31 *SS*, III, 714–15. Zolyan, ' "Vot ya ves' . . ." ', 97–104. Zabolotsky, *The Life of Zabolotsky*, 249.
32 *SS*, V, 703–8, 898–9. Letter of 1 July 1958 to V. V. Ivanov, *SS*, V, 566.
33 *Vil'yam Shekspir v perevode Borisa Pasternaka*, ed. M. M. Morozov (Moscow-Leningrad, 1949–50). See above chapter 8, on Christ and Hamlet, pp. 171–2.
34 Letter of 5 October 1946 to O. M. Freidenberg, *Perepiska*, 243. See also letter of 15 July 1946 to S. Chikovani, 'Pis'ma druz'yam', *Literaturnaya Gruziya*, 2 (1966), 85. The 15 March dateline seems mistaken.
35 'Zamechaniya k perevodam iz Shekspira', *SS*, IV, 413–31. See Ann Pasternak Slater's commentary notes incorporated in Barnes, 'Introduction', in B. Pasternak, *People and Propositions* (Edinburgh, 1990), 22–3.
36 'Some Remarks by a Translator of Shakespeare', *Soviet Literature*, 9 (September

1946), 51–7. Letter of 18 June 1946 to V. M. Sayanov in 'Pis'ma k V. M. Sayanovu', 201. A fuller (although still condensed) version appeared in Russian only in 1956: 'Zametki k perevodam shekspirovskikh tragedii', *Literaturnaya Moskva*, 1 (1956), 794–809.

37 O. M. Freidenberg, letter to B. L. Pasternak of 11 October 1946, *Perepiska*, 246–7.

38 Haight, *Anna Akhmatova*, 136.

39 Gershtein, 'O Pasternake i ob Akhmatovoi', 397–9.

40 *EBP*, 583.

41 *EBP*, 583. Vilenkin, 'O Borise Leonidoviche Pasternake', 468–9.

42 Letter of 26 June 1946 to L. L. Pasternak Slater (APT).

43 Undated telegram draft (Pasternak's English) (PFA). Letter of 25 June 1946 to R. N. Lomonosova, *PPL, Minuvshee*, 17 (1995), 403.

44 Letter of 26 June 1946 to R. N. Lomonosova, *PPL, Minuvshee*, 17 (1995), 404.

45 Letter of 5 October 1946 to O. M. Freidenberg, *Perepiska*, 243.

46 Petrovskaya, 'Vospominaniya', ms. (PFA).

47 'Pis'ma B. L. Pasternaka–K. A. Fedinu', 168.

48 Letter of 26 August 1946 to K. A. Fedin, *ibid.*

49 'O zhurnalakh *Zvezda* i *Leningrad*: iz postanovleniya TsVKP(b) ot 14–ogo avgusta 1946 g.', *Zvezda*, 7–8 (1946), 3–6.

50 'Rezolyutsiya obshchegorodskogo sobraniya leningradskikh pisatelei po dokladu tov.Zhdanova', *LG*, 24 August 1946.'Doklad t.Zhdanova o zhurnalakh *Zvezda* i *Leningrad*', *Znamya*, 10 (1946), 7–22; *LG*, 21 September 1946.

51 Vickery, 'Zhdanovism 1946–53', in Hayward and Labedz (eds.), *Literature and Revolution in Soviet Russia 1917–62*, 99–124. 'Rezolyutsiya Prezidiuma Pravleniya Soyuza sovetskikh pisatelei SSSR ot 4 sentyabrya 1946 g.', *LG*, 7 September 1946.

52 N. Mandel'shtam, *Vtoraya kniga*, 419–23.

53 'O repertuare dramaticheskikh teatrov i merakh po ego uluchsheniyu' (24 August 1946), *Bol'shevik*, 16 (1946), 45–9; on the cinema, see *ibid.*, 50–53.

54 *Perepiska*, 242.

55 Danin, *Bremya styda*, 269–70.

56 'M. Sholokhov – kandidat na nobelevskuyu premiyu', *LG*, 19 October 1946. *EBP*, 585.

57 On Tikhonov as establishment figure, see N. Mandel'shtam, *Vospominaniya*, 250–3.

58 See *Vospominaniya*, 208.

59 Ivanov, 'Perevernutoe zerkalo', 202.

60 'Iz vystupleniya A. Fadeeva', *LG*, 7 September 1946. 'Bol'shevistskaya ideinost' – osnova sovetskoi literatury. Na obshchemoskovskom sobranii pisatelei', *ibid.*, 21 September 1946.

61 *EBP*, 585.

62 Ivinskaya, *V plenu vremeni*, 135.

63 A. Sinyavsky, cited discussion in Aucouturier (ed.), *Boris Pasternak 1890–1960*, 351.

64 Letter of 1 October 1946 to L. and N. O. Gudiashvili, 'Pis'ma gruzinskim druz'yam', *Literaturnaya Gruziya*, 2 (1980), 36. *EBP*, 586.
65 Chukovsky, 'Iz dnevnika', 267.
66 *Ibid.*, 267–8.
67 Letter of 5 October 1946 to O. M. Freidenberg, *Perepiska*, 243–4. See also letter of 4 December 1946 to N. A. Tabidze, *SS*, V, 456.
68 *LG* for 27 July and 3 and 10 August 1946 nevertheless carried some articles on Blok by G. Blok, I. Sergievsky, Antokol'sky, V. Orlov and N. Vengrov.
69 Hingley, *Pasternak*, 154–5.
70 Kun, 'Iz vospominanii'. Babichenko (ed.), '*Literaturnyi front*', 186–7.
71 Chukovskaya, 'Otryvki iz dnevnika', 411.

12 FAUSTIAN PURSUITS IN LIFE AND LETTERS

1 G. S. Neigauz, 'Boris Pasternak v povsednevnoi zhizni', *Vospominaniya*, 550.
2 Krotkov, 'Pasternaki', *Grani*, 60 (1966), 72. Z. Pasternak, 'Vospominaniya', 214. G. S. Neigauz, 'Boris Pasternak', 551–2, 554.
3 Z. Pasternak, 'Vospominaniya', 214. Muravina, *Vstrechi s Pasternakom*, 89.
4 Gershtein, 'O Pasternake i ob Akhmatovoi', 399.
5 Ivinskaya, *V plenu vremeni*, 19–20, 26.
6 Z. Pasternak, 'Vospominaniya', 214. Ivinskaya, *V plenu vremeni*, 17.
7 Ivinskaya, *V plenu vremeni*, 24, 28.
8 Emel'yanova, 'Moskva, Potapovsky', 51. Ivinskaya, *V plenu vremeni*, 28.
9 *Ibid.*, 29–31.
10 *Ibid.*, 33–4.
11 Emel'yanova, 'Moskva, Potapovsky', 52.
12 *EBP*, 594.
13 Z. Pasternak, 'Vospominaniya', 214. On Asmus' second marriage, see Muravina, 83–4.
14 Letter of 2 March 1947 to O. M. Freidenberg, *Perepiska*, 259.
15 Neigauz, 'Boris Pasternak v povsednevnoi zhizni', 548–63.
16 M. Polivanov, 'Tainaya svoboda', *Vospominaniya*, 493. *DZh*, 530; *SS*, III, 510.
17 *EPIV*, 156. Polivanova, 'Iz razgovorov', 487. M. Polivanov, 'Tainaya svoboda', 496–7. Letter of 3 February 1953 to M. K. Baranovich, *SS*, V, 507.
18 L. Chukovskaya, 'Otryvki iz dnevnika', 408–9. *EBP*, 590. Ivinskaya, *V plenu vremeni*, 195–6.
19 L. Chukovskaya, 'Otryvki iz dnevnika', 410. E. Gershtein, 'O Pasternake i ob Akhmatovoi', 400–2. 'Perepiska s Evgeniei Pasternak', *Znamya*, 2 (1996), 185.
20 Gershtein, 'O Pasternake i ob Akhmatovoi', 402–5.
21 Letter of 2 April 1955 to B. S. Kuzin, ' "Vtorzhenie voli v sud'bu" (Pis'ma Borisa Pasternaka o sozdanii romana "Doktor Zhivago")', publ. E. Pasternak and K. Polivanov, *Literaturnoe obozrenie*, 5 (1988), 8.
22 *EBP*, 592. Gershtein, 'O Pasternake i ob Akhmatovoi', 411.

23 B. Turbin, 'Konets "Zhivagovskogo" doma', *Russkaya mysl'*, 22/29 July 1982. *EBP*, 593. Salys, 'A Tale of Two Artists', 82-6.
24 Muravina, *Vstrechi s Pasternakom*, 41-51.
25 *Ibid.*, 47.
26 Gladkov, *Vstrechi s Pasternakom*, 114. *DZh*, 294; *SS*, III, 282-3.
27 N. Mandel'shtam, *Vtoraya kniga*, 421-2.
28 M. Polivanov, 'Tainaya svoboda', 504.
29 Gladkov, *Vstrechi s Pasternakom*, 120-1.
30 *EBP*, 593-4.
31 Letter of 21 May 1948 to V. D. Avdeev, M. Rashkovskaya (publ.), 'Pasternak v poslevoennye gody (novye dokumenty)', *Literaturnaya ucheba*, 6 (1988), 116.
32 Kun, 'Iz vospominanii o B. L. Pasternake'. Letter of 7 March 1948 to B. S. Kuzin, *SS*, V, 464-5.
33 *EBP*, 586. *DZh*, 541-2. *SS*, III, 519.
34 Letter of 13 October 1946 to O. M. Freidenberg, *Perepiska*, 244-5.
35 Z. Pasternak, 'Vospominaniya', 215. *EPIV*, 157.
36 Gladkov, *Vstrechi s Pasternakom*, 108.
37 *EBP*, 589-90.
38 L. Chukovskaya, *Zapiski*, II, 336-9.
39 Ivinskaya, *V plenu vremeni*, 25. *EBP*, 590. Chukovskaya, 'Otryvki iz dnevnika', 410; *Zapiski*, II, 336-9.
40 *Perepiska*, 254-6.
41 Levin, *Iz glubin pamyati*, 92-6.
42 Gladkov, *Vstrechi s Pasternakom*, 109-10.
43 Pertsov, 'Russkaya poeziya', 187. 'Sodoklad V. Pertsova: o putyakh razvitiya poezii', *LG*, 8 March 1947.
44 Fadeev, 'Za vysokuyu ideinost' sovetskoi literatury'.
45 Surkov, 'O poezii B. Pasternaka'. See also, Gladkov, *Vstrechi s Pasternakom*, 109-10; Surkov, 'Zhizn' – istochnik poeticheskogo vdokhnoveniya', *Molodoi bol'shevik*, 4 (1947), 29.
46 E.g. 'Za vysokuyu ideinost' sovetskoi literatury', *LG*, 21 June 1947. Fadeev: 'Sovetskaya literatura posle Postanovleniya'; 'Sovetskaya literatura na pod"eme'; 'O literaturnoi kritike', *Bol'shevik*, 13 (1947), 18-9 and 'Zadachi literaturnoi kritiki', 157-8.
47 Plotkin, 'Partiya i literatura', 161.
48 Gladkov, *Vstrechi s Pasternakom*, 110.
49 Letter of 26 March 1947 to O. M. Freidenberg, *Perepiska*, 259.
50 See *Soch.*III, 295. Conquest, *Courage of Genius*, 86-7.
51 A. Fadeev, 'Sovetskaya literatura posle Postanovleniya TsK VKP(b) ot 14 avgusta 1946 goda o zhurnalakh "Zvezda" i "Leningrad"', *LG*, 29 June 1947, and 'Nashi ideinye protivniki'. See *FBPPP*, 252.
52 Quoted in L. Chukovskaya, 'Otryvki iz dnevnika', 411-12.
53 Gladkov, *Vstrechi s Pasternakom*, 50.

54 *Ibid.*, 111.
55 *FBPPP*, 252–3.
56 Pertsov, 'Original i portret'.
57 Letter of 20 May 1947, to O. M. Freidenberg, *Perepiska*, 264.
58 L. Chukovskaya, 'Otryvki iz dnevnika', 412.
59 *EBP*, 596. Ivinskaya, *V plenu vremeni*, 37–9. For comparison of their translated work in the 1950s, see Kiasashvili, 'Rabota B. L. Pasternaka', in Podgaetskaya (ed.), *Pasternakovskie chteniya* (Moscow, 1992), 256–7.
60 Letter of 16 February 1947 to O. M. Freidenberg, *Perepiska*, 258.
61 Letter of 30 September 1947 to M. M. Morozov, in 'K perevodam shekspirovskikh dram', 363.
62 Letter of 8 September 1947 to O. M. Freidenberg, *Perepiska*, 264–5.
63 Chudakova, 'Neizvestnyi korrekturnyi ekzemplyar', 110. 'Writers in Exile: A Conference of Soviet and East European Dissidents', *Partisan Review*, 3 (1983), 353. Miłosz, *The History of Polish Literature*, 451.
64 Kun, 'Iz vospominanii o B. L. Pasternake', and 'Memories of Pasternak', 102.
65 *Ibid.* Ivinskaya, *V plenu vremeni*, 38.
66 Letter of 8 September 1947 to O. M. Freidenberg, *Perepiska*, 264–5.
67 L. Chukovskaya, 'Otryvki iz dnevnika', 415.
68 *Ibid.*, 414–15.
69 Danin, 'Eto prebudet s nami', 320. See ' "Molodaya gvardiya" na stsene nashikh teatrov', *Pravda*, 3 December 1947; 'Novoe izdanie romana A. Fadeeva "Molodaya gvardiya" ', *Pravda*, 23 December 1947; Vickery, 'Zhdanovism 1946–53', 114–15.
70 Livanov, 'Nevydumannyi Boris Pasternak', *Moskva*, 11 (1993), 172.
71 L. Chukovskaya, 'Otryvki iz dnevnika', 417–18.
72 Gladkov, *Vstrechi s Pasternakom*, 116–20.
73 M. Polivanov, 'Tainaya svoboda', 496.
74 Hayward, *Writers in Russia*, 204–7. 'Za mir, za demokratiyu!', *LG*, 14 February 1947. *EBP*, 593.
75 Wilson, *Shostakovich: A Life Remembered*, 199–200, 203, 207–8. MacDonald, *The New Shostakovich*, 190–4. G. Neigauz, 'Razmyshleniya muzykanta (Iz dnevnikovykh zapisei G. G. Neigauza)', pub. I. M. Leble, *Vstrechi s proshlym*, 6 (1988), 390. Ivinskaya, *V plenu vremeni*, 135.
76 'Ob opere "Velikaya druzhba" V. Muradeli', *LG*, 3 March 1948. *EBP*, 596–7.
77 Maslin, 'Mayakovsky i nasha sovremennost'', 154–6.
78 Yakovlev, 'Poet dlya estetov', 225–6.
79 Polivanov, ' "Izbrannye" Pasternaka i raznye redaktsii "Marburga" ', in Dorzweiler and Harder (eds.), *Pasternak-Studien I*, 124–5. Muravina, *Vstrechi s Pasternakom*, 63.
80 Chudakova, 'Neizvestnyi korrekturnyi ekzemplyar', 106–18.
81 L. Chukovskaya, 'Otryvki iz dnevnika', 419.
82 Letter of June 1948 (n.d.) to Z. N. Pasternak, *BPZNP*, 160.

83 L. Gornung, 'Vstrecha za vstrechei', 85. Letters of 16, 22, 24 June 1948 to Z. N. Pasternak, *BPZNP*, 161–4.

84 See *EBP*, 578, 598.

85 Muravina, *Vstrechi s Pasternakom*, 83. *EPIV*, 157.

86 Chudakova, 'Neizvestnyi korrekturnyi ekzemplyar', 111. *EBP*, 600.

87 Letter of 1st October 1948 to O. M. Freidenberg, *Perepiska*, 267.

88 *EBP*, 601.

89 See vol. I, 265. Kopelev, 'Faustovskii mir Borisa Pasternaka', in Aucouturier (ed.), *Boris Pasternak 1890–1960*, 497. A. Livingstone, ' "Fausta cho li, Gamleta li": Faustovskie motivy v rannikh stikhotvoreniyakh Pasternaka', in Dorzweiler and Harder (eds.), *Pasternak-Studien I*, 91–6.

90 Efron, 'Stranitsy bylogo', 166. Letter of 15 July 1929 to L. O. and R. I. Pasternak (APT). Letter of 6 November 1948 to O. M. Freidenberg, *Perepiska*, 272.

91 Markov, 'An Unnoticed Aspect', 507–8.

92 Kopelev, 'Faustovskii mir', 510.

93 *EBP*, 601.

94 Gershtein, 'O Pasternake i ob Akhmatovoi', 404.

95 Quoted in Kopelev, 'Faustovskii mir', 498.

96 On Pasternak and *Faust* see also: 'Ein faustisches Schicksal', in R. Orlowa and L. Kopelew, *Boris Pasternak* (Stuttgart, 1986), 31–6; Pohl, *Russische Faust-Überset-zungen*, 123–67; Baevsky, ' "Faust" ', 341–52; Livingstone, 'Pasternak and Faust', 353–69; and 'A Transformation of Goethe's *Faust*', 81–92.

97 Letters of 12 and 20 July, 14 August 1948 to S. D. Spassky, *SS*, V, 468–71. *EBP*, 598–600.

98 *EPIV*, 158. Lekić, 'Pasternak's *Doktor Zivago*', 177–91.

99 Belkina, *Skreshchenie sudeb*, 439 ff.

100 Efron, letters of 28 November and 15 December 1948 to B. L. Pasternak, in *Pis'ma iz ssylki*, 21–32.

101 'Boris Pasternak i Kaisyn Kuliev', 260, 266. Letter of 25 May 1950 to V. D. Avdeev, M. Rashkovskaya (publ.), 'Boris Pasternak v poslevoennye gody', 116.

102 O. M. Freidenberg, letter of 29 November 1948 to B. L. Pasternak, *Perepiska*, 273.

103 *DZh*, 67–9; *SS*, III, 68–70.

13 THE DARKNESS BEFORE DAWN

1 Letter of 12 December 1948 to F. K. Pasternak and family (APT).

2 'Ob odnoi antipatrioticheskoi gruppe teatral'nykh kritikov', *Pravda*, 28 January 1949.

3 Rapoport, *Stalin's War*, 82. Conquest, *The Great Terror*, 431. B. Pinkus, *The Soviet Government and the Jews 1948–1967: A Documentary Study* (Cambridge, 1984), 147–92.

4 Vickery, 'Zhdanovism 1946–53', 105–11. *Perepiska*, 282–3.

5   A. Makarov, 'Tikhoi sapoi', *LG*, 19 February 1949.
6   M. Lukonin, 'Problemy sovetskoi poezii (itogi 1948 goda)', *Zvezda*, 3 (1949), 184–5.
7   'Sovetskaya poeziya v 1948 godu', *LG*, 23 March 1949. See also Zakharenko (ed.), *Russkie Pisateli-Poety*, 175.
8   Rapoport, *Stalin's War*, 111.
9   Muravina, *Vstrechi s Pasternakom*, 103. *EBP*, 602.
10 Livanov, 'Ne vydumannyi Pasternak ', *Moskva*, 10 (1993), 178–9.
11 Letter of 27 March 1949 to M. V. Yudina, in 'Pis'ma B. L. Pasternaka k M. V. Yudinoi', *Zapiski otdela rukopisei*, 29 (1967), 255.
12 . G. G. Neigauz, letter of 2 April 1949 to L. A. Pogosova, in Rikhter (ed.), *Genrikh Neigauz*, 233.
13 I. V. Gete (Goethe), *Izbrannye proizvedeniya* (Moscow, 1950).
14 Letter of 20 July 1949 to A. A. Fadeev, 'Pis'ma k Aleksandru Fadeevu', *Moskva*, 9 (1967), 198.
15 Letter of 7 August 1949 to O. M. Freidenberg, *Perepiska*, 280–1.
16 See above, p. 226. Gershtein, 'O Pasternake i ob Akhmatovoi', 404–5. *DZh*, 124–6; *SS*, III, 123–5.
17 *EPIV*, 156–7, 169.
18 Muravina, *Vstrechi s Pasternakom*, 93, 112–15, 119.
19 Letter of 7 August 1949 to O. M. Freidenberg, *Perepiska*, 279; 'here' and 'there' referred to Russia and Western Europe.
20 Ivinskaya, *V plenu vremeni*, 97.
21 *EBP*, 605. Letter of 7 May 1958 to R. Schweitzer, in Schweitzer, *Freundschaft*, 43.
22 · Muravina, *Vstrechi s Pasternakom*, 95–6. Chukovskaya, *Zapiski*, II, 552.
23 See Krotkov, 'Pasternaki', and *The Nobel Prize* (London, 1980). Barron, *KGB*, 123–40.
24 Ivinskaya, *V plenu vremeni*, 97–100. *EBP*, 605. Ivinskaya's dating is contradicted by correspondence.
25 *EBP*, 605. Haight, *Anna Akhmatova*, 159–63.
26 Ivinskaya, *V plenu vremeni*, 109 ff. A. Grant, 'Ot peremeny mesta kukhon' summa razgovorov v nikh ne menyaetsya . . .' *Novoe russkoe slovo*, 13 May 1994.
27 Ivinskaya, *V plenu vremeni*, 117–20. Emel'yanova, 'Moskva, Potapovsky', 53.
28 See Ivinskaya, *V plenu vremeni*, 107–8, 120–1.
29 Letter of 7 May 1958 to R. Schweitzer, in Schweitzer, *Freundschaft*, 43. On Ivinskaya's interrogation, see V. Kovalev, ' "Chem byla vyzvana vasha svyaz' s Pasternakom?" – "Lyubov'yu": Iz sledstevnnogo dela O. Ivinskoi 1949–1950 gg.', *LG*, 16 March 1994.
30 Hingley, *Pasternak*, 175.
31 Muravina, *Vstrechi s Pasternakom*, 121. Letter of 9 December 1949 to O. M. Freidenberg, *Perepiska*, 286.
32 Letter of 15 October 1949 to N. A. Tabidze, *SS*, V, 479–80. 'Boris Pasternak i Kaisyn Kuliev', 265. Ivinskaya, *V plenu vremeni*, 44.

33 Muravina, *Vstrechi s Pasternakom*, 122.
34 Ivinskaya, *V plenu vremeni*, 121–3.
35 Muravina, *Vstrechi s Pasternakom*, 57.
36 Grant, 'Ot peremeny mest'.
37 Rayfield, 'Unicorns and Gazelles', 374.
38 Ivinskaya, *V plenu vremeni*, 114.
39 Letter of 29 March 1950 to A. S. Efron, *Pis'ma iz ssylki*, 53.
40 L. Chukovskaya, *Zapiski*, II, 123.
41 Haight, *Anna Akhmatova*, 159.
42 Letter of 6 April 1950 to N. A. Tabidze, *SS*, V, 487–8.
43 Ivinskaya, *V plenu vremeni*, 130–1.
44 *Ibid.*, 35, 133.
45 *Ibid.*, 35.
46 Letter of 6 April 1950 to N. A. Tabidze, *SS*, V, 488.
47 Letter of 2 January 1953 to M. N. Kostko, quoted in Ivinskaya, *V plenu vremeni*, 134.
48 Emel'yanova, 'Moskva, Potapovsky', 53. Letter of 2 January 1953 to M. N. Kostko, Ivinskaya, *V plenu vremeni*, 134.
49 Emel'yanova,'Moskva, Potapovsky', 53.
50 Ivinskaya, *V plenu vremeni*, 137–45. 'Dusha', *Soch.*III, 63; *SS*, II, 75.
51 Z. N. Pasternak, in Zimyanina (ed.), *Stanislav Neigauz*, 25. G. S. Neigauz, *ibid.*, 56.
52 M. Polivanov, 'Tainaya svoboda', 502. *EPIV*, 158–63.
53 G. S. Neigauz, in Zimyanina (ed.), *Stanislav Neigauz*, 59–60. T. G. Suvorova, in *ibid.*, 15; Ts. A. Voskresenskaya, in *ibid.*, 42; E. V. Malinin, in *ibid.*, 81–2.
54 Muravina, *Vstrechi s Pasternakom*, 139.
55 *Ibid.*, 57, 131–2.
56 Muravina, *Vstrechi s Pasternakom*, 143–5. Cf.Ivinskaya, *V plenu vremeni*, 54–5. 'Bez nazvaniya', *SS*, II, 77.
57 Muravina, *Vstrechi s Pasternakom*, 158.
58 Motyleva, 'Faust v perevode B. Pasternaka', 239–43.
59 Dymshits, 'Kniga o Gete'.
60 Letter of 21 September 1950 to A. S. Efron, *Pis'ma iz ssylki*, 75.
61 *EBP*, 609.
62 Letter of 21 September 1950 to A. S. Efron, *Pis'ma iz ssylki*, 75.
63 Letter of 19 November 1950 to N. A. Tabidze, *SS*, V, 492.
64 See vol. I, 229–30. N. Mandel'shtam, *Vtoraya kniga*, 33.
65 Ivanova, 'Boris Leonidovich Pasternak', 248.
66 M. Polivanov, 'Tainaya svoboda', 501. N. Mandel'shtam, *Vtoraya kniga*, 92. Muravina, *Vstrechi s Pasternakom*, 145 ff.
67 M. Polivanov, 'Tainaya svoboda', 501. *DZh*, 169; *SS*, III, 165.'
68 See vol. I, 238.
69 Letter of 18 November 1950, to R. K. Mikadze, *SS*, V, 490. Letter of 19 November 1950 to N. A. Tabidze, *SS*, V, 492.

70 Muravina, *Vstrechi s Pasternakom*, 134, 155. Letter of 11 October 1951 to O. M. Freidenberg, *Perepiska*, 291. Kun, 'Iz vospominanii'.

71 Letter of 5 December 1950 to Efron, *Pis'ma iz ssylki*, 93.

72 Letter of 16 September 1953 to V. P. Zhuravleva, in Zhuravlev, *Zhizn', iskusstvo, vstrechi*, 342. Letter of 13 November 1953 to V. T. Shalamov, in ' "Nad starymi tetradyami . . ." (Pis'ma B. L. Pasternaka i vospominaniya o nem V. T. Shalamova)', pub. I. P. Sirotinskaya, *Vstrechi s proshlym*, 6 (1988), 293.

73 Letter of 11 October 1951 to E. D. Orlovskaya, 'Boris Pasternak i Kaisyn Kuliev', 267.

74 Letter of 5 October 1951 to N. A. Tabidze, 'Pis'ma gruzinskim druz'yam', 23.

75 Letter of 21 April 1952 to E. D. Orlovskaya, 'Boris Pasternak i Kaisyn Kuliev', 268.

76 Erastova, 'Moi razgovor s Pasternakom', *Vospominaniya*, 570. *EBP*, 613.

77 Letter of 3 June 1952 to N. A. Tabidze, *SS*, V, 495.

78 Letter of 29 April 1951 to S. Chikovani, *SS*, V, 494.

79 Quoted in *SS*, V, 665.

80 Letter of 9 July 1952 to V. T. Shalamov, *SS*, V, 497–505, 665

81 V. V. Ivanov, 'Vikhr'', in Kasack (ed.), *Konstantin Bogatyrev*, (1982), 180 ff.

82 On Bogatyrev, see Kasack (ed.), *Konstantin Bogatyrev*. Ivinskaya, *V plenu vremeni*, 141.

83 Voznesensky, 'Mne 14 let', 574 ff.

84 *Ibid.*, 574–8. Gornung, 'Vstrecha za vstrechei', 81. On Pasternak's coterie, see also G. S. Neigauz, in Zimyanina (ed.), *Stanislav Neigauz*, 59.

85 Voznesensky, 'Mne 14 let', 576–9. Letter of 4 January 1952 to N. A. Tabidze, 'Pis'ma gruzinskim druz'yam', 25.

86 Letters of 22 June and 30 July 1952 to F. A. Tvaltvadze, 'Pis'ma gruzinskim druz'yam', 33–5. Letter of 14 June 1952 to S. I. and M. N. Chikovani, ' "Krai, stavshii mne vtoroi rodinoi" ', 193.

87 Letter of 9 April 1952 to G. N. Leonidze, *ibid.*, 191–2. Letter of 3 June 1952 to N. A. Tabidze, 'Pis'ma gruzinskim druz'yam', 26. *EBP*, 610–11.

88 Letter of 14 June 1952 to S. I. and M. N. Chikovani, ' "Krai, stavshii mne vtoroi rodinoi" ', 193.

89 Letter of 2 August 1952 to V. Kaverin, quoted in Kaverin, 'Pis'mennyi stol', 148.

90 Borisov and Pasternak, 'Materialy', 239.

14 CREATIONS OF THE THAW

1 Borisov and Pasternak, 'Materialy', 239.

2 Letter of 17 January 1953 to N. A. Tabidze, *SS*, V, 502. See also letter of 20 January 1953 to O. M. Freidenberg, *Perepiska*, 297. N. Mandel'shtam, *Vtoraya kniga*, 260, 264.

3 L. Chukovskaya, *Zapiski*, II, 14.

4 Letter of 19 January 1953 to N. Muravina, Muravina, *Vstrechi s Pasternakom*, 166–79.

5 Letter of 3 January 1953 to O. M. Freidenberg, *Perepiska*, 294.
6 *EBP*, 614.
7 Rapoport, *Stalin's War*, 65, 133, 146ff., 183, 101.
8 *Ibid.*, 176ff.
9 Letter of 4 April 1953 to N. A. Tabidze, *SS*, V, 511.
10 Letter of 3 March 1953 to V. F. Asmus, *SS*, V, 510–11.
11 Letter of 5 February 1953 to N. N. Aseev, *SS*, V, 508.
12 Borisov and Pasternak, 'Materialy', 240.
13 Letter of 7 March to G. I. Gudz', *PBP*, 537–8.
14 *Ibid.*
15 V. Kaverin, *Epilog. Memuary* (Moscow, 1989), 312. 'Pis'ma na "Olimp"', 213.
16 Letter of 7 January 1954 to O. M. Freidenberg, *Perepiska*, 305.
17 Letter of 30 December 1953 to O. M. Freidenberg, *Perepiska*, 303.
18 Shalamov, 'Pasternak', *Vospominaniya*, 610.
19 Letters of 4 April and 7 July 1953 to N. A. Tabidze, *SS*, V, 511–12.
20 Letter of 30 July 1954 to Z. N. Pasternak, *BPZNP*, 173, 240.
21 Letter of 12 July 1954 to O. M. Freidenberg, *Perepiska*, 317. Chukovsky, 'Iz dnevnika', 268.
22 Letter of 4 April 1953 to N. A. Tabidze, *SS*, V, 511. Letter of 13 April 1953 to K. A. Fedin, 'Pis'ma B. L. Pasternaka – K. A. Fedinu', 168–9.
23 Letter of 26 December 1953 to N. A. Tabidze, 'Pis'ma gruzinskim druz'yam', 29.
24 Zabolotsky, *The Life of Zabolotsky*, 306–8.
25 Letter of 12 July 1953 to O. M. Freidenberg, *Perepiska*, 301.
26 Letter of 15 December 1953 to M. S. Volynsky, Kedrov, 'Prigovor B. Pasternaka sovremennoi literature'.
27 Etkind, *Poeziya i perevod*, 210–11. See also *EBP*, 620–1.
28 Letter of 18 January 1954 to M. V. Yudina, 'Pis'ma B. L. Pasternaka k M. V. Yudinoi', 256. Letter of 15 September 1953 to D. N. and V. P. Zhuravlev, in Zhuravlev, *Zhizn', iskusstvo, vstrechi*, 341. See also letter of 12 July 1953 to O. M. Freidenberg, *Perepiska*, 302.
29 Letter of 9 August 1953 to M. K. Baranovich, *SS*, V, 516. See letters extracted in *EBP*, 618.
30 Etkind, *Poeziya i perevod*, 206–14.
31 W. Pohl, *Russische Faust-Übersetzungen*, 127ff.
32 Gete (Goethe), *Faust* (Moscow, 1953), 535.
33 V. Markov, 'An Unnoticed Aspect', 507–8. Hingley, *Pasternak*, 177–8. Yurchenko, 'Anafema', 161–8.
34 Fedin, *Pisatel', iskusstvo, vremya*, 389–90.
35 Letter of 30 December 1953 to O. M. Freidenberg, *Perepiska*, 303.
36 Letter of 7 January 1954 to O. M. Freidenberg, *Perepiska*, 306. See also letter of 4 January 1954 to E. D. Orlovskaya, 'Boris Pasternak i Kaisyn Kuliev', 269–70.
37 N. Vil'mont, 'Gete i ego "Faust"', in Gete, *Faust* (Moscow, 1953), 3–32.
38 Letter of 30 December 1953 to O. M. Freidenberg, *Perepiska*, 303.

39 Letter of 9 August 1953 to M. K. Baranovich, *SS*, V, 517.
40 *DZh*, 535–6. *SS*, III, 514. Ivinskaya, *V plenu vremeni*, 29.
41 *DZh*, 536–7. *SS*, III, 515.
42 *EBP*, 616 See also Fleishman, 'Avtobiograficheskoe i "Avgust" Pasternaka', in *Stat'i o Pasternake*, 103–12; Ivinskaya, *V plenu vremeni*, 56–7; *SS*, III, 725.
43 Letter of 29 October 1953 to N. A. Tabidze, quoted in Bodin, *Nine Poems*, 51–2. *DZh*, 545–8; *SS*, III, 522–4. Ivinskaya, *V plenu vremeni*, 36.
44 Chukovsky, 'Iz dnevnika', 268. Letter of 18 September 1953 to N. A. Tabidze, 'Pis'ma gruzinskim druz'yam', 27.
45 Borisov and Pasternak, 'Materialy', 241.
46 Ivinskaya, *V plenu vremeni*, 35.
47 *Ibid.*
48 Emel'yanova, 'Moskva, Potapovsky', 57.
49 Ivinskaya, *V plenu vremeni*, 35.
50 *Ibid.*, 43–4. Letter of 30 September 1953 to Nina Tabidze, *SS*, V, 519–20.
51 *EPIV*, 169.
52 Letter of 30 September 1953 to Nina Tabidze, *SS*, V, 520.
53 Letter of 27 October 1953 to N. A. Tabidze, 'Pis'ma gruzinskim druz'yam', 28.
54 Letter of 30 September 1953 to N. A. Tabidze, *SS*, V, 518.
55 Letter of 29 October 1953 to N. A. Tabidze, 'Pis'ma gruzinskim druz'yam', 27. Letter of 17 December 1953 to M. V. Yudina, *SS*, V, 521–2.
56 Letter of 30 September 1953 to N. A. Tabidze, *SS*, V, 520. See also letter of 1 October 1953 to D. N. and V. P. Zhuravlev, *ibid.*, 520–1.
57 Letter of 16 November 1953 to N. A. Tabidze, 'Pis'ma gruzinskim druz'yam', 29.
58 S. G. Neigauz, 'Avtobiografiya', in Zimyanina (ed.), *Stanislav Neigauz*, 9. Z. N. Pasternak, *ibid.*, 25–6. E. V. Malinin, *ibid.*, 82–3.
59 O. Berggol'ts, 'Razgovor o lirike', *LG*, 16 April 1953. I. Erenburg, 'O rabote pisatelya', *Znamya*, 10 (1953), 160–83. V. Pomerantsev, 'Ob iskrennosti v literature', *Novyi mir*, 12 (1953), 218–45.
60 Chukovsky, 'Iz dnevnika', 268.
61 Letter of 31 December 1953 to O. M. Freidenberg, *Perepiska*, 305.
62 Letter of 15 December 1953 to M. S. Volynsky, in Kedrov, 'Prigovor B. Pasternaka'.
63 Letter of 31 December 1953 to O. M. Freidenberg, *Perepiska*, 304.
64 'Stikhi iz "Doktora Zhivago"', *Znamya*, 4 (1954), 92–5.
65 Voznesensky, 'Mne 14 let', 596–8.
66 L. Chukovskaya, *Zapiski*, II, 50. Emel'yanova, 'Moskva, Potapovsky', 56.
67 Letter of 12 July 1854 to O. Freidenberg, *Perepiska*, 316.
68 Letter of 31 July 1954 to O. M. Freidenberg, *Perepiska*, 323.
69 Letter of 18 January 1954 to M. V. Yudina, *SS*, V, 527.
70 G. M. Kozintsev, letter of 26 February 1954 to B. L. Pasternak. Letters of 4 and 14 March 1954 to G. M. Kozintsev, 'Pis'ma o "Gamlete"', *Voprosy literatury*, 1 (1975), 218–21. Letter of 16 April 1954 to O. M. Freidenberg, *Perepiska*, 316.

71 Letter of 20 March 1954 to O. M. Freidenberg, *Perepiska*, 309–10.
72 Letters of 20 and 27 October 1953 to G. M. Kozintsev, 'Pis'ma o "Gamlete"', 215–16.
73 Letter of 15 March 1954 to G. M. Kozintsev, 'Pis'ma o "Gamlete"', 221. Letters of 27 March and 4 April 1954 to O. M. Freidenberg, *Perepiska*, 310–11.
74 O. M. Freidenberg, letter of 11 April 1954 to B. L. Pasternak, *Perepiska*, 312–15.
75 Emel'yanova, 'Moskva, Potapovsky', 55.
76 *Ibid.*, 56.
77 L. Chukovskaya, *Zapiski*, II, 51.
78 Letter of 12 July 1954 to O. M. Freidenberg, *Perepiska*, 317.
79 Borisov and Pasternak, 'Materialy', 242.
80 Letter of 9 November 1954 to T. M. Nekrasova, quoted in Borisov and Pasternak, 'Materialy', 242–3.
81 *DZh*, 376–7; *SS*, III, 361–2. Livingstone, *Boris Pasternak*, 94–5.
82 Letter of 22 August 1959 to S. Spender, 'B. Pasternak. Three Letters', *Encounter*, August 1960, 5.
83 Jones, 'History and Chronology', 160–63.
84 Gladkov, *Vstrechi s Pasternakom*, 54.
85 Deutscher, 'Pasternak and the Calendar of Revolution', in Davie and Livingstone (eds.), *Pasternak: Modern Judgements*, 254.
86 *DZh*, 427; *SS*, III, 411.
87 *BPZNP*, 172ff., 240. Ivinskaya, *V plenu vremeni*, 48.
88 Ivinskaya, *V plenu vremeni*, 48–9.
89 Simonov, 'Chelovek v poezii', and *Na literaturnye temy*, 277.
90 Ermilov, 'Za sotsialisticheskii realizm'.
91 O. M. Freidenberg, postcard of 4 November 1954 to B. L. Pasternak; Letter of 12 November 1954 to O. M. Freidenberg, *Perepiska*, 324.
92 Letter of 12 November 1954 to O. M. Freidenberg, *ibid.*, 324–5.
93 *Ibid.*, 324.
94 A. Surkov, 'O sostoyanii i zadachakh sovetskoi literatury', *LG*, 16 December 1954. S. Vurgun [sodoklad], *Vtoroi Vsesoyuznyi S"ezd sovetskikh pisatelei* (Moscow, 1956), 75. Kaverin, *Epilog, Memuary*, 324–5.
95 L. Chukovskaya, *Zapiski*, II, 59, 69–70.
96 Letter of 22 January 1955 to M. V. Yudina, quoted in Borisov and Pasternak, 'Materialy', 243.
97 Ivanova, 'Boris Leonidovich Pasternak', 251.
98 Letter of 2 April 1955 to N. P. Smirnov, *SS*, V, 536–8.
99 Kunina, 'Vospominaniya o vstrechakh s B. L. Pasternakom'.
100 Letter of 26 May 1955 to M. Ya. Apletin; I am grateful to M. A. Rashkovskaya for showing me this item. Ruge, *Pasternak*, 89.
101 Ivinskaya, *V plenu vremeni*, 49. Emel'yanova, 'Moskva, Potapovsky', 55, 58.
102 Ivinskaya, *V plenu vremeni*, 49–50.

103 *Perepiska*, 307.
104 *Perepiska*, 326.
105 *EBP*, 623.
106 *Perepiska*, 333–4.
107 *EBP*, 624.
108 Borisov and Pasternak, 'Materialy', 243.
109 *EPIV*, 166. Vaksberg, *Stalin's Prosecutor*, 183–4. Letters of 7 September and 4 October 1955 to N. A. Tabidze, 'Pis'ma druz'yam', *Literaturnaya Gruziya*, 2 (1966), 93–4.
110 Letter of 18 September 1955 to M. K. Baranovich, *SS*, V, 538.
111 Borisov and Pasternak, 'Materialy', 243.
112 *Ibid.*, 244.
113 Letter of 10 December 1955 to V. T. Shalamov, *PBP*, 556–7. Letter of 10 December 1955 to Z. F. Ruoff, *SS*, V, 539–40.
114 Letter of 10 December 1955 to N. A. Tabidze, *SS*, V, 541.
115 Ivinskaya, *V plenu vremeni*, 213. Borisov and Pasternak, 'Materialy', 245.

15 THE SKIES CLEAR . . . AND DARKEN

1 Ivinskaya, *V plenu vremeni*, 230.
2 Letter of 10 December 1955 to N. A. Tabidze, *SS*, V, 541–2.
3 *Literaturnaya Moskva*, 1 (1956), 794–809.
4 Kaverin, 'Literator. Iz knigi vospominanii', 114.
5 Letter of 12 July 1956 to K. G. Paustovsky, *SS*, V, 547. Kaverin, 'Literator', 114.
6 Ivinskaya, *V plenu vremeni*, 138. Letter of 10 December 1955 to Nina Tabidze, *SS*, V, 540–1.
7 G. D. Zlenko and N. N. Chernego, *Boris Pasternak. Bibliograficheskii ukazatel'* (Odessa, 1990), 25–7.
8 Ivinskaya, *V plenu vremeni*, 57, 71. See above, pp. 297–8.
9 'Kul't lichnosti zabryzgan gryaz'yu . . .', *SS*, II, 558. See Ivinskaya, *V plenu vremeni*, 156, for a longer variant.
10 Ivinskaya, *V plenu vremeni*, 155–6.
11 'Predsmertnoe pis'mo Aleksandra Fadeeva i vokrug nego', *LG*, 10 October 1990.
12 Ivinskaya, *V plenu vremeni*, 154. Chukovskaya, *Zapiski*, II, 155–6. Belkina, *Skreshchenie sudeb*, 502. For 'liberal' verdicts on Fadeev's death, see Chukovsky, *Dnevnik 1930–1969*, 237–8; Kaverin, *Epilog*, 312–14. See also see *Soch*.II, 38–9; *VP*, 451–3; *SS*, IV, 332–3.
13 L. Chukovskaya, *Zapiski*, II, 551–2. Hingley, *Pasternak*, 184–5. Ivinskaya, *V plenu vremeni*, 379. See also *Dossier*, 220–9.
14 *EBP*, 622.
15 A. V. Abasheli, *Izbrannoe* (Moscow, 1957). R. Tagor, *Sochineniya* (Moscow, 1957). G. Tabidze, *Stikhotvoreniya i poemy* (Moscow, 1958). Ivinskaya, *V plenu vremeni*, 40–43.

16 Letter of 2 April 1955 to N. P. Smirnov, *SS*, V, 537.
17 Letter of 12 July 1954 to E. B. Pasternak, *SS*, V, 531–2. See E. B. Pasternak's verses in Aucouturier (ed.), *Boris Pasternak 1890–1960*, [5–7]. *EPIV*, 163–5.
18 Letter of 15 December 1955 to M. G. Vatagin, *SS*, V, 542–4.
19 L. Chukovskaya, *Zapiski*, II, 70. Ivinskaya, *V plenu vremeni*, 57. *EBP*, 634. Chukovsky, 'Iz dnevnika', 270.
20 Shalamov, 'Pasternak', 622.
21 Gifford, 'Pasternak and the "Realism" of Blok', 96–106.
22 *Soch.*II, 52; *SS*, IV, 346.
23 S. P. Bobrov, letter of 15 April 1967 to C. J. Barnes. *Soch.*II, 45. Belkina, *Skreshchenie sudeb*, 486. Maslenikova, *Portret*, 206–7. Kryukova, ' "Razgovor s neizvestnym drugom" ', 526–7.
24 Barnes, 'Biography, Autobiography and "Sister Life" ', 51–2. *SS*, IV, 827–34. L. Chukovskaya, *Zapiski*, II, 178, 560. Verbal testimony of V. V. Ivanov.
25 *Izbrannoe*, II, 496–9.
26 *DZh*, 465–6. *SS*, III, 448.
27 *Izbrannoe*, II, 496.
28 *EBP*, 629, 634.
29 Letter of 17 August 1965 to A. M. Ripellino, 'Boris L. Pasternak: Pis'ma k A. M. Ripellino', *Rossiya/Russia*, 4 (1980), 318.
30 *Soch.*II, 352.
31 *Soch.*II, 32. *VP*, 446. *SS*, IV, 326–7.
32 Ivanova, *Moi sovremenniki*, 414–15; and 'Boris Leonidovich Pasternak', 251.
33 On various textual changes, see *Soch.*I, 444ff., and III, 240ff.; *SS*, I, 637ff. and II, 618ff.
34 Letter of 10 July 1956 to S. I. Chikovani, quoted in *EBP*, 633.
35 Quoted in E. B. Pasternak, 'Priblizit' chas', 26.
36 *Ibid.*, 26–7. *EBP*, 628.
37 *EBP*, 629–30.
38 Ivanova, *Moi sovremenniki*, 417.
39 *Soch.*III, 62–3; *SP*, 447–8; *SS*, II, 74.
40 *SS*, II, 78. E. B. Pasternak, 'Priblizit' chas', 27–8. See K. Chukovsky, *Chukokkola* (Moscow, 1979), 413–15.
41 *Soch.*III, 79–80. *SP*, 461–2. *SS*, II, 94–5.
42 S. Pollak, 'Relyatsiya', ms. (PFA) 'V redaktsiyu "Tribuna lyudu" ', *SS*, IV, 667, 890–91.
43 *Soch.*III, 85–7; *SP*, 467–8; *SS*, II, 102–3. L. Chukovskaya, *Zapiski*, II, 201–2. On Pasternak's late verse, see also: Gifford, *Boris Pasternak*, 219–30; Proyart, 'La nature et l'actualité', in Aucouturier (ed.), *Boris Pasternak, 1890–1960*, 373–409; Girzheva, 'Nekotorye osobennosti', 54–9; Zh. A. Dozorets, 'B. L. Pasternak. Kogda razgulyaetsya (kniga stikhov kak tseloe)', *Russkii yazyk v shkole*, 1 (1990), 60–6.
44 V. Veidle, 'Zavershenie puti', in *Soch.*III, xiv.

45 A. Livingstone, 'Pasternak's Last Poetry', *Meanjin Quarterly* (December, 1963), 395.
46 Proyart, 'La nature et l'actualité', 377–80.
47 *EBP*, 629.
48 Shtut, 'U karty nashei literatury', 245. B. Solov'ev, 'Smelost' podlinnaya i mnimaya', *LG*, 19 May 1957.
49 See Alexander, '*Dr Zhivago* and *The Leopard*', 384–5. D'Angelo, 'Der Roman des Romans', 490.
50 D'Angelo, 'Der Roman des Romans'. Ivinskaya, *V plenu vremeni*, 215–18.
51 H. Shapiro's verbal communication to C. J. Barnes, March 1964.
52 Kaverin, 'Literator', 115.
53 Neigauz, 'Boris Pasternak v povsednevnoi zhizni', 561.
54 Ivinskaya, *V plenu vremeni*, 216–17.
55 Letter of 12 July 1956 to K. G. Paustovsky, *SS*, V, 547.
56 Ivinskaya, *V plenu vremeni*, 219–22.
57 *Ibid.*, 222–3.
58 Proyart, 'Introduction', in *Lettres*, 21, 24–6.
59 *EBP*, 631.
60 Letter of 12 July 1956 to K. G. Paustovsky, 'Pozitsiya khudozhnika', *Literaturnoe obozrenie*, 2 (1990), 14.
61 *Dossier*, 13–21.
62 L. Chukovskaya, *Zapiski*, II, 175.
63 *Dossier*, 40.
64 'B. L. Pasternaku', appendix in *Novyi mir*, 11 (1958), III-XVI.
65 Simonov, 'Uroki Fedina', 169–70.
66 *FBPPP*, 278.
67 Pasternak's silence led some to assume erroneously that the letter, which was published two years later, was backdated to September 1956. See d'Angelo, 'Der Roman des Romans', 491, and Ivinskaya, *V plenu vremeni*, 227.
68 L. Chukovskaya, *Zapiski*, II, 174–5.
69 Chukovsky, 'Iz dnevnika', 271.
70 *EBP*, 633.
71 Letter of 20 September 1956 to K. A. Fedin, 'Pis'ma B. L. Pasternaka – K. A. Fedinu', 169.
72 *EBP*, 633. L. Chukovskaya, *Zapiski*, II, 176–7. T. Ivanova, 'Boris Leonidovich Pasternak', 252.
73 Letter of 26 September 1956, to T. V. Ivanova, quoted in her 'Boris Leonidovich Pasternak', 253.
74 Berlin, 'Vstrechi', 531–3.
75 Letter of 14 August 1956 to L. L. Pasternak Slater, Zh. L. and F. K. Pasternak (APT).
76 Letter of 4 November 1956 to L. L. Pasternak Slater (APT). B. Pasternak, *An Essay in Autobiography*, trans. Manya Harari, introd. Edward Crankshaw (London,

1959). B. Pasternak, *Kogda razgulyaetsya. Poems 1955–1959*, trans. Michael Harari (London, 1960).

77 P. Blake, 'Introduction', in M. Hayward, *Writers in Russia*, xlixff. Pasternak's letter of 21 October 1956 to L. L. Pasternak Slater (APT) mistakenly underestimated Katkov's enthusiasm for the novel.

78 Chukovsky, 'Iz dnevnika', 271. Ivanova, 'Boris Leonidovich Pasternak', 252.

79 E. g. B. Ryurikov, 'Literatura i zhizn' naroda', *Pravda*, 26 August 1956.

80 Polivanova, 'Iz razgovorov', 490. Emel'yanova, 'Moskva, Potapovsky', 55.

81 Proyart, 'Introduction', *Lettres*, 17.

82 *Ibid.*, 21. *Dossier*, 51.

83 Proyart, 'Introduction', *Lettres*, 24–5.

84 A. Efron, *O Marine Tsvetaevoi*, 254ff.

85 J. de Proyart, 'Introduction', *Lettres*, 17–21.

86 Letter of 17 January 1957 (?) to H. Peltier, *Lettres*, 63–4.

87 Letter of 6 February 1957 to H. Peltier, *Lettres*, 66. Letters of 6 February 1957 to G. Gallimard and G. Feltrinelli, *Dossier*, figs 15 and 17.

16 THE PRINTING AND THE PRIZE

1 L. Chukovskaya, 'Otryvki iz dnevnika', 422.

2 Zhuravlev, *Zhizn', iskusstvo, vstrechi*, 335. Voznesensky, 'Mne 14 let', 579–80.

3 See allusion to this in *NNVV*, 7. Ivinskaya, *V plenu vremeni*, 44–5.

4 *Alla Konstantinovna Tarasova.Dokumenty i vospominaniya* (Moscow, 1978), 100–4. Letter of 21 August 1957 to N. A. Tabidze, *SS*, V, 549. On 'Vakkhanaliya', see Yakobson, ' "Vakkhanaliya" '.

5 'Anastasii Platonovne Zuevoi', *SS*, II, 165–6, 644; also *ibid.*, 543, 657. Ivinskaya, *V plenu vremeni*, 66.

6 Letters of 6, 9, 10, 13 and 17 February 1957 to Z. N. Pasternak, *BPZNP*, 178–88.

7 Letter of 5 August 1957 to A. K. Tarasova, *Alla Konstantinovna Tarasova*, 319. *EBP*, 636–7. E. B. Pasternak, 'Priblizit' chas', 28–9.

8 *EBP*, 636–7. Ivanova, *Moi sovremenniki*, 431.

9 *SS*, II, 582. See *EBP*, 637; E. B. Pasternak, 'Priblizit' chas', 29; also his 'Reading Pasternak – Some Errors Corrected', 43–4. 'Pered krasoi zemli v aprele . . .', *SS*, II, 598.

10 Letter of 5 November 1930 to L. O and R. I. Pasternak (APT). Ivinskaya, *V plenu vremeni*, 44. Barnes, 'Boris Pasternak and Mary Queen of Scots', 25–38. *Soch*.III, 94–6; *SP*, 475–7; *SS*, II, 113–15.

11 Letter of 7 May 1957 to A. K. Tarasova, *Alla Konstantinovna Tarasova*, 318–19.

12 G. S. Neigauz, 'Boris Pasternak v povsednevnoi zhizni', 559.

13 E. B. Pasternak, 'Priblizit' chas', 30. *EBP*, 639–40. *EPIV*, 169.

14 Ivinskaya, *V plenu vremeni*, 393–8. Proyart, 'La nature et l'actualité', 406. Chukovsky, 'Iz dnevnika', 270–1.

15 *EBP*, 64.

16 See Zakharenko (ed.), *Russkie Pisateli-Poety*, 72.
17 *EBP*, 640. Ivinskaya, *V plenu vremeni*, 224–6. Proyart, 'Introduction', *Lettres*, 45.
18 *Dossier*, 22–3. Letter of 21 August 1957 to N. A. Tabidze, *SS*, V, 550. *EBP*, 640.
19 Letter of 6 February 1957 to G. Feltrinelli, *Dossier*, facsimile illustration 17. See p. 320 above.
20 *Dossier*, 25–6. *EBP*, 640.
21 Letter of 23 August 1957 to S. I. Chikovani, *SS*, V, 553.
22 Letter of 21 August 1957 to N. A. Tabidze, *SS*, V, 550.
23 Letter of 18 August 1957 to K. A. Fedin, 'Pis'ma B. L. Pasternaka – K. A. Fedinu', 170. Ivinskaya, *V plenu vremeni*, 236–40; Ivinskaya wrongly dates this event to 1958. Letter of 21 August 1957 to N. A. Tabidze, *SS*, V, 550–1.
24 Letter of 21 August 1957 to N. A. Tabidze, *SS*, V, 550.
25 *EPIV*, 170.
26 *Ibid.*, 551.
27 Ivinskaya, *V plenu vremeni*, 230–1.
28 L. Chukovskaya, *Zapiski*, II, 203.
29 *Dossier*, 31. M. H. Berlin, 'A Visit to Pasternak', 333.
30 Letter of 6 February 1957 to G. Bebutov, in G. Bebutov, 'Po stranitskam odnoi perepiski', 74. Letter of 23 August 1957 to S. Chikovani, *SS*, V, 553.
31 See J. de Proyart, 'La nature et l'actualité', 373–409; E. B. Pasternak, 'Priblizit' chas', 26–32; and 'Pered krasoi zemli . . .', 31–3; Ivinskaya, *V plenu vremeni*, 411–33. See also *SS*, II, 580–98.
32 E. B. Pasternak, 'Priblizit' chas', 27. *EBP*, 642–3. Maslenikova, *Portret*, 185.
33 *Grani*, 34–35 (1957), 3–13; also *ibid.*, 36 (1957), 3–10.
34 *Dossier*, 32–34.
35 L. A. Ozerov, 'Eshche o Fedine i Pasternake', *'Naiti svoi lad . . .'*, 23, 25–6.
36 *Dossier*, 37–8.
37 K. Zelinsky, 'O naznachenii poezii', *Inostrannaya literatura*, 4 (1958), 200–1. Ripellino, 'Vystuplenie', *ibid.*, 212.
38 Conquest, *Courage of Genius*, 66–7.
39 'Vsegda s partiei, vsegda s narodom. Na sobranii tvorcheskoi intelligentsii Moskvy', *LG*, 28 November 1957.
40 S. Khrushchev, *Khrushchev on Khrushchev. An Inside Account of the Man and his Era*, ed. and trans. William Taubman (Boston-Toronto-London, 1990), 208. *Khrushchev Remembers: The Last Testament*, trans. Strobe Talbot (Boston-Toronto, 1974), 76–7.
41 Ivinskaya, *V plenu vremeni*, 231–2. *EBP*, 641. *Dossier*, 37–8.
42 *Dossier*, 35–6.
43 *Ibid.*, 38–9.
44 Ruge, *Pasternak*, 95–6.
45 Letter of 19 January 1958 to J. de Proyart, *Lettres*, 88 (Pasternak's emphasis).
46 Letter of 16 December 1957 to E. A. Blaginina, *SS*, V, 558.

47 B. Makarov (president of 'Mezhdunarodnaya kniga'), letter of 5 February 1958 to CPSU Central Committee, *Dossier*, 55. *Ibid.*, 41–54, 57–65.

48 *Ibid.*, 65–6.

49 Letter of 6 October 1957 to S. Chikovani, *SS*, V, 554.

50 *SS*, IV, 346, 827. A. Sinyavsky, 'Odin den' s Pasternakom', in Aucouturier (ed.), *Boris Pasternak 1890–1960*, 11–17. See Sinyavsky 'Poeziya Pasternaka', *SP*, 9–62.

51 'Druz'yam na vostoke i zapade. Novogodnee pozhelanie', *SS*, IV, 669–70. Cf. N. Nilsson, 'Pasternak: We are the Guests of Existence', *Reporter*, 19 (27 November, 1957), 34–5.

52 Proyart, 'Introduction', 41.

53 Letter of 2 May 1958 to M. K. Baranovich, quoted in *EBP*, 643.

54 Postcards of 14 and 23 January 1957 to L. L. Pasternak Slater (APT).

55 Letter of 19 January 1958 to I. Utenkov, *Dossier*, 57. *Lettres*, 87.

56 G. Feltrinelli, letter of 30 October 1958 to F. D. Wieck of University of Michigan Press (Archive of University of Michigan Press). Proyart, 'Introduction', 41–2.

57 Letter of 8 July 1958 to H. Peltier-Zamoyska, *Lettres*, 104.

58 Reuter (The Hague), 4 November 1958. *Dossier*, 142.

59 Proffer, *The Widows of Russia*, 136–8. C. S., 'Ma chi fu il primo editore del "Dottor Zivago"?', *Corriere dell sera*, 14 January 1988. J. de Proyart, 'Introduction', 41–4.

60 Proyart, 'Introduction', 44–7. Letter of 30 March 1959 to J. de Proyart, *Lettres*, 152.

61 Proyart, 'La nature et l'actualité', 407–8; and 'Introduction', *Lettres*, 47–8.

62 Chukovsky, 'Iz dnevnika', 271–3. L. Chukovskaya, *Zapiski*, II, 574–6.

63 L. Chukovskaya, *Zapiski*, II, 217–18.

64 Ivinskaya, *V plenu vremeni*, 234–5. Letter of 12 July to L. L. Pasternak Slater (APT).

65 Postcards of 24 February, 5 and 25 March, 1 April 1958 to L. L. Pasternak Slater; postcard of 3 May 1958 to Zh. L. Pasternak (APT). L. L. Pasternak Slater, postcard of 6 October 1958 to B. L. Pasternak (PFA).

66 Letter of 12 May 1958 to Zh. L. Pasternak (APT).

67 Postcard of 6/13 October 1958 to Zh. L. Pasternak (APT).

68 Letter of 12 December 1958 to L. A. Voskresenskaya, *SS*, V, 568. Letter of 6 September 1958 to J. de Proyart, *Lettres*, 125.

69 Boris Pasternak/Thomas Merton, *Six Letters*, introd. L. Pasternak Slater (Lexington KY, 1973). Wolff, *Briefwechsel eines Verlegers*, 477–82.

70 Letter of 28 September 1958 to Zh. L. Pasternak (PFA). *Poems of Boris Pasternak*, trans. and introd. E. Kayden (London-Ann Arbor MI, 1959).

71 E. Tall (ed.), 'Correspondence', 274–8. Letter of 25 June 1958 to K. I. Chukovsky, *SS*, V, 563.

72 The Tagore text, if written, has been lost. 'Für die Faust-Gedenkstätte Knittlingen (18 June 1958), quoted in Schweitzer, *Freundschaft*, 22–4. See also *ibid.*, 20–1.

73 Proyart, 'Introduction', 40. Letter of 18 August 1958 to J. de Proyart, *Lettres*, 117.

74 Letter of 28 September 1958 (unsent) to Zh. L. Pasternak (PFA). Pasternak had meanwhile turned down the idea of Nabokov as translator of the Zhivago poems;

see A. Field, *The Life and Art of Vladimir Nabokov* (New York, 1987), 302. See also P. Blake, 'Introduction', in M. Hayward, *Writers in Russia*, 1.
75 Z. A. Maslenikova, *Portret Borisa Pasternaka* (Moscow, 1990). G. S. Neigauz, 'Boris Pasternak v povsednevnoi zhizni', 556.
76 Hingley, *Pasternak*, 234–5. G. S. Neigauz, 'Boris Paternak v povsednevnoi zhizni', 561. Evtushenko, 'Pocherk, pokhozhii na zhuravlei', 641–3.
77 Letter of 10 July 1958 to L. L. Pasternak Slater (APT).
78 Letter of 2 May 1958 to M. K. Baranovich, quoted *EBP*, 643.
79 Letter of 11 June 1958 to N. A. Tabidze, *SS*, V, 561–2. Letter of 1 July 1958 to V. V. Ivanov, *SS*, V, 565.
80 *SS*, II, 632.
81 E. B. Pasternak, 'Pered krasoi zemli', 32.
82 *EBP*, 644, 646. E. B. Pasternak, 'Priblizit' chas', 31.
83 *Soch*.III, 100–1; *SP*, 481; *SS*, II, 119. E. B. Pasternak, 'Pered krasoi zemli', 32.
84 L. Chukovskaya, *Zapiski*, II, 247. *Dossier*, 65–7.
85 Letter of 1 May 1958 to Zh. L. Pasternak (APT). *Lettres*, 124–5.
86 Chukovsky, 'Iz dnevnika', 274.
87 Ivinskaya, *V plenu vremeni*, 252. Letter of 6 September 1958 to J. de Proyart, *Lettres*, 125.
88 Pertsov, 'Golosa zhizni'.
89 Ivinskaya, *V plenu vremeni*, 240.
90 Letter of 8/13 October 1958 to Zh. L. Pasternak (APT). Letter of 9 October 1958 to R. Schweitzer, in Schweitzer, *Freundschaft*, 53.
91 Letter of 8/13 October 1958 to Zh. L. Pasternak (APT).
92 *Dossier*, 68–70.
93 *Ibid.*, 70–1.
94 Gyllensten, 'Some Notes', 112; cf.inaccurate data in Mallac, *Boris Pasternak*, 225.
95 Espmark, *The Nobel Prize in Literature*, 78.
96 Gyllensten, 'Some Notes', 113. Espmark, *The Nobel Prize in Literature*, 110.

17 'OTHER NEW GOALS': THE FINAL YEAR

1 M. Frankel, 'Soviet calls Nobel Award to Pasternak a Hostile Act', *New York Times*, 25 October 1958.
2 Mallac, *Boris Pasternak*, 226. See accounts of media coverage, etc., in Conquest, *Courage of Genius*; Hingley, *Pasternak*; Mallac, *Boris Pasternak*.
3 Ruge, *Pasternak*, 110. Ivanova, 'Boris Leonidovich Pasternak', 254–5. Z. Pasternak, 'Vospominaniya', 219–20.
4 Ivanova, 'Boris Leonidovich Pasternak', 255. *Dossier*, 100–1.
5 *EBP*, 648. T. Ivanova, 'Boris Leonidovich Pasternak', 255. E. Chukovskaya, 'Nobelevskaya premiya', *Vospominaniya*, 287. Chukovsky, 'Iz dnevnika', 277. *Dossier*, 101.
6 E. Chukovskaya, 'Nobelevskaya premiya', 286–7. Mallac, *Boris Pasternak*, 230–1.

7 Chukovsky, *Dnevnik 1930–1969*, 261.
8 Ivinskaya, *V plenu vremeni*, 242–3. Ivanova, 'Boris Leonidovich Pasternak', 255–7.
9 Conquest, *Courage of Genius*, 89. *FBPPP*, 288.
10 'A za mnoyu shum pogoni', 103–4. *Dossier*, 72–4. Mallac, *Boris Pasternak*, 228–9.
11 Conquest, *Courage of Genius*, 89. 'Provokatsionannaya vylazka mezhdunarodnoi reaktsii', *LG*, 25 October 1958.
12 Ivinskaya, *V plenu vremeni*, 244–5. Mallac, *Boris Pasternak*, 232.
13 Zaslavsky, 'Shumikha reaktsionnoi propagandy'; *Pravda*, 26 October 1958.
14 Ivinskaya, *V plenu vremeni*, 250–1. 'Na literaturnom chetverge', *Kurortnaya gazeta* (Yalta), 31 October 1958. Chukovskaya, *Zapiski*, II, 594–5.
15 *EBP*, 648–9. *EPIV*, 172.
16 *EPIV*, 172–3. Ivinskaya, *V plenu vremeni*, 247–8. *Dossier*, 101–3. *EBP*, 649. Mallac, *Boris Pasternak*, 233. E. B. Pasternak, 'Priblizit' chas', 26.
17 *Dossier*, 103–5.
18 *Dossier*, 105–8. Mallac, *Boris Pasternak*, 233. Ivinskaya, *V plenu vremeni*, 249–50. Vanshenkin, 'Kak isklyuchali Pasternaka', *Vospominaniya*, 632–7. Conquest, *Courage of Genius*, 90–1.
19 V. Soloukhin, 'Pora ob"yasnit'sya', *Sovetskaya kul'tura*, 6 October 1988. G. Pozhenyan, ' "Pora ob"yasnit'sya"? Nu chto zhe. . .', *ibid.*, 13 October 1988. E. Evtushenko, 'Kazn' sobstvennoi sovest'yu', *ibid.* Kaverin, *Epilog*, 368.
20 'O deistviyakh chlena Soyuza pisatelei SSSR B. L. Pasternaka, nesovmestimikh so zvaniem sovetskogo pisatelya', *LG*, 28 October 1958.
21 L. Chukovskaya, *Zapiski*, II, 251–7.
22 *Dossier*, 108–9. Ivinskaya, *V plenu vremeni*, 255–7.
23 Krotkov, 'Pasternaki', *Grani*, 60 (1966), 45–6. Z. Pasternak, 'Vospominaniya', 222. Ruge, *Pasternak*, 122.
24 Ivinskaya, *V plenu vremeni*, 253. Mallac, *Boris Pasternak*, 235–6. *FBPPP*, 290–2. *Dossier*, 115–17. *EPIV*, 174.
25 I. A. Kurchatov *et al.*, 'Vydayushchiesya nauchnye otkrytiya sovetskikh fizikov', *Pravda*, 29 October 1958.
26 *EBP*, 649–50.
27 *EBP*, 650. *EPIV*, 173. Conquest, *Courage of Genius*, 94. Z. Pasternak, 'Vospominaniya', 223–4.
28 Semichastny, '40 let Vsesuyuznomu Leninskomu kommunisticheskomu soyuzu molodezhi', *Komsomol'skaya pravda*, 30 October 1958.
29 Z. Pasternak, 'Vospominaniya', 223–4. Ivinskaya, *V plenu vremeni*, 258. *EPIV*, 175.
30 Ivinskaya, *V plenu vremeni*, 259. Mallac, *Boris Pasternak*, 236. Mamiofa, 'O pis'makh B. Pasternaka'.
31 Ivinskaya, *V plenu vremeni*, 261–2, 282; also *ibid.*, 262–71. *FBPPP*, 297–8. Spelling of Gringolts' name corrected from Mamiofa, 'O pis'makh B. Pasternaka'.

32 'Pis'mo N. S. Khrushchevu, *Pravda*, 2 November 1958; *LG*, 4 November 1958; *Soch*.III, 227.

33 Ivinskaya, *V plenu vremeni*, 260–1. Conquest, *Courage of Genius*, 93. Mallac, *Boris Pasternak*, 237. *Dossier*, 119–20.

43 'B. Pasternak i Soyuz Sovetskikh Pisatelei', *Novyi zhurnal*, 83 (1966), 204. L. Chukovskaya, *Zapiski*, II, 582–4. Chukovsky, 'Iz dnevnika', 278. *FBPPP*, 296.

35 Conquest, *Courage of Genius*, 91–2. Ivinskaya, *V plenu vremeni*, 271–9. 'B. Pasternak i Soyuz Sovetskikh Pisatelei', 185–227. Vanshenkin, 'Kak isklyuchali Pasternaka', 637–8. 'Golos moskovskikh pisatelei', *LG*, 1 November 1958.

36 Kaverin, 'Literator', 116. Rayfield, *The Literature of Georgia*, 296.

37 Ivinskaya, *V plenu vremeni*, 285. Schewe, *Pasternak privat*, 28.

38 Ivinskaya, *V plenu vremeni*, 281–8. Schewe, *Pasternak privat*, 26–9.

39 Ivinskaya, *V plenu vremeni*, 298–9.

40 'V redaktsiyu gazety "Pravda" ', *Soch*.III, 228–9.

41 *FBPPP*, 300.

42 'Gnev i vozmushchenie', *LG*, 1 November 1958. Ivinskaya, *V plenu vremeni*, 288–91.

43 Letter of 12 December 1958 to L. A. Voskresenskaya, quoted *EBP*, 651. Ivinskaya, *V plenu vremeni*, 292.

44 *Dossier*, 123–5. *Saturday Review*, 3 October 1959. See *Dossier*, 206–8.

45 *Dossier*, 185–94. Maslenikova, *Portret*, 147.

46 M. Aliger, 'Pishi!', *Oktyabr'*, 7 (1979), 109–10.

47 Mallac, *Boris Pasternak*, 242.

48 *Ibid.*, 241–2.

49 *Dossier*, 126, 127–8, 142–3.

50 Ivinskaya, *V plenu vremeni*, 296–7. R. Conquest, *Courage of Genius*, 97–100. *Dossier*, 129. Letter of 11 December 1958 to L. L. Pasternak Slater (APT).

51 Gladkov, *Vstrechi s Pasternakom*, 145. Ivinskaya, *V plenu vremeni*, 303–5.

52 Ivanova, 'Boris Leonidovich Pasternak', 257. Ivinskaya, *V plenu vremeni*, 306.

53 Schewe, *Pasternak privat*, 77–8, 83. Ruge, *Pasternak*.

54 Ruge, *Pasternak*, 96. Ivinskaya, *V plenu vremeni*, 314–17.

55 Proyart, 'Introduction', 48. Ivinskaya, *V plenu vremeni*, 316. Schewe, *Pasternak privat*, 91. Ivinskaya, *V plenu vremeni*, 315.

56 *EBP*, 650. Letter of 11 December 1958 to L. L. Pasternak Slater (APT).

57 M. Hayward, 'Conflict and Change in Soviet Literature', in Hayward and Labedz (eds.), 214. Conquest, *Courage of Genius*, 95.

58 A. M. Williams, 'Pasternak will have to "Apologise" ', *The News Chronicle*, 19 January 1959.

59 A. Shelepin, report of 18 February 1959 to the Central Committee, *Dossier*, 173.

60 Conquest, *Courage of Genius*, 96. Ivinskaya, *V plenu vremeni*, 317–19. See also M. Hayward, notes in O. Ivinskaya, *A Captive of Time: My Years with Pasternak* (London, 1978), 319–20, 432–3.

61 *Soch*.III, 107–8; *SS*, II, 128, See above, p. 341. E. B. Pasternak, 'Pered krasoi zemli' 31; and 'Priblizit' chas', 32.

62 ' "Napadki na menya prodolzhayutsya". Neizvestnoe pis'mo Borisa Pasternaka N. S. Khrushchevu', publ. M. Feinberg, *LG*, 5 September 1990. Letter of 3 February 1959 to J. de Proyart, *Lettres*, 141.

63 *Dossier*, 161–3. A. Brown, 'Pasternak: On My Life Now', *Daily Mail*, 11 February 1959.

64 *New York Herald Tribune* (international edn), 14–15 February 1959. Conquest, *Courage of Genius*, 96. *Dossier*, 164–6. Z. Pasternak, 'Vospominaniya', 226.

65 Ivinskaya, *V plenu vremeni*, 320–1, 398–406. *EBP*, 652.

66 Dzhaparidze, 'Dorogoi nashemu serdtsu', 183–6. Krotkov, 'Pasternaki', *Grani*, 60 (1966), 36–50. Z. Pasternak, 'Vospominaniya', 226–7.

67 Letters of 22 February and 2 March 1959 to O. V. Ivinskaya, Ivinskaya, *V plenu vremeni*, 399, 404.

68 Dzhaparidze, 'Dorogoi nashemu serdtsu' 187. Maslenikova, *Portret*, 175–7. *EBP*, 653.

69 Verbal testimony of V. V. Ivanov. Rayfield, *The Literature of Georgia*, 289.

70 ' "Krai, stavshii mne vtoroi rodinoi" ', 169–70. *EBP*, 653. Maslenikova, *Portret*, 163.

71 'A za mnoyu shum pogoni', 109–11. *Dossier*, 175–7.

72 Ivinskaya, *V plenu vremeni*, 313–14. 'A za mnoyu shum pogoni', 111–12. *Dossier*, 177–80. *Vospominaniya*, 729.

73 'A za mnoyu shum pogoni', 111. *Dossier*, 177. Postcard of 15 March 1959 to L. L. Pasternak Slater and Zh. L. Pasternak (APT).

74 *Dossier*, 182–3. Letters of 2 and 10 May 1959 to J. de Proyart, *Lettres*, 167, 170. P. Blake, 'We don't Breathe Easily', *Harper's Magazine*, May 1961, 121. Schweitzer, *Freundschaft*, 75–6. Chukovsky, 'Iz dnevnika', 279.

75 'A za mnoyu shum pogoni', 106–9. *Dossier*, 168, 173.

76 Letter of 19 March 1959 to T. T. and N. A. Tabidze, *SS*, V, 570. Schewe, *Pasternak privat*, 15–16. *EPIV*, 178.

77 K. Chukovsky, 'Iz dnevnika', 278. See also *Vospominaniya*, 729. Hayward, 'Conflict and Change', 215–20. *FBPPP*, 306–7. M. Dewhirst and R. Farrell (eds.), *The Soviet Censorship* (New York, 1973), 13.

78 *Dossier*, 194–5. See above p. 351. Hayward, 'Conflict and Change', 220.

79 L. Chukovskaya, *Zapiski*, II, 292. M. Polivanov, 'Tainaya svoboda', 506–8. See also A. Zholkovsky, '21 avgusta 1959 goda', in Loseff (ed.), *Boris Pasternak*, 296–9. *EPIV*, 185–6.

80 *Vospominaniya*, 700. *SS*, V, 571–3, 575, 577–8. 'Three Letters', *Encounter*, 83 (1960), 3–6. *Quarto*, 6 (May 1980), 12. A. Chakravarty, 'Pasternak: Poet of Humanity', *The Christian Century*, 6 July 1960; and 'Reflections on Pierre Teilhard de Chardin and Excerpts from a Letter from Boris Pasternak', *The Forum*, I (New York, March 1981), 18–19.

81 Mallac, *Boris Pasternak*, 246. *Dossier*, 203–5. *Lettres*, 144, 207. *EPIV*, 178.

82 Mallac, *Boris Pasternak*, 250. Schweitzer, 105–6.

83 V. Berestov, 'Srazu posle voiny', *Vospominaniya*, 516. E. Evtushenko, 'Pocherk, pokhozhii na zhuravlei', 642. Maslenikova, *Portret*, 50. Ivanov, 'Sestra moya – zhizn''. A. Yashin, 'Rychagi', *Literaturnaya Moskva*, 2 (1956), 502–13.
84 Postcard of 11 December 1958 to L. L. Pasternak Slater (APT).
85 Postcard of 22 January 1959 to Zh. L. Pasternak (APT), Pasternak's English. *The Poetry of Boris Pasternak: 1917–1959*, ed. and trans. G. Reavey (New York, 1959). *In the Interval 1945–1960*, trans. Henry Kamen, introd. Maurice Bowra, notes by George Katkov (Oxford, 1962).
86 Letter of 8 December 1959 to Kurt Wolff. K. Chukovsky, 'Iz dnevnika', 283–4. Letter of 26 July 1959 to R. Schweitzer, Schweitzer, 86–7. 'Boris Pasternaks Briefe an Rolf-Dietrich Keil' in Orlowa and Kopelev, *Boris Pasternak*, 37–50, 58–61.
87 Ivanov, 'Sestra moya – zhizn'', *LG*. Ivinskaya, *V plenu vremeni*, 312.
88 Yu. Glazov, 'Vstrechi s B. L. Pasternakom', ms. Quoted in *EBP*, 654. Letter of 3 November 1959 to R. Schweitzer, Schweitzer, *Freundschaft*, 104. Letter of 4 November 1959 to L. L. Pasternak Slater (APT). P. Kal'deron, *P'esy* (Moscow, 1961), I, 47–142.
89 J. Lindsay, 'Dr. Zhivago', *Anglo-Soviet Journal*, winter 1958–59, 20–3.
90 Nilsson, 'Besuch bei Boris Pasternak. September 1958', 111–12. Letter of 20 May 1959 to J. de Proyart, *Lettres*, 172. See also letter of 12 May 1959 to K. Wolff; letter of 14 May 1959 to R. Schweitzer, Schweitzer, *Freundschaft*, 79. E. Wilson, 'Doctor Life and his Guardian Angel', *New Yorker*, 34 (November 15), 1958, 201–26; and 'Legend and Symbol in *Doctor Zhivago*', *Nation*, 25 April 1959, 263–73; reprinted in *Encounter*, June 1959, 5–16.
91 Letter of 22 August 1959 to S. Spender, 'Three Letters', 4–5.
92 Maslenikova, *Portret*, 174. Letter of 30 July 1959 to H. Peltier-Zamoyska, *Lettres*, 182.
93 Letter of 9 November 1959 to L. L. Pasternak Slater (APT). Letter of 14 May 1958 to R. Schweitzer, Schweitzer, *Freundschaft*, 80. Letter of 22 December 1959 to J. de Proyart, *Lettres*, 209–10. B. Pasternak, 'Chopin', *Die Zeit*, 13 November 1959.
94 *FBPPP, 308.*
95 Letter of 31 July 1959 to L. L. Pasternak Slater (APT).
96 *Ibid.* Letter of 4 October 1959 to B. K. Zaitsev, *SS*, V, 575.
97 *EBP*, 654. A. Bely, *Masterstvo Gogolya: issledovanie* (Moscow-Leningrad, 1934), 296.
98 Carlisle, 'Three Visits with Boris Pasternak', 61–6; also in her *Voices in the Snow* (London, 1963), 201–8.
99 'To a French Musician', *Pasternak Speaks*, Discurio Record L7/001, William Lennard Concerts, n.d.
100 Ivinskaya, *V plenu vremeni*, 337. *EBP*, 656.
101 Carlisle, 'Three Visits', 66.
102 B. Jangfeldt, 'My very dear Mr Svensson . . .', *Boris Pasternak och hans tid*

(Stockholm, 1991), 163–7. Letter of 24 January 1960 to L. L. Pasternak Slater (APT).

103 Letter of 14 November 1959 to J. de Proyart, *Lettres*, 204. Letter of 5 February 1960 to L. L. Pasternak Slater (APT). In fact it was another Italian publisher, Vigorelli of 'Il Dramma' who, though lacking a Russian text, published an Italian version in 1969 establishing world rights; the Collins & Harvill and other foreign-language editions were produced from a text held by the present writer. On *Slepaya krasavitsa*, see also M. Hayward, 'Foreword', in Boris Pasternak, *The Blind Beauty* (London, 1969), 5–12; Mossman, 'Pasternak's *Blind Beauty*'.

104 Letter of 14 November 1959 to J. de Proyart, *Lettres*, 206. *Dossier*, 147–8.

105 *EBP*, 651. K. Chukovsky, 'Iz dnevnika', 280. Letter to J. de Proyart of 30 March 1959, *Lettres*, 153.

106 Letter of 11 January 1959 to G. B. Khesin, *Dossier*, 160–1. ' "Napadki na menya prodolzhayutsya": Neizvestnoe pis'mo B. Pasternak N. S. Khrushchevu', *LG*, 5 September 1990. *Dossier*, 183–5. Ivinskaya, *V plenu vremeni*, 358. See also *Lettres*, 146–7.

107 Schewe, *Pasternak privat*, 83. *Lettres*, 169, 188, 191.

108 Schewe, *Pasternak privat*, 81, 87–7. *Lettres*, 136–8, 141–2. Schweitzer, *Freundschaft*, 99.

109 Letter of 31 July 1959 to L. L. Pasternak Slater (APT).

110 Letter of 21 July 1959 to H. Peltier-Zamoyska. Letter of 17 January 1960 to J. de Proyart, *Lettres*, 179–81, 217–20. Proyart, 'Introduction', *Lettres* 48–9, 51, 229.

111 Letter of 6 April 1959 to J. de Proyart, *ibid.*, 154–5.

112 Letter of 15 November 1959 to K. N. Bugaeva, *SS*, V, 576.

113 H. Burton, *Leonard Bernstein* (New York, 1995), 108–11. *EBP*, 656. *EPIV*, 186.

114 A. Terts, 'Literaturnyi protsess v Rossii', *Kontinent*, 1 (1974), 156. See correction of this in E. B. Pasternak, 'Reading Pasternak – Some Errors Corrected', 38–9.

115 Letter of 22 December 1959 to J. de Proyart, *Lettres*, 212.

116 'Was ist der Mensch?', *Magnum*, 27 (1959), 37.

117 Letters of 4 November 1959 and 24 January 1960 to L. L. Pasternak Slater (APT).

118 G. S. Neigauz, 'Boris Pasternak v povsednevnoi zhizni', 563.

119 *Ibid*. Ivinskaya, *V plenu vremeni*, 323.

120 Schweitzer, *Freundschaft*, 108. Schewe, *Pasternak privat*, 35–42. Ivinskaya, *V plenu vremeni*, 335–6.

121 Letter of 30 September 1959 to R. Schweitzer, Schweitzer, *Freundschaft*, 57.

122 Ivinskaya, *V plenu vremeni*, 322 ff. Z. Pasternak, 'Vospominaniya', 217.

123 Livanov, 'Ne vydumannyi Boris Pasternak', *Moskva*, 11 (1993), 185–7. Maslenikova, *Portret*, 188–9, 231–2. Ivinskaya, *V plenu vremeni*, 325.

124 Letter of 5 February 1960 to Ch. Gudiashvili, 'Pis'ma gruzinskim druz'yam, 40.

125 Ivinskaya, *V plenu vremeni*, 334–5. Schewe, *Pasternak*, 17–20. E. B. Tager, *Izbrannye raboty o literature* (Moscow, 1988), 491–2. Ivanova, *Moi sovremenniki*, 423. Maslenikova, *Portret*, 241.

126 Schweitzer, *Freundschaft*, 127–8.

127 *Ibid.*, 127, 131–2. Ivinskaya, *V plenu vremeni*, 338–9, 408. Z. Pasternak, 'Vospominaniya', 228.

128 Schewe, *Pasternak privat*, 52, 76–7, 83.

129 *Ibid.*, 54–7, 75.

130 Ivinskaya, *V plenu vremeni*, 340, 354–7.

131 Mallac, *Boris Pasternak*, 256.

132 *EBP*, 657. Z. Pasternak, 'Vospominaniya', 228.

133 F. Stepun, 'Boris Leonidowitsch Pasternak. Der "Fall" Pasternak', *Die Neue Rundschau*, 70 (1959), 145–61. Chudakova and Lebedushkina, 'Poslednee pis'mo B. L. Pasternaka k F. A. Stepunu', 40–1; revised reprint in Podgaetskaya (ed.) *Pasternakovskie chteniya*. Zh. Sheron (G. Cheron), 'K publikatsii poslednego pis'ma Pasternaka', *De visu*, 5–6 (1994), 92–3.

134 Schewe, *Pasternak privat*, 43–5. Ivinskaya, *V plenu vremeni*, 341. Z. Pasternak, 'Vospominaniya', 228.

135 Schewe, *Pasternak privat*, 45–6. Ivinskaya, *V plenu vremeni*, 341–4. Z. Pasternak, 'Vospominaniya', 228. *EPIV*, 189. N. Tabidze, 'Raduga', 307.

136 Z. Pasternak, 'Vospominaniya', 228.

137 G. S. Neigauz, 'Boris Pasternak v povsednevnoi zhizni', 562. Z. Pasternak, 'Vospominaniya', 228–9. Ivanova, 'Boris Leonidovich Pasternak', 238, 260. A. Golodets, 'Poslednie dni', *Vospominaniya*, 673–4.

138 Ivinskaya, *V plenu vremeni*, 342. M. Polivanov, 'Tainaya svoboda', 508. Ivanova, 'Boris Leonidovich Pasternak', 260–1. Golodets, 'Poslednie dni', 675–9. *EPIV*, 190.

139 M. Polivanov, 'Tainaya svoboda', 508.

140 *EBP*, 658.

141 *Ibid.*

142 Kosachevsky, 'Posleslovie k romanu', 147. See also Grieser, *Glückliche Erben*, 55–66.

Bibliography

The following bibliography is selective and confined mainly to works specifically referred to in the text and notes of the present volume. The section of Works by Pasternak does not include any of his translations; information on these can be found in the bibliographies of Troitsky, Zakharenko, and Zlenko and Chernego (below), as well as in various monographic and specialised secondary sources. More exhaustive bibliography on many aspects of Pasternak's life and work can be found in various publications indicated under Secondary Works, particularly in the following book-length studies and symposiums: Aucouturier (ed.) (1979), Barnes (ed.) (1990), Cornwell (1986), Fleishman (1977, 1981, 1984, [ed.] 1989, 1990), Gifford (1977), Loseff (ed.) (1991), Mallac (1981), Nilsson (ed.) (1976), E. B. Pasternak (1989) Podgaetskaya (ed.) (1992). The following bibliographies devoted to Pasternak should be consulted:.

'Boris Pasternak: A Selected Annotated Bibliography of Literary Criticism (1914–1990)', *Russian Language Journal*, 150 (1991), 41–259.

'Boris Pasternak in Literary Criticism (1914–1990): An Analysis', *Russian Language Journal*, 151–2 (1991), 129–83.

'Pasternak's *Doktor Živago*: An International Bibliography of Criticism, 1957–1978', *Bulletin of Bibliography*, 37 no.3 (1980), 105–26.

Sendich, M. 'Pasternak's *Doktor Živago*. An International Bibliography of Criticism (1957–1974)', *Russian Language Journal*, 105 (1976), 109–52.

'Supplementary Bibliography to M. Sendich's International Bibliography of Criticism of *Doktor Zivago*: 1957–77', *Russian Language Journal*, 113 (1978), 193–205.

Troitsky, N. A. *Boris Leonidovich Pasternak 1890–1960. Bibliografiya*. Ithaca, NY, 1969.

Zakharenko, N. G. (ed.) *Russkie Pisateli-Poety. Bibliograficheskii ukazatel'. 18. B. Pasternak*. St Petersburg, 1995.

Zlenko, G. D. and Chernego, N. N. *Boris Pasternak. Bibliograficheskii ukazatel'*. Odessa, 1990.

WORKS BY BORIS PASTERNAK

Editions referred to (in order of publication)

Doktor Zhivago. Milan, 1957.

Sochineniya, ed. G. P. Struve and B. A. Filippov, 3 vols. Ann Arbor, Michigan, 1961.

Bibliography

Stikhotvoreniya i poemy, ed. L. A. Ozerov. Moscow-Leningrad, 1965.
Vozdushnye puti. Proza raznykh let, ed.E. B. Pasternak and E. V. Pasternak. Moscow, 1982.
Izbrannoe v dvukh tomakh, ed. E. B. Pasternak and E. V. Pasternak. Moscow, 1985.
Sobranie sochinenii v pyati tomakh, compiled with commentary by E. V. Pasternak and K. M. Polivanov. Moscow, 1989–1992.
Boris Pasternak ob iskusstve, compiled with commentary by E. B. and E. V. Pasternak. Moscow, 1990.

Additional writings and statements not included in collected editions

'Andrei Bely (nekrolog)' (co-authored with B. Pil'nyak and G. A. Sannikov), *Izvestiya*, 9 January 1934.
'Mayakovsky v moei zhizni' (publ. M. A. Rashkovskaya), *Literaturnaya gazeta*, 4 October 1989.
'Rech' B. L. Pasternaka na pervom vsesoyuznom soveshchanii perevodchikov', *Literaturnaya Gruziya*, 8 (1968), 38–41.
' "Namerennyi risk". Vystuplenie B. L. Pasternaka na diskussii o formalizme v 1936 godu' (publ. E. B. Pasternak), *Literaturnoe obozrenie*, 3 (1990), 86–91.

CORRESPONDENCE

The most complete representative edition under one cover is in volume 5 of *Sobranie sochinenii v pyati tomakh*. Selected significant letters also appear in volume 2 of *Izbrannoe v dvukh tomakh*, and in *Boris Pasternak ob iskusstve* (see above under *Editions*). Various correspondences referred to in the present book have been collected and published as below:

(a) Book editions (in order of publication)

R. Schweitzer, *Freundschaft mit Boris Pasternak*. Munich-Vienna-Basel, 1963.
Boris Pasternak/Thomas Merton: Six Letters, intro. L. Pasternak Slater. Lexington, Kentucky, 1973.
Perepiska s Ol'goi Freidenberg. New York, 1981.
A. Efron–B. Pasternaku. Pis'ma iz ssylki (1948–1957). Paris, 1982.
Iz pisem raznykh let, compiled E. B. Pasternak. Biblioteka 'Ogon'ka', vypusk 6. Moscow, 1990.
Perepiska Borisa Pasternaka, compiled and ed. E. B. and E. V. Pasternak. Moscow, 1990.
Rainer Maria Ril'ke, Boris Pasternak, Marina Tsvetaeva, *Pis'ma 1926 goda*, publ. K. M. Azadovsky, E. B. and E. V. Pasternak. Moscow, 1990.

Pis'ma B. L. Pasternaka k zhene Z. N. Neigauz-Pasternak, ed. K. Polivanov. Moscow, 1993.

Lettres à mes amies françaises, intro. and ed. J. de Proyart. Paris, 1994.

(b) Journal and other publications (alphabetical order)

'B. L. Pasternak. Pis'ma k G. E. Sorokinu', publ. A. V. Lavrov, E. B. and E. V. Pasternak. *Ezhegodnik Rukopisnogo otdela Pushkinskogo doma na 1979 god.* Leningrad, 1981, 199–227.

'B. Pasternak i G. Kozintsev: pis'ma o "Gamlete"', publ. V. Kozintseva and E. B. Pasternak, *Voprosy literatury*, 1 (1975), 212–23.

'Boris L. Pasternak: pis'ma k A. M. Ripellino', *Rossiya/Russia*, 4 (1980), 317–21.

'Boris Pasternak et Romain Rolland: Correspondance (1930)', publ. M. Aucouturier. *Europe*, 767 (March, 1993), 104–18.

'Boris Pasternak i Kaisyn Kuliev', publ. E. B. and E. V. Pasternak. *Druzhba narodov*, 2 (1990), 259–70.

'Boris Pasternak: Letters to an English Correspondent', publ. J. P. Harris, C. J. Barnes, D. Ward, *Scottish Slavonic Review*, 3 (1984), 82–94.

'Boris Pasternak. Pis'ma k I. A. Gruzdevu', publ. E. V. Pasternak. *Zvezda*, 9 (1994), 92–107.

'Boris Pasternak v perepiske s Maksimom Gor'kim', publ. E. B. and E. V. Pasternak. *Izvestiya Akademii Nauk SSSR (Seriya literatury i yazyka)*, 45 no.3 (1986), 261–83.

'Dva pis'ma Fedoru Stepunu', publ. R. Guerra, in Z. N. Shakhovskaya (ed.), *Russkii al'manakh*. Paris, 1981, 475–77.

'Dve sud'by (B. L. Pasternak i S. N. Durylin. Perepiska)', publ. M. A. Rashkovskaya. *Vstrechi s proshlym*, 7 (Moscow, 1990), 366–407.

'Gor'ky – B. L. Pasternak'. *Literaturnoe nasledstvo*, 70 (1963), 259–310.

'Iozef Gora i Boris Pasternak', publ. O. Malevich and E. V. Pasternak. *Voprosy literatury*, 78 (1979), 182–5.

'Iz perepiski Borisa Pasternaka s Andreem Belym', publ. E. B. and E. V. Pasternak, in *Andrei Bely: problemy tvorchestva*. Moscow, 1988, 686–706.

'Iz perepiski s pisatelyami', publ. E. B. and E. V. Pasternak. *Literaturnoe nasledstvo*, 93 (1983), 649–737.

'Iz pisem B. Pasternaka k S. Spasskomu', publ. V. Spasskaya. *Voprosy literatury*, 9 (1969), 165–81.

'K perevodam shekspirovskikh dram', publ. E. B. Pasternak. *Masterstvo perevoda, 1969*, 6 (1970), 341–63.

' "Krai, stavshii mne vtoroi rodinoi" (Pis'ma B. Pasternaka k gruzinskim pisatelyam)', publ. G. G. Margvelashvili. *Voprosy literatury*, 1 (1966), 166–200.

' "Napadki na menya prodolzhayutsya". Neizvestnoe pis'mo Borisa Pasternaka N. S. Khrushchevu', publ. M. Feinberg. *Literaturnaya gazeta*, 5 September 1990.

' "Neotsenimyi podarok". Perepiska Pasternakov i Lomonosovykh (1925–1970)', publ. C. Barnes and R. Davies. *Minuvshee*, 15 (1993), 193–247; 16 (1994), 150–208; 17 (1995), 358–408.

' "Nesvoboda prednaznacheniya": iz pisem', publ. E. B. Pasternak. *Znamya*, 2 (1990), 194–204.

' "Neumenie zhit'" '. Nepublikovannye pis'ma B. L. Pasternaka'. *Novoe vremya*, 7 (1990), 46–7.

'Pasternak: Unpublished Letters'. *Quarto*, 6 (May 1980), 10–12.

'Perepiska s Evgeniei Pasternak', publ. E. B. Pasternak. *Znamya*, 1 (1996), 136–67; 2 (1996), 137–86.

'Pis'ma B. L. Pasternaka D. E. Maksimovu', publ. Z. G. Mints. *Tezisy I Vsesoyuznoi (III) konferentsii 'Tvorchestvo A. A. Bloka i russkaya kul'tura XX veka*. Tartu, 1975, 11–13.

'Pis'ma B. L. Pasternaka–K. A. Fedinu', publ. E. B. Pasternak and R. Likht. *Volga*, 2 (1990), 164–76.

'Pis'ma B. L. Pasternaka k M. V. Yudinoi', publ. A. L. Panina. *Zapiski otdela rukopisei*, 29 (1967), 255–7.

'Pis'ma druz'yam', publ. G. G. Margvelashvili. *Literaturnaya Gruziya*, 1 (1966), 75–83; 2 (1966), 83–96.

'Pis'ma gruzinskim druz'yam', publ. G. G. Margvelashvili. *Literaturnaya Gruziya*, 2 (1980), 15–40.

'Pis'ma k Aleksandru Fadeevu', *Moskva*, 9 (1967), 194–201.

'Pis'ma k I. A. Gruzdevu', publ. E. V. Pasternak. *Zvezda*, 9 (1994), 92–107.

'Pis'ma k V. M. Sayanovu', publ. A. V. Lavrov. *Ezhegodnik Rukopisnogo otdela Pushkinskogo doma na 1977 god* (Leningrad, 1979), 195–202.

'Pis'ma na "Olimp" ', publ. M. A. Rashkovskaya. *Kontinent*, 90 (1996), 199–213.

'Poslednee pis'mo B. L. Pasternaka k F. A. Stepunu', publ. M. O. Chudakova and O. P. Lebedushkina. *Pyatye tynyanovskie chteniya* (Riga, 1990), 40–1; expanded version in Podgaetskaya (ed.) (1992), 269–79.

'Pozitsiya khudozhnika. Pis'ma Borisa Pasternaka', publ. K. M. Pomerantsev, K. M. Azadovsky, A. Semenov. *Literaturnoe obozrenie*, 2 (1990), 3–24.

' "Razgovory o samom glavnom . . .": Perepiska B. L. Pasternaka i V. T. Shalamova', publ. I. Sirotinskaya. *Yunost'*, 10 (1988), 54–67.

'Three Letters', publ. Stephen Spender. *Encounter*, 83 (August 1960), 3–6.

' "Vtorzhenie voli v sud'bu" (Pis'ma Borisa Pasternaka o sozdanii romana "Doktor Zhivago")', publ. E. Pasternak and M. Polivanov. *Literaturnoe obozrenie*, 5 (1988), 97–107.

' "Vysokii stoikii dukh": perepiska B. L. Pasternaka i M. V. Yudinoi', publ. E. B. Pasternak and A. M. Kuznetsov. *Novyi mir*, 2 (1990), 166–91.

'Zhivym i tol'ko do kontsa', publ. E. B. Pasternak. *Ogonek*, 16 (1987), 26–28.

(c) Collectively signed letters (in order of publication)

'N. S. Allilueva', *Literaturnaya gazeta*, 17 November 1932.

'Ruki proch' ot geroicheskogo rabochego klassa Avstrii!' *Literaturnaya gazeta*, 22 February 1934.

'Vchera vecherom v Moskvu prileteli tovarishchi Dmitrov, Popov i Tanev', *Literaturnaya gazeta*, 28 February 1934.

'Ponesem ego znamya vpered!', *Novyi mir*, 12 (1934), 5.

'Skorb' i gnev', *Pisateli Kirovu*. Moscow, 1934, 23.

'Kollektivnyi golos mirovoi literatury', *Literaturnaya gazeta*, 5 July 1935.

* 'Steret' s litsa zemli!' *Pravda*, 21 August 1936.

'Mezhdunarodnomu kongressu mira', *Literaturnaya gazeta*, 5 September 1936.

* 'Ne dadim zhit' vragam Sovetskogo Soyuza', *Literaturnaya gazeta*, 15 June 1937.

Additional items of correspondence referred to are contained in the following publications listed alphabetically in the general bibliography section: Aucouturier (ed.) (1979), Bebutov (1966, 1968, 1979), *Dossier* (1994), Efron (1982)(1989), Fleishman (1981, 1984) (1991), Kasack (ed.) (1982), Kedrov (1995), Kozovoi (1986), Levin (1973), Malevich and Pasternak (1979), Margvelashvili (1972), Mukhanov (ed.) (1987), Muravina (1990), Nemirovich-Danchenko (1979), Orlowa and Kopelev (1986) E. B. and E. V. Pasternak (1990), E. V. Pasternak (1990), Pushkin (1990), Rashkovskaya (1988), Rashkovsky (1990), Schewe (1974), Sirotinskaya (1988), Struve (1967), T. Tabidze (1964), Tall (1990), *Vek Pasternaka* (1990) *Vospominaniya* (1993), Wolff (1966), 'Zametki o peresechenii . . .' (1981).

SECONDARY WORKS

'A za mnoyu shum pogoni . . .', publ. M. Rashkovskaya et al., *Istochnik*, 1 (1993), 101–3.

Adalis, A. 'Golos chitatelya', *Literaturnaya gazeta*, 20 March 1936.

Adamovich, G. 'Literaturnye zametki', *Poslednie novosti*, 26 September 1929.

Afinogenov, A. *Stat'i, dnevniki, pis'ma, vospominaniya*. Moscow, 1950.

   'Iz dnevnika 1937 goda', in *Vospominaniya* (1993), 376–87.

Akhmatova, A. *Sochineniya*, ed. G. P. Struve and B. A. Filippov, 2 vols. Washington DC: I:1965; II:1968.

Aleksandrov, A. I. 'B. L. Pasternak na "Chelyabtraktorstroe" v 1931 g.' (manuscript).

Aleksandrov, V. 'Nashe poeticheskoe segodnya', *Na literaturnom postu*, 3 (1929), 13–24.

   'Chastnaya zhizn'', *Literaturnyi kritik*, 3 (1937), 55–81.

Alekseev, M. ' "Gamlet" Borisa Pasternaka', *Iskusstvo i zhizn'*, 8 (1940), 14–16.

Alexander, M. ' "Dr Zhivago" and "The Leopard" ', *The Listener*, 84 (9 September 1965), 384–5.

Alla Konstantinovna Tarasova: Dokumenty i vospominaniya. Moscow, 1978.

Aloits, A. 'Podvig ili predatel'stvo?' *Novoe russkoe slovo*, 30 March 1990.

Altauzen, D. 'Za Mayakovskogo! Rech' tov. Altauzena', *Literaturnaya gazeta*, 16 February 1936.

    * Pasternak's signature was affixed to these items without his permission or assent.

'Ne otstavat' ot zhizni. Rech' tov. Dzh. Altauzena', *Literaturnaya gazeta*, 26 February 1937.

Anastas'eva, M. 'Boris Leonidovich Pasternak v zhizni nashei sem'i', in *Vospominaniya* (1993), 364–75.

Andronikashvili-Pil'nyak, B. 'O moem ottse', *Druzhba narodov*, 1 (1989), 147–55.

'Dva izgoya, dva muchenika: B. Pil'nyak i E. Zamyatin', *Znamya*, 9 (1994), 123–53.

Annenkov, Yu. *Dnevnik moikh vstrech*, 2 vols. New York, 1966.

Antokol'sky, P. 'Boris Pasternak. Na rannikh poezdakh. Novye stikhotvoreniya. Moskva, Sovetskii pisatel', 1943', *Znamya*, 9–10 (1943), 312–16.

Ispytanie vremenem. Moscow, 1945.

Aseev, N. 'Iskusstvo na "kholostom khodu". Iz rechi tov. N. Aseeva', *Literaturnaya gazeta*, 20 March 1936.

Asmus, V. F. 'Rech' na pokhoronakh Pasternaka', *Vek Pasternaka*, 30.

Aucouturier, M. 'Ob odnom klyuche k *Okhrannoi gramote*', in Aucouturier (ed.) (1979), 337–48.

'Pasternak and Proust', in Barnes (ed.) (1990), 342–51.

Aucouturier, M. (ed.) *Boris Pasternak 1890–1960. Colloque de Cérisy-la-Salle*. Paris, 1979.

Avdeev, V. 'Vspominaya Pasternaka', in *Vospominaniya* (1993), 342–6.

Averintsev, S. 'Pasternak i Mandel'shtam. Opyt sopostavleniya', *Vek Pasternaka*, 20–1.

'B. L. Pasternaku'. *Novyi mir*, 11 (1958), III–XVI.

B. N. 'Poet i ego okruzhenie. Na vechere B. Pasternaka', *Literaturnaya gazeta*, 11 April 1932.

'Pshavela i Pasternak', *Literaturnaya gazeta*, 30 March 1935.

'B. Pasternak i Soyuz sovetskikh pisatelei. Stenogramma Obshchemoskovskogo sobraniya pisatelei, 31 oktyabrya 1958 goda', *Novyi zhurnal*, 83 (1966), 185–227.

'B. Pasternak. "Spektorsky"', *Kniga stroitelyam sotsializma*, 24 (1931), 101.

Babaev, E. 'Gde vozdukh sin' . . .' in *Vospominaniya* (1993), 536–47.

Babichenko, D. L. (ed.). *'Literaturnyi front'. Istoriya politicheskoi tsenzury 1932–1946 gg. Sbornik dokumentov*. Moscow, 1944.

Baevsky, V. S. '. . . Chestnost' privetstvovat' prezhde vsego', *Literaturnaya Gruziya*, 7 (1988), 144–9.

' "Faust" Gete v perevode Pasternaka', *Izvestiya Akademii Nauk SSSR (Seriya literatury i yazyka)*, 49 no.4 (1990), 341–52.

Bakhrakh, A. 'Po pamyati, po zapisyam. Andre Zhid', *Kontinent*, 8 (1976), 349–86.

Po pamyati, po zapisyam. Literaturnye portrety. Paris, 1980.

Baluashvili. V. 'Vdokhnovennyi poet-patriot', *Literaturnaya Gruziya*, 7 (1964), 81–9.

Barnes, C. J. 'Boris Pasternak: A Review of Nikolaj Aseev's "Oksana"', *Slavica Hierosolymitana*, 1 (1977), 293–305.

'The Original text of "O skromnosti i smelosti"', *Slavic Hierosolymitana*, 4 (1979), 294–303.

'Biography, Autobiography and "Sister Life": Some Problems in Chronicling Pasternak's Early Years'. *Irish Slavonic Studies*, 4 (1983), 48–58.

Boris Pasternak: A Literary Biography. Vol.I: 1890–1928. Cambridge, 1989.
'Pasternak, Dickens and the Novel Tradition', in Barnes (ed.) (1990), 326–41.
'Introduction' in Boris Pasternak. *People and Propositions.* Edinburgh, 1990, 12–25.
'Boris Pasternak and Mary Queen of Scots: An Aspect of the Female Image', *Scotland and the Slavs. Papers from the Glasgow-90 East-West Forum.* Nottingham, 1993, 25–38; trans. as [Barns, K.], 'Boris Pasternak i Mariya Styuart', *Problemy istorii, filologii, kul'tury* (Magnitogorsk), 3 pt. 2 (1996), 293–304.

[Barns, K.] 'Suitsidal'nye motivy v poetike i zhizni (Pasternak i Mayakovsky)', *Problemy istorii, filologii, kul'tury* (Magnitogorsk), 2 (1995), 286–91.

Barnes, C. J. (ed.). *Pasternak and European Literature. Forum for Modern Language Studies,* 26 no.4 (October 1990).

Barnes [see also under Correspondence].

Barron, J. *KGB. The Secret Work of Soviet Secret Agents.* New York, 1974.

Bebutov, G. 'Po stranitsam odnoi perepiski', *Literaturnaya Gruziya,* 3 (1966), 70–77; reprinted in his *Sodruzhestvo poetov. Vospominaniya i stat'i.* Tbilisi, 1979, 58–81.

Bebutov, G. (ed.). 'Eto obmen opytom, eto zhiznennoe dykhanie nashikh respublik', *Literaturnaya Gruziya,* 8 (1968), 37–41.

Belkina, M. *Skreshchenie sudeb,* 2nd edition. Moscow, 1992.

Berberova, N. *Kursiv moi,* 2 vols. New York, 1983.

Berestov, V. 'Srazu posle voiny', in *Vospominaniya* (1993), 511–17.

Berezov, P. 'Okhrannaya gramota. L.IPL.1931' *Proletarskaya literatura,* 2 (1932), 177.

Berlin, I. 'The Energy of Pasternak', *Partisan Review,* 17 (1950), 748–51.

'Vstrechi s russkimi pisatelyami 1945 i 1956', in *Vospominaniya* (1993), 518–35 [translated version of 'Meetings with Russian Writers in 1945 and 1956', in his *Personal Impressions.* London, 1980, 156–210].

Berlin, M. H. 'A Visit to Pasternak', *American Scholar* (summer 1983), 327–35.

Betser, D. M. 'Neskol'ko shtrikhov k portretu B. L. Pasternaka' (manuscript).

Bezymensky, A. 'Vo imya bol'shevistskoi druzhby. Rech' tov. A. Bezymenskogo', *Literaturnaya gazeta,* 16 February 1936.

Bodin, P. A. *Nine Poems from Doktor Živago: A Study of Christian Motifs in Boris Pasternak's Poetry.* Stockholm, 1976.

'Boris Pasternak and the Christian Tradition', in Barnes (ed.) (1990), 382–401.

Bokov, V. 'Sobesednik roshch', in *Vospominaniya* (1993), 347–52.

Borisov, V. and Pasternak, E. B. 'Materialy k tvorcheskoi istorii romana B. Pasternaka "Doktor Zhivago" ', *Novyi mir,* 6 (1988), 205–48.

Borovoi, L. 'Dvadtsat' chetvertyi "Gamlet" ', *Literaturnaya gazeta,* 20 April 1940.

Bowra, M. 'Boris Pasternak 1917–23', in his *The Creative Experiment.* London, 1949, 128–58.

Bragin, A. 'Boris Pasternak. Poverkh bar'erov. Stikhi raznykh let. GIZ, 1929 g. str.158. Boris Pasternak. Izbrannye stikhi. Akts.Izd.O-vo "Ogonek", M. 1929 g.' *Na pod"eme,* 12 (1929), 90–1.

Brown, C. *Mandelstam.* Cambridge, 1973.

Brown, E. J. *Mayakovsky: A Poet in the Revolution*. Princeton NJ, 1973.

'The Year of Acquiescence', in Hayward, M. and Labedz, L. (eds) (1963), 44–61.

Brügel, F. [Bryugel', F.] 'Razgovor s Borisom Pasternakom', *Voprosy literatury*, 7 (1979), 179–82.

Buckman, D. *Leonid Pasternak: A Russian Impressionist 1862–1945*. London, 1974.

Bukharin, N. I. 'O poezii, poetike i zadachakh poeticheskogo tvorchestva v SSSR. Doklad na I s"ezde sovetskikh pisatelei 1934 g.' in *Pervyi vsesoyuznyi s"ezd sovetskikh pisatelei* (1934), 479–503.

Buromskaya-Morozova, E. 'Perevodya Shekspira', *Nashe nasledie*, 1 (1990), 49–50.

Carlisle, O. 'Three Visits with Boris Pasternak', *Paris Review*, 24 (1960), 61–6.

Chernyak, E. 'Pasternak. Iz vospominanii', in *Vospominaniya* (1993), 127–42.

Chikovani, S. 'Svyashchennye uzy bratstva', *Literaturnaya Gruziya*, 9 (1968), 93–100.

Chudakova, M. O. 'Neizvestnyi korrekturnyi ekzemplyar sbornika perevodov B. L. Pasternaka', *Zapiski Otdela rukopisei*, 39 (1978), 106–18.

Zhizneopisanie Mikhaila Bulgakova, 1st edn. Moscow 1988.

'Bez gneva i pristrastiya', *Novyi mir*, 9 (1988), 240–60.

'Pasternak and Bulgakov', *Russian Studies in Literature*, 23 no.1 (winter 1995–6), 83–102.

Chudakova, M. O. and Lebedushkina, O. P. 'Poslednee pis'mo B. L. Pasternaka F. A. Stepunu', in Podgaetskaya (ed.) (1992), 269–79.

Chukovskaya, E. 'Nobelevskaya premiya', in *Vospominaniya* (1993), 286–8.

Chukovskaya, L. *Zapiski ob Anne Akhmatovoi*, I: Paris, 1976; II: Paris, 1980.

'Otryvki iz dnevnika', in *Vospominaniya* (1993), 408–42.

Chukovsky, K. *Chukokkala*. Moscow, 1979.

Dnevnik 1930–1969. Moscow, 1994; extracted in 'Iz dnevnika (O B. L. Pasternake)', in *Vospominaniya* (1993), 263–85.

Cockrell, R. 'Two Writers in Soviet Society: Fadeev and Pasternak', *Journal of Russian Studies*, 51 (1986), 12–20.

Cohen, J. M. 'The Poetry of Pasternak', *Horizon*, 55 (1944), 23–36.

Cohen, S. [Koèn, S.] *Bukharin. Politicheskaya biografiya 1888–1938*. Moscow, 1988.

Conquest, R. *Courage of Genius*. London, 1961.

The Great Terror. London-Johannesburg-Melbourne, 1968.

Cornwell, N. *Pasternak's Novel: Perspectives on Doctor Zhivago*. Keele, 1986.

Dadashidze, I. 'Ya ni v maloi stepeni ne chuvstvuyu sebya zhenoi prestupnika', *Moskovskie novosti*, 14 November 1993.

d'Angelo, S. 'Der Roman des Romans', *Ost-Europa*, 7 (1968), 489–501.

Danin, D. 'Vospominaniya o nevernom druge', *Nauka i zhizn'*, 10 (1988), 118–32.

'Eto prebudet s nami', in *Vospominaniya* (1993), 308–20.

Bremya styda. Moscow, 1996.

Davie, D. and Livingstone, A. (eds.) *Pasternak: Modern Judgements*. London, 1969.

Davies [see under Correspondence].

Deutscher, I. 'Pasternak and the Calendar of the Revolution', in Davie and Livingstone (eds.), 240–58.

447

Djurčinov, M. 'Antonimiya "romantizm – realizm" v poetike Pasternaka', in Aucouturier (ed.) (1979), 95–102.

Dolmatovsky, E. 'Protiv ravnodushiya i khaltury. Iz rechi E. Dolmatovkogo na Obshchemoskovskom sobranii pisatelei', *Literaturnaya gazeta*, 20 March 1936.

Bylo. Zapiski poeta. Moscow, 1982.

Dorzweiler, S. and Harder, H.-B. (eds.) *Pasternak-Studien I. Beiträge zum Internationalen Pasternak-Kongreß 1991 in Marburg*. Munich, 1993.

dossier de l'affaire Pasternak, Le. Preface J. de Proyart. Paris, 1994.

Druzin, V. 'Na poeticheskie temy', *Zvezda*, 1 (1936), 242–7.

Durylin, S. N. 'Zemnoi prostor', *Literaturnaya ucheba*, 6 (1988), 110–114.

V svoem uglu. Iz starykh tetradei. Moscow, 1991.

'Iz avtobiograficheskikh zapisei "V svoem uglu"', in *Vospominaniya* (1993), 54–8.

'Dve vynuzhdennye repliki', *Komsomol'skaya pravda*, 16 March 1936.

Dymshits, A. 'Kniga o Gete', *Literaturnaya gazeta*, 19 December 1950.

Dzhaparidze, M. 'Dorogoi nashemu serdtsu dom', *Literaturnaya Gruziya*, 5 (1986), 183–8.

Dzyubinskaya, O. 'Gorod serdtsa moego . . .' in Mukhanov (ed.), 165–78.

E. F. 'Pechat' o "Gamlete" v perevode B. Pasternaka', *Literatura v shkole*, 6 (1940), 93–5.

Efron, A. 'Stranitsy bylogo', *Zvezda*, 6 (1975), 148–89.

Pis'ma iz ssylki (1948–1957). Paris, 1982.

O Marine Tsvetaevoi. Vospominaniya docheri. Moscow, 1989.

Eidel'man, Ya. 'Dnevnik diskussii', *Literaturnaya gazeta*, 15 March 1936.

Eideman, R. 'Literatura i oborona', *Literaturnaya gazeta*, 29 February 1936.

Elagin, Yu. *Temnyi genii (Vsevolod Meierkhol'd)*. New York, 1955.

Emel'yanova, I. 'Moskva, Potapovsky', *Nashe nasledie*, 1(1990), 51–63.

Erastova, T. 'Moi razgovor s Pasternakom', in *Vospominaniya* (1993), 568–73.

Erenburg, I. 'Pis'mo s kongressa', *Izvestiya*, 26 June 1935.

'Pis'ma s Mezhdunarodnogo kongressa pisatelei', *Literaturnyi kritik*, 8 (1935).

Lyudi, gody, zhizn', bks 3 and 4. Moscow, 1963.

Erlich, V. (ed.) *Pasternak: A Collection of Critical Essays*. New Jersey, 1978. .

Ermilov, V. 'Za sotsialisticheskii realizm', *Pravda*, 4 June 1954.

Ermolaev, H. *Soviet Literary Theories 1917–1934. The Genesis of Socialist Realism*. Berkeley-Los Angeles, 1963.

Espmark, K. *The Nobel Prize in Literature: A Study of the Criteria behind the Choices*. Boston MA, 1991.

'Est' li krizis v sovremennoi lirike?' *Molodaya gvardiya*, 12 (1928), 191–201.

Etkind, E. G. *Poeziya i perevod*. Moscow-Leningrad, 1963.

'"Eto tramplin, doping, zaryadka . . ." (Iz dnevnikov A. M. Faiko)', *Vstrechi s proshlym*, 5 (1984), 296–320.

Evgen'ev, A. 'Perevody B. Pasternaka', *Literaturnoe obozrenie*, 3 (1939), 12–15.

Evtushenko, E. 'Pocherk, pokhozhii na zhuravlei', in *Vospominaniya* (1993), 639–45.

Fadeev, A. 'Za podlinnuyu demokratiyu. Rech' tov.A.Fadeeva', *Literaturnaya gazeta*, 10 March 1937.

'Iz rechi tov.A. Fadeeva', *Literaturnaya gazeta*, 6 May 1939.

'Iz vystupleniya A. Fadeeva', *Literaturnaya gazeta*, 7 September 1946.

'Bol'shevistskaya ideinost' – osnova sovetskoi literatury. Na obshchemoskovskom sobranii pisatelei', *Literaturnaya gazeta*, 21 September 1946.

'Za vysokuyu ideinost' sovetskoi literatury', *Literaturnaya gazeta*, 8 March 1947.

'Sovetskaya literatura posle Postanovleniya TsK VKP(b) ot 15 avgusta 1946 g.', *Literaturnaya gazeta*, 29 June 1947.

'Sovetskaya literatura na pod"eme', *Pravda*, 1 July 1947.

'Zadachi literaturnoi kritiki', *Oktyabr'*, 7 (1947), 148–63.

Fedin, K. 'Dva vida oruzhiya', *Literaturnaya gazeta*, 29 February 1937.

Pisatel', iskusstvo, vremya. Moscow, 1957.

Fedina, N. K. 'Dom oknami na Kamu', in Mukhanov (ed.), 221–34.

'Iz istorii gorodka pisatelei v Peredelkine (1936–41 gody)', in '*Naiti svoi lad*' (1992), 3–14.

Feinberg, M. I. and Pasternak, E. V. (eds.) [see under *Vospominaniya* (1993)].

Filina, M. A. 'Soyuz Borisa Pasternaka s Titsianom Tabidze i Paolo Yashvili', in Podgaetskaya (ed.) (1992), 245–52.

Filina-Ramishvili, M. and Kiasashvili, E. 'Solnechnomu poetu Titsianu Tabidze . . .' *Literaturnaya Gruziya*, 10 (1985), 161–76.

Fleishman, L. 'B. Pasternak i A. Belyi', *Russian Literature Triquarterly*, 13 (Fall 1975), 545–51.

Stat'i o Pasternake. Bremen, 1977.

Boris Pasternak v dvadtsatye gody. Munich, 1981.

Boris Pasternak v tridtsatye gody. Jerusalem, 1984.

'Pasternak and Bukharin in the 1930s', in Fleishman (ed.) (1989), 171–88.

Boris Pasternak: The Poet and His Politics. Cambridge MA-London, 1990.

'Pis'mo Pasternaka Stalinu', *Russkaya mysl'*, 28 June 1991.

Fleishman, L. (ed.). *Boris Pasternak and His Times. Selected Papers from the Second International Symposium on Pasternak*. Berkeley, 1989.

France, A. K. 'Boris Pasternak's Interpretation of *Hamlet*', *Russian Literature Triquarterly*, 7 (Fall 1973), 201–23.

Boris Pasternak's Translations of Shakespeare. Berkeley-Los Angeles-London, 1978.

France, P. 'Pasternak et le romantisme', in Aucouturier (ed.) (1979), 83–91.

'Pasternak and the English Romantics', in Barnes (ed.) (1990), 315–25.

Frank, V. *Izbrannye stat'i*. London, 1974.

Frolovskaya, T. 'Nekotorye nablyudeniya nad obraznoi sistemoi stikhotvornogo tsikla B. Pasternaka "Poverkh bar'erov"', *Kazakhskii gosudarstvennyi universitet im. S. M. Kirova. Studencheskie nauchnye raboty. Sbornik statei*, vyp.1, ch.2. *Filologiya, Iskusstvo*. Alma-Ata, 1970, 29–48.

Gaprindashvili, V. 'Perevod – dvoinik originala', *Literaturnaya gazeta*, 15 January 1936.

Gasparov, M. L. ' "Bliznets v tuchakh" i "nachal'naya pora" B. Pasternaka: ot kompozitsii sbornika k kompozitsii tsikla', *Izvestiya Akademii Nauk, Seriya literatury i yazyka*, 49 no.3 (1990), 218–22.

Geller, M. 'Poet i vozhd' ', *Kontinent*, 16 (1978), 227–40.

Andrei Platonov v poiskakh schast'ya. Paris, 1982.

Gershtein, E. 'O Pasternake i ob Akhmatovoi', in *Vospominaniya* (1993), 388–407.

Gidash, A. [Hidas Antal] 'Poeziya dlya millionov. Iz rechi tov. A. Gidash', *Literaturnaya gazeta*, 20 March 1936.

Gide, A. *Retour de l'U. R. S. S.* Paris, 1936.

[Zhid, A.] 'Novaya pishcha' [Les nouvelles nourritures], *Znamya*, 1 (1936), 161–90.

Gifford, H. 'Pasternak and the "Realism" of Blok', *Oxford Slavonic Papers*, 13 (1967), 96–106.

Boris Pasternak: A Critical Study. Cambridge, 1977.

Ginzburg, L. *Chelovek za pis'mennym stolom*. Leningrad, 1989.

Girzheva, G. N. 'Nekotorye osobennosti pozdnei liriki Borisa Pasternaka', *Russkii yazyk v shkole*, 1 (1990), 54–9.

Gladkov, A. *Vstrechi s Pasternakom*. Paris, 1973.

Goldberg, A. M. *Ilya Ehrenburg, Revolutionary, Novelist, Poet, War Correspondent, Propagandist: The Extraordinary Epic of a Russian Survivor*. New York, 1984.

Goldman, H. A. 'Shakespeare's Hamlet in the Work of Boris Pasternak and Other Modern Russian Poets'. Unpublished PhD thesis, Indiana University, 1975.

Golodets, A. 'Poslednie dni', in *Vospominaniya* (1993), 672–84.

Golodny, M. 'Partiinoe pristrastie v poezii', *Literaturnaya gazeta*, 27 March 1936.

Gol'tsev, V. 'Poety Gruzii i Boris Pasternak', *Krasnaya nov'*, 1 (1936), 228–37.

Gonta, M. 'Martirik', in *Vospominaniya* (1993), 232–7.

Gorbunov, A. N. 'K istorii russkogo "Gamleta" ', in U. Shekspir [W. Shakespeare], *Izbrannye perevody*. Moscow, 1985, 7–26.

Gor'ky, M. *Sobranie sochinenii v 30 tomakh*. Moscow, 1949–56.

Gornung, L. V. 'Vstrecha za vstrechei (po dnevnikovym zapisyam)', in *Vospominaniya* (1993), 67–89.

Graf, O. M. *Reise in die Sowjetunion 1934*. Darmstadt-Neuwied, 1974.

Grant, A. 'Ot peremeny mesta kukhon' summa razgovorov v nikh ne menyaetsya', *Novoe russkoe slovo*, 13 May 1994.

Grieser, D. *Glückliche Erben. Der Dichter und sein Testament*. Munich-Vienna, 1983.

Gromov, P. 'Boris Pasternak. Zemnoi prostor', *Zvezda*, 5–6 (1945), 157–9.

Gudiashvili, L. *Kniga vospominanii. Stat'i. Iz perepiski. Sovremenniki o khudozhnike*. Moscow, 1987.

Gutner, M. 'Proza poeta', *Literaturnyi sovremennik*, 1 (1936), 118–131.

'O putyakh liriki', *Literaturnyi sovremennik*, 1 (1936).

'Tvorcheskaya deklaratsiya', *Literaturnyi Leningrad*, 11 October 1936.

Gyllensten, L. 'On Pasternak's Nobel Prize', *Rysk Kulturrevy*, 4 (1981).

'Some Notes on Pasternak's Nobel Prize in 1958', *Artes*, 1 (1983), 112–13.

Haight, A. *Anna Akhmatova: A Poetic Pilgrimage.* New York-London. 1976.

Hayward, M. 'Pilnyak and Zamyatin: Two Tragedies of the Twenties', *Survey*, 36 (1961), 85–91.

Writers in Russia 1917–1978. London, 1983.

Hayward, M. and Labedz, L. (eds.) *Literature and Revolution in Soviet Russia 1917–62.* London-New York-Toronto, 1963.

Hidas [see under Gidash].

Hingley, R. *Pasternak: A Biography.* London, 1983.

Inber, V. 'Literatura i deistvitel'nost'. Rech' tov. V. Inber', *Literaturnaya gazeta*, 29 February 1936.

Inge, Yu. 'Otkrytoe pis'mo poetu Borisu Pasternaku', *Udarnik*, 6 (1932), 84–6.

'Iskusstvo sotsializma i burzhuaznoe restavratorstvo', *Literaturnaya gazeta*, 18 December 1931.

Ivanov, V. V. 'Akhmatova i Pasternak: Osnovnye problemy izucheniya ikh literaturnykh vzaimootnoshenii', *Izvestiya Akademii Nauk SSSR. Seriya literatury i yazyka.* 48 no.5 (1989), 410–18.

'Perevernutoe nebo', *Soglasie*, 1 (1990), 199–212.

'Sestra moya – zhizn'', *Literaturnaya gazeta*, 31 January 1990.

'Pochemu Stalin ubil Gor'kogo?' *Voprosy literatury*, 1 (1993), 91–134.

Ivanova, T. *Moi sovremenniki, kakimi ya ikh znala.* Moscow, 1987.

'Boris Leonidovich Pasternak', in *Vospominaniya* (1993), 238–62.

Ivinskaya, O. *V plenu vremeni. Gody s Borisom Pasternakom.* Paris, 1978.

Izgoev, N. 'Boris Pasternak', *Oktyabr'*, 5 (1937), 251–7.

Jakobson, R. 'Randbemerkungen zur Prosa des Dichters Pasternak', *Slavische Rundschau*, 6 (1935), 357–74.

'Kontury "Glejtu"' in Boris Pasternak. *Glejt.* Prague, 1935, 149–62.

Jakobson [see also under Yakobson].

Jangfeldt, B. 'My very dear Mr Svensson . . . Boris Pasternaks brev till Georg Svensson', in *Boris Pasternak och hans tid* (eds. P. A. Jensen, P.-A. Bodin, N. A. Nilsson). Stockholm, 1991, 163–7.

Jones, D. L. 'History and Chronology in Pasternak's "Doctor Zhivago"', *Slavic and East European Journal*, 23 no.1 (spring 1979), 160–63.

K. 'O Pasternake', *Literaturnaya gazeta*, 29 May 1932.

Kal'm, D. ' "Spektorsky" B. Pasternaka. Moskva-Leningrad. Gos.izd-vo khudozh.lit-ry, 1931', *Literaturnaya gazeta*, 19 March 1931.

'Na tvorcheskoi diskussii VSSP o poezii', *Literaturnaya gazeta*, 18 December 1931.

'Poeticheskoe tvorchestvo' *Literaturnaya gazeta*, 16 May 1934.

Karlinsky, S. *Marina Cvetaeva: Her Life and Art.* Berkeley, 1966.

Marina Tsvetaeva: The Woman, Her World and Her Poetry. Cambridge, 1985.

Kasack, W. (ed.) *Poet-perevodchik Konstantin Bogatyrev: drug nemetskoi literatury.* Munich, 1982.

Kassil', L. *Mayakovsky – sam.* Moscow, 1963.

Katanyan, V. A. *Mayakovsky. Literaturnaya khronika*, 4th edn. Moscow, 1961.

'O Mayakovskom i Pasternake', *Russian Literature Triquarterly*, 13 (Fall 1975), 499–518.

Kaverin, V. 'Pis'mennyi stol', *Oktyabr'*, 9 (1984), 95–164.

'Literator. Iz knigi vospominanii', *Znamya*, 8 (1987), 109–21.

Epilog. Memuary. Moscow, 1989.

Kedrov, K. 'Prigovor B. Pasternaka sovremennoi literature', *Izvestiya*, 11 March 1995.

Khardzhiev, N. I. 'Istoriya odnoi stat'i ("O Borise Pasternake")', in Nilsson (ed.) (1976), 7–8.

Khardzhiev, N. I. and Trenin, V. V. 'O Borise Pasternake', in Nilsson (ed.) (1976), 9–25.

Khelemsky, Ya. 'Ozhivshaya freska', *Znamya*, 10 (1980), 123–41.

Khokhlov, G. 'Sud'by, naidennye na snegu', *Literaturnaya gazeta*, 29 September 1934.

Kiasashvili, E. N. 'Rabota B. L. Pasternaka nad podstrochnikami (po arkhivnym materialam)', in Podgaetskaya (ed.) (1992), 153–65.

Kirpotin, V. Ya. 'Za iskusstvo pobedivshego naroda. Rech' tov. V. Kirpotina na obshchemoskovskom sobranii pisatelei', *Literaturnaya gazeta*, 15 March 1936.

'Literatura i sovetskii narod', *Oktyabr'*, 6 (1936), 210–25.

Klychkov, S. 'Lysaya gora', *Krasnaya nov'*, 5 (1936), 387–90.

Koen [see under Cohen].

Kolonsky, W. 'Pasternak and Proust: Towards a Comparison', *Russian Literature Triquarterly*, 22 (1988), 183–93.

Kopelev, L. 'Faustovskii mir Borisa Pasternaka', in Aucouturier (ed.) (1979), 491–515.

Kopelev [see also with Orlowa].

Kosachevsky, V. 'Posleslovie k romanu: iz zapisok advokata', *Moskva*, 10 (1988), 139–47.

Kovalev, V. ' "Chem byla vyzvana vasha svyaz' s Pasternakom?' – 'Lyubov'yu": iz sledstvennogo dela O. Ivinskoi 1949–1950 gg.', *Literaturnaya gazeta*, 16 March 1994.

Kozovoi, V. (ed.). 'Iz perepiski B. Pasternaka i P. Suvchinskogo' *Revue des études slaves*, tome 58 fascicule 4 (1986), 637–48.

Krotkov, Yu. 'Pasternaki', *Grani*, 60 (1966), 36–74; 63 (1967), 58–96.

Kryukova, A. M. ' "Razgovor s neizvestnym drugom" (Aseev i Pasternak)', *Literaturnoe nasledstvo*, 93 (1983), 516–30.

Krzhevsky, B. 'Iz novykh perevodov B. Pasternaka', *Leningrad*, 13–14 (1945), 16.

Kun, A. 'Memories of Pasternak', *New Hungarian Quarterly*, 27 no.104 (1986), 90–109.

'Iz vospominanii o B. L. Pasternake' (manuscript).

Kunina, E. 'O vstrechakh s Borisom Pasternakom', in *Vospominaniya* (1993), 106–18.

'Vospominaniya o vstrechakh s B. L. Pasternakom' (manuscript).

Kuznetsov, A. M. (ed.) *Mariya Veniaminovna Yudina: stat'i, vospominaniya, materialy.* Moscow, 1978.

Labedz [see under Hayward and Labedz].

Larina, A. M. *Nezabyvaemoe.* Moscow, 1989.

Lang, D. M. *A Modern History of Georgia*. London, 1962.

Leach, R. *Vsevolod Meyerhold*. Cambridge-New York-Melbourne, 1989.

Leble, I. M. (publ.) 'Razmyshleniya muzykanta (Iz dnevnikovykh zapisei G. G. Neigauza)', *Vstrechi s proshlym*, 6 (1988), 322–31.

Leites, A. 'Malen'kie nedorazumeniya v ser'eznom razgovore', *Novyi mir*, 10 (1945), 156–67.

Lekić, M. D. 'Pasternak's *Doktor Živago*: the novel and its title', *Russian Language Journal*, 141–143 (1988), 177–91.

'Pasternak's "Na etom svete" and the genealogy of "Doktor Živago"', *Russian Language Journal*, 150 (1991), 17–38.

Leneman, L. 'Begegnung mit Boris Pasternak', in Boris Pasternak. *Bescheidenheit und Kühnheit: Gespräche, Dichtungen, Dokumente*, ed. R. E. Meister. Zurich, 1959, 96–101.

Levin, F. *Iz glubin pamyati. Vospominaniya*. Moscow, 1973.

Levin, M. 'Neskol'ko vstrech', in *Vospominaniya* (1993), 353–63.

Levin, Yu. I. 'Zametki k stikhotvoreniyu B. Pasternaka "Vse nakloneniya i zalogi"', in Podgaetskaya (ed.) (1992), 67–75.

Levina, T. M. 'Energiya kholsta', in *Vek Pasternaka* (1990), 7.

Lezhnev, A. 'Boris Pasternak (k vykhodu "Dvukh knig" i "1905 goda")', in his *Literaturnye budni*. Moscow, 1929, 310–13.

Likht [see with E. B. Pasternak under Correspondence].

Livanov, V. 'Ne vydumannyi Boris Pasternak: vospominaniya i vpechatleniya', *Moskva*, 10 (1993), 164–80; 11 (1993), 170–92.

Livingstone, A. 'Pasternak's Last Poetry', *Meanjin Quarterly*, 4 (1963), 388–96; reprinted in Erlich (ed.)(1978), 166–76.

Boris Pasternak: Doctor Zhivago. Cambridge, 1989.

'Pasternak and Faust' in Barnes (ed.)(1990), 353–69.

'A Transformation of Goethe's *Faust* (Remarks on Pasternak's Translation of *Faust*, with a Survey of the Criticism)', in *Themes and Variations: In Honor of Lazar Fleishman*, Stanford Slavic Studies, vol. 8. Stanford CA, 1994, 81–92.

Loks, K. 'Boris Pasternak. "Poverkh bar'erov". GIZ, 1929, str. 159', *Literaturnaya gazeta*, 28 October 1929.

Loseff, L. (ed.). *Boris Pasternak 1890–1960*. Norwich Symposia on Russian Literature and Culture, vol. 1. Northfield VE, 1991.

Lozinskaya, L. 'Novyi perevod "Romeo i Dzhul'etty"', *Ogonek*, 46 (1942), 13.

Lukonin, M. 'Problemy sovetskoi poezii (itogi 1948 goda)', *Zvezda*, 3 (1949), 181–99.

MacDonald, I. *The New Shostakovich*. London, 1990.

MacKinnon, J. E. 'Boris Pasternak's Conception of Realism', *Philosophy and Literature*, 12 no.2 (1988), 211–31.

Makarov, A. 'Tikhoi sapoi', *Literaturnaya gazeta*, 19 February 1949.

Malevich, O. and Pasternak, E. V. (eds.) 'Iozef Gora i Boris Pasternak (K istorii odnogo perevoda)', *Voprosy literatury*, 7 (1979), 177–87.

Mallac, G. de. *Boris Pasternak: His Life and Art*. Norman OK, 1981.

Malmstad, J. E. 'Binary Opposites: The Case of Xodasevic and Pasternak', in Fleishman (ed.) (1989), 91–120.

Mamiofa, I. 'O pis'makh B. Pasternaka i klevete O. Ivinskoi', *Novoe russkoe slovo*, 18 February 1994.

Mandel'shtam, N. *Vospominaniya*. New York, 1970.

Vtoraya kniga. Paris, 1972.

Mandel'shtam, O. E. *Sobranie sochinenii v dvukh tomakh*. Washington, 1966.

Sobranie sochinenii v trekh tomakh, vol. I, 2nd edn. Washington, 1967.

Manfred, A. 'B. Pasternak. Poverkh bar'erov. M. L. GIZ, 1929', *Kniga i revolyutsiya*, 23 (1929), 56.

Margvelashvili, G. 'Vykhod v Gruziyu', *Literaturnaya Gruziya*, 11 (1972), 23–47.

Markov, V. 'An Unnoticed Aspect of Pasternak's Translations', *Slavic Review*, 20 no.3 (October 1961), 503–8.

Maslenikova, Z. A. *Portret Borisa Pasternaka*. Moscow, 1990.

Maslin, N. 'Mayakovsky i nasha sovremennost'', *Oktyabr'*, 4 (1948), 148–60.

Mathewson, R. 'The First Writers' Congress. A Second Look', in Hayward and Labedz (eds.) (1963), 62–73.

Mayakovsky, V. V. *Polnoe sobranie sochinenii*, 13 vols. Moscow, 1976.

Medvedev, R. *Nikolai Bukharin. The Last Years*. New York-London, 1980.

Meilakh, M. ' "Vnutrennyaya svoboda – eto samoe vazhnoe . . ." Beseda s serom Isaiei Berlinom', *Russkaya mysl'*, 22 June 1990.

Mezhdunarodnyi kongress pisatelei v zashchitu kul'tury. Parizh, iyun' 1935. Doklady i vystupleniya. Moscow, 1936.

Mikulich, B. 'Povest' ne dlya sebya', *Neman*, 3 (1987), 62–105.

Miller-Budnitskaya, R. 'O "filosofii iskusstva" B. Pasternaka i R. -M. Ril'ke', *Zvezda*, 5 (1932), 160–8.

'B. Pasternak. "Stikhotvoreniya v odnom tome", Leningrad. Izd-vo IPL, 1933; "Vozdushnye puti", GIKhL, 1933', *Literaturnyi sovremennik*, 11 (1933), 159–61.

Milne, L. *Mikhail Bulgakov. A Critical Biography*. Cambridge, 1990.

Miłosz, C. *The History of Polish Literature*. London-Toronto, 1969.

Mil'shtein, Ya. I. (ed.). *G. G. Neigauz. Razmyshleniya, vospominaniya, dnevniki. Izbrannye stat'i. Pis'ma k roditelyam*. Moscow, 1975.

Mindlin, E. *Neobyknovennye sobesedniki*. Moscow, 1968.

Mirsky, D. 'Pasternak i gruzinskie poety', *Literaturnaya gazeta*, 24 October 1935.

'Zametki o poezii', *Znamya*, 12 (1935), 231–6.

'Poeziya Gruzii. Rech' tov.D. Mirskogo', *Literaturnaya gazeta*, 29 February 1936.

Molochko, M. and Molova, A. *Tebe, moya zhizn'*. Moscow, 1965.

Moravia, A. 'Entretien avec Pasternak', *Preuves*, 88 (July 1958), 3–7; translated as 'Vstrecha s Pasternakom: sedoi yunosha', *Inostrannaya literatura*, 6 (1989), 216–18.

Morozov, M. M. '*Gamlet* v perevode B. Pasternaka', *Teatr*, 2 (1941), 144–7.

'Novyi perevod "Romeo i Dzhul'etty" ', *Literatura i iskusstvo*, 21 November 1942.

'Predislovie' in Shekspir, V. *Gamlet prints datskii* (transl. B. Pasternak). Moscow-Leningrad, 1942, 5-16.

'Shekspir v perevodakh B. Pasternaka', *Literatura i iskusstvo*, 7 August 1943.

'Novyi perevod "Antoniya i Kleopatry" ', *Pravda*, 2 October 1944.

Mossman, E. 'Pasternak's "Blind Beauty" ', *Russian Literature Triquarterly*, 7 (1974), 227-42.

Motyleva, T. L. 'Faust v perevode B. Pasternaka', *Novyi mir*, 8 (1950), 239-43.

Mukhanov, G. S. (ed.) *Chistopol'skie stranitsy – stikhi, rasskazy, povesti, dnevniki, pis'ma, vospominaniya*. Kazan, 1987.

Muravina, N. *Vstrechi s Pasternakom*. Tenafly NJ, 1990.

Mustangova, E. 'Vershiny mirovoi poezii. Rech' tov. Mustangovoi', *Literaturnaya gazeta*, 24 February 1936.

N. N. 'Poety sovetskoi Gruzii', *Literaturnaya gazeta*, 5 February 1935.

N. V. 'O novykh stikhotvoreniyakh Borisa Pasternaka', *Novyi mir*, 7-8 (1943), 157-60.

'Na obshchemoskovskom sobranii pisatelei 16 marta', *Literaturnaya gazeta*, 20 March 1936.

'Na pushkinskom plenume pravleniya Soyuza sovetskikh pisatelei', *Izvestiya*, 28 February 1937.

Nagibin, Yu. 'Bliz chelovecheskogo serdtsa. Popytka vospominanii', *Ogonek*, 2 (1987), 9-11.

'Naiti svoi lad . . .' Fedinskie chteniya, No. 2. Saratov, 1992.

'Nakanune plenuma. V Prezidiume pravleniya SSP', *Literaturnaya gazeta*, 20 February 1935.

Nei, Anna [pseudonym of Josephine/Zhozefina Pasternak] *Koordinaty*. Berlin, n.d.[1938].

Neigauz, G. G. [see Leble, I. M. (pub.) and Mil'shtein, Ya.I. (ed.)]

Neigauz, G. S. 'O Borise Pasternake', *Literaturnaya Gruziya*, 2 (1988), 194-212; revised version: 'Boris Pasternak v povsednevnoi zhizn', *Vospominaniya* (1993), 548-63.

Neigauz, S. G. 'Avtobiografiya', in Zimyanina (ed.), 9-10.

Nekhoroshev, G. [untitled notes on D. S. Mirsky], *Pamyatnye knizhnye daty*, 1990, 109-11.

Nemirovich-Danchenko, V. I. *Izbrannye pis'ma v dvukh tomakh*. Moscow, 1979.

Neznamov, P. 'Dva Kavkaza (Aseev i Pasternak)', *Vechernyaya Moskva*, 5 January 1935.

Nikulin, L. V. 'Men'she pretenzii – bol'she knig', *Literaturnaya gazeta*, 27 March 1936.

'Vladimir Mayakovsky', in Reformatskaya (ed.)(1963), 494-511.

Nilsson, N. A. 'Besuch bei Boris Pasternak. September 1958', in Boris Pasternak. *Bescheidenheit und Kühnheit*, ed. R. E. Meister. Zurich, 1959, 102-113.

Nilsson, N. A. (ed.) *Boris Pasternak. Essays*. Stockholm, 1976.

Nivat, G. 'Pasternak dans l'Oural en 1932', in Aucouturier (ed.) (1979), 521-2.

'Une lettre d'Andrej Belyj à Boris Pasternak', *Cahiers du monde russe et soviétique*, 25 no.1 (1984), 89–91.

Novikov, V. ' "Otzvuki i grimasy". Pasternak v parodiyakh i epigrammakh', *Literaturnoe obozrenie*, 3 (1990), 104–12.

Novikova, E. A. 'Iz proshlogo' (manuscript).

Nusinov, I. 'Masterskaya starykh obraztsov. B. Pasternak. Vozdushnye puti. GIKhL, 1933', *Khudozhestvennaya literatura*, 9 (1933), 7–9.

'O deistviyakh chlena Soyuza pisatelei SSSR B. L. Pasternaka, nesovmestimykh so zvaniem sovetskogo pisatelya', *Literaturnaya gazeta*, 28 October 1958.

Oblomievsky, D. 'Boris Pasternak', *Literaturnyi sovremennik*, 5 (1934), 127–42.

Oksenov, I. 'Bor'ba za liriku', *Novyi mir*, 7–8 (1933), 390–407.

Orlowa, R. and Kopelev, L. *Boris Pasternak*. Stuttgart, 1986.

Osborn, M. *Leonid Pasternak*. Warsaw, 1932.

'Otkrovennyi razgovor. O tvorchestve Borisa Pasternaka', *Komsomol'skaya pravda*, 23 February 1936.

Ozerov, L. Preface to Z. Pasternak, 'Vospominaniya', *Neva*, 2 (1990), 130–1.

'Fedin i Pasternak', in *'Naiti svoi lad'* (1992), 14–27.

'Sestra moya – zhizn'', in *Vospominaniya* (1993), 443–63.

'Pasternak, B. Izbrannye stikhi. Moskva, Sovetskaya literatura, 1933', *Khudozhestvennaya literatura*, 6 (1933), 63.

'Pasternak, B. Poverkh bar'erov. M.-L. , 1929', *Rekomendatel'nyi byulleten' bibliograficheskogo otdela Glavpolitprosveta*, 20 (1929), 159.

'Pasternak, B. Poverkh bar'erov. 2-oe dop. izd. M.-L., GIKhL, 1931', *Kniga stroitelyam sotsializma*, 23 (1931), 94.

'Pasternak, B. 1905 god. M.-L. GIZ, 1930, *Rekomendatel'nyi byulleten' bibliograficheskogo otdela Glavpolitprosveta*, 15–16 (1930), 75.

Pasternak, E. B. 'Posleslovie', in Yu.Slovatsky [Juliusz Słowacki]. *Stikhi. Mariya Styuart*, transl. B. Pasternak. Moscow, 1975, 171–5.

Preface in Boris Pasternak. 'Istoriya odnoi kontroktavy', *Slavica Hierosolymitana*, 1 (1977), 251–6.

'Reading Pasternak – Some Errors Corrected', *Irish Slavonic Studies*, 4 (1983), 38–46.

'Priblizit' chas . . .', *V mire knig*, 5 (1987), 26–32.

'Pered krasoi zemli . . .' *V mire knig*, 6 (1987), 31–3.

'Poleta vol'noe uporstvo: B. Pasternak o romane "Doktor Zhivago" ', *Novoe vremya*, 29 (1987), 28–30.

Boris Pasternak. Materialy dlya biografii. Moscow, 1989.

'Rasskaz o khudozhnitse Evgenii Pasternak', in *Vek Pasternaka* (1990), 7–8.

'Koordinaty liricheskogo prostranstva', *Literaturnoe obozrenie*, 2 (1990), 44–51; 3 (1990), 91–100.

'Iz vospominanii', *Zvezda*, 7 (1996), 125–91.

Pasternak, E. B. and E. V. 'Koordinaty liricheskogo prostranstva', *Literaturnoe obozrenie*, 2 (1990), 44–51; 3 (1990), 91–100.

Pasternak, E. B. [see also with Borisov, V. M. and under Works by Boris Pasternak, and Correspondence].

Pasternak, E. V. 'Rabota Borisa Pasternaka nad tsiklom "Nachal'naya pora" ', *Russkoe i zarubezhnoe yazykoznanie* (Alma Ata), 4 (1970), 121–41.

'Leto 1917 ("Sestra moya – zhizn'" i "Doktor Zhivago")', *Zvezda*, 2 (1990), 158–66.

' "Novaya faza khristianstva". Znachenie propovedi L'va Tolstogo v dukhovnom mire Borisa Pasternaka', *Literaturnoe obozrenie*, 2 (1990), 25–9.

'O chistopol'skoi p'ese Borisa Pasternaka', *Teatral'naya zhizn'*, 3 (1990), 22–3.

' "Ty – tsar': zhivi odin . . ." (Boris Pasternak i Vladimir Mayakovsky)', *Scandoslavica*, 38 (1992), 64–76.

'Znachenie nravstvennoi propovedi L. Tolstogo v formirovanii Pasternaka', in Podgaetskaya (ed.) (1992), 154–63.

'Znachenie avtobiograficheskogo momenta v romane "Doktor Zhivago" ', in Dorzweiler and Harder (eds.) (1993), 97–106.

Pasternak, E. V. (ed. and publ.) 'Boris Pasternak: ankety, zayavleniya, khodataistva 1920-kh godov', *Russkaya rech'*, 4 (1992), 38–49.

Pasternak, E. V. and Feinberg, M. I. (eds.) *Vospominaniya o Borise Pasternake.* Moscow, 1993.

Pasternak, E. V. [see also with Malevich, O. and under Works by Pasternak, and Correspondence].

Pasternak, J. 'Patior', *The London Magazine*, 6 (September 1964), 42–57; translated in *Vospominaniya* (1993), 25–31.

'Introduction' in *The Memoirs of Leonid Pasternak* (trans. J. Bradshaw). London-Melbourne-New York, 1982, 1–14.

[see also under: Nei, Anna and Pasternak, Zh.].

Pasternak, L. O. *Zapisi raznykh let.* Moscow, 1975.

Pasternak, Z. 'Vospominaniya', in *Vospominaniya* (1993), 175–231.

Pasternak, Zh. *Pamyati Pedro.* Paris, 1981.

Pasternak Slater, A. (trans. and introd.) A. Pasternak, *A Vanished Present.* Oxford-Melbourne, 1984.

Pasternak Slater, L. *Before Sunrise.* London, 1971.

Vspyshki magniya. Geneva, 1974.

Pertsov, V. 'Vymyshlennaya figura', *Na postu*, 1 (1924), 209–24.

'Novyi Pasternak', *Na literaturnom postu*, 2 (1927), 33–9.

'Literaturnye zapiski', *Literaturnaya gazeta*, 27 October 1936.

'Literaturnye zapiski (1936)', *God dvadtsatyi. Al'manakh*, 11 (1937), 350–80.

'Original i portret. Nikolai Baratashvili v perevodakh Borisa Pasternaka', *Literaturnaya gazeta*, 8 March 1947.

'Russkaya poeziya v 1946 godu', *Novyi mir*, 3 (1947), 172–88.

'Sodoklad V. Pertsova: o putyakh razvitiya poezii', *Literaturnaya gazeta*, 8 March 1947.

'Golosa zhizni', *Literaturnaya gazeta*, 9 September 1958.

Mayakovsky: zhizn' i tvorchestvo v poslednie gody 1925–1930. Moscow, 1965.

Mayakovsky v poslednie gody. Moscow, 1965.

Pervyi Vsesoyuznyi s"ezd sovetskikh pisatelei 1934. Stenograficheskii otchet. Moscow, 1934.

Petrovskaya, O. 'Vospominaniya o Borise Leonidoviche Pasternake', in *Vospominaniya* (1993), 90–105.

'Vospominaniya' (manuscript).

Pirozhkova, A. N. 'Years at His Side (1932–1939) and Beyond', *Canadian Slavonic Papers*, 36 nos.1–2 (1994), 169–240.

'Plenum tvorcheskoi druzhby', *Literaturnaya gazeta*, 24 February 1936.

Plotkin, L. 'Partiya i literatura', *Zvezda*, 10 (1947); reprinted in his *Partiya i literatura*. Leningrad, 1947.

Podgaetskaya, I. Yu. 'Pasternak i Verlen', *De visu*, 1 [2] (1991), 47–56; reprinted in Dorzweiler and Harder (eds.) (1993), 107–21.

Podgaetskaya, I. Yu. (ed.). *'Byt' znamenitym nekrasivo . . .' Pasternakovskie chteniya, vypusk I.* Moscow, 1992.

Pohl, W. *Russische Faust-Übersetzungen.* Meisenheim am Glan, 1962.

Polivanov, K. 'Marina Tsvetaeva v romane Borisa Pasternaka "Doktor Zhivago": neskol'ko parallelei', *De visu*, 3 (1992), 52–8.

' "Izbrannye" Pasternaka i raznye redaktsii "Marburga" ', in Dorzweiler and Harder (eds.) (1993), 125–33.

'Zametki i materialy k "politicheskoi" biografii Borisa Pasternaka (1934–1937)', *De visu*, 4 (1993), 70–79.

Polivanov, M. K. 'Tainaya svoboda', in *Vospominaniya* (1993), 492–510.

Polivanova, A. A. 'Iz razgovorov Pasternaka', in *Vospominaniya* (1993), 487–91.

Pollak, S. 'Pol'skie stikhi v perevodakh Borisa Pasternaka', in Aucouturier (ed.) (1979), 475–89.

'Relyatsiya' (manuscript).

Pol'sky, I. 'Boris Pasternak. Izbrannye perevody. Izd. "Sovetskii pisatel'"', M. 1940', *Leningrad*, 3 (1941), 24.

Polyanina, S. 'Neopublikovannoe pis'mo M. I. Tsvetaevoi k N. S. Tikhonovu', *Maria Cvetaeva. Studien und Materialien. Wiener slawistischer Almanach.* Sonderband 3 (1981), 209–11.

Porman, R. 'B. L. Pasternak v Chistopole', *Russkaya literatura*, 3 (1966), 193–5.

'Priem v Soyuz sovetskikh pisatelei', *Literaturnaya gazeta*, 16 May 1934.

Proffer, C. R. 'A Footnote to the Zhivago Affair', in his *The Widows of Russia and Other Writings.* Ann Arbor MI, 1987, 132–41.

'Proletarskaya poeziya na pod"eme', *Literaturnaya gazeta*, 23. April 1932.

'Protiv politicheskikh makhinatsii v prisuzhdenii nobelevskikh premii po literature', *Pravda*, 29 October 1958.

'Provokatsionnaya vylazka mezhdunarodnoi reaktsii', *Literaturnaya gazeta*, 25 October 1958.

Proyart, J. de. 'Une amitié d'enfance', in Aucouturier (ed.) (1979), 517–20.

'La nature et l'actualité dans l'oeuvre de Pasternak. Réflexions sur la structure du cycle Kogda razguljaetsja', in Aucouturier (ed.) (1979), 373–409.

'Introduction', in Pasternak, B. *Lettres à mes amies françaises 1956–1960*. Paris, 1994, 13–52.

Prozorov, A. 'Tragediya sub″ektivnogo idealista', *Na literaturnom postu*, 7 (1932), 26–35.

'Tezisy dushi', *Khudozhestvennaya literatura*, 24 (1932), 5–7.

'B. Pasternak. "Vtoroe rozhdenie". M. Federatsiya, 1932', *Kniga stroitelyam sotsializma*, 24 (1932), 5–7.

Pushkin, A. K. ' "Mirskontsa". Iz arkhiva A. E. Kruchenykh: stat′i, vospominaniya, pis′ma B. L. Pasternaka', *Vstrechi s proshlym*, 7 (1990), 497–524.

Rannit, A. 'Neizvestnyi Boris Pasternak v sobranii Tomasa P. Uitni', *Novyi zhurnal*, 156 (1984), 7–50.

Rapoport, L. *Stalin's War Against the Jews: The Doctors' Plot and the Soviet Solution*. New York-Toronto, 1990.

Rashkovskaya, M. 'Dve sud′by (Pasternak i Durylin. K istorii vzaimootnoshenii)', in Podgaetskaya (ed.) (1992), 235–44.

Rashkovskaya, M. (publ.) 'Boris Pasternak v poslevoennye gody (novye dokumenty)' *Literaturnaya ucheba*, 6 (1988), 108–16.

Rashkovskaya [see also under Additional Writings].

Rashkovsky, E. B. 'Pasternak i Teiyar de Sharden [Teilhard de Chardin]', *Voprosy filosofii*, 8 (1990), 160–66.

Rayfield, D. 'Pasternak and the Georgians', *Irish Slavonic Studies*, 3 (1982), 39–46.

'Unicorns and Gazelles: Pasternak, Rilke and the Georgian Poets', in Barnes (ed.) (1990), 370–81.

'The Killing of Paolo Iashvili', *Index on Censorship*, 19 no.6 (1990), 9–14.

'The Death of Paolo Iashvili', *Slavonic and East European Review*, 68 no.3 (October 1990), 631–64.

'Stalin, Beria and the Poets', *Poetry Nation Review*, 92 (1993), 22–30.

The Literature of Georgia. Oxford, 1994.

Reavey, G. 'A First Essay Towards Pasternak', *Experiment*, 6 (1930), 14–17.

Reformatskaya, N. V. (ed.) *V. Mayakovsky v vospominaniyakh sovremennikov*. Moscow, 1963.

Regler, G. *The Owl of Minerva. The Autobiography of Gustav Regler*. London, 1959.

Reztsov, L. 'Prints datskii v novom osveshchenii', *Literaturnoe obozrenie*, 20 (1940), 52–5.

Rikhter, E. R. (ed.) *Genrikh Neigauz: vospominaniya, pis′ma, materialy*. Moscow, 1992.

Ripellino, A. M. 'Vystuplenie', *Inostrannaya literatura*, 4 (1958), 212–13.

Rowe, E. *Hamlet: A Window on Russia*. New York, 1977.

Rozanov, I. *Russkie liriki. Ocherki*. Moscow, 1929.

Ruge, G. *Pasternak. A Pictorial Biography*. London, 1959.

Ryabinina, A. P. [memoirs] (manuscript).

'S obshchemoskovskogo sobraniya pistelei', *Pravda*, 16 March 1936.

Salys, R. 'A Tale of Two Artists: Valentin Serov and Leonid Pasternak', *Oxford Slavonic Papers*, 26 (1993), 75–86.

'Leonid Pasternak's *Moi proizvedenija*. Text and Commentary', *Russian Language Journal*, 47 nos.156–8 (1993), 159–322.

'From the Pale to the University: The Memoirs of Vladimir Osipovich Garkavi', *Canadian-American Slavic Studies*, 28 no.4 (1994), 445–72.

'Love, Death and Creation: Boris Pasternak and Two Rilke Requiems', *Russian Review*, 55 no.2 (1996), 265–78.

Sbornik statei, posvyashchennykh tvorchestvu B. L. Pasternaka. Munich, 1962.

Schewe, H. *Pasternak privat*. Hamburg, 1974.

Schimanski, S. 'The Duty of the Younger Writer', *Life and Letters Today*, 36 (February 1943).

'The Prose Works of Boris Pasternak', in B. Pasternak, *The Collected Prose Works*. London, 1945, 11–44.

Schweitzer, R. *Freundschaft mit Boris Pasternak*. Vienna-Munich-Basel, 1963.

Selivanovsky, A. 'Poeziya opasna?', *Literaturnaya gazeta*, 15 August 1931.

'Poet i revolyutsiya. O tvorchestve B. Pasternaka', *Literaturnaya gazeta*, 5 December 1932.

'O burzhuaznom restavratorstve i sotsialisticheskoi lirike', *Krasnaya nov'*, 2 (1932), 156–8.

'Razgovor o poezii', *Literaturnaya gazeta*, 11 November 1932.

'Boris Pasternak'. *Krasnaya nov'*, 1 (1933), 210–19; reprinted in his *Poeziya i poety. Kriticheskie stat'i*. Moscow, 1933, 155–78.

'Pasternak, B. L.' *Literaturnaya entsiklopediya*, vol. 8. Moscow 1934, 465–71.

'Boris Pasternak', in his *Ocherki po istorii russkoi sovetskoi poezii*. Moscow, 1936, 185–203.

'V zashchitu sovetskoi kul'tury', *Literaturanaya gazeta*, 20 July 1936.

Selyutsky, N. 'Eshche odna versiya zvonka Stalina Pasternaku', *Pamyat'*, 2 (1979), 438–41.

Semenov, Ya. 'Boris Pasternak', *Literaturnaya gazeta*, 24/29 August 1935.

Sergievsky, I. 'Boris Pasternak. "Dve knigi", "Devyat'sot pyatyi god", GIZ, 1927 g.', *Molodaya gvardiya*, 2 (1928), 199–200.

Serman, I. '"Vysokaya bolezn'" i problema eposa v 1920–e gody', in Loseff (ed.) (1991), 75–94.

Shalamov, V. 'Pasternak', in *Vospominaniya* (1993), 608–31.

Shklovsky, V. 'Syuzhet v stikhakh (V. Mayakovsky i B. Pasternak)', in *Poeticheskii sbornik*. Moscow, 1934, 173–94.

O Mayakovskom. Moscow, 1940.

Shostakovich, D. *Testimony. The Memoirs of Dmitrii Shostakovich as Related to and Edited by Solomon Volkov*. New York, 1979.

Shtein, A. '"I ne tol'ko o nem . . ." Dokumental'naya povest'', *Teatr*, 1 (1988), 171–90; 2 (1988), 166–85; 3 (1988), 169–86.

Shtut, S. 'U karty nashei literatury', *Novyi mir*, 9 (1956), 239–49.

Shugal, M. 'Pervaya vstrecha s gruzinskoi poeziei' (manuscript).

Shugrin, Yu. 'Takoi nastoyashchii, talantlivyi i neozhidannyi', *Sovetskaya kul'tura*, 4 August 1990.

Shvartsman, S. 'Odna vstrecha' (manuscript).

Simonov, K. 'Pravil'nyi put'', *Ogonek*, 34–35 (1943), 13.

'Chelovek v poezii', *Literaturnaya gazeta*, 4 November 1954.

Na literaturnye temy. Moscow, 1956.

'Uroki Fedina', *Druzhba narodov*, 1 (1979), 169–70.

Sinyavsky, A. 'Poeziya Pasternaka', in B. Pasternak, *Stikhotvoreniya i poemy*, Moscow-Leningrad, 1965, 9–62.

'Odin den's Pasternakom', in Aucouturier (ed.)(1979), 11–17.

Sirotinskaya, I. P. (publ.) ' "Nad starymi tetradyami . . ." ' (Pis'ma B. L. Pasternaka i vospominaniya o nem V. T. Shalamova)', *Vstrechi s proshlym*, 6 (1988), 291–305.

Sletova, V. A. 'Tverskaya 25, 1932 g.' (manuscript).

Smolitsky, V. G. 'B. Pasternak – sobiratel' narodnykh rechenii', *Russkaya rech'*, 1 (1990), 23–8.

Smol'yakov, G. 'Zametki o poezii. B. Pasternak. Vtoroe rozhdenie', *Rezets*, 28 (1932), 25.

Sollertinsky, I. I. ' "Gamlet" Shekspira i evropeiskii gamletizm', in L. V. Mikheeva (ed.); *Pamyati I. I. Sollertinskogo*, Leningrad-Moscow, 1974, 211–31.

Solov'ev, B. 'V poiskakh Gamleta', *Literaturnyi sovremennik*, 12 (1940), 140–8.

Solov'ev, V. 'Telefonnyi razgovor: analiticheskii rasskaz', *Novoe russkoe slovo*, 10–11 February 1990.

'Sovetskaya poeziya pered s"ezdom. Na vsesoyuznom poeticheskom soveshchanii', *Literaturnaya gazeta*, 24 May 1934.

Spassky, S. 'Pis'ma o poezii: pis'mo pervoe', *Zvezda*, 1 (1945), 118–23.

'B. Pasternak. "Zemnoi prostor", Izdatel'stvo "Sovetskii pisatel'". M. 1945 g.' *Leningrad*, 21–22 (1945), 31–2.

Stavrov, P. 'B. Pasternak. Vtoroe rozhdenie. Izd-vo Federatsiya', *Chisla* (Paris), 10 (1934), 290–1.

Stavsky, V. 'O formalizme i naturalizme v literature'. *Literaturnaya gazeta*, 15 March 1936.

'Na obshchemoskovskom sobranii pisatelei. Doklad V. P. Stavskogo o Chrezvychainom S"ezde Sovetov na obshchem sobranii chlenov SSP SSSR 16 dekabrya 1936 goda', *Literaturnaya gazeta*, 20 December 1936.

'Reshitel'no uluchshit' rabotu Soyuza pisatelei. Iz soobshcheniya tov.Stavskogo na IV plenume Pravleniya Soyuza pisatelei SSSR', *Literaturnaya gazeta*, 20 March 1937.

Stolovich, L. Preface to V. Asmus, 'Pasternak ob iskusstve', *Raduga* (Tallinn), 8 (1987), 60–1.

Struve, G. P. 'Boris Pasternak. Slovo o poezii', in *Sbornik statei* (1962), 9–15.

461

'Dnevnik chitatelya: Pasternak i ego cheshskii perevodchik', *Russkaya mysl'*, 29 April 1967.

Superfin, G. G. (publ.) 'B. L. Pasternak – kritik "formal'nogo metoda"', *Trudy po znakovym sistemam, V, Uchenye zapiski Tartuskogo Gosudarstvennogo Universiteta*, 284 (1971), 528–31.

Surkov, A. 'O sovetskoi poezii. Doklad A. Surkova na III plenume Pravleniya SSP SSSR', *Literaturnaya gazeta*, 16 February 1936.

'Vliyanie formalizma v poezii. Iz rechi tov. A. Surkova', *Literaturnaya gazeta*, 20 March 1936.

'O poezii B. Pasternaka', *Kul'tura i zhizn'*, 8 (21 March 1947), 8.

'Vsegda s partiei, vsegda s narodom. Na sobranii tvorcheskoi intelligentsii Moskvy', *Literaturnaya gazeta*, 28 November 1957.

Tabidze, G. *Stikhotvoreniya i poemy*. Moscow, 1958.

Polveka. Stikhi i poemy. Tbilisi, 1959.

Tabidze, N. 'Raduga na rassvete', in *Vospominaniya* (1993), 289–307.

Tabidze, T. *Stat'i, ocherki, perepiska*. Tbilisi, 1964.

Tall, E. (publ.). 'Correspondence Between Albert Camus and Boris Pasternak', *Canadian Slavonic Papers*, 22 no.2 (1980), 274–8.

Tarasenkov, A. 'Okhrannaya gramota idealizma', *Literaturnaya gazeta*, 18 December 1931.

'Boris Pasternak', *Zvezda*, 5 (1931), 228–35.

'B. Pasternak. "Okhrannaya gramota". L. IPL, 1931', *Kniga stroitelyam sotsializma*, 34 (1931), 101.

'"Vtoroe rozhdenie" B. Pasternaka', *Literaturnaya gazeta*, 11 December 1932.

'Tvorchestvo B. Pasternaka', in B. Pasternak, *Izbrannye stikhotvoreniya*. Moscow, 1933, 3–13.

'Polden' liriki', *Literaturnaya gazeta*, 20 March 1934.

'"Gruzinskie liriki". Moskva. Sovetskii pisatel' 1935', *Znamya*, 9 (1935), 201–9.

'O gruzinskikh perevodakh Pasternaka', *Znamya*, 9 (1935), 201–9.

'Pasternak v krivom zerkale', *Znamya*, 10 (1935), 228–35.

'V redaktsiyu zhurnala "Znamya"', *Znamya*, 6 (1937), 284–5.

'Novye stikhi Borisa Pasternaka', *Znamya*, 4 (1945), 136–9.

'Zametki kritika', *Znamya*, 10 (1949), 167–8.

'Znachenie poetiki Mayakovskogo dlya sovetskoi poezii', *Znamya*, 4 (1950), 171–82.

'Pasternak. Chernovye zapisi. 1930–1939' in *Vospominaniya* (1993), 150–74.

Thomson, B. *The Premature Revolution*. London, 1972.

Tizengauzen, V. 'Gamlet v perevode B. Pasternaka', *Sovetskoe iskusstvo*, 30 April 1940.

Tregub, S. 'Voenno-polevoi soyuz pisatelei', in his *Sputniki serdtsa*. Moscow, 1964, 197–203.

Trenin, V. V. [see with Khardzhiev, N. I.].

Tsvetaeva, M. *Pis'ma k A. Teskovoi*. Prague, 1969.

Sobranie sochinenii v semi tomakh, Moscow 1994.

Bibliography

Tsybulevsky, A. S. *Vysokie uroki (Poemy Vazha Pshavela v perevodakh russkikh poetov)*. Tbilisi, 1980.

Turbin, B. 'Konets "Zhivagovskogo" doma', *Russkaya mysl'*, 22/29 July 1982.

Tynyanov, Yu. 'Promezhutok (o poezii)', *Russky sovremennik*, 4 (1924), 209–21; reprinted in his *Arkhaisty i novatory*. Leningrad, 1929, 563–8.

Usievich, E. 'K sporam o politicheskoi poezii', *Literaturnyi kritik*, 5 (1937), 62–102.

'V storone ot zhizni. O tvorchestve Borisa Pasternaka', *Vechernyaya Moskva*, 19 December 1936.

Vaksberg, A. *Stalin's Prosecutor: The Life of Andrei Vyshinsky*. London, 1990.

Vanshenkin, K. 'Kak isklyuchali Pasternaka', *Vospominaniya* (1993), 632–8.

Vasil'eva, L. *Kremlevskie zheny*. Moscow-Minsk, 1993.

'Vecher gruzinskoi poezii', *Literaturnaya gazeta*, 24 August 1934.

Veidle, V. 'Zavershenie puti', in B. Pasternak, *Sochineniya*, vol.3. Ann Arbor MI, 1961, vii–xv.

'Vek Pasternaka'. *Literaturnaya gazeta. Dos'e 'Vek Pasternaka'* (February 1990).

Vickery, W. 'Zhdanovism 1946–53', in Hayward and Labedz (eds.) (1963), 99–124.

Vilenkin, V. *Vospominaniya s kommentariyami*. Moscow, 1982.

'O Borise Leonidoviche Pasternake', in *Vospominaniya* (1993), 464–86.

Vil'mont, N. 'Gete i ego "Faust" ', in Gete [Goethe], *Faust*. Leningrad, 1953, 3–32.

O Borise Pasternake. Vospominaniya i mysli. Moscow, 1989.

Vil'mont, N. [see also as Vil'yam-Vil'mont, N. N.].

Vil'yam-Vil'mont, N. N. ' "Gamlet" v perevode Borisa Pasternaka', *Internatsional'naya literatura*, 7–8 (1940), 288–91.

Vospominaniya o Borise Pasternake, ed. E. V. Pasternak and M. I. Feinberg. Moscow, 1993.

Voznesensky, A. 'Mne chetyrnadtsat' let', *Novyi mir*, 8 (1980); reprinted as 'Mne 14 let' in *Vospominaniya* (1993), 574–607.

Vygodsky, D. ' "Gruzinskie liriki". Moskva. Sovetskii pisatel', 1935', *Literaturnyi sovremennik*, 1 (1936), 235–6.

Vysheslavsky, L. *Naizust': vospominaniya*. Moscow, 1989.

Wilson, E. *Shostakovich: A Life Remembered*. London-Boston, 1994.

Wolff, K. *Briefwechsel eines Verlegers: 1911–1963*. Frankfurt a.M., 1966.

Wrenn, C. L. [Renn, K.] 'Shekspir v perevodakh B. Pasternaka', *Britanskii soyuznik*, 22 (3 June 1945).

'Boris Pasternak', *Oxford Slavonic Papers*, 2 (1951), 82–97.

Wright, A. C. *Mikhail Bulgakov: Life and Interpretations*. Toronto, 1978.

Ya. E[idel'man]. 'Na vechere Dm.Petrovskogo', *Literaturnaya gazeta*, 30 January 1935.

'Preniya po dokladu tov. V. Stavskogo', *Literaturnaya gazeta*, 5 March 1937.

Ya. En.[Eidel'man] 'Zametki i vpechatleniya. Na chetvertom plenume pravleniya SSP', *Literaturnaya gazeta*, 26 February 1937.

Yakobson, A. ' "Vakkhanaliya" v kontekste pozdnego Pasternaka', *Slavica Hierosolymitana*, 3 (1978), 302–79.

Yakovlev, B. 'Poet dlya estetov (Zametki o Velemire Khlebnikove i formalizme v poezii)', *Novyi mir*, 5 (1948), 207–31.

Yurchenko, Yu. 'Anafema', *Literaturnaya ucheba*, 5 (1988), 161–8.

Zabolotsky, N. *The Life of Zabolotsky*, ed. R. R. Milner-Gulland, trans. R. R. Milner-Gulland and C. G. Bearne. Cardiff, 1994.

'Zametki o peresechenii biografii Osipa Mandel'shtama i Borisa Pasternaka', *Pamyat'* 4 (1981), 283–337. [Revised version see under E. B. and E. V. Pasternak, 'Koordinaty liricheskogo prostranstva'].

Zaslavsky, D. 'Shumikha reaktsionnoi propagandy vokrug literaturnogo sornyaka', *Pravda*, 26 October 1958.

Zazubrin, V. Ya. *Khudozhestvennye proizvedeniya, stat'i, doklady, rechi*. Literaturnoe nasledstvo Sibiri, 2. Novosibirsk, 1972.

Zelinsky, K. 'Liricheskaya tetrad'', *God shestnadtsatyi. Al'manakh pervyi*. Moscow, 1933, 383–427.

Kriticheskie pis'ma. Kniga vtoraya. Moscow, 1934.

'O lirike', *Znamya*, 8–9 (1946), 179–99.

Zhdanov, N. 'Boris Pasternak – "krasnomu flotu"', *Druzhba narodov*, 11 (1979), 268–9.

Zholkovsky, A. 'Mekhanizmy vtorogo rozhdeniya', *Literaturnoe obozrenie*, 2 (1990), 35–41.

'21 avgusta 1959 goda', in Loseff (ed.) (1991), 296–9.

Zhuravlev, D. N. *Zhizn', iskusstvo, vstrechi*. Moscow, 1985.

Zimyanina, N. (ed.) *Stanislav Neigauz: vospominaniya, pis'ma, materialy*. Moscow 1988.

Zingerman, B. *Teatr Chekhova i ego mirovoe znachenie* (ed. A. Anikst). Moscow, 1988.

Zolyan, S. '"Vot ya ves'..." K analizu "Gamleta" Pasternaka', *Daugava*, 137 (1988), 97–104.

Index of works by Boris Pasternak

Page references are given for the Russian titles of Pasternak's works, with cross-references to English titles used in text or commentary. Ellipsis at the end of an item indicates the first line of an untitled poem. Cross-reference is made to commonly used alternative translated titles. Titles beginning with numerals are placed after the alphabetical entries. References to authors and works *translated* by Pasternak can be found in the general index.

General Index

470

323, 356, 369; translations by Pasternak,
111, 225, 269, 275
*Leonov, Leonid, 19, 102, 123, 127, 133,
135, 159, 163, 181, 188, 193, 205, 233
Leontovich, Mikhail Aleksandrovich
(b. 1903), 346
*Lermontov, Mikhail, 16, 18, 35, 52, 53, 98,
152, 155, 161
Leskov, Nikolai Semyonovich (1831–95),
207
Levin, Fyodor Markovich (b. 1901), 246, 259
*Levin, Dr Lev, 14, 62, 71, 157–8, 196
Levin, Dr Georgii Lvovich, 158
Levin, Vladimir Lvovich, 158
Lewis, Sinclair (1885–1951), 104
Lezhnev (Altshuler), Isai Grigoryevich
(1891–1955), 95
Li Tai-Po (c. 700–762), 359
Lidin (Gomberg), Vladimir Germanovich
(1894–1979), 102, 127
Life and Letters Today (London), 201
Likhotal, Aleksandr Vasilyevich, 343
Linde, Fyodor Fyodorovich (?–1917), 270
Lindsay, Jack (1900–90), 361
Literatura i iskusstvo, 205, 209, 211, 214
Literaturnaya Entsiklopediya, 74
Literaturnaya gazeta, 4, 7, 9, 19, 21, 28, 41,
60, 61, 62, 66, 68, 73, 74, 75, 85, 86,
87, 111, 117, 123, 126, 132, 135, 136,
137, 148, 149, 153, 154, 156, 162, 183,
210, 232, 269, 324, 337, 339, 343, 344,
345, 348, 349–50, 358
Literaturnaya Gruziya, 324, 328, 337
Literaturnaya Moskva, 301, 314, 318
Literaturny Leningrad, 135
Litfond (Literary Fund), 65, 127, 162, 165,
180, 197, 253, 345, 364, 371, 374, 375
Livanov, Boris Nikolaevich (1904–72), 167,
205, 270, 274, 276, 286, 319, 367–8,
373
Livanova, Evgeniya Kazimirovna (1911–78),
270, 276, 286, 319
*Livingstone, Angela, 311
*Livshitz, Benedikt, 112
Lo Gatto, Ettore (1890–1983), 297, 313
Loiter, Elizaveta Emmanuilovna (1906–73),
190
*Loks, Konstantin, 4, 204, 296
*Lomonosov, Yurii, 62, 109
*Lomonosova, Raisa, 11, 12, 13, 15, 28, 35,
36, 37, 62, 76, 93, 98, 104, 109, 130,
151, 155, 159, 230

London, 71, 108, 109, 113, 128, 164, 322,
330, 336, 372
Lozinsky, Mikhail Leonidovich (1886–1955),
112, 170, 191, 223, 295
Lubyanka (Moscow), 89, 142, 186, 262, 263,
264, 279, 297, 357
Lugovskoi, Vladimir Aleksandrovich
(1901–57), 65, 101, 305, 311
Lukonin, Mikhail Kuzmich (1918–76), 259
*Lunacharsky, Anatolii, 21, 37, 70, 79
Lyaskovsky, Dmitrii Vladimirovich, 151, 160
'Lyonya' *see* Pasternak L. B.
Łysohorsky, Óndra (real name: Ervin Goj)
(1905–1989), 205–6
lyric (literary genre), 2–5, 33, 34, 60, 82, 132,
204, 289
Lyubimov, Nikolai Mikhailovich, 360
Lyubimov, Yurii Petrovich (b. 1917), 322

Macauley, Thomas Babington, Lord
(1800–59), 132, 144, 153
Macbeth see Shakespeare
Macmillan, Harold (1894–1986), 355
Madame Bovary (Flaubert), 133
Maisky, Ivan Mikhailovich (1884–1975),
219
*Mallac, Guy de, 359
Malraux, André (1901–76), 93–5, 104–7,
115, 124
Maly Theatre (Moscow), 186, 200, 213, 297,
322, 351
Malyshkin, Aleksandr Grigoryevich
(1892–1938), 50, 158, 162
*Mandelstam, Nadezhda, 72, 83, 84, 89–92,
144–5, 152, 158, 190, 204, 216, 227,
271
*Mandelstam, Osip, 2, 4, 7, 57, 65, 72–3, 82,
83–4, 89–93, 99, 143, 144–5, 156, 158,
174, 216, 227, 253, 302
Manet, Édouard (1832–83), 233
Manfred, Albert Zakharovich (1906–76), 44
Mann, Heinrich (1871–1950), 104, 107
Mann, Klaus (1906–49), 94, 107
*Mann, Thomas, 244
Marburg, 32, 33, 52
*Margulius, Aleksandr, 72
*Margulius, Klara (1869–1949), 14, 72, 179
*Margulius, Maria *see* Markova, M. A.
Margvelashvili, Georgii Georgievich
(1923–90), 307, 356
Maria Stuart (Schiller), 297, 322–3, 358
Maria Stuart (Słowacki), 344, 357, 364

Österling, Anders Johan (1884–1981), 341
Ostrovskaya, Raisa Porfiryevna (18?–1963),
    206
Ostrovsky, Nikolai Alekseyevich (1904–36),
    206
Othello see Shakespeare
Oxford, 128, 145, 164, 165, 178, 198, 219,
    225, 226, 228, 235, 247, 257, 319, 334,
    352, 371
Oxford Book of Russian Verse, The, 223
Oxford University, 317, 336, 360
*Ozerov, Lev, 49, 209

Palladini, Leo, 369
Panfyorov, Fyodor Ivanovich (1896–1960),
    80, 104, 106, 133, 182, 334
Pankratov, Yurii Ivanovich (b. 1935), 351,
    352, 358
Panova, Vera Fyodorovna (1905–73), 289,
    345
Pantheon Books (publisher), 335, 336, 351
Parain, Brice (1897–1971), 319, 357
Paris, 11, 30, 49, 62, 93, 104–8, 109, 111,
    115, 128, 136, 149, 150, 289, 330, 332,
    350, 359, 362
Paris Congress of Writers in Defence of
    Culture (1935), 104–7, 110, 111, 118,
    124, 129, 130, 201
Party *see* Communist Party
*Pasternak, Aleksandr ('Shura'), 14, 37, 38,
    51–2, 63, 64, 65, 94, 145, 178, 179,
    181, 196, 197, 205, 250, 340, 346, 371,
    372, 375
Pasternak, Boris Evgenyevich (b. 1961), 376
*Pasternak, Boris Leonidovich: late 1920s
    literary ambiance, 1–3, 19–21, 28–9;
    socio-political events, 5–7; *Over the
    Barriers* (1929), 3–4; *The Story*, 7–11;
    Rilke translations, 11–12; *Spektorsky, 7,
    21–4*; reception of *Spektorsky*, 46, 61; *Safe
    Conduct*, 11, 32–5, 42, 47; reception of
    Safe Conduct, 61, 78–9; relations with
    Mayakovsky, 29–32, 34–5, 46–7, 80,
    113; *Second Birth*, 45, 56–8, 73–4; 1930s
    prose, 99–100, 152–5, 174–5; *see
    also* 'Zapiski Patrika'; verse of mid 1930s,
    125–6, 131–2, 135, 175–7; poetic style
    change, 177–8; family life and vacations
    1929–30, 14–17, 18, 24, 37–40;
    relations with wife Evgeniya, 43–5, 48–9,
    59, 62–5, 71, 78, 130, 151, 203; travel
    plans, 8, 13–14, 35–7; Berlin family

links, 14, 43, 49, 70–1, 77–8, 105–6,
    112–13, 127, 149–50, 159–60; family
    contacts during and after removal to
    England, 113, 127, 178–9, 235, 257–8,
    317–18, 334–5, 368, 374–5; mother's
    death, 164–5; father's death, 219; sister
    Josephine's poetry, 99, 159; relations
    with second wife Zinaida, 26–8, 39–41,
    43–5, 49–52, 59, 62–5, 71–2, 101–2,
    103–4, 108–10, 130–1, 150–1, 174–5,
    218–19, 237–8; relations with sons and
    stepsons, *see* Pasternak, E. B.; Pasternak
    L. B.; Neigauz, A. G.; Neigauz, S. G.;
    links with Asmus family, 26–8, 37–40;
    links with Neigauz family, 26–8, 37–41,
    43–5, 49, 51, 63–4, *see also* Neigauz, G.
    G.; reputation and critical reception in
    1930s, 60–2, 65–8, 73–4, 88–9, 111,
    135–8, 142–3, 149, 160–1; anti-
    formalist campaign, 117–18, 121–4,
    126; poetic addresses and dialogue with
    Stalin, 47–8, 74–6, 90–3, 114–16; Stalin
    Constitution, 128–9; visit to Urals
    (1931), 50–1, (1932), 69–70; visits to
    Georgia (1931), 52–5, (1933), 80–2;
    Georgian literary contacts *see* Georgia;
    Georgian literature; Georgian
    translations; Tabidze; Yashvili, *et al.*;
    Writers' Union membership in 1930s,
    79ff, 86–7, 97–8, 101, 129–30; First
    Writers' Congress, 93–8; Paris Congress
    1935, 106–8; Minsk conference 1936,
    118–20; Pushkin Plenum 1937, 140–2;
    nervous depression (1935), 103–4,
    108–10; London visit, 109; terror and
    trials, 133, 138–40; arrest of Georgians,
    Pilnyak, Meyerhold, 145–7, 147, 157–9,
    163–4; support of victims of Stalinism,
    76, 146–7, 225; rehousing in Moscow,
    127–8; Peredelkino life, 127–8, 130–1,
    133, 160, 162–3, 174–7; World War 2,
    166ff, 178–81, 197–200, 203ff, 232–4;
    evacuation to Chistopol, 180–1, 185–6,
    187–90; wartime verse, 183–4, 208–11,
    217–18; wartime drama, 183–4, 192–6;
    wartime reportage, 206–8, 219; *On
    Early Trains*, 199, 204; wartime
    translations, *see* Shakespeare; postwar
    ambiance, 211–12, 216, 219; 1945
    Georgian visit, 223–4; Zhdanovism,
    231–5, 145–7, 252–3; anti-cosmopolitan
    campaign, 258–60, 279–80; public

Tabidze, Tanit Titsianovna (b. 1922), 147, 298, 355–6, 367

Tabidze, Titsian Yustinovich (1895–1937), 53–5, 60, 81–2, 88, 94, 95, 101, 102, 104, 111, 115, 118, 125, 126, 128, 131, 134, 136, 146–7, 156, 224, 226, 264, 281–2, 302, 305, 308; Pasternak's translations, 81–2, 90, 95, 111, 132, 302, 303

Tager, Elena Efimovna (1908–81), 172, 368, 372

*Tager, Evgenii, 172, 368

Tagore, Rabindranath (1861–1941), 37, 303, 336, 359

*Tairov, Aleksandr, 196

Tal, Boris Markovich 1898–1938), 133

Tamm, Igor Evgenyevich (1885–1971), 346

Tanev, Vasil Konstantinov (1897–1941), 86

Tankhilevich (Erastova), Tatyana Danilovna, 273

Tarasenkov, Anatolii Kuzmich (1905–56), 46, 62, 68, 73, 88–9, 111, 123, 129, 134, 136–7, 140, 142, 164, 196, 210, 217, 218, 232, 235, 259, 303

Tarasov-Rodionov, Aleksandr Ignatyevich (1885–1938), 134

Tarasova, Alla Konstantinovna (1898–1973), 213, 322, 323

Tarkovsky, Arsenii Aleksandrovich (1907–89), 304

Tashkent, 180, 184, 185, 190, 192, 204, 205, 216

Tbilisi, 26, 52–5, 81, 87–8, 104, 126, 131–2, 147, 169, 223–5, 276, 307, 355–6, 367

Teatr, 322

Teilhard de Chardin, Pierre (1881–1955), 359

Tempy (Tbilisi), 55, 57

Third Congress of the Writers' Union, 358

Thomson, Boris (b. 1933), 210

Tiflis *see* Tbilisi

*Tikhonov, Nikolai, 5, 12, 17, 20, 21, 73, 81–2, 88, 95, 96, 104, 106, 107, 108, 112, 139, 140, 206, 216, 219, 222, 232, 250, 342, 345

Times Literary Supplement, The, 226

Togliatti, Palmiro (1893–1964), 325

Toller, Ernst (1893–1939), 94, 104

Tolstaya, Sofia Andreyevna (1900–75), 242

*Tolstoy, Aleksei, 11, 51, 76, 89, 104, 107, 149, 190, 193, 206

*Tolstoy, Lev, 12, 102, 153, 155, 201, 215, 242, 253, 288, 305, 330, 359, 361

Tolstoyanism, 66, 70, 119, 148, 162, 177, 242, 244, 307, 315

Tomashevsky, Boris Viktorovich (1890–1957), 204

Tomasi di Lampedusa, Giuseppe (1896–1957), 311

Tomsky, Mikhail Pavlovich (1880–1936), 133

Tonya Gromeko (character in 1930s prose), 154

Toroshelidze, Malakhia Georgievich (1880–1938), 95

Transformations, 220

Treece, Henry (1911–66), 220

Trenin, Vladimir Vladimirovich (1904–41), 74

Trenyov, Konstantin Andreyevich (1876–1945), 127, 166, 187, 188, 193

Trenyova, Larisa Ivanovna, 102, 237, 294

Tretyakov Gallery (Moscow), 127, 186

Tribuna Ljudu (Warsaw), 310

Tridtsat' dnei, 87, 170

Troshchenko, Ekaterina Dmitrievna (1902–44), 67, 134

*Trotsky, Lev, 233

Trotskyism/Trotskyist(s), 5, 116, 134, 139, 142, 145, 158

Troyanovskaya, Anna Ivanovna (1885–1977), 37

Troyat, Henri (Lev Tarasov) (b. 1911), 351

Trubnikovsky Lane, Moscow, 27, 44, 63, 71

Trud, 207, 210

Tselikovskaya, Lyudmila Vasilyevna (b. 1919), 322, 367

Tsereteli, Akakii (1840–1915), 225, 275

*Tsvetaeva, Anastasia, 13, 165, 225, 255, 282

*Tsvetaeva, Marina, 2, 8, 9, 13, 22, 36, 51, 106, 107–110, 134, 165, 169, 172–3, 184–5, 186, 188, 192, 211, 214, 241, 254, 302, 305, 306, 330

Tukhachevsky, Mikhail Nikolaevich, General (1893–1937), 148

Turgenev, Ivan Sergeyevich (1818–83), 207

Tvardovsky, Aleksandr Trifonovich (1910–71), 159, 208, 222, 259, 294, 327, 329, 345, 358

Tverskoi Boulevard, Moscow, 65, 68, 71, 72, 78, 130, 151, 185, 204

Twentieth Party Congress, 301, 303, 309, 312, 316

Tychina, Pavlo (1891–1967), 156, 269
*Tynyanov, Yurii, 18, 19, 81, 94, 152
*Tyutchev, Fyodor, 119

Uborevich, Ieronim Petrovich, General
    (1896–1937), 148
Ugrimov family, 154–5
Union of Soviet Writers, 67, 70, 72, 79,
    85–6, 88, 93–4, 97–8, 101–3, 105,
    109–10, 112, 118, 120, 122, 124, 126,
    129–30, 133–5, 137, 139, 141, 142,
    144, 148, 158, 159, 163, 169, 172, 180,
    184, 188, 193, 199, 203–4, 212, 216,
    231–4, 235, 237, 246, 253–4, 259, 291,
    296, 314, 326–7, 333, 342–5, 348, 352,
    358, 366; *see variously* All-Russian Union
    of Writers; First/Second/Third
    Congress; Leningrad Union of Writers;
    Moscow Union of Writers
Urals, 50, 51, 68–70, 99, 154, 180, 186, 270,
    275
Ushakov, Nikolai Nikolaevich (1899–1973),
    38
Usievich, Elena Feliksovna (1893–1968),
    135
Utkin, Iosif Pavlovich (1903–44), 141
Uzkoye sanatorium, 103, 324

Vakhtangov Theatre (Moscow), 171, 172,
    186, 305, 322, 367
*Valéry, Paul, 107
Vasilyev, Pavel Nikolaevich (1910–37), 79,
    129, 134
Vasilyev, Sergei Aleksandrovich (1911–75),
    250
Vatagin (Vainshtein) Mark Germanovich, 304
Vazha Pshavela (Luka Pavlovich Razikashvili)
    (1861–1915), 87, 88, 98, 112, 225, 302
Vechernyaya Moskva, 60, 126, 137, 151
Vedenyapin, Nikolai (character in *Doktor
    Zhivago*), 226, 242, 271, 293, 366
Veidle *see* Weidlé
Venice, 32, 34, 52, 61, 97, 359
*Veresaev, Vikentii, 102
*Verhaeren, Émile, 215
*Verlaine, Paul, 156, 170, 214, 215, 223
Vertinsky, Aleksandr Nikolaevich
    (1889–1957), 247
Vesyoly, Artem (Kochkurov, Nikolai
    Ivanovich) (1899–1939), 6, 139
Vildrac, Charles (Charles Messager)
    (1882–1971), 12

Vilenkin, Vitalii Yakovlevich (b. 1910), 46,
    167, 176, 200, 204, 213
*Vilyam-Vilmont, Nikolai, 10, 37, 38–9, 45,
    63, 91, 99, 100, 171–2, 182, 225, 234,
    260, 269, 283, 285, 291, 322
*Vinograd, Elena, 204
Vinogradov, Dmitrii Aleksandrovich
    (b. 1942), 238–9, 266, 294, 296
Vinokurov, Evgenii Mikhailovich (b. 1925),
    359
Vishnevsky, Vsevolod Vitalyevich (1900–52),
    46, 66, 101, 132, 133, 135, 139, 149,
    154, 203, 232
Vityazev (Ferapont Ivanovich Sedenko)
    (1886–1938), 4
Vkhutein (Higher Art and Technical
    Institute), 38
Vkhutemas (Higher Artistic and Technical
    Studios), 16
VOKS *see* All-Union Society for Cultural
    Links
Volin, Boris Mikhailovich (1886–1957), 134
Volkhonka Street, Moscow, 17, 27–8, 44, 48,
    59–60, 63–5, 71–3, 89, 94, 99, 114, 151
*Voloshin, Maksimilian, 160
Volya Rossii, 18
Volynsky, Mark Semyonovich, 289–90
Voronkov, Konstantin Vasilyevich
    (1911–84), 343, 348
*Voronsky, Aleksandr, 47
Voroshilov, Kliment Efremovich
    (1881–1969), 75, 351
Votchal, Dr Boris Evgenyevich (1895–1971),
    279, 370
Vovsi, Dr Miron Semyonovich (1897–1960),
    279–80, 333
*Voznesensky, Andrei, 274, 301, 318, 319,
    322, 351, 360
Vysheslavsky, Leonid Nikolaevich, 38
Vyshinsky, Andrei Yanuarovich (1883–1954),
    133
*Vysotskaya, Ida, 107, 287
Vysotsky family, 1, 2

*Wagner, Richard, 87
Warsaw, 14; *see also* Poland
Weidlé (Veidle), Vladimir Vasilyevich
    (1895–1979), 311
Weigel, Helene (1900–71), 296
Weinert, Erich (1890–1953), 107
Wells, Herbert George (1866–1946), 225
Westhoff *see* Rilke (née Westhoff)

Williams, Alan Moray (1913–96), 352
Wilson, Edmund (1885–1972), 361
Wolff, Kurt (1887–1963), 335, 351, 361, 364
Woolf, Virginia (1882–1941), 318, 359
World War One/Two *see* First/Second World
    War
Writers' Club (Moscow), 169, 196, 200, 228
Writers' House *see* House of Writers

Y-3 (character in *Povest'*), 10, 363
Yagoda, Genrikh Grigoryevich (1891–1938),
    19, 89, 90, 144, 154
Yakhontov, Vladimir Nikolaevich
    (1899–1945), 356
Yakir, Ionna Emmanuilovich, General (1896–
    1937), 148
Yakovleva, Tatyana Alekseyevna (1906–91),
    30
Yarzhemskaya *see* Neigauz, G. S.
Yashin, Aleksandr Yakovlevich (1913–68),
    360
Yashvili, Paolo Dzhibraelovich (1895–1937),
    51, 52, 53–5, 60, 66, 69, 72, 81–2, 88,
    90, 95, 101, 102, 118, 131, 145–7, 156,
    305, 308; Pasternak's translations, 81–2,
    90, 93, 95, 112
Yashvili, Tamara Georgievna (1904–82), 51,
    53, 146
Yudina, Maria Veniaminovna (1899–1970),
    27, 101, 165, 203, 240, 241, 259, 288,
    291, 317, 373
yurodivy (holy fool) syndrome, 76, 92, 94,
    109, 140, 143

Zabolotsky, Nikolai Alekseyevich (1903–58),
    58, 112, 227, 282, 302, 359
*Zaitsev, Boris, 336, 359, 362
Zakgiz (publishers), 81, 88, 223
Zakkniga (publishers), 55
Zalka, Máté (1896–1937), 66
Zamoyska, Hélène *see* Peltier-Zamoyska, H.
*Zamyatin, Evgenii, 18, 19–21, 28, 45, 90,
    107, 126
Zarya Vostoka, 215, 224

Zarya Vostoka (publishers), 224
Zaslavsky, David Osipovich (1880–1965), 7,
    122, 343–4
*Zbarsky, Boris ('Pepa'), 10, 14, 71, 112–13,
    127, 151, 180
Zbarsky, Lev Borisovich (Feliks) (b. 1931),
    113
Zelinsky, Kornelii Lyutsianovich
    (1896–1970), 68, 74, 112, 173, 205,
    234, 329, 348
Zenkevich, Mikhail Aleksandrovich
    (1891–1973), 112
Zharov, Aleksandr Alekseyevich (1904–84),
    79, 96, 116, 141, 158, 216
Zhdanov, Andrei Aleksandrovich
    (1896–1948), 94, 231–3, 242, 246,
    252, 258, 280, 318
'Zhenya' *see* Pasternak, E. B.
Zhgenti, Bessarion ('Besso') (1903–76), 54,
    81, 82
Zhivago, Evgraf (character in *Doktor Zhivago*),
    270, 292–3
Zhivago, Yurii (hero of *Doktor Zhivago*), 1–2,
    20, 73, 177, 194, 219, 226, 240–5, 254,
    256, 270–1, 275, 279, 282, 285–6,
    288–90, 292–3, 294, 305, 306, 315–16
Zhuravlyov, Dmitrii Nikolaevich (1900–91),
    242, 274–5, 283, 298
Zilbershtein, Ilya Samoilovich (1905–88),
    241
'Zina' *see* Pasternak, Z. N.
*Zinovyev, Grigorii, 102, 133
Znamya, 66, 111, 115–16, 125, 132, 134–5,
    142, 154, 204, 208, 217, 269, 289, 290,
    299, 308, 311, 313
*Zoshchenko, Mikhail, 58, 212, 231–2, 234,
    246, 345
Zubovsky Boulevard, Moscow, 27, 44, 197
Zueva, Anastasiya Platonovna (b. 1896),
    322
Zvezda, 11, 18, 46, 62, 111, 122, 173, 223,
    228, 231, 234
Zvyagintseva, Vera Klavdievna (1894–1972),
    245